EVER THE TEACHER
William G. Bowen

Ever the Teacher

Ever
the
Teacher

* * * * *

WILLIAM G. BOWEN'S
WRITINGS
AS PRESIDENT OF PRINCETON

Princeton University Press
Princeton, New Jersey
1987

Contents

Introduction

During his fifteen years as President of Princeton University (1972–87), William G. Bowen published fifteen annual reports, spoke at fifteen Opening Exercises ceremonies, delivered concluding remarks at fifteen Commencements, and prepared statements, speeches, and testimony on a wide range of topics whose significance extended well beyond his own institution.

These writings provided a medium through which he could communicate his aspirations for Princeton and his perspectives on the central educational issues of his time. His principal audience, more often than not, encompassed Princetonians of many affiliations, including faculty, students, staff, alumni, parents, and friends. But the breadth of his vision and the acuteness of his analysis spoke powerfully to another audience as well: presidents of other colleges and universities, federal and state officials, and other educational leaders who came to look forward to the clear delineations of difficult topics and the thoughtful prescriptions for institutional and national policy that characterized so many of his works.

From each of these audiences came the suggestion that some convenient compilation of these writings would constitute a valuable resource for anyone hoping to understand the Princeton of this era or anyone interested in important questions of policy that continue to dominate the agenda for American higher education.

This volume attempts to provide a selective compilation, drawn from the more complete listing of works that are annotated in Appendix B. It is organized into seven topical chapters:

(1) The nature of the university and its role in the society.

(2) The purposes of education, and particularly of liberal education, at a university like Princeton.

(3) The nature and purposes of graduate education, scholarship, and research.

(4) Concerns of the faculty.

(5) The implications and importance of diversity, of opportunity, and of the availability of financial aid.

(6) The economics of the private research university.

(7) Reflections on the goals of education, and the ways in which those goals are served at Princeton.

Each of the works in this collection was written to stand by itself, in the context of its own time. While I have made every effort to minimize duplication (and have included only about half of the total compilation represented by Appendix B), some repetition is inevitable as recurring themes are addressed, even if from slightly different perspectives. My goal was to produce a useful *reference* volume that would be comprehensive enough to provide a full menu, and would offer at least some flavor of how topics evolved over time, without completely overwhelming the reader. In the end, the responsibility for what has been included and how it has been organized is mine, as are the brief explications that introduce each chapter.

In addition to these topical works (all of which are available in their entirety from the University's Archives), President Bowen also prepared remarks for a number of memorial services. Four of these more personal reminiscences are included as Appendix A.

Brief biographical information is provided in Appendix C.

President Bowen welcomed his opportunities to put pen to paper, or in later years to put keyboard to computer, just as he welcomed his opportunities throughout his presidency to spend time in the classroom teaching a section of Economics 101. His usual style was to do his own drafting after consulting widely with colleagues whose views he respected, with research support from a member of his office employed for that purpose on a part-time basis. First drafts were circulated for editorial and substantive comment among a circle of associates whose candor was actively encouraged and genuinely appreciated. Later drafts also were circulated, and final editing (or ''piddling'') frequently continued until the moment when the text was finally delivered—from a podium, or to a printer.

This high level of engagement did not mesh easily with the many other demands of a presidential calendar. Fortunately, President Bowen was able to work in moving vehicles, so while most Opening Exercises addresses could be drafted in the stationary seclusion of a home at the New Jersey shore, most annual reports were prepared, at least in part, at altitudes above thirty thousand feet or while traversing the New Jersey Turnpike.

Perhaps the premier example was the 1975 report, which was written in large measure on the way to, from, and in the Los Angeles, Tokyo, and Hong Kong airports in connection with a pioneering visit to China. He would write while flying to Los Angeles; mail back the handwritten draft from his hotel and then write more en route to Tokyo; mail back this new section from Tokyo while receiving a typed version of an earlier section that had been mailed to him there for editing; emerge from China to edit the section he had mailed from Los Angeles that was now awaiting him in Hong Kong; and so on. While more global than usual, this general pattern would be repeated again and again over the years, helping to explain why the publication date for his annual reports— November in his first year, then January, then March, then April—had finally been extended to May by the time he published his fifteenth.

Those who had the opportunity to work with President Bowen on these materials know what a careful craftsman he was, challenges of schedule notwithstanding; know of his passionate regard for both precision and felicity of expression; know that he saw his writing as an extension of the teaching that he always considered his principal calling. At their most fundamental levels, his writings and his teaching shared a common motivation—to provoke thought, to sharpen understanding, and to communicate the exhilaration of wrestling hard with ideas that matter.

Robert K. Durkee
Vice President for Public Affairs
Princeton University

December 1987

Ever the Teacher

PART ONE

The University
in Society

Princeton's president is also the presiding officer of the Board of Trustees, and President Bowen keenly felt the trustee's obligation to protect the integrity and independence of the university as a center of learning. Thus it is not surprising that a central and recurring theme of the Bowen presidency concerned the nature of the university and its roles and responsibilities in the larger society.

This theme was developed most fully in the September 1985 Opening Exercises address, entitled "At a Slight Angle to the World." That address begins this chapter, followed by what are, in effect, three case studies:

> • an excerpt from the 1975 annual report that discusses the implications for freedom of speech of a visit to Princeton by Dr. William Shockley, a scientist at Stanford whose views on matters of race were offensive to many;
> • a statement issued in January 1978 in response to a proposed boycott at Princeton of textiles manufactured by the J. P. Stevens Company, which was alleged to have engaged in unfair labor practices; and
> • the opening statement from a May 1985 forum on divestment and South Africa.

The chapter then looks at relationships between the university and the federal government, turning first to a 1987 speech to the Princeton Club of Washington that asked whether higher education is "just another special interest?" and then to a 1982 paper on the role of the federal government that was prepared at a time when many in Washington were proposing a substantial redefinition of that role.

The final section in this chapter reviews the role of the university and the role of the government from the perspective of President Bowen's visit to China in November 1974 as a member of the first delegation of college and university presidents to travel in China following the enormous dislocations of the Cultural Revolution. The talk, delivered at the Princeton Club of New York, is fascinating both for its initial impressions of an elusive and reclusive China and for the light shed by those impressions on American universities and the society they serve.

At a Slight Angle to the World

OPENING EXERCISES ADDRESS
SEPTEMBER 1985

. . . I wish to explore with you the nature of the University—and, more specifically, its relationship to the society it seeks to serve. I want to begin by contrasting the openness and independence of the University you are entering with the much more authoritarian character of higher education in other times and places.

If you had attended Princeton a century ago, the faculty who taught you would have been chosen, at least in part, on the basis of their religious beliefs as well as their competence as teachers and scholars. You would have found that there were real limits to the range of opinions thought acceptable.

Colleges and universities in this country today enjoy a degree of autonomy, and especially of freedom from the application of political as well as religious tests, that is almost unique when viewed historically or when compared with universities right now in most other parts of the world.

The treatment of the Chinese universities during the Cultural Revolution is the most extreme recent example of ideological domination of higher education. I was in the People's Republic of China in 1974, after the start of efforts to resuscitate the universities, and even then, when I asked one university president to identify his principal problem, he was quick to respond: "Getting the faculty to think right."

In Chile, immediately following the coup of 1973, the universities were purged of known Marxists and put under the control of military rectors. One of the many faculty members subsequently dismissed had committed the "crime" of producing research critical of government figures on economic growth and income distribution. By that test, economics departments in this country would be depopulated overnight!

The Greek universities suffered severely under the juntas from 1967 to 1974; and then, when civilian rule was restored, militant students called for "catharsis"—the purging of professors who had collaborated with the military dictatorship. They denounced as well, it was reported in the *New York Times*, "professors they considered too conservative politically or too strict academically." Many other examples could be cited to demonstrate that even democratic forms of government often provide no assurance of freedom for universities from ideological intervention.

In all universities, at all times, the same fundamental questions have to be answered. On the basis of what criteria are students and faculty to be chosen? What subject matter should be taught and studied? Should one or many points of view be presented? Who should decide what are the "right" answers to controversial questions? In short, what educational philosophy should be followed? And, how should society exercise its strong and altogether legitimate interest in the way universities function?

You will not expect me (I hope!) to provide anything purporting to be comprehensive answers to those large questions today. I will try only to give you some sense of how responses have changed over time, and some understanding of the principles that underlie how this University—now *your* University—seeks to serve the societal purposes for which it was chartered.

Underlying all else are of course the values of the society itself. A distinguished faculty member of ours, Professor Bernard Lewis, has recently published a brilliant book called *The Jews of Islam* in which he describes the interactions between these two religious traditions over nearly thirteen centuries. Early on he observes that "tolerance is a new virtue, intolerance a new crime. . . . Until comparatively modern times, Christian Europe neither prized nor practiced tolerance itself, and was not greatly offended by its absence in others. The charge that was always brought against Islam was not that its doctrines were imposed by force—something seen as normal and natural—but that its doctrines were false."

A reading of Richard Hofstadter and Walter Metzger's classic history of the development of academic freedom in the United States, with its European roots, underscores the relevance of Professor Lewis's observation for universities. Whereas it is common today simply to assume the right of free inquiry, the driving assumption throughout most of history has been a very different one. The medieval academic community, for instance, while self-governing in many respects, took for granted "the right of some authority to exercise censorship and proscription in theology and on such conclusions of philosophy as were deemed to encroach upon theology." Heretics were expelled—and sometimes burned.

In America, the struggles for religious tolerance and academic freedom were closely entwined. Both were affected profoundly in the second half of the nineteenth century by the work of Charles Darwin and, more generally, by the growing acceptance of the scientific method. The ensuing debates over doctrine and the nature of Truth itself were often exceedingly painful. American universities were also affected powerfully by the impressive accomplishments of the German universities and by the growing interest in higher education of the federal and state governments, as reflected in the establishment of the land-grant universities.

Private universities were of course particularly susceptible to pressures from their own constituents. The increasing generosity of individuals of means meant that colleges and universities were beginning to be subject to the strong will of donors. A famous case of this kind occurred at Stanford when in 1900 an outspoken critic of big business, Professor Edward A. Ross, was forced to resign at the direct instigation of Mrs. Stanford herself.

The tensions associated with World War I affected many campuses, including this one, as I learned just this spring through a profile in the *Princeton Alumni Weekly* of an extraordinary alumnus of ours, Henry Strater '19. Strater, a pacifist as an undergraduate, joined with several other students to bring the most famous anti-war personality of the time, William Jennings Bryan, to speak at Princeton. Mr. Strater offers this recollection. "The president of Princeton called me into his office when he found out about Bryan. President Hibben said that he couldn't allow Bryan to speak on campus because he had already committed Princeton to a war policy. Eventually we were able to have Bryan speak at a little church that adjoined the campus, and he spoke to a full house."

Ahistorical as so many of us are these days, we may forget that the famous statement on academic freedom adopted by the American Association of University Professors and subsequently endorsed by many educational associations was not drafted until 1915, was not endorsed by the American Council on Education until 1925, and was not approved in its final form until 1940. And then, of course, the sad legacy of the McCarthy period in America in the early 1950s is a forceful reminder of how easy it seems to be, even in the second half of the twentieth century, to slip back into efforts at thought control.

Let me now move to the present and outline as briefly as I can the philosophy and policies that guide us today, the reasons for them, and what I believe is required if they are to be kept secure.

Princeton's obligations to society are to educate students for responsible citizenship and to advance the frontiers of knowledge. The educational philosophy adopted to achieve these goals has three principal roots: first, an unqualified commitment to the most vigorous possible search for truth in all of its cultural, spiritual, social, and physical manifestations; second, a belief that openness to conflicting viewpoints and free debate is central to this search; and, third, a faith in the individual and a corresponding insistence on the importance of fostering independent thinking.

Implicit in this educational philosophy is acknowledgment of the ever-present possibility of being wrong, a willingness to change one's mind, and an ability to respect viewpoints other than one's own—in short, a reasonable degree of intellectual as well as personal humility. It is salutary to remember the number of errors and even crimes that have been committed in the names of Truth and Conscience.

For many years, one of the faculty members at Princeton who most successfully challenged students and faculty alike to reexamine their assumptions and confront their prejudices was H. H. Wilson of the Politics Department. Professor Wilson once described education as "the opposite of indoctrination." He explained: "In all societies efforts are made to use the schools for indoctrination, to propagandize, to inculcate beliefs, to produce cheerleaders for the status quo. Learning how to think is a wholly different operation from being told what to think. . . . The teacher expresses respect for the student; the indoctrinator holds the student in contempt." This is not to say that Princeton abjures efforts to distinguish right from wrong, truth from falsehood, but rather that it believes, with John Milton, that given an opportunity, truth and right will eventually triumph over falsehood and wrong.

Viewed against either the norm today worldwide or even against our own recent past in this country, the concept of education that I have just outlined is a very radical one: teachers and students alike are to be permitted—and, in some sense, even encouraged—to be critical of the very individuals, organizations, and agencies that are providing their sustenance. It is certainly not hard to understand why anyone in a position of authority would be tempted to use educational institutions to indoctrinate, to insist that they hew to the party line, to be sure that faculty "think right." Indeed, the interesting question is the opposite one: what accounts for the rather peculiar willingness of our society to support institutions that can be the home of so much contrariness?

There are, I think, two explanations. First, we are fortunate to live in a country in which democratic values predominate; in which a Constitution and its "Bill of Rights" protect dissenters. The second explanation is more practical but no less important. The freedom to think freshly, and for one's self, is essential to deeper understanding of all subjects, to scientific and technological progress, and to the full development of the capacities of our people. In short, teaching and research are done better when they are unfettered than when ideological constraints are applied, and the society has a very pragmatic interest in the quality of a place like Princeton.

What is required of us if this philosophy of openness is to be sustained? I would like to suggest four elements that, working together, seem to me to constitute the essential foundation for the independence of the University and the effective exercise of freedom within it.

First is clarity on our part concerning our mission and integrity in carrying it out. This includes an unwillingness, especially in recruiting and promoting faculty, to subordinate the single-minded pursuit of excellence and integrity to anything else. Cronyism or favoritism of any kind (related to friendship, to shared political sympathies, to religious affiliation, or even to the apparent advantages of "comfortable" relationships within a department) have no place in the appointment process.

Second is an unwillingness to be "bought." Governments and private donors alike must understand that support cannot be conditioned on ideological conformity. The University is not for sale. Furthermore, to allow such assertions of independence to be powerful realities, the University must have flexible resources of its own. Inevitably, and with the greatest regard for the "not for sale" principle, many funds provided to the University will reflect the greater interests of grant-making entities and other donors in some aspects of the University's mission than in others. Accordingly, the University must have the funds to achieve at least some balance in its activities and to retain, finally, the capacity to determine what kind of place it is to be. As someone once said: "To be great, an institution must be free; and to be free, it must be solvent."

Third, the University as an institution must exercise a significant degree of institutional restraint if its individual members are to enjoy the maximum degree of freedom. This seeming paradox is somewhat complex, and I want to take a few minutes to explore its ramifications.

The idea that the university *as an institution* should consciously distance itself somewhat from the political and social conflicts of the day developed only in this century, and as a concomitant with greater academic freedom for faculty and students. From medieval times through the early 1900s, it was normal for universities in their institutional capacities to serve as defenders and propagandists of the official religious and political systems, and for administrators, faculty, and students to be expected to support these positions. This earlier pattern emphasized more institutional involvement in the outside world, and less individual freedom of expression. Religious, political, and intellectual radicals have always found refuge in the interstices of the university, but until very recently they have often been liable to discrimination and expulsion. The relatively recent reversal of this relationship—restraining collective university positions on issues of public policy but expanding the range of individual opinions—has proved to be critically important in the building of modern research universities with the highest academic standards.

Institutional restraint, then, has been an essential corollary to the strengthening of freedom of expression for individuals. The reluctance of universities to take institutional stands on issues has not stemmed from indifference, from any sense of being in a privileged position "above the fray," or from any lack of awareness that all the institutions of the society are implicated in its imperfections and should seek to avoid adding to them. Rather, this reluctance has been viewed as a positive thing: a direct demonstration of the institutions' openness to all points of view. Internally, the absence of an institutional statement of "orthodoxy" lessens the risk that faculty or students will be favored in some way—or will think that they may be favored—by taking the "right" position on a controversial question.

In fact, the more agreement within the University there is on a particular issue of political or social policy, the more important it may be not to take an institutional position. That is because a key obligation of the University is protection of minority viewpoints, and such protection is needed especially when the minority feels itself beleaguered. This point was made—though not always successfully—in the later stages of the Vietnam War when the people on campus who often felt most oppressed were the small group in favor of U.S. policy. It is very important that we do nothing that might, in H. H. Wilson's phrase, "drive disagreement under cover."

While it is essential that individuals within the University have the freedom to be as frank as they wish to be in expressing unpopular opinions, it is equally important that the society accept expressions of belief by individuals that many will see as "outrages" without punishing the

University itself. Defending provocative points of view can be done most credibly when the institution itself has a reputation for evenhandedness and impartiality.

It is inevitable that the University as an institution will enrage from time to time one or another powerful interest or constituency. If it is a place of integrity, it will do so simply by defending the very forms of freedom that we have been considering. The University must also speak strongly, and, if need be, act politically, if its central mission or independence is threatened. In short, the University must never fear controversy; but its willingness to be contentious should grow directly out of its educational responsibilities and be consistent with them.

Institutional restraint is an expression of institutional tolerance, and it is unfortunately true that tolerance is often regarded as a lowest common denominator kind of value, important only to those who don't care very much anyway or who are afraid to take positions for fear of offending someone. "Doesn't the University believe in anything?" is a question sometimes raised. The answer is a resounding "Yes." This is a value-laden institution, and it is for that reason that I avoid using the word "neutrality" to describe its aims, even in areas outside the academic. But the University's core values emanate from its character as a university. In this setting, the unrelenting, open-minded search for truth is itself the highest value; it is not to be sacrificed to anything else.

It is one thing for the University to espouse central human values, including freedom of inquiry and respect for the rights and dignity of each person. It is quite another for the University as an institution to advocate particular political strategies. That is a task for each of us, as Richard Hofstadter explained so well at the Columbia commencement of 1968 when he said: "While I hope I am speaking in the interest of my university, it would be wrong to suggest that I am precisely speaking for it. It is in fact of the very essence of the conception of the modern university that . . . no one is authorized to speak for it. . . . It does not have corporate views of public questions. . . . This fact of our all speaking separately is in itself a thing of great consequence, because in this age of rather overwhelming organizations and collectivities, the university is singular in being a collectivity that serves as a citadel of intellectual individualism."

Fourth and last on my list of elements necessary to the effective carrying out of our philosophy of openness is what I would call simply a good temper on the campus, and among those off the campus who care about Princeton. The issues I have been discussing—and many others—stir the passions. We will argue mightily about them. We should. Indeed, our openness virtually guarantees disputes and perhaps even conflicts among us. But we must conduct ourselves, and our debates, with the same spirit of open-mindedness and with the same commitment to close reasoning that should be evident in our academic undertakings. We should be calm in our disagreements, generous in our imputations of motives, and respectful of the institution itself. Civility, good humor, and a capacity for sustaining friendships in spite of disagreements are important values in all institutional cultures. They are absolutely indispensable in this one. Otherwise, pluralism can collapse into anarchy, and the very educational values we are here to celebrate will be jeopardized.

*   *   *   *   *

This kind of university is poised delicately between what Professor Hofstadter described as "its position in the external world, with all its corruption and evils and cruelties, and the splendid world of our imagination." It stands, as someone once said of the poet Cavafy, "at a slight angle to the world." It has clear responsibilities to the society, but it discharges them in important degree by means that are sometimes as likely to provoke as to reassure. The modern university is a unique entity, fundamentally different from agencies of government, from churches, businesses, labor organizations, political parties, and social clubs. Far more than any of these, it flourishes by maintaining a climate of freedom.

It is up to each of you to *exercise* this hard-won freedom, to experience the joys as well as the frustrations of opening yourselves to new ideas, but without forgetting that you need to remain rooted in the values that give meaning to your lives. Only as you put your sturdiest qualities to work on behalf of others, in the service of those commitments and shared efforts that will do so much to shape the world, will the restraints and other obligations that the University accepts achieve their full value. . . .

Freedom of Speech—and the Appearance of Dr. Shockley

EXCERPTED FROM THE
REPORT OF THE PRESIDENT
JANUARY 1975

As important to any university as the quality and character of the individual students and faculty members that it attracts is the climate for learning that characterizes it. The opportunity to hear, and to consider, the views of a wide variety of speakers, however objectionable their views may be to some, is so central to the climate for learning for which we strive that any challenge to the right of members of our community to hear whom they please has to be viewed as a serious challenge to the very nature of the University. It is for this reason that the appearance of Dr. Shockley on our campus last year deserves comment in this report.

The Whig-Cliosophic Society decided in October 1973 to invite Dr. William Shockley, a professor at Stanford, and Mr. Roy Innis, National Director of the Congress of Racial Equality, to come to Princeton to debate Dr. Shockley's views concerning genetic differences related to race—views exceedingly offensive to black people, and to many of the rest of us, for reasons that are easily understood. The widely publicized difficulties that Dr. Shockley had experienced in attempting to speak on other campuses made it obvious from the outset that this was not going to be an easy situation.

In an effort to prevent any possible misunderstanding, and to encourage people to think through the basic questions at issue, I made a statement expressing both official University policy and my own view of the principles at stake. Rather than paraphrase it, I take the liberty of reproducing that statement here; it continues to reflect what I believe:

> Let me begin with two personal observations. First, I find nothing more offensive than doctrines of supremacy, be they stated in racial terms or in terms of any of the other categories that have been used historically in an effort to relegate people to an inferior status. Second, neither Mr. Innis nor Mr. Shockley seems to me to have much in the way of professional credentials when the subject to be discussed is genetics.

Neither of these observations, however, speaks to the fundamental issues of policy that have been raised for Princeton as an educational institution as a consequence of the Whig-Cliosophic Society's invitation to Messrs. Innis and Shockley to speak here. The test of whether an individual can be invited to this campus, and can receive a hearing, is not, and in my view cannot be, agreement with the individual's point of view or endorsement of his professional qualifications by the President of the University or by anyone else. We are not that kind of institution.

It is important that we understand the special concerns felt by some black students and others at Princeton about the scheduling of this debate. Black Americans carry with them a particular history of victimization for which various doctrines of racial inferiority have been advanced as justification. The reiteration of such doctrines is bound to trigger deep-rooted suspicions and to raise questions about the intent of organizations that arrange for their discussion.

It cannot be emphasized too strongly, however, that the presence of a speaker on campus in no way denotes support for the speaker's views on the part of either the organization that issued the invitation or the University. An invitation to speak here carries with it no presumption that the views of the speaker are legitimate or valid—or even that many people will find that they are worth hearing. An organization may invite a speaker who will express views that are widely shared; on the other hand, an organization may invite a speaker simply to become familiar at first hand with what might be extremely distasteful views, precisely in order to challenge vigorously those views, or to demonstrate their shallowness. Whatever the circumstances, the University must remain a place where even the most heretical ideas can be discussed in ways that help sharpen our insights and deepen our understanding.

The University's position with regard to speakers is as clear as it is longstanding: (1) Any organization on campus is free to invite any speaker its members choose to hear. (2) Furthermore, the right of speakers to speak and to be heard by those who wish to hear them is protected explicitly by established rules and procedures of the University.

These two policies are fundamental to any community dedicated, as this one is, to the unimpeded investigation of ideas. They are not policies imposed on the campus by any external body. Rather, they are policies evolved over the years by the community itself for the protection of what is surely one of our core values: the freedom of inquiry. We will do all that we can to ensure that these policies are carried out and that the rights of those who have invited speakers, of the speakers themselves, and of those who wish to hear, are protected.

Underlying these policies is an unwillingness to delegate to anyone or to any group the power to determine who may not be heard or what may not be said on this campus. As a direct consequence of this attitude, Princeton has a long and proud history of being open to many points of view. Over the past decade alone, various organizations, including Whig-Clio, the Association of Black Collegians, and Undergraduates for a Stable America have brought controversial speakers as diverse as Ross Barnett, William F. Buckley, Jr., Al Capp, Stokely Carmichael, Angela Davis, Daniel Ellsberg, Huey Newton, Madam Nhu, Arthur Schlesinger, Jr., and George Wallace, to name only ten of many.

Some of us have found the views of one or more of these speakers, or of other speakers, revolting, foolish, or just plain wrong. But that has been—and is—for each of us to decide individually. There is no mechanism within the University for declaring a speaker or a topic out of bounds, and for good reason.

No one has been able to define such a mechanism in ways that would not invite abuse or threaten basic rights of each of us. There is also a more positive and even more fundamental consideration. Not alone, but perhaps especially among the institutions of the society, universities need to have faith in the power of truth. How does one overturn an idea? Not by repressing it or even by trying to ignore it. Bad ideas yield only to better ideas, and it is in that spirit that we must continue to stand together as a community committed to the widest exchange of views, to the rule of reason, and to the ultimate sanction of truth itself.

Finally, there is a practical consideration that should be noted. Most people in this country, and certainly most members of a university community, have a natural sympathy for the person who can't seem to get a hearing. A speaker deprived of a chance to be heard often appears more attractive than he or she may otherwise appear to be; conversely, no speaker appears less attractive than when given every opportunity to make a case and then, when challenged in a calm and reasonable way, fails to respond effectively to a well-put question.

I am sure there are others who remember the day, ten years ago, when Ross Barnett, then Governor of Mississippi, spoke at Princeton in what now seems a different era. One moment during that evening made a particular impression, I believe, on the audience. After Governor Barnett had stated his case for racial segregation in educational institutions, in the midst of the ensuing discussion an undergraduate rose to ask a question. In a pronounced southern drawl the student asked: "Governor, what harm will befall me from attending classes with black students?" For what seemed a very long time there was nothing but silence from the podium. Finally, Governor Barnett replied: "That's hard to say, son, that's hard to say." The meeting adjourned shortly thereafter.

It would take too much space to recount in this report all of the reasons behind the many particular decisions made by Whig-Clio in arranging for the debate (time and location; seating on a first-come, first-served basis, with only members of the University community admitted; limitations on the number of seats reserved for the press; refusal to permit television coverage; and so on); nor shall I describe the security arrangements made by the University or the content of the discussion itself. There was a last minute change in participants when Mr. Innis, who was interested in reaching a wider audience, announced that the arrangements determined by Whig-Clio were unacceptable and withdrew from the debate several hours before it was to take place. He was replaced by Dr. Ashley Montagu, a distinguished anthropologist residing in Princeton, and the original debate format was followed.

Suffice it to say for the purpose of this report that Dr. Shockley and Dr. Montagu spoke without disruption before an audience of approximately four hundred that filled McCosh 10. In addition, the debate was broadcast over WHWH radio in Princeton so that those who were not able to be there in person were able to hear what was said. Outside McCosh 10, students and others (including some people from off campus) demonstrated their opposition to Dr. Shockley and his views, but they did so in lawful ways and did not interfere in any way with the debate itself. A small group calling itself the Attica Brigade, consisting largely of non-students, made one effort to enter the hall after it was full and the debate had begun, but they were unsuccessful, as they also were unsuccessful in attempts to persuade the other anti-Shockley demonstrators to go beyond expressing their own views in the peaceful, nondisruptive ways permitted by our national Constitution as well as by the regulations of the University.

It is noteworthy that the overwhelming majority of persons on the campus, including faculty members of all persuasions, the managing board of the *Daily Princetonian*, the Undergraduate Assembly, and the Council of the Princeton University Community, gave strong and visible support to applicable University policies. It is noteworthy also that in the discussions that preceded the appearance of Dr. Shockley on our campus, there was widespread concern about insensitivity to the feelings of black people. I think it is important that all of us recognize the difficult and unenviable position that black students and faculty members at Princeton were in, not only because of their own strong feelings about the implications of Dr. Shockley's message, but also in view of the pressures brought to bear on them from groups at other colleges and universities and from other off-campus groups to respond as others had at other places. It is to their great credit that, while many of them opposed strongly not just Dr. Shockley's views but Whig-Clio's judgment in inviting him in the first place, they did not think it right to try to prevent others from hearing him. Dr. Shockley's appearance produced an emotional, highly charged situation, and I was very proud of the way so many people associated with Princeton conducted themselves.

Clearly the outcome this time was different from in 1970 when a speech by Secretary of the Interior Walter Hickel was disrupted. I think it is useful to ask why.

There is no one answer. First, there has been a change in the temper of the times, with people generally less inclined than before to arrogate to themselves a "right" to violate the rights of others. However, the very difficulties experienced by Dr. Shockley himself on other campuses, before and after his appearance at Princeton, indicate that this is certainly not a full explanation.

At a more practical level, we have learned some lessons from previous experiences, and better and more careful planning this time no doubt helped. We took pains in advance of Dr. Shockley's appearance to restate our continuing commitment to freedom of expression and to make clear our readiness to pursue disciplinary measures if disruption did occur.

I believe, however, that far more important than any of these considerations was a more subtle influence—the widely shared consensus on campus that disrupting speeches is simply wrong. This consensus has grown with experience and with greater understanding of the importance of the principles at issue for the rights of all of us. In this instance it was encouraged and strengthened by the leadership of a number of faculty members, deans, and students, including importantly Michael Shepard '74, President of the Whig-Cliosophic Society, Andrew Strenio '74, President of the Undergraduate Assembly, Professor Marvin Bressler, who moderated the debate, those faculty members and others who went to the debate primarily because they thought their presence might help the tone, and, finally, Dean Simmons and Provost Hackney, who had primary administrative responsibility and who played a central role in planning for the event. Rules are necessary and their enforcement is important, but the discipline exerted by a shared set of values within a university community matters more than anything else.

Among recent generations of students there have been some who would have qualified the University's commitment to freedom of speech. They argued that because they strongly opposed what a speaker might say or would represent, they were justified in preventing him from speaking—a notion not unique to them, or to young people generally, but nonetheless a notion that threatens the core values of any community such as ours to which freedom of expression and inquiry is essential. Happily, this view that the ends justify the means has been countered vigorously—and I think effectively—by the overwhelming majority of students, by the faculty, by many alumni, by my colleagues in the administration, and by the Trustees. It is a view that finds few adherents today, and, on campus at least, I think there is no uncertainty about where this University stands on freedom of expression—both for those who are offered a platform and for those who, without violating the rights of others, would exercise their rights to dissent.

It would be comforting to think that now that the Shockley experience is behind us we have no more need to be concerned about sustaining free speech, but it would be dangerous—indeed foolish—to hold that view. A historical perspective is useful in reminding us that threats to free speech did not originate with the anti-war protests of the late 1960s. Many faculty as well as alumni will remember the attempts by some to force cancellation of Whig-Clio's invitation to Alger Hiss in 1956. One of our older alumni has told me of attempts by a group of students to silence a socialist in the early 1920s. And those familiar with Princeton's history will remember that a century ago even the President of the College was prevented from proceeding on at least one occasion by the explosion of fireworks and the systematic tapping of heels.

A great many speakers come to our campus every year, and it is of course true that most of them, whatever their viewpoints, come and go without attracting any unusual attention. But whenever emotions run high, there is risk of wrong conduct, and it is well to recognize that it takes only a very few people—some of whom, in some cases, may not even be members of the University community—to cause considerable difficulty. This is, of course, not a problem peculiar to a university, as some participants in meetings of school boards and other community groups can attest. Princeton cannot expect to be immune from the characteristics of the larger society, although we can be expected to lean strongly against the forces of intolerance and ill will—as we are determined to do. Finally, it is of course true that the population of a university is constantly changing, and it is risky to assume that every new student and faculty member automatically and instantly will be aware of the values which have developed over time in the community which he or she is joining.

Thus, we need to keep reminding ourselves and others of what kind of community we are—of the need for fair play, free discussion, and mutual respect, and of the dangerous implications of allowing any group to limit who can speak at Princeton. The freedom to listen to whom one will, and then to make up one's own mind, is far too precious to take for granted.

The Role of the University as an
Institution in Confronting External Issues

STATEMENT ON A PROPOSED
BOYCOTT OF J. P. STEVENS
JANUARY 1978

A group of students and faculty members has petitioned the University to discontinue any acquisition or rental of the products of the J. P. Stevens Company, thereby asking that the University participate in a national boycott of the products of this company. This petition raises directly the larger question of the role of the University as an institution in responding to concerns expressed by students, faculty members, or others regarding issues in the society at large of a social, economic, legal, moral, or political character.

Perhaps the best way to begin this discussion is with an examination of institutional purpose. As the Charter of the University indicates, the purposes for which Princeton is chartered have to do fundamentally with learning and the advancement of knowledge. The University's mission is defined in terms of "the promotion, advancement, evaluation and dissemination of learning by instruction, study and research. . . ." This formal language commits us to a continuing search for deeper understanding of ourselves and the world around us, which must include the constant reexamination of both inherited assumptions and new orthodoxies, as well as to the education of new generations who will in turn improve on our understanding and correct our errors.

As can be seen from the history of education in this country and in other countries, this basic mission can be pursued in many different ways, depending on one's philosophy of education. Central to the philosophy of education at Princeton is the proposition that the University has a responsibility to expose students and faculty members to a wide variety of views on controversial questions, to stimulate careful and critical thinking, to encourage an openness to new ideas, and, finally, to make clear that ultimately it is up to each individual to decide what he or she believes about the issues that confront all of us personally and as citizens.

This conception of education, with its stress on opening minds and encouraging independent thought, is both a more radical and a more recent conception than most of us realize. Professor Lawrence Stone, internationally known for his studies in the history of education, has argued forcefully that from the middle ages through most of the seventeenth, eighteenth, and even nineteenth centuries, a primary purpose of education in Europe and in America was more or less straightforward indoctrination in accepted values as well as in accepted ideas. People who held what were thought to be odd views were often repressed if not dismissed, and academic freedom as we know it now did not exist. It was not until the early 1900s that the twin notions of the open mind as a goal of education and of academic freedom as a necessary instrument in the pursuit of truth became generally accepted.

Even in recent years in this country, our conception of educational purpose has been attacked from both the right and the left—witness the McCarthy period in the 1950s and the activities of some radical groups in the late 1960s. The ability of the University to continue to be a place genuinely open to all points of view is not something that can be taken for granted.

This philosophy of education has a number of corollaries and consequences. The positive educational case for having a student body that is diverse in terms of backgrounds, experiences, interests, and predilections is rooted directly in the notion that learning is stimulated when different perspectives are represented and expressed. The strong commitment of the University to the right of any group on campus to hear speakers of its choice is another corollary. Perhaps most important of all is the proposition that no current or prospective member of the University community—student, member of the faculty or staff—should be penalized or rewarded within the institution as a consequence of that individual's views on the political or social issues of the day. This view of the educational mission of the University is also strongly value-laden. It depends on a shared acceptance of certain core values including commitment to the pursuit of truth, respect for evidence, a belief in the worth and integrity of each person, and concern for fairness in our relationships with others.

Put simply, the University's ability to carry out its basic educational mission requires an environment conducive to the maximum possible freedom of thought and expression for each individual student and faculty member. We are not talking here about something that is merely desirable; we are talking about something that is essential. In this crucial respect the University has a special role in the society—a special responsibility for creating a milieu in which every individual, whether the steadiest proponent of the majority viewpoint or the loneliest dissenter, is encouraged to think independently. In its dependence on this kind of environment for the achievement of its central purposes, the University is different in nature from churches, labor unions, businesses, political organizations, social clubs, and all other entities.

It is primarily because of an overrriding commitment to this philosophy of education that there is a strong presumption against the University as an institution taking a position or playing an active role with respect to external issues of a political, economic, social, moral, or legal character. Before discussing the kinds of special considerations that could be so compelling as to warrant setting aside this presumption, it is important to understand the reasons why the presumption itself is such a strong one.

First, there is a direct conflict between institutional expressions of opinion on external issues and the clear need to create and sustain the kind of learning environment within the University described above. Any time that the University as an institution begins to play an active role with respect to an external issue, by boycotting a product or in some other way, the commitment of the University to be as open as possible to all points of view is inevitably compromised in some degree. For the institution to take sides, to suggest that there is a single "right" answer or a single right way to proceed, can only discourage those within who hold dissenting views. In extreme cases, pressures that are either subtle or overt can in effect stifle dissent.

There is an associated danger. Whether their fears are grounded in fact or not, individuals may come to feel that their status, or their chances for advancement, could be affected by their agreement or disagreement with the "official," institutional position on an issue that does not seem central to the purposes of the University or to their reasons for being at the University. It is precisely to protect against this danger that many people in universities have insisted, for example, that while faculty members must be free to express their views *as individual citizens* on any or all questions, the University itself should signify its openness to various positions by declining to be identified in an institutional sense with any one position.

This viewpoint has not always prevailed historically and indeed does not prevail throughout the world today; and it is instructive to see what can happen when universities become politicized. Many people would agree that in recent years important educational values have been damaged or actually lost in countries as different as West Germany, Brazil, and the People's Republic of China when decisions on such key questions as admissions, appointments, and curriculum have been conditioned by considerations that are not primarily academic.

A second problem of an extremely serious nature is that if the University as an institution were to play a more active role vis-à-vis external issues, it would become much more difficult to protect the internal academic freedom of the University from outside interference. At present the University argues vigorously against attempts by external bodies (donors or sponsors, private or public) to condition support of the University on our institutional acceptance of their views on matters ranging from the private enterprise system to appropriate foreign policy in the Middle East. What is at stake here, of course, is not merely "acceptance of views" in an abstract sense but who is to influence, or even decide, questions in areas as vital to the University as admissions, appointments, and the teaching process—and on the basis of what criteria.

The legal prohibition against partisan political activity by the University as a tax-exempt organization chartered for educational purposes represents just one manifestation of a much broader "understanding" between the academy and the larger society. We are given certain privileges, receive certain kinds of support, and are permitted important fundamental freedoms on the condition that as an institution we shall stand apart from contemporary controversies that are not primarily educational in character. This can be seen as a kind of "social contract." Our strongly defended right to make our own faculty appointments, to make our own admission decisions, to shape our own curriculum—all of these hard-won prerogatives depend finally on our ability to persuade society that we are indeed firm and consistent in upholding our commitment to a University atmosphere that encourages a genuine diversity of views, including importantly those of people who may feel out of step with most others on the campus or in the society generally.

We should also recognize that it is not possible for the University to play an active role in one situation, no matter how meritorious the cause may seem to a great many people, without being asked to take actions or to "declare itself" in any number of other situations. Action in one instance would lead inevitably to a request that the University offer a convincing account of its general policy on similar issues; such an account would also have to address the general question of the role of the University in the society and the responsibility of the University to adhere to its side of the "social contract."

A third problem associated with taking institutional positions is also rooted in a basic characteristic of the University. As a community we are exceptionally diverse, individualistic, and argumentative. That is our nature, and if we were none of these things, we would be much less effective as a place of learning. It follows, however, that any attempt to secure agreement within a community such as ours on external questions is likely to be very difficult. How does one determine and weigh the views of students, faculty, staff, and alumni—especially given different degrees of knowledge and interest? Moreover, the process of reaching such decisions can create antagonisms and divert significant amounts of time and energy from our central commitment to teaching and scholarship.

Fourth and last, the credibility of the University as an institution in the society is an exceedingly valuable asset. It is of particular importance in those special situations (discussed below) when the University must defend its freedom or must speak on other questions that are essential to its mission. Credibility and effectiveness depend on speaking only when the special capabilities of the institution relate to the question at issue; and it must be recognized that the University as such (as distinguished from many individuals within it) has neither any charge nor any special competence to make judgments outside the fields of education and research. Even within its own domain, there is a strong case to be made for concentrating the institutional efforts of the University on those issues which we believe we can address most effectively.

It is for the reasons given above, rooted in both the nature of the educational process and the special role of the University in the society, that there is such a strong presumption against institutional involvement in issues that are primarily external to our purposes. At the same time it is possible to distinguish three sets of situations in which it seems proper or even necessary in certain circumstances for the University as an institution to speak beyond the campus. Even in these situations, however, the basic arguments against institutional involvement usually apply, and a decision to take an institutional position therefore requires a careful balancing of conflicting considerations.

The first set of situations in which the University has reasons for overcoming its strong presumption against institutional positions involves questions related directly to the educational mission of the University. Here the University has direct factual information to provide, some special competence, and perhaps even an obligation to make its views known. An example is the area of graduate education in which we have tried hard to identify ways in which national policies might serve what we believe to be national needs. Similarly, we have not hesitated to make our views known on questions concerning government regulation of academic research, financial aid for students at the undergraduate level, the future of research libraries, the implications for education of some proposed changes in the tax code, the likely effects of changes in the age of retirement, or any issue in which we have seen a threat to the autonomy or educational quality of the University. To be sure, these are matters in which we have a clear self-interest; but they are also matters about which we have first-hand knowledge, and on which the educational community's voice must be heard if there is to be informed public discussion.

There can be differences of view within the institution on these issues as on others, and careful consideration must be given to possible effects on the perceived freedom of faculty and students to hold contrary views. Also, there may be some outside the University who will be antagonized by positions taken. An "institutional view" may be difficult or divisive to obtain. And the risk of diminishing institutional credibility is ever present. Nevertheless, when all these considerations are weighed, the potential benefits of institutional action may be judged to outweigh the potential harm in situations in which the educational mission of the University is directly involved. There is less likely to be serious division within the University in most cases of this kind; those outside are likely to be more tolerant because of more understanding of the University's need to assert its own position; and University credibility is inherently greatest in such situations. Accordingly, the presumption against institutional involvement may be overcome.

There is a second set of situations quite different in character which should be recognized conceptually even though they occur exceedingly infrequently and can be hard to identify with confidence in particular instances. Involved here are potential threats to the fabric of the entire society that are so serious that if the "wrong" outcome occurs, the survival of the University itself would be threatened—or, in the most extreme situations, would not even matter. The development of Nazi Germany is generally cited as perhaps the clearest example. A number of people felt that the Vietnam War justified truly exceptional actions by the University, and those who were on campus then will remember all of the meetings and discussions that occurred on that subject. Some special arrangements were made (especially concerning academic schedules), but this was done primarily for the purpose of allowing individuals or groups of individuals to express their own opinions; the University as an institution did not take a position.

Finally, there are situations that are essentially internal, in that they grow out of the University's responsibilities as an institutional resident of several municipalities, as an employer, or as an owner of securities, and which *require* decisions to be made that can be construed as having significance beyond the educational program of the University. For example, from time to time the University takes positions on local land-use and zoning questions. The University is engaged in collective bargaining relationships with some groups of employees and in that context must demonstrate, as we do, what our own views are on the right of employees to organize, on what constitutes fair labor practices, and so on. Similarly, in discharging its legal responsibilities as an owner of shares of stock, the University votes in proxy disputes presented to us and communicates its views on various questions to the managements of the companies concerned.

Some have argued that decisions concerning products to be purchased are analogous to voting proxies. There is, however, a very significant distinction. When the University buys shares of stocks, it inevitably accepts part of the responsibility for the company that accompanies ownership, even if the shares represent a very small fraction of the company's stock. Purchasing the product of a company, on the other hand, conveys no similar right or responsibility to participate in policy decisions of the kind raised explicitly by proxy resolutions. Also, when the University buys products, it can specify—as it does— the bid specifications that suppliers must meet (quality, delivery date, and so on) without instructing the Purchasing Office to buy or not to buy from a particular company for other reasons unrelated to the use which the University is to make of the product. This is our basic policy.

It should be emphasized that in purchasing products from suppliers, who in turn may buy from various manufacturers, the University as an institution neither approves nor disapproves of the policies followed by any of the firms involved in manufacturing or distributing the products. Neither the presence nor the absence on the campus of the product of a firm should be viewed as a decision either supporting or condemning the firm. It has been argued, for example, that because there is an organized boycott of J. P. Stevens, the University supports the firm if it does not participate in the boycott. A major difficulty with this argument is the very troubling implication that any time any group organizes a boycott (or takes any one of a number of other actions against a firm or a union), it could in effect require the University to choose one side of the dispute or the other. To accept this line of argument would be to take out of the hands of the University one of the most fundamental decisions of all—namely, the decision as to its proper role in society. The University must retain for itself the right to decide which external issues are and are not appropriate for determination by the University as an institution; and it must therefore reject arguments that would impute a position to the University when no position has in fact been taken.

More generally, in considering what response to make in a dispute between contending parties that takes the form of an effort to organize a boycott, any organization has three distinct options: (1) to join the boycott by explicitly enjoining the purchase of the products in question; (2) to oppose the boycott by explicitly instructing its agents to purchase the products in question; or (3) to take no position in the controversy. The option of deciding to take no position is clearly available, and for all of the reasons given earlier this seems the appropriate policy for the University as an institution. Such an approach does not imply anything about the merits of the case, its importance, or what individuals should do as individuals. What it does imply is that taking an institutional position on such a matter is thought to be inconsistent with the essential role of the University in society.

At the same time that the University tries to avoid *institutional* involvement in issues that seem inappropriate to the University as such, it not only recognizes the right of *individual* members of the University community to take positions on current issues, it encourages its members to be informed and effective citizens. In the case of the J. P. Stevens controversy, for example, it is right and proper for students and others to express the views they hold, to try directly to persuade the company to change its policies if that is what they believe should be done, or to work for changes in the law if that is what seems wise to them.

But what is right and proper for individuals may be wrong and damaging for the institution. If the University is to serve well the purposes for which it exists, there must be a continuing commitment to the freedom of each individual to think freshly and independently, to be as free as possible of every form of coercion, of every pressure to join a position because others—even a substantial majority—happen to hold it. Required too is a large measure of forbearance on the part of students, faculty, and alumni, who will naturally and properly feel strongly about a great many causes that are extremely significant to them. The University itself advances important causes by assuring that both their champions *and* their opponents have a full opportunity to argue their cases. This requires institutional restraint and a willingness to differentiate between the right of the individual to argue vigorously for what he or she believes and the obligation of the institution to remain open in fact and in appearance to different points of view.

In almost all cases of this kind, those who argue for a boycott or some other form of action by the University stress what are for them important moral concerns. All of us can respect such concerns. At the same time, respect is also due the University as a unique institution in the society, with an abiding commitment to improve the lot of all people through the ideas it stimulates and the individuals it educates. It is an institution with a peculiar need for a degree of detachment from the controversies of the moment, not because it is indifferent to the values being debated but because of the fundamental importance of maintaining an atmosphere of maximum freedom and intellectual diversity for the benefit of all who study and learn within it.

Those of us who are deeply concerned about any tendency to ''politicize'' the University, in the broadest sense of that term, are by no means opposed to controversy or uninterested in ultimate values or moral precepts. In fact, the depth of our concern stems directly from a strong commitment to the educative influence of conflicting opinions, a strong belief in the power of the ideas that can emerge from the exchange of opinions, and a strong belief in the potential for good of a university that is true to its own highest principles. It stems from what are really moral convictions about the values to be served by education.

Divestment and South Africa

REMARKS AT A CAMPUS FORUM
MAY 1985

I am pleased that the Council of the Princeton University Community is sponsoring this meeting, which has been called to give interested members of the University community an opportunity to hear directly the reasons for the University's current policies on investments in companies doing any part of their business in South Africa and to provide an opportunity for questions.

A number of students, faculty members, and others have told me that they find aspects of the current debate perplexing, and I am glad to have this opportunity to clarify, as best I can, some of the underlying issues as seen from the perspective of the Trustees. This year, more than in some previous years, the focus of much of the discussion has been squarely on arguments for and against divestiture as a general approach, and I think we take fullest advantage of this gathering if we concentrate on that specific question rather than on other aspects of University policy (including the ways in which the University has sought to act as a responsible shareholder by encouraging companies to follow practices in South Africa that have seemed to offer the possibility of a constructive, if limited, impact).

My starting point is a conundrum that we might all ponder: Given the widespread agreement among so many of us on the basic values—the dignity of each human being, a revulsion at repression and violence, a commitment to building relationships among people that transcend race—why are many of us nonetheless at such an impasse on the issue of divestiture?

There are, I think, two parts to the answer. First, there are significant differences of opinion as to what policies toward South Africa provide the best chance of ending apartheid, and of doing so in a way that offers some hope of building a better society for all. The second, and in some ways more fundamental, answer is that what may be right action for an *individual* may not be right action for this kind of *university*.

This key distinction dominated much of the discussion at the last meeting of the Board of Trustees, and I will come back to it several times in these remarks. Let me begin, however, by reiterating a central point of agreement: those of us who have participated in this debate within the Board and on the campus are, I believe, unanimous in our condemnation of apartheid. I cannot convey adequately how strongly the Trustees feel about this. Some of them have spent significant parts of their lives fighting for civil rights in this country and abroad, and a number have direct experience of South Africa. For me personally, apartheid is a violation of every principle of decency and of right relationships among people. To pile on adjectives is superfluous and even demeaning. The point is clear without embellishment.

What is at issue, then, is not how we feel about apartheid. Nor is the issue what we should do about apartheid as *individuals* (even though there are obviously differences of opinion about that). What *is* at issue is what this *University*, as an educational institution, can and should do.

To sharpen my own thinking, I have listed eight considerations that have led the Board of Trustees (with different Trustees naturally giving different weights to different considerations) to conclude that divestiture is not the right means, for this University, to an end that many support strongly.

1. The first consideration is not peculiar to the University as a shareholder but applies equally to all who are concerned about the future of South Africa. Even if divestiture of stock by Princeton were to lead American companies to withdraw from South Africa (which is itself a far from evident proposition, to say the least), many members of the Board are much less certain than many advocates of divestiture that such withdrawals would improve rather than retard the prospects for an eventual solution to the problem of racism in South Africa—and especially for a solution that holds out at least some hope of reconciliation. No one whom I know believes—or ever has believed—that the Sullivan Principles, in and of themselves, are capable of bringing about an end to apartheid; but it certainly can be argued that they make conditions marginally better rather than marginally worse. More generally, and at least in part for reasons of economic self-interest, the business community in South Africa is widely regarded as one of the more progressive elements there; more generally yet, the very process of economic development may prove, over time, to be among the most powerful enemies of apartheid. At the minimum, it seems clear that the near-term and long-term effects of economic withdrawal cannot be assessed unambiguously.

2. Many Trustees, and many others, are much more skeptical than proponents of divestiture about the likely effects of such action on the

policies of the companies themselves, let alone on apartheid in South Africa. The sale of shares of stock is quite removed from the real objective sought by the proponents (major political change in South Africa), and the connections may not be nearly as tight as some assume. Quite apart from the fact that Princeton holds only a very small fraction of the stock of any of the companies in question, it is the experience of many of us that companies are much more responsive to reasoned argument, based on special knowledge or special competence, than to apparently dramatic actions of a once-and-for-all character that can be dismissed as bowing to local pressures and that, in any event, allow for no follow-through.

3. If part of the resistance to divestiture rests on serious doubts about one or the other of the two key premises just mentioned, another part rests on real reservations about arguments that relate to "moral purity." It is sometimes argued that, whatever the actual effects or lack of effects of divestiture, it is wrong in principle for the University to hold stock in a company that can be seen as in any degree participating or acquiescing in apartheid. Some Trustees reject this argument because they believe, as noted earlier, that the companies in question are more positive than negative in their actual impacts and are therefore acting in morally responsible ways. But other Trustees reject the moral purity argument on more general grounds. They believe that the quest for "clean hands" is an impossible one, in a world too full of imperfection, and that it can even lead to narrow, self-congratulatory acts that do not in fact address the full range of moral issues that need to be taken into account.

There is, for example, the problem for the University of how to treat the many companies that sell products to South Africa—or that buy from South Africa—without actually having offices there. Are they less involved in the complicity that we would be seeking to avoid? Should not their stock be sold too? What about gifts that the University receives from this same, very large, set of companies—or from the even larger number of individuals who hold their stock? It would be hard for many Trustees to justify requesting support for scholarships, professorships, or any other University needs from companies that have been found unacceptable as investment vehicles on moral grounds. There is, in addition, the fact that the University uses products from these same companies. If we really wish to dissociate ourselves from IBM, for example, is it sufficient to sell IBM stock? Can we, in good conscience, simultaneously accept money from IBM for a professorship (as we have just done), or matching gifts that go into Annual Giving, or—as we have also done recently—computers used by faculty and students all across the campus?

Please do not misunderstand me. I have great respect for those who are concerned about the moral issues presented here. Indeed, the moral issues are, for me, the most fundamental. But they are far from simple.

From my point of view, actions taken on moral grounds are most credible when any negative consequences are felt directly by the individuals urging the actions, rather than by others now at Princeton who may have very different views as to the correct policy, or by still others, future students and faculty members, not even here yet. From this perspective, what should be the position of the current faculty and staff whose personal pension funds are invested in a large, national portfolio (TIAA-CREF) that holds vastly greater amounts of stock in these same companies than any university? There would seem to be a case for making a maximum effort to dissociate one's own pension funds from such investments before asking the University—with its much broader institutional mission—to take similar actions. When an argument is couched strongly in moral terms, there is a special obligation, I think, to consider the full range of implications—personal as well as institutional—and not just to say "enough" when the lines become extremely difficult to draw or the implications too pervasive.

The next group of considerations, 4, 5, 6, and 7, all have a common theme: whatever the effects of divestiture on racism in South Africa—and to many they seem either negative or very uncertain or ambiguous at best—the effects of divestiture on the long-term welfare of the University could be very damaging. It is natural, I suppose, that the Trustees take this set of considerations particularly seriously. It is their clear responsibility to do so.

4. Trustees are fiduciaries, which means that they have been entrusted by others, many no longer living, with seeing that the resources which have been given to Princeton to advance the educational and scholarly purposes of the University are employed as productively as possible for those specific purposes. Whatever a Trustee may feel *personally* about the propriety of investing in a particular company, when acting as Trustee for Princeton University there is an obligation to be scrupulous in not allowing personal convictions to constrain inappropriately the investment of funds that have been entrusted to the University. That too is a moral obligation.

To rule out, as potential investments, classes of securities in industries such as banking, or, still more generally, in large multinational companies, would almost certainly have a long-term financial effect that would limit the ability of the University to serve its most central purposes. Such actions would also make it difficult to convince prospective donors that the University was prepared to be a good fiduciary in the future. What additional constraints might be imposed next, would be an obvious query.

5. Another problem with divestiture that is particularly serious for Trustees—and that is often not well understood—involves the obligation to be fair and consistent in the application of University policy. An individual can say perfectly well, "I feel very strongly about A, and I am going to act accordingly by selling my holdings in the stock of A," without being terribly concerned about fitting that act into some larger policy that has a demonstrable consistency. That approach is not possible for this University, however, at least not without harming its credibility. Thus, the Trustees have been resistant to the notion that we should "make an example" of Company A, unless we are really persuaded that Company A is so bad, judged overall and compared with all other companies, that it deserves such censure.

Over the years, we have spent a great deal of time and energy trying to persuade others—outside the University—who have disagreed with one aspect or another of life at Princeton, that they should judge the University *overall*, not on the basis of their attitudes toward, for example, coeducation, vigorous minority recruitment efforts, the alleged political views of faculty, or any other specific issues which may have troubled them. Surely we have an obligation to apply the same standard to those who displease us on one ground or another. This is why the Trustees have not thought that it was right in principle to sell the stock of a company solely because that company has not agreed with the University on a particular proxy question or some other policy issue.

Every action that the University takes becomes a precedent, and therefore it is important for the Trustees to be sure that the precedent is one that they and their successors can—and should—follow faithfully in other situations. It is perfectly understandable that groups who feel intensely about a particular issue such as apartheid in South Africa may not be immediately concerned about whether the University treats all companies consistently, or whether it addresses another issue at some future time in the same way that it responded to a particular set of proposals for divestiture; but the Trustees have to take seriously precisely such questions of consistency if they are to discharge faithfully their responsibilities for the long-term governance of the University.

6. A sixth consideration for many Trustees concerns their attitude toward the use of economic pressure. Some who have advocated divestiture have been clear in saying that they want the University to use its "clout" in seeking to compel a particular company to comply with Princeton's sense of how it ought to conduct itself. Putting aside the question of how much "clout" the University really has, it has seemed to many of us that to use the economic resources of Princeton as a weapon in this way is to invite one of the things that we ourselves have worked hardest to discourage—namely, the use of economic coercion by those outside the University to pressure us to conform to their ideas of (for instance) what we should teach, whom we should appoint to our faculty, and whom we should admit. Once *we* concede the legitimacy of economic pressure as a weapon in defining relationships between the University and corporations (or others), we will have opened a box that, I fear, we will very much wish were closed.

7. The seventh reason for concern with divestiture has to do with the political connotations of any decision to boycott the securities of a particular company or group of companies. Some of those advocating divestiture have been explicit in saying that it is precisely the "announcement," "embarrassment" effect which they are seeking, an effect that they hope will mobilize others to follow suit, will energize lawmakers, and so on. I have been warned by faculty colleagues and others about exaggerating the power of the University in this arena, but the issue for the Trustees is not really the degree of the University's power in any case. The concern rather is with maintaining our independence—and especially maintaining the openness of the University to a range of viewpoints on all matters—which in turn depends on keeping a certain institutional distance from political debates that are not primarily about educational matters, including debates about U.S. policy toward South Africa.

The purpose of Princeton as a university is not, ultimately, to determine the right constitutional policy for other countries, the right economic policy for this country, or any other broad public policies. It is, rather, to be an educational institution of the highest quality, that probes and studies such issues, that stimulates independent thinking on the part of students and faculty alike, and that takes pride in the contributions that its students, faculty, and alumni make, *as individuals*, in addressing such compelling problems as ignorance, inequality, racism, hunger, and the threat of war. But the University is in a much stronger position to be the home of outspoken critics and scholars expressing a variety of points of view—as it must be in a free society—if the University itself does not try to assume the role of political and social actor, attempting to promulgate "official institutional" views outside the University or within it.*

The university is unique among institutions in the degree to which it depends on an environment of academic freedom or "openness." Its nonpartisan, nonpolitical character is, therefore, not just "nice" to preserve: it is absolutely essential. In this fundamental respect, universities differ sharply from political parties, churches, civic groups, businesses, foundations, and other organizational entities that may quite properly have political, doctrinal, or partisan goals. It is for this reason, among others, that Trustees who serve on the boards or in leadership capacities in these other organizations may feel much freer in those contexts to advocate divestiture or to take other actions intended to have political effects. This leads to another distinction: it is quite proper, in my view, for the University to speak out strongly in favor of core values such as an end to racism; it is quite another thing for the University, as an institution, to advocate particular political strategies such as corporate withdrawal from South Africa.

8. Finally, a number of Trustees have seen proposals for divestiture as deflecting energies and attention from actions and arenas that seem more appropriate both to the University and to the ends being sought. Universities function best when they are true to their own calling, when they encourage their individual scholars, teachers, and students to develop a deeper understanding of South Africa and of possibilities for change there. We are now actively exploring whether there is more the University can do, consistent with its character, to support a number of such efforts.

Many of us also believe that in a democracy it is action by government that is the most effective—and most appropriate—way of communicating clearly what the citizens feel about apartheid. The renewed debate in Congress on legislation that would redefine the relationship

---

* From this standpoint as well as from others, voting proxies is very different from selling stock. Voting proxies can be seen as accepting responsibilities placed upon the University by dint of being a shareholder: it is a way of expressing views when one has standing to do so. Divestiture—actively boycotting a particular security—is a step that requires the University to initiate a political action, and that has seemed to the Trustees to press the University over a very important threshold. It is also true, of course, that proxies can be voted without constraining the portfolio, and thereby without raising the questions of fiduciary responsibility raised directly by divestiture.

between U.S. businesses and South Africa seems to me to offer new opportunities for the members of this University, as for other citizens, to express forcefully the views that they hold. And it affords an opportunity to do so without compromising the mission of an institution— the University—that has its own, different, but I think vital, role to play.

*　*　*　*　*

For many of us used to debating a variety of issues, this one is fundamentally different. It is, for me at least, particularly gripping, frustrating, and saddening. A number of you, I suspect, share these feelings even as you may have come to exactly the opposite conclusion as to what ought to be done.

The fundamental difficulty, I believe, is that the wrong proximate issue—divestiture—has come to carry tremendous emotional and symbolic significance. I wish it were otherwise. There are positive contributions the University can make, but they are limited and neither dramatic nor immediate in their effects. This is not easy to accept, for any of us. What I see as the necessary restraints on *institutional* action implies, for me, that the burden of conscience rests all the more heavily on each of us as an individual. That makes it harder for all of us, but surely the inhumanity of what we are really opposing justifies the acceptance of that burden.

Just Another Special Interest?

SPEECH BEFORE THE
PRINCETON CLUB OF WASHINGTON, D. C.
MARCH 1987

Each time that I am in Washington, I feel the temptation to reflect on points of intersection between the world of higher education and the world of government. I hope you will allow me, once again this year, to succumb.

In our society—unlike so many other societies—these two worlds remain somewhat separate, despite the substantial degree to which each is dependent on and serves the other. That is, I believe, all to the good.

The federal interest in higher education was certainly well understood by those who gathered two hundred years ago to establish a constitution under the leadership of a Princetonian, James Madison, at a convention so populated by graduates of the College of New Jersey that one of our faculty members has described it as Princeton's first alumni college. Among the proposals under consideration at that convention was the creation of a national university—a proposal whose principal advocates included an eighteenth-century Princeton parent by the name of George Washington.

Despite this determined advocacy, and the good intentions of its proponents, the proposal was never adopted—in my view, a wise result. What has evolved instead has been a rather remarkable partnership, punctuated by such milestones as the land grants of the nineteenth century that gave birth to our great state universities; the GI Bill, Pell Grants, and other federal programs to expand educational opportunity; and the substantial post-war federal investment in academic science and technology.

The world of higher education has grown and diversified dramatically, but its fundamental contributions to the society remain what they have always been: the discovery of new ideas, the integration of new knowledge into the corpus of what was known before, the transmission of this assimilated body of learning through the teaching process, and the concurrent preparation of succeeding generations for responsible citizenship and the assumption of positions of leadership. Different educational institutions pursue these goals with different emphases and with different degrees of success. But the overall system that has been created is the envy of many people, and many governments, through-out the world.

One of the comments heard with worrying frequency these days in Washington, and elsewhere, is that somehow this traditional, mutually reinforcing, partnership between the federal government and higher education has changed—that colleges and universities have become, in one of the most pejorative phrases that can be uttered on this Hill, "just another special interest."

It is of course true that colleges and universities have a special interest in certain appropriations, in specific provisions of the tax code, and in those legislative or regulatory proposals that directly affect their capacity to serve the purposes for which they are chartered. But the implication of those who utter the phrase is more than that. It is that there is somehow something selfish, or "greedy," or unseemly either about the interests being represented or the purposes being served.

What are these interests? What are these purposes? Who, in the end, is being served?

Colleges and universities do not come to Washington to line their own pockets. In fact, and in contrast to many other organizations, they have, finally, no significant personal or private pockets of their own to line. Self-evident as it is, perhaps it should be noted that colleges and universities have no shareholders aspiring to higher dividends or to appreciating stock values. We do not have investment bankers ripe with insider information who see our competitors (or us) as appealing morsels, and we do not have faculty or administrators who can anticipate bonuses attendant on achieving some financially defined bottom line.

What we *do* have are teachers, scholars, students, and staff members working hard for what they perceive to be, at least in large part, important public purposes. We also have alumni and friends who expect to give rather than to take (in this sense the flow of monetary "dividends" is all negative), and Boards of Trustees who not only, in the vernacular, fail to "rip off" their institutions but are instead quite regularly ripped off by them. All of this seems to many quite odd, which it is, but it is also quite American and, if I may say so, quite wonderful.

Of course the university world has its share of egomaniacs, selfish people, and even some who do seek to profit personally and improperly from their associations with places like Princeton. How unreal life would be otherwise! Our halo is very loose-fitting indeed, but at least we can take comfort from the fact that institutional priorities and rewards are directed overwhelmingly to the service of societal interests and societal purposes.

Far from being "just another special interest" in a pejorative sense, universities are national assets that in this country serve to channel a unique blend of private and public resources to the fulfillment of goals that transcend any set of special interests.

One of these goals is, as I have said, the discovery of new knowledge, and the latest issue of the *Princeton Weekly Bulletin* reports the contributions of one of Princeton's Nobel Laureates, Physics Professor Philip Anderson, to recently announced breakthroughs in the area of superconductivity. The potential benefits of these advances range from enhanced medical imaging and 300 mph trains (suspended over rather than bumping along their tracks) to providing a critical ingredient in efforts at our Plasma Physics Laboratory to derive energy from the fusion of hydrogen nuclei. But the more pertinent point of the story is that these recent developments have their origins in discoveries that date back at least to 1911, and that represent the fruits of many decades of basic research, carried out quite apart from any sense of what might result.

As we look to the future, all of us are concerned with maintaining the strength of the nation's scientific establishment by recruiting and retaining outstanding young scientists. The same issue of the *Bulletin* features nine young scientists and engineers at Princeton who have won Presidential Young Investigator awards this year from the National Science Foundation. Princeton has now won twenty-five of these highly competitive awards since the program's inception in 1984 (the highest total, I might add, on a per capita basis of any university). These awards provide flat grants over five years plus matching funds to encourage industrial support. They allow their recipients, at early points in their careers, to meet costs for equipment, assistance, and other needs that otherwise could not be met. The result is not only a greater national investment in talent, but an essential counterweight to the more sophisticated equipment, greater resources, and certainly higher salaries available to these young people in industry.

When universities come to Washington for funds to support basic research, or for such major scientific enterprises as the Plasma Physics Laboratory and our new supercomputer center, they are motivated not by some invidious form of "special interest," but by the staggering costs of modern science, often by the lack of other appropriate places to turn, and by the pressing needs of individual scientists whose ideas will shape our world, and whose students will shape the world that we leave to others.

When we look for support for libraries, it is so our faculty and students will have the resources they need at a time when knowledge is proliferating rapidly (both in this country and overseas).

When we look for support for international education, it is because our programs of teaching and research in fields such as East Asian and Near Eastern studies, and the specialized resources necessary to support them, constitute a priceless national resource that no university could justify through any narrow, institutionally oriented, cost-benefit analysis. As I point out in my annual report for this year, direct expenditures for library resources alone at Princeton are more than $6,000 per student each year in East Asian studies, and over $5,500 per student each year in Near Eastern studies. If our overriding objective were some kind of measure like earnings/share, we would surely jettison such extraordinarily expensive "product lines."

We persevere in sustaining such programs because of their intrinsic merits and because of their importance to a nation far more deficient than it ought to be in its understanding of other cultures. As a recent report sponsored by the Social Science Research Council noted, the network of regional studies centers at American universities is "unparalleled anywhere else in the world. . . . We tend to take it for granted, but if it did not exist we would be trying desperately to create it, and at a cost that would be almost unimaginable."

As compelling as all of these concerns are, in some ways the most compelling interest that any college or university represents is the individual student—including those students whose financial circumstances or backgrounds would otherwise limit their opportunities to be educated up to their true potential and to live full and productive lives. Universities differ—yet again—from the profit-making sector in that *we care enormously about the nature of our clientele.* How much easier—and how much less rewarding—our lives would be if we were indifferent to the quality or the variety of the students whom we admit.

Roughly half of the quite remarkable number of Princeton undergraduates who have won Rhodes and Marshall scholarships in recent years have been students who were able to attend Princeton only because of the availability of financial aid. Most of that aid has been contributed by alumni and friends—in term gifts for this purpose, as endowment, or through Annual Giving dollars allocated to this priority area. But critically important funds also come from the federal government in the form of scholarships, loans, and work study, and at the graduate level in the form of fellowships, traineeships, and research grants.

One of the undergraduates who has been supported by these aid programs is this year's Pyne Prize winner, Kirsten Bibbins, an absolutely remarkable young woman from Maryland who is majoring in molecular biology while also earning a certificate in the Woodrow Wilson School. An outstanding resident adviser, she has been active in Student Pugwash, an organization concerned with ethical issues in science, the Aquinas Institute and the Catholic community on campus, the Student Volunteers Council, and a number of other groups. One faculty member said simply that she is "the single most effective student I have known in my fourteen years at Princeton." She is planning to spend next year in Africa working on problems of technology transfer in agriculture.

Another noteworthy beneficiary of financial aid in this year's senior class is Joel Barrera, who came to Princeton from a high school in Texas that was 80 percent Chicano and 20 percent black. Joel came to our campus without, as he put it, ever having really known an Anglo. Talk about culture shock! Joel has been an outstanding contributor to Princeton, and, like Kirsten Bibbins, has won one of the top prizes available to a senior—in Joel's case, the Daniel M. Sachs Class of 1960 Graduating Scholarship for study at Oxford (after which he expects to return to Texas to work with the poverty-stricken residents of the unincorporated towns along the border with Mexico). Dan Sachs was himself a person of many accomplishments at Princeton and afterward—a football star, a Rhodes Scholar, and a graduate of Harvard Law School—who died tragically of cancer at the age of twenty-eight. The Sachs Scholarship is given annually to that senior who most exemplifies Dan's qualities of character, intelligence, and commitment, and "in whose prospective career the scholarship would be deemed most likely to have consequences of value to the public." Joel Barrera meets that exacting standard very well, and his accomplishments to date and promise for the future are an eloquent testimonial to the role of Princeton in advancing goals that certainly ought to be high on the nation's agenda.

May I dispel one dangerous myth about the relationship between federal support of financial aid and tuition charges? No less highly placed a person than the Secretary of Education has opined that federal support of financial aid programs only makes it easier for colleges and universities to raise tuition. In the Princeton context, the actual cause and effect relationship is precisely the opposite. Scholarship and fellowship dollars are budget expenditures for us ($26 million, in all, in the current year), and any failure of federal programs to keep pace with rising costs only increases the upward pressure on tuition, which is of course a source of revenue that can be used, as required, to sustain Princeton's commitment to need-blind admissions.

I leave to others the cheerless task of explaining the origins of this confusion. Perhaps it is rooted in the view that it doesn't really matter, finally, who comes to places like Princeton as long as they pay their bills. In my view it matters enormously that Princeton, and other places like it, continue to admit students of the greatest promise without regard to their financial circumstances. This is important not only for the individuals whose aspirations are directly at risk, but for all of us who believe that enrolling students from diverse backgrounds is educationally invigorating and essential to the health of a democracy. This is, for me, a matter of high principle as well as an educational imperative.

Our "interests," then, as I perceive them, are both moral and intellectual; and it is my faith that, as Professor Gregory Vlastos once argued in a memorable Baccalaureate address, at their deepest levels they converge. It is a great privilege to be part of a University whose "special interest" is in uniting the pursuit of the highest standards of teaching and scholarship with an equally firm commitment to respect for the individual and to opportunity for all. My thanks to those of you gathered here today, and to so many others, for your staunch support—for giving life to this shared vision of Princeton and its role in our democracy.

The Role of the Federal Government in Higher Education

PAPER PREPARED FOR DISTRIBUTION
IN WASHINGTON
JANUARY 1982

Any time that a need to economize stimulates a far-reaching review of federal programs in an area such as higher education, there is both an opportunity and a danger. The opportunity is to consider freshly what overall set of objectives should guide policy; the danger is that budgetary pressures will lead to ad hoc decisions on particular programs that fail to reflect broad principles or long-term national interests. The purpose of this paper is to suggest an overall framework, and a set of basic principles, that can help us think systematically about specific proposals affecting higher education.

The appropriate role of the federal government in higher education, as I envision it, is a limited but extremely significant one. My starting point is a general belief that the federal government should act in a particular area if all three of the following conditions are met:

1. There is a clear *national interest* to be served;
2. There is a *need for federal involvement*, since state and private efforts, however welcome, will not meet the national need adequately without complementary federal actions;
3. There is a *workable mechanism* that can be used effectively by the federal government to accomplish its purposes.

There are four broad areas in which I believe the federal government has a proper—indeed indispensable—role. They are:

A. Support of basic research;
B. Support of graduate education and advanced training;
C. Encouragement of individual opportunity and diversity within the educational system; and
D. Maintenance of an environment that encourages private support of education and the decentralized exercise of responsibility for educational decisions.

Let me now discuss the reasons why each of these areas satisfies the three-pronged test stated above.

A. SUPPORT OF BASIC RESEARCH

1. *National Interest*

There is a strong and long-standing consensus on the national stake in promoting basic research of the highest quality, much of which is conducted in universities. On what is this consensus based?

• Such research is critically important for the nation's economy, and especially for the rate of economic growth over the long run. This nation's "comparative advantage" is in new ideas, technology, and our capacity to innovate. Thus, basic research in a wide variety of fields is essential to our ability to compete with countries such as Japan that are themselves investing heavily in research. Some observers believe that the momentum of research accomplishment, especially in high technology areas, has already started to swing away from the United States. Failure to make substantial investments in the discovery of new knowledge is a sure route to economic stagnation. And there are grounds for serious concern that current efforts to increase investments in capital goods and in industrial research and development will not be matched by equivalent efforts to strengthen the basic research that must provide their foundation.

• Basic research is also essential to further progress in medicine, in the health sciences generally, and in a great many other areas, such as transportation, where new ideas can generate far greater national benefits and may be far more productive in the long run than simple additions to expenditures in support of current technologies and practices.

• Basic research is vital to the defense capability of the nation. Any number of examples can be cited to show how weapons systems, new modes of communication, and other devices central to the defense effort have stemmed from fundamental advances in mathematics, astrophysics, and many other subjects—advances often achieved without any thought of specific applications.

• Basic research—including scholarship of the highest order in the humanities and social sciences as well as in science and engineering—is important if the United States is to continue to enjoy a position of international leadership in the world of ideas, and is to be regarded as a country concerned about human values as well as technical proficiency. At a practical level, the wise governing of the nation depends on an understanding of our own society, and our effective interactions with other countries depend importantly on the depth of our understanding of other cultures and societies. The deterioration in the nation's language capabilities and in research related to international affairs surely weakens our country's ability to play an effective role in world affairs.

2. Need for Federal Involvement

But why must the federal government act, as distinct from the states and private enterprises, if the compelling national interest in basic research is to be served? The answer lies in the nature of basic research and in the concept known to economists as "spill-over benefits." Basic research is an inherently less predictable enterprise than many others; there can never be a guarantee that valuable results will be obtained from any one undertaking; the benefits from successful efforts are likely to be realized fully only over long periods of time; and these benefits often turn out to be surprisingly different—and to have a far greater variety of applications—than could have been anticipated. Accordingly, those responsible for the discoveries cannot expect to capture for themselves all of the benefits that flow from basic research. In short, the benefits of a powerful new idea in, say, mathematics inevitably "spill over," as they should, to many individuals, companies, activities, and uses. Consequently, the nation at large has a far stronger economic incentive to invest heavily in basic research than does any individual enterprise or any individual state.

It should also be recognized that traditional attitudes toward competition in the United States, as reflected in our stringent antitrust laws, make it less likely here than in some other countries (Japan is again a useful example) that groups of companies will band together to fund basic research. Of course, as one moves along the scale from basic research toward more applied work, the economic incentive for business to do the investing increases, since results are more predictable, potential applications are clearer, and processes and products can be patented. For this reason, the economic case for governmental involvement is not nearly as strong at the "applied" end of the research spectrum as at the "basic" end.

3. Mechanisms

In considering the availability of mechanisms to serve the federal interest in the promotion of basic research, we can point to proven experience with two complementary modes of support:

(a) Sponsored research linking particular agencies of government with particular projects (through contracts and grants) has worked well since it was introduced on a large scale after World War II. This mode of support is flexible, in that it allows the government to reflect its greater interest in some fields than in others through the amounts of money provided. The "project" mode of support also allows sponsoring agencies to provide funding to those individuals and groups that it believes will do the best work, while simultaneously taking advantage of existing research facilities.

(b) Programs designed to provide "core" support for laboratories, libraries, and other shared research facilities in leading universities can complement the beneficial effects of project support. The recent deterioration of scientific laboratories and facilities, in particular, is widely seen as a major handicap to the basic research effort in the United States, and it is clear that institutional resources alone will be inadequate to remedy the situation. Nor can support awarded on an individual "project" basis be expected to meet this broader need to preserve the underlying foundations for both outstanding research and advanced training.

B. Graduate Education and Advanced Training

1. *National Interest*

Excellence in graduate education is related directly to research and scholarship of the highest quality. Research benefits immeasurably from the active involvement of the brightest young minds; strong graduate programs, in turn, are essential if we are to educate the leaders of the next generation in the sciences, in engineering, in international studies, and in all other fields. Thus, the long-term national interest in a vigorous research enterprise requires that we insure a steady flow of the most capable young people into advanced training.

The United States today has an enviable reputation all over the world for the quality of both its graduate education and its research (as illustrated, for example, by the large number of foreign students who come here for advanced training and by this country's remarkable success in winning Nobel prizes). But this reputation is both more recent and more fragile than many realize, having been built largely over the past forty years. A substantial federal investment has been critical in this process, and it is imperative that it be continued—not for the purpose of educating large numbers of graduate students in fields in which job prospects are bleak, but to assure that the country will continue to educate its most outstanding potential candidates.

It is important to the nation that we make full use of the talents of all of our citizens, including women and members of minority groups.

This is an essential objective at the graduate level because it is advanced training that qualifies individuals for academic positions and many other leadership roles.

2. Need for Federal Involvement

The case for the assumption of some measure of federal responsibility for graduate education (especially in certain fields) is derived in large part from the case for support of basic research. The two activities are mutually reinforcing and together provide major spill-over benefits for the country as a whole that extend beyond the rewards that will accrue to the individuals being educated or to particular states.

Financial assistance to graduate students, in the form of fellowships, research assistantships, and some relief from market rates of interest on loans, is essential if we are to attract strong candidates—especially in fields where the lure of alternative career paths is all too clear. In engineering, for example, where there are currently 2,000 vacant faculty positions, we are enrolling such a limited number of well-qualified candidates in graduate programs that we face a serious risk of failing to replenish our educational "seed corn." In other fields as well, the ablest candidates have many other attractive options. But it is essential to the future of basic research and the advancement of learning that graduate education be attractive to those who have the ability to work at the forefront of the search for knowledge in the years ahead—and who must also be counted on to educate their own successors in the following generation.

There is a special case to be made for federal guarantees of student loans. It is difficult for individual graduate students without substantial resources to obtain funds from private capital markets for the simple reason that they have no collateral to offer. Students seeking to invest in their own "human capital" face obstacles fundamentally different from those faced by borrowers seeking to finance acquisition of an asset that can be used to secure the loan (the house in the typical case of the home mortgage). Thus, there is a compelling reason for government loan guarantees here that does not apply in many other instances.

In a limited number of specialized fields, there is also a strong need for federal assistance that extends beyond support for outstanding graduate students. Universities alone simply do not have the resources needed to offer excellent graduate programs (or to do the necessary research) in fields that are as inordinately expensive as, for example, plasma physics and Chinese studies. Yet outstanding work in such fields is vital to the national interest.

3. *Mechanisms*

Here again effective mechanisms for federal participation already exist. Perhaps the most successful has been the portable, merit-based fellowship program of the National Science Foundation. This highly regarded program has concentrated support on the most promising candidates, has given them recognition as well as financial support, and thus has played a major role in sustaining the flow of outstanding future scientists into mathematics, physics, and many other fields. The ability of students to use these fellowships at whichever university seems to them best (hence the designation "portable") is an extremely important feature, in that it provides a market test of graduate programs, as their quality is perceived by the strongest candidates. Also, fellowship programs of this kind can be kept deliberately small, thereby encouraging the ablest students without simultaneously stimulating overly large graduate populations in fields where the national interest may not require large numbers.

Sponsored research has also provided valuable support for graduate students, who are trained as they contribute to the research projects. Here again quality (this time as determined by panels of leading scholars) has dictated the allocation of funds. The "training grants" of the NIH, which combine some of the features of fellowship programs with some of the features of sponsored research grants, have been especially useful in enabling excellent students to pursue advanced training in the health sciences.

As noted above, the guaranteed loan program has also proved to be an effective means for enabling graduate students to invest in themselves, under terms that they can afford and with assured access to capital. At the same time, I believe that the definition and administration of this program can be improved.

Finally, there are also existing mechanisms that provide the more general support for graduate education required in special fields that are both extremely costly and essential to the national interest. Project support (defined broadly) and training grants can continue to serve this purpose in the sciences. A certain amount of general support has been critically important to the development of international and regional studies in universities and should be maintained on a competitive basis through the Language and Area Centers Program.

C. Individual Opportunity and Diversity

1. *National Interest*

One of our most significant national characteristics is our commitment to the philosophy of advancement by merit and to the proposition that in this country individuals should be able to move up the ladder of accomplishment as far as their energies and abilities will take them. Educational opportunity is a key to this philosophy. By pursuing this commitment, we have taken advantage of talent that otherwise would have been lost to the nation and have given substance to this aspect of what is often referred to as "the American Dream." It cannot be claimed that we have served this high purpose perfectly. Plainly, barriers of many kinds continue to limit the upward mobility of many deserving young people. But we have done better in this respect than most countries, and now is no time to abandon an objective that seems so right in principle as well as so very important in its practical effects.

"Diversity" within our educational institutions is a related but different concept that has become something of a catchword. But we should not lose sight of what it means and why we should care about it. As Justice Powell observed in the Bakke decision, the quality of the educational process is enhanced when individuals from different backgrounds, with different perspectives, learn together—and from each other. This would be important in any society, but it is especially important in the United States, where we pride ourselves on our pluralism. There is surely a strong national interest in avoiding the resegregation of many educational institutions on the basis of economic status, race, or geography. The social fabric would be harmed greatly if this were to occur, and the quality of education would be diminished for all.

2. *Need for Federal Involvement*

Educational opportunities should be available nationally, not just within the students' home states, and that is an important reason for federal involvement in this broad area. The educational purposes of the country as a whole will be served most effectively if students are able to attend the colleges and universities best suited to their individual needs, and if there is a considerable degree of mobility across state lines.

In my judgment, students (and their families) should be expected to invest heavily in the pursuit of their own educational goals. That is why many of us insist so strongly on "self-help" contributions and on scholarship aid provided only on the basis of remaining need. In addition, both state and private sources should be expected to provide scholarship assistance, as they have historically. But with tuition and other charges now over $10,000 per year at a number of private colleges and universities and over $7,000 for out-of-state students at some state universities, these sources alone will not promote adequately the twin national goals of individual opportunity based on merit and diversity within the educational system. Accordingly, there is an important supplementary role—not a dominant one but more a supporting role—for the federal government in this area.

3. *Mechanisms*

While these large purposes are relevant to both graduate and undergraduate education (albeit in different degrees), the comments that follow apply mainly to undergraduate financial aid. (Comments on graduate student support were made earlier.) It is fortunate, in my view, that a basic structure of federal support for undergraduate students already exists. It is composed of a carefully crafted mix of programs involving: (a) direct grants to students based primarily on family circumstances; (b) campus-based programs including work-study that allow additional support to go to needy students in relation to their educational costs; and (c) guaranteed loan programs. For reasons mentioned already, and for reasons related to the desirability of maintaining strong private as well as public institutions (discussed below), it is important to preserve this basic structure. It has been built up carefully over time to offer students from all economic backgrounds some real choice—including the option of attending more expensive, and often more selective, institutions if they can meet the academic standards *and* are willing to make the personal financial sacrifices required.

This is not the place for detailed comments on specific elements of present federal financial aid programs. Let me add only these observations. First, I agree that the administration—and even the construction—of parts of these programs had become too lax and, consequently, too expensive. It was understandable that reductions in support and redefinitions of programs should occur, especially at a time of such overall budgetary stringency. Even now, it may be possible to achieve some additional economies—in particular by basing student aid even more fully on demonstrated need and by requiring larger self-help contributions. But it would be a serious error, in my judgment, if in the pursuit of economies, we were to lose sight of our broad national purposes. I would hate to see us reach a point where we would say, in effect, to those of ability but limited means: "Yes, you can go on to college, but be sure it is not too expensive a place; the more costly educational opportunities are reserved largely for those whose families are affluent enough to pay the bills." That message would be clear—and clearly read—as a significant retreat from major national goals. The long-term effects on education in America, and on our society, would be damaging in the extreme.

D. Maintenance of an Environment that Encourages Private Support of Education and the Decentralized Exercise of Responsibility for Educational Decisions

1. *National Interest*

Beyond the provision of direct governmental support for the purposes listed above, the national interest also requires the maintenance of a setting, a set of incentives, and a philosophical orientation conducive to private initiative and decentralized processes of decision-making. This entails:

• Encouraging private contributions (from individuals, corporations, and foundations) for the educational purposes served by all colleges and universities, public and private;

• Sustaining a healthy variety of educational institutions by promoting the continuing vitality of strong privately administered colleges and universities as well as those responsible to state authorities; and

• Insuring that those regulatory actions deemed necessary are carried out as non-intrusively as possible.

2. *Need for Federal Involvement*

Each of these objectives is affected by actions taken—and not taken—by the federal government. It is the federal government's taxing power that can create (and diminish) the most powerful economic incentives for charitable contributions by the private sector; federal programs inevitably affect the sometimes delicate balance between public and private institutions; and federal regulations affect directly the degree of autonomy enjoyed by individual colleges and universities in both the public and private sectors. More generally, it is only the federal government that has a sufficiently broad perspective to give force to a national philosophy that encourages a variety of educational approaches, that respects individual choice, and that therefore seeks to avoid imposing any one model of education on our society.

3. Mechanisms

Tax incentives for private philanthropy have served the national interest in higher education well for many decades, and it is all the more important that they be preserved—indeed strengthened—at a time when more of the burden of support for higher education is being shifted to the private sector. Of immediate concern are the likely side effects on private giving caused by the reductions in income tax rates and other provisions of the Economic Recovery Tax Act of 1981.

To achieve the second objective—sustaining strong private as well as public institutions—it is essential that the government not only preserve tax incentives for charitable giving but also look carefully at the implications for the various sectors of higher education of modifications in key programs. An important case in point is the array of student aid programs now being reviewed once more. The Supplemental Educational Opportunity Grant Program, for example, was designed specifically to allow talented students some real choice among colleges by making up *part* of the differential in costs entailed in attending a more expensive institution. Recent proposals for ending it entirely would have particularly severe effects on private institutions. Proposed reductions in other student aid programs would also have disproportionately severe consequences for the private sector of higher education. It would be ironic—and tragic, in my view—if during a time when there is a growing commitment to the philosophy of private initiative, we were to adopt measures that had the de facto effect of eroding the capacity of private institutions to serve essential public purposes.

Finally, with regard to regulation, most of us would agree that the federal government has both a right and an obligation to insist on accountability for public monies, to safeguard the health of citizens, to guard against discrimination, and to encourage affirmative action. But the hope of many in higher education is that regulations will not be insensitive to the variety of circumstances within the educational sector or so detailed that they distract institutions from their main purposes.

*   *   *   *   *

The preceding discussion has sought to define the role of the federal government in terms of those responsibilities that I believe represent an irreducible minimum. While there are, of course, other programs and services that the government might usefully provide—some existing now and some new initiatives that might be considered—it is equally clear that in the present economic climate we must be prepared to make hard choices. It is in that spirit that this paper has been written. And it has been written, too, with the conviction that, even in the present budgetary environment, the federal government must not neglect objectives that are absolutely essential to the long-term well-being of our society.

University Education in the People's Republic of China: A Visitor's Impressions

SPEECH BEFORE THE
PRINCETON CLUB OF NEW YORK
JANUARY 1975

I am very pleased to have this opportunity to discuss with you some of my impressions of university education in the People's Republic of China—impressions formed during a fascinating and always instructive, if at times frustrating, twenty-one-day visit in November of 1974. I went to China as a member of a delegation of eleven American college and university presidents, accompanied by an able historian of China and by an administrative officer with a considerable knowledge of the language and the people. Our visit was under the auspices of the National Committee on U.S.–China Relations, our leader was Roger Heyns, President of the American Council on Education, and we were meant in some terribly imprecise way to represent the variety of four-year colleges and universities in America today.

Before leaving on this trip I received three pieces of advice from a friend who had been part of an earlier delegation: savor the gracious hospitality, listen carefully, and always separate the myth from the reality. This was all excellent advice, but it proved far easier to put into practice the first two injunctions than the last. Certainly we were received not just courteously but warmly wherever we went; certainly we tried to listen carefully and to learn as much as we could from the opportunities for informal conversation as well as from the many official visits and discussions; but "reality" is always an elusive concept, and I would mislead you as well as myself if I were to claim to have returned with more than impressions, hunches, and conjectures about some of the most important questions.

The processes of university education, in all their subtlety, are difficult to comprehend in any society. But firm conclusions about university education in China today are especially difficult, in part because of the unsettled nature of the universities (more on this shortly), in part because of the intimate relationship between university education and the rest of that society (about which we also know far less than we should), and of course because of the all too real problems of communicating through interpreters and with people who start with very different outlooks on the world and very different assumptions. For these reasons, among others, I have no reason to believe that the various members of our delegation would describe the "reality" of any given meeting, never mind our stay as a whole, in the same terms. You should also know that I came to this visit as a person with no prior scholarly or personal experience of China. Therefore, I am simply not in a position to make the kinds of comparative judgments that might have been possible had I been there before or had I been more familiar with the history and the culture of China. So, you are all warned!

As a final preliminary, perhaps I should say a word about the places we visited. In terms of geography, we started out in Beijing, went from there to Shenyang and Anshan in the northeast, then to Nanjing, Suzhou, Shanghai, and Canton. We talked with people at six universities, the Institute of Physics, the Academy of Sciences, a leading observatory, a middle school, several primary schools, a children's Cultural Palace, a May 7 Cadre School, a number of factories, two factory-run universities, two communes, and a major hospital. In addition, we spent time with government and party officials including Vice-Premier Deng Xiaoping (recently also named deputy chairman of the Party), leading persons in the provinces and cities, and of course our host from the Foreign Affairs Bureau of the Science and Education Group under the State Council, and the interpreters who were with us throughout our stay.

In my remarks today I am going to try to avoid the temptation to relate anecdotes about everything from acupuncture to crowd behavior and forms of political dissent and concentrate instead on the one large subject of higher education. Wherever possible I shall suggest, or at least imply, comparisons between China and the United States. Time is too short, however, to do more than hint at many things that could be, and should be, discussed at considerable length.

THE PURPOSES OF HIGHER EDUCATION

Any system of higher education can be understood only in terms of the purposes it is intended to serve within the society of which it is a part. That simple—indeed obvious—proposition is driven home with special force when one visits the People's Republic of China, for many features of that country's system of higher education that differ drastically from what is familiar to us are related directly to fundamental differences in purposes and in values.

"Education must serve the proletarian revolution; we must train successors for revolutionary leadership." Phrases of that kind appear over and over in my notebooks as statements of the fundamental purpose to be served by higher education in China. To be sure, the pursuit of scientific discovery is also mentioned explicitly as one of the three great "struggles" (the others being the class struggle and the struggle for production), and Zhou Peiyuan, a leading physicist in Peking, made quite a point of emphasizing to us this strong commitment to science by Chairman Mao and the party.

Still, I think it fair to say that even this commitment seemed in general not just derived from, but clearly subordinate to, clear ideological objectives. To illustrate, a specific objective of the Cultural Revolution, applied to education, has been to prevent the intellectuals from becoming an elite group, cut off from, inclined to look down on, the mass of people. The slogan "learn from the workers, peasants, and soldiers—and serve them" is certainly meant to apply to people in universities; and students and teachers of science are by no means exempt from the specific measures (which I shall describe in a moment) that are intended to give substance to this injunction.

Objectives have a way of colliding, in China as in this country, and while there may well be instances in which scientific needs of one kind or other (e.g., related to work in atomic physics) may be treated as preeminent, the overall tendency is to resolve conflicts in favor of the ideological rather than the scientific or strictly educational imperative.

This dominance of political purpose, as defined and spelled out in some detail by the party, is one clear difference between the Chinese system of higher education and ours. There has been a good deal of discussion in this country about the possible politicization of our universities (especially when Vietnam was so much on our minds and our consciences), and I among others have argued strongly against allowing our universities to become instruments of any political party or viewpoint. But it was only as a result of my visit to China that I came to see what real politicization of higher education could mean—how it could not only affect but nearly determine every aspect of university life from admissions to course content, teaching methods, recruitment of faculty, research, and placement of students.

One other major, and closely related, difference between our respective statements of purpose for higher education has to do with the role of the individual vis-à-vis the state. Conspicuous by its absence in China was any reference to developing the capabilities of the individual, as an end in itself—an end to which we attach, needless to say, great importance.

THE SCALE OF THE EFFORT: ENROLLMENT

If it is impossible, in the nature of the case, to quantify differences in purpose, it is possible to quantify differences in the scale of the effort in higher education being made in the two societies, as approximated by differences in enrollment. The numbers—and I am going to give them to you for primary and secondary education as well as for higher education—are simply staggering.

In the People's Republic of China now there are about 130 million people in primary schools and about 34 million in what they call middle schools, what we would regard as a combination of junior and senior high school. (Since the Cultural Revolution the norm for each of these levels is a five-year course, ages 7 to 12 in primary school and 12 to 17 in middle school.) In universities, on the other hand, the total regular enrollment was said to be 400,000—in a country with a total population of about 800 million.

That is a dramatically different educational pyramid from anything we know. To give you a rough point of comparison, the 400,000 number is roughly equivalent to college and university enrollment in the State of Ohio. The overall numbers for the United States are in the order of 37 million primary school students, about 18 million high school students, and a little over 8 million in colleges and universities. (Our periods of study, especially in primary and secondary schools, are of different lengths, so these figures should be adjusted for this. On a "China scale," the U.S. figures might be something like 29 million and 26 million for primary and secondary schools.)

These figures suggest—and they are consistent with a number of other impressions—that university education is seen to be much less important in China than it is here. This is true, I believe, both for some very good reasons related to differences in levels of real income and stages of economic development, and for some reasons that may not be so good, related to the ideological imperatives I mentioned earlier.

Higher education was affected very dramatically by the Cultural Revolution in the 1966–69 period when almost all of the universities were closed in an effort to curb elitist tendencies and reform their orientation. They have since reopened, but they are still troubled institutions. They are still in the midst of what was described to us as "the continuing revolution in education." An answer one receives over and over, and in response to a great many different kinds of queries, is: "that is still under study," or "we are still in an experimental stage."

While I can't give you enrollment statistics for the whole of China pre- and post-Cultural Revolution, I do have figures for some individual institutions that I think are revealing. At Fudan University in Shanghai, for example, enrollment now is 2,800 compared with 6,000 prior to the Cultural Revolution. At Peking University there are about 5,000 students now compared with 10,000 prior to the Cultural Revolution. The comparable numbers at Liaoning University in the northeast are 1,800 now as compared with 4,000 before; and at Sun Yatsen University in Canton, 2,600 now as compared with 4,000 earlier. While in interpreting all such figures allowance needs to be made for the shortening of the period of study since the Cultural Revolution (from five or six years to three or three and a half or four years in most cases), it seems clear that at the universities we visited only about half as many regular students are enrolled now as were enrolled in the mid-1960s.

Enrollment this year was said to be larger than enrollment last year, and further increases are expected. When we asked if persons responsible for planning higher education in China thought that universities were turning out enough graduates now, the answer given was an unequivocal "no." However, in response to a direct question about plans for increasing enrollment, we were told that decisions have not yet been made, the question is still under study, and so on. It seemed to me at the time at least slightly ironic that in this unplanned society of ours I could make a better estimate of enrollment five years from now than apparently was possible in their planned society—but then this is no doubt more of a commentary on the unsettled state of higher education in China than anything else.

One last comment on enrollment. So far as we could learn, all, or very nearly all, of the 400,000 students in the universities of China are enrolled in *undergraduate* programs of study. For all intents and purposes there are at present no regular programs of graduate study. And this lack seems to me to have implications that are potentially exceedingly serious for the future of higher education in China—indeed for the future of the society as a whole.

SELECTION OF STUDENTS

Now, however, I want to talk a bit about undergraduate education, beginning with the selection of students. One of the important changes made as a consequence of the Cultural Revolution is that students no longer go directly from secondary school to the university. All students completing secondary school are assigned to a task somewhere in the society and are required to spend at least two years gaining practical experience and relating directly to the masses of the people. The numbers I quoted to you earlier indicated that only a tiny minority of secondary school graduates can in fact expect to continue their education in any event. (Remember that there are at present 34 million secondary school students and 400,000 university students. Even allowing for differences in periods of study and some further increases in university enrollment, the chances of a secondary school student going on to a university would seem to be no more than about one in forty or fifty.)

How is this very select group chosen? At Peking University, where we had the longest discussion of admission, we were told that there is a four-stage process: (1) the prospective student indicates his or her desire to apply at the commune, factory, or wherever the person works; (2) the suitability of the individual is discussed among the workers or peasants in the locality and recommendations are passed up, via the local Revolutionary Committee, to the higher (usually district) level; (3) a further screening takes place at this higher level and some of the applications are approved; (4) the applications are reapproved by the university to which the application has been sent. In point of fact, there also appear to be some opportunities for discussion among representatives of the university and the officials at the local levels as the process develops.

We were told that preference is given to applicants from worker and peasant backgrounds, and that Chairman Mao has made it plain that the universities are not to be filled up with the children of officials, army leaders, teachers, or other elites. Special efforts seem to have been made to enroll larger numbers of women students and students from ''minority'' or ''nationality'' cultures. The criteria for selection stress possession of the right revolutionary spirit and outlook, as well as good performance in the current job, good health, and some aptitude for university work. We were informed that examinations are not used any longer because now those associated with the applicants know them so well that this kind of check would be redundant.

The more we talked with students and with persons in the universities, the more convinced some of us became that this approach to admission (which differs so significantly from what we know in terms of both process and criteria) probably does result in the selection of individuals who will be effective political leaders in that society—"successors to the revolutionary leadership," in their terms. It is, after all, the ability to function well in the society, to work effectively with workers and peasants, and to conform to party directives that is so important in the selection process.

At the same time, many of us were—and are—highly skeptical that this approach necessarily leads to the recruitment of individuals with exceptional minds, or with strong creative powers. I kept posing what I called the "Einstein question": will this approach pick up the relatively few Einsteins in any society, who may be persons with unusual temperaments, who may not be very good workers or "team players," and who may have no interest whatsoever in criticizing Confucius? The answer I usually received amounted to a denial that there are any such people or to a simple assertion that the Einsteins would somehow be chosen by their process. One or two university teachers, in private conversations, acknowledged the existence of the problem but said candidly that a decision had been made to make some sacrifices along this line in the pursuit of other goals.

We were also told by some teachers, again in quiet conversations, that the combination of the new selection process and the requirement that secondary school students spend at least two years out of school before continuing their education meant that students in general were not as well prepared for university work now as before (particularly in the sciences). At the same time, we were told that students work much harder now, an assertion that also seemed credible.

CURRICULUM AND COURSE CONTENT

Curriculum and course content were affected dramatically by the Cultural Revolution, and the effects certainly were evident in our visits to universities. The basic disciplines covered in a "comprehensive university" remain much the same: for example, Chinese literature, foreign languages, philosophy, history, economics, mathematics, physics, chemistry, biology, and so on. (Psychology and sociology are notable for their absence.) All students continue to be admitted, as in many European universities, to study one discipline, not to study the liberal arts, broadly defined.

However, as I have already noted, the period of undergraduate study has been shortened substantially—from about five or six years to three or three and a half or four years depending on the subject studied and the university. In addition, all students are now required to spend a significant portion of the school year working on a commune or in a factory. Thus, the time available to learn course content has been reduced greatly. When I asked about the effects of this great compression of the period of formal study in a discipline like mathematics, I was told that the number of courses taken has dropped from 23–26 to 13–14. A good deal of work at more advanced levels has plainly been sacrificed.

A second effect of the Cultural Revolution has been to unsettle the course content in many fields. We were told that a great deal of the time of teachers continues to be devoted to reforming textbooks, developing new teaching materials, and so on. In the case of some topics (genetics is apparently an example), no decision has yet been made as to how they are to be taught in accord with current orthodoxy, and so at present they simply are not taught, or are not taught in any depth. In the case of other subjects (ancient history, for example), the appropriate course content is clear (criticize Confucius and study and popularize the writings of the so-called legalists), and there are no such problems. The extent of political domination of course content is at first shocking to someone from our country, but it is entirely consistent with the current Chinese sense of the purposes of higher education.

Another striking characteristic of Chinese education today is how China-centered it is. History students seem to spend a good 80 percent of their time studying Chinese history, and even the teaching of English makes use of materials translated into English that reflect Chinese thought or are about particular international or domestic questions of interest to China. Several members of our group noted that when we teach Chinese we generally try to use materials written by Chinese, or at least about China. For their part, however, they seem to make very little effort to teach their students anything about other cultures. This powerful tendency to look inward—and the consequent lack of knowledge about and interest in other places—was also reflected in the fact that very few of the Chinese with whom we came in contact asked questions about the United States or the rest of the world. In this important sense, as in others, the education offered in Chinese universities today is very narrow and focused quite directly on current concerns.

A word about the treatment of minority (or "nationality") cultures seems appropriate here. At all levels of education one sees evidence of what at first glance seems a strong interest in minority cultures. For instance, music and dance programs consist to a very large degree of performances related to minorities—in, say, Korean or Tibetan costumes. What seemed significant to many of us, however, was that the *content* of these numbers was almost always contemporary and consistent with current political themes. A Korean dance, for example, showed peasant women collecting manure and shoveling it into a great pot in the center of the stage from which a sheaf of wheat arose at the end of the number! I remember too a song "from Tibet" which reported the warm feelings of the Tibetan people for Chairman Mao. In short, here again what we saw was very China-centered, and intended not to celebrate other cultures but to stress the common commitment of all the Chinese peoples to the present objectives of the state. The contrast with some of our efforts to enable minority groups of various kinds to retain their own identities is obvious.

A final note on one thing we did not see at any university we visited and that we had expected to see: I refer to academic work in economic planning. Given the nature of the Chinese economy, with its emphasis on planning, it is surprising to say the least that so little instruction in this field seems to be taking place. It may be that the reaction during the Cultural Revolution against technocrats of all kinds is still having inhibiting effects here, but that is only speculation. In any event, as a sometime economist with a quantitative bent I was disappointed at being unable to see at first hand how the Chinese treat this subject matter, and I was more than a little puzzled by the apparent lack of attention to planning in a thoroughly planned economy.

TEACHING METHODS

Teaching methods, as well as course content, were reformed as a result of the Cultural Revolution. Today there is, first, a great emphasis on "teaching in the open doorway" and maintaining contact with the masses of the people. This goal is served in several ways: by sending students out to the factories, communes, and neighborhoods to join in the campaign to criticize Confucius and Lin Piao; by inviting workers, soldiers, and others to come to the universities to participate with teachers and regularly enrolled students in "short courses," usually of a political nature; by inviting some workers to come to the universities to teach; and by having the universities themselves operate some small factories and farms.

In the regular courses taught in the universities special efforts are made to combine theory and practice. Indeed, that refrain is heard over and over. In mathematics, it often takes the form of emphasizing applications to computers; in architecture, applications to achieving certain spatial standards in housing. Nor are subjects like ancient literature immune from this injunction. Annotating the texts of classical writers to make political points thought to be important now is cited as a clear example of combining theory and practice. A leading person at one university told us that before the Cultural Revolution teachers were able to "grow rice only on the blackboard." Now all is said to be changed.

At present there is also a great deal of stress placed on reasoning, self-study, discussion, and analysis—all meant to represent the rejection of the old "rote learning." Students are encouraged to correct each other—and their teachers—and use is made of open-book examinations, assignment of papers, and so on.

One recurring question about teaching methods in use now is whether they encourage real creativity. Students are encouraged to find for themselves new ways of explicating, furthering, and applying official doctrine, but all of this must take place within narrowly prescribed limits. Students are certainly not encouraged to ask fundamental questions about the rightness of a policy, or to challenge commonly held perceptions, and in the arts and in literature the price of conformity seems to be especially high. A student from the United States whom we met in Beijing spoke eloquently about the dampening effects on creative writing of the insistence that all characters be portrayed as either totally good or totally bad rather than as the all-too-human mixture of these elements that is in fact characteristic of all of us.

Dormitory Life and Placement

Let me conclude this discussion of undergraduate education with just a word about two very different subjects: dormitory life and job placement.

The next Princeton student who complains about either cramped quarters in the dormitories or an incompatible roommate is going to have some new data with which to contend. In the Chinese universities we visited the norm seemed to be six to eight students sharing one room, with bunk beds lining *both* sides of the room. Students are assigned rooms and roommates, and when I asked what happens when conflicts develop I was told that the revolutionary consciousness of the students is raised by discussion and the problem resolved in that way. In some respects, at least, it is plainly easier—if perhaps less invigorating—to administer a Chinese than an American university!

As far as placement is concerned, students about to graduate are able to express an interest in one career line or another. If what the student wants to do coincides with the needs of the state, fine; if not, it is the attitude of the student that is adjusted, not the needs of the state. When asked what they want to do when they finish school, students invariably respond: "to serve the people," or "do whatever the state needs to have done."

RESEARCH

Research in China is carried out partly in universities, partly in institutes affiliated with the National Academy of Sciences, and partly in government departments, in factories, and in communes. Just as the combination of theory and practice is stressed in teaching, so in research it is applications that receive great emphasis. We saw very little "basic research" being done, as we would use that term, and much of what is called research in China would be called "development" here.

The conscious downplaying of abstraction and of theory was evident many times. In Shanghai, for example, a mathematician explained to me that while prior to the Cultural Revolution he had done abstract analyses he now saw how foolish that had been. His most recent research project, he went on to explain, had been the development of a new train schedule between Nanjing and Shanghai. At the Institute of Physics in Beijing, the theoretical unit that existed prior to the Cultural Revolution has now been dispersed, in the main, among the applied research groups. A small theoretical group remains, and even does some work on general relativity, but our Chinese friends seemed somewhat annoyed when I pressed a question concerning the justification for studying general relativity in the face of their stress on combining theory and practice.

Political orthodoxy is of course reflected directly in the content of scholarship and research in sensitive fields like philosophy, history, economics, and now ancient literature. In the sciences and engineering, on the other hand, political goals determine the *direction* of research (which projects are undertaken), but the research itself, on electric power, for example, is in its nature less subject to political influence. Individual scientists can and do prepare their own projects, but all such proposals must be approved by higher authorities, who may instead indicate a different project that they want undertaken. In short, as one would expect, research in China is carried out on a far more closely directed basis than in this country.

I am not qualified to assess the level of the scientific research which we saw, but I can note that the equipment was very primitive, that a number of the leaders of research projects appear to have had some of their education abroad, and that there is little indication that many new lines of research are being started now.

Needless to say, the virtual ending of graduate education at the time of the Cultural Revolution has had a profound effect. One lab we saw in which numerous graduate students used to work is operating at a greatly reduced level now. And at the Institute of Physics we were told directly and unequivocally that the lack of graduate students finishing advanced programs meant that the Institute had received no "fresh blood" for some years and that this was obviously a serious matter. Certainly it seemed so to us.

FACULTY

Our group spent many hours talking with faculty members in Chinese universities. A first impression is that there are a great many of them, relative to the number of students. Indeed, it was only after we had heard the figures for student-teacher ratios several times that we could really believe them. At Peking University, for example, there are about 2,600 teachers for 5,000 students; at Nanjing, 1,300 teachers for 3,380 students; at Fudan University in Shanghai, 1,900 teachers for 2,800 students; and at Sun Yatsen University in Canton, 1,085 teachers for 2,600 students. In short, student-teacher ratios seemed to range from about 1.5:1 to just under 3:1.

When we expressed amazement at the generosity of these ratios we were told that all of the teachers were very busy indeed doing a variety of things in addition to classroom teaching. Teachers go out to the countryside or to factories for periods of time and, more important, they are still devoting a great deal of effort to reforming the curriculum and course content as well as to doing applied research. It was hard for us, as outsiders, to judge how hard people were in fact working, or what they were accomplishing, but then that is not a problem peculiar to China.

We asked many questions about the recruitment of new teachers, and a fairly clear pattern of response emerged. Each university seemed to recruit heavily from among its own graduates. We also asked about criteria, and the answer we were given at Liaoning University was that knowledge of Marxism/Leninism and the ability to follow the right line counted most. Personal qualities of various kinds and knowledge of the subject matter were also said to be important.

Once a person has been assigned to a teaching position in a Chinese university the presumption is that the individual will make his or her career there. There is nothing like the turnover, and the high degree of competition for tenure positions, that characterize many of the American colleges and universities with the highest standards. In fact, as far as we could determine, almost no one is ever terminated. People who are not performing as well as they might are helped by their students and colleagues to do better, but they are rarely, if ever, asked to go elsewhere or to do something else. A policy of this kind (which is, I should add, characteristic of China generally, not just of the universities) puts an enormous burden on the wisdom of the initial placement process, and one could not help but wonder if the placement process was really that reliable, especially now that there is no experience in graduate school to take into account.

The lack of graduate education, coupled with the compression of the undergraduate program of study, must have a pronounced effect on the preparation which new teachers bring with them to the universities. We spent much time and effort trying to find out to what extent new teachers really undergo an informal kind of graduate training in their first years as teachers. We were not very successful, however, in eliciting precise answers. Plainly some informal instruction does occur, with senior personnel helping the new teachers, and there may be somewhat more of an apprentice relationship in Chinese universities than in our universities. But I am not sure of this, and I am skeptical that this kind of on-the-job training, to the extent that it occurs, is any real substitute for the lack of graduate education.

The advancement and compensation of teachers in Chinese universities proved to be an enormously sensitive subject—as indeed did the larger subject of salary differentials in factories and throughout the society. In point of fact, salary differentials at present are substantial, with new teachers earning perhaps 60 yuan per month and some persons with the title of Professor earning around 300 yuan per month. These are appreciably larger differentials than are common in the United States, especially when the lack of a progressive income tax in China is taken into account.

This somewhat ironical situation seems to be a result of the general policy in China of never firing anyone, never taking away a title once it has been bestowed, and never reducing an individual's salary. Both the title of Professor and the salary associated with the title pre-date the Cultural Revolution, and no one has been made a professor or an associate professor since then.

We asked repeatedly what future system of faculty ranks they expected to use, and we were told time and again that this question is under study, that no decision has been made yet, and that a central determination at higher levels is awaited. At Sun Yatsen University, in particular, there seemed to be almost an obsession with this subject, judging from the length of the response to our question. The general impression one gets is that from now on everyone will be called "teacher," that formal ranks will not be used. I presume, however, that they see a need for some structure; otherwise it is hard to see why they seem to be having so much trouble resolving the question.

It is unnecessary for me to say much about the most striking difference between Chinese and American faculties because its existence stems so directly and inexorably from fundamental differences in the societies. I refer of course to freedom of expression and dissent. Teachers in Chinese universities are very careful not to deviate from the official line on any question, and there was more than one occasion during our visit when it seemed clear that teachers were responding to a question with ideological overtones more for the benefit of other Chinese in the room—showing the correctness of their own thinking—than for our benefit. This was always depressing and even at times a bit chilling. Differences of opinion can be expressed only within the most carefully prescribed boundaries.

One final comment on teachers in China. When we asked on several occasions what was the most difficult problem faced by the leadership of the universities, we were told: "remolding the ideology of the teachers." Teachers, like other members of the society, have been sent to May 7 Cadre Schools for ideological remolding, and it is obvious that great efforts have been made within the universities as well. Indeed, we sensed from time to time what seemed to be a real tension between older teachers (some of whom have been abroad and may harbor, or be thought to harbor, revisionist views) and younger people who have grown up under Chairman Mao's tutelage and who see themselves as guardians of the revolution. Perhaps for this reason the universities often seemed tenser, less relaxed, places than other institutions we visited. And perhaps this speaks more eloquently than we realized at the time of our visit to the long-term cost in any society of trying to discourage people in universities from thinking for themselves.

ADMINISTRATION AND FINANCE

As university presidents, our group had at least a mild curiosity about how the Chinese universities were run. "Mild" is, I think, the right adjective, and it is an interesting—and perhaps even favorable—commentary on us that this set of questions ranked well down on the list of topics of greatest interest to us.

In brief, the situation is as follows. The Chinese universities, like all other institutions and organizations in the society, are run by "revolutionary committees." The size and composition of these committees vary from place to place, but invariably the composition is far broader than just representatives from the administration and the teaching staff of the university. Workers and government or party cadres are always involved, and often members of the People's Liberation Army as well.

Students are frequently on the revolutionary committee too, but we gained the distinct impression that they are much less important now than they were in the immediate aftermath of the Cultural Revolution. We learned that as a general rule students are not now on the "standing" or "executive" committee of the revolutionary committee; moreover, we were told by several people at different universities that experience had shown that the ability of students to contribute effectively to the governing of universities was limited by their relatively short stay at the university, their lack of knowledge of many things, and their need to concentrate on their studies. When we heard this, certain members of our group exchanged what looked to be knowing glances!

Leadership seemed to be a collective responsibility, although it was often hard for us to determine who constituted the key group. We did notice, however, that the person who seemed to be in charge was often an individual whose background was not mainly academic. Persons who had been active in government positions of one kind or another often seemed to be the spokesmen for the local university groups. More generally, the obvious role of the party in determining the leadership of the universities was acknowledged explicitly and readily. Interestingly, while the Cultural Revolution certainly shook the leadership structure of the universities, a number of the people who seem to be in influential positions now also had been influential before the Cultural Revolution. I have no way of measuring the success of pre-Cultural Revolution leaders in holding on to, or regaining, important positions, but I would guess it has been quite high.

Leaders of the universities naturally feel the need to be true to the official line even more strongly, if anything, than do teachers. Not only the same ideas, but the same phrases, were repeated over and over in the briefings given us at the various universities. By the end of the trip several members of our group, I felt confident, could have given the briefings without missing a syllable.

We also noticed another, rather more frightening, phenomenon. At one university, in particular, we were struck by the fact that the same person was very open and candid with some of us in one setting and almost unbelievably evasive and obscurantist in another setting. One of our group who had been present at both of these discussions had trouble believing that it was in fact the same person. There were many more Chinese, including a number of students, present at the "evasive" session, and it was hard to avoid the conclusion that it was their presence that had made the difference.

Now, just one word on finance. When we asked our Chinese counterparts to name their most serious problems, finance was never mentioned, to my knowledge. It is hard to imagine a much more striking contrast with the United States, and one of the most pleasurable aspects of the visit for our delegation was the opportunity to spend twenty-one days without being reminded of the terrific financial problems all our colleges and universities face here in the United States. This relative "freedom" from financial anxiety that our Chinese friends enjoy has been acquired, needless to say, at a cost in terms of other freedoms that is incalculable.

Concluding Observations and Questions for the Future

I want now, in concluding these remarks, to raise some questions for the future, even if I can't answer them. But first let me offer two general observations about higher education in China.

1. As I thought more and more about what our hosts kept referring to as "the continuing revolution in education" in China, I came to feel that there were really two revolutions taking place simultaneously, and that they were very different in character. One is a revolution directed at what most if not all of us would agree are fundamental problems for education in any society: how to teach people to analyze, to avoid rote learning, and to relate what they are learning in the classroom to the world around them. In an effort to cope with these problems the Chinese have moved toward more emphasis on discussion in classes, term papers, open-book examinations, and so on. This kind of reform—this kind of "revolution"—is quite consistent with developments in this country and made good sense to us. Indeed, we plainly have more to accomplish along these lines ourselves. But there is also a second part of the educational revolution, which is much more political than educational in character, centering as it does on the effort to inculcate a tight orthodoxy, which reflects some anti-intellectual bent, and many of us found this both frightening in and of itself and threatening to the very educational goals being pursued simultaneously.

2. It is largely because of these pervasive political effects and tensions, I suspect, that a number of members of our group felt that higher education in China was the most disturbing—the least promising—part of the society. Certainly that was my view. This is not the occasion to talk about other aspects of Chinese society, but I left China very impressed by what has been accomplished in feeding and clothing the masses of the people. I saw for myself why Americans come back from China very enthusiastic about what has been done in agriculture, for example. The same ideological imperatives that create real problems in education may in fact have been necessary—or at least helpful—in transforming agricultural production. But then perhaps this is just to say again that higher education has a peculiarly strong need for a climate of openness and freedom.

Thinking now about the future, four questions come to my mind, three about China and one about the United States. First, how will the Chinese cope with the rising expectations regarding educational opportunities that seem almost certain to be generated by the great emphasis on education at the elementary and secondary levels? The primary and secondary schools that we saw seemed to be marked by a very good spirit, and the students seemed to enjoy learning. The number of pre-university students should be expected to continue to rise, and one can't help but wonder if it will be possible indefinitely to preclude the possibility of university education for so many well-educated and strongly motivated people. The power of the "serve the state" ethos helps greatly with this problem now, but it may weaken as material needs are met more fully and as the society itself moves further from the time of revolution and from so many personal memories of what life was like in the old China.

A second question presumes that the further expansion of educational and cultural exchanges to which everyone refers will in fact occur. (This seems somewhat less clear to me than the official pronouncements suggest because further developments of this kind could be difficult to reconcile with the exceedingly China-centered character of education in China to which I referred earlier.) If more contact does occur, will it be possible for the Chinese to continue to discourage so fully the consideration of alternative views of the world and of China? Greater contact would certainly seem to imply at least the possibility of more challenges to accepted orthodoxy.

My third question about the future of China is whether the society will have the educated leadership that it is going to need. This question is based in part on the small scale of the current system of higher education, on the compression in the amount of academic study, and even more on the lack of graduate study and basic research. It was hard for us to see how under these circumstances the current leadership is to be replaced, let alone how growing demands are to be met.

Moreover, the problem does not seem to me to be quantitative only. As I indicated before, the selection process used to fill the existing number of openings puts such stress on political and personal criteria that one has to wonder whether the most exceptionally talented individuals will be able to go on with their education. An even more fundamental aspect of the question has to do with the long-term effects on creativity, on the capacity to generate new ideas and to adapt one's own thinking to changing circumstances, of a system of education that puts such stress on conformity. Those of us who believe, as I do, that leadership in the full sense of the term is nurtured and encouraged when individuals are challenged to think for themselves, and to accept pronouncements only on the basis of evidence, must wonder if a real price is not going to have to be paid in the long run for achieving so much acquiescence in the short run.

To put what I am trying to say in economic terms, China now seems to me to be living heavily off the intellectual capital of the past and, to some extent at least, off intellectual capital formed in other countries. To what extent—and for how long—and with what consequences—can this continue? This is, I think, a question of fundamental importance for the Chinese and for all of us who will be watching what they do.

My question for the United States is of a different nature. It is, however, really the other side of some of the questions I have just posed for China. While one has the most serious questions about the effects of limiting freedom in China, one cannot help but be impressed by the sense of shared commitment that so many of their people seem to feel. And as I was thinking about my own country while I was in China I could not help but wonder whether those of us in the United States are going to be able to combine our freedom with enough sense of common purpose to make us more than a society of isolated and all too selfish individuals. Combining freedom and responsibility has never been easy, but it has never been unimportant either; certainly it is not now.

PART TWO

Purposes of Education/
Liberal Education

In the 1970s, concerns about the economy and the job market for college graduates fueled an impassioned national debate over the purposes of education, and particularly over the "practicality" of the kind of liberal education characteristic of Princeton.

A decade later, the focus of the debate had shifted dramatically. The concern now was not that colleges were paying too much attention to the liberal arts but that there was too little concern for the kinds of values and habits of mind traditionally associated with liberal education at its best.

President Bowen addressed the broad topic of "Liberal Education at Princeton" in his 1977 annual report, which provides a general introduction to this chapter. The report sketches a brief historical context and then discusses: (1) the content of the curriculum; (2) the structure of the undergraduate program; (3) course patterns; (4) teaching methods and teaching staff; (5) residential and extracurricular aspects of undergraduate life; and (6) liberal education as preparation for careers and later life.

The chapter then explores particular aspects of the educational experience at Princeton, including:

• preparation for citizenship, from the 1979 Opening Exercises address entitled "The Skills of Freedom";

• the role of the university in developing and strengthening personal values, from the 1973 Opening Exercises address on "The University and Moral Values," and from the 1975 Opening Exercises address on "Academic Pressures and Purposes";

• the growing role of the creative arts, from the 1985 annual report on that topic;

• the importance of "Capturing 'Otherness,'" from the 1984 Opening Exercises address with that title, and from the 1987 annual report on "International Studies at Princeton";

• the importance of an ethos conducive to learning and personal growth, from the 1980 Commencement remarks on "The Texture of the Effort."

The chapter turns next to outcomes, to what Princeton aims to accomplish in and through its graduates. These outcomes are discussed, first, in the 1977 Commencement remarks entitled "A Quiet Confidence"; and then in the 1985 Commencement remarks entitled "OTSOG" (On the Shoulders of Giants).

The chapter concludes with a broad discussion of the purposes of education from the 1981 Opening Exercises address, which had its origins in a trip that summer to the Oracle at Delphi. Taking its inspiration from the travels of Odysseus, the address suggests goals for a student's journey through Princeton in its explication of Constantine Cavafy's poem "Ithaka."

Liberal Education at Princeton

REPORT OF THE PRESIDENT

MARCH 1977

On October 22, 1746, the Great Seal of the Province of New Jersey was affixed to Princeton's original Charter, authorizing a college in New Jersey "wherein Youth may be instructed in the learned Languages, and in the Liberal Arts and Sciences." Seven months later, the College's first undergraduates assembled in Elizabeth, New Jersey, to begin their studies at the home of Jonathan Dickinson, the institution's first president.

The changes that have occurred over the ensuing 230 years can be described only as monumental: Princeton has become a university, with major responsibilities for scholarship, research, and graduate education, as well as for undergraduate education; there are now professional schools of engineering and applied science, of architecture and urban planning, and of public and international affairs, as well as a variety of other special programs which supplement and complement work in the humanities and in the natural and social sciences; within the arts and sciences alone the curriculum has grown to encompass new disciplines and new approaches to old subjects; there have been pronounced changes in the competition for admission and in the composition of the student body; the faculty now numbers over six hundred and includes many individuals of international standing in their disciplines; extracurricular activities have grown in size and scope; there have been evident changes in the physical facilities (as well as the physical location) of the University; and there have been critically important increases in financial resources. Yet, for all of these changes, the essential and fundamental commitment of this institution to liberal education in the arts and sciences remains constant.

I propose in this report to discuss this traditional and continuing commitment as we see it now. . . . My emphasis will be on undergraduate education, not because similar questions do not exist at the graduate level, indeed in some respects in even sharper form, but because so much of the current controversy over liberal education (and "careerism") is centered on undergraduate studies. In a brief concluding section I want to express some concerns for the future in light of broad educational, demographic, financial, and political trends. Before attempting to cover any of this ground, however, I want to try to provide some historical perspective.

THE HISTORICAL CONTEXT

Debate over liberal education—its nature, purposes, and value—goes back more than two thousand years, at least to Aristotle, who asked: "Should the useful in life, or should virtue, or should the higher knowledge be the aim of our training?" It seemed particularly appropriate, therefore, that last spring when I asked the heads of departments and programs at Princeton for their thoughts on liberal education, one of the first responses I received was from Robert Connor, chairman of our Classics Department. Professor Connor provided an interesting historical comment:

> The term "liberal arts" (*eleutherai technai*) to my knowledge first occurs in Greece of the fourth century B.C. It means the skills that a free man ought to have, and assumes that other skills, e.g. technical know-how, and even a lot of management skills can be left to slaves. Hence the liberal arts are those required for activities from which slaves were barred, above all the governing of the city-states. Hence the strong emphasis on rhetoric, a field which included (or subordinated) ethical judgment, historical and geopolitical analysis, and the law as well as what some would today call "communication skills." The concept of liberal arts originates, then, from a slave-based society and indeed from an acceptance of the necessity of slavery. But its survival and relevance depend, it seems to me, on its focus on skills that have to be acquired if free governments are to persist. The liberal arts, in other words, are historically the arts of the citizen. We might even do better to talk about "the skills of freedom" (an equally tolerable translation of the Greek) rather than the shop-worn and misunderstood phrase "liberal arts."*

In the middle ages, clergymen were educated in the seven "liberal arts" of the literary trivium (grammar, rhetoric, and logic) and the sci-

---

* Such a translation would be consistent with an observation by Harold R. Medina '09, one of our most distinguished alumni and still a practicing senior circuit judge, in a lecture on "Liberal Arts and the Professions" delivered some twenty years ago. Judge Medina observed: "Whatever one may think of Plato and the Pythagoreans and the very early days, there seems no reason to doubt that the phrases 'a liberal education' and 'the liberal arts,' from the middle ages down to the present times, have had a connotation of freedom. For only a man whose mind is free may follow the path of truth, wherever it may lead."

entific quadrivium (arithmetic, geometry, astronomy, and music). Later, the curricula of the European universities were broadened, consistent with the Renaissance ideal of the educated layman. Not surprisingly, the earliest American colleges reflected their European precursors, as well as the special needs of the colonies. From its earliest days, Harvard (which had been founded in 1636 to promote piety, civility, and learning) was preparing more than half of its graduates for careers outside the ministry, and by the middle of the eighteenth century American colleges generally were introducing their students to such subjects as moral and natural philosophy and belles lettres. One of the most important leaders of this movement was John Witherspoon, sixth president of Princeton. By the turn of the century, however, a reaction set in, and the American curriculum reverted in large part to a more classical form. As late as 1850, with only one half of one percent of the college-age population in the United States attending college, the classical trivium and quadrivium for the most part were considered quite adequate to train citizens properly for the professions as well as for the more general responsibilities of citizenship.*

But economic and sociological changes of far-reaching significance coincided at the midpoint of the nineteenth century to challenge colleges and curricula. New technologies and growing urban centers—and the increased learning that they both required and supported—were opening new horizons and leading to demands for more practical training, especially in the sciences. The new set of pressures for change was considered seriously and with some sympathy by the newly-inaugurated president of the College of New Jersey, James McCosh. Arguing in his 1868 inaugural address that "every study should, as far as possible, leave not a distaste, but a relish on the palate of the young, so that they may be inclined to return to it," McCosh went on to say: "It is not imperative now to resort to profitless studies when such rich and

---

* While it is obviously impossible to summarize adequately developments spanning centuries in a paragraph or two, it does seem important to recognize that the various questions we confront today have important antecedents of striking similarity. As Lawrence Stone of our faculty has noted, for example, during the middle years of the seventeenth century there was great concern over much of Eruope "that far too many men were being educated at far too high a level in far too non-vocational subjects such as the classics for these underdeveloped societies to find them satisfactory employment afterward. The state began to worry about the threat to social stability of a class of alienated intellectuals . . ." (Lawrence Stone, "The Ninnyversity?" *The New York Review of Books*, January 28, 1971, p. 25). James McLachlan, editor of *Princetonians: A Bibliographical Dictionary*, has referred to the ambivalence concerning the nature of the college as an institution at the beginning of the nineteenth century, noting that: "Neither educators nor the public could decide whether college students were citizens, or children" (*The University in Society*, Vol. II, edited by Lawrence Stone, Princeton University Press, 1974, p. 464).

fertile fields are evidently lying all around us . . . [I do not hold] that practical fruits are better than knowledge, but that knowledge cannot be genuine when it does not yield such fruits. So, using the same distinction, I hold that in study, while the true end is the elevation of the faculties, they never will be improved by what is in itself useless, or bound to be profitless in the future life. And I am prepared to show that the sciences, physical and moral, not only supply nutriment and strength to the intellect, they give life to it.''

In 1862 the first Morrill Act was passed, offering an endowment for a college in each state with funds derived from the sale of federal lands. These "land-grant" colleges, designed to "promote the liberal and practical education of the industrial classes in the several pursuits and professions of life," fostered instruction in fields such as agriculture and engineering. Shortly thereafter, in 1873, the John C. Green School of Science became a division of the College of New Jersey.

With new institutions to the west beginning to attract large enrollments, some of the older colleges of the east were modifying their curricula in response. At the same time, many of the American universities were feeling the influence of their European, and especially German, counterparts. The research laboratories of Europe were increasing the academic respectability of new technical fields, and a number of American faculty members had either studied in Germany or earned Ph.D.'s modeled on the German approach, and were pursuing sub-specialties and new fields. With the establishment of Johns Hopkins University in 1876, graduate education on a new scale, and a new conception of scholarship, came to the United States. At this juncture an important development occurred: by associating graduate schools directly with undergraduate colleges, American institutions pioneered an arrangement that gave promise of uniting in one place a commitment to both broad studies at the undergraduate level and rigorous advanced training.*

Perhaps the single most dramatic and influential development in undergraduate education in the nineteenth century was the adoption in 1871 of a very free elective system at Harvard, as proposed by Charles Eliot. By giving the students wide-ranging choice in the subjects they would take—greater than at many universities today—this approach

---

* To skip ahead in terms of chronology, the Association of American Universities (AAU) was founded in 1900 to advance the causes of research and graduate education. While Princeton's graduate school has never been large numerically, it is significant to note that Princeton was one of the fourteen original members of the AAU.

rejected the notion that only a certain few subjects had intrinsic value, and it encouraged diversification in the curriculum and specialization on the part of the faculty. Despite its widespread popularity, this system was not instituted at Princeton, as President McCosh warned of the educational "crimes and cruelties [that] have been perpetrated" in the name of liberty. Nonetheless, there were some significant modifications in the Princeton program of study under McCosh, consistent with a philosophy which bears striking similarities to the educational philosophy that prevails today at both Princeton and Harvard. In his inaugural, for example, McCosh said: "The question is often discussed whether it is better to have a general knowledge of various subjects or a thorough acquaintance with one. . . . In these days, when all the forces are seen to be correlated and all the sciences to be connected, I would have every educated man acquire a broad, general acquaintance with a number and variety of branches, and I would have this followed up by a devoted study of a few or of one."

By 1900, four percent of the American college-age population was enrolled in institutions of higher education, and as student bodies grew larger and became more diverse, so did the educational institutions themselves. As a result of the second Morrill Act in 1890, state universities expanded rapidly. These universities were meant to serve an increasingly broad public, and they began to develop programs in professional fields ranging from journalism and architecture to public health and finance. Most importantly, both universities and colleges were affected by the emergence of new academic fields: anthropology, sociology, political science, modern literature, and subdivisions of the natural sciences. At Princeton, the transformation to a university, first proposed to the Trustees by James McCosh in 1877, was consummated officially at the sesquicentennial ceremonies in 1896 when The College of New Jersey became Princeton University.

During the early years of this century, the attention of colleges and universities was focused for the first time not just on the curriculum itself but on methods of instruction. Under the leadership of President Wilson at Princeton (with his "preceptor guys") and others, tutorials, preceptorials, and seminars were developed. The debate over electives, and the structure of the undergraduate program more generally, continued (as it has ever since), accelerated by the decision of incoming President Lowell at Harvard in 1909 to transform the unrestricted free elective system into one combining distribution requirements and concentration in a major field of study. This change was meant to correct a perceived abuse of freedom and an apparent decline in the quality of undergraduate scholarship. There was general agreement that the new plan did provide a greater sense of direction while preserving some elements of freedom, but there were those who lamented its required specialization and those who regretted that the study of at least some particular subjects and materials could be avoided.

Such modifications of the extremely free elective system and the introduction of improved instructional methods, when added to the richer curriculum, higher admission standards, and greater selectivity in admission, had a beneficial effect on student scholarship. At the same time, the growth in size of the student population, its increasing diversity in background and in preparation, concern with the specialization of faculty members, and a variety of cultural changes, all led to increased discussion of the responsibility of colleges for the full range of their students' personal development—moral, cultural, and social as well as intellectual. This discussion, along with the continuing controversy over electives and specialization, underlay a growing interest in, first, the so-called "general education" movement and then, later, a counter-movement led by those followers of John Dewey known as "progressives."

"General education" programs at various times and places have ranged from a particular set of courses that attempts to expose all undergraduates to what is agreed upon as an essential interdisciplinary core of knowledge, to entire curricula organized around a selection of "great books." The "general education" movement began at Columbia in 1917 with a course on "war issues" (which after the war became a course on "peace issues" and then "contemporary civilization"). It was spearheaded in the 1920s by Robert Hutchins of Chicago, and took on its most comprehensive form at St. John's College in Maryland where every undergraduate program entailed the study of the same limited number of "great books." The "progressives," on the other hand, tended to view knowledge not as something that resides in one specific group of "perennial" texts but as a set of intellectual processes or problem-solving skills; knowledge was seen not as fixed but as evolving, and liberal studies were to be applied to specific problems of the society. Dewey favored the social and natural sciences, with active, experimental pursuit of one's studies in the laboratory, studio, or workshop.

Clearly there was merit in both conceptions of education; and clearly both, if carried too far, had dangers and limitations. Many institutions, including Princeton, attempted to build programs which incorporated elements of both approaches, as the national debate (more on form and emphasis than on the extreme possibilities) continued, highlighted by a widely discussed report from Harvard in 1945 entitled *General Education in a Free Society.* *

This debate, and more generally the nature of American higher education, were influenced decisively by changes brought about by World War II. One major influence was the sudden increase in college attendance as the G.I. Bill of Rights sent almost five million veterans to (or back to) college. These veterans brought with them a wide variety of backgrounds, experiences, and ambitions and, in many cases, a greater maturity, a determination to make their own decisions, and considerable impatience with courses that they thought were unrelated to their particular career goals. The unprecedented diversity represented by this group seemed to accentuate the need for some common academic experience while at the same time rendering more difficult the definition and imposition of a common program.

A second important development was the rapid growth in federal grants for training and research, a factor which of course gave great encouragement to specialized research, particularly in the sciences. While the postwar boom in sponsored research had far more pronounced direct effects on graduate than on undergraduate education, it had large indirect effects on the whole of higher education because of its broad impact on the work of faculty members, especially in the sciences.

Third, there had been, and there continued to be, an extraordinarily rapid rate of increase in knowledge, an aroused curiosity about other cultures and societies, and an elevated set of expectations regarding what colleges and universities might accomplish in the service of society. Important breakthroughs in a number of fields, the expanded American role in world affairs, and the nation's vigorous commitment to science and technology in the post-Sputnik era accelerated the growth of knowledge and led simultaneously to a greater uncertainty than ever before as to which pieces of knowledge or which fields should

* *General Education in a Free Society: Report of the Harvard Committee*, by the President and Fellows of Harvard College, 1945. The report noted "a supreme need" for a "unifying purpose and idea" in American higher education. "The true task of education," it said, "is . . . to reconcile the sense of pattern and direction deriving from heritage with the sense of experiment and innovation deriving from science that they may exist fruitfully together, as in varying degrees they have never ceased to do throughout Western history. . . . It must uphold at the same time tradition and experiment, the ideal and the means, subserving, like our culture itself, change within commitment. . . ."

be considered essential, and therefore which, if any, ought to be required of all students.

This sense of uncertainty about what, if anything, should be common to all of higher education became even greater as undergraduate enrollments reached 34 percent of the college-age population in 1963 and 45 percent in 1972. The unprecedented increase in total enrollments was accompanied by much greater diversity than ever before of racial and cultural backgrounds, of socio-economic backgrounds, and of formal academic preparations. An important part of the country's response to larger numbers of students and to a far wider variety of interests and preparations was of course the rapid development of the community college movement, the growth of state college systems, and dramatic changes in the sense of mission of some municipal colleges such as the City College of New York. A direct consequence of these changes has been a sharp decline in the percentage of the total enrollment in postsecondary education that is in private colleges and universities; there also has been a decline in the percentage of the total enrollment in institutions of higher education, public or private, that are seen as primarily committed to the liberal arts and sciences.

Other developments in recent years also have had important effects on educational policy and practice. The age at which society recognizes individuals to be adults has been lowered, as marked particularly by the drop in the voting age to eighteen, and this change, combined with broad social changes affecting the whole society, has led colleges and universities throughout the country to accept less of an *in loco parentis* role than once was the case. The awakened sense of injustice inspired by the civil rights movement, the anger and frustration growing out of the Vietnam War, and changing perceptions of the role of women in society, all have raised questions of fundamental importance as well as controversies of a more transitory nature. Still more recently, the economic problems of the country, and especially the presence of a high rate of inflation at the same time that unemployment is high, have created serious financial problems for institutions, for families, and for students—and have led to considerable questioning of educational approaches viewed as insufficiently utilitarian.

It is against this background that I want now to discuss the educational objectives of Princeton today at the undergraduate level, and the ways in which we try to serve what we conceive to be our purposes within a system of higher education that is far more complex than our predecessors could have foreseen.

Undergraduate Education in the 1970s

Broad Purposes

In a paper entitled "What is the Central Purpose of Princeton University?" which was appended to the September 1974 report of the Trustee Subcommittee on Residential Life, former Trustee Philip H. Schaff, Jr. '42 offered the following summary of our aspirations as an educational institution: "Broadly, our purpose is to advance the cause of the human race, to benefit mankind. We aim to accomplish this through *the leverage of uncommon individuals and through the leverage of important ideas.*"

This perceptive statement has the important advantages of applying to graduate and undergraduate education alike and of recognizing explicitly our commitment to the advancement of knowledge as well as to the education of individuals who will make contributions of many kinds. Undergraduate education at Princeton has to be seen within the context of a University that seeks to serve these large purposes and is committed to the cause of liberal education in the arts and sciences.

It also can be said of Princeton that:

1. We are perhaps the smallest of the universities of great distinction, not just within the United States, but worldwide.

2. As a consequence, our contributions never will be primarily quantitative; it is through the quality of our students and of our scholarship and research, not through numbers of degrees awarded or papers published, that we hope to serve useful purposes.

3. We put particular stress on seeking to promote the integration of graduate and undergraduate teaching, scholarship, and research; having a single faculty, responsible for serving all of these purposes more or less simultaneously, is one of the very important means toward this end.

4. We are a residential university, offering many opportunities to learn and to grow outside as well as within the structures of formal teaching, for we believe that education involves the development of strong personal qualities as well as the acquisition and application of knowledge.

We seek to serve our broad purposes at the undergraduate level through a faculty, a curriculum, a set of requirements, methods of instruction, and an overall milieu that encourage undergraduates to become active participants in the educational process, to pursue their own interests as far as their abilities will carry them, and to move well beyond their own special fields of interest. We hope that they will gain a basic knowledge of the human condition, the societies human beings have created, and the physical world we inhabit—a knowledge that is historical as well as contemporary, that includes an appreciation for languages and cultures other than one's own, that reflects some rigorous understanding of the principles and methods of modern science, and that encourages thoughtful consideration of ultimate values.

There always has been argument over what ought to be included in and what can be excluded from a liberal arts curriculum, and the surest way to guarantee a long, disputatious, unsettled, and unsettling faculty meeting is to bring to the floor almost *any* proposal for a change in the nature or content of the requirements governing the undergraduate program. Yet disagreements as to what should and should not be required of candidates for a liberal arts degree, as strongly felt and expressed as they sometimes are, would be far sharper if the content of the curriculum *per se* were seen as the one defining characteristic of a liberal education. Professor Theodore Ziolkowski, chairman of our Department of Germanic Languages and Literatures, responded to my request for thoughts on liberal education last spring by suggesting a rather different approach to the problem of definition:

> I prefer to think of a liberal education in terms of attitude rather than subject matter. In this sense a liberal education can be distinguished from pre-professional or vocational training to the extent that it produces questions rather than providing answers. It inspires the student with a critical attitude and equips him with the best tools and methods available at the moment. But the attitude is what really matters. Tools and methods change and develop very rapidly. We must nurture in our students the imagination to adapt to new conditions, and we must attempt to preserve this kind of flexibility and resourcefulness in our own work. In this sense I know colleagues in engineering who provide a more "liberal" education than some colleagues in the humanities.

For my own part, I conceive of liberal education very much in terms of certain ways of thinking, of certain habits of mind, habits which I would like to believe can become quite compulsive. . . .

A liberal education ought to encourage the development of a tough and disciplined mind, a mind that is both persistent and resilient. But I believe it ought to do much more than that. It ought to serve a genuinely "liberating" function—it should help to foster a critical independence and to free us from our own forms of slavery, from the parochialisms of our own time and place and station. It should help us to develop those habits of thought which always ask why, which believe in evidence, which welcome new ideas, which seek to understand the perspectives of others, which accept complexity and grapple with it, which admit error, and which pursue truth, wherever it may lead, however uncomfortable it may be. It should help us to be compassionate and sensitive human beings, of service to others. It should help us to develop, and then demonstrate, a concern for ultimate values that are more than superficial signposts and that reflect more than the rote repetition of someone else's formula for living a good life.

Particularly important, I believe, is the desire—and the ability—to keep on learning. In this vein, a favorite quotation of mine, for which I am indebted to Dean Rudenstine, is from *The Education of Henry Adams*:

> Perhaps Henry Adams was not worth educating; most keen judges incline to think that barely one man in a hundred owns a mind capable of reacting to any purpose on the forces that surround him, and fully half of these react wrongly. The object of education for that mind should be the teaching itself how to react with vigor and economy. No doubt the world at large will always lag so far behind the active mind as to make a soft cushion of inertia to drop upon, as it did for Henry Adams; but education should try to lessen the obstacles, diminish the friction, invigorate the energy, and should train minds to react, not at haphazard, but by choice, on the lines of force that attract their world. What one knows is, in youth, of little moment; they know enough who know how to learn.

Since this long has been an objective of our programs of study, it was reassuring to hear testimony last fall from a distinguished graduate of ours, Dr. John Kemeny, president of Dartmouth and a mathematician who has made important contributions in the computational sciences. President Kemeny noted that while an undergraduate and then a graduate student at Princeton he never took a course in computer science for the simple reason that there were no computers when he was in college. "Yet when computers came," he said, "I was able to make a contribution to their development, not because of any one particular thing I had learned, but because of the breadth of a liberal arts education I was fortunate enough to acquire, because of learning to think in a certain way, and having been prepared to react to totally unexpected challenges."

*   *   *   *   *

How do we endeavor to serve these important, if elusive, purposes? Let me try to summarize under five headings: (1) *The Content of the Curriculum*, which defines the range of academic choices open to undergraduates at Princeton; (2) *The Structure of the Undergraduate Program*, by which I mean primarily the numbers of courses to be taken, the writing, language, and distribution requirements, and the requirements concerning the choice of a major field and independent work— all of which constrain the choices students may make; (3) *Course Patterns*, which means simply the combinations of courses that are in fact selected; (4) *Teaching Methods and Teaching Staff*, including class size, the use made of precepts, and the respective roles of faculty and graduate students in the instructional process; and (5) *The Residential and Extracurricular Aspects of Undergraduate Life*.

The Content of the Curriculum

At Princeton, as at every other American university of distinction, the curriculum has been expanded and enriched significantly over the past twenty-five years. Accordingly, undergraduates today have a far greater range of choice in terms of subject matter than heretofore, even though Princeton remains more selective, and less comprehensive, in its course offerings than many other, generally much larger, universities. It is now possible for a student to "major" in any one of 32 departments, to do special work in any one of 20 interdisciplinary academic programs, or to develop an "independent major" if his or her academic interests cannot be served adequately within existing programs. By comparison, in the immediate post-World War II period there were some 26 departments and 4 interdisciplinary programs.

The evolution of the academic departments since World War II is depicted in Table 1. Noteworthy, first, is the more or less "balanced" nature of the growth that has occurred. Significant changes have taken place within every division of the University in response to essentially the same phenomena: the expansion of knowledge; the development of important new disciplines; a general broadening of intellectual perspectives.

Also noteworthy is how frequently new departments have evolved quite directly from disciplines (or combinations of disciplines) that

Table 1
Evolution of Academic Departments, 1948-49 to 1976-77

1948-49   *1976–77*

Humanities

Art & Archaeology ——————→ Art & Archaeology
                        ——————→ Architecture & Urban Planning
Classics ————————————→ Classics
English ————————————→ English
                        ——————→ Germanic Languages & Literatures
Modern Languages & Literatures ——→ Romance Languages & Literatures
                        ——————→ Slavic Languages & Literatures
Music ————————————————→ Music
                        ——————→ East Asian Studies
Oriental Studies ——————→ Near Eastern Studies
Philosophy ————————————→ Philosophy
Religion ————————————→ Religion
                        ——————→ Comparative Literature

Social Sciences

                        ——————→ Anthropology
Economics & Social Institutions ——→ Economics
                        ——————→ Sociology
History ————————————————→ History
Politics ————————————————→ Politics
Woodrow Wilson School ——————→ Woodrow Wilson School

Natural Sciences

Astronomy ————————————→ Astrophysical Sciences
                                    (includes Astronomy &
                                    Plasma Physics)
Biology ————————————————→ Biology
                        ——————→ Biochemical Sciences
Chemistry ————————————→ Chemistry
Geology ————————————————→ Geological & Geophysical Sciences
                        ——————→ Mathematics
Mathematics ————————————→ Statistics
Physics ————————————————→ Physics
Psychology ————————————→ Psychology

Engineering and Applied Science

Aeronautical ——————
Mechanical ————————————→ Aerospace & Mechanical Sciences
Chemical ————————————→ Chemical Engineering
Civil ——————
Geological ————————————→ Civil Engineering (includes programs in
Basic ——————   Geological & Basic Engineering)
Electrical ————————————→ Electrical Engineering &
                                    Computer Sciences

were once more broadly defined. For example, Sociology and Economics are now separate departments rather than a single Department of Economics and Social Institutions; and what was called Oriental Studies is now two separate departments: East Asian Studies and Near Eastern Studies. In other cases, elements of particular disciplines have grown into separate departments of their own; thus, Statistics was once part of Mathematics, and Biochemistry has grown out of Biology and Chemistry. Our newest department, Comparative Literature, represents an effort, not to achieve greater specialization, but to bring together work from a large number of separate departments that can, and should, enjoy a certain unity.

While they are not departments (in that their course offerings are more limited in number, and students do not "major" in these fields), the Creative Writing Program, the Program in Theatre and Dance, and the Visual Arts Program must be included in any discussion of important curricular changes at Princeton. These three programs evolved from what was a single program in Creative Arts, and today offer a far wider range of educational opportunities than used to be the case. For example, whereas there was only a single course in creative writing in 1950, the Creative Writing Program today, with instruction in poetry, fiction, nonfiction, and translation, provides opportunities for credit work in creative writing throughout an undergraduate's four-year program of study—supplemented by courses in playwriting offered by the Program in Theatre and Dance.

The establishment of area studies programs and committees which coordinate work in such areas as Medieval Studies and Renaissance Studies constitutes a series of developments that has been designed to encourage interdisciplinary work in the humanities. To cite a parallel development, there also has been a significant increase in interdisciplinary offerings within the School of Engineering and Applied Science, as social, economic, and political aspects of technological questions are studied more fully, both within the school itself and through joint efforts with other schools and departments. Among these interdisciplinary efforts are topical programs in Energy, Transportation, Bioengineering, and Environmental Studies, which complement and bind together studies in the traditional disciplines.

The content of the curriculum, then, as defined by the major fields of knowledge we pursue, has grown in a genuinely evolutionary way, and many of the changes that have occurred represent efforts to integrate new developments within the same basic and fundamental set of academic disciplines that are today, as earlier, central to liberal learning in the arts and sciences. The fields that we do cover seem important in and of themselves, consistent with our broad objectives; in addition, they offer the possibility, though never a certainty, that study in them will contribute to the habits of mind and the kinds of general perspective to which I referred earlier.

Equally important changes have occurred *within* established fields of study, representing in most instances both a broader and deeper academic content. In Art and Archaeology, for example, most courses twenty-five years ago dealt with ancient and medieval art, Renaissance art and architecture, and European painting from 1600 to 1800. There was one course in Chinese art, one in modern painting, and one in modern architecture. Today there are five courses in Chinese and Japanese art, two in pre-Columbian art, nine courses that treat art after 1800—and a separate School of Architecture and Urban Planning.

The University's most popular department in terms of undergraduate concentrators, History, has added courses in early and modern Japanese and Chinese history; the Near East and North Africa in the nineteenth and twentieth centuries; and Islamic history. There also has been considerable growth in courses dealing with the modern era—in Britain, in Europe more generally, in Russia, in South Africa, and in America. Finally, courses which reflect new perspectives have been added (the history of the city, of science, and of medicine), along with courses related to the intellectual thought of different eras and nations.

Within the social sciences, the most significant general change has reflected the development of mathematical and quantitative approaches. This is particularly apparent in Economics, in which enrollments have increased by more than 50 percent over the past decade. Similar trends in the use of quantitative techniques also can be seen in Politics and Sociology.

The changes within established departments in the natural sciences have been no less spectacular. A comparison of Biology 201 and 202, in 1950 and in 1976, shows the course in 1950 covering "the fundamental properties of living things, their functions, structure, classification, life histories and evolution," while in 1976 it covers "cell structure and function, genetics, evolution . . . physiology, behavior and ecology." Even more startling is a comparison of the course offerings of the Department of Astronomy twenty-five years ago with the offerings of the Department of Astrophysical Sciences today, which shows that virtually all the subject matter previously taught in the entire

Astronomy Department is covered today in the two beginning courses in Astrophysics.

Engineering courses over the recent period have grown not only in number, complexity, scope, and sophistication, but in their attractiveness to students majoring in the liberal arts and sciences. After years of negligible enrollment of A.B. students in engineering courses, in 1975–76 there were 450 such enrollments. This significant change is a tribute to the determination of Dean Robert G. Jahn '51 and his colleagues in the School of Engineering and Applied Science to contribute directly to the broad educational purposes of Princeton and to the efforts mentioned earlier to relate the study of science and technology to economic, social, political and humanistic concerns.

One cause—and one result—of this expansion in the curriculum has been an increased specialization in all academic fields. In thinking about the implications of this development, it seems to me essential that we recognize the inevitability of increased specialization as knowledge proliferates and as disciplines mature. This does not mean, however, that every course will be narrowly focused, nor does it imply that those pursuing specialized interests will not also be interested in broader and more fundamental questions, and in the capacity of their particular pursuits to shed light on such questions.

Our efforts to see that undergraduates continue to pursue a reasonably broad program of studies are described in the next section of this report. Here I would observe only that while undergraduates today do push further in many academic fields than they did even a decade or two ago, that is explained far more by the nature of their secondary school preparation and by what has happened to the disciplines themselves than by their election of a narrower concentration of courses at Princeton. In fact, a number of developments in recent years, ranging from the many new interdisciplinary offerings to options in the creative and performing arts (and including a provision for limited pass-fail grading), have been designed to encourage a larger and broader perspective. Nor is it clear that an additional course focused solely on a major figure such as Aristotle or Rembrandt need be a step toward fragmentation of knowledge in any pejorative sense; indeed, I suspect that courses attempting to cover vast expanses of material sometimes provide no more than a string of fragments connected only tenuously.

I do not mean to suggest that overspecialization cannot occur. It can and I am sure it does, at Princeton as elsewhere. However, no constructive purpose would be served by trying to prevent fundamental changes in disciplines from infiltrating, and altering, the undergraduate course of study—even if this were possible, which it is not. Indeed, it is precisely this kind of penetration that we must not merely welcome, but must insist on. It is, after all, one of the principal ways in which the quality of the undergraduate program benefits directly from our being a major university. The right response to the problem posed by the increasing complexity of academic subjects lies primarily, I believe, in continuing to attract faculty members—and students—with broad perspectives, in encouraging fresh, integrating approaches to the subjects that we study and teach, and in scrutinizing carefully all proposed changes to the curriculum with this concern in mind.

It is worth emphasizing that Princeton differs from some other universities in that individual faculty members and departments are by no means autonomous in deciding what courses are to be offered. First, for budgetary as well as educational reasons, each department is authorized to offer no more than a set number of courses each year, and this limitation itself militates against easy proliferation of course offerings. In addition, any proposal from a department or program to initiate a new course, to drop a course, or to modify a course in a substantial way, is reviewed carefully by the Faculty Committee on the Course of Study, which is composed of three deans *ex officio* (including the dean of the college as chairman) and nine elected members of the faculty, including at least one tenured member and one non-tenured member from each of the four divisions of the University (humanities, social sciences, natural sciences, and engineering).

This committee also considers and recommends to the faculty appropriate action on all other matters pertaining to educational policy at the undergraduate level, including requirements for degrees, methods of instruction, programs of study, and regulations concerning scholastic standing. By concentrating this important set of responsibilities in one committee, chaired by the dean of the college, we have sought to insure that particular decisions concerning courses and all other aspects of the academic program are made within the context of our overall educational objectives.

The Structure of the Undergraduate Program

The structure of the undergraduate program is defined by a series of requirements intended to insure that each student has acquired certain basic skills, has studied a reasonably broad spectrum of disciplines, and has demonstrated an ability to pursue one discipline (the major field of concentration) in some depth.

There is, first of all, a minimum course requirement, which is today thirty courses spread over four years for a student working toward a Bachelor of Arts degree (generally four a term during the first three years and three a term during senior year when the senior thesis also must be written).* The number of required courses has declined over the decades, from five a term during all four years in the 1920s, to five a term for underclass students and four a term for upperclass students in the 1930s, to the present requirement, which dates from 1967. This evolution reflects two main developments: (1) an increase in the work expected in most courses as knowledge has expanded and academic standards have become more demanding; and (2) increased emphasis on paper writing and independent work of various kinds.

Recently, some sentiment was expressed for reducing course requirements in junior year to ease what many consider to be a very heavy workload, since junior independent work is required in addition to the same course requirements that pertain to the first two years. The Committee on the Course of Study decided against any reduction, however, because of a concern that what would be sacrificed would be the electives which students need if they are to take advantage of the breadth of the Princeton curriculum. It is also worth noting that a significant number of students (347 members of the Class of 1977), following consultation with their advisers, take more than the required number of courses during their years at Princeton.

A second general requirement is that all students concentrate in a particular department or program (or devise and obtain approval for an "independent major"). There are both a minimum and a maximum number of courses to be taken in the department of concentration (normally eight and twelve, respectively, out of the required thirty), the objective being to insure that a reasonable balance is struck between the need to do enough work in one department to gain the benefits of study in depth, and the sense that a liberal education ought not to consist of too heavy a concentration in any one field. Students normally begin to concentrate in a department in their junior year, but it is also possible to begin departmental work earlier.

---

* Candidates for the Bachelor of Science in Engineering degree normally enroll in four courses a term as freshmen, and then may enroll in four or five courses a term during their other three years to satisfy a total requirement of thirty-six courses over four years. Independent work, in lieu of a course, is encouraged for upperclass students and may be undertaken by sophomores as well.

Every student must, of course, satisfy the requirements of the department in which he or she concentrates, and this normally includes a senior comprehensive examination. Independent work is a central feature of departmental requirements; indeed, it is so important at Princeton that it is, deservedly, identified separately as a major requirement for graduation. All arts and sciences departments require their juniors to do independent study of some kind, and all seniors are required to complete a thesis or another comparable major project.

Concentration in the upperclass years—along with the various independent work requirements—not only provides important skills and experiences, but helps students to develop intellectual confidence, maturity, and depth, and to gain some insight into the practice of scholarship and the discipline it entails. Princeton continues to be unique in the extent to which it expects concentrated independent work from *all* undergraduates (not just those who are "honors" candidates), and in the extent to which it commits the enormous amount of faculty time needed to provide the individual attention that undergraduate independent work of high quality requires.

Princeton also continues to retain composition, foreign language, and distribution requirements that are among the most stringent in the country.* Approximately 90 percent of our undergraduates are required to take a course in English composition and literature, and most satisfy this requirement by taking one of a small core of introductory courses focused on great writers: Literature 121, Homer and the Tragic Vision; 131, Shakespeare; 141, Modern European Writers; 122, Classical Mythology; 132, Major American Writers; 142, European Fiction. This past fall, 605 freshmen enrolled in the three fall semester courses, as did 37 sophomores. All of these courses require extensive writing—generally five essays plus a midterm exercise. There also is a Literature 151 course on Exposition and Literature, required of all students who need further experience in writing, which last fall enrolled some 188 students.

In a major post-World War II revision of the undergraduate program, which established distribution requirements in a form similar to that prescribed today, basic proficiency in a foreign language or in mathe-

---

* As the *New York Times* observed recently in an article on the consideration being given at Harvard and at a number of other colleges and universities to proposals to reimpose stronger requirements, following their relaxation during the late 1960s and early 1970s in the face of general pressures against requirements, Princeton and Columbia are noteworthy for having retained their requirements throughout this period.

matics was required. In the late 1960s, this requirement was altered to pertain solely to foreign language as the mathematics option was removed. Thus, almost all A.B. students now are required either to demonstrate proficiency in a foreign language at entrance or to gain proficiency through completing work at the sophomore level.*

Beyond the language and literature requirements, all A.B. undergraduates except a small number of "University Scholars" are required to complete two one-term courses in each of four areas: natural science; social science; arts and letters; and history, philosophy, religion. In addition to meeting departmental prescriptions and the University's writing requirement, engineering students are expected to complete at least seven supporting technical courses in mathematics, science, and engineering, and a minimum of seven courses in the humanities and social sciences.

The merit of distribution requirements—and of alternative approaches, including the abolition of requirements—continues to be debated, as it has been for generations.** Writing in *University* magazine in the fall of 1975, Dean Rudenstine discussed some of these questions very perceptively:

> It is difficult to see how any curriculum which does not demand some substantial study in each of the major divisions of knowledge, plus advanced work in at least one major field, plus serious work in English and in a foreign language, can be termed "liberal." Beyond this, however, I myself would not regard it as a sign of crisis if some students graduated from excellent institutions without having been specifically *required* to read Freud or Aristotle or Montaigne, so

---

* Some of the 40 to 50 students selected as "University Scholars" are relieved of the language requirement, and a few students with demonstrable disabilities in language study have this requirement waived. Some students who demonstrate exceptional writing ability at entrance are exempted from the writing requirement.

** A report of the Carnegie Council on Policy Studies in Higher Education, "Changing Practices in Undergraduate Education," last spring found that on a nationwide basis general education requirements have decreased and free electives have correspondingly increased over the past decade to the point where "the proportion of a student's undergraduate program in general education is about 22% less today than it was in 1967," in the 271 institutions sampled as part of the study. The overwhelming move over this period has been from prescribed courses to distribution requirements. The report found that students increasingly were electing courses outside their major departments but within the division in which they were concentrating, that courses elected outside the major division were more likely to be in the humanities or social sciences than the natural sciences, and that natural science majors were more likely to select electives from the social sciences than from the humanities. The study also found that the number of institutions among those surveyed requiring English, a foreign language, and mathematics had declined appreciably from 1967 to 1974—from 90 percent to 72 percent for English, from 72 percent to 53 percent for foreign language, and from 38 percent to 20 percent for mathematics.

long as they *had* read Plato, Darwin, and Voltaire; or St. Augustine, Cervantes and Marx—or any number of other combinations. Perhaps even more important, I would want to feel confident that students knew something about the intellectual and historical context of the great books they had read.

For what is pertinent, finally, is not that any four or five or even dozen particular books shall have been required in formal course work during one's college years, but that all students should encounter some considerable number of significant works; that they should be stimulated to read these works intensively enough to develop much more than a superficial response to them; and that their education should take place in an atmosphere that provokes them not only to explore further, but also to do something effective with what they learn.

The total pattern is what counts, not any single ingredient—or any single deficiency. Moreover, our best planning certainly needs to take a healthy account of human idiosyncrasy and waywardness. Many people will become superbly educated by following unpredictable and irregular paths, acquiring their liberal and general learning outside the classroom as much as inside. Conversely, large numbers of students will continue to resist, annually, the most delectable great books presented in elegantly structured and prescribed courses. Not everything can be done by curricular means; and not everything can be done in one's youth.

As always, we must continue to consider these questions and see if we wish to make further modifications—either in our requirements or in the courses that do serve as relatively broad introductory surveys.* But in any event, we have to accept the fact that there is far more fundamental knowledge than anyone can hope to acquire in four years, and ultimately we have to rely on the curiosity of our students, and on their eagerness to learn and to explore various branches of knowledge.

Beyond distribution requirements, the University has developed a

---

* One particular question that has been raised by several members of the faculty, and especially by Dean Jahn of our School of Engineering and Applied Science, is whether we might not, in Dean Jahn's words, "now question typical university attitudes which have long insisted on 'cultural breadth' for science and engineering students, but have blandly awarded degrees in the humanities and social sciences to graduates ignorant as savages of the most rudimentary concepts of modern technology." There have been some efforts to remedy this situation in recent years, including a conference under the auspices of the American Studies Program last year entitled "Technology and American Society" in which one of the faculty members was from the Engineering School. Some engineering courses may be taken to fulfill the science part of the distribution requirements, which of course all A.B. students must satisfy.

number of programs over the past decade to facilitate exploration and to provide some flexibility within the undergraduate course of study. One of these programs is the pass-fail option, under which B.S.E. and A.B. students may elect up to six courses over four years to be taken pass-fail. Certain courses, ordinarily including departmental courses, may not be taken pass-fail, and a few others, especially in the creative and performing arts, are offered only on a pass-fail basis. The main purpose of this limited option is of course to encourage students to take courses in new fields, or in fields in which they feel unsure of their preparation, without worrying excessively about the effects on their academic record.

Another option available to all undergraduates is the student-initiated seminar. Under this program, students may conceive a new course, develop a reading list, and solicit faculty guidance and participation prior to making application to the Course of Study Committee, which then reviews the proposal. Seminars that are approved are carried as regular courses by those students who elect them. Among the student-initiated seminars offered last spring were: Spark Ignited Internal Combustion Automotive Engines; The Development of Arthurian Literature; *Vergangenheitsbewaltigung*: West Germany's Attempt to Cope with its National Socialist Past; Selected Topics in Canadian History; Immigration and Assimilation in the United States; Women in Twentieth Century Third World Revolutions; Spoken Arabic of Cairo; and World Order and its Spiritual Foundations. In addition, students with particular interests may develop or participate in a wide variety of reading courses which may amount to no more than one or two students working under the direction of a member of the faculty who shares their interests.

Undergraduates also may elect graduate level courses for which they are qualified, and last year undergraduates were enrolled in half of all regular graduate courses given at Princeton. The flow of students is in both directions, as I believe it should be, and last year almost 30 percent of all undergraduate courses had graduate students enrolled in them. We try to avoid duplication of work whenever possible and to encourage undergraduates and graduate students alike to elect courses that meet their particular needs, regardless of the particular level at which they happen to be offered. The high quality of the undergraduate body at Princeton makes these crossovers feasible, and I believe there is still more progress to be made along these lines.

Finally, there are several special programs, in addition to the Independent Concentration and University Scholar programs referred to earlier, which provide additional flexibility. These include programs of foreign study, field study, and urban work assignment, all of which are small and carefully monitored. Applications are reviewed individually by the office of the dean of the college and the faculty Committee on Examinations and Standing, which look for evidence that particular projects have been well thought out, that they are supported by sufficient faculty involvement, and that the applicants have a serious commitment to the program of study being proposed.

Course Patterns

Whatever a university's expectations and requirements, there always is a chance that there will be some considerable discrepancy between policy and practice, or that within relatively consistent requirements of a general nature there will be significant changes in the patterns of choice over some period of time.

One question that has been raised in recent years is whether students are meeting their distribution requirements with obscure and specialized courses, i.e., whether general introductory courses are being ignored. In fact, that seems quite emphatically not to be the case. In the fall of 1975, for example, four out of five freshman course selections for the entire college were introductory courses in language, literature, mathematics, the natural sciences, economics, history, politics, and sociology. The spring semester counterparts of these courses, along with introductory courses in art, music, philosophy, and English, accounted for 68 percent of all freshman spring enrollments.

If we examine total undergraduate enrollments in the largest departments in 1966–77, 1971–72, and 1975–76, we find that there has been relatively little change. Indeed, the top six departments in terms of enrollment are the same in each of the three years studied (Economics, English, History, Mathematics, Politics, and Romance Languages and Literatures), except that Psychology pushed Mathematics down to seventh place in 1971–72 (see Table 2). Art and Archaeology and Chemistry appear consistently within the next six. The sciences are represented somewhat more strongly in 1975–76 than in the two earlier years (perhaps because of greater interest in premedical programs and in engineering), but even this change is a modest one. It is interesting to note that the largest twelve departments, *as a group*, account for a smaller proportion of all course enrollments in 1975–76 than in 1971–

Table 2

Twelve Largest Departments, By Course Enrollment

	1966-67			1971-72			1975-76	
Total No. of Course Enrollments	28,248			31,576			34,364	

Department	No. of Course Enroll- ments	% of Total Enroll- ments	Department	No. of Course Enroll- ments	% of Total Enroll- ments	Department	No. of Course Enroll- ments	% of Total Enroll- ments
History	2716	10	English	2613	8	Economics	2806	8
English	2442	9	History	2210	7	English	2536	7
Politics	2098	7	Romance			Romance		
Romance			Lang. & Lit.	1972	6	Lang. & Lit.	2188	6
Lang. & Lit.	1952	7	Psychology	1943	6	History	2121	6
Economics	1841	7	Politics	1879	6	Mathematics	1979	6
Mathematics	1835	7	Economics	1767	6	Politics	1979	6
Chemistry	1372	5	Mathematics	1765	6	Physics	1578	5
Religion	1322	5	Religion	1544	5	Psychology	1571	5
Physics	1298	5	Chemistry	1448	5	Chemistry	1505	4
Art & Arch.	1052	4	Sociology	1238	4	Art. & Arch.	1172	3
Psychology	1034	4	Art & Arch.	1180	4	Biology	1136	3
Philosophy	931	3	Philosophy	1170	4	Civil Engr.	1099	3
Total	19,893	70*		20,729	66*		21,670	63*

 * Columns do not add due to rounding.

72, and a smaller proportion in 1971–72 than in 1966–67 (63 percent, 66 percent, and 70 percent respectively).

There were eight departments (out of thirty-two) in which more than half of the Class of 1976 took at least one course before graduating: Economics, English, History, Mathematics, Philosophy, Politics, Psychology, and Romance Languages and Literatures. There were twelve other departments and programs to which more than a quarter of the class was exposed: Anthropology, Art and Archaeology, Biology, Chemistry, Classics, Creative Arts, Civil Engineering, Humanistic Studies, Music, Physics, Religion, and Sociology.

Patterns of undergraduate concentration have also remained relatively stable (see Table 3). History and English continue to have more majors than any other departments; also included in the top six in each of the years studied are Economics, Politics, and the Woodrow Wilson School. The proportion of all upperclass students majoring in the

Table 3
Twelve Largest Departments,
By Number of Undergraduate Concentrators

	1966-67			1971-72			1976-77	
Total Enrollment	3213			3953			4360	
Total No. of Jrs. & Srs.	1557			1873			2141	
Department	No. of Concentrators	% of Total Jrs. & Srs.	Department	No. of Concentrators	% of Total Jrs. & Srs.	Department	No. of Concentrators	% of Total Jrs. & Srs.
History	203	13	History	251	13	History	243	11
English	158	10	English	200	11	English	178	8
Politics	156	10	Politics	138	7	Economics	159	7
Biology	110	7	Economics	117	6	Politics	151	7
Woodrow Wilson	106	7	Woodrow Wilson	110	6	Civil Engr.	126	6
Economics	96	6	Psychology	85	5	Woodrow Wilson	120	6
Civil Engr.	81	5	Biology	83	4	Psychology	104	5
Chemistry	61	4	Sociology	77	4	Elect. Engr. & Comp. Sci.	103	5
Aerospace & Mech. Sci.	60	4	Civil Engr.	76	4	Biology	92	4
Psychology	51	3	Religion	64	3	Chem. Engr.	77	4
Religion	51	3	Architecture	62	3	Biochemistry	69	3
Elect. Engr.	51	3	Biochemistry	57	3	Aerospace & Mech. Sci.	68	3
			Philosophy	57*	3			
Total	1184	76**		1320	70**		1490	70**

 * Excluded from total (thirteenth department).
** Columns do not add due to rounding.

twelve largest departments dropped from 76 percent in 1966–67 to 70 percent in 1971–72, and remains at 70 percent in 1976–77.

Table 4 represents an effort to analyze the extent to which students in the Class of 1976 majoring in eight large and representative departments concentrated their course elections within the broad division of the University in which their own department was located* (humani-

* There are several departments whose divisional status is ambiguous. In preparing Table 4 and the following analysis, we have relied on the divisional definitions used by the faculty for purposes of representation on faculty committees (except that, as indicated in the text, Architecture and Mathematics, which would be assigned to the humanities and natural sciences respectively, are shown separately). Accordingly, East Asian Studies and Near Eastern Studies are assigned to the

Table 4

Average Number of Courses Taken in Academic Divisions
By Students Majoring in Eight Selected Departments: Class of 1976

*Department of Concentration**

Division	Art	English	Politics	Economics	Biology	Chemistry	Civil Engineering	Aerospace & Mech. Sci.
Humanities	**22.0**	**21.9**	8.7	8.3	7.5	8.3	4.2	4.2
Social Sciences	3.6	3.9	**17.7**	**17.8**	2.9	2.7	5.0	2.9
Natural Sciences (excluding Mathematics)	2.6	3.2	3.0	3.8	**18.9**	**17.4**	4.7	6.0
Engineering	0.1	0.1	0.4	1.0	0.4	0.4	**14.1**	**16.1**
Mathematics	0.2	0.5	0.4	2.0	1.7	2.6	4.0	3.6
Architecture	0.4	0.2	0.2	0.2	0.1	0.1	1.8	0.2
Average Total	28.9	29.8	30.4	33.1	31.4	31.4	33.7	33.0

* Numbers of courses in the "home" division are in bold. Some special courses, *e.g.*, in teacher preparation, are excluded.

ties, social sciences, natural sciences, and engineering) and the extent to which they took courses in each of the other divisions, or in Mathematics or Architecture, which are shown separately. According to these data, the average student in the two humanities departments was the most heavily "concentrated," with about 22 courses (over two thirds of all courses) in the humanities. At the same time, these students took an average of between 3½ and 4 courses in the social sciences and roughly 3 to 3½ courses in the natural sciences and mathematics combined. Students majoring in the two social science departments shown on the table took a little more than half their courses in that division, with 8 to 9 courses in the humanities and approximately 3-plus courses in the natural sciences. Students majoring in Biology and Chemistry took more than half their courses in the natural science division, and yet also took between 7½ and 8½ courses on average in the humanities.* Students majoring in Civil Engineering and Aerospace and Me-

humanities, History is assigned to the social sciences, and Psychology is assigned to the natural sciences. All four of these departments contain a mix of courses which cross the inevitably rather arbitrary divisional lines which have been used in this analysis.

* This pattern at Princeton contradicts the finding in the national survey that students in the

chanical Sciences averaged more than 4 courses in the humanities, from 3 to 5 courses in the social sciences, from 4½ to 6 courses in the natural sciences, and between 3½ and 4 courses in mathematics.

Before attempting to interpret—and qualify—these findings, let me note that similar data have been collected for the Classes of 1956 and 1966. In these classes, the total number of courses was greater, but for the most part the additional courses were spread fairly evenly over the various divisions. Thus, while the pattern of course elections does not seem to have changed appreciably, this kind of comparison does illustrate the obvious effect on free electives of reducing the minimum course requirement.

In thinking about the significance of the broad pattern of course elections depicted in Table 4 from the perspective of our concern for liberal education, it is tempting to conclude (as I did when I looked at these data initially) that students in the humanities are being less adventurous than students in other disciplines in taking courses outside their own major field of interest. Given the tendency to identify the humanities particularly strongly with a commitment to breadth in undergraduate education, it would be ironic if we were to find that it is the humanities students themselves who come closest to following a course of study confined rather largely to one set of academic interests.

Before reaching this—or any other—sweeping conclusion, however, one must take into account several important considerations. First, the system of distribution requirements at Princeton is itself weighted significantly toward the humanities, and the differential pattern of elections by division must be seen more as a consequence of these requirements than as revealing intrinsically different degrees of desire for breadth. We should remember that the language requirement for A.B. candidates may entail up to 4 courses in a language, depending on the student's preparation and the language chosen, and that the distribution requirements for A.B. candidates call for 2 courses in arts and letters (generally including the literature course chosen to meet the writing requirement) and 2 courses in religion/philosophy/history. This means that as many as 8 courses may be taken in the humanities simply to meet requirements (with 5 to 6 about average, Dean Rudenstine estimates), as compared with 2 or 3 in the social sciences and 2 in the natural sciences. If we set aside these required courses, we find that

natural sciences tend to concentrate the courses that they take outside their division in the social sciences rather than the humanities. The different pattern at Princeton is due primarily to our distribution requirements.

there is really very little variation by division in the number of courses freely elected outside of the division.

A secondary set of considerations has to do with the range of subject matters, and even disciplinary approaches, to be found within our four very broad divisional groups, marked as they are by quite arbitrary boundaries. While there is a significant degree of range within each division, the humanities are especially diverse. Students can elect a very broad set of courses within this division, encompassing as it does a spectrum of studies that includes, for example, classical archaeology, analytical philosophy, Russian literature, Japanese culture, African religions, creative writing, and electronic music.

Finally, and most important of all, there are significant differences among divisions in the opportunities for students to "crossover" in choosing courses. Courses in science and engineering (and in parts of economics), for example, are more sequential or "laddered" than most courses in the humanities and social sciences. As a consequence, students in the humanities and social sciences (and even in other sciences, albeit to a lesser degree) are often precluded from electing advanced courses in these disciplines because they have not completed the prior courses in the sequence. In the humanities and social sciences, on the other hand, there are few prerequisites and a great many upper-level courses can be taken by students with little prior study in the field in question.

A closely related factor is the differential effect of what Dean Rudenstine calls "linguistic barriers," defined broadly to include mathematics and related skills as well as foreign languages. Modern mathematics has made such an impact on the natural sciences and on engineering, as well as on economics, that it is very hard for a person who lacks good training and a reasonable aptitude in mathematics to do advanced work in those subjects.

Acquiring the necessary mathematical skills requires the kind of special attention, rigor, and continuing effort that is involved in learning the foreign languages that are so central to many of the humanistic disciplines. But for perhaps a century now, the humanities have been easing their linguistic barriers, while disciplines on the mathematics/science side of the spectrum have become increasingly demanding. For example, early in this century (and before), it was extremely difficult for students to take any courses in such fields as classics, French, German, Russian, and even parts of history and art history, without being able to read materials in the original languages. There has been a veritable revolution since then, and the humanities have adopted the general position that their "special languages" need not constitute a major barrier to undergraduate study in their fields, especially when it comes to offering a broad range of courses open to non-majors; a considerable growth of courses-in-translation, using texts in English, has resulted.

The fact that the humanities, overall, have moved in a general direction different from that of the science/engineering/economics group does not mean that either change has been wrong. (Nor have the changes been monolithic on either side.) My own feeling is that in all likelihood both directions have been right ones for the respective groups of disciplines, taking into account the missions they serve and the substantive changes that have occurred within the various disciplines.

A genuine dilemma is posed, however, by conflicting objectives. On the one hand, we want to make the substance of all disciplines as accessible as possible to undergraduates who are interested in obtaining a broad education but who may be unable, because of time constraints if nothing else, to master all relevant "languages" and to complete large numbers of prerequisites. On the other hand, we want to teach disciplines in sufficient depth so that students who do have the inclination and preparation will be able to stretch themselves intellectually and benefit fully from advances in the disciplines and from the talent represented by faculty who are themselves contributing new insights and developing new techniques.

"Some of both" is appropriate to a liberal arts institution with our objectives, and that is why we have worked to develop general courses such as Physics for Poets as well as Modern European Writers (in translation). Meeting these large objectives within the constraints imposed by finances and limits on the time available to students and faculty alike is no easy task, but it is one that we must continue to address directly if students who graduate from Princeton are to have an appropriate sense of both the arts and the sciences, and of the perspectives that each offers.

Teaching Methods and Teaching Staff

In addition to defining the content and the structure of the course of study in ways we believe most appropriate to a liberal education, Princeton places great emphasis on the value of certain methods of teaching and learning. The habits of mind that are so central to a liberal education cannot be acquired by passive learning. They require the active engagement of the student with the material and with other students and teachers. It can be exciting as well as enlightening to have to try out one's ideas, to have to articulate a line of argument, to have to defend one's best efforts against serious criticism, to have to start over again, and finally, if one is fortunate, to enjoy the very special pleasure that comes from really understanding something for the first time.

For this reason we emphasize—and at a considerable cost—precepts, seminars, class discussions, laboratories, workshops, conferences, and independent work, in the form of papers and projects of various kinds, including the senior thesis. We also continue to schedule a reading period at the end of each semester which provides an opportunity for reflection and consolidation of materials that have been learned, an opportunity to pursue independent or supplementary reading, and an opportunity to prepare materials for those courses which require regular papers, or offer papers in lieu of examinations.

If we believed that the purposes of a liberal education could be served simply by transmitting a stock of knowledge from teacher to student, we would proceed very differently. By the same token, if we believed that one particular teaching format worked best in all circumstances, we would want all courses to follow that format. We have found, however, that different formats work best for different purposes. Thus an upperclass course that involves research papers and extensive discussion may follow the format of a seminar that meets for several hours every week or two, whereas a course concerned primarily with the transfer of information or the development of quantitative skills may make much greater use of a combination of lectures and classes (which ordinarily have some fifteen to twenty students). In the humanities, however, and to a large extent in the social sciences, especially at the upperclass level, the basic teaching tool remains the precept, as it has been since it was introduced by President Wilson.

As the size of the undergraduate body has increased by some 40 percent over the recent period as a result of coeducation, the average size of courses, classes, and precepts also has increased somewhat. However, Princeton's tradition of small-group teaching remains very strong, and class and precept sizes in even the largest courses have not changed appreciably. Since 1972, the average number of students per course has increased by about 4 students, and the average number of students per precept has increased by less than one student (about 0.8). Since the beginning of coeducation in 1969, we have added an average of about 1.5 students per precept.

Many of the largest introductory courses in the college—including Economics 101–102, Psychology 101, and Mathematics 101—use classes, not precepts, as their basic teaching formats, and they have done so for decades. An analysis of 15 of the largest introductory courses last year showed that since 1972 the average class (not precept) size in these courses had grown from 16.0 to 17.5 students.

An analysis of precept size in 26 of the largest upperclass courses—those with the largest precepts—revealed that since 1972 the average size of precepts in these courses had declined from 11.4 to 10.7 students. Again, this was a sample of the largest courses; most precepts in several hundred other 300-level courses have been smaller.*

In the fall of 1975, Princeton offered 431 undergraduate courses. More than three quarters of these courses had total enrollments below 50 students. Only 32 courses in the entire college had more than 100 students enrolled. Many of these are of course the introductory courses, and one of our continuing concerns is that freshmen and sophomores, in the nature of the case, are less likely to be in small courses than are upperclass students.

Let me turn now to the composition of the teaching staff and specifically to the instructional role played by graduate students. This is an important subject, which was considered carefully by the Patterson Committee, which assessed the desirability and feasibility of coeducation at Princeton. As that committee anticipated, there has been some increase in graduate student teaching in conjunction with the expansion of enrollment associated with coeducation.

In the 1960s, graduate students did some 11.6 percent of the University's teaching. They served primarily as laboratory assistants in science courses and, to a lesser extent, as teachers of class sections and precepts. The Patterson Committee recommended that the graduate student share of teaching be allowed to increase from 11.6 percent to about 16.5 percent as total enrollment increased from 3,200 to 4,400. The actual situation as of 1975–76 was that graduate students were responsible for 16.1 percent of all classroom and laboratory teaching hours, with total enrollment at 4,364. (It continues to be true that graduate students at Princeton are not asked to be in charge of courses, to

---

* For example, in the fall of 1975 the Art Department offered a total of 21 precepts and seminar-groups in nine 300-level and 400-level courses. The average precept and seminar size was 8.8 students. Five precepts had 5 or 6 students each, and fifteen had 9 or 10. One precept had 12 students. In Classics, twenty-one precepts were offered in four 300-level courses; the enrollment was 8 students per precept, with essentially no variation. In History, there were sixty-six precepts in twelve courses, and the average precept size was 9.6 students.

lecture, to give seminars, or to supervise either junior or senior independent work. Thus their teaching remains devoted entirely to assisting in laboratories and to being responsible for classes and precepts.)

In addition to reflecting increased enrollment and the financial pressures common to all of higher education, the relatively modest increase that has occurred in graduate student teaching also represents certain efforts to improve instruction and to increase small-group teaching. In some departments, improving instruction has meant breaking larger teaching units into smaller ones; in some cases, classes and precepts have replaced lectures, an adjustment which, while offering more individual attention and greater flexibility, also requires an increased commitment of teaching time that can be quite substantial in larger courses. Under such circumstances, the number of graduate students teaching in a course may be increased without necessarily changing the ratio between students and professorial faculty.*

Except for some who are assisting in laboratories, most graduate student teachers are in their third or fourth years of graduate study and are therefore only a year or two away from being assistant professors. As many undergraduates will attest, some graduate students are outstanding teachers just as others are disappointing. At their best, graduate students bring a fresh perspective to preceptorial and classroom discussions of material being presented in lecture by older faculty members; moreover, many graduate students are particularly effective in working closely with undergraduates who wish extra help. It is important to our graduate students—and ultimately to those students whom they will teach one day as faculty members in courses of their own—that they have experience in the classroom as part of their graduate training. But it also is important to them, and to Princeton, that they be carefully supervised and trained while here. A number of efforts have been made recently to improve our performance in this regard, including an orientation session for all teachers involved in the introductory composition-literature courses, and training programs in several departments intended to encourage regular observation and consultation by accomplished teachers. Still, the results of graduate student teaching are more

* One department in which this has happened in recent years is Music, a field which in addition to becoming more technical and complex, has had to accommodate a much greater spectrum of abilities and preparations as the University has actively sought undergraduates with special talents in music. A similar situation has developed in Mathematics, as the number of introductory levels has been increased over recent years from two to four to accommodate different levels of preparation.

mixed than we would like, and we are continuing to look for ways of doing better.

Ultimately, of course, the quality of instruction at Princeton, and our success in achieving in some measure the higher purposes of a liberal education, depend primarily on our regular faculty: on their knowledge and their skills, to be sure, but also on the spirit with which they approach teaching and learning. In response to my request for comments on the general subject of this report, I received the following response from Professor John T. Bonner, who is this year completing his twelfth year of service as chairman of the Department of Biology:

> My view on education and on all intellectual matters is one of an unabashed purist. By this I mean I really believe in knowledge for its own sake even though I am always interested in its applications. I have no objection with starting off with an application and working back to the basic principle. Louis Pasteur, among others, showed that this was not only a reputable, but an extraordinarily effective way to do science. All I care is that one attend to the basic principles and whether the application precedes, follows, or is not mentioned is immaterial to me. A liberal education involves the searching and understanding of those basic principles; the rest is up to the tastes and whims of the individuals involved. And this is the very reason why a great university needs to be strong in both teaching and research, for without the research one may soon lose contact with the fundamentals of a subject. That is so, of course, because those fundamentals are always changing, always going deeper, and only an involved scholar can see this. This is why I think . . . Princeton is so right to teach and do research in biology rather than in ''premedicine.'' By sticking to this we do our students a large service no matter what careers they may choose. They will have left here with something upon which to build.

This perception of teaching and research as two elements of the same process is widely shared, and it is reflected again in the following observation by Dean Jahn:

> If we aspire simply to transmit existing knowledge to our students, no matter how thorough and profound that knowledge may be, then a good case can be made for the overriding importance of pedagogical experience, skill, and charisma in the faculty. However, if we aspire to something more in the teaching/learning relationship—and

given the quality of our students, I feel we should so aspire—that is, to prepare and stimulate our students to become creative thinkers in their own right, to be able throughout their careers to break new ground, to deal with unforeseen problems, and to uncover new knowledge, then it follows that we must immerse those students in a creative environment. Just as budding artists and composers seek instruction from accomplished, active practitioners, so students destined for creative careers in many other fields need generous exposure to active, contemporary scholarship on the part of their faculty. Only insofar as a teacher creates can he inspire his students to create. It is in this sense that good teaching and good scholarship are inseparable, and that any attempt to evaluate them separately misses the highest definition of teaching.

We seek to attract to the Princeton faculty individuals who not only care deeply about their own subjects, and are very good at them, but who also care about their students as people and who have a broad view of what it means to be a faculty member in a university. We seek individuals who have an irresistible penchant for sharing with others what they themselves are learning. This desire to share one's knowledge, and even one's uncertainties, takes many forms. It is expressed in both publishing and teaching, as well as through a great deal of conversation with colleagues and students.

It is very important, in my view, that these conversations reach across disciplinary boundaries and that they involve beginning students as well as graduate students and faculty colleagues. In a university committed to liberal education, we need to feel a particular responsibility to encourage the interpenetration of fields and to consider the large questions that it is sometimes so convenient to push aside. As many faculty members will testify, able and interested students, with a predilection for asking the most fundamental questions, are major contributors to this process, as well as major beneficiaries of it.

The Residential and Extracurricular Aspects of Undergraduate Life

As an academic institution, we attach great importance, as I have said, to the curriculum, the structure of the undergraduate course of study, the methods by which the formal academic program is conducted, and the intellectual quality of our faculty and student body. We also attach great importance to the informal opportunities for learning that are available at Princeton: our open stack libraries, our computer facilities, our art museum, and so on, all of which can contribute so importantly to intellectual growth and to the deepening and broadening of academic interests.

But of course it is not just to academic development that we are committed. Our larger concern is for the overall development of the individual—including the development of qualities of character and judgment, of an ability to sort out the important from the trivial, of a capacity for commitment to the service of large causes, and of the personal skills and attributes that are necessary if one is to work effectively with other people.

These are qualities that we believe are nurtured through every aspect of our educational program. It is a serious mistake, in my view, to assume that there is one part of a student's life at Princeton (an "academic" part) that serves to develop intellectual muscle, and another, separate part that serves to develop other personal qualities. As I have tried to say more fully in other contexts, I believe that the content of the academic program itself, methods of instruction, and the interactions between teacher and student all help students to consider and to develop values as well as to acquire knowledge and skills. Our academic policies and procedures, and the approach to learning of our faculty, are meant to reflect such values central to the University as honesty, integrity, and respect for the individual.*

To resist what seems to me to be a false dichotomy is not, of course, to downgrade in any way the major contributions made by the less formal, less strictly academic, aspects of undergraduate life at Princeton. We are a residential university, and we devote very considerable resources to extracurricular activities and supporting services of many kinds precisely because we do attach such a high value to informal discussions in dormitories and dining halls, opportunities to perform in as well as to attend cultural events, the benefits of participation in intercollegiate and intramural athletics, the experiences to be gained through involvement with Whig-Clio, the Student Volunteers Council, and any number of other campus-based organizations, and the oppor-

---

* A similar observation is found in the report of the Commission on the Future of the College, in which Professor Bressler and his colleagues argued that "an undergraduate curriculum should expose students to the range of ethical prescriptions in the literature of philosophy and religion which throughout the centuries have defined the nature of moral choice. Moreover, whenever relevant, every significant aspect of individual and social behavior should be examined from a moral perspective. Scholars have no special gifts as moral seers but they can claim superior expertise in specifying the consequences of alternate courses of action." The Commission went on to point out: "It may well be that the most influential moral instruction is achieved through example and by introducing students into the thoughtways of scholarship. It is difficult to imagine a more bountiful ethical system than is implicit in the norms that sustain the process of inquiry."

tunities to examine oneself and one's beliefs through a wide variety of religious and counseling programs. More generally, we believe strongly that there are significant benefits to be derived simply from being part, day in and day out, of an academic milieu that is conducive to reflective thought and personal growth and of a community that sets the highest standards even as it helps each of us to learn that we never meet them fully.

To discuss any of these aspects of undergraduate life in any detail would require far more space than is available here; each is really a subject all its own. I do want to say, however, that the increasing academic pressures felt by so many students in recent years make it all the more important that we do not undervalue the positive significance of the residential and extracurricular aspects of undergraduate life.

Liberal Education as Preparation for Careers and Later Life

Let me turn now, as I did at Opening Exercises last September, to a consideration of what undergraduate students, their parents, and the society at large should expect—and not expect—from a liberal education in terms of preparation for careers and for later life.

The last few years have seen renewed debate over the vocational implications, and obligations, of different kinds of education, in this country and throughout the world. A French government document last winter concluded: "It is now no longer possible to let the majority of students follow courses that lead to nowhere." The former United States Commissioner of Education, T. H. Bell, made the following comment in a widely publicized speech just about a year ago:

> I feel that the college that devotes itself totally and unequivocally to the liberal arts today is just kidding itself. Today we in education must recognize that it is our duty to provide our students also with salable skills.

Of course, other points of view have also been stated. Shortly after Commissioner Bell's speech, Robert Goldwin, then a member of the President's White House staff, took sharp exception to this position, and many statements have appeared in the press and in popular magazines since then. On one factual matter there is no dispute: we are witnessing a marked trend within American higher education toward what has been called "careerism." The issues that divide people center on the desirability of this development.

Having mentioned the national character of the current debate, I want to disavow quickly any intention in this report of addressing such important questions of public policy as the relative emphasis that should be given to various forms of postsecondary education or the proper content of educational programs designed to serve immediate vocational ends. Perhaps I should declare myself to this limited extent, however: in company with many others, I believe that a great strength of American higher education, as contrasted with educational systems in almost all other countries, is the wide variety of options that it offers. Moreover, I believe that one salutary result of the recent discussion is an increasing recognition that higher education is not right for every-one, especially immediately after high school, and that within the broad scope of "postsecondary education" a crucial objective must be to achieve the best possible match between the talents and interests of individuals and the considerable range of educational opportunities that exist.

So, I am a strong supporter of the community college movement and of well-designed programs of vocational education. But it would be a tragedy in my view, nothing less than that, if in supporting a wider range of choice among educational programs, we were to undervalue the contributions of strong programs of liberal education—or if we were to allow the quality of colleges and universities offering such pro-grams to be endangered.

In much of this debate there is the implicit assumption of a necessary conflict, and a rather sharp one, between the kind of education that will prepare someone for a career and the kind of liberal education we offer here. Much depends, of course, on the kind of work one expects to be doing. There are many, many skills, crucial to various occupations, which we do not teach here, and many specific vocations for which a student cannot be prepared at Princeton in any direct and precise way. On the other hand, we offer some courses that are quite directly related to specific vocations, and a number of the components of the education we offer have a clear value from the narrow perspective of an ability to do well vocationally. I am convinced that a good liberal education, if it "takes," has great practical, vocational advantages.

In many fields, including those of most interest to many of our un-dergraduates, there is nothing more important than an ability to apply fundamental principles, to analyze, to weigh evidence, to listen intelligently, to argue persuasively, to write clearly, to learn new techniques and new approaches, to adjust to new circumstances. Even more generally, some sensitivity to other people, and their feelings, and a reasonably broad perspective on the world and its inhabitants, can be of enormous value in many callings.

I was interested to read last summer in *University* magazine an interview with David E. Lilienthal, a person who has distinguished himself over many years as a highly successful businessman and public servant. He said: "Leadership qualities can be inculcated in people better by a good liberal education than by special courses in public administration, or industrial administration, or any other kind of special 'training for leadership.'" And, judging from the responses of a number of leading business organizations to a letter on this subject sent out by my office last summer, and from the continuing presence on our campus of interviewers for employers from both the private and public sectors, many others agree with Mr. Lilienthal.*

As far as the professions of law and medicine are concerned, I am firmly convinced that a good liberal education is a more important preparation now than ever before. The most outstanding members of these professions are not narrow technicians; they are people with real breadth of vision and strong personal qualities, including a sense of values, as well as technical competence. Let me refer here, as I did at Opening Exercises, to a very interesting article by Richard Neely, a justice of the West Virginia Supreme Court of Appeals. He wrote as follows about a decision concerning the insanity defense in criminal matters:

> We knew that regardless of the scientific research, this question was as much moral and philosophical as it was medical. To what extent a society excuses crime because of "irresistible impulses" or "mental diseases or defects" is determined by how that society answers the age-old question of whether men have free will or are predestined. Science can help us find an answer, particularly where re-

---

* Newell Brown '39, director of Career Services at Princeton, has told me that recently four of the eight major accounting firms have begun to recruit at Princeton. More generally, Mr. Brown's perception is that about half of the companies that recruit at Princeton are not particularly concerned about a student's major, although many of them like to see some courses in economics, statistics, mathematics or accounting, which are thought to demonstrate some aptitude and interest in disciplines important to business. For the most part, companies are interested in a candidate's maturity and sense of direction, evidence of leadership, competitiveness, energy, and persistence. Also, Mr. Brown has observed that the great selectivity in admissions at Princeton, and the rigor of the educational program, contribute to the employability of our students.

habilitation and alternatives to imprisonment are concerned. But to the balanced answer we can give now must be added insights from Raskolnikov's crime and punishment or Don Quixote's catastrophic release of the galley slaves.

There are more than enough personal testimonials and examples that illustrate the power of a good liberal education to discourage, even as it cannot prevent in every instance, what one of my friends has called an " 'illiberal,' isolated professionalism.'' In this regard, I am encouraged by the extent to which the transcripts of members of the Classes of 1975 and 1976 who entered law schools and medical schools reveal a more broadly defined group of curricular choices than one might expect. This set of preprofessional students elected courses in *every* department and *every* major academic program at Princeton, and those who majored in "unlikely" departments (for example, Comparative Literature) often did particularly well in the competition for admission to schools of law and medicine.

As have those who graduated from Princeton in earlier days, this generation of Princeton undergraduates, I am confident, will find that Princeton has prepared them—and prepared them well—for a variety of occupations as well as for the stiff competition for places in professional schools.* My own worry, in fact, is not so much that many of our present students will fail to appreciate what a good education can do for them in strictly vocational or occupational terms; it is rather that our students, and their parents, will think about undergraduate education here too much in those terms.

For my own part, I back away from basing the case for liberal education on these grounds, valid as I believe the line of argument to be. My main objection to emphasizing the vocational contributions of a liberal education is that this emphasis can detract from what may well be far more important contributions: to the society at large and to ourselves as individuals with lives to lead as well as jobs to hold.

More than 60 years ago Woodrow Wilson wrote about Princeton:

* The variety of jobs taken by recent Princeton graduates is illustrated well by the Fifth Reunion book of the Class of 1971. While the largest numbers of graduates in this class have pursued traditional careers in law, medicine, banking and investments, and education (the four largest job groups, in that order), the class also includes a fisherman, a director of exhibitions at a zoo, and a producer of half-time shows for a professional football team.

It should also be noted that our alumni over the years have been able and willing to move among jobs. They have displayed an adaptability that is enhanced, I believe, by a good liberal education. For example, the Twentieth Reunion book of the Class of 1953 revealed that, as of that time (1973), 21 percent of the class had held one job since graduation, 26 percent had held two, 20 percent had held three, 14 percent had held four, and 17 percent had held five or more.

"This is not the place to teach men their specific tasks . . . it is the place in which to teach them the relations which all tasks bear to the work of the world." The historic commitment of this University to the nation's service should not be seen just as educating future public servants—though I hope, of course, that we shall continue to contribute more than our share, and I was delighted to see, among many in government, two more alumni of the undergraduate college elected to the United States Senate this fall (Jack Danforth '58 and Paul Sarbanes '54), and an alumnus of the graduate school chosen to be Secretary of the Treasury (W. Michael Blumenthal *56). More generally, we hope to contribute ideas through the scholarship and research that are done here, and to educate people who will be constructive, effective citizens, whatever their specific vocations.

Numerous studies have found that college graduates in general participate more actively than others in the many voluntary activities that are so important to the society, that they are more likely to vote and to be better informed about public issues, and that they are more likely to be concerned about conserving the resources of the country. While I know of no studies that provide documentation, I would also like to think—indeed I do think—that persons with a good liberal education are especially likely to be concerned about the broad directions in which this society is moving, about questions of importance to peoples everywhere that transcend national boundaries, and about the long-run consequences of actions that may seem easy to accept in the short run. The age we are living in now, characterized by high degrees of technical sophistication, specialization, and interdependence, makes it all the more important that there be citizens who do possess "the skills of freedom" (to use Professor Connor's phrase), who are concerned about interrelations among both ideas and people, and who will give thoughtful consideration to what we ought to be doing as well as how to do it.

The contribution of a liberal education that continues to seem most important to me, however, is not preparation for a career, even a distinguished one, or preparation for citizenship, even when exercised with the utmost sense of responsibility: it is an enhanced capacity for developing one's own personal qualities to the fullest extent, for enjoying things of beauty, for sympathetic understanding of other people, and for the development of constructive relationships with others—an enhanced capacity, in short, to do nothing less than lead a full life.

Please do not think of me as suggesting that even if one makes the most of the great opportunities which a good liberal education offers (and too few of us do), "happiness" in some easily understood sense is sure to follow. The world is not like that; human beings are not like that. I think Jacob Neusner, professor of religious studies at Brown, was right when he suggested that students who have been successful at college "should feel slightly discontented: discontented with yourselves, therefore capable of continued growth; discontented with your field of work, therefore capable of critical judgment and improvement; discontented with the world at large, therefore capable of taking up the world's tasks as a personal and individual challenge."

I do believe, however, that one may find joy as well as discontent in learning, that a good liberal education, pursued in the right spirit and seen as opening windows on the world and even on oneself, offers great opportunities for personal fulfillment, as well as for service to others; and I hope that the strongly practical and materialistic tone of so much of American life these days will not dissuade us from believing in the importance of such benefits, however intangible and immeasurable they may seem to be.

Concerns for the Future

Having begun this report with some historical commentary, I want to end by noting briefly several broad educational, demographic, economic, and political considerations that could have significant consequences for the future of liberal education.

First, of course, there is the continuing, and inevitable, growth in knowledge itself, with an accompanying increase in the need for specialization if subjects are to be studied in depth—indeed, if they are to be understood. A direct implication is that we may well encounter more and more difficulty finding faculty members, especially young faculty members, whose perspective is broad enough to enable them to teach effectively at the undergraduate level. Also, we must be prepared to pay careful attention to the design of both individual courses and the curriculum as a whole if we are to succeed in retaining a broad approach to disciplines, and to their interrelationships, without becoming superficial in our treatment of them.

This is hardly a new problem, and serious as it is today, I am encouraged by what I believe to be a wider recognition of it by faculty members and graduate students alike—a recognition that has been stimulated in part by the difficult academic job market and the attendant need for graduate students to be able to teach a variety of topics if they are to compete successfully for openings at many colleges. I am encouraged too by the fact that many of today's most exciting intellectual developments seem to be occurring either in the spaces between disciplines or in the places where they overlap, thus encouraging interpenetration of fields of knowledge rather than more fragmentation. Recent developments at Princeton in comparative literature, medieval studies, biochemistry, the neurosciences, and energy serve to illustrate this point.

A second, very different, source of concern for the future is demographic in nature. As is well known, the dramatic drop in the birth rate has created a situation in which the number of persons between 18 and 21 is going to fall significantly. Between 1978 and 1988, the 18 to 21 age group will decline from approximately 16 million to about 13 million. While the growth of continuing education may offset this decline in part, it is widely agreed that we must anticipate a drop in college enrollment in the 1980s.

This projection causes many colleges and universities to worry, understandably enough, that they may not be able to attract enough good students to continue to operate satisfactorily. From the standpoint of liberal education, there are at least three dangers. First, there may be some institutions that will not survive, or at least not maintain their commitments to the liberal arts and sciences. Second, if the quality of the student body at some places does in fact decline, it may be more difficult for such institutions to teach in as demanding a way, thus making it easier for students to avoid both broader and more fundamental questions. Third, there may be considerable temptation on the part of a number of colleges and universities to compete for students by not requiring them to take things they might not like, by shifting to a more vocational orientation in the hope of promising a more immediate and more easily understood reward for having gone to college, or by doing both.

Plainly each institution, faced with its own circumstances, will have to find its own way; the pressures growing out of these demographic changes will vary tremendously, and we should recognize that Princeton is very fortunate in having such a large number of well-qualified applicants that even substantial changes in the total college-age population are not likely to present us with enrollment problems that could be threatening to our purposes as a liberal arts institution. More generally, however, the increasing competition on a national scale to enroll students is likely to mean some further reduction in the overall proportion of students attending colleges and universities committed to the liberal arts.

The implications for Princeton will depend, to some extent, on which of two countervailing forces proves to be the more powerful. On the one hand, these developments would increase the "scarcity value" of the kind of liberal education that I hope and believe Princeton will continue to offer. On the other hand, a further reduction in the overall number of students pursuing programs of liberal education could erode the general support for all such institutions.

Having devoted all of my last annual report to a detailed discussion of the implications of another general set of forces—those associated with economic constraints—I shall do no more here than restate a central point: as the inexorable increases in costs make themselves felt, we shall have to consider carefully what our priorities are, what trade-offs we are prepared to accept. My own conviction is that we shall prove capable of resisting the temptation to give up the essential, albeit costly, features of our commitment to a liberal education, including importantly a strong emphasis on independent work, on close contacts between faculty and students, on concentrating our efforts in teaching and scholarship in the most basic disciplines within the arts and sciences (including engineering), and on providing scholarship funds sufficient to enable the most outstanding applicants from every background to attend Princeton. In this respect, at least, I am an incorrigible optimist—perhaps because I believe so strongly in the importance of what we are trying to do and because of the strong consensus concerning priorities that I believe exists among those associated with Princeton.

What is less certain, to my mind, is whether, or to what extent, large numbers of people, and the society in general, will be willing to support liberal education, costly as it is, into the future. To answer this fundamental question would require a greater ability to analyze trends in broad social and political attitudes than I can claim. One clear danger, as I noted above, is that the relative number of students pursuing liberal arts programs will decrease further, with a corresponding reduction in the numbers of people who feel the most direct and most personal involvement with programs of this kind and with the institutions committed to them.

The situation is aggravated by the tendency of some to attack as "elitist," in a pejorative sense, any educational program that, in seeking to serve the large, inevitably nebulous and high-sounding objectives that are in fact ours, is both expensive and selective. I do not think that this viewpoint should be ignored or obscured. I think that many of us have not been sufficiently effective or persistent in arguing the general case for liberal education in terms that are not parochial and that do involve a vision of what will serve the society as well as our own students. If we are reluctant to present the case for these objectives, whom can we expect to speak on their behalf?

Let me stress that I am not talking about special educational opportunities restricted by family income and past advantages. There is a crucial difference, of course, between that conception and what I am urging—namely, the preservation of educational opportunities of the highest quality designed to encourage the achievement of each person's fullest potential, with access to such opportunities based on conscientious efforts to make even-handed assessments of each individual's ability to benefit from them and then to make constructive use of what has been learned. Viewed in this way, the ends we seek must be seen, I believe, as not just acceptable, but essential, to the well-being of the whole society.

At the same time that we join with others in an effort to gain greater recognition of the national interest in colleges and universities committed to excellence in liberal education, we need also to assure that Princeton retains both the strength and the confidence to chart its own educational course, to pursue its own instincts and priorities, and to preserve into the years ahead its own special character. Much depends, needless to say, on the willingness of alumni and other friends to sustain their commitment to Princeton and, if anything, to be even more generous in their support. Here again I am an optimist, because I know how deeply committed so many are to this University and to the purposes we seek to serve.

The Skills of Freedom

. . . My subject this morning is your education here seen as preparation for citizenship. This seems to me a timely topic, given the large questions concerning the obligations of citizens, the processes of government, and the uncertainties facing this country and the world that have been—and are—so much on our minds.

I hasten to reassure you. I do not propose to use, or rather to abuse, this setting by inflicting on you personal views concerning such important issues of the day as energy and inflation, SALT II, the dilemmas of the Middle East and Northern Ireland, the future of Southern Africa, or the proper role of police in the urban centers of this country. But it does seem appropriate to recognize directly the obvious fact that as citizens we confront an extremely unsettling set of problems.

At the same time, there is today, for whatever reasons, a mood in this country that often seems to me a mixture of pessimism, cynicism, self-serving efforts to evade issues or oversimplify them, and blame-fixing that I find neither attractive nor encouraging. It is in many ways a somber time, and I think we do well to recognize that reality—not as a justification for opting out, but as a prelude to considering how various individuals and institutions, including this University, can make a constructive difference.

In addition to being timely, education for citizenship seems to me a subject particularly appropriate to Princeton. This University's historic commitment to public service is evident from its earliest days in the careers of individuals such as Witherspoon, Madison, and Rush; and then it was of course given enduring verbal form through Woodrow Wilson's famous phrase ''Princeton in the Nation's Service.''

This is a tradition of which we can be proud, on which we can seek to build—and, let me emphasize, without feeling that we must thereby be constrained by any unnecessarily narrow, overly confining constructions of either our history or Wilson's phrase. Indeed, the phrase seems to me subject to abuses of at least three kinds, which I hope we can avoid; first, thinking in too nationalistic or parochial a way about the problems of the world, a mistake Wilson certainly did not make in his day; second, assuming, without earning it, a special claim on the opportunities of citizenship; third, accepting too limited a conception of either the purposes of education or, for that matter, of what constitutes service to the nation. Needless to say, the nation needs its poets every bit as much as its diplomats; and this University stands for a philosophy of education that exalts learning as something vitally important in its own right, not simply as a means to any more utilitarian end, even "the nation's service" however defined.

It is important to remember, too, that we are a university, not just an undergraduate college. Thus, our institutional contributions to the society take the form of ideas as well as educated individuals. Scholarship and research, and graduate education seen in large part as the incubator for the ideas of the future, may well be of more long-run significance now than at any time in the recent past. I wish only that I were more confident that their value was appreciated broadly.

As we think about the extraordinarily perplexing problems before the nation, it seems to me that what is required is not a "quick fix" or even just the application of what is known already, but rather the exercise of imagination, fresh ways of thinking about issues and interrelationships, and a renewed capacity for innovation, as well as a collective determination to get hold of ourselves and address our problems in a forthright way. While universities certainly have no monopoly on the generation of new ideas, they have made major contributions in the past and can continue to do so if given proper support and encouragement. Certainly it is our obligation within the universities to hold fast to this responsibility.

In returning to our principal subject this morning—the education of students as preparation for citizenship—I want to stress, first, the central importance of the formal course of study. Sometimes we are so quick to extoll the virtues of extracurricular activities, the experience of living in a residential community, and the general civilizing possibilities of the university milieu (all of which I in fact propose to do shortly), that we understate the significance of the academic program itself.

When we describe the educational philosophy of Princeton in terms of liberal education, we have in mind not so much the explicit lack of a vocational or pre-professional orientation as a strong affirmative commitment to the study of the basic arts and sciences, and to a conception of education that exalts the individual, that is concerned with values, and that is meant to encompass an appreciation of the nature of citizenship in a republic. . . .

Consistent with this large view of our purposes, the structure and content of the curriculum, including the distribution requirements, impose on each student the obligation to obtain at least some familiarity with the principal branches of knowledge. More generally, it is our hope that students will graduate from Princeton with at least a reasonable understanding of the human condition, of the ways people express themselves through art, literature, and music, the ways they relate to each other through organizations, the vagaries as well as the patterns of history, the characteristics of the natural world and the universe in which we live, the nature of modern technology, the languages and cultures of other people, the role of religion in shaping the lives of individuals and societies, and the rigor and beauty of mathematics. You can add to the list.

As you do, it will be ever more apparent that there is no way that even the most intelligently designed course of study, pursued by the best-prepared, most hardworking student, can provide anything like complete "coverage" of all the subjects with which each of us should have at least some acquaintance. It is possible, however, to learn enough to see the most important questions in a fuller context; and to develop a broader framework of knowledge and understanding that may serve to ward off at least the most outrageous errors and, perhaps even more important, enable you to develop an appreciation for the views of others. You can acquire, if you will, more, and better, and more sensitive, antennae.

The inability of any college or university to provide a truly comprehensive educational content—sufficient to today's needs—can be offset, and in large part, I believe, by combining hard substantive work with an emphasis on understanding basic methodologies, mastering techniques of analysis, and, even more fundamentally, learning how to learn what one does not know or has forgotten. Certainly the experience of doing independent research is very important from this perspective, as are the ability to write well and the capacity to argue a position effectively in the company of other knowledgeable people. It is because of the importance we attach to these kinds of skills that we put so much emphasis on written work, directed study, laboratory and library research, precept and seminar discussions, and the preparation of a senior thesis.

Perhaps even more nebulous, but probably at least as important, are the habits of mind that we hope to see you develop as you learn for yourselves what it is like to take a difficult problem, break it down into its components, examine them in light of relevant principles and available evidence, and develop conclusions that you are prepared to defend—and then, I hope, to modify in light of criticism, new evidence, and better ideas. Required is self-discipline, a certain humility, and more than a little willingness to start over again.

One of our objectives is the development of a capacity for critical thinking that depends in part on what John Dewey referred to as the ability to suspend judgment—to avoid being captured prematurely by the first suggestion that comes to one's mind; to continue trying out alternative explanations; to resist efforts to propose solutions until the problem itself is understood.

In addition to knowing how—and when—to suspend judgment, it is important to learn to cope with complexity, not to try to will it away, and not to give up in the face of it. Now I recognize that we academics sometimes try to pass off a high level of confusion for profundity. Nor is this a new tendency. There was an eighteenth-century poet, Sir Richard Blackmore, who warned against it, writing: "Let students on their volumes pore, to cloud with learning what was clear before." To this, a teacher of mine, Jacob Viner, offered the following reply in kind: "Let unlearned laymen not be too sure that what seems simple is not obscure"—an even more important warning, I think, especially for those who would reduce what really are hard problems to the level of argument by epithet or by assertion of moral or intellectual superiority.

Important as it is to see problems whole, with a decent respect for their complexity, that is, of course, not enough: finally we have to decide, as citizens, what we believe should be done. And in almost all interesting cases, analysis by itself, however sophisticated, cannot provide the answers to the largest questions. A sense of purpose—and a set of values—are essential, and another aspect of education for citizenship is that it should stimulate us to think as hard about our purposes and values as about the means we use to advance them. Important parts of the curriculum itself serve this objective, but then of course so do many other aspects of life in a residential university community.

Plainly this chapel, its dean, and the denominational chaplains are very important in this respect. We do not believe it is the role of the University to seek to impose a particular set of religious beliefs on anyone, and we respect—we insist on—the right of each person to come to his or her own conclusions concerning such matters. At the same time, we believe strongly in encouraging students, as well as others, to grapple with such issues as the relationship of faith to reason and the nature of an ultimate allegiance to a spirit that transcends day-to-day concerns. . . .

As I hope is evident, neither in the classroom nor out of it do we seek to do more of your work for you than would be consistent with an emphasis on independent thinking. You should not expect to find a single opinion on any genuinely difficult issue. In part for this reason, in part to sustain the openness of the campus to many points of view, and in part to protect our own independence, the University as an institution seeks to avoid being used to declare a single, "proper" position on the many vexing issues of the day. In contrast to the practice in many other countries, with different forms of government and different educational philosophies, we do not believe that educating for citizenship gives the University the responsibility—or, for that matter, the right—to tell you what to believe. That is for you to decide, consistent with our commitment to the kind of freedom that depends on the exercise of judgment by each one of us.

Many of the qualities and skills essential to enlightened citizenship can be nurtured through participation in the myriad organizations and activities on campus, including music, drama, debate, athletic teams, various forms of journalism, service groups such as the Student Volunteers Council, and student government. We have chosen to give students opportunities to participate in the conduct of various aspects of University life, in part because of the relevance for effective citizenship of direct experience in the process of arriving at communal decisions and in accepting responsibility for them.

At the same time, we ask all to remember that we are first and foremost a university; we are not a political entity, and the governance of the University is clearly a means to an end—the advancement of knowledge—not an end in itself. I remember well a meeting in 1971 involving Trustees and a number of student government leaders. Perhaps in the hope of sparking a lively political debate, one participant asked a student leader what was the most important issue on campus. The response was "how to learn"—and that has always seemed to me to be an answer for all seasons.

We also need to recognize that participation in decision-making processes can produce frustrations as well as satisfactions, and in committing time to such activities you should understand that your views will not always prevail and that your best efforts and best ideas may be unproductive for reasons that may seem (and in some instances may even be) obscure if not clearly wrong-headed. But then perhaps you can take some comfort from knowing that there are more than a few occasions when the rest of us feel the same way. A certain amount of irritation, as well as inefficiency of a kind, are inherent in almost any participatory process, and they are, in general, a cost that we have chosen to accept in this country to obtain the protections even cumbersome processes offer against the capricious exercise of power. In a slightly different vein, our distinguished alumnus, Adlai Stevenson of the Class of 1922, once remarked that "the sound of tireless voices is the price we pay for the right to hear the music of our own opinions." . . .

There is one further way in which the University seeks to educate for citizenship. It is difficult to describe, but perhaps in some respects even more important than any of the more tangible elements of one's experience here. The University as an institution stands for certain principles, and reflects certain ideals, that can have a powerful impact on you, all your lives, if you will let them—and sometimes even if you would resist them. Many are implicit in what has been said already, including importantly a commitment to personal integrity evident in the Honor System and respect for the search for a religious dimension to life.

In addition, this University certainly stands for the uncompromising pursuit of truth even as we recognize its elusiveness, a belief in the liberating power of ideas, freedom of thought and expression, respect for the individual, acceptance of responsibility by the individual for his or her own acts, and service to others. These are in large measure self-evident, though of no less consequence for that. They require no extensive elaboration. I would ask, however, that you not fall prey to the temptation to take them too much for granted.

As one looks about the world, and as one reads about other times and places, it is evident that freedom is not the natural human condition; universities are not inevitably centers of free inquiry; individual rights are not always even assumed to have standing—never mind being respected in fact. And so we have to be ready to work for our ideals, to defend what has been given to us as a trust, and to seek to improve on what we have, to make things better, even if only by a little bit, in what can be inhospitable circumstances. The 1980s are going to be hard years, requiring, I suspect, significant changes in some of our more comfortable assumptions. Citizenship is going to be a most demanding responsibility.

I referred a few minutes ago to Adlai Stevenson, who in his career of public service said so many things relevant to our subject this morning. Just last spring I read again some words he spoke in 1954: "We look to the free universities whose function is a search for truth and its communication to succeeding generations. Men may be born free; they cannot be born wise; and it is the duty of the university to make the free wise."

It is a right task for us. We recommit ourselves to it again this September. We do so humbly, knowing how limited is our ability finally to know what wisdom is. But we do so confident in the importance of the effort, grateful for the opportunities to study and to learn here, and determined to do our best to acquire "the skills of freedom" so that we may, in our turn, exercise them responsibly.

The University and Moral Values

EXCERPTED FROM THE
OPENING EXERCISES ADDRESS
SEPTEMBER 1973

. . . In the literature on moral education one proposition at any rate comes through very clearly: attempts to teach character directly fail. Professors Kohlberg and Turiel of Harvard have noted that the traditional American approach to character development, which at the turn of the century consisted of teaching conventional virtues, rules, manners, and beliefs by the exercise of authority and sermonizing, fell from favor in the 1930s, not because people were any less interested in character development, but because this approach simply did not work. Experimental research by several scholars showed that "character-education classes in the schools . . . had no appreciable effect in raising the child's level of actual honesty or altruism in experimental replicas of life situations."

Robert Hutchins, in an address made when he was president of the University of Chicago in the mid-1930s, observed that, "All attempts to teach character directly . . . degenerate into vague exhortations to be good which leave the bored listener with a desire to commit outrages which would otherwise never have occurred to him."

There is a sense in which the inability to "teach character" by such means in our society is comforting, at least to me. It says something about the independence of the mind. And that, in turn, offers some hope that efforts to impose any kind of "state orthodoxy," under the guise of character education, would be less successful in this country than apparently has been the case in some other places. It is at least mildly ironic, I think, that some of those in the United States who have been the most critical of the schools for failing to teach "character" and "patriotism" have also been the most opposed to societies in which this has been standard practice.

The inappropriateness of seeking to teach character directly does not mean of course that the teaching process has nothing to contribute to the development of moral values. On the contrary, I believe that both the *substance* of the curriculum and, even more importantly, the *ways* in which we teach and learn can have profound effects on moral development.

First, as to substance, students here, as at other colleges and universities, have opportunities to read, to discuss, and to think about the range of religious, philosophical, and ethical doctrines that have engaged man down through the centuries. Of course, it is hardly through the study of abstract concepts and doctrines alone that moral questions are encountered. Some of the most profound and discriminating teaching of morality takes place through the study of art, music, and man's fictions. In plays, poetry, and novels, the moral dilemmas are often presented most sharply precisely because they are seen in all their ambiguity and particularity. In history and the social sciences too there are opportunities to think about the conflicting pushes and pulls that have tested human beings and shaped events, and, in the process, to refine one's own sense of right conduct. And the history and the application of science and technology are no less rich in insights of a peculiarly moral kind; indeed, it would be hard to think of a more important—or more difficult—set of moral questions than those springing from new developments in biology, biochemistry, and bioengineering.

Now, I am certainly not proposing that the various disciplines I have mentioned be viewed by teacher or student mainly as vehicles for teaching virtue (somehow defined). Each discipline makes its own demands on those who study it, and those demands must be met. But I believe it is possible to be rigorous in approach and, at the same time, take advantage of the opportunities offered to encourage thoughtful consideration of the large questions of values that are so often present. This can be done, and in my view should be done, without taking unfair advantage of the teaching situation to try to impose one's own views on others.

More generally, in pursuing our intellectual goals we seek to help our students, and to encourage them to help us as well as each other, to develop those habits of thought which always ask why, which believe in evidence, which welcome new ideas, which seek to understand the perspectives of others, which accept complexity and grapple with it, which admit error, and which pursue truth, wherever it may lead, however uncomfortable it may be. To the extent that the processes of teaching and scholarship serve these basic objectives, they contribute importantly, I believe, to moral ends as well as purely intellectual ends.

It is frequently pointed out that bright, well-trained people have proved themselves capable of grossly immoral acts. That is so. It would be foolish to argue that a well-trained mind guarantees ''goodness'' by anyone's definition. There is no guarantee of ''goodness.'' But surely the capacity—and the willingness—to think at least can help the well-intentioned to act out his or her better instincts. As Harold Dodds, fifteenth president of Princeton, put it at the Opening Exercises that began the University's 187th year: "A thick head can do as much harm as a hard heart." So, I do not think we should be apologetic, in a world as obviously in need of moral strength as ours, in stressing our own peculiar obligation to hard intellectual effort. The one central, fundamental commitment of a university—of *this* University—is to the life of the mind. In this respect the university differs from the family, the church, and every other institution in the society.

The obligation of education to make just this kind of contribution was stated cogently by Jacques Maritain, the great Roman Catholic philosopher and theologian who was a member of our Philosophy Department, who cared deeply about values and about education, and who died only this year. In his book *Education at the Crossroads*, published in 1943 when, as now, moral questions were much discussed, he wrote that, "it is chiefly through the instrumentality of intelligence and truth that the school and college may affect the powers of desire, will, and love. . . . The main duty in the educational spheres of the school as well as of the state is not to shape the will and directly to develop moral virtues . . . but to enlighten and strengthen reason; so it is that an indirect influence is exerted on the will, by a sound equipment of knowledge and a sound development of the powers of thinking." Thus, Maritain gives, as his "first rule" for the teacher, "to foster those fundamental dispositions which enable the individual to grow in the life of the mind."

Now let me turn, if I may, to other ways in which we may assist in the process of personal growth and development.

A residential university like Princeton is, of course, much more than a set of lecture halls and laboratories. We are a community of people privileged to live and learn together outside the classroom as well as inside it.

We should recognize candidly the view of some that the general milieu of the University, with its considerable, and I think proper, emphasis on independence and personal responsibility is responsible for corrupting rather than improving the moral qualities of students. In some cases that may be so, but in general I do not think it is at all a correct assessment. For one thing, I suspect the University as an institution receives both too much credit and too much blame for what all of us do. I remember well the complaint of one mother who wrote to the *Alumni Weekly* some years ago chastising the University for allowing her son to live, as she put it, "like a pig." And I remember the reply in the next issue from another mother who asked how the first mother could possibly expect the University to do in four years what she had obviously failed to do in eighteen.

Looking historically at the question of the degree of regulation of the personal lives of students, it is clear that for at least the last three quarters of a century there has been a steady reduction in the extent to which the University has sought to impose a detailed personal code of conduct on its students. The change has been gradual, not sudden, and in part it no doubt reflects shifts in the general status of persons of college age; eighteen is now the legal age of majority in New Jersey and many other states. In part this change reflects changes in societal norms and, in particular, a greater reluctance by society at large to limit the freedom of individuals as long as they do not harm others. (We gave up some years ago, for example, a University prohibition of dancing that, I am told, was highly controversial in the 1920s. And in earlier days, even the theater was denounced for its wickedness. On a wall of the registrar's office there is, as some of you may have noticed, an excerpt from a work by John Witherspoon, Princeton's sixth president, in which he argued, in 1762, that "the stage is not merely an unprofitable consumption of time, it is further improper as a recreation, because it agitates the passions too violently, and interests too deeply, so as, in some cases, to bring people into a real, while they behold an imaginary distress.")

One thing the decrease in detailed rules and regulations does *not* reflect, in my opinion, is any less interest in the personal development of students. On the contrary, as Dean Halcy Bohen has pointed out, one of the ironies of the much-noted demise of the concept of *in loco parentis* is that it has been accompanied by a significant *increase* in the efforts made by the University to help undergraduates seeking answers to hard questions of personal adjustment and often of personal morality. In this sense—seeking to provide the positive assistance that parents generally provide—the University seems more committed to an *in loco parentis* role now than formerly.

Surely one of the main reasons for the shift from detailed regulations to greater emphasis on helping individuals to find their own way is, as in the case of shifts in attitudes toward character-education courses, a changed sense of what *works*, not just in preventing actions of which one disapproves, but of encouraging the positive virtues that are so important—and so far beyond the reach of any simple list of dos and don'ts.

Prohibition taught the whole of society a good deal about the consequences of trying to over-regulate personal behavior, in terms not only of the failure of the effort itself but also in terms of the hypocrisy and disrespect for law that were engendered. The change in the chapel rule at Princeton illustrates well the general change in approach that I have been describing. President-emeritus Goheen, in an interview in the spring of 1971, put the point very well when he said: "We—the Trustees, myself, the dean of the chapel—came to see that this requirement was proving counterproductive; that instead of advancing our view of religion as an important dimension of life it was actually building up resentment of religious observances. So we dropped the requirement—not because we didn't care about religion but because we *did!*"

What I have just said is hardly an argument against rules in general. We need regulations that protect the common rights and common needs of all of us; otherwise the bully has his way. But we ought not to confuse, in my view, the need for protection of such core values as free expression and privacy and freedom from intimidation with the far larger and much harder task of encouraging the development of an abiding and compelling sense of personal morality on the part of each of us.

A distinguished professor of ethics, James Gustafson, has observed that, "The practical interest in moral education . . . is to make possible the development of persons who are capable of responsible moral action. . . . We want them to be agents and initiators, not merely passive reactors, in the lifestream of which they are part. This sort of person is to be preferred to the excessively scrupulous keeper of a clean conscience, who seeks authoritative moral prescriptions from some person or institution by which to govern his conduct, and thus denies his autonomy, and incidentally is probably a boring and ineffectual member of the human community."

This is hardly a new idea. In *Harper's Weekly* of January 26, 1895, there appeared a story on Princeton's achievements and aims that included the following statement: "Her aim is to cultivate manhood rather than to enforce innocence. . . ."

Again, the hard question, now as then, is how to do this. There is no magic formula, as far as I know, but there are a number of things that can help. I have already mentioned both the substance and the general approach of the processes of teaching and scholarship, as we hope they will be carried on here. I have already alluded to the need for regulations designed to protect our core values and for appropriate means of enforcing such regulations (the Honor Code being a good case in point). And I have mentioned the provision of personal counseling of all kinds. Through the work of this chapel and the chaplains of the many faiths represented here at Princeton we seek to provide opportunities for religious growth and discovery and renewal. Extracurricular activities of all kinds—from competitive athletics to Theatre Intime to student government—afford significant learning opportunities.

But beyond, or perhaps beneath, all of these forms and organized efforts are two elements that I believe are of fundamental importance. The first is the people themselves. We try to assemble here individuals from every background and representing widely varying points of view who will not see themselves simply as teachers or as students or as staff members in any narrow sense, but who will have much more to contribute to the general life of the University. The second and closely related element is the attitudes toward each other and toward our common mission that characterize the members of our community: in particular the extent to which we really do care about each other as individuals.

Uniting us, I hope, will be shared commitments to integrity, humility, and a goodly measure of compassion. But beyond these fundamental personal values, which are themselves subject to somewhat different statement, we should expect normative questions to be answered in a wide variety of ways. Even among individuals who have the same, or a similar, set of basic beliefs, there will be far more than a single answer to the question of what really constitutes the right judgment or the right action at a particular time—especially in complex situations in which principles collide. And of course in any free society, which is committed to the principle of pluralism, we should expect different weights to be attached to different values. As an English educator, Professor Richard Peters, has put it: "In this sphere of 'the good' or of personal ideals . . . there are any number of options open to individuals. And the principle of freedom demands that there should be."

It is for this very reason that we put our stress on such fundamental concepts as fairness and consideration of the interests of others. The value of these abstract criteria is limited, because they have to be interpreted in concrete situations. But then so do principles of any kind, including the most powerful principles of modern science, and these fundamental principles do perform the essential function of prescribing what sorts of considerations are to count as *reasons* for the specific judgments we make.

This need for interpretation, and for hard thought, and for a good deal of agonizing, far from creating a setting free of moral concerns, creates a setting in which there is the possibility of real personal growth and development. A woman graduate of last year's senior class at Princeton, who had once considered transferring, wrote to me in the spring as follows: "By transferring from Princeton I would only have turned my back on the very challenges that have been the essence of my personal growth. Princeton has taught me that discovery without times of frustration, happiness without periods of doubt, and friendships without occasions of loneliness and isolation are no longer worth seeking."

As we now enter a new academic year, may each of us, in our various ways, take advantage of the opportunities for personal growth as well as intellectual growth that are here; may we recognize our limitations, may we celebrate our possibilities, and may we never stop striving, not only to improve ourselves, but to contribute what we can to the lives of others.

Academic Pressures and Purposes

EXCERPTED FROM THE
OPENING EXERCISES ADDRESS
SEPTEMBER 1975

. . . Perhaps most important of all, we can reaffirm, as an institution, the values of liberal education for which we stand. Any student who thinks that we believe that high grades are all that matter is simply wrong. All too often transcripts do not begin to reflect what students have learned. I have had students in my own sections of Economics 101 who have received C's but who learned far more of lasting value from the course, and for whom I had greater respect, than some other students who got A's. Our commitment is to learning, to the development of the still mysterious capacity to use one's mind in new ways, to think independently, to live responsibly, to form and reform values which will be more than superficial signposts, to be of service to others. These are lofty objectives, and no one knows better than I do that we often serve them less well than we should; but we do need to remind ourselves, and all of you who join us this September, what it is that we seek even if our actual attainments fall short of our reach.

We do put great stress on the pursuit of academic excellence. We are, after all, an academic community. But we are also a very human community, dedicated to personal as well as academic growth. Please do not think that we believe that it is possible—even if it were desirable—to pursue ''academics'' in such a single-minded way as to leave no room for anything else. In admitting students to Princeton each year we turn down many candidates with higher test scores and better grades than others whom we admit, and we do so precisely because we are interested in our students as individuals capable of contributing to the society in many ways—as individuals with courage, character, and even a sense of humor, as well as good minds.

I want now to end these remarks by saying just a few words about the contributions I believe each of us as individuals can make to enabling more members of this community to cope more successfully with the pressures and anxieties which are bound to be felt.

One thing all of us can do is to remind ourselves as well as others of the importance of organizing our lives here with the purposes and long-term values of a truly liberal education very much in mind. While Adlai

Stevenson did not compile an outstanding record in terms of grades, by his own testimony and the testimony of others he learned an enormous amount at Princeton. He took the courses that interested him, even if he did not always do as well as he might have in them. He found time for extracurricular activities and for friends, and he developed habits of thought and ways of approaching problems and relating to people that were important for the rest of his life, that enabled him to keep on learning and to keep on growing. A classmate of his, T. S. Matthews, visited then Governor Stevenson years later in Springfield, Illinois, and he commented: ''What I could hardly fail to notice . . . was the rate and extent of his development since our college days; in comparison the majority of our classmates seemed to have stood still.''

Please do not misunderstand. I am in no way trying to downgrade academic achievement. I am not suggesting that the way to prepare for success as a statesman is to accumulate a mediocre grade record. And I am certainly not trying to excuse the sloppy thinking and just plain laziness that poor grades sometimes reflect all too accurately. What I am trying to do is urge that grades not be seen as ends in themselves, that courses be approached in terms of what they can contribute to your development as a liberally educated person, and that a sensible balance be found between course work and other pursuits. Deciding what you are going to do here, and how you are going to do it, requires a constant series of hard choices that will test and test again your own values. But that is as it should be. After all, one of the most important things all of us must learn is how to set priorities for ourselves, how to choose, and how to live with the consequences of the choices we have made. . . .

In seeking to find your own way here, I hope too that you will be willing to take some chances in your relations with others. Getting to know other people, learning to care for them, involves risks. I hope you will accept those risks. Times of solitude can be times of discovery, and there are times when each of us needs to be alone; but we should remember that this is a community, and that we depend on each other to a greater extent than we sometimes realize.

Competition needs to be balanced by cooperation. This past summer a friend of mine described for me a vision of hell in which a number of desperately hungry people were gathered around a big table. In the middle of the table was a great abundance of delicious food. However, each person had only a very long fork—a fork so long that it was impossible for anyone to feed himself. Unfortunately, they did not understand that it was possible for them to be fed by feeding each other.

As we now enter a new academic year—a year in which considerable thought should be given to old values as this country approaches its bicentennial, as many of us begin and others continue an association with Princeton—may we remember one of the oldest lessons: that it is so often by giving that we receive. May we recognize that it is by seeking to help others respond sensibly and humanely to the pressures and anxieties which we share that we often achieve for ourselves the strength and the humility to cope with our own problems. And may each of you experience for yourself the joy that can come from learning and growing as a person—and from being part of a community that *is* very exacting in the demands it makes of us, but that also offers so much, especially to those who would give to it and take from it with a broad sense of purpose, with an openness to new ideas and new people, and with a generosity of spirit.

The Creative Arts at Princeton

EXCERPTED FROM CHAPTERS 1 AND 3 OF THE
REPORT OF THE PRESIDENT
APRIL 1985*

. . . As we now approach the mid-century mark for the establishment of the Creative Arts Program at Princeton, I would like to review what has been accomplished, some of the major issues that are still before us, and the prospects for further development. Along the way, I hope also to provide some sense of the role of the creative arts in a research university dedicated to liberal education—while acknowledging directly the tensions (healthy tensions, I believe) that are ever present.

The tremendous amounts of time, energy, and resources that have been devoted to the sciences at Princeton in recent years have allowed the University to make much-needed progress in these vitally important fields of knowledge. It is no less important, in my view, that we strengthen the University's capacity to contribute through other fields, including the creative arts, and we are now witnessing some significant steps forward in these areas. They deserve more attention than they sometimes receive, and one of my objectives in writing this report is to cast a brighter light on activities in creative writing, theater, dance, film, painting, sculpture, photography, the other visual arts, music, and architecture.

Activities in these fields—in both their curricular and extracurricular aspects—complement teaching and scholarship in the more traditional subjects within the humanities and enrich the overall program of the University in essential ways. To anticipate something I want to say at the end of this report, if Princeton is to remain a university in the full meaning of the word, it must continue to seek an appropriate balance among its central subjects, and excellence in each.

A Brief History . . . and a Point of View

In responding to my request for help in preparing this report, Professor Edward T. Cone '39 of our Department of Music adopted a historical approach and labeled the epoch at Princeton that lasted until the

* Chapter 2 described the various creative arts programs at Princeton.

mid-1930s "The Dark Ages." With the notable exception of several excellent student groups (Triangle, Intime, and the *Nassau Lit*, among others), this was a period with essentially no organized work in the creative arts. There was then what Professor Cone calls "The Gradual Awakening," from 1935 to 1942, a period that included the formal establishment of the Creative Arts Program in 1939. Allen Tate arrived in that year as Poet-in-Residence, and there were some studio courses (noncredit) in drawing, painting, and sculpture. Credit courses in composition already existed in the Music Department, largely as a result of the pioneering efforts of Roy Dickenson Welch, who had come to Princeton in 1934. But the general situation in the arts was perhaps typified by the fact that the person teaching sculpture (Joseph Brown) had a more permanent position at the University as boxing coach.

World War II caused this early, experimental period to be artificially prolonged, and it was not until 1947 that real expansion began. The arrival of Richard P. Blackmur in 1940 had by this time given a great lift to creative writing, and after the war courses in the creative arts were regularized and some distinguished visiting lecturers were recruited. At the same time, informal and extracurricular activities continued to be very important.

The present-day role of the creative arts at Princeton was defined largely by the report of a special committee appointed in 1965 by President Robert F. Goheen '40 and chaired by Professor Rensselaer Lee '20 *26. This committee concluded that four major aims would be served by expansion of the Creative Arts Program: (1) to permit artistically talented undergraduates to receive a liberal education while continuing work in the arts; (2) to allow students with artistic talent (whether or not they had professional aspirations) to broaden their experience and develop their creative faculties as undergraduates; (3) to help counter the movement toward ever greater specialization in education; and (4) to provide a means of bringing a larger number of visiting writers and artists to campus each year. Administrative responsibility for the creative arts (outside of music and architecture) was vested in the Council of the Humanities, an arrangement that has worked very well to this day.

In 1966, a wing of the newly acquired Nassau Street School was assigned to the creative arts, and in this way space was found for painting and sculpture studios (including the old gymnasium for larger sculptures), for playwriting, for a print shop and a graphics studio, and for ceramics. There was also a reading room for the arts and office space for visiting faculty, while other classrooms in the building accommodated overflow sections of economics and language courses. The space was far from elegant, but it at least met basic needs.

As student interest continued to increase, the decision was made in 1971 to divide the Creative Arts Program into two separate programs, the Program in Creative Writing and the Performing Arts and the Visual Arts Program; later (in 1975) the Program in Theater and Dance was separated from Creative Writing and given equal status.

Each of these programs has its own director, who is responsible to the chairman of the Humanities Council and to an interdisciplinary faculty committee. A major objective has been to provide both course offerings in the arts for all interested students, whatever their majors, and opportunities for more intensive work by advanced students whose creative arts work combines with disciplinary courses to constitute specializations within departments such as English, Comparative Literature, and Art and Archaeology.

The advent of coeducation in 1969 had a substantial impact on the arts, not only in numbers of interested students, but also in spirit and in the availability of new talent. Theater, dance, and choral singing benefited immeasurably from the presence of women, as did academic and extracurricular activities generally. Since external perceptions often lag behind realities, the next section of this report is intended to convey some of the flavor of present-day activities.

First, however, I would like to state explicitly, if briefly, the general point of view that informs the University's approach to the creative arts. They are not a "frill," or something that it is nice to have alongside "serious" subjects. Rather, the creative arts are a central component of a liberal education, worthy of rigorous pursuit in their own right, and with much to contribute to deeper understanding of other subjects just as they, in turn, draw strength from work that is more historical or critical in character.

This point of view was expressed with particular clarity in an essay written in 1947 by our distinguished colleague Professor Cone when he was an instructor in music at Princeton:

> Knowledge is not covered by historical scholarship alone—nor, going one step further, by critical, interpretive evaluation. *Creation itself opens a unique channel of knowledge, and as such is in the proper sphere of the university.*
>
> I am not speaking only of the profound knowledge of his medium

which every artist must possess, although this aspect is important. When I speak of creation in relation to knowledge, I mean that the process of writing a poem, of painting a picture, of composing a song, involves discovery on the part of the artist, which is in turn communicated to his audience through the work of art. Every poem, picture or song, insofar as it has any value, contributes to human knowledge in a unique way. When Liszt wrote his B minor piano sonata, he discovered something about the relationship of triads separated by a tritone. And when Michelangelo painted and chiseled, he contributed to our knowledge of the expressiveness of the human figure.

The paradox is, indeed, that the artist should be forced to prove his fitness to join the community of scholars. Who should know more about poetry than the poet, about music than the musician? Yet historians and critics presume to teach the artist his trade, under the assumption that he is an inspired fool who knows not what he does. Granted that he sometimes is—yet is he not just as often a man with the profoundest insight into his medium, gained by careful study and constant practice? Granted that he may have something to learn from the scholars, should they not learn from him as well?

It is encouraging that the University has come such a long way along that path that Professor Cone proposed. In my view, however, the current level of activity, and the current degree of integration of the creative arts into the larger university, are only steps—albeit important ones—toward the fuller realization of the potential of the creative arts at Princeton. . . .

THE CREATIVE ARTS IN A LIBERAL ARTS CURRICULUM

Contributions of the Arts to Liberal Education

One of the principal objectives of a liberal education is to give students an enhanced appreciation of their own culture, as well as other cultures, all seen in their many dimensions. This is accomplished through the study of history, language, literature, and critical interpretation, along with the study of other subjects ranging from philosophy to psychology to physics. Today, few would disagree that active engagement with the creative arts, with the processes of artistic creativity, also has much to contribute beyond simply the acquisition of certain kinds of technical proficiency.

My longtime friend and colleague Professor William J. Baumol of the Department of Economics has been one of the strongest advocates of the arts at Princeton. Recently he wrote to me:

Any student of history or criticism who has never struggled with the problems with which the great artists have had to grapple and were to some degree able to solve must inevitably be handicapped seriously in dealing with his subject. . . . The study of art history and the study of the techniques and artistic goals of painting or sculpture are inherently complementary, each benefiting substantially from the other.

Similarly, the production of a Shakespearean play is much more than an exercise in the techniques of acting, directing, staging, and costuming; it is primarily an opportunity to learn more about the play itself—the nature of its characters, the design of its action, and the meaning of the work as a whole. This kind of artistic activity—making a play come alive in a fresh way—also serves an integrating function by allowing those involved most intimately to see the often subtle connections between the underlying ideas and the forms through which they have been communicated in the past and are communicated today.

Professor Edmund M. Keeley '48, teacher of creative writing at Princeton for nearly three decades, believes that in an era in which critical theory in literature has moved away from a focus on the writer as craftsman, students derive special educational benefits from creative writing. As the student learns the specific techniques of the writer, he is much better able to see other works from the writer's perspective as well as from the perspective of the scholar. James Richardson '71, who directs the Program in Creative Writing, underscores this important point:

Though I as an amphibious writer-scholar would no more have all literature courses taught by writers than all writing courses taught by scholars, I do think that writers provide critical insights that supplement the work of literature departments. There may be aspects of literature that writers *tend* to understand better than non-writing critics (just as there are things scholars understand better than writers—often the things that readers, most of whom are not writers, need and want to know). Writers often have special understanding of how works achieve their effects—that is, of style. Style is the literary equivalent of personality, and it is as inseparable from our response to a literary work as personality is from our response to a person. Writers also tend to have a particularly strong sense of how ordinary personal experience is transformed into art. This is often interesting to younger readers, who may regard literature as a means of self-discovery, and who may have difficulty finding anything directly relevant to them in historically or stylistically "distant" works unless told how to "dig it out."

Liberal education is also concerned, in a more general sense, with the development of critical faculties of all kinds, and here again the opportunity to try one's own hand at creating a work of art can be highly instructive. Students in the various creative arts programs are helped to develop a heightened critical sense by evaluating the works of their peers as well as by having their own efforts subjected to the scrutiny of both teachers and fellow students. Standards of excellence developed in this way are indispensable counterparts to other kinds of learning aimed at serving this same objective.

The arts may also provide unusually good opportunities for personal growth. Studying acting and acting on stage, for example, often enable students to learn many things about themselves, their intuitions, and their perspectives as well as their limitations and their fears. Having to complete a painting by a certain date, or having to write a prescribed number of poems by the end of term, can also teach self-discipline—often much more powerfully than simply having to study for an examination. As a colleague remarked: "When ten people expect to hear your poem tomorrow, it concentrates the mind wonderfully."

A group of students who wrote to me earlier this fall on behalf of a newly formed Theatre Arts Council suggested another important contribution of the arts to life in a residential university. Productions and performances of all kinds are one way of bringing together students from all classes. The establishment of the residential college system for freshmen and sophomores has made it all the more important to encourage interactions among the classes, and the myriad activities in the arts described earlier in this report certainly offer opportunities for undergraduates to get to know each other as well as faculty, graduate students, staff, and, in some cases, residents of the local community. The arts can be a strongly unifying set of activities.

The student authors of the Theatre Arts Council report go on to speak eloquently of the benefits of (in their words) the "hands-on experience for those who participate":

The architecture student can both design and build a set; the future businessman or advertising executive can gain invaluable experience in budgeting and promoting a production; a visual artist can design posters and programs; a budding writer can write material and have it performed and critiqued. Any person who participates in the production end of theatre receives very concentrated lessons in the management of people and resources.

Finally, the burgeoning development of the arts in recent years has enriched the life of the entire University community by attracting a far larger number of students for whom the arts are important. When we talk about diversity and its educational benefits, we often have in mind differences in economic background, in race or religion, in political persuasion, or in geographic region or country of origin. But surely differences in interests—the presence on campus of both artists and athletes (including some who are artists *and* athletes)—contribute greatly to the overall learning environment of Princeton.

Similarly, the significantly larger number of professional artists who have come to Princeton to teach in recent years has added vitality to the entire University community. Many faculty colleagues have remarked on what a much more interesting place Princeton is as a result of the rich variety of exhibitions, plays, concerts, and performances of all kinds now available. The University at large benefits immeasurably, in many indirect as well as direct ways, from this most welcome outpouring of activity in the arts.

Contributions of Princeton to the Arts

Relationships that are genuinely reciprocal are often the strongest ones. In this spirit, it is the hope of many of us that, just as the arts contribute much to liberal education at Princeton, so the liberal arts character of this University will make a significant contribution to the arts.

The first and most obvious way in which Princeton can contribute to the arts is through the careers—and lives—of our graduates. I recall a conversation a year or two ago with Jimmy Stewart '32, who remembered clearly (and very affectionately) *both* the time he had spent in Triangle and the lasting value of the broad, liberal education that he received at Princeton. Frank Stella '58 made progress as an artist at Princeton in spite of the very limited commitment of Princeton to the visual arts when he was an undergraduate. Among writers, W. S. Merwin '48 in poetry and John McPhee '53 in nonfiction have gone on to enjoy distinguished careers. In music, Milton Babbitt *42, who earned one of our earliest M.F.A. degrees, has contributed his formidable talents in teaching as well as in composing. Robert Venturi '47 *50 is one of a number of distinguished graduates in architecture.

Even more relevant, I suspect, are the accomplishments of recent graduates who have studied here under more favorable circumstances than their predecessors. To cite a few examples: innovative sculptor and sound artist Christopher Janney '73 was named by *Esquire* magazine to the 1984 register of "men and women under forty who are changing America" in the category of Arts and Letters; Barbara Shottenfeld '78 had her senior thesis, an original musical show, produced at an off-Broadway theater in New York as *I Can't Keep Running in Place*; Maria Katzenbach '76 published her senior thesis as a widely acclaimed novel entitled *The Grab*; Julio Rivera '76, a professional dancer in New York, has worked extensively with the Alvin Ailey Company; and Mark Nelson '77, who has regularly acted in the New York theater, now plays the leading role in Neil Simon's *Brighton Beach Memoirs* on Broadway.

Perhaps just as important as what they are doing is the perspective that recent graduates have on the character of their experience at Princeton. A visual arts graduate now enrolled in an internship program at the Whitney Museum in New York, Mary K. Weatherford '84, observed that the small scale of Princeton's program, the rich resources of courses in the humanities, and the opportunity for close contact with faculty who are themselves active in the arts were, from her point of view, the most salient features of her program of study. "For me," she concluded, "I don't think there was a better place to study art."

A recent letter to Ze'eva Cohen speaks for itself:

> Ze'eva, I'm very happy. You said once that a person must give his all to become a dancer. Well I don't think about it much; I can't imagine being anything else. Money doesn't concern me even though it's scarce; just as long as it keeps me alive, that's all I ask for right now.
>
> And to think . . . without you I might still be a physicist. . . .

Without in any way deprecating the value of professional programs in conservatories, art institutes, and other colleges and universities that have different educational philosophies, I am persuaded that the intellectual and personal interactions possible at Princeton can have powerful long-term effects on artists. John McPhee '53, whose own work has done so much to shape the literary genre that is now associated with him, has commented that writers need "enough grist for their mills," and that this vital resource is offered Princeton students through an "incomparable feast of courses." "When else," he asks, "will individuals have such an opportunity to get the factual basis for their creative work?"

Even more is involved than just the professional experience of the artists, important as that is. Artists can be just as narrow and parochial as the rest of us, and one of the objectives of Princeton should be to educate artists who will appreciate other points of view and the relevance of their own work as artists to the society in which they live.

Finally, however, the most fundamental contribution of Princeton to students who are aspiring artists is the same contribution that the University seeks to make in the case of all students: to provide an overall education that is broad, stimulating, and liberating. It was encouraging to see precisely this kind of contribution applauded by George Hartman, Jr., FAIA, who had served on the jury for 1984 senior theses, in an article published last year in *Architecture*. Mr. Hartman was quoted as saying that he preferred Princeton graduates to any others because "these students are learning to think; Princeton educates people more than it trains them. And this is fine. Give me a year in an office with them, and I'll make them architects. That's *my* job. Educating them is Princeton's job. Training ends with skill development. Education begins lifelong learning, and *that's* what makes excellence in architecture."

Princeton also contributes to the arts through its graduates who do not become professional artists. An appreciation of the arts developed as a student can have lasting effects no matter what the individual's career path. Princetonians in the future, as in the past, will no doubt have many opportunities to serve on arts councils and on the boards of theater companies, symphonies, and museums. As citizens, and in some cases as legislators and government officials, they will also have opportunities to influence national policy in this as in other areas.

In this vein, Professor John Shearman, chairman of the Department of Art and Archaeology, has observed:

> The special thing we can contribute beyond a training of the mind might be, therefore, the planting in innumerable other careers of young people who are visually critical and educated; the world does not need everyone to be like that, but it certainly needs more than it

has at present. Further, I think that the generation we train now will have one responsibility which has never weighed so heavily on an earlier one, that is in conservation. To decide what shall be retained of the past, and how, is a great issue, and it is partly economic, partly political; but I for one want those decisions taken or influenced by people who know what they are talking about. If Princeton is producing future leaders, it is important that a proportion should be visually informed, or at least know where information exists.

Princeton also contributes to the arts by providing opportunities for artists in residence to be part of a university community, with daily contact with students as well as faculty colleagues. We should be careful not to underestimate the reciprocal value of the teaching process, nor to undervalue the bonds that are forged along the way. John McPhee remarked recently that teaching forces him to articulate what it is that he does, and "takes me out of myself" for a while to think about the writing of other individuals. As a result, he finds it possible to "go back to my own writing refreshed."

In addition, Princeton, like other universities, can contribute to the arts by serving as a locale for experimentation and the testing of ideas. As indicated earlier, the economic problems that beset the arts in most commercialized surroundings put a premium on avoiding risk. While there are at times similar pressures in the University, they are much attenuated here; and there are (fortunately) offsetting pressures to take chances, to explore new approaches, to be provocative.

From this perspective, universities can be seen as important patrons of the arts. To be sure, universities will never be able to be the sites for activities such as those that take place at such large, specialized institutions as the Metropolitan Opera and the Art Institute of Chicago. But perhaps Princeton can complement the work of such organizations by serving as a supportive "home" for activities that can be done on a smaller scale, at an earlier stage in their development, and with more of a commitment to the learning that can come from a partial success (or even a monumental failure!).

Issues

It would be surprising (and even disappointing) if the success of the arts in becoming much more central to all aspects of the life of the University were not accompanied by some continuing debates. Apart from ever-present questions about resources and priorities, there is continuing discussion of three important issues: (1) Where should the line be drawn between "credit" and "noncredit" activities, between what is part of the curriculum and what is extracurricular? (2) What status should be conferred on those who teach in the arts—should they be regular faculty, with tenure-track appointments, or should their careers be seen differently? (3) Should Princeton offer graduate programs in more areas of the arts than music and architecture?

At a much earlier point in Princeton's history, arguments were made against giving credit for any work in the arts (excepting architecture), the feeling being that the extracurricular activities available to undergraduates were adequate to satisfy their interests. If students could participate in music groups of many kinds, write for literary magazines and newspapers, and act, direct, and design sets in a variety of student musical and dramatic productions, why should they need courses to provide them with similar opportunities? The response, of course, is that more "formal" instruction provides quite a different kind of opportunity—an opportunity to extend one's knowledge and to perfect one's skills under the supervision of experienced practitioners who have the same commitment to excellence as instructors in other subjects taught at Princeton.

It seems to me highly desirable that there continue to be strong curricular *and* strong extracurricular opportunities in the arts, permitting the arts at Princeton to meet more than one kind of need and to fit more than one kind of temperament. Within courses in the arts, students must be prepared not merely to be creative at the same level of artistry they have already achieved, but to sharpen their creative and critical faculties in a highly disciplined way—to *stretch* themselves through a carefully designed process of constructive criticism. Extracurricular activities often reach high standards of quality and can impose a healthy discipline of their own, but they allow for a greater degree of flexibility and a somewhat less formal approach.

I should add that there is one important area within the arts where the question of credit versus noncredit has not yet been resolved. At issue is credit for certain specific kinds of musical performance. It has been suggested informally that Princeton consider establishing a Program in Musical Performance, in which some formula involving participation in ensembles, private instrumental or vocal instruction, and a written component might combine to equal one course. The arguments for such an arrangement are that: (1) it would add a crucial dimension to the teaching of music at Princeton; (2) it would lessen the academic "penalty" (in the form of time not devoted to course work) attached to practicing and performing on a regular basis; and (3) it would enable faculty instructors in musical performance to participate more in the essential educational mission of the University.

The question becomes: Would it be wise to extend the range of credit offerings in the arts in this way, perhaps building on the University's experience with theater and dance? We have here, in any case, a good example of the kind of healthy tension between artistic commitments and more traditional conceptions of liberal education to which I referred at the start of this report.

The dilemmas that confront us in faculty staffing are different in character but no less important. It has been generally agreed that the teachers of courses in the arts should be active practitioners. As noted earlier, Princeton has been fortunate to attract many fine artists, in all fields, to teach undergraduate courses on a part-time basis while pursuing active artistic careers off the campus (especially in New York and environs). This is ideal from many standpoints. It brings a wide range of techniques and viewpoints to the campus, it assures a constant "freshness" of outlook, and it avoids the problem of teachers getting into routines that bore them as well as their students.

However, work on a short-term and part-time basis has meant that this group of teachers cannot acquire the security of tenure available to regular faculty, and some may feel distanced from the customary practices of the institution. A particular danger is that such teachers may think of themselves as peripheral, and, as a result, their students may assume that the pursuit of the arts is not "serious" at Princeton. To alleviate aspects of this problem, it has been suggested that at least one position in each program—presumably that of director—should be on a tenure track, providing not only a regular faculty status for that position but also a reasonable continuity of leadership for the program. The current compromise has been to provide full-time positions for the directors of programs and to allow individuals holding these positions, as well as some others, to be eligible for reappointment without limit as to number of terms.

A new proposal that I believe deserves serious consideration is to make provision for a limited number of continuing appointments as "Fellows of the Council of the Humanities" for part-time teachers in the arts of exceptionally high standing with whom the University wishes to maintain a long-term association. Such appointments could enjoy a status all their own and might confer some of the benefits of more permanent ties. Obviously, a good deal more thought needs to be given to this idea, including the exact specifications of such positions and the process to be followed in making appointments of this kind.

The question of whether Princeton should offer graduate programs in more areas of the arts than music and architecture is different again from either the question of credit or the question of faculty status. It is certainly true that a master of fine arts degree could draw on considerable existing resources at Princeton. Supporters of such an extension of the University's teaching programs in these fields see work at a higher level as a natural continuation of the search for excellence in all fields studied at the University.

Others have observed that the goals of an M.F.A. program are intrinsically different from those of an A.B. program in a liberal arts context. M.F.A. programs exist primarily to further the professional careers of aspiring artists in a quite practical way. As a consequence, students and instructors alike become involved in making contacts and arranging for students' work to be seen or read or heard. The vocational objectives reflected in such concentration on career advancement could detract from the broader educational goals of Princeton, and graduate programs of this kind would also inevitably put more pressure on scarce resources. For these reasons, there is at present no consideration being given to additional master's programs in the arts.

Princeton has always been very selective about new ventures, and particularly cautious about proposals that would take it outside its traditional emphasis on the liberal arts and sciences. The formal creative arts programs that now exist are designed to provide a rigorous introduction to the creative process as an integral part of that tradition. Our goal, it seems to me, ought not to involve an increased professional orientation, but further improvement in the quality of existing programs and the development of even stronger ties between these programs and other parts of the curriculum.

*   *   *   *   *

Working on this annual report has provided an opportunity to review within a single document a series of developments in the creative arts that in their totality constitute, I believe, a quiet revolution at Princeton. Looking back over what has transpired, especially in recent years, I am particularly pleased by:

• The *vitality and infectious good spirit* of teachers and students alike, a group hard to discourage and eager to share their excitement with others.

• The *range* of activity, extending from poetry to drama, from musical composition and performance to dance, from sculpture and painting to design, from photography to film.

• The *diversity* of students as well as of art forms, with engineers and English majors working side by side in creative writing workshops, on stage, and in artistic activities of every kind.

• The extraordinarily *high quality* of what has been accomplished—in the face of severe limitations of facilities, resources, and (if we are to be frank) a somewhat inhospitable early history.

• The exceptional degree of *personal attention* and *individual supervision* that has characterized these programs.

• The development of the creative arts *within the context of a liberal arts and sciences institution*, with a premium placed on ideas, on appreciating the creative process, and on reinforcing other forms of learning rather than fighting against them or believing that it is narrow technical goals that are to be served.

Professor W. Robert Connor *61, whose leadership of the Council of the humanities is critical to the future of the arts at Princeton, has described our prospects well:

> In the long run one of the great opportunities for the humanities and for Princeton is to move toward a closer integration of the creative and the scholarly talents of our students. Literature, architecture, indeed all the visual arts, even historical studies, might benefit from a closer involvement with the arts. We need students who have not merely read plays but have experienced them, who have not only studied historical periods but who can imagine them as living realities. Conversely, if Princeton has a role to play in strengthening the creative arts in this country, it is surely not in attempting to duplicate what conservatories or professional schools do, but in bringing the arts closer together with the formidable scholarly resources of this institution.

The long-term strength of Princeton as a university depends on nurturing the creative spirit in all of its forms. This requires an energetic effort in the arts that complements scholarship in other areas and that reflects the same capacity to see beauty and the same excitement over new discoveries that stimulate the most outstanding teachers and scholars in every field of knowledge.

Capturing "Otherness"

. . . Addresses, as well as sermons, sometimes have texts, and today I would like to consider the broad implications for education of a passage from Professor Robert Darnton's widely acclaimed book, *The Great Cat Massacre and Other Episodes in French Cultural History*. Professor Darnton (who is, I am pleased to say, a member of this faculty) comments on anthropology and the study of history as follows:

> One thing seems clear to everyone who returns from field work: other people are other. They do not think the way we do. And if we want to understand their way of thinking, we should set out with the idea of capturing otherness. Translated into the terms of the historian's craft, that may merely sound like the familiar injunction against anachronism. It is worth repeating, nonetheless; for nothing is easier than to slip into the comfortable assumption that Europeans thought and felt two centuries ago just as we do today—allowing for the wigs and wooden shoes. We constantly need to be shaken out of a false sense of familiarity with the past, to be administered doses of culture shock.

How did ordinary Frenchmen in the eighteenth century construe their world, invest it with meaning, and infuse it with emotion? These are the questions Professor Darnton investigates, and the principal actors in his drama are peasants, artisans, and petty bourgeois; his source materials include folktales (among others, a singularly gruesome version of Little Red Riding Hood), diaries, and police files. As his title suggests, a centerpiece of the book is a detailed account of a massacre of cats carried out with gleeful abandon by the apprentices and journeymen in a Paris print shop—and then reenacted over and over for the pleasure of the perpetrators as they mock their ungenerous master. To "get the joke" requires appreciating its various levels of meaning, being aware of the nature of relationships between artisans and their masters, knowing something about attitudes toward the treatment of animals in Europe at the time, and understanding as well the symbolic significance of cats in that society. To read the story only from our perspective is to becloud its meaning and to consign ourselves to the role of puzzled outsiders.

Another distinguished member of our history faculty, Professor Natalie Davis, has enriched our understanding of a still earlier period in French society by retelling the tale of a sixteenth-century peasant, Martin Guerre, who deserts his wife and disappears from his village. Some years later, a "stranger" arrives in the village claiming to be the same Martin Guerre, returning to his family. A complex legal case over his identity and property rights ensues, and the stranger is proved an imposter only upon the return of the real Martin Guerre. Professor Davis's research not only resulted in an excellent book, but also provided invaluable guidance for the creators of a fine movie that some of you may have seen.

Those of us who have heard Professor Davis describe her attempts to get the movie producer to "tell the story right" have been both entertained and instructed. She is not just a good storyteller, though she certainly is that, but a shrewd analyst who argues persuasively, for example, that some of the simplest interpretations of the complicity of Martin Guerre's wife in the deception, which make sense to us today, would have had no meaning in a sixteenth-century French village.

Seeking to capture "otherness" is, in my view, much more than a powerful approach to the study of history. Given broad definition—to encompass not only other times but also other cultures in our own time, other disciplines, other groups within our own society, and other individuals within one's own group (however specified)—an appreciation for "otherness" is central to the very idea of liberal education. We aim always to understand, but we cannot truly understand if we allow ourselves to look at other peoples, at events new to us, at academic subjects with which we are unfamiliar, and even at fellow students, from a preestablished viewpoint that is often, if we are honest enough to acknowledge it, terribly parochial.

To be sure, it is not easy to appreciate properly perspectives different from our own, and we have to guard against adopting an oversimplified conception of another society or another field of study. Most societies, for example, are likely on examination to turn out to be as complex and as pluralistic as our own, and it will not do simply to substitute one stereotype for another. The image of the Chinese box puzzle comes to mind: clearing up one conundrum often leads directly to another. But the alternative to developing a suitably complex understanding of various ways of thinking is to accept a limiting myopia: a nearly impenetrable barrier to learning.

As easy as it is to misread European history by failing to comprehend other angles of vision, it is, of course, easier yet to misunderstand the history and culture of non-Western societies. Last spring our Art Museum had a splendid exhibit of Chinese painting and calligraphy that spanned the eleventh to the twentieth centuries. Wen Fong, professor of art history at Princeton, wrote an accompanying catalog that painstakingly demonstrated the respects in which Chinese painting, calligraphy, and poetry have developed out of ways of thinking very different from ours. That exhibition was not only beautiful, it was extraordinarily educational.

Works of art generally can be powerfully revealing. As John Shearman, chairman of our Department of Art and Archaeology, recently observed: ''Art history allows the study of the concrete historical product . . .; not a reconstruction, visualization, interpretation of a situation or event, but the Sistine Ceiling or the Parthenon in fact. This brings with it proportionally exceptional opportunities and responsibilities: the opportunity, for example, to be more precise and to apply tests to our conclusions, the responsibility to be vigorously critical with the evidence.'' Our own museum, which is in the process of a long overdue expansion, is dedicated to precisely the kind of study Professor Shearman describes. It is a *teaching* museum, and I hope that you will take advantage of the great learning opportunities that it offers.

Colleagues in the School of Architecture are quick to point out that the buildings and spaces all around us, including those on this campus, can provide not only immediate pleasure, but deep insights into the aspirations, the aesthetic convictions, and the technologies of different periods as well as different architects. Both colonial America and the British Parliament are represented in Nassau Hall. This chapel, in its rich detail, reveals many elements of the vision that inspired Gothic architecture. The molecular biology laboratory now under construction will be seen as the modern-day offspring of Guyot Hall, its scientific neighbor to the north. Please do not walk past Wu Hall for four years without reflecting on (and asking about) the Elizabethan mode of decoration over the entrance and the allusion to an Italian piazza at the base of the monument capped by Mr. Venturi's wonderfully whimsical outline of a tiger. The ''why'' questions about architecture are just as interesting—and just as important—as the corresponding questions about the meaning of a painting or historical document.

An inquiring mind, and open eyes, then, are two indispensable aids to capturing otherness. But additional aids are needed too, and I would put an appreciation for language—including English—right near the top of any list we might construct. In my view, our frequent failure to understand other contemporary societies has many roots, but surely lack of proficiency in languages contributes mightily to lack of insight into distant cultures and different traditions. For reasons both geographic and historical, our country is particularly ill served in this regard, and the consequences of this national neglect can be very serious.

You will think of historical examples as readily as I will. Sad to say, the long history of this country's relations with Latin America provides a far too extensive record of the effects of fundamental misperceptions. It has been said that "Americans will do anything for Latin America except read about it." The current interest in a number of distinguished Latin American authors offers at least some hope that this will begin to change.

Just as literature, art, and architecture can reveal much about the history, the culture, and even the present-day politics of a region, an understanding of diverse fields of knowledge can open up entirely new realms of thought and experience. Thus, in urging an appreciation of otherness, I am as concerned about our approach to academic disciplines that seem difficult and threatening as I am about the way we view other societies.

This University's distribution requirements for undergraduates testify to the importance we attach to breadth in education. But it is not enough simply to do what you are required to do for the sake of satisfying requirements. The problem is not that most of us fail to recognize the "otherness" in subjects that are uncomfortable for us; it is rather that too often we seek to protect ourselves from such subjects—to keep away from them and to keep them away from us. If you are to take full advantage of your educational opportunities here, you must try to get "inside" subjects that for you have an aura of "otherness" about them, whether that means the study of poetry, physics, or twelve-tone music.

Getting "inside" a subject is made easier if you try hard to understand its appeal, not if you treat it simply as something to acquire or to overcome. Mathematicians, for example, are understandably irritated when we think of their subject as consisting of a bunch of tricks to be learned so that we can perform other necessary operations. Mathematics is in fact one of the most aesthetically satisfying and cumulative of subjects, with a rich history and a power to excite the imagination that is very special. Bertrand Russell once tried to explain the essence of his lifelong love affair with mathematics in these terms:

Mathematics, rightly viewed, possesses . . . supreme beauty—a beauty cold and austere, like that of sculpture, without appeal to any part of our weaker nature, without the gorgeous trappings of painting or music, yet sublimely pure, and capable of a stern perfection such as only the greatest art can show. The true spirit of delight, the exaltation, the sense of being more than man, which is the touchstone of the highest excellence, is to be found in mathematics as surely as in poetry.

History records that Archimedes, the great Greek mathematician and scientist, was killed in 212 B.C. by Roman soldiers who burst in on him while he was too absorbed in studying a diagram etched in sand to escape. I do not recommend—or expect—that degree of absorption. Moreover, I recognize that mathematics is frightening to many of us. Indeed, fear of mathematics may be more responsible than any other single factor for discouraging many Princeton students from pursuing not just mathematics itself but subjects that use it—and one result is that too many graduates of this University have much less of an appreciation for other fields (especially the sciences and engineering) than they should have.

Those of us on the faculty need to keep working to find ways to make all of our subjects as accessible as possible, without sacrificing either their subtlety or their rigor. I hope that you will urge us on. Otherwise, all of us will be tacit participants—conspirators really—in the modern-day separation between modes of thought that diminishes our capacity to see fundamental interrelationships, or even to believe, any longer, in the unity of knowledge that the Greeks took so much for granted.

There is one further dimension to ''otherness'' that I want to mention specifically: in this residential University, you are members of what will almost certainly prove to be the most marvelously diverse human community that the great majority of you will ever know again. While you will have much in common with those you will meet here, you will also be aware right away that there are many manifestations of ''otherness.'' And I do not refer simply to such obvious differences as gender, race, socio-economic background, and state (or country) of origin, even though all of these are very important. I have in mind as well differences in interests (athletics, the arts, and music, to cite just three examples), in religion and politics, and in outlook and personality defined in a multiplicity of ways.

You are given a special opportunity to get to know these other talented people close up, warts and all; to see them grow and develop and change—as you yourself grow and develop and change. You have so much to learn from each other, but both effort and risk-taking will be required. Please do not encapsulate yourself with those here who have the least to teach you (and you them) because you are already the most alike. Celebrate, at the same time, the *individuality* that ultimately contradicts all group labels.

I would like to conclude by referring to a personal experience. Ten years ago, I was a member of one of the earliest delegations of Americans to travel to the People's Republic of China following the Cultural Revolution. Our group consisted of eleven presidents of American colleges and universities invited to visit a number of Chinese universities at a time when foreign visitors—and especially American visitors—were very rare. That trip, which lasted three weeks, was one of the most intensive, most revealing, learning experiences of my life. I was driven to cope with all of the levels of "otherness" that we have been discussing. Immersed in a radically different society, operating on assumptions at variance with any I had known, I was also obliged to talk about fields of knowledge that were often unfamiliar (how many times I wished that I knew more about technology), and I was thrown together, literally every waking hour, with a small group of people who had been largely strangers to me before.

What did I learn? In part, surely, to appreciate another society, even though I certainly did not acquire more than a surface familiarity with any aspect of life in China, including university life. The dose of culture shock that I received was substantial by any reckoning. Interestingly, however, I think that the main consequence for my own education was not so much greater familiarity with China as it was a far sharper understanding of my own country, my own University, and myself.

Perhaps there is a kind of paradox here: the greater the opportunity to capture "otherness" (and it would be hard to imagine a trip better calculated to serve that purpose than the one I have described), the more fully we come to know our own society and ourselves. In my case at least, the harder I tried to get outside myself, to see things from perspectives different from my own, the more aware I became of what were really the central features—often taken for granted—of my own everyday pattern of life. Never before had such elemental concepts as freedom of expression and individual choice presented themselves to me in such stark relief. Never before had I been so aware of the pervasive effects of severe resource constraints, demography, and centuries of history.

It may be, then, that we give greatest effect to the ancient dictum "know thyself" by making the most vigorous effort to know others, and on their terms. Contrast sharpens perceptions of all kinds, and a determined quest to capture "otherness" may serve to increase your own self-awareness at the same time that it allows you to develop a far richer understanding of places and peoples around you.

May this University stimulate just such a quest. And in doing so, may it offer you an education that is enlightening and enjoyable: an education, moreover, that can be profoundly rewarding in the opportunities it offers to be of service in a world very much in need of both breadth of outlook and generosity of spirit.

International Studies at Princeton

EXCERPTED FROM THE THIRD AND FINAL CHAPTER OF
THE REPORT OF THE PRESIDENT
MAY 1987*

. . . Not even the most cynical among us could deny that a great deal has been accomplished in the last three decades in strengthening international studies, at Princeton and elsewhere, and in breaking down tendencies toward provincialism, which must always be recognized. Still, I am even more conscious of what must yet be done.

In a generic sense, the tasks ahead are of two kinds: first, to make further progress in *integrating* forms of teaching and of scholarship in international studies that are still too innocent of each other; second, to find, nationally as well as within particular universities, the substantial resources that are required if we are to discharge our responsibilities adequately.

The Intellectual Challenge: Fusing Ancient and Modern, Cultural and Economic/Political

At Princeton, as at most universities, the natural organization of the institution reinforces certain kinds of intellectual separatism that are, I believe, at odds with the way things ought to be. The departmental structure of universities, with its manifold advantages, contributes to this problem. So too does the pressure of specialization. Nor has the prevailing pattern of funding worked against the forces of compartmentalization.

The two principal forms of "separatism" that seem to me especially dangerous are: (1) the dichotomy sometimes present between the study of ancient and modern aspects of a culture or a region; and (2) the often even more pronounced division between the study of language/literature/culture/history and the rigorous study of contemporary economic and political developments.

It is trite and not terribly helpful to preach against specialization when all of us recognize the value of digging deeply into a particular historical period, culture, or discipline. At the same time, there are

* The first two chapters described international and regional studies programs at Princeton and the increasing internationalization of its faculty and student body.

obvious advantages to avoiding a compartmentalization of knowledge that robs students and scholars of larger perspectives.

How are we to increase our institutional capacity to connect the study of ancient and modern periods? One way is by recognizing and rewarding examples of faculty breadth that are, fortunately, already present at universities such as Princeton. For example, Professor Martin Collcutt works with both early and modern Japanese literatures and, in addition, knows a great deal about Chinese thought. Our most recent appointment in East Asian Studies, Professor Ying-shih Yü, is a distinguished scholar of thirteenth- to seventeenth-century Chinese history while also enjoying an enviable reputation as a poet. In making additional appointments, at both junior and senior levels, it clearly behooves us to seek scholars who are themselves "connectors" of subspecialties.

A longer-term approach is to give more emphasis in graduate training to appropriate kinds of complementarities—across periods, styles of research, cultures, and disciplines. This is much easier said than done, and many of the incentives (at least the short-term ones) work in the other direction. But there is a growing recognition, I think, that this kind of breadth will enrich an individual's scholarship and will also enable a young faculty member to teach a wider variety of courses in, one hopes, a more interesting fashion.*

Bridging the gulf that often exists between contemporary social science and the study of history, culture, and language is even more difficult. To be sure, universities generally have a few individuals who are both distinguished in their disciplines and competent in the use of a difficult language such as Chinese or Japanese. Princeton is fortunate, for example, to have on its faculty Professor Gregory Chow, an eminent economist, whose personal knowledge of China has led him to write about economic reform in China and to participate actively in programs within China to improve the teaching of economics and to introduce more of the concepts of the price system to that country. Professor Chow is clearly an exception, however, to the general rule

---

* The general examination required of all Ph.D. candidates in the Department of Germanic Languages and Literatures represents one effort to reverse the trend toward overspecialization of graduate studies. The general examination is specifically designed to encourage students to make connections between history and literature and to demonstrate an understanding of the relationship among historical periods in German culture, as well as knowledge of one period. To accomplish these ends, the general examination requires the student to prepare two topics for discussion: one is a "diachronic" or historical topic, i.e., a question that pertains to the changes in a literature over some period of time; and the other is a "synchronic" or period topic, i.e., a question that pertains to the literature at one specific point as seen in its broader cultural context.

that outstanding economists (in particular) often seem to lack detailed knowledge of non-Western languages and cultures.

The other social sciences are somewhat better off in this regard. The objectives to be served are illustrated by the activities of two exceedingly well-trained faculty members in our Departments of Sociology and Politics, both of whom also participate in the Program in East Asian Studies.

Professor Gilbert Rozman in the Sociology Department has a deep interest in the comparative historical development of the Chinese, Japanese, and Russian societies. His extensive knowledge of the languages and cultures of all three of these countries has enabled the Program in East Asian Studies to offer a sequence of comparative courses on China, Japan, and Russia: "The Impact of Communism on China and Russia," "The Asian Legacy: China and Japan and Rapid Modernization," and "Rapid Modernization: Japan and Russia." There are, needless to say, few social scientists with Professor Rozman's grasp of Chinese, Japanese, and Russian.

Assistant Professor Kent Calder, who holds a joint appointment in the Department of Politics and the Woodrow Wilson School, reads and speaks Japanese fluently. His scholarly interests include the political economy of East Asia, the politics of international trade, U.S.-Japan economic and technological relations, and the domestic determinants of foreign policy in the United States, Japan, and Western Europe. One can hope that Professor Calder represents an emerging generation of scholars who are at home in both foreign cultures and the social sciences.

In an effort to prepare more scholars of this kind, the Harvard Academy for International and Area Studies offers the Ira Kukin Scholarships, intended "for those who are pursuing an academic career involving both a social science discipline and a particular area of the world. It is the intent of the program to assist those who, having developed significant expertise in a given geographical area, require further training in an established discipline or those who, having achieved a high level of competence in a discipline, wish to gain further mastery of a given geographical area." More programs of this kind, and more interest on the part of academics in programs of this kind, would be very helpful.

In our own setting, it is not evident that we have as yet found all of the right organizational structures to promote the cross-disciplinary learning that is required. It might be possible for the Humanities Council (which has a distinguished history of breaking down barriers between departments within the humanities) and the Woodrow Wilson School (which plays a similar role within the social sciences) to collaborate in building a new program directed specifically to melding competence in language, history, and culture with rigorous training in the social sciences. Postdoctoral programs, and visiting scholar programs, may make particularly good sense in this context.

Also, I believe that the Center of International Studies—which already does more than any other entity at Princeton to unite regional studies and social science research—can play an even larger role in the future. The recent Center proposal (to be funded by the J. Howard Pew Freedom Trust) on "Integrating Economics and National Security" not only has important analytical and disciplinary emphases, but also a major regional focus—East Asia.

THE FINANCIAL CHALLENGE: PAYING FOR INTRINSICALLY EXPENSIVE PROGRAMS

One of the major barriers to greater accomplishments in international and regional studies is the very high costs that are involved. Some things that might seem like "extras" in other fields (foreign travel and research abroad, for example) are essentials here, yet it is very hard to find the funding needed for students or for faculty members. It is certainly not desirable, on any grounds, that pursuit of studies in these fields be limited to individuals from affluent backgrounds who can cover such costs themselves.

Readily identifiable costs of this kind are, however, the proverbial tip of the iceberg. The truly major investments that must be made by universities interested in international and regional studies fall into two broad categories: (1) support for the core faculty required to provide the necessary coverage of fields, even though enrollments will never, in and of themselves, justify so many positions; and (2) library resources.

It is useful to compare expenditures for East Asian Studies and Near Eastern Studies with comparable figures for the rest of the University. The results of a recent analysis that related faculty positions in each department and program to student enrollments are striking. Economics is the department at Princeton with the largest student population per faculty position, and if we set our index of students per faculty position at one hundred for Economics, we find that the comparable index for East Asian Studies is thirty-three, and for Near Eastern Studies, twenty. That is, *three* times more faculty resources per student are required in East Asian Studies than in Economics, and *five* times more faculty resources per student are required in Near Eastern Studies than in Economics. (Lest anyone think that Economics is such an extreme case as to skew these comparisons, the median value of this same index of students per faculty position for all departments was fifty-six.)

In the case of library costs, East Asian Studies is even more expensive than Near Eastern Studies, and expenditures for both of these libraries dwarf the comparable figures for the University at large. Specifically, if we restrict the comparison to actual expenditures for staff and acquisitions in 1985–86 (ignoring space costs entirely), we find that direct expenditures for library resources alone were more than $6,000 per student in East Asian Studies, $5,500 per student in Near Eastern Studies, and approximately $2,100 per student in all other fields. Yet, without library resources of these kinds, our programs of teaching and research simply could not go forward.

Resource requirements in the relevant social science departments are different in character and scale, but hardly negligible. In the case of the Center of International Studies, for example, we have been engaged in raising over $5 million for desperately needed new space. Fortunately, we are now very close to achieving this objective. In addition, while the Center is very successful in competing for ''project'' grants from foundations and government agencies, it badly needs a core endowment to give it financial flexibility and genuine freedom of action. Such funding is far from easy to attract.

The Office of Population Research is another example of an entity of exceptional strength that is handicapped in its efforts to mount an important new program by the lack of assured support for faculty teaching time and graduate student support. Sponsored research funds, which OPR attracts very successfully, do not meet these needs.

Private Fund Raising

How is the University to cope? In part by doing what we always do: making the best case we can for generous contributions from alumni, parents, and friends interested in international and regional studies. This traditional approach will serve some needs better than others, and it seems particularly appropriate to ask individual donors to provide undergirding endowment for the Center of International Studies and for the key regional programs.

We should not, however, underestimate the difficulty of this task. Princeton was fortunate to receive a challenge grant from the Andrew W. Mellon Foundation for the support of East Asian Studies, which requires the University to raise an additional $1.8 million over four years. Vigorous efforts to satisfy this obligation have resulted in gifts totaling less than $700,000 to date, and we are now appreciably more humble about our ability to raise such funds than we were before this experience. Still, the gift of $10 million by Averill Harriman to endow the Harriman Institute for Advanced Study of the Soviet Union at Columbia University is a welcome illustration of what is possible under especially favorable circumstances.

Fund raising from private resources in the international area must include special efforts directed at those foundations whose charters include international affairs. In the mid-1960s foundations were major sources of support, and the Ford Foundation alone spent over $100 million in 1965 and 1966 to establish and strengthen a large number of area studies programs as well as other programs in international affairs. Immediately thereafter, there was a sharp drop in foundation support, with annual grants for such purposes from the Ford Foundation, for instance, plateauing at about $10 million to $12 million during most of the 1970s and the early part of the 1980s. (Of course, *total* foundation expenditures by a number of foundations, including Ford, also declined during much of this period, even in nominal dollars.) As Frank Sutton, who was vice president of the international division of the Ford Foundation, has noted, there was also a substantial shift in the character of support. Much more emphasis was given to studies of policy questions than to the study of regions of the world.

In Princeton's own case, foundation support for international and regional studies during A Campaign for Princeton represented just over 4 percent of total foundation grants. Almost two thirds of the contributions by foundations to international affairs supported research projects, and just over one third supported regional studies and language training. Of the amount received for regional studies programs, virtually all came from two foundations, the William and Flora Hewlett Foundation and the Andrew W. Mellon Foundation.

Recently there have been signs of growing interest on the part of a number of foundations, including the Carnegie Corporation of New York, the John D. and Catherine M. MacArthur Foundation, and the Pew Charitable Trusts, in areas such as disarmament and national security. This is encouraging, and our Center of International Studies is an active participant in these programs. However, as I noted earlier, project support needs to be complemented by endowment and flexible funds.

New efforts to strengthen the teaching of foreign languages and regional studies have also been undertaken. Princeton is one of eleven major research universities that have joined together to form the Consortium for Language Teaching and Learning, which has identified three areas of greatest need: (1) the development of curricular materials, particularly at the intermediate and advanced level in less common languages; (2) the exploration of ways to use technology to improve foreign language teaching; and (3) the training of teachers of foreign languages in the most effective methodologies. The Consortium received initial planning grants from the Exxon Education Foundation, the Andrew W. Mellon Foundation, the National Endowment for the Humanities, and the Pew Memorial Trust; currently it has operating and program support from the Pew Memorial Trust, the Charles E. Culpeper Foundation, and the Andrew W. Mellon Foundation.

It was also announced last fall that grants from the Pew Memorial Trust, the Ford Foundation, and the Exxon Education Foundation have permitted the establishment of a National Foreign Language Center at the Johns Hopkins School of Advanced International Studies in Washington, D.C. The goal of this Center is to develop ''a coherent national strategy for improving the quality of our foreign language teaching both in and out of our formal educational system.''

The Government Role

There have also been recent discussions of the role that government ought to play in helping the nation to meet its needs for both broad understanding and specialized training in foreign languages, in area studies, and in international policy questions. Some of this discussion was stimulated by the release last fall of a draft report by the Association of American Universities (AAU) titled ''To Strengthen the Nation's Investment in Foreign Languages and International Studies: A Legislative Proposal to Create a National Foundation for Foreign Languages and International Studies.''

Such a federal agency, modeled after the National Science Foundation and the National Endowments for the Arts and the Humanities, would be expected ''to formulate a coherent policy on international education'' for the government. It also would aim ''to assure comprehensive, high-quality language and area competency across all world areas; to encourage stable, long-term funding; and to foster effective linkages among academic scholars, government policy makers, and international business executives.''

Currently, 196 international studies and exchange programs exist in 35 departments of the federal government. Some of these programs are designed to encourage a broad national awareness of other languages, other societies, and the global context in which we live. Others support more advanced teaching and research, recognizing both the critical role of foreign languages and cultural studies in a liberal arts education, and our strong national interest in a more sophisticated understanding of societies and cultures throughout the world. Still other programs support policy studies, language training, exchanges for faculty or students, and efforts to apply international perspectives in fields ranging from business to agriculture to science, law, and health.

The national foundation described by the AAU is meant to encourage a higher degree of coordination among these programs. It is also meant to provide a sharper focus in Washington on the resources needed to accomplish our goals.

The present situation is described bluntly in the AAU report: ''[The] erosion in the quality and capacity of our language and area studies centers is the result of diversity carried to disorganization in national policies as well as twenty years of unstable and inadequate funding.'' The Title VI program in international education has become largely invisible within the array of programs administered by the Department of Education. This is the only federal program supporting campus-based language and area studies centers (including Princeton's Program in Near Eastern Studies). It also supports graduate fellowships, faculty and doctoral dissertation research abroad, intensive summer language institutes, and more general outreach programs.

Unfortunately, with a total appropriation of just over $30 million, this program is unable to support an adequate number or range of centers. For those it does support, the average grant covers only about 5 percent of the center's costs—far less than in the post-Sputnik era when this program was inaugurated. Rather than seek additional resources, however, the present Administration has called for the elimination of all Title VI funding in every budget request since 1981.

This has been true despite a growing recognition that understanding foreign languages and cultures is an important dimension of ''international competitiveness'' (the new catch phrase) as well as international citizenship, and despite the urgent requests of such cabinet-level departments as State, Defense, and Commerce for greater expertise in foreign languages and international studies. The AAU proposal last fall was drafted at the request of the Department of Defense. One of the specific programs highlighted in the proposal is a $5 million Soviet-European Research and Training Act that was established by the State Department in 1984 in response to what it perceived as an alarming decline in our national capacity to monitor and interpret Soviet behavior. This program has quickly become something of a model. It supports research, graduate and postdoctoral training, exchanges, and the broad dissemination of research results through the awarding of funds to national scholarly organizations that in turn make grants to individuals.

The Administration's requests to terminate Title VI have been soundly rejected by a Congress that, by contrast, has joined the academic community—and increasingly the business community—in exploring ways to strengthen our national investment in international education. Stimulated in part by an earlier recommendation by President Michael Sovern of Columbia University, the Congress enacted an amendment last fall, sponsored by Paul Simon, Senator from Illinois, that called upon the Secretary of Education, in consultation with the Secretaries of State and Defense and the Directors of the United States Information Agency and the Agency for International Development, to study the feasibility of establishing a National Endowment for International Studies—an organizational structure that, at least in general concept, is similar to the one proposed by the AAU.

The challenge is to find a national policy, an organizational structure, and the resources necessary to do two things: (1) to sustain and build on existing programs related to the study of languages and cultures, area studies, and international affairs generally, while also (2) developing new strengths in teaching and research in fields ranging from international finance and modernization to diplomacy and national security. Such an effort will need to recognize the substantial and growing costs of first-rate teaching and research; the sizable spectrum of languages and areas in which we as a nation have interests; and the importance nationally—as well as on individual campuses—of cross-disciplinary initiatives that can provide the knowledge necessary to make critical distinctions and reliable judgments.

In an effort to assure the widest possible discussion, the AAU has joined with various disciplinary groups, associations, business leaders, and others to form a Coalition for the Advancement of Foreign Language and International Studies. The Coalition's main task is to seek broad agreement on a specific agenda for action and on the organizational structure most likely to promote "high and broadly based competence in the languages of the world and knowledge of the cultures and social arrangements of those with whom we both cooperate and compete, often simultaneously."

In my view, there is a clear need for a range of governmental actions that will reinforce and augment the contributions of individuals, foundations, corporations, and universities. Individuals and private institutions must commit even more of their own resources to the international arena, but they simply cannot be expected to do on their own everything that needs to be done. We must also marshal national resources and be guided by national leadership. It is no mere rhetorical device to suggest that peace in the world and the welfare of all people depend on our capacity to do so.

The Texture of the Effort

EXCERPTED FROM
COMMENCEMENT REMARKS
JUNE 1980

. . . Last September, one of our Trustees, Nicholas Katzenbach, gave a talk to the entering class that was reprinted subsequently in the *Princeton Alumni Weekly*. Part of that talk is so relevant to what I am trying to say that I want to repeat it. He said: "Now not all of you, or even very many of you, are going to push back the frontiers of knowledge in significant ways except—and this is an important exception—*for yourselves*. Very few Nobel prizes are awarded to undergraduates. But the process of learning, the experience of expanding your own frontiers, your own understanding, is the same for each one of you, whatever your capacities."

What counts for so much is what another distinguished alumnus and former Trustee, George Kennan of the Class of 1925, once called "the texture of the effort." Adversity, the overcoming of obstacles, surviving in tough competition—all these have their uses. Among other things, they can teach humility. . . .

While it is of course a clear advantage, in most respects, to possess great natural ability, sailing along so very easily can also have disadvantages. It can be harder for the extraordinarily gifted person not only to appreciate his own limitations, but also to grasp the need for patience, persistence, and hard work, and to develop the sense of humor that makes life so much more sustainable; it can also be harder for such a person to understand our common frailties and to have faith in things not seen.

Now I certainly do not mean to suggest an inverse relationship between effort and achievement. I know all too well that many who have earned the highest distinctions have done so because of determination as well as talent; and I also suspect that there may be at least a few others some distance down the scale about whom other remarks would be appropriate—or, even if not appropriate, especially in the presence of parents on Commencement Day, justified nonetheless!

Be that as it may, I believe that a vigorous encounter with one's education, some real struggle with one's own confusions as well as the confusions of others, can yield important insights, whatever the immediate outcome in terms of grades. For one thing, if every idea that you eventually came to hold was not immediately obvious, if you went through occasional bouts of indecision (perhaps even reverberating from error to error at times), if you had to change your mind every now and then and sometimes had to reverse your field entirely, you may have acquired a considerable tolerance for complexity. I hope so, because that is very important in its own right always; and it seems to me especially important now, as all of us in this country wrestle with issues that are intrinsically very difficult. There is often a limit, a low limit, to the value of the "instant answer" or the "obvious conclusion"— and sloganeering is rarely the solution to any problem of consequence. As Einstein once said: "Everything should be made as simple as possible, but not more so."

Above all, I hope that in the course of your education here each of you has struggled enough—has had to think hard enough—to have gained a real appreciation for learning, in both its broad and its more precise forms. Just two weeks ago, I received a letter from a member of this year's senior class in which the writer commented appreciatively on the extent to which the breadth of his studies here has led him to feel that he can leave as "an educated man"; but with, he went on, "an intense awareness of the limits of my knowledge and understanding." He then added: "It is a heartening irony that only as graduates do we realize that we will always be students."

The pursuit of learning, approached with a certain ration of fear and trembling as well as zest, can have profound effects on one's development as a person—on one's vistas and moral sensibilities as well as on one's intellectual capacity. That need not be so, and you may not even know if it is so, certainly not right away. But I would not underrate the possibilities, particularly for those of you who have had both the courage to test yourselves in ways that often escape the reckonings of the registrar's office and the honesty to acknowledge imperfect results.

Woodrow Wilson once commented on education and character in these words: "Character . . . is a by-product. It comes, whether you will or not, as a consequence of a life devoted to the nearest duty; and the place in which character would be cultivated, if it be a place of study, is a place where study is the object and character is the result."

My plea, let me stress, is for a balanced view of learning. Let us not overstate what we or others know, or what learning has in fact done for us. Let us not allow ourselves to be objectionably "learned." A great teacher of mine, Jacob Viner, who was a truly learned man, loved to tell the story of a woman who went into a shop and asked for a drinking bowl for her dog. When the clerk replied that he had no drinking bowls especially for dogs, the woman replied that any drinking bowl would do. The clerk found one for her and then suggested that if she would wait a moment he would have the word "dog" lettered on it. "No thanks," said the woman. "It's not necessary. My husband doesn't drink water and my dog can't read." As Viner wisely concluded, "Learning should be kept in its place."

But its place should be, in my view, a large and lasting one, consistent in character and scale with the values and aspirations of this University from which you are now to take your leave. May it be a place able to accommodate the fun of learning as well as the effort all true learning requires. May its boundaries be set not by what we think we know now, but by a lifelong curiosity and an abiding appreciation for ideas—for their elusiveness, to be sure, but also for their power, their beauty, and their capacity to enrich our lives and the lives of others.

A Quiet Confidence

COMMENCEMENT REMARKS
JUNE 1977

. . . I would not try to impose an easy ordering on your experiences here, on your various senses of Princeton, even if I could—which I cannot. But I do want to suggest one thing that I think many of you, if not all, will take from Princeton; to say a few words about how its development may have been encouraged here; and then to suggest a few of its implications for you as you go forth from this place. I refer to what I can call only a reasonable degree of confidence—thought of as self-assurance; or, even more fundamentally, as trust, to go back to the Latin root of the word, in one's self and in one's capacity to understand the world about us.

I certainly do not mean to equate confidence with a belief that one is always right. On the contrary, it has been my experience that people with a reasonable degree of confidence are generally better able to admit their errors and to acknowledge their limitations than are most others. It is the insecure person who most often tries to hide behind a facade of arrogance that he hopes will protect him from having even to discuss the possibility that he may be wrong.

Dean Rudenstine described to me recently conversations he had earlier this spring with seniors, in which he asked them what they thought they would be taking with them from Princeton. There was a great diversity in terms of backgrounds, personalities, interests, accomplishments, and aspirations. But there was also, Dean Rudenstine reported, a remarkably common sense that they were going forth feeling like reasonably competent, confident people who could do something with their lives—a feeling akin to what Henry Adams called "self-possession" in describing his perceptions of his own days at Harvard College in the 1830s.

Plainly the University cannot take anything like full credit for developing this sense of self. We are fortunate in being able to attract some extraordinarily talented people to this campus in the first place, and no one could look out on this gathering today and fail to feel the power of family ties, of "upbringing" in the largest, most completely non-snobbish sense.

It may be true—I suspect it is—that the initial effect of coming to a highly selective university like Princeton is to erode rather than to build confidence. A number of you may have wondered, as I know I did when I first came to Princeton as a graduate student, what malevolent deities had conspired to make me the least competent, most confused, member of an entering class that, with my single exception, consisted entirely of paragons.

But then, through some mysterious alchemy, a deeper kind of confidence develops, at least in many cases—a confidence that is not based on being first in one's class or on earning some other externally defined distinction. The development of this deeper kind of confidence is helped, of course, by the acquisition of competence—a competence that is not of the narrow, vocational kind, but which consists rather of an enlarged capacity to understand and to apply principles; to read and to think critically; to recognize, to marshal, and to respect evidence; and to express one's self effectively. It is helped, too, and very greatly, by the personal associations that are formed through athletics, extra-curricular activities, the simple act of living in this kind of community—learning that it is possible not just to cope with all those other able people who are students and faculty members here, but even to enjoy them, to recognize their frailties as well as their strengths, to contribute to their understanding.

There is, in addition, a still larger, more amorphous, but perhaps even more important way in which a university such as this builds confidence. I am not sure I can explain it very well in the few moments we have together today, but I want to try. It derives from what Dean Alvin Kernan has argued so brilliantly is the most fundamental function of a university such as this: to reassure us that, in his words, "for all its multiplicity, the world is ultimately a whole, that it is structured and coherent."

The University provides this reassurance in many ways—importantly through the questions that are studied by its faculty and students, ranging from the nature of black holes, to forms of language, to genetics, to the kinds of technologies, social structures, and institutions people have created in various times and places, to religious concerns as expressed in art and literature as well as in theology and history. What really matters, I think, is not so much the individual subjects as the sum total of all that we do in the arts and sciences, and especially the ways in which fields such as mathematics and music, engineering and economics, biology and philosophy, interact with one another. It is this sum total that becomes an institutional statement—an institutional affirmation that, in Dean Kernan's words, "the world, for all its manifold parts . . . does finally hang together, does make sense, is comprehensible to, and therefore can potentially be controlled by, the human mind."

Nor is this kind of reassurance, this sense of wholeness, provided only through the curriculum. It is conveyed also through the quality of the faculty and the way faculty members are seen to engage their material as well as their students, through personal experiences that are often profoundly spiritual, through the arrangement of space and the architecture of buildings, through the paths and plantings that unify the campus, through the relatively small scale of Princeton, through a sense of institutional continuity to which alumni contribute greatly, and, finally, through the feeling that this is, in some non-trivial sense, a community that can still come together, as we do today in front of Nassau Hall.

This conception of the University as satisfying what can be seen as an "almost metaphysical need for cosmic orientation" explains in no small part, I think, what it is about the University, at the deepest level, that enables it to impart to so many graduates a reasonable sense of confidence in themselves and in their ability to relate to their universe. We are helped to come to believe that the world is ultimately understandable; that, as Einstein put it in a famous quotation inscribed over a fireplace in Jones Hall, "The Lord God is subtle, but he is not malicious"; the world does not play tricks on us. There is something in the ethos of this place that many of us internalize quite powerfully—and that gives us a confidence, a strength, many of us never knew we could possess. It is a curious kind of strength, born in part of a deeper understanding of our ignorance and of our weakness; but it can help us, if we will let it, to continue to grow and to learn.

What are its uses?

First, the kind of confidence I am describing, far from breeding arrogance, should enable us to be genuinely humble, to be able to welcome new insights and new ideas, to be secure enough that we do not have to hold on to old conceptions no matter what. It is a confidence that permits—that is in fact essential to—continuing intellectual growth.

Secondly, a right sense of confidence should enable us to take some risks in our associations with other people as well as in our contacts with new ideas. No one likes to be rebuffed, and I am afraid that too often on this campus, as well as off it, we are reluctant to reach out to others, especially if they seem different from us in terms of race, or background, or outlook, for fear that we will be rejected or made to feel rejected. This is a particular problem for sensitive people, and many of us are sensitive. But I am convinced that our ability to keep growing as individuals depends greatly on our having enough faith in ourselves, and in others, to accept the possibility of being hurt. And I am also convinced that your ability to contribute to society—to a society that needs desperately the human qualities as well as the academic qualities that I hope you have developed here—depends on your ability to reach out to others, to accept some risks, and perhaps even to fail now and again, without losing your fundamental trust in yourself.

Finally, a reasonable degree of confidence can enable us, should enable us, to allow ourselves to feel as well as to think—and to do so unselfconsciously and without embarrassment. Sometimes very well educated people seem afraid to confront their emotions, afraid to share their feelings with others, afraid to be warm, loving, even at times sentimental. Happily, there are also outstanding examples of an entirely opposite set of tendencies. One of the most distinguished graduates of Princeton, one of my great personal heroes—Adlai Stevenson of the Class of 1922—appeals to me so much in part because he was so human, so capable of crying and laughing as well as thinking. I think of him often at commencement time because he loved this University, and especially the commencement season, so much—and also because he represented so well the personal qualities that I hope many of you will represent in your lifetimes.

May you go from this place with a quiet confidence that will grow as you grow, and may you continue to derive strength from knowing that you are part of this University—a University that will continue to speak to us, and to our deepest needs, if we will let it.

OTSOG

COMMENCEMENT REMARKS
JUNE 1985

. . . While some of you, especially those undertaking academic careers, will spend much of the rest of your lives in universities, most of you will not. In either case, I hope that you will retain an appreciation for learning, as scholars understand that quite complicated, if simple-sounding, word, and a respect for the values associated with it.

A marvelously light-hearted but subversively serious book on this subject has just been reissued this spring, twenty years after it first appeared. It is by Professor Robert K. Merton and is known to its many addicts (I am one) by the acronym "OTSOG." The phrase beneath the acronym, "On the Shoulders of Giants," is often associated with Sir Isaac Newton's response to Robert Hooke in a seventeenth-century debate over the priority of discovery of properties of light and color. Newton wrote: "You defer too much to my ability for searching into this subject. What Descartes did was a good step. You have added much. . . . *If I have seen further, it is by standing on ye sholders of Giants.*" Professor Merton then devotes well over two hundred pages to tracing the lineage of this expression, and I follow him no further today than to report that he finally settles on Bernard of Chartres, in the twelfth century, as the originator of the aphorism.

It is, I think, the continuity of knowledge, the linkage between what were accepted truths and what may prove to be new truths, that is the very essence of learning—and, for that matter, the essence of a university. It is in places like this where the "building" of ideas takes place, and where the accompanying intellectual tensions are most productive.

From this perspective, the university is properly seen as both one of the most conservative and one of the most radical of institutions. Poised delicately—and sometimes quite uncomfortably—between the old and the new, it seeks both to preserve and to create. Just as this Commencement celebrates an important form of torch-passing, so the University has the awesome responsibility of transmitting the learning we have inherited while simultaneously challenging the very same body of knowledge, and—at the same time—educating those of you who will, in your turn, correct our newly created errors.

This is a never-ending process, vital to society and even to what most of us mean by civilization. It depends utterly on certain things we are prone to take for granted: first, the luxury of time . . . to think, to learn, to dream; second, the resources of library, laboratory, faculty, and fellow students; third, the precious gift of the freedom to think new thoughts, to advocate what may seem to others the most outrageous points of view, without worrying that such offenses against orthodoxy might be subject to retribution; and, finally, the shared conviction that this peculiar form of exercise, this hard work of learning, is ultimately worthwhile.

One of my Princeton colleagues whom I admire most, Professor Emeritus W. Arthur Lewis, Nobel Laureate in Economics, once said: "The supremely important task of receiving . . . knowledge, adding to it, and handing it down to the next generation has always devolved on a very small body of people, who specialized in using their brains. They were known as 'clerks'. . . ." He continues: "Here we come to the fundamental purpose of education: to produce young men and women who will join the small band of clerks stretching backwards through history and forward through generations yet unborn. Who will receive our truths, embellish them, defend them against numerous and powerful enemies, and pass them on to the next generation? If our graduates do not help to keep civilization together, to reduce the sum of human misery . . . then our university will have laboured in vain."

This conception of the responsibility of educated people—of all of you—seems to me ever more compelling in a world that is extraordinarily complicated, frequently obsessed with narrow concerns, and terribly fragmented in so many different ways. Bigotry, racism, repression, injustice are not just words, they are harsh realities for people in every part of the world . . . including, of course, some people in this most privileged of all countries. Ideas, the fruits of education, will plainly not solve all problems, and they will often seem agonizingly remote from immediate concerns; but in the long run they matter more than we may realize.

A decade after publishing his prophetic book, *The Economic Consequences of Mr. Churchill*, Lord Keynes wrote: "The ideas of economists and political philosophers, both when they are right and when they are wrong, are more powerful than is commonly understood. Indeed the world is ruled by little else. Practical men, who believe themselves to be quite exempt from any intellectual influences, are usually the slaves of some defunct economist. Madmen in authority, who hear voices in the air, are distilling their frenzy from some academic scribbler of a few years back.''

There are, of course, many forms of knowledge, and many kinds of schools, colleges, and universities. At this Commencement it is right to reaffirm the faith of this University in an avowedly non-vocational, liberal education that recognizes the contributions of the Giants on whose shoulders we stand—and that, in addition, stresses the integrating power of an approach to learning intended to make connections, emphasize values, and respect subtleties. A weary friend of mine, on leaving a high government position some years ago, said that the principal lesson he had learned was to fear decisions made on the basis of an ahistorical, one-problem-at-a-time, compartmentalized approach that deferred to the presumed ''expert'' and ridiculed anything purporting to be a larger world view.

For you to go forth from this place as I am suggesting—purposefully, confidently, and yet with respect for our limitations and for the limitations of all knowledge—will require qualities of character no less than qualities of intellect. It is qualities of character that will help you to act effectively, on your own and in collaboration with others. Let me suggest two such qualities, one through the medium of a tale from *The 1001 Nights*, and one through the medium of a poem.

Some of you may have read that *The 1001 Nights* was banned recently in Egypt, and lest you harbor false expectations, I should quickly assure you that my tale from this great collection is nothing like those racy enough to have prompted such censure. I heard this particular story from a Princeton parent, Ezra Zilkha, who prefaced it by saying that he had confessed to a friend that he believed all proposed solutions to the international debt crisis were in fact impossible to achieve. Mr. Zilkha was then accused by his friend of being a pessimist, to which he replied: ''Sure I am a pessimist, but I am an adapting pessimist.''

Mr. Zilkha then related the story of the condemned prisoner who was asked by the sultan if he had a last wish: ''The prisoner said that if he were given a year's reprieve, he could make the sultan's favorite black horse talk. So the sultan reprieved him for a year, and as the prisoner returned to fetch his clothes from the jail, his friends asked him how it was that he had been set free. He told them the reason the sultan had reprieved him, and they asked how it was possible for him to accomplish this. He replied, 'Well in one year I could die naturally, the sultan could die, the horse could die, or, who knows, I might make the black horse talk.' '' Mr. Zilkha went on: ''That is the reason I am in favor of improvising. . . . Time, if we use it, might make us adapt and maybe, who knows, find solutions." He concluded: "The Princetons of this world must be preserved and encouraged for in places like Princeton it is possible that we might educate people who could make the black horse talk."

If that is a tale about patience and adaptability, the poem to which I referred a moment ago is about forms of courage. I saw it in a recent *New Yorker*, though it dates from the 1960s. It is by Jack Gilbert and is entitled: "The Abnormal Is Not Courage." The reference point of the poem is September 1, 1939, in Poland. It begins:

> The Poles rode out from Warsaw
> against the German
> Tanks on horses. Rode knowing, in
> sunlight, with sabers.
> A magnitude of beauty that allows
> me no peace.
>
> And yet this poem would lessen that
> day. Question
> The bravery. Say it's not courage.
>
> . . .
>
> It was impossible, and with form.
> They rode in sunlight.
> Were mangled. But I say courage is
> not the abnormal.
>
> Not the marvelous act . . .
> The worthless can manage in public,
> or for the moment.

The poet goes on to say that courage is not "the bounty of impulse"; it is rather (and I return to his words):

> . . . The beauty
> That is of many days. Steady and
> clear.
> It is the normal excellence, of long
> accomplishment.

There are, of course, many kinds of courage. What this poem suggests is that courage is above all a result of studied conviction, that the firmness and resolution we associate with it generally derive from a distillation of experiences and sustained reflection. Courage, in this sense, cannot be separated from thoughtfulness and steadiness.

What is required, then, if you are to use your education to the full? A blend, I believe, of continuing respect for learning, a capacity to take the long view, and the courage of persistence. Knowing that you are part of Professor Lewis's "small band of clerks" may give you a somewhat heightened sense of obligation; and knowing that you can see further because you stand on the shoulders of those who have preceded you should provide at least some measure of reassurance. But it is to your own inner resources, finally, to your own values, that you will have to look for strength as well as for generosity of spirit.

It is my hope that this University, in ways mysterious as well as obvious, has helped to prepare you. We are fortunate to have had you here, we admire what you have accomplished, we are optimistic about your future, and we wish you well.

Ithaka

OPENING EXERCISES ADDRESS
SEPTEMBER 1981

. . . Just prior to graduation, a member of the Class of 1981 came up to me and said rather wistfully that he wished that he could start over as a freshman—and that, if he could, he would take much fuller advantage of his time at the University.

His was not an isolated comment. In fact, quite similar sentiments have been voiced over the years by a number of other seniors. That general lament was much on my mind when, immediately after Commencement, I went to Greece to attend meetings and to vacation with my family. In the course of a bus trip to Delphi (where, I should confess, the dean of the faculty and I took the opportunity to consult the Oracle about one of our more troubled departments), a faculty colleague, Professor Keeley, read a poem to our group. It led me to think again of that Commencement conversation, and it is my text today.

The poem is by a Greek who lived in Alexandria in the early 1900s, Constantine P. Cavafy, and it is titled "Ithaka." I would like to read it to you as Professor Keeley has translated it. First, however, I should note that the Ithaka to which Cavafy refers is the island home to which Odysseus returned in Homer's *Odyssey*, following ten years of fighting in the Trojan War and ten more years of wandering. The only other annotations I will supply are identifications: the Laistrygonians (cannibal giants encountered by Odysseus), Cyclops (the one-eyed giant who was blinded by Odysseus in a famous scene that all readers of the *Odyssey* will recall), and Poseidon (the god of the sea who was infuriated because of the blinding of his son, the Cyclops, and did his best to prevent Odysseus from returning to Ithaka).

Here is the poem:

> As you set out for Ithaka
> hope your road is a long one,
> full of adventure, full of discovery.
> Laistrygonians, Cyclops,
> angry Poseidon—don't be afraid of them:
> you'll never find things like that on your way
> as long as you keep your thoughts raised high,

as long as a rare excitement
stirs your spirit and your body.
Laistrygonians, Cyclops,
wild Poseidon—you won't encounter them
unless you bring them along inside your soul,
unless your soul sets them up in front of you.

Hope your road is a long one.
May there be many summer mornings when
with what pleasure, what joy,
you enter harbours you're seeing for the first time;
may you stop at Phoenician trading stations
to buy fine things,
mother of pearl and coral, amber and ebony,
sensual perfume of every kind—
as many sensual perfumes as you can;
and may you visit many Egyptian cities
to learn and go on learning from scholars.

Keep Ithaka always in your mind.
Arriving there is what you're destined for.
But don't hurry the journey at all.
Better if it lasts for years,
so you're old by the time you reach the island,
wealthy with all you've gained on the way,
not expecting Ithaka to make you rich.

Ithaka gave you the marvellous journey.
Without her you wouldn't have set out.
She has nothing left to give you now.

And if you find her poor, Ithaka won't have fooled you.
Wise as you will have become, so full of experience,
you'll have understood by then what these Ithakas mean.*

The more I thought about the poem, in the very land of Odysseus,
the more relevance it seemed to have for the beginning of the academic
year—and especially for those of you who are freshmen. You are beginning an entirely new journey, and no doubt many of you are think-

* "Ithaka," in *C.P. Cavafy: Collected Poems*, trans. Edmund Keeley and Philip Sherrard, ed.
George Savidis, copyright © 1975 by Edmund Keeley and Philip Sherrard. Reprinted with permission of Princeton University Press.

ing about where it will lead—about the goals that will give direction to your own days at Princeton.

"Ithaka," I believe, has much to teach us. First, it reminds us of the need to have destinations in mind so that we do not simply wander aimlessly—so that we have at least some general sense of why we are here. Each of us is left, however, to determine his or her own "Ithaka," which is as it should be. It is certainly not for me to define your highest, most personal, aspirations; I would not even if I could, for that is one of life's most important tasks for each individual.

Please allow me, nonetheless, to say just a few words about the character of the goals you will choose as you continue your education. I hope you will not fix on objectives that are too easily achieved, too utilitarian, too self-serving, or too rigid. Of course it is important to receive a degree; of course you will want to do your best to get good grades along the way; and of course many of you will seek credentials sufficiently compelling to assure admission to medical or law or business school, or to start you along whatever vocational path you wish to pursue. But none of these, in my judgment, should be your real source of direction here.

The most worthwhile goals are often elusive and almost always just beyond reach. "Hope your road is a long one," Cavafy writes, and that will be true only if your destination is not too easily seen or too close at hand. Goals that are narrowly defined and rather limited often seem, once achieved, disappointing and unfulfilling—in part, perhaps, because they did not require a journey that was sufficiently adventuresome and stimulating. When you look back on them, such goals can turn out to be trivial and even unworthy.

My daughter said that this theme in the poem reminded her of a quotation from *Walden*. "In the long run," Thoreau wrote, "men hit only what they aim at. Therefore, though they should fail immediately, they had better aim at something high."

In the setting of this University, "something high" can include, in my judgment should include, the most vigorous pursuit of learning. Learning pursued for its own sake—and not merely as a means to some more prosaic end—can be a source of great enjoyment and personal satisfaction; it can also serve as the soundest preparation for citizenship and for what I hope will be lives lived generously, in service to others. It is this kind of learning that we are here to promote.

About eight years ago, I had a student in my section of beginning economics who was without doubt both one of the worst students of economics I have ever had and, at the same time, one of the most appealing. It was evident right away that she was going to have great difficulty with the subject. And she did. I remember well the conversation in which I suggested as gently as possible that she might consider dropping the course and taking it later. She replied: "It may not be obvious to you, Mr. Bowen, but I am learning a great deal from this course; that's why I came to Princeton, and so I'll stay. If I get an F, I get an F." What could I say? She stayed . . . and received her earned D. She is, I might add, a gifted writer and a person of no little courage. She understood her purposes—and Princeton's—very well indeed.

While "Ithaka" speaks to us of destinations, it speaks even more powerfully about journeys themselves. *How* we seek our individual Ithakas, with what vision, and in what spirit, matters enormously. Part of what the senior was telling me last June was that he had not allowed himself to be educated broadly. He had pursued his particular objectives so single-mindedly that it was not until he was about to graduate that he realized what Princeton really had to offer. To be sure, he had fulfilled distribution requirements and participated in some extracurricular activities—but without, I suspect, any of the "rare excitement" to which Cavafy refers. It was almost as if the student had gone through Princeton wearing blinders. And it was very sad to see him discover his blinders, and remove them, only as he was leaving.

Remember the passage in the poem: "Hope your road is a long one. May there be many summer mornings when, with what pleasure, what joy, you enter harbours you're seeing for the first time. . . ." There is so much here to see for the first time. The "harbours" of Princeton include, most importantly, ideas. There is nothing quite like the experience of encountering a new idea, wrestling with it, turning it over in your mind, testing your comprehension of it—and, finally, if you are fortunate, coming to understand it and to appreciate its beauty. But you have to be open to such experiences; no one can force them on you. Avoiding subjects because they are unfamiliar, and might result in a modestly lower grade-point average, is not the path of openness; and neither is approaching the courses you do take with the primary objective of doing precisely what you have to do, and no more, in order to fare well on examinations. Don't miss, please, the pleasure, the joy of learning.

Our "harbours" also include the campus itself: the buildings, the trees, the courtyards, the walks. It saddens me to see people going to class with eyes down and apparently neither time nor inclination to observe the things about them. Your journey here should include moments spent looking at the flowers in Prospect Garden, listening to the magnificent organ in this chapel, tracking down the gargoyles to be found all about the campus, and reflecting on the history of this place as it is given tangible expression in Cannon Green, FitzRandolph Gate, and the inscriptions on dormitories and archways. This is to be your home for a time now; and I hope you will always feel that it is your home in at least some sense. So, please get to know it; make it yours in the only way that you can: through familiarity and affection.

If both ideas and the setting of Princeton are to be parts of your journey, so too are the people who make up this University—your classmates, other students, faculty, staff, and alumni. You will miss a great deal if in experiencing this personal dimension of Princeton you keep your blinders on and are satisfied with making only easy friendships. We often say—because it is true—that the human resources of this place are remarkable. But they will in fact prove to be remarkable to you only if you take the initiative to discover them, and make the special effort that will allow them to enrich your time here. Cavafy expresses the hope that the journey to Ithaka will be "full of adventure." And surely there are few adventures more significant than really getting to know someone else.

I sometimes feel that in developing friendships, especially those that require us to reach across such complex boundaries as race and religion, we are too self-protecting. The adventure of forming new friendships, and deepening old ones, has to include a willingness to accept the risks of bruised feelings that result from being rebuffed. Real friendship, and warmth, and love, carry with them great vulnerability; as all of us learn, they often entail much pain as well as much happiness. You can spare yourselves discomfort by keeping your distance, by remaining safely aloof, by maintaining what are largely superficial friendships. But if you do, you will deprive yourselves, and others, of one of the greatest opportunities for learning and for personal growth.

No aspect of your journey here is terribly predictable, and in all of your encounters—with new ideas, new places, new people—I hope you will be prepared to welcome, and not merely to accept, the inevitable surprises. Sometimes we work too hard to force the events of the day to conform to our design. As Dean Aaron Lemonick, my companion on the way to Delphi, is fond of saying: "Life is what happens to you when you're planning something else." Odysseus certainly came to understand that—as all of us must, to one degree or another.

We must also contend with obstacles along the way, though for most of us—fortunately!—they take on appreciably less dramatic form than Laistrygonians, Cyclops, and Poseidon. Odysseus was tested much more severely than I hope any of you will be, but we should recognize that there are analogues to cannibalistic giants and vengeful gods on every road, including the walkways of Princeton.

Thus, the third, and last, theme of our poem that I would like to encourage you to think about concerns how we are to view such distressing creatures. Cavafy writes: "Laistrygonians, Cyclops, wild Poseidon—you won't encounter them unless you bring them along inside your soul, unless your soul sets them up in front of you." If we are to read those words as saying that all barriers are self-imposed, then I would have to disagree. Many obstacles that we confront are real and they cannot be simply wished or willed away. I think, for example, of serious illnesses. Or, some of us may find our journey impeded by professors who seem unfair, by a grade that surely should have been an A but was somehow inexplicably transformed into a C, by failure to secure a position on a team or a place in the orchestra, by the presumed friend who turns out to be unreliable and uncaring.

It is also true, however—and I think this is the real meaning to be gleaned here—that each of us creates his or her own climate to a considerable extent. Many of our problems *are* self-imposed. We carry them with us as a kind of "baggage" that weights us down, dulls our spirits, and drains us of energy. On the other hand, if we are genuinely excited about what we are doing, about the people around us, we can often surmount obstacles that otherwise might have been crushing. Thus, while there surely are Poseidons at Princeton (I hope I do not have to concede Cyclops as well!), they are overwhelming only if we allow them to be. Opponents, difficulties of every kind, generally become too powerful, too much for us, only if we allow them that ascendancy.

It is easy—indeed, natural and inevitable—to become discouraged sometimes. On such days, perhaps it will help to recall that discouragement is no stranger to any of us. Perhaps it will help, too, to remember that wonderful Italian expression: "meno male"—"It could have been worse." That expression comes to my mind on occasion, I must say, and it has a vividness for me that stems from the first time I heard it used. I was having lunch in a café in Florence when a waiter tripped and spilled a pitcher of water over the head of a woman sitting at the next table. She leaped up, gestured dramatically, and exclaimed:

"meno male"—which I understood to mean, in that setting, it could have been hot coffee.

I have just one other, very modest, suggestion concerning how you approach whatever problems you may encounter here. If you believe you have a Laistrygonian in your dormitory—or, worse yet, teaching one of your courses—do not keep this insight to yourself. Talk with a friend, with a counselor, with someone who can help you prevent such difficulties, or other difficulties, from overwhelming you. Please don't be afraid to ask for help; and, of course, please respond as well as you can when others make you aware of their needs and worries.

Our journeys here, while they may lead to as many Ithakas as there are individuals at Princeton, are not undertaken alone. Universities exist today, as they have since the middle ages, as *communities* of scholars. We are here to engage in the shared pursuit of knowledge and of the wisdom that sometimes comes afterwards. We are here to laugh and to cry together, as well as to reason with each other. We are here, above all, to enjoy the wonderful privilege of learning.

May each of you contribute your own freshness, your own "rare excitement," to this never-ending quest. And may you take full advantage of the riches this place offers to those who will seek them out.

> Hope your road is a long one,
> full of adventure, full of discovery.

PART THREE

Graduate Education, Scholarship, Research

While the previous chapter is concerned largely with Princeton as undergraduate college, this chapter focuses on Princeton as major research university—an institution recognized throughout the world for the quality of its graduate education, scholarship, and research.

The chapter begins with the 1981 annual report on "Graduate Education in the Arts and Sciences: Prospects for the Future." After a brief account of the defining characteristics of the graduate school at Princeton, the report examines national trends threatening graduate education and reviews the principal policy questions facing Princeton, universities generally, the government, and other institutions of society.

The 1979 annual report then assesses the importance of scholarship and research, for the society and for universities, and identifies a number of problems and concerns.

Finally, the 1986 annual report concentrates on one of the principal resources of any college or university, its library. The report looks first at the role of the library and the ways it has changed over time, and then at the challenges confronting the Princeton library—and all libraries—for the rest of the 1980s, and beyond.

Graduate Education
in the Arts and Sciences:
Prospects for the Future

REPORT OF THE PRESIDENT
APRIL 1981

INTRODUCTION

In the United States, Princeton is thought of most often in terms of its undergraduate college. This is hardly surprising, in part because Princeton, like other early American colleges, offered essentially no regular instruction at the graduate level for the first 150 years of its history. Although there are records as early as 1748–49 of "resident graduates" (including James Madison who stayed on to pursue advanced studies in theology), all such cases were exceptional. The graduate school was not constituted formally until 1901, and between that date and the onset of World War II, fifteen baccalaureate degrees were awarded for every doctoral degree. After the war, the graduate school grew much more rapidly than the college; even so, three of every four students at Princeton today are candidates for undergraduate degrees.

Yet in much of the world Princeton is known principally for its standing as a leading research university, offering graduate programs of distinction in fields ranging from physics to philosophy. In fact, one foreign visitor to the campus recently expressed to Dean Theodore Ziolkowski his astonishment at the fact that Princeton actually teaches *undergraduates*.

One purpose of this report is to give a broader audience a sense of the importance—and the distinctive characteristics—of graduate education at Princeton. There is also a larger purpose: to draw increased attention to critical issues confronting graduate education in the arts and sciences at essentially all doctorate-granting universities in the United States.

Dramatically declining employment opportunities in academia, combined with rising costs and reduced financial aid for graduate students, threaten the continuity of scholarship in basic fields of knowledge. Paradoxically, American universities are likely to award too many Ph.D. degrees in the arts and sciences relative to job opportunities over the next fifteen years, while at the same time failing to educate and place enough truly outstanding individuals. From a national stand-point, I believe our objective over this difficult period should be to improve the quality of graduate education (or, at the minimum, to maintain quality) while reducing overall numbers of graduate students and Ph.D. programs in an orderly way.

These concerns are of such moment, and the attendant dilemmas so difficult, that the welfare of graduate education in the arts and sciences is arguably the most serious single issue of educational policy facing American universities today. The major part of this report, accord-ingly, discusses the underlying trends forcing these issues upon us and the related questions of policy that simply must be addressed by Prince-ton, by universities generally, and by the federal government and other institutions of society. First, however, by way of introduction, there is a brief account of the defining characteristics of the graduate school at Princeton.

It is my hope that by discussing a major national problem from the perspective of a particular university, this report will encourage more active consideration of questions of general importance. While I am of course interested in making as good a case as I can for graduate edu-cation at Princeton, it is not my purpose simply to argue for maintain-ing the status quo. All major universities, including this one, must ad-just to rapidly changing realities. Moreover, all of us have an obligation to think hard about the future of graduate education nationwide and about ways in which each of our universities can contribute most ap-propriately to the resolution of problems that transcend local concerns.

THE PRINCETON GRADUATE SCHOOL: DEFINING CHARACTERISTICS

As a result of its unique history, American higher education displays a wider spectrum of institutional types than can be found in any other country in the world—types as confusing to some observers in their variety as they are useful to students for the range of options they offer.

This country's educational institutions have resulted from the amal-gamation of two utterly different models. Early American colleges emerged along lines developed in England—that is, as institutions ded-icated to the instruction of undergraduates. When Americans began going abroad in the nineteenth century to pursue more advanced stud-ies, they went mainly to Germany, where a wholly different institu-tional form had developed after the founding of the University of Berlin in 1810—a university devoted mainly to scholarship and to training students for research. In the last quarter of the nineteenth century, when a need for post-graduate education was perceived in this country, an attempt was made to graft the German university system onto the existing undergraduate college. The result today is a wide variety of institutional types, ranging from two-year community colleges to such institutions as Rockefeller University, which consists entirely of a small and rather specialized graduate school.

Most of the major research universities of the country represent a blending of the earlier models, combining one or more four-year colleges with a variety of graduate and professional schools. Even within this group of institutions there are, of course, major differences. Some of the great state universities combine a veritable multiplicity of schools, colleges, programs, campuses, and faculties. Other universities, like Columbia and Chicago, have developed relatively large graduate and professional schools on top of relatively small liberal arts colleges of distinction.

At Princeton a unique combination has evolved: a graduate school devoted almost entirely to arts and sciences, which is small relative not only to other graduate schools but also to its undergraduate college. The more readily quantifiable respects in which Princeton differs in size and mission from a number of other major universities are summarized in Table 1. Of the universities listed, Princeton's graduate enrollment is smaller than the graduate enrollment at all except Brown. At the same time, Princeton has none of the most common professional schools—notably law, business, medicine, or education. As a result, Princeton's graduate school enrolls a conspicuously high percentage of students in the arts and sciences (72 percent), and the arts and sciences therefore set the tone of the institution. At Harvard and Yale, in contrast, 30 percent and 41 percent (respectively) of all graduate students are enrolled in the arts and sciences; at M.I.T. and Columbia, the comparable figure is 35 percent.

Looked at from another perspective, the graduate school at Princeton is smaller in proportion to the undergraduate college than is the case at nearly all other universities of comparable scale. Of a total student population of approximately 6,000, the graduate school accounts for 24 percent, or just under 1,500 students. This ratio is appreciably higher at Stanford (44 percent), Harvard (58 percent), Columbia (64 percent), and Chicago (71 percent).

The stress on the basic arts and sciences is so central to the graduate

Table 1

Characteristics of Selected Major Universities, 1979

	Total Enrollment			% of Total Graduate Enrollment in Arts & Sciences	Professional Schools		
	Underg.	Grad.[1]	% Grad.		Law	Bus.	Med.
Brown University	5,230	1,350	21%	77%			x
Columbia University	5,366	9,360	64%	35%	x	x	x
Cornell University	13,319	3,381	20%	30%	x	x	x
Duke University	5,609	3,904	41%	38%	x	x	x
Harvard University	6,557	9,159	58%	30%	x	x	x
Massachusetts Institute of Technology	4,547	4,165	48%	35%		x	
Princeton University	**4,440**	**1,436**	**24%**	**72%**			
Stanford University	6,560	5,170	44%	30%	x	x	x
University of California– Berkeley	21,000	9,000	30%	36%	x	x	
University of Chicago	2,653	6,442	71%	39%	x	x	x
University of Michigan	22,076	13,748	38%	29%	x	x	x
University of Pennsylvania	11,776	8,380	42%	32%	x	x	x
University of Texas at Austin	34,617	7,959	19%	34%	x	x	
University of Virginia	10,300	5,200	34%	33%	x	x	x
University of Washington	25,106	7,933	24%	37%	x	x	x
University of Wisconsin– Madison	30,461	8,969	23%	47%	x	x	x
Yale University	4,984	4,631	48%	41%	x	x	x

[1] Includes enrollments in professional schools.

Source: *Peterson's Annual Guides to Graduate Study* and information supplied directly by the institutions.

school at Princeton—and such a distinguishing characteristic—that it deserves special emphasis. As noted, Princeton does not have a full panoply of professional schools, and it is unlikely to develop them. This decision is not based on any lack of appreciation for what are obviously extremely important programs of study; it is based, rather, on a conviction that we are well advised to concentrate on what we believe to be our comparative advantage—namely, to remain relatively small in size and to maintain a single faculty of distinction committed to scholarship and research and to the teaching of both undergraduates and graduate students within a range of disciplines that conform to un-derlying notions of what constitutes a liberal education.

The weight of this general orientation also affects the three profes-sional schools that exist as important parts of the graduate school at Princeton: the Woodrow Wilson School of Public and International Affairs, the School of Architecture and Urban Planning, and the School of Engineering and Applied Science. Graduate programs in all three of these schools tend to display a rather more theoretical orientation than similar programs at many other institutions. Also, each professional school maintains strong ties to arts and science departments through shared course enrollments, joint faculty appointments, and overlapping areas of research.

Like any other institution that has developed over the years, many of Princeton's present characteristics are foreshadowed in its history. Andrew Fleming West was the dominant figure in the establishment of the graduate school in 1901, as well as during the formative years of its development, and his strong personality has left marks that are visible today. This is of course true of the location and character of the Graduate College (the principal residential part of the graduate school), which is set apart from the main campus—one visible result of the titanic struggle between Dean West and President Woodrow Wilson that has been recounted so often. It is, however, the less tangible manifestations of Dean West's convictions that are perhaps most important. A classics scholar with an unshakable commitment to the highest academic standards, Dean West regarded as ideal a small graduate school in which the students would be bound together by certain common interests and academic commitments.

Even though the graduate school has grown well beyond the two hundred full-time students that Dean West regarded as a suitable maximum, it is still committed primarily to preparing a relatively small number of the very best advanced students for scholarship, teaching, and research. The average department today numbers roughly thirty-five graduate students (approximately eight to ten in each entering "class"), with the larger programs in Economics, Chemistry, and Physics enrolling as many as eighty to eighty-five students at the same time that some of the smaller departments like Anthropology and Religion have only about ten to twelve students in residence.

The small overall size of the graduate school should not lead us, however, to underestimate even its purely quantitative importance, especially in those fields in which Princeton has been strong for many years. For instance, while ranking thirtieth among American graduate schools in the total number of Ph.D.'s awarded between 1920 and 1974, Princeton awarded 1,101 doctorates in mathematics and physics, placing ninth among all graduate schools in these fields; 451 doctorates were awarded in foreign languages and literatures, placing Princeton eighth nationally.

In any event, the fundamental case for graduate education at Princeton has been understood since Dean West's time to rest on aspirations that are qualitative, not on numbers of students enrolled or degrees awarded. While judgments about quality are notoriously difficult, defying precise calibration, there is no lack of evidence to suggest that Princeton offers a number of graduate programs of the highest distinction.

One partial test is the number and quality of applications, seen in relation to fields covered and the number of places available. Despite the national decrease in graduate school applicants (discussed in the next section of this report), and recognizing that our own applications have declined moderately since 1976–77, the Princeton graduate school nonetheless received last year over 4,000 applications for approximately 450 places. Among these applicants were many of the nation's most talented prospective graduate students. For example, last year only four much larger universities (University of California at Berkeley, Harvard, M.I.T., and Stanford) attracted more winners of National Science Foundation fellowships than did Princeton. Over the twenty-eight-year history of the Danforth Program, which awarded fellowships primarily in the humanities and social sciences, Princeton ranked third nationally in the number of Danforth Fellows enrolled.

The ratings of graduate programs compiled over the years serve as another rough source of evidence concerning quality. In the 1969 Roose-Andersen evaluations of the effectiveness of graduate programs, fifteen of Princeton's programs were ranked among the top five, including two that were first. In the more restricted Ladd-Lipset survey of 1977, which evaluated only fourteen fields covered at Princeton, our departments fared equally well, with five departments among the top five and three more among the top seven nationally.

It is, finally, the individual recipients of advanced degrees who are the true tests of the graduate school and the extent to which it does in fact serve its purposes. Dean of the Faculty Aaron Lemonick, himself a distinguished graduate alumnus of Princeton's Physics Department, is fond of ticking off on his fingers the seven graduate alumni of that department who among themselves have won eight Nobel prizes. And the chairmen of other departments, if given an opportunity, would cite with pride the names of their distinguished graduate alumni who are recognized in *Who's Who*, the *Directory of American Scholars*, and many other national and international records of professional achievement.

The flexibility of programs of study is another defining characteristic of graduate education at Princeton that dates to Dean West's time. It is a characteristic both important in and of itself—related, we believe, to the quality of programs—and consistent with the opportunities offered by small scale. There are no general course or credit requirements (although departments may suggest certain core courses as preparation for the General Examination); instead, students arrange their individual programs with the departmental director of graduate studies in an effort to design courses of study that will enable them to prepare most efficiently for the General Examination and the writing of a dissertation. We know from correspondence with applicants and from conversations with students that this flexibility is one of the most attractive features of the graduate school.

Another long-standing characteristic of Princeton's graduate school is that it encourages students to complete their degrees in relatively short periods of time. Data collected by the National Research Council indicate that this policy has had effect: in all of the fields in which Princeton offers doctoral degrees, the average elapsed time from B.A. to Ph.D. degree is much less for recipients of Princeton degrees than for students at universities generally. In fact, Princeton and M.I.T. are clearly first among all major universities by this measure.*

In summary, Princeton offers a rather special option: a small graduate school of high quality with a principal orientation, even in its professional components, toward the liberal arts and sciences, and with an unusual degree of flexibility. Because of the significant contribution our graduate programs make, on an international as well as a national scale, I believe it is essential that Princeton sustain its basic commitment to graduate education. At the same time, the University must, of course, continue to examine and reexamine particular graduate programs as well as more general questions of educational policy, scale, and finance.

In addition to being extremely important in its own right, the gradu-

---

* National Research Council, *A Century of Doctorates* (National Academy of Sciences, Washington, D.C., 1978), Table 42. The average elapsed time from B.A. to Ph.D. for male graduates in the engineering-mathematics-physical sciences fields at Princeton is 5.8 years compared with an average for all universities of 7.52 years; the corresponding figures for the bio-behavioral sciences are 7.3 at Princeton and 9.22 nationwide; for the humanities, 7.8 at Princeton and 10.81 nationally. Of course, elapsed time from undergraduate degree to doctorate exaggerates time in graduate school because it includes time away from school as well as time spent in doctoral study.

ate school is also indispensable to the quality of undergraduate studies. Princeton takes pride in having a single faculty rather than separate graduate and undergraduate faculties, as is the practice at some other universities. Senior faculty members teach undergraduate courses; conversely, assistant professors are often entrusted with graduate seminars. We act in the belief, first, that effective teaching is not only compatible with continuing scholarship but dependent on it if teaching is to remain vigorous and responsible; and, second, that scholarship can be invigorated and enhanced by teaching.

The existence of strong graduate programs is an essential element in enabling Princeton to recruit and retain a faculty of unusual distinction. Although most faculty members are here because they also want to work with talented undergraduates, many would soon go elsewhere—as they often have more than ample opportunity to do—if they were deprived of the opportunity to pursue their scholarship and research in a stimulating environment. This in turn implies having graduate students with whom to work in seminars and laboratories, on experiments and scholarly projects.

If these professors were to elect to accept other offers because Princeton had no graduate school, or retained only a seriously weakened graduate school, undergraduates would lose the opportunity of studying with some of the most distinguished scholars to be found anywhere. And it is not only the eminence of the faculty and the variety of curricular offerings that would suffer. At Princeton there is no intellectual ceiling for talented undergraduates. Able students can move past the normal undergraduate course of study, and indeed in every semester more than 250 undergraduates register for graduate courses that take them well beyond the offerings available in even the finest undergraduate colleges. A recent survey of Princeton seniors who won such prestigious outside awards as Rhodes, Marshall, Danforth, and Fulbright fellowships revealed that almost all had taken graduate courses. (This healthy traffic, I should add, is by no means all one way: in the fall term of 1979, 431 graduate students registered in undergraduate courses.)

Beyond these obvious curricular implications, the presence of the graduate school also affects undergraduates through the availability of facilities and other academic resources. Without major graduate programs, the science and engineering departments would have little chance of building and sustaining the extensive research laboratories that are available to undergraduate students as well. Students in all departments would have to accommodate themselves to a relatively small undergraduate "college" library rather than a first-rate research library. But perhaps the most significant effect of all is one that is difficult to describe except in the broadest terms: without the graduate school, Princeton simply would not be able to sustain the overall academic vitality and intellectual milieu that make such a difference, in so many subtle ways, to its fundamental character.

This brief restatement of the significance of the graduate school to Princeton, and of graduate education at Princeton to the advancement of learning, seems especially appropriate under present circumstances, when factors that lie beyond the direct control of individual institutions are so threatening. It is to an analysis of these factors, as they affect graduate education generally, that we now turn.

NATIONAL TRENDS THREATENING GRADUATE EDUCATION

The Outlook for Academic Employment

As mentioned earlier, the two most ominous developments threatening graduate education in the arts and sciences nationally are dramatically declining job opportunities in many fields and rapidly rising net costs for those students who nonetheless elect to seek advanced degrees. These trends combine to threaten the quality and continuity of scholarship by: (1) discouraging many of the ablest students from considering academic careers (at the same time that the overall number of Ph.D. candidates is too large); and (2) eroding the ability of even the strongest universities to offer distinguished programs of graduate education in some fields. Another characteristic of much of modern graduate education—intense specialization—also is worrisome, both on educational grounds and as a complicating factor in attempting to match Ph.D. recipients with evolving job opportunities. It is discussed at the end of this section of the report.

In sharp contrast to most students seeking graduate degrees in professional fields such as medicine, law, and business, the clear majority of students working for doctorates in the arts and sciences have in mind careers in teaching and research. The proportion is highest in the humanities. According to a recent survey conducted by the National Research Council, of the 46,000 humanists employed full-time in their field of study, over 95 percent held academic appointments. In addition, there were 8,400 humanists working outside their field of graduate study, and over 50 percent of them were also in academic employment.*

In recent years, there has been some increase in the number of Ph.D. recipients in essentially all fields, including the humanities and social sciences, who have taken positions in business and other places outside academia. But the numbers are still quite small, and the fundamental situation remains much as it was before. While there are excellent opportunities outside education in fields such as chemistry, economics, geology, statistics, and engineering, it remains true that academic employment is of primary importance for most Ph.D. candidates in the arts and sciences. For this simple reason, any pronounced change in the outlook for academic employment is certain to have major effects on graduate students and graduate schools.

THE PLACEMENT SITUATION. Difficult as it may be to describe with precision as broad and amorphous a concept as "opportunities for academic employment," the changes that have occurred in recent years are so dramatic as to override all problems of definition. It is obvious to any observer that the prospects today of finding a desirable job—often any job at all related to one's graduate training—are nothing like what they were when most current faculty members were completing their own graduate work.

If I may be both impressionistic and personal for a moment, I recall vividly that when I was a graduate student at Princeton in 1955–58, the one thing almost none of us worried about was the availability of jobs. Our concerns centered rather on our own ability to meet the intellectual demands of rigorous Ph.D. programs, on the need to make decisions concerning fields of concentration, and in some cases on the *kind* of position that would be most appealing. In those halcyon days of rapid increases in enrollments and "shortages" of teachers, the idea that there could ever be a serious problem finding a job would have seemed odd indeed. It was clearly a seller's market, and at meetings of many professional associations in the 1950s and 1960s, department chairmen literally stood in line to interview job candidates.

The contrast with the present situation could hardly be more stark. English or history will elicit several hundred applications from desperate job seekers. A survey by the Modern Language Association conducted last spring revealed that of the 965 graduate students who earned

---

* *Employment of Humanities Ph.D.'s: A departure from traditional jobs*, National Research Council, National Academy of Sciences, Washington, D.C., 1980, p. 24.

doctoral degrees in foreign languages in 1978–79, 45 percent had not found full-time academic jobs by February 1980. Furthermore, of the 55 percent who had taken full-time teaching or research positions, only two thirds held positions that could lead to tenure.

The situation is appreciably less bleak in a number of fields within science and engineering. In chemical engineering, for example, the problem is precisely the obverse—the number of Ph.D.'s being awarded falls far short of the needs of academic institutions, and industrial and government laboratories are strong competitors for those candidates who are available.* But there are other areas of science, such as mathematical physics, where the problem of finding a suitable position is all too real. It is not the case that severe problems of placement exist only in the humanities and in certain social sciences, although the problems in these fields are certainly most acute.

Although Princeton's placement rate is better than the rate for the nation as a whole, it too is lower now than it has been in the past. In 1978–79 there were 223 job seekers in the graduate school as a whole, 93 percent of whom found employment. This summary figure seems to compare reasonably well with Princeton's overall placement rate of 96 percent in 1971–72. What it conceals, however, is the fact that all of the students not placed (with but one exception) were in the humanities and social sciences. Indeed, a comparison of placement percentages in the humanities over the past decade shows that, while 96 percent of job seekers were placed in 1971–72, only 82 percent found jobs in 1978–79. The pattern in the social sciences is similar, with the rate of placement declining from 92 percent to 86 percent over the same period. (These percentages appear to be representative for major private universities.) What all of these statistics ignore, of course, is the fact that many of those students who are "placed" have secured only temporary, part-time, or fill-in positions and will be back in the market again the next year, competing for positions with all the new Ph.D.'s then emerging from the graduate schools.

The most important question is what the future holds. Planning for graduate education must be based on an especially long time horizon since five years or more often elapse between the time of entry to grad-

* A recent issue of the American Chemical Society news magazine (*Chemical and Engineering News*, Nov. 10, 1980, pp. 37ff) reports that 309 Ph.D. degrees in chemical engineering were awarded throughout the United States in 1979. However, about half of the recipients were foreign students, a number of whom will be returning to their countries. Thus, the American Institute of Chemical Engineers estimates that only about 175 Ph.D.'s were available to fill all open positions in universities, industry, and government. The report noted 172 vacant teaching positions alone.

uate school and an initial job placement. Unfortunately for those who will be seeking academic employment, there are compelling reasons to expect the grim conditions of recent years to worsen, and perhaps to worsen appreciably, for some considerable period of time. In fact, *no major, lasting improvement in the outlook for academic employment is in sight until the mid- to late 1990s.*

This proposition is so critical to our understanding of the problems facing graduate education that I am going to discuss in some detail the evidence for it, considering in turn: population and enrollment projections; faculty retirement patterns; other factors affecting job prospects (including student-faculty ratios); and, finally, the "supply" of Ph.D.'s who will be competing for available positions. The threads of this analysis are then drawn together in the form of an assessment of the overall relationship between job opportunities and the supply of new Ph.D.'s that can be expected between now and the year 2000.

POPULATION AND ENROLLMENT PROJECTIONS. The single most powerful force contributing to such a sobering prognosis is demographic: We have just witnessed a fall in the birth rate so dramatic as to overwhelm almost all other relevant factors. As can be seen from Figure 1, annual births fell from roughly 4.3 million in the early 1960s to about 3.5 million in the late 1960s, and then, after a brief period of increasing births around 1970, to slightly more than 3.1 million in 1973–76. In the last three years there has been a modest rise to just over 3.3 million births per year—still 1 million below the level of the early 1960s. To summarize these basic demographic data another way, the Carnegie Council has calculated that the 18–24 age cohort will decline 23.3 percent between 1978 and 1997.

The potential consequences of such an unprecedented drop in the traditional college-age population are so staggering for higher education—threatening the very survival of many institutions—that great efforts have been made to translate these rather straightforward population data into projections of enrollment. This has proved to be a complicated and highly controversial undertaking. The projections depend greatly on how much of an offset to the essentially certain decline in the 18–24-year-old population one believes can be expected from such other factors as: (1) the increasing enrollment of older people as a consequence of both their larger relative numbers and their increased propensity to go to school on at least a part-time basis; (2) the rate of attrition of college students (as schools desperate for students seek

Figure 1
Population Data: Annual Births in the United States, 1951-1979

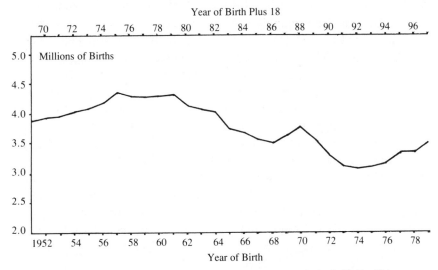

Source: U.S. Bureau of the Census, *Current Population Reports,* Series P-25, No. 704,
"Projections of the Population of the United States: 1977 to 2050," 1977.

Figure 2
Projected Full-Time-Equivalent Enrollments in Higher Education, 1980-2000

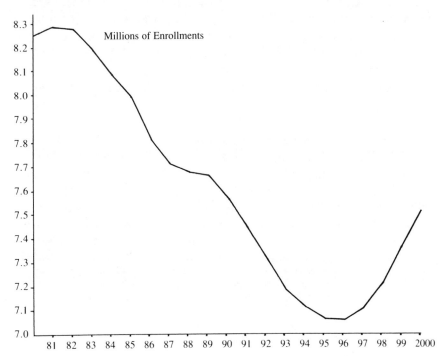

ways, good and bad, to reduce attrition); (3)·the high school graduation rate—which has been roughly constant at about 75 percent for some years now; and finally, (4) the fraction of the traditional college-age population that will decide to go on to college—recognizing that in recent years the tendency for some large groups (especially white males) to continue their education beyond high school has decreased, ending the pronounced upward trend in college attendance for all groups that characterized our entire history until about 1970.

No one can be sure about all such factors, and it is therefore hardly surprising that the enrollment projections that have been developed vary widely—reflecting in part, no doubt, the hopes of some authors as well as differing assessments of key factors. The final report of the Carnegie Council on Policy Studies in Higher Education contains a useful survey of both "high" and "low" projections as well as its own conclusion: that undergraduate enrollment will decline within a range of 5 percent to 15 percent between 1978 and 1997.

As the Carnegie Council itself states, this projection is close to the "optimistic end" of the spectrum, and the Council is also candid in warning readers that its own earlier projections are now seen to have overestimated enrollments. Fred Crossland of the Ford Foundation has been critical of the even more favorable assessment of possibilities published recently by the American Council on Education, and he has expressed forcefully his concern that wishful thinking not be allowed to shield us from harsh realities. Crossland's own estimate (which he regards as, if anything, also too optimistic) is that by the mid- to late 1990s, "full-time equivalent enrollment probably will fall somewhat more than 15 percent from the anticipated 1981 high."*

Because the outlook for enrollment is so critical to an understanding of what the future holds for Ph.D. recipients, those of us who have worked on this report have attempted rough projections of our own, based on separate calculations for six different age groups (17-year-olds, 18–21, 22–24, 25–29, 30–34, and 35–59). This approach has the advantage of isolating effects due to year-to-year changes in the age structure of the population from effects due to changes in enrollment within age groups. The results of this exercise are shown in Figure 2 in terms of "full-time equivalent" enrollments (using the normal convention that three part-time students are defined as equivalent to one full-

---

* Fred E. Crossland, "Learning to Cope with a Downward Slope," *Change*, July/August, 1980. The same issue of *Change* contains a reply to Crossland's position by Carol Frances of the American Council on Education titled "Apocalyptic vs. Strategic Planning."

time student). As can be seen from the figure, these projections suggest a rather steady fall from a high of about 8¼ million full-time equivalent enrollments in 1981 to a low of just over 7 million in 1996, a result consistent in the aggregate with some of the other figures cited above in that the overall decline is approximately 15 percent.

It is important to note that these projections are rough, and it would be a mistake to invest them with specious precision. Even the broad trends suggested here could of course be affected significantly by economic, social, or political developments. We have not tried to foresee, much less take into account, possible changes in student aid policies, the tax laws, or the multitude of other factors that could prove to be highly relevant. In any event, it is the general magnitude of the changes and the general patterns of the enrollment figures that deserve attention.

In the context of already depressed employment opportunities, and seen against a background of two centuries of rising enrollments, a projected decline of approximately 15 percent over a fifteen-year period is *very* substantial. In addition, we can be fairly confident that this expected general decline in ''full-time equivalent'' enrollment will be accompanied by significant changes in the *composition* of the student population that also will have negative implications for the future employment prospects of Ph.D. candidates in the arts and sciences. Our aggregate enrollment figures, for example, encompass a marked increase in the number of older students relative to those who are in the 18–24 age range (with the full-time equivalent enrollment of older students rising from just over one quarter of the total in 1980 to about one third in 2000). The absolute numbers of older students will of course rise even more rapidly, relative to other students, since approximately 80 percent of all older students study on a part-time basis. Accordingly, we should expect the educational system to include a much larger number of part-time students relative to full-time students, and we should also expect more pronounced declines in enrollment at four-year colleges and universities than at two-year schools.*

* See National Center for Education Statistics, ''Early Release,'' March 19, 1980. This publication projects decreases in enrollment from 7.3 million in 1981 to 6.7 in 1988 for four-year schools while simultaneously projecting essentially no decline at two-year colleges (from 4.38 million to 4.35 million).

It would have been possible to project an even greater increase in the number of older students if we had chosen to assume that the proportion attending school would continue to increase at the rate evident between 1973 and 1978. This seems rather unlikely, however, because so much of the overall increase observed between 1973 and 1978 was due to a dramatic upsurge in the enrollment of women. Indeed, between 1968 and 1978 the proportion of women enrolled in higher education rose from 40 percent to 50 percent. Much of the increased enrollment in the 30–34 and

Such shifts in relative "shares" of enrollment work against Ph.D. candidates in the arts and sciences because of differences in the general pattern of course elections at the two types of institutions and differences in the kinds of courses taken by part-time and full-time students. In addition, there has been a reluctance on the part of some two-year colleges to hire candidates with Ph.D.'s (on the grounds that such candidates are "over-qualified" and less interested in teaching than research). Some four-year colleges have also been reluctant to hire as many Ph.D.'s as they otherwise might because of budgetary limitations and unwillingness to make long-term commitments.

We must also anticipate significant variations among regions in enrollment trends. Declines in enrollment in the northeast over the period in question may well be *twice* the national rate—that is, roughly 30 percent rather than 15 percent. Since many educational institutions continue to express some regional preference in hiring decisions, this is an additional reason for concern about opportunities for graduate students at Princeton and other universities in our part of the country.

The broad trends in enrollment depicted in Chart 2 suggest, first, that the overall decline should be expected to occur in two stages, with a short plateau intervening in the late 1980s. The subsequent sharp drop provides graphic warning that it would be a mistake to interpret the arrival of this plateau as signaling the end of downward pressure on enrollments. That cannot be expected until about 1995–96. (Our figures suggest that enrollment within the traditional 18–21 age group may actually rise slightly about 1989, but here again the danger is that this temporary change will be misread.)

Equally important is the projection of significant recovery in the latter half of the 1990s. The length and magnitude of this recovery cannot be projected with confidence (in part because it is so hard to know what will happen to birth rates). Still, in planning for the future it is important to recognize the likelihood of a major increase in enrollment fol-

---

35–39 age ranges was almost certainly due to a "catching-up" phenomenon, whereby women who had missed schooling opportunities earlier (or had been deprived of them) went back to school. But now that women are enrolling in the same percentages as men, there seems little reason to believe that influxes of similar magnitude will occur in the future. This line of reasoning could lead to a downward revision of projected attendance estimates in some age groups. We have not made such revisions, and in fact have assumed a continuation of the historically high rate of attendance achieved in the late 1970s by persons in the 30–34 and 35–39 age ranges. Nor have we assumed that recent declines in the percentages of "younger students" (17–21) attending college will continue into the future; thus, we have based our projections on somewhat higher school enrollment percentages for 17-year-olds, and for those in the 18–21 age bracket, than were observed most recently. We note these assumptions only to suggest that the projections presented here could well be off in either direction.

lowing what are sure to be fifteen extraordinarily difficult years for both institutions and teachers.

FACULTY RETIREMENTS, DEATHS, AND RESIGNATIONS. Openings for new faculty depend importantly on the number of current faculty members vacating their positions, as well as on changes in enrollment, and here too it is necessary to confront objective realities that are far from comforting. The key development historically is the rapid expansion of American higher education that occurred in the late 1950s and during almost all of the 1960s. The large numbers of faculty members hired in those years are still relatively young; consequently, the retirement rate to be anticipated over most of the next two decades is well below normal. This would be true, it should be stressed, even if Congress had not recently changed the law to prohibit mandatory retirement prior to age 70. The major consequence of that change, which takes effect for tenured faculty in 1983, is to delay for three to five years the point at which faculty hired in the expansion years of the 1950s and 1960s begin to reach retirement age.

The extent to which the age distribution of faculties nationwide is skewed to the younger age groups is shown dramatically in Figure 3. In 1978, almost 60 percent of all faculty members were under 45 years of age, and a full 73 percent were under 50. At the other end of the age distribution, about 16 percent were 55 or over and only 7 percent were 60 or older.

By using more or less standard techniques, we have combined estimates of vacancies to be created through retirements (assuming a fairly gradual increase in the average age at retirement, not an instant shift to age 70), through mortality, and through resignations and terminations. In brief, we project a total of just under 50,000 "replacement vacancies" during the five years from 1980 to 1985, about 56,000 between 1985 and 1990, approximately 62,500 between 1990 and 1995, and about 67,500 between 1995 and 2000. Thus, starting from a low point at the present time, there should be a reasonably steady, although modest, increase in replacement demand for faculty over the next two decades. Of course, as a result of declining enrollments as well as other factors, colleges and universities will in all likelihood not fill all of these positions, a reality recognized in the overall projections we present below.

OTHER FACTORS AFFECTING THE NUMBER OF OPENINGS. The number of new openings for faculty members also depends on student-fac-

Figure 3
Age Distribution of Faculty in Institutions of Higher Education, 1978

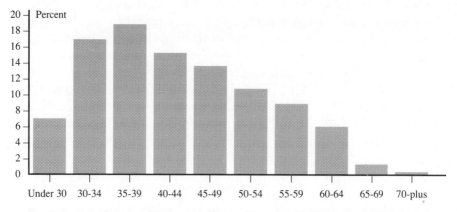

Source: Paula R. Knepper and Thomas M. Corwin, *Finance and Employment Implications of Raising the Mandatory Retirement Age for Faculty,* Policy Analysis Service Reports, American Council on Education, 1978.

Figure 4
Doctorates Granted by U.S. Universities, 1940-1980

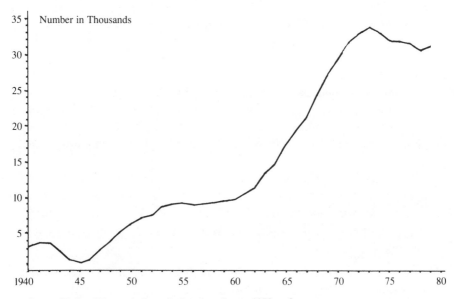

Source: National Research Council, *Summary Report 1979,* p. 3.

ulty ratios. The Carnegie Council reports that this ratio has risen by more than 10 percent in recent years, and suggests that it could well rise by an additional 10 percent—another development that hardly augurs well for the future prospects of aspiring graduate students. One reason for this trend is that higher proportions of all students have been attending two-year colleges that have relatively high student-faculty ratios. Student-faculty ratios have also been driven up at some institutions by budgetary pressures. These pressures are likely to continue, and perhaps become even more intense, as payroll costs increase with larger numbers of older, and better paid, faculty staying on until age 70. Nevertheless, recent data from the National Center for Educational Statistics fail to indicate any significant upward drift in the student-faculty ratio, and we have therefore elected to maintain a constant ratio of 17:1 in constructing our overall estimates of faculty openings. If anything, use of this assumption may make our estimates of faculty openings somewhat too optimistic.

Among the many other factors that will affect academic job prospects for new Ph.D.'s, let me mention just one: the extent to which reductions in enrollment force a considerable number of institutions to close, as contrasted with a situation in which most institutions survive, albeit with all (or nearly all) adjusting in some respects to declining enrollments. Paradoxical as it may seem at first glance, graduate students will be better off if sizable numbers of institutions cease operations entirely than if the effects of declining enrollments are spread more evenly. The reason is that closing will impose more of the burden of adjustment on current faculty members who will lose their jobs (with many no doubt leaving academic employment altogether). New recipients of Ph.D.'s will probably have a better chance than most of these displaced faculty members of securing positions in the remaining colleges and universities, which will be making more appointments than would have been the case if the impact of the enrollment decline had been more uniform.

THE NUMBER OF PH.D.'S COMPETING FOR POSITIONS. Exacerbating the problems just described is the fact that the number of newly graduating Ph.D.'s—direct competitors for scarce positions—is so very large. In 1979, the most recent year for which data are available, the total number of Ph.D. recipients was 31,200.* This number is down

* National Research Council, *Summary Report 1979, Doctorate Recipients from United States*

modestly from the peak of 33,756 reached in 1973, but it is still far above the levels characteristic of earlier years; indeed, in 1979 there were roughly *twice* as many Ph.D.'s awarded as in 1964 and roughly *three* times as many as in 1960. (See Figure 4.)

While it may seem odd, it is true that even after the present difficulties in the academic labor market were being felt—and well after they had been anticipated by many—the number of new Ph.D.'s continued to increase. This is due in part to the fact that graduate education can be such a long process; many students emerging with degrees when retrenchment was well under way had begun their work when conditions in the academic labor market were still relatively favorable. In any case, of the 60,000 humanities Ph.D.'s in the American labor force in 1977, more than 25 percent were awarded in the 1960s—and over 44 percent were awarded in the 1970s!

These numbers reflect dramatic—and relatively recent—increases in the number of institutions granting doctorates. In 1974 there were 307 regionally accredited institutions granting the doctorate, compared to 61 Ph.D.-granting institutions in the 1920–24 period, 107 in the early 1940s, and 208 in the early 1960s.*

We have made no systematic effort to project the future supply of Ph.D.'s. Obviously, much depends on "market factors" (trends in salaries, how grim the job market in fact becomes, and so on) as well as on the responses of *both* potential graduate students and universities as they determine the future of their Ph.D. programs. What can be said is that the number of Ph.D.'s awarded each year shows no sign of continuing to accelerate (as some suggested prior to the high point reached in 1973); in fact, other things being equal, we probably can expect some further modest reductions in the annual number of Ph.D. recipients.

One other point deserves emphasis. Competition for academic positions available in any one year comes not only from those receiving advanced degrees in that year but from earlier graduates as well. Thus, in thinking about the outlook for Ph.D. programs and Ph.D. candidates, careful attention has to be given to the accumulated "stock" of individuals holding doctorates, many of whom may be in temporary positions waiting to apply for a permanent opening if one should occur.

THE OVERALL RELATIONSHIP BETWEEN OPENINGS AND APPLICANTS. Important as it is to recognize individual factors affecting job pros-

---

Universities, p. 3. This report and another entitled *A Century of Doctorates* are the source of all the data cited here on Ph.D.'s awarded.

* *A Century of Doctorates*, p. 3. According to Peter Syverson of the National Research Council, there are currently 324 doctorate-granting institutions.

pects, it is even more important to understand the relationships they bear to each other and to the overall supply of candidates. For a variety of reasons (conceptual and statistical), these are not easy tasks. It is possible, however, to approximate the overall relationship between job opportunities and job seekers.

Perhaps the best analysis of this historical relationship was made by Alan Cartter, and Figure 5 is reproduced from his study published in 1976. Cartter interprets an approximate equality of doctorates awarded and new appointments as constituting a rough equilibrium, reflecting the fact that traditionally there has been an approximate balance between the number of Ph.D. recipients who have not sought academic jobs and the number of openings that have been filled by persons without Ph.D.'s. He then notes that whereas there was a significant shortage of Ph.D.'s between 1962 and 1968, the curves crossed dramatically in 1969. A large "excess supply" of Ph.D.'s is evident in the 1970s, and the situation he projected for the mid- to late 1980s can be described only as dismal from the standpoint of job seekers.

We have attempted to update and extend Cartter's analysis, taking advantage of what is known now about developments that occurred after he had completed his work. Our conclusions are summarized graphically on Figure 6 (which also reproduces a portion of Cartter's graph to facilitate comparisons).

It is clear, first, that Cartter's estimates for the "supply side" of the academic labor market were appreciably too high. (Cartter projected 43,000 Ph.D. recipients in 1980; the actual number is likely to be just over 30,000.) His estimates of the likely number of new jobs, on the other hand, continue to seem roughly correct, even though we project somewhat more openings in certain years than Cartter did. *The important conclusion is simply that there is a very large gap between even the appreciably smaller number of new Ph.D.'s now projected and the likely number of academic openings over the next fifteen years.*

According to our projections, only about 100,000 academic positions will be filled during the entire *fifteen*-year period from 1980 to 1995. Some perspective on this number is provided by noting that there were about 60,000 positions filled in the *five* years from 1971 through 1975, generally regarded as a "lean" period. Put another way, this projection of the total demand for new faculty during these fifteen years is about equal to the total demand for faculty in 1965–67, the *three* peak years of the past. At the same time, roughly 30,000 new Ph.D.'s are now completing their work each year, as contrasted with an annual rate of less than 20,000 in 1965–67. Moreover, there is obviously

Figure 5
Comparison of Junior Faculty Openings with Earned Doctorates Awarded (Actual: 1948-1973, Projected: 1974-1990)

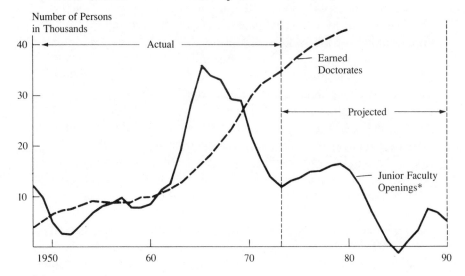

*Three-year moving average.
Copyright 1976 by The Carnegie Foundation for the Advancement of Teaching, reproduced with permission.

Figure 6
Projected Faculty Demand, 1981-2000, Compared with Cartter's Projections for 1975-1990

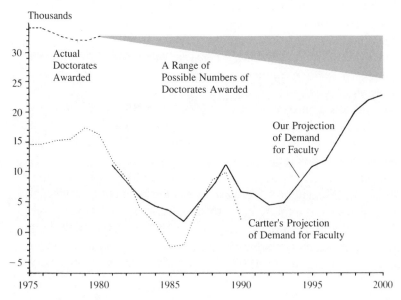

going to be an accumulating "stock" of Ph.D.'s educated in prior years, some of whom will compete with each year's new graduates for whatever positions are available.*

It is figures such as these that force the conclusion that the next fifteen years will not be at all like the past, however much some of us may wish them to be. As the modest decline in the number of new Ph.D.'s awarded since 1973 attests, both individuals and institutions can react to changed circumstances. But the response to date can fairly be described as minimal.

New circumstances, including new policy decisions as well as the response of potential graduate students, will of course modify all projections of this kind. So too will unanticipated fluctuations in enrollments, faculty retirements, and developments in other areas of the economy. Still, the overall picture is sufficiently clear, and the outlook sufficiently worrisome, to put us well beyond the point at which modest differences in assumptions can make the underlying problem of the next decade and a half disappear. At no time over this period do we expect the total demand for Ph.D.'s in academia to come close to matching the corresponding supply of Ph.D.'s.

A strong upturn in job opportunities, caused both by increases in the college-age population and by increases in the number of faculty retirements, is projected for the mid- to late 1990s. As we now consider necessary modifications in graduate programs, we must be careful to avoid damaging our fundamental capacity to satisfy the needs of the future, as they will begin to be felt then. In this light, some have cautioned against significant retrenchment, noting that with the lags involved in the educational process the classes of students beginning graduate study in the mid-1980s might expect tenure decisions just as job prospects begin to brighten somewhat ten to twelve years later. Others are worried that the projected surge in demand for teachers will occur just as supply turns down, creating an imbalance in the other direction as occurred in the 1960s.

It must be recognized, however, that being considered for tenure in 1995 requires one to have secured an initial appointment in, say, 1988

---

* The aggregate figure for this category of unemployed or "underemployed" holders of doctorates over these fifteen years could be as high as 200,000 (the difference between total degrees awarded and the total number of junior faculty openings). However, as a result of both some inevitable obsolescence of knowledge as well as intervening experiences with alternative careers, by no means all of these individuals could be considered serious candidates for new faculty positions. Our rough analysis suggests a net stock availability of perhaps 30,000 to 40,000 Ph.D.'s over most of this period.

or 1989—when the competition for the limited number of available positions will be extremely keen. Moreover, in contrast with the situation that existed in the 1960s, a considerable part of the expected increase in job opportunities in the late 1990s may be satisfied by the very large stock of Ph.D.'s who were educated relatively recently but will be unemployed or underemployed at that time. Thus, recognition that conditions will improve approximately fifteen years from now should not obscure the need to respond to present and prospective realities.

As discouraging as these realities are, our projections do not suggest that there will be any year in which there are no job opportunities whatsoever. Even in the most unfavorable years, some positions will be available, including positions in universities whose stringent tenure policies ensure turnover. Thus, there is reason to expect that a limited number of candidates—one hopes the very best candidates—will be placed. Our concern, therefore, should be with the quality of Ph.D. recipients, even as we recognize the serious overall quantitative imbalance in the academic labor market.

Rising Costs and Changing Patterns of Financial Support for Graduate Students

Compounding the difficulties created for graduate students by a shrinking academic labor market is the high—and rapidly rising—cost of a graduate education. At Princeton, for instance, annual tuition charges have gone from $2,600 in 1970–71 to $6,400 in 1980–81, and these figures are representative of the situation at most private universities. Costs have risen at state universities as well. At the University of Michigan, for example, tuition for state residents has increased from $660 to $2,100 over this same period (and from $1,940 to $4,600 for out-of-state students).

Unfortunately, at the same time that inflation and other economic factors have driven up the cost of graduate tuition, major sources of support for graduate students have fallen off precipitously. The result is that the net cost of graduate education to students and their families has grown astronomically.*

Since the beginning of graduate education in this country, doctoral candidates have received much more financial support than undergrad-

---

* Costs to universities of providing graduate education are of course far greater than tuition, and these "institutional costs" are also rising rapidly. This too is a most serious matter, but it is part of the more general problem of institutional finance and is not the subject of this report.

uates, perhaps because they have been seen as "apprentice scholars" making a direct and immediate contribution to programs of teaching and research as well as to the overall intellectual quality of their institutions and disciplines. In 1915–16, for instance, there were 630 recipients of Ph.D.'s in the United States; of the 530 who responded to a survey, only 49 had not received a fellowship or assistantship of some sort. In 1960, only 12 percent of all doctoral students (8 percent in the arts and sciences) received no stipends. Within the past decade, however, important sources of graduate student support either have been reduced significantly or have disappeared entirely.

The number of federal fellowships, after growing steadily for almost a decade, fell off sharply after 1968 as program after program established in the 1950s and early 1960s was dismantled. A study conducted by the National Board of Graduate Education found that between 1968 and 1974 the number of federally supported fellowships and traineeships for doctoral students decreased from 51,500 to 6,600. And 1974 was not the low point. The National Science Foundation, which has long supported the most promising students in the sciences, engineering, and some of the social sciences, awarded 1,941 fellowships in 1970–71; in 1981–82 this number will be 450. The few remaining fellowships funded by governmental monies are almost entirely in scientific and health-related fields; today there is essentially no federal investment in the support of doctoral students in the humanities, arts, and social sciences.

In addition to providing stipends for students, federal fellowship programs generally also include cost-of-education allowances that are paid to institutions in lieu of tuition. Unfortunately, while tuitions have escalated over recent years, cost-of-education allowances have lagged far behind. For example, the NSF now contributes only $3,400 toward Princeton's tuition of $6,400, while stipulating that the University absorb the difference. As a result, each year universities—and especially the major private universities—are faced with a need to cover an increasingly large proportion of the total educational expense for students receiving prestigious national awards.

This drastic decline in federal support has come at the same time that privately funded national fellowship support has almost disappeared. Over the past five years, the Ford Foundation has eliminated all 600 individual graduate fellowships previously awarded in domestic fields of study and has reduced its international fellowships by a third. The Woodrow Wilson National Fellowship Foundation terminated a program in the early 1970s that had, for the preceding twenty years, supported some 18,000 graduate students, 70 percent of whom were in the humanities and social sciences. And the last class of Danforth Foundation Fellows—a group that has included some 3,500 students over the past twenty-eight years, with a substantial majority in the humanities and social sciences—entered graduate school this fall. The demise of these three programs has poignant connotations for me personally, I might add, since I benefited from the generosity of all three during my own graduate study at Princeton. Their termination is a particularly vivid reminder for me of the dramatic changes that have occurred.

The impact of these decreases in outside support can perhaps be seen more clearly if we examine shifts in support patterns at Princeton over the past ten years. A comparison of the sources of support for degree candidates in 1970–71 and 1979–80 shows that the number of non-university fellowships fell almost 50 percent. A large proportion of this decline was due to the phasing out of the Ford Foundation fellowships; whereas 135 students were supported by these fellowships at the beginning of the decade, none were last year. Some of the slack has been taken up by a necessarily large increase in the number of fellowships financed by University funds. In addition, the numbers of students who support themselves as assistants in instruction and assistants in research have increased sharply. Finally, the number of students coming to Princeton with no support whatsoever from either outside sources or University funds has jumped dramatically despite the rise in tuition.

One obvious concomitant of these shifts has been a large increase in University "general funds" expended for direct support of graduate students—the annual commitment having risen from $2.5 million to $6.7 million over this decade. Yet, despite this increase, there has been a precipitous fall in the level of financial aid received by a typical graduate student.

One consequence of this decline in support during years of steep inflation is that students are now borrowing larger and larger amounts of money. In 1970–71, Princeton graduate students as a group borrowed only $70,000. In 1979–80, the total amount borrowed was $1.2 million. At the current rate of borrowing, the average indebtedness incurred in graduate school for a humanities student who receives his Ph.D. in 1985 will be $7,500—a considerable sum by most standards, but a particularly formidable figure when one considers the typical beginning salary at colleges and universities and when one adds in the large debts already incurred by many graduate students while they were undergraduates. At Princeton last year, 21 percent of entering graduate students in all fields who were eligible to borrow were carrying undergraduate loans, compared with 10 percent five years before.

Effects on the Pool of Candidates for the Ph.D. and the Vitality of Fields of Study

Over time, the combination of grim job prospects and accelerating costs is certain to have a major impact on the composition and quality of the group going on to graduate study, and, in turn, on the vitality of fields of study. Already, as is hardly surprising, the pool of applicants is declining, with the degree of contraction varying significantly from field to field.

Just how significant a decline has occurred already in the pools of candidates can be seen by comparing the number of students across the country taking the Graduate Record Examination (GRE) in 1970–71 and in 1978–79: the overall number fell from 309,000 to 280,000. The figures for specific fields are even more revealing. For example, the number of students taking the GRE Advanced Test in French declined from 2,500 to 1,000 during this eight-year period; the number taking the Advanced Test in Spanish dropped from 2,000 to 900; and the German test drew only 350 candidates compared with 700 at the beginning of the decade. Nor are languages the only fields affected. In philosophy and geography there has also been a decline of approximately 50 percent, and the number of students who took the Advanced Tests in mathematics and history decreased 63 percent and 72 percent respectively.*

These national trends have begun to take hold at Princeton, where this year the total number of applications was 4 percent less than last year. Applications to the Woodrow Wilson School and to the School of Architecture and Urban Planning actually increased by 2 percent and 13 percent respectively, while the natural sciences decreased by 3 percent, engineering by 5 percent, the social sciences by 8 percent, and the humanities by 11 percent. A somewhat more startling comparison shows that, although Princeton received roughly the same number of applications for 1970–71 and 1980–81, this stable total conceals a decline over the decade of 27 percent in the humanities, and 33 percent

---

* It should be noted that there need be no close correspondence between numbers of test-takers, or even numbers of applicants, and the eventual number of entering Ph.D. candidates in any year. Some students take aptitude and achievement tests and then do not apply for graduate study or, if they do apply, decide to take jobs and pursue other careers instead of enrolling in Ph.D. programs. However, reductions in applicant pools by definition reduce the selectivity of the graduate admission process and almost certainly affect the quality of candidates actually enrolled.

in the social sciences. It needs to be said that our experience is not idiosyncratic; indeed, it has paralleled that of comparable universities. (I should add that we are unable to determine to what degree, if at all, these declines in numbers of applications result from individual students applying to fewer universities.)

Needless to say, it is not the numerical decline in and of itself that should preoccupy us. Indeed, it would be worrying, as well as astonishing, if the dramatic decline in job opportunities and financial support did not elicit some such response from potential students. "Signals" as strong as these should be both heard and heeded, and in these circumstances some substantial decrease in the number of applicants is surely healthy from a national perspective. There are, however, three serious questions raised by the decrease in numbers. First, what effect will this decrease have on the quality and composition of the graduate student body? Second, to what degree will the declining numbers threaten the viability of particular academic programs? And third, how serious a negative effect will these changes have on the quality of undergraduate teaching, on the nature of scholarship and research, and on the advancement of knowledge?

The danger of losing the most talented students to other pursuits is already more than hypothetical, since it is evident that by no means are only the marginal students self-selecting themselves out of the applicant pool. Often the best prospective graduate students choose other careers. At Dartmouth, for example, a comparison of the top 100 students in 1977 and 1978 showed a 25 percent decline in the number going on to graduate study in the arts and sciences. At Harvard/Radcliffe, more than 75 percent of all *summa* graduates planned immediate graduate study in the arts and sciences in the mid-1960s, compared to 34 percent last year.

The chairman of Princeton's History Department, Professor Robert L. Tignor, described the situation as follows in his most recent annual report:

> In the humanities and some of the social sciences graduate education is in a state of crisis. This is the case in history. The dearth of jobs makes graduate study of history unpopular. Ten years ago, for example, it was common for one third to one half of this department's highest honors graduates to go on for graduate study. At present there is usually one very hardy and courageous soul among the highest honors recipients who is so committed to history that he or

she is willing to brush aside all the gloomy predictions about the state of the job market and to embark upon graduate training in this field.

Although most fields still have an adequate number of applicants from which to choose, and although Princeton's incoming graduate students continue on the whole to be talented and well prepared, no graduate school can expect immunity from an almost inevitable fall-off in quality if the number of applicants continues to plummet. In such circumstances, the temptation to admit less well qualified candidates in order to attract enough students to constitute a "critical mass"—or the number which, at some point in time, was believed necessary to give a program vitality and breadth—is a real one, hard to resist.

Although most of the developments mentioned thus far apply fairly generally to students in all fields, there are other developments that affect particular academic areas. In the field of engineering, paradoxically, a strong demand for engineers has had serious negative effects on the national pool of graduate students. As undergraduate engineering students are offered attractive and very well-paying jobs, even if they have not gone beyond the B.S.E. level, fewer are attracted to graduate study with its high costs and the modest salary levels for those who then pursue academic careers. The resulting loss of talented graduate students is now widely perceived as a serious threat to research and teaching, and it has been widely noted—not only by deans of engineering schools but also by the National Science Foundation, industry publications, and the popular press.

In addition to concern for the overall quality of the applicant pool, there is also growing apprehension that current circumstances are having particularly negative effects on the willingness of minority students to attend graduate school. Reports from a number of institutions indicate that, despite strenuous efforts in recruiting, their minority applicant pools last year either decreased or showed no significant increase. This was our experience. Nationwide, the lure of professional schools and immediate job opportunities often outweighs the attractions of graduate school; in engineering the job offers for black students, for example, are especially attractive. The realities of growing indebtedness and discouraging job prospects are extremely difficult to counter. Yet it is clear that these factors simply must be overcome if there are to be qualified minority applicants sufficient to enable the nation's colleges and universities to broaden the composition of their faculties.

Otherwise, important efforts to promote affirmative action will continue to be impeded by *very* small pools of candidates.

From a long-term perspective, the most disturbing possibility raised by the trends affecting graduate education is that the vitality of entire fields of knowledge may be weakened for extended periods of time—a development that, if it occurred, would be serious and difficult to reverse. To be sure, some fields are not yet threatened. At Princeton, for example, applications to our three professional schools (Engineering and Applied Science, Public and International Affairs, and Architecture and Urban Planning) have in general either remained reasonably constant or have increased over the past ten years, a pattern consistent with national trends. Among the arts and sciences departments, Economics has shown a spectacular increase in applications. But these examples are manifest exceptions; in many departments, reduced applications coupled with declining support pose real dangers.

In departments like English or History, major reductions in scale can harm the educational structure of programs even if they do not threaten the existence of graduate programs per se. Fewer students mean fewer courses; fewer courses mean less adequate coverage of fields generally regarded as necessary; and less interaction and more parochialism can result. In the case of some smaller departments, the danger is even greater. As Professor John F. Wilson, former chairman of the Department of Religion, has noted: "Princeton's special situation is that its small scale makes very difficult a reduction in the scope of departmental graduate programs much beyond their current orders of operation without altogether eliminating them."

Related to these concerns is the risk of counterproductive competition among institutions. If there is an adequate supply of qualified candidates, then strong departments can easily attract enough students to sustain their programs at educationally viable levels. But if the national pool becomes significantly smaller, competition among the universities can lead to an academically undesirable situation in which students are in effect encouraged to choose graduate schools by accepting the highest bids—not by selecting the most suitable programs. If qualified students are then spread too thinly over too many departments, all of the major departments may be hurt. Within individual institutions, if students are distributed too unevenly from field to field, the intellectual integrity of the institution can suffer. As Dean West recognized so clearly—and as Dean Ziolkowski testifies today—the strength of any university comes not only from the quality of individual departments, but from the joint strength of many departments working within neighboring fields of knowledge.

The largest question raised by the possible disappearance, or real weakening, of high-quality graduate programs has to do with the overall future of research, scholarship, and teaching in this country. Most basic research is done in universities and, more specifically, by faculty and research staff working closely with able graduate students. Programs of advanced study cannot simply be turned on and off at will; years are required to develop the capacity to train scholars and teachers to the point where they can make genuine contributions, and the continuing vitality of fields of knowledge depends on regular replenishment by the most talented students of succeeding generations who bring with them new perspectives and new ideas. If the continuity of a field—the flow of students through the educational systems to its highest reaches—is interrupted at any point, it cannot simply be "turned on" ten or fifteen years later when circumstances have changed.

Unless we can maintain our graduate schools and unless we can continue to attract and find opportunities for outstanding graduate students, we must contemplate the prospect of universities in which increasingly elderly professors teach without the stimulation of advanced students and younger colleagues. This would be a grim future for students and professors alike—and it would be catastrophic in fields in which the most extraordinary advances are often made by young scholars.

The Problem of Specialization

For as long as there have been graduate schools, tension has existed between the demands for special competence within a relatively narrow field of study and the importance of a broader perspective on learning. But if the debate is an old one, never capable of full resolution, it does seem to me that the other trends described above require us to think freshly about pressures for specialization and their significance.

The consequences of highly specialized graduate training for learning, for scholarship itself, and for teaching—especially in colleges committed to liberal education—have never been described better than they were by Jacob Viner, under whose tutelage I studied the history of economic thought. In a memorable address before the Graduate Convocation at Brown University in 1950, Viner described as "the major barrier to the promotion of true scholarship in our graduate schools":

> . . . the ever-growing specialization not only as between departments but even within departments, a specialization carried so far

that very often professors within even the same department can scarcely communicate with each other on intellectual matters except through the mediation at seminars and doctoral examinations of their as yet incompletely specialized students. This development has not been capricious or without function. The growth in the accumulation of data, in the refinement and delicacy of tools for their analysis so that great application and concentration are necessary for mastery of their use, has not only ended the day of the polymath with all knowledge in his province, but seems steadily to be cutting down the number of those who would sacrifice even an inch of depth of knowledge for a mile of breadth.

I am told, and do not disbelieve, that this intensive specialization is frequently necessary for discovery, and especially for the improvement of techniques of discovery. To be able to keep on discovering things not known before it seems often to be necessary to work in a narrow groove, and to look always straight ahead in that groove without even glances at the once delectable knowledge in one's scholarly neighbor's rival garden. For our liberal colleges we preach synthesis of disciplines, breadth of view, and historical perspective, and in our liberal colleges there are still teachers who practice it. But when, by fellowships or other blandishments, we have enticed the college graduate into our graduate schools, we at once encourage him to grow the professional blinders which will confine his vision to the narrow research track, and we endeavor—often successfully— to make out of him a trufflehound, or, if you prefer, a race-horse, finely trained for a single small purpose and not much good for any other. We then let him loose on the undergraduates.

Not even Viner's eloquence—or his example—could reverse the trend, at least in many fields. I wonder what he would say about undergraduate training in many subjects today, thirty years later. Whatever may have happened to our pursuit of a broader, more generous sense of what constitutes knowledge, it is my conviction that the constricting opportunities for academic employment, combined with a resurgence of interest in "general education" in at least some colleges and universities, provide an occasion to reassert old claims for greater breadth in graduate education. And, in fact, the growth of some interdepartmental programs over the last decade or so, especially in areas of the humanities, suggests that some countervailing trends favoring broader combinations of subjects are already being felt.

If it is true that a higher and higher fraction of Ph.D. recipients will enter non-academic callings, they will surely need some of the larger talents and broader vision to which Viner alluded. Also, with academic institutions able to choose carefully among the many aspiring candidates for teaching positions, many will want teachers who are not so limited as those whose highly specialized graduate training left no room for anything but the study of a single specialty. Finally, the graduate students themselves may, if given at least minimal encouragement, choose to learn more about neighboring subjects, as something desirable in its own right, and to prepare themselves for a wider range of possible positions.

In any event, there is much to be said for our making a real effort to take whatever educational advantage we can of present and prospective circumstances. I am persuaded that if we fail to resist at least some of the pressures of specialization, we shall make it still harder for the future holder of doctorates to find ways to spend their lives that are both useful and satisfying.

Questions of Policy

The outlook for graduate education raises major questions of policy—for Princeton, for universities generally, and for government and society at large. While there are some who believe that the outlook is not all that bleak, the trends and projections described above seem to me to make a compelling case for consideration of major adjustments all through the system of higher education. Of course it is always possible to be overly pessimistic. In my view, however, there is much more to be feared from inaction, from assuming that the expected problems will not materialize or will somehow take care of themselves (as they surely will, though perhaps in extremely damaging ways), than from making decisions that address forthrightly problems too obvious and too serious to ignore.

It is fair to ask whether we have the institutional capacity, in particular universities and nationwide, to cope intelligently with a need to retrench following a century of uninterrupted expansion of graduate education. Given our history, and the inherent conservatism of our institutions and decision-making processes, there seems to me little danger of overreaction, at least on the part of universities. At the level of the individual institutions, all of the biases press in the other direction. Governments (state and federal), on the other hand, generally seem to me to have overreacted already—or to have failed to react in appropriate ways; and I believe that the same comment applies to some foundations, though by no means all of them.

For Princeton

Before considering what others might do to respond constructively, we have an obligation to look first to ourselves and our own options. We need to do so, I believe, not simply in a spirit of doing the best we can to fend off disaster, but with the objective of taking maximum advantage of our need to think afresh about large issues of educational policy as well as finance.

To the most fundamental question—should Princeton maintain a major commitment to graduate education—I have already given my own answer: an emphatic "yes."

To the next question, however, which has to do with the right size of the graduate school and the fields to be covered, my answer is much more equivocal. It is hard to be an absolutist in light of the marked changes over time in what various people were sure was "optimal." The total number of graduate students has increased from the 200 preferred by Dean West at the turn of the century, to the 500 considered just right shortly after World War II, to a peak of almost 1,500 in the 1970s.

These changes in total numbers reflect a substantial growth in fields of study. Princeton awarded graduate degrees in 1980 in some fifteen fields not even listed in the Graduate School Announcement of twenty years ago, including anthropology, biochemistry, comparative literature, computer science, statistics, and urban planning—subjects hardly regarded as esoteric today. We could not conceive of going back to anything resembling the numerical levels of earlier years without a drastic reduction in coverage of major fields, which in turn would have a devastating impact on the quality and eminence of the University.

Since we have been so selective in the fields we cover, it is also very hard to identify subjects which are easy targets for elimination because they can be regarded as peripheral. Thus, any significant reduction in fields of graduate study is a more difficult, and less plausible, option for Princeton than for many—in fact, most—other universities. Our dilemma is compounded by the fact that we must continue to be prepared, even under the most difficult conditions, to move into carefully chosen new fields (or recombinations of old fields) as new ideas, and new branches of knowledge, evolve. If this had not been our practice, we would still be teaching alchemy rather than chemistry and "natural philosophy" rather than biology.

But we must continue to choose carefully what we will do, and we must be prepared, if need be, to suspend graduate work in some subjects as the academic structure of the University continues to change. Our capacity to make painful decisions of this kind—and to sustain them—was tested when we decided in 1970 to suspend graduate work in Slavic languages and literatures.

That painful decision was made in spite of the fact that the Slavic graduate program was then ranked eleventh nationally. The reasoning was that a graduate program at Princeton in Slavic languages and literatures was not necessary from a national standpoint at a time when the trends in applications and employment opportunities described above were already evident and when even stronger programs existed at some other universities in our region. Strengthening Princeton's efforts would have required more resources than we could commit, and we believed that the needs and interests of other Princeton graduate students for work in Russian language, literature, culture, and history could be satisfied within the context of programs in Russian studies and (later) in comparative literature. (The University continues to have an excellent undergraduate program in Slavic languages and literatures.) It is certainly possible that similar decisions to suspend programs will prove to be the most sensible solution in other fields, but these are plainly not decisions that should be taken without the most careful assessment of all ramifications.

Another approach is phased retrenchment within specific departments. A decade ago the Department of Religion undertook a major revision of its graduate program, cutting back the number of sub-fields. As a result, the program is at present quite small and highly selective, but noted for its excellence and for its emphasis on the individual student. The Department of Biology made the decision some years ago to focus on only four areas, just as the Department of Psychology has done. Similarly, our Department of Germanic Languages and Literatures, while it has offered instruction in Dutch or Scandinavian languages on request, has made no effort to "cover" those closely related fields. And the same concentration of effort is evident in many other parts of the University. Princeton engineering departments, for instance, can compete with much larger departments elsewhere only by maintaining a high degree of selectivity in the fields they choose to emphasize.

Increasingly, departments at all universities will have to ask themselves if they should become more selective in their major offerings in order to concentrate their strengths. Such decisions should not be construed to imply value judgments about the absolute merits of various areas of specialization. They should be seen, rather, as a realistic recognition of the limitations of any single department's resources—and of a consequent need to choose. In an ideal world, perhaps a university might be expected to reflect the entire universe of knowledge through its offerings. But intellectual horizons have expanded so rapidly in the past two centuries that that ideal has become unrealizable by any institution. Moreover, it has long been Princeton's philosophy to concentrate on trying to do a relatively small number of things well, and that principle will almost surely become increasingly important in graduate education over the next decade or two.

If we adopt the assumption that what is important is to stimulate intellectual vitality rather than simply to maintain existing academic structures or patterns of graduate education, then it is possible to consider a number of other approaches to the problems of the next fifteen to twenty years. As noted earlier, the essential features of the graduate school at Princeton were established early in the century under Dean West. As new fields were added to the original core of seventeen that existed through the 1920s, the established pattern was maintained, at least to the extent possible. This rather monolithic model worked well as long as there were enough qualified students and enough money to support all candidates until they received their Ph.D.'s—and as long as many colleges and universities were eagerly waiting to employ them.

Today the realities are obviously different. Rather than seeking to perpetuate the more or less uniform academic structure that is still largely the rule at Princeton, it may well be sensible to respond in a more differentiated way to the varied circumstances of individual disciplines.

One norm for Ph.D. programs at Princeton has been that they should entail four years of study. This number is not random; it is based on an explicit conception of graduate education. A first premise is that we should admit to graduate programs students who have both sufficient talent and sufficient preparation to be ready to take the General Examination by the end of the second year. (The notable exceptions to the four-year rule have been those fields, such as East Asian studies and comparative literature, in which students have had to learn new and difficult languages.) The student is then expected to devote two additional years to a dissertation that is seen, not as a final *magnum opus*, but as a demonstration that the student has mastered the tools of independent research and has made at least a modest contribution to knowledge.

This approach distinguishes Princeton from many other institutions, and there is much to be said for it—both on the merits and to preserve an educational option not widely available. Especially in present circumstances, we should be admitting only the very best students—the ones who will need only two years to prepare for their General Examinations and who will be able to write the dissertation in two more years. But the policy of four years of graduate work was based on the assumption that students would be able to find academic employment even if the dissertation was not quite finished and the degree not yet awarded—an assumption that is no longer valid. The job competition is so demanding that students in many of the humanities and social sciences fare badly if they cannot show both a completed degree and the likelihood of attendant publications. For this reason there is already considerable pressure in some fields for a five-year program. Princeton may want to move in that direction in the case of selected departments—as long as the move is coupled with the admission of fewer students at the beginning, a greater willingness to choose among students after the first year or two of graduate study (an approach discussed more fully below), or both.

The likelihood of at least some general decline in student numbers, in a graduate school already as small in most fields as Princeton's, also could require changes in teaching methods. Some departments may need to move away from such heavy reliance on the present seminar or "course" system to more of an apprenticeship approach with greater emphasis on tutorials and reading courses. This is already the normal mode of graduate study in many of the sciences, where it generally works well; but it is less clear how well it would work if used more extensively in the humanities and social sciences. The attractions include an earlier introduction to independent work and an even closer relation between teacher and student. At the same time, there are dangers. As Professor T. James Luce, chairman of the Classics Department, has noted, the abandonment of seminars could "shift the entire nature of graduate education from the give-and-take among a group to tutoring and discipleship. . . . The latter prospect is blinkered, creates an unhealthy dependency, and takes place in an atmosphere of isolation."

As always, much depends on both the determination of departments to assure balanced educational programs and the real alternatives (recognizing that it is probably unrealistic in many fields to expect to maintain current numbers of graduate students over the next fifteen years). Under at least some circumstances, the need to consider such basic questions can lead to positive outcomes—to programs of high quality even as they include fewer students. For example, the Sociology Department at Princeton has recently restructured its entire program in this spirit, emphasizing independent research and the acquisition of methodological skills rather than "coverage" in a traditional sense. Other departments (Anthropology, for example) have compensated for small numbers by designing basic courses that can be taken by graduate students and advanced undergraduates alike.

Historically, Princeton has been an almost entirely Ph.D.-oriented graduate school, and in general it seems to me that there should continue to be a strong presumption in favor of our stressing the Ph.D. degree. This judgment is based on the premise that there will continue to be a need for excellently trained scholars in the forefront of all major fields and that Princeton's comparative advantage is in providing this kind of advanced education. But we could be less rigid, taking fuller account of differences among departments and of differences in aptitude and inclination among very able students—differences evident, in some cases, only after some graduate work has been completed.

Even if we maintain our emphasis on doctoral programs, as I believe we should, it may make excellent sense to encourage the concurrent development of additional master's programs (or non-degree programs) in certain fields. Such steps can serve real national needs and also sustain seminar programs in departments where the number of Ph.D. candidates is very small. In statistics, Near Eastern studies, and East Asian studies, for example, mid-career programs might be a service to professionals in other fields who can benefit from intensive training in these areas. In engineering, also, it may be desirable to provide opportunities to return to graduate school for some of those who went directly to industry following their undergraduate education.

Thinking along these lines raises another question: to what degree is it wise for Princeton to continue to insist on full-time commitments from almost all graduate students? We make exceptions to this rule now, but they are genuine exceptions. Again, re-examination of current assumptions is certainly proper. My own suspicion, however, is that a decision to admit large numbers of part-time students would alter the character of the graduate school in undesirable ways. The full-time student, even if he or she is present only for one year or arrives following other kinds of experience, nevertheless usually participates fully in all activities of the University and in ways not always possible for the part-time student—in seminars, group research projects, lectures, colloquiums, and the informal conversations and discussions that can contribute so much to one's education. The result is a rather special learning environment—one that provides at least some protection against the excessive narrowness of outlook that I continue to see as a major problem in graduate education generally.

While considering the possibility of being more flexible at the master's degree level, Princeton may also want to examine the possibility of expanding its opportunities at the postdoctoral level, particularly in the humanities and social sciences. Several department chairmen have suggested placing emphasis on the admission of at least a small number of extremely able postdoctoral fellows in the humanities and in some social science departments as a way of sustaining the flow of new ideas, and the active interchange among scholars of varying ages, in the face of dwindling numbers of Ph.D. candidates. This approach has the advantage of serving these purposes by improving the qualifications of those who have already completed the Ph.D., rather than by increasing the numbers of competitors for positions in fields already overpopulated.

Finally, it seems to me essential that, individually and collectively, we begin to develop new attitudes toward graduate education. In part it is as simple as coming to recognize that, in an era when graduate education is becoming progressively more expensive and the Ph.D. degree no longer confers job security, it is both inappropriate and potentially very damaging for graduate students to feel that they must strive to complete the Ph.D. no matter what. Thus the decision of a student to discontinue his or her graduate education after the first or second year needs to be seen not necessarily as evidence of failure but often as an indication of a more realistic self-assessment. Indeed, the balance of expectations should be shifted so that continuation toward the Ph.D. is no longer an automatic assumption. Each student should ask routinely: Am I doing so well, is my commitment so strong, that I ought to continue to the full completion of the doctorate?

Faculty members can help students with these difficult decisions by advising them frankly of their abilities and by avoiding any suggestion that withdrawal from pursuit of the Ph.D. is tantamount to failure in life. There are unmistakable signs of increased psychological pressures on graduate students for all of the obvious reasons, and faculty members can provide real assistance by listening closely, by offering constructive advice, and simply by being aware of the stresses that affect so many.

In my own view, faculty members also should be more willing than many are at present to insist that some students *not* continue after the first year or two of graduate study. While it is easy to understand the reasons why departments are reluctant to recommend against readmission (including an understandable desire to avoid creating an even more oppressive atmosphere than now exists), I am persuaded that the balance of interests is generally served best by readmission decisions that may seem harsher in the short run but will be fairer to all concerned, as well as more sensible, in the long run.

A necessary corollary to such an approach is some modification in the attitudes toward non-academic pursuits. It has been suggested that in the past some faculty members, especially in the humanities and social sciences, tended to look down on students who did not pursue academic careers. However prevalent such attitudes may have been (and it would be surprising and even disturbing if academics, like people in other professions, did not have at least *some* positive bias toward their own calling), perspectives clearly have been changing. Our History Department, for instance, has sought to prepare students to serve as editors of historical documents, working in a variety of non-academic settings. To cite another example, Edward Sullivan, Avalon Professor of the Humanities, has been active nationally in programs designed to provide opportunities in business for students with graduate training in the humanities. Still, there is more to be done as we seek a balance between the continuing desirability of exciting students about academic life—an excitement we must continue to communicate as well as to feel—and the need to encourage positive consideration of other opportunities as well.

Running through most of these suggestions for possible change in our own policies toward graduate education is the belief that greater flexibility across departments and within departments is necessary. Much as we want to preserve a sense of common purpose, much as we want to resist the pressures toward fragmentation, circumstances vary so greatly that it is no longer possible to operate on the basis of a single set of assumptions for either all departments or all students. Of course every department must seek to maintain the highest standards, and to do so within the context of a small university that prides itself on a certain coherence. However, this single large goal will almost certainly have to be pursued in a variety of ways.

We should recognize candidly one consequence of this approach: the existence of more differences among departments and students—differences bound to be visible. Differences of all kinds are especially obvious in the setting of a small and rather closely knit university; and they inevitably seem invidious to some, especially when they involve such matters as stipends, readmission decisions, the duration of graduate study, and assumptions about job prospects. Avoiding such tensions by pursuing more uniform approaches can be tempting, but it is an artificial solution likely to lead to far worse problems, including both greater frustration for many and the waste of scarce resources. It could even call into question our ability to come to terms with realities so powerful that no university can ignore them.

For Universities Generally

While all universities offering graduate programs in the arts and sciences must confront roughly the same external realities, and answer roughly the same questions, there is no reason whatsoever to expect all to come to the same conclusions. There are of course great differences among institutions in missions, resources, and circumstances; and even universities that are similar in these respects may well elect different approaches as a result of different decision-making processes. Individual departments will often have preferences that vary markedly from what a dean of the graduate school or a faculty committee will think best from the perspective of the institution as a whole. Decisions can be expected to reflect in part the degree of decentralization that characterizes the institution.

There is much to be said for this kind of pattern—or "nonpattern"—of decision-making, for leaving these decisions to individual institutions. The classic arguments against uniformity and centralized control apply here as elsewhere, and they apply with special force when one is dealing with educational questions and hoping to preserve a variety of educational options. Moreover, it is also far from clear that there is a single "right" policy or set of policies in any event. Experimentation should most definitely be welcomed.

Unfortunately, however, there is no assurance that the sum total of decisions reached separately by the more than 300 institutions now offering Ph.D.'s in the arts and sciences will make sense from a national standpoint. An obvious worry is that each institution will elect to leave the hard decisions to others. Graduate programs of significant size benefit institutions through the prestige they confer, through greater ability to recruit faculty, and through the livelier intellectual environment they can create. The natural interest of universities in appropriating such benefits inevitably discourages necessary reductions in the overall number of graduate students.

Another complication is the heavy use often made of graduate students as teaching assistants in undergraduate courses. The need to staff undergraduate courses can exert great pressure to maintain large graduate programs for that reason alone. Princeton probably makes less use of graduate students in undergraduate teaching than any other major university; yet even in our situation this kind of pressure is felt. The problem is much more acute, and more difficult to address, at many other places.

There is a good argument for replacing at least some teaching assistants with full-time faculty, thereby improving opportunities for those graduate students who do receive Ph.D.'s while simultaneously enhancing the quality of teaching (at least in some instances) and removing one source of pressure for overly large graduate student populations. Such a shift in teaching patterns would involve some increases in cost, however, and would have to be accompanied by increased financial support from other sources for the smaller number of graduate students still enrolled who otherwise would have relied on teaching assistantships as a major source of financial aid.

While an adverse "market" will itself discourage some students from pursuing Ph.D. programs, as we can see from recent experience, it is far from obvious that the response will be sufficient or sufficiently selective. This is true from at least two perspectives: which students go on to advanced study and the distribution of cutbacks among graduate programs. Nor, as suggested earlier, is it realistic to expect voluntary restraint on the part of institutions, in and of itself, to produce a desirable pattern of response nationally.

One particular risk, as numbers of applicants continue to decline and departments begin to feel squeezed, is that institutions will engage in "price-wars" in offering financial aid to graduate students. Strong believer that I am in competition, and in relying on market forces to give signals, I believe that this form of competition is likely to serve mainly negative purposes: it can be expected to demoralize students, to absorb precious fellowship resources that could be allocated more wisely, and to encourage students to choose graduate programs for financial rather than educational reasons. Thus, in the area of financial aid I am an advocate of cooperative approaches that will conserve resources and promote healthier forms of academic competition, while ensuring that stipends are generally adequate.

I do not believe, however, that it is right to expect uniformity of stipends across fields. If enough able students are to pursue Ph.D.'s in engineering, for example, financial incentives simply must be adequate to offset (in at least small part) the pull of immediate job opportunities in industry; at the same time, similar stipends in other fields, offered on an across-the-board basis, could well attract far more students to those fields than one would want. Cooperative approaches need to recognize such powerful market realities.

Carefully conceived inter-institutional programs of other kinds can simultaneously encourage the efficient use of resources and offer real educational advantages—for example, by providing a breadth of offerings that could not be made available otherwise. Princeton already enjoys successful exchange agreements with other universities: the Department of Religion exchanges students and faculty on a modest basis with Columbia University; the Department of Near Eastern Studies works closely with colleagues at New York University; and the joint degree of Master of Public Affairs–Doctor of Jurisprudence in the Woodrow Wilson School is based on close collaboration with the law schools of Columbia and N.Y.U. Similarly, Princeton and Rutgers have long maintained an agreement allowing students from either institution to take courses at the other. To the extent that students benefit from exposure to new professors, different methods, and competing ideas, they profit from spending at least part of their time at another institution.

Inter-institutional cooperation has long been taken for granted in the sciences, where students travel routinely to other institutions in order to learn techniques that have been perfected by scholars there or to use specialized equipment. It is a concept capable of at least somewhat broader application. Professor Bruce W. Arden, chairman of the Department of Electrical Engineering and Computer Science at Princeton, writes encouragingly of the manner in which " 'disciplinary computer networks' now being contemplated make possible a kind of collegiality that was formerly possible only by physical proximity." In the past, excessively grandiose ideas about cooperation often dulled the willingness to consider more modest possibilities, but there is reason to hope that more can now be achieved along these lines—and not just in science and engineering.

For the Government and Private Sources of Support

While there is much that universities themselves can do to address the major problems facing graduate education, the shape of the future will depend significantly on actions taken, and not taken, by government, foundations, corporations, and other private donors. To my mind, it is right in principle to look to these entities for constructive assistance. Graduate education provides benefits to the larger society that are clearly national in character, that cannot be "captured" by states or even regions, and that do not accrue only to the individuals being educated. Thus, it is appropriate for the federal government, and those foundations, corporations, and individuals that take the broadest outlook, to come to conscious decisions as to what they believe ought to happen and what roles they should play. This point of view is reinforced by the powerful interaction between graduate education and the nation's research effort—the strength of which also has clear implications for the future of our society.

The national stake in graduate education has been recognized explicitly by many countries. There has been considerable discussion, for example, of state support—and direction—of graduate education in the Soviet Union, where assistance is shifted from field to field, and back and forth from predoctoral to postdoctoral students, as job prospects and the needs of the state dictate. In West Germany and a number of other countries far less subject to detailed state regulation than the Soviet Union, it is still the practice to operate on the basis of a more or less strict system of disciplinary quotas (known in Germany as *numerus clausus*). Manpower surveys are generally used to determine how many new people will be needed to fill projected job openings in various fields, and student enrollments are then determined accordingly.

I have serious reservations about this general approach, especially in its more rigid forms. Some of these reservations are philosophical, centering on the degree of freedom of choice left to individuals, including the freedom to pursue particular callings even in the face of great obstacles and potential frustrations. On a more pragmatic level, such systems, for all their apparent rationality, make decisions that are extremely weighty for both individuals and the state on the basis of manpower projections that can be, and have been, notoriously off target. (This is partly because most such projections fail to allow for the feedback response of demand to variations in the numbers of candidates for positions—and, in market economies, to the salaries individuals can command. Also, it is exceedingly difficult to forecast the manpower implications of changing technologies, shifts in trade patterns, and the myriad other factors at work.)

My own preference is for an approach that is less prescriptive but that can at least encourage individuals and institutions to act in ways intended to serve broadly defined national objectives. *Maintaining a continuity of excellent scholarship and research in all major fields of knowledge seems to me to be one such objective of paramount importance. Another is the assurance that opportunities for graduate study of the highest quality will be available to outstanding individuals of all races, both sexes, and varying economic circumstances.*

As is evident from what has been said earlier in this report, I am no advocate of large-scale support of expansive graduate programs. On the contrary, I agree with those who believe that reductions in the numbers of Ph.D. candidates are called for in many fields. But I certainly do not believe that the number should be reduced to zero in any field, however discouraging the immediate job prospects. Nor do I believe that we can manage without the most able students in all fields, including students from a variety of backgrounds. The major task in designing policy, then, is to avoid stimulating too large a *quantitative* interest in graduate study while not simultaneously discouraging the necessary *qualitative* interest.

The rapid disestablishment in recent years of major programs of graduate student support by government and foundations has served the quantitative imperative by reducing the overall incentive for graduate study by large numbers of students. But the sharp downtrend in external support has certainly *not* served the qualitative imperative of ensuring a minimal flow of exceptionally talented students to all fields.

How is this delicate combination of policy objectives to be served? I believe the best approach is to provide attractive incentives for limited numbers of very capable candidates to pursue advanced work at those universities best suited to their educational needs. Fortunately, there is already a tested model which we know works: portable national fellowships awarded on the basis of merit that allow the successful candidates to attend the universities of their choice. The National Science Foundation has awarded fellowships of this kind for a number of years, and the Woodrow Wilson and Danforth Foundation fellowship programs (both now terminated) worked in essentially the same way.

Even beyond providing support to particularly promising students, fellowship programs of this kind have a further advantage. They make a strong statement of the importance the society attaches to outstanding intellectual accomplishment, and these "recognition effects" themselves stimulate able people to continue their studies. To achieve this end, the programs need not be large, and indeed should not be. The objective is to identify and encourage a relatively small number of the most promising individuals without simultaneously encouraging larger numbers of candidates in fields already almost certain to be overcrowded for at least the next fifteen years.

From the standpoint of effects on universities, there is also much to be said for such fellowship programs. If the fellowships are portable, students will take them to departments most likely to meet their needs. This stimulates the right kind of competition among programs, and it allows distinctions to be drawn between stronger and weaker programs on the basis of a series of decisions by individual students rather than on the basis of some single governmental (or institutional) judgment. It also helps to assure that the strongest departments will be able to enroll enough first-rate students over time to create the kind of learning environment that is important to the quality of graduate work.

One of the most serious dangers is that cutbacks in programs will occur more or less across the board, with the result that we will end up with roughly the same number of graduate programs as we have now, but with each program limping along at a level that is hard to defend from the standpoint of either educational values or a sensible allocation of resources. Portable fellowships awarded on the basis of merit would help reduce this risk—and without centralized determination of how many programs, and which ones, should be allowed to exist.

Thus, it was most heartening to see formal legislative recognition of the importance to the nation of a merit-based fellowship program in the last session of Congress. In enacting a law to extend most federal higher education programs over the next five years, the Congress (with the strong encouragement of Senator Claiborne Pell '40) authorized a new "National Graduate Fellows Program" that provides for up to 450 four-year nationally competitive portable fellowships "for graduate study in the arts, humanities, and social sciences by students of superior ability selected on the basis of demonstrated achievement and exceptional promise." The fellowships are to be awarded by distinguished national panels in fields designated by a presidentially-appointed National Graduate Fellowship Board.

As important as this program can be, it is of course by itself no panacea. One difficulty with relying solely on portable fellowships is that single, very strong departments may be nourished while neighboring departments necessary for intellectual interchange may not attract sufficient students. Excellent graduate education and research do not occur in isolation, and so attention must be given to sustaining overall institutional strength. Also, there are good arguments that are not solely political for ensuring a reasonable degree of regional balance among graduate programs—another objective not necessarily served fully by portable fellowships alone. One way of addressing these additional concerns would be to make a series of modest institutional grants to a specified number of leading graduate institutions.

Beyond meeting the needs of outstanding students during their periods of graduate study, we also need to make special efforts to increase the likelihood that the most promising young scholars will have opportunities to begin their scholarly careers—the generally depressed conditions that will prevail during the next fifteen years notwithstanding. Fortunately, as noted earlier, we can expect there to be at least some openings every year as a result of normal turnover and replacement demand. In addition, the Andrew W. Mellon Foundation has taken a strong lead in financing a limited number of additional opportunities for the appointment and promotion of young scholars in the humanities. Other efforts of a similar kind can do much to assure the continuity of scholarship and research in all fields of knowledge.

The general tenor of these comments is meant to have at least some applicability to all external sources of support even as we recognize that government, corporations, foundations, and individual donors operate under varying constraints and will naturally differ in what they can do to be helpful. The responsibility for the future of graduate education should be seen as broadly shared, and it seems important for all of the obvious reasons that support come in varying forms and from a variety of sources.

One encouraging sign, in addition to the recent inclusion of a merit-based portable fellowship program in the Higher Education Act, is a growing expression of corporate interest in the general strengthening of graduate programs. Understandably enough, companies often identify most closely with the need for effective graduate education within the particular areas of science and engineering most pertinent to their activities. Many corporations have a long history of supporting graduate fellowships and assistantships in areas of particular relevance to them, as well as providing research support for faculty that in turn supports graduate programs in various direct and indirect ways. Such arrangements have worked well in the past and certainly should continue. At the same time, some corporations now seem more inclined than before to consider broader forms of support, less tied to particular projects, and of sufficient magnitude and duration to allow well-planned improvements in programs.

More help of this kind would be most welcome, and it is my hope that mutually beneficial relationships between universities and corporations will continue to develop. It is no exaggeration to say that the future scientific leadership within companies, as well as within universities and other institutions, is at stake.

It is hard to predict to what extent foundations generally will elect the qualitative support of graduate education as a priority. The important leadership role played by the Andrew W. Mellon Foundation has already been noted. The Whiting Foundation, working with a group of seven universities, continues to provide distinguished fellowships for exceptional humanities students. And the Charlotte W. Newcombe Foundation has just announced the first major new program of foundation-supported fellowships in the humanities in more than a decade: forty-five Newcombe Fellowships are to be awarded annually for doctoral dissertation research and writing.

Those of us convinced of the long-term importance of sustaining quality in graduate programs need to work harder, however, to explain the seriousness of the immediate situation to other foundations. Especially at a time when what is required is not massive support but programs tailored to promote quality, based on a willingness to be selective, the potential contribution of foundations is very great indeed.

Private donors can also be extremely helpful, as they have been historically. Until World War II, the support of graduate education was sustained almost entirely by individual donors and a relatively small number of corporate sponsors. The first three graduate fellowships at Princeton open to students from other colleges, announced by President McCosh in 1877, were supported by funds donated, respectively, by individuals, a class, and a private club.

For individuals or organizations to support graduate work, especially in fields that seem either so established as to be unexciting or so lacking in immediate practicality as to appear unrelated to the needs of the day, requires, as Dean Ziolkowski has put it, ''imagination and faith.''

What is necessary is a belief that intellectual pursuits are important, and that the search for knowledge is itself a worthy end.

* * * * *

On what, finally, does the case for graduate education in the arts and sciences depend? On important practical considerations, to be sure, ranging from preparing future teachers, to providing the technical competence necessary to increase the nation's productivity, to learning enough about other cultures and languages to avoid serious errors of foreign policy. But it is not only, or even primarily, on such grounds that I believe the ultimate argument rests.

The chairman of our Biology Department, Professor Edward Cox, has written:

> The [importance of graduate education] springs directly from my belief that gaining new knowledge about the universe and man's place in it is a central human activity that cannot be suppressed for very long. Why this is so is not altogether clear, but it probably has its roots in our evolution as a species. . . . Our curiosity is so deeply imbedded in our biological make-up that rather than deny it we have to cultivate it.

And, from a somewhat different but complementary perspective, Lewis Thomas '33, chancellor of the Memorial Sloan-Kettering Cancer Center in New York, has observed:

> As long as we are bewildered by the mystery of ourselves, and confused by the strangeness of our uncomfortable connection to all the rest of life, and dumb-founded by the inscrutability of our own minds, we cannot be said to be healthy animals in today's world.
>
> We need to know more . . . not for [the sake of] technology, not for leisure, not even for health or longevity, but for the hope of wisdom which our kind of culture must acquire for its survival.

It is this conception of the role of learning, and of graduate education, that speaks to many of us at deeper levels. For me, at least, it is compelling.

Scholarship and Research

REPORT OF THE PRESIDENT

APRIL 1979

In the *Princeton Companion* published last fall, the legacy to the University from Woodrow Wilson is described as "a vision of an institution dedicated both to things of the mind and the nation's service."

That continues to be our vision, and we fulfill it in essential ways through our commitment to scholarship and research of the highest quality. In the context of Princeton, this commitment is widely understood as an indispensable element in an overall educational philosophy that stresses the continuing interaction between the search for new knowledge and teaching at both undergraduate and graduate levels.

Princeton has recognized the importance of scholarship and research, and the vitality that they can impart to the intellectual life of the campus, over much of its history. Scholarly work in the humanities dates back to the earliest days of the College of New Jersey, and experimental science goes back at least as far as Joseph Henry, who in 1841 sent the first telegraph signal on record across the Princeton campus to notify his household that he was ready for lunch. As early as 1881, Professor Allan Marquand had constructed a "logical machine," a forerunner of the computer.

In devoting this year's annual report to scholarship and research, I want first to discuss their importance, both in the society and on this campus. I want then to discuss some recent trends that raise the most serious questions about the future of scholarship and research—in universities generally and at Princeton.

THE IMPORTANCE OF SCHOLARSHIP AND RESEARCH

Scholarship and research contribute importantly to the society. On one level, they yield insights and discoveries that increase productivity, that enhance the competitive position of American industry, and that can serve to improve standards of living all over the world. While precise calculations of economic effects are not possible, careful studies suggest that advances in knowledge have accounted for roughly one quarter to one third of the increases in national income in the United States since 1929. It was recognition of these effects, along with great concern for inflation and for the implications of lagging productivity, that led President Carter to make such a strong plea for research in his most recent budget message. Stating the need for "investing in the nation's future," he called for an increase of 9 percent in federal support for basic research even at a time of severe budgetary constraint and reduced budgetary provision for many politically popular programs.

Apart from the economic benefits they confer, advances in knowledge are directly and critically important to national security. This is self-evident in the case of science and technology, but the same proposition also holds for other branches of knowledge, including importantly our understanding of other peoples and societies. If "national security" is read properly as shorthand for the much larger issues of war and peace, and relationships among nations, then it is no less evident that a deep understanding of languages and cultures can minimize the risk of confrontations of force that take such a terrible human toll. Even more generally, the pursuit of peace and the achievement of more just relationships among people may be aided most fundamentally by studies in the humanities and the arts that enable us to see ourselves and our place in life more humbly and with greater understanding of the human condition.

Science, too, needs to be seen in terms of the broad possibilities that it presents. Dr. Frank Press, Science Advisor to the President, made an eloquent speech to the American Association for the Advancement of Science just a year ago in which he put the matter this way:

> Everywhere one looks today, it is apparent that the success of science is essential to human survival. Human numbers, human institutions, and human expectations demand the extension and application of human knowledge. Not to meet that demand does not mean limiting growth or moving toward any kind of stability. In the dynamic world we have created, it means fomenting human misery, economic collapse, social upheaval and, at worst, war. The choice before us then is not one of growth or no growth—as was popular to debate a few years ago—but between various approaches to controlling and directing growth in the most constructive and humane manner. It is toward this end that science and government and industry and the public must all work together, building not only the technological systems but the institutional ones that will make our complex society serve the best interests of all.

There is also a powerful connection between scholarship and research and the very concept of freedom. I do not believe I exaggerate when I say that all the freedoms of our society depend importantly on the critical exercise of scholarship and research, unfettered by any ideological or political harness and uncompromising in the pursuit of truth.

Finally, scholarship and research matter greatly for reasons that are intangible and hard to capture in words. These reasons have to do with our zest for learning—about ourselves, the world in which we live, the historical record of our failures and partial achievements, the institutions and societies in which we band together, the ways we express ourselves artistically, and the hopes, the fears, and the spiritual concerns that drive us. Any literate society, interested in human values, needs its poets and philosophers, its art historians and its scholars of religion, no less than its physicists, mathematicians, and engineers. All are necessary for our health and vitality—and perhaps even more for our individual and collective sanity.

Fortunately, there is today in the United States an enviable capacity for outstanding scholarly accomplishment in many disciplines. Much of this collective capacity, especially in scientific fields, has been developed relatively recently. Scientists from the United States have received 94 of the 185 Nobel prizes awarded in their fields since 1945; before the awards were suspended at the outbreak of the second world war, American scientists had received only 20 of the 102 prizes awarded up to that time. According to figures compiled by the National Science Foundation, it is also true that, of 492 major technological innovations in the period 1953–1973, 65 percent resulted from work in the United States. (Great Britain was second with 17 percent; Japan was third.)

Francis Bacon counseled three and one half centuries ago that we must "from experience of every kind first endeavor to discover true causes and axioms; and seek for experiments of Light, not for experiments of Fruit. For axioms, rightly discovered and established, supply practice with its instruments not one by one, but in clusters, and draw after them trains and troops of works."

While the task of finding applications of new knowledge is obviously of enormous importance, it is worth stressing that the applications and the technologies of any given age depend critically on the intellectual capital painstakingly developed in earlier times—generally by people interested in understanding the fundamental "axioms" of their fields without the deliberate intention of solving a practical problem or achieving a specific utilitarian end. Moreover, the path to application of the discoveries of scholarship and research is not always predictable and rarely obvious. Frequently it is irregular and filled with detours and surprises, with each set of findings building on an earlier set and with the practical benefits flowing from a particular field of research often manifesting themselves only years after the initial discoveries were made.

An excellent illustration of the relationship between basic research over time and some of the extraordinary medical breakthroughs of this century is provided by a distinguished alumnus of ours, Lewis Thomas '33, president of the Sloan-Kettering Memorial Hospital:

> Starting in the last decade of the nineteenth century, the basic science needed for a future science of medicine got under way. The role of bacteria and viruses in illness was discerned, and research on the details of this connection began in earnest. The major pathogenic organisms, most notably the tubercle bacillus and the syphilis spirochete, were recognized for what they were and did. By the late 1930s this research had already paid off; the techniques of active and passive immunization had been worked out for diphtheria, tetanus, lobar pneumonia, and a few other bacterial infections; the taxonomy of infectious disease had become an orderly discipline; and the time was ready for sulfanilamide, penicillin, streptomycin, and all the rest. But it needs emphasizing that *it took about fifty years of concentrated effort in basic research to reach this level*; if this research had not been done we could not have guessed that streptococci and pneumococci exist, and the search for antibiotics would have made no sense at all. Without the long, painstaking research on the tubercle bacillus, we would still be thinking that tuberculosis was due to night air, and we would still be trying to cure it by sunlight. . . . We need reminding, now more than ever, that the capacity of medicine to deal with infectious disease was not a lucky fluke, nor was it something that happened simply as the result of the passage of time. It was the direct outcome of many years of hard work, done by imaginative and skilled scientists, none of whom had the faintest idea that penicillin and streptomycin lay somewhere in the decades ahead. It was basic science of a very high order, storing up a great mass of interesting knowledge for its own sake, creating, so to speak, a bank of information, ready for drawing on when the time for intelligent use arrived. . . . The great need now, for the medicine of the future, is for more information at the most fundamental levels of the living

process. We are nowhere near ready for large-scale programs of applied science in medicine, for we do not yet know enough.*

Princeton, of course, has no medical school, but our biologists and biochemists have worked—and continue to work—at "the most fundamental levels of the living process." Applied work in agriculture (which the land grant colleges and universities have done so well for more than a hundred years) is another field in which Princeton has not been active. But in this field, too, members of our faculty have contributed in essential and seminal ways, not least George Shull, who came to Princeton in 1915 as Professor of Genetics and Botany to pursue a life-long fascination with the evening primrose and to refine his earlier work that led to the development of hybrid corn. Even today, with more nations than ever importing food, with fewer exporting it, with population growth in developing countries exceeding food supplies, and with our country supplying half the grain traded worldwide, Princeton faculty members continue to explore questions that increasingly are recognized as fundamental to the adequate production of food—questions in such areas as genetics, cell growth and development, photosynthesis, weather variability and climatic fluctuation, and population.

Without a clear understanding of what purposes projects are seeking to serve, and why, it is frequently easy to ridicule particular research efforts. Perhaps the most prominent example of such ridicule is Senator William Proxmire's "Golden Fleece Awards," one of which was presented last fall in the field of agriculture. It went to researchers at the University of Georgia for a project concerned with the effects of exercise on pregnant sows. In a good humored letter of "acceptance," the University noted that the research was similar to work being done around the world and that it was designed to "find ways to reduce farrowing problems in sows kept in confinement housing. There is reason

---

* "Biomedical Science and Human Health: The Long-Range Prospect," *Daedalus*, Spring 1977, pp. 164–69. I was reminded earlier this year that just as "basic" research can yield practical applications, so "applied" research can yield fundamental insights and new knowledge. In remarks to the members of the Association of American Universities, Dr. Roland W. Schmitt, vice president, corporate research and development, of the General Electric Company said: "A great deal of work undertaken with the intended outcome of improvements in existing products and processes is done by methods indistinguishable from those used in the most 'pure' research, and such work can often yield fundamental scientific discoveries. After all, Irving Langmuir's Nobel Prize winning work on surface chemistry began as an effort to improve light bulbs; Louis Pasteur's work on microbiology began as a consulting project for the French beer industry; Arno Penzias and Robert Wilson were able to detect the remnants of microwave radiation from the origin of the universe using a radio antenna designed for use in developing satellite communications."

to believe that exercising sows will improve reproductive performance. These experiments could result in lowering the costs of producing pork, and consumers will be the greatest beneficiaries.'' Moreover, the University noted, the total federal investment in the project was less than $1,000. It is also noteworthy that the modern field of genetics received more than a small push forward as a result of a study by Gregor Mendel that could well have been titled ''How to Segregate Round from Wrinkled Peas''—a surefire candidate for a ''Golden Fleece Award'' in its time!

A field more commonly identified with Princeton than either medicine or agriculture—and certainly one of high national, indeed international, priority—is energy. Next fall we shall be dedicating the new Energy Laboratory of the School of Engineering and Applied Science. Faculty members in engineering, along with faculty in many other fields (ranging from architecture and urban planning to economics, politics, physics, sociology, statistics, geology, and psychology), are involved in efforts to explore the production and use of energy from sources such as geothermal reservoirs, fission reactors, nuclear fusion, and solar devices, as well as more conventional sources such as gas, oil, and coal. In addition, there is interest in methods of conservation and in environmental considerations.

In many of these areas, the University's current work is based on a long history of basic research. Certainly this is true of our largest and most dramatic undertaking—the effort at our Plasma Physics Laboratory to harness the energy produced when isotopes of hydrogen are fused to form helium (the source of energy for the sun). Controlled thermonuclear research at Princeton began in 1951 under the code name Project Matterhorn. At that time, Professor Lyman Spitzer convinced the Atomic Energy Commission to invest in the possibility that his studies of interstellar gas might yield clues that could lead to a safe and environmentally acceptable method of producing energy from an inexpensive and essentially inexhaustible fuel available from sea water. The Plasma Physics Laboratory continues to develop the implications of that insight, said to have come to Professor Spitzer almost thirty years ago as he was skiing on a sunny day—working in a mode designed to confound those determined to apportion precisely all the costs of research! . . .

In the social sciences and humanities, too, Princeton has a history of exceptional work in many fields, some done entirely by individual scholars working alone and some organized through such entities as the

Center of International Studies, the International Finance Section, the Industrial Relations Section, the Shelby Cullom Davis Center for Historical Studies, and the Office of Population Research. The Office of Population Research, founded in 1936 as the first major effort in its field by an American university, is a particularly interesting example of what can be accomplished with good leadership, able faculty members, and strong financial support. Beyond expanding our understanding of the most basic principles of demography in fundamental ways, the office has helped to shape public policy both in this country and abroad through its studies of population trends in developing countries, its theoretical work in the structure of populations, and its fertility studies, which continue to provide information on which to base the estimates necessary to make responsible policy judgments. It also publishes the widely regarded *Population Index*.

In the study of languages, literature, history, and culture, Princeton has made exceptional contributions over many years through work in East Asian, Near Eastern, and other area studies, as have a number of other major research universities. But the level of support for such work has never been commensurate with the needs, and the capacities of universities to contribute in this field have been woefully underutilized, especially recently, as both public and private support have diminished. . . .

Discussions of large projects and work organized through research entities of one kind or another run the considerable risk of leading us to overlook the fundamental contributions of the individual scholar—whether it be a William Thurston in mathematics, who recently solved the Smith conjecture, a thirty-year-old problem involving transformations of three-dimensional manifolds, or a Lewis Lockwood in music, whose historical research has resulted in new discoveries about the nature of Beethoven's work as a composer and the development of music in Italy at the time of the Renaissance. The bibliography of faculty publications published regularly through the office of the dean of the faculty is an impressive reminder of the range of scholarly activity, and there is no way even to begin to indicate the dimensions of that terrain in this report.

Perhaps it is in order, however, to mention at least one scholarly publication in the humanities that won a major prize recently: Victor Brombert, Henry Putnam University Professor of Romance Languages and Comparative Literature, was awarded the first Harry Levin Prize in Comparative Literature for *The Romantic Prison*, a work that was cited for its "distinguished scholarship, impressive historical breadth, and acute critical sensitivity, enlivened by an awareness of the urgency of the theme for our time as well as for the nineteenth century.'' Different as it is from work in plasma physics, the study of imprisonment as a symbol of the human condition reflects a deeply rooted need to understand individuals and institutions as well as the ordering of particles and the properties of matter when heated to temperatures higher than that of the sun. There is even the chance that on occasion such understanding will lead to changes in behavior that improve the functioning—and extend the civility—of our society.

The Special Environment of Universities

Scholarship and research are, of course, conducted in many places other than universities, and much significant work is done in industrial and government laboratories, as well as in less formidable locations where individuals may seek solace to think and to write. But universities do offer important advantages, and evidence suggests that the university environment has proved to be exceptionally conducive to major advances in knowledge.

To cite just one set of findings: when the National Science Foundation recently compiled a list of eighty-five significant advances over the past twenty years in four fields (mathematics, chemistry, astronomy, and earth sciences), university scientists were found to have been responsible for more than 70 percent of them. (A tabulation of where the university scientists received their highest degrees showed that Princeton ranked fifth, and was one of only four universities—with Harvard, the University of California at Berkeley, and Columbia—to have educated at least one person in each of the four fields. A tabulation of where the work was done showed that Princeton ranked second, behind only the California Institute of Technology.)

There are, I believe, several characteristics of universities which account in large degree for this record of accomplishment. First, universities are committed to the twin concepts of academic freedom and the pursuit of the most fundamental questions, however unsettling or controversial they may be. Much of the most exciting work done on our campus, as at other major universities, tends to be in highly abstract and theoretical areas, with knowledge pursued for its own sake, not for its immediate utility. As Dennis Thompson, the chairman of our Department of Politics, wrote in a memorandum to me last year:

> To qualify as a scholar in the eyes of one's colleagues, one must not simply master certain skills and a body of accepted knowledge, but one must make an original contribution to knowledge. Since it is

not always possible to predict what form such contributions might take, our profession must permit considerable independence and diversity. The great virtue of the modern university is that it has provided an environment where original research can be conducted without the pressures of an immediate judgment about its significance. Sometimes such freedom has been abused and sometimes it has not been productive, but on the whole scholarship has probably flourished more in the modern university than in any other institution in history.

It is also true that both the processes of the university (which are decentralized and heavily dependent on the judgment of peers) and the qualities that tend to motivate faculty members in their scholarship and research (including intellectual curiosity and independence) encourage a considerable degree of objectivity. This is not to say that individuals in universities are any more inherently "objective" than other individuals. In my experience they are not. Commitments to predetermined points of view—and sometimes especially to one's earlier publications!—can take a toll on the thinking of faculty members as on the thinking of all mortals. Universities are rather special, however, in that they are communities of individuals who are charged with a particular responsibility to think for themselves, to challenge each other as well as orthodoxies old and new, and to feel no obligation to follow anyone else's sense of the right way to attack a particular problem.

This generalized—perhaps idealized—concept of the university has to be qualified to take account of the need for orderly conduct of large projects (where each individual cannot proceed entirely independently of colleagues) and of the inevitable pressures, however subtle, present in any institutional setting. Still, the university retains a uniqueness in both its determination to avoid taking institutional positions, thus encouraging independence, and in its ambience, which fosters an irreverent spirit that celebrates the achievements of individuals who correct the errors of professional colleagues and which is meant to stimulate creativity.

Another characteristic of universities is that they encompass work in a great variety of disciplines. Thus it is possible—though no one should claim that it happens always or necessarily—for faculty members in various fields to "kibitz" on the work of colleagues in other fields, thereby providing fresh perspectives and some hope of avoiding overly narrow approaches to fundamental problems. Interdisciplinary or multidisciplinary work is never easy to encourage, and always runs the risk of operating at the lowest common denominator for all participants; but it can also be extremely important in fields ranging from the life sciences to literature. The relatively small size and cohesiveness of Princeton offer special opportunities in this regard, and the cross-departmental programs we have established in such areas as energy and environmental studies, transportation and urban studies, East Asian and Near Eastern studies, and economic development and modernization represent efforts to take advantage of this characteristic.

Finally, universities are "special" because of the interrelationship between research and teaching which is as important as it is evident. The involvement of graduate students in advanced research—and frequently at Princeton of undergraduates as well—not only provides exceptional opportunities to prepare the next generation of scholars, but benefits the scholarship and research of this generation by subjecting it to new sources of criticism. Almost every faculty member on this campus, I suspect, can cite examples where students have asked a question or made a suggestion that opened a promising new line of inquiry, clarified a puzzle, or called into question a convention that ultimately proved to be deficient.

What this means, in part, is that the investment in university research produces a double benefit: not only is the research accomplished in an unusually conducive environment, but those who will be the research leaders of the next generation are prepared and encouraged at the same time. Moreover, many students, especially at the graduate level, make direct contributions of a highly substantive character. To cite just one example, two years ago a graduate student in aerospace and mechanical sciences, E. Michael Campbell, demonstrated plasmadynamic, steady-recombination lasing for the first time, thereby achieving a breakthrough that promises to have wide application in industry, communications, and space exploration.

The Relationship to Teaching

The relationship between scholarship and research, on the one hand, and teaching, on the other, is one in which benefits flow strongly in both directions: just as the presence of students contributes importantly to the advancement of knowledge, so scholarship and research contribute importantly to the education of students. Moreover, this proposition holds, in my judgment, not only for those students who may themselves go on to careers in scholarship and research, but for students generally, whatever professions they pursue. This is why scholarship and research matter so greatly to the educational purposes of a university such as Princeton, as well as in their own right.

Chairmen of departments and directors of academic programs are acutely aware of these interactions. In a long and thoughtful commentary last year on the role of scholarship and research in a university community, Professor Theodore J. Ziolkowski, chairman of our Department of Germanic Languages and Literatures and newly appointed dean of the graduate school, wrote:

> Above all . . . it is the dedication to scholarship and research—the commitment to the *process* of knowledge rather than merely to its product—that contributes the intellectual tension and excitement to life in a university. It is scholarship that makes of Princeton a major world university and not simply—as fine as it may be—an undergraduate college that transmits knowledge. It is ultimately the principle of scholarship and research that unites an otherwise disparate faculty. For astrophysics, economics, and literary history as fields of knowledge are worlds apart. But the process of discovery in those fields, their intellectual rigor, and the moral discipline that they demand is remarkably similar. It is the similarities among the disciplines, produced by scholarship, that justify the Romantic ideal vision of the university as a unified universe.

Professor Charles C. Gillispie of our Department of History, who also serves as director of the Program in History and Philosophy of Science, described the importance of scholarship in another way:

> There are few scholars who do things that really are going to make a discrete and measurable difference in some aspect of the world, in its practical affairs or in the knowledge available to persons capable of assimilating it. But even for those of us who do not produce that kind of applicable scholarship, or those deep and profound contributions to a discipline that change it somehow, scholarship and research are still important. They are important, as is often said, for keeping members of the faculty alive in their own thinking. That is obvious. But it is not just a question of keeping them alive. It is a question of keeping them honest, or at least as honest as we can be kept. Our scholarship can be evaluated in a way that our teaching cannot. . . . In short, I think an important aspect of insisting on

scholarship and research is that only so can one be confident of the validity and integrity of the teaching process.

Still a third perspective was offered by Gregory Vlastos, a distinguished emeritus member of our Department of Philosophy, in his 1975 Baccalaureate address. He noted that the four processes necessary to advance and disseminate knowledge are: (1) the discovery of new ideas and new forms; (2) the critical scrutiny of these innovations; (3) the assimilation of these very new results with the vast inheritance of previously discovered knowledge; and (4) the transmission of appropriate portions of this aggregate to succeeding generations of incoming students. "The excellences at the two extremes—of research and teaching," he said, "have essential bonds with what comes in between—with criticism and erudition: without excellence in each of these the creator's work would be wild and the teacher's shallow."

Scholarship and research invigorate and discipline teaching of all kinds, often in the most subtle ways. But at Princeton there is a particularly acute dependence on the continuing engagement of faculty with new work in their fields of study. The emphasis we place on independent work at the undergraduate level, and especially on the senior thesis, as well as the inherently "independent" nature of advanced graduate work, leaves us no real option but to insist on close interaction between teaching and research. All of our faculty members are expected to be able to supervise junior independent work and senior theses, as well as graduate dissertations, and surely it is engagement with one's own scholarly work that provides the best assurance of a capacity to assist students in coming to terms with the demands of their scholarship and research.

Examples of the mutual dependence between teaching and research are mentioned frequently in science and engineering, but they can be found as readily in the social sciences and humanities. John Wilson, chairman of our Department of Religion, provides interesting testimony:

> I think the best of our undergraduates and the more promising of our graduate students are scholars and researchers in their own right. . . . In the humanities, as well as the sciences, undergraduates are drawn up into doing first-rate research on a relatively regular basis. An example or two of this from the Religion Department, of all places, might interest you. A graduating senior last year wrote a junior paper on an aspect of DNA research under Paul Ramsey. The

piece was published by the *New York State Journal of Medicine*, and we have been rather amused and pleased at the number of requests for offprints which have arrived at the departmental office on the assumption that our senior student was a medical doctor and a member of the faculty. Our ranking senior will have her thesis, "Ibn 'Arabi's Lights with Extracts from a Commentary of Jili," published in a monograph series. A third example is a senior thesis I directed for the History Department this year which turned out to be a superior analysis of the reorganization of Princeton Theological Seminary half a century ago in the broader cultural setting of fundamental struggles within American culture. I think without doubt it is better than anything else that has been written on an important cultural event.

At various levels and in all fields, the scholarship and research of our universities constitute an invaluable national resource, contributing to the advancement and enrichment of society, and to some sharper illumination of the forces that shape our lives.

CONCERNS FOR THE FUTURE

The successful pursuit of scholarship and research within the University depends on many things: first and most fundamentally, the quality of the people involved—faculty, research and technical staff, students, and support personnel; second, facilities and equipment, including laboratories and libraries; third, the funds necessary to free time for scholarship and research, to hire research personnel, and to cover all of the other direct and indirect costs; and fourth, an ambience that stimulates and encourages each individual to make the most of the intellectual and physical resources that are available.

We are very conscious of the need to pay careful attention to all of these factors, and especially to the recruitment, retention, and motivation of those rare individuals who are genuinely creative as well as committed to the hard work that is indispensable to first-rate scholarship and research. In the absence of such people the finest facilities and unlimited budgets will not lead to significant accomplishments. Unfortunately, however, it is almost always true that terribly tangible forms of support are also a necessary condition—though never sufficient—for work of the highest quality. It is the discouraging trend in financial support, especially from external sources, that poses the greatest danger to scholarship and research right now.

The Level of External Support

Between 1968 and 1978, the overall dollar volume of external support for sponsored research at Princeton, from private and public resources, increased dramatically: from $30 million to $90 million. Moreover, approximately $40 million of this increase in annual expenditures has occurred over the last two years.

Aggregate comparisons of this kind, however, are not only superficial; they are grossly misleading. The main reason is that these totals are dominated by the expenditures of the Plasma Physics Laboratory, which is largely self-contained. A far more accurate picture of what has happened generally to external support for scholarship and research at Princeton emerges when we subtract expenditures at the Plasma Physics Laboratory (and, in earlier years, at the Princeton-Pennsylvania Accelerator). As can be seen from Figure 1, annual support for sponsored research in all parts of the University *except* the Plasma Physics Laboratory and the Accelerator increased by only about $4.5 million over this entire eleven-year period: from $16.2 million to $20.7 million.

"Only" seems the correct modifier, especially when we take account of the severe inflationary pressures that have cut so seriously into the purchasing power of the dollar. A much more realistic picture of the trend in the value of external support is seen in Figure 2, where the figures in actual dollars have been corrected for changes in the price level.* Thus, for the University generally, the *real* value of external support for scholarship and research has declined by more than 30 percent during this eleven-year period. A fundamental problem, then, is that increases in external support have not even come close to keeping pace with increases in the cost of doing research.

During the whole of this period the federal government has of course provided the bulk of the external support for research at Princeton as at every other major university, and it is the erosion in the real value of this support that has been so pronounced. In the face of an 85 percent increase in the cost of living between 1968 and 1978 (measured by the GNP implicit price deflator), federal government support for research at Princeton, excluding again the Plasma Physics Laboratory, increased

* The figures in actual (current) dollars have been converted into constant dollars (with 1968 as base year) by using the GNP implicit price deflator. A more sophisticated price index, based explicitly on the cost of doing research, might well show an appreciably greater erosion in the real value of support.

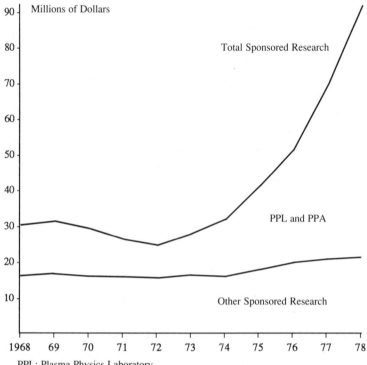

Figure 1
Sponsored Research at Princeton, 1968-1978,
in Current Dollars

PPL: Plasma Physics Laboratory
PPA: Princeton-Pennsylvania Accelerator

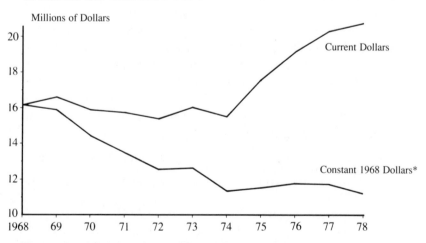

Figure 2
Sponsored Research at Princeton, excluding PPL and PPA, 1968-1978,
in Current and Constant Dollars

*Converted to 1968 dollars using the GNP Implicit Price Deflator

just 22 percent. Although support at Princeton from foundations, industry, and other non-governmental sources increased 97 percent over this same period, and has been critically important to work in a number of fields, it still amounted to only about 11 percent of all of our sponsored research in 1978 ($2.3 million out of a total of $20.7 million for all departments and programs exclusive of the Plasma Physics Laboratory).

It should be stressed that the problem for us has *not* been an inability on the part of Princeton faculty to secure approval of proposals submitted for review by panels of their peers. On the contrary, for the past four years (the only time period for which these data have been compiled systematically), the "success rate" of Princeton proposals has held steady at 70 percent—one of the highest in the country. Moreover, this has been true despite increasing competition for available funds, making these results all the more noteworthy.

The increased competition is due to a number of factors, including: (1) widespread financial pressures within higher education; (2) a wider distribution of talented faculty members among colleges and universities owing to the very limited number of new positions at many of the most prestigious institutions; and (3) the presence of large numbers of talented, grant-seeking individuals in non-academic institutions as a result of these same job market considerations. In addition, there have been continuing political pressures to spread available funds more broadly among geographic areas, institutions, and individuals.

While our faculty members have continued to fare exceptionally well in securing general approval of their proposals, this greater degree of competition, combined with severe limitations on the total funds available (see below), has had a serious impact on their research by reducing significantly the dollars awarded in relation to dollars sought in funded proposals—from 64 percent in 1975 to 48 percent in 1978. This decline in the dollar value of successful proposals threatens the quality of our research efforts in a number of ways, some of which I shall mention below. First, however, I think it may be helpful to try to examine these local facts in the context of the general trend in federal support for research.

The total amount of federal support for basic research rose steadily from the end of World War II until the late 1960s, largely as a consequence of an appreciation within the government (and especially within the Department of Defense) of the great value to the country of our stock of basic knowledge. This "knowledge base" was widely seen as an extraordinarily valuable national asset which needed to be preserved and enhanced. Since the late 1960s, however, federal support for basic research has not increased nearly fast enough to keep pace with inflation. As can be seen from Figure 3, there has been an overall decline, measured in constant 1968 dollars, of roughly 5 percent between 1968 and 1978. Even though the President's budget last year called for an investment in basic research greater than the rate of inflation, a series of Congressional appropriations decisions had the effect of undercutting that initiative. This year the President again has proposed a real increase in federal support for basic research, with a budget that calls for a 9 percent rise in such support and assumes a 7 percent rate of inflation.

Another perspective is gained when we examine the federal expenditures for all forms of research and development, as well as for basic research, in relation to the Gross National Product. (See Figure 4.) In 1968, .27 percent of the GNP was spent on basic research; in 1978, .20 percent. While these figures must be interpreted with great care, especially since defense spending accounts for nearly half of total R & D, they are worrying—particularly in light of recent studies by the NSF which show that a number of other countries, including such major trading partners of ours as West Germany and Japan, have increased their emphasis on research substantially.*

The role of government in supporting basic research, in particular, is rooted in the character of the activity: basic research confers benefits in the form of new ideas which no private entity can keep entirely to itself, but which naturally and inevitably "spill over" to the entire society. Accordingly, economists, businessmen, members of Congress, and others—whatever their political persuasions, whatever their differences on other questions concerning the proper role for government, and whatever their views concerning the right magnitude and form of support—have agreed overwhelmingly with the principle that government has a clear responsibility to foster advances in knowledge that are the common property of all. . . .

External support from the private sector must also be encouraged. While it has been relatively modest in amount, compared with govern-

---

* The most recent available statistics show that between 1962 and 1975 the fraction of GNP spent on R & D in West Germany increased by 80 percent, while in Japan the comparable fraction grew by 31 percent. In the U.S., however, there was a 15 percent decline in the share of GNP spent on R & D during that same period. (*Science Indicators 1976*, Report of the National Science Board 1977, p. 184.)

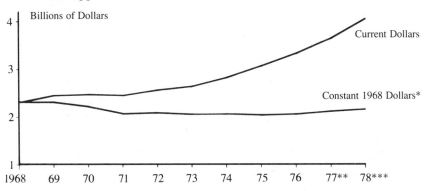

Figure 3
Federal Support for Basic Research, 1968-1978

Source: *Science Indicators 1976,* Report of the National Science Board, 1977, U.S. Government Printing Office, Washington, D.C., p. 211, and Robert R. Wright, Division of Science Resources Studies at NSF.

*Converted to 1968 dollars using   **Preliminary
the GNP Implicit Price Deflator   ***Estimated

Figure 4
Federal Expenditures on Basic Research
and Total R&D as a Percentage of GNP

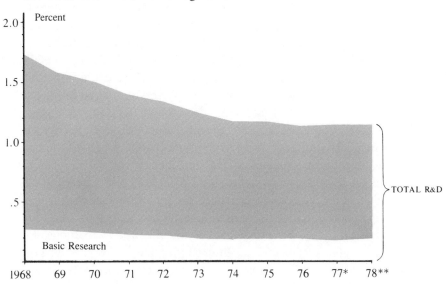

Source: *Science Indicators 1976, op. cit.,* pp. 207, 211, and 185, and Robert R. Wright, NSF.
*Preliminary   **Estimated

mental funding, it has been more flexible and for that reason has had disproportionately powerful effects. . . . In the specific case of scholarship and research, private sources may often be willing to support work, especially in the humanities and social sciences, that seems too controversial, too value-laden, or too lacking in immediate "relevance" for a governmental sponsor. In addition, private sources of support are freer of general political pressures and thus more capable of directing limited funds to particular purposes, institutions, and individuals thought to be especially meritorious. Finally, the broad field of · research offers fruitful opportunities for mutually beneficial forms of collaboration in circumstances where the interests of business and education overlap.

Internal University Support

It is not, of course, only external funding that supports scholarship and research at Princeton. Because of both their intrinsic importance and their complementarity with the kind of teaching (especially the emphasis on independent work) that is so distinguishing a characteristic of Princeton, we devote considerable University resources to these purposes.

There are both explicitly defined research funds (such as the Higgins Fund and the budget of the University Committee on Research in the Humanities and Social Sciences) and a wide variety of other more or less visible ways in which research is supported at both departmental and University levels. Endowed funds support particular research centers. A combination of endowed funds and general funds supports the library, which is the major tool of scholarship and research in the humanities and social sciences as well as being very important in science and engineering. Even in individual departments with heavy engagement in sponsored research, facilities and supporting services critical to research activities cost appreciably more than is provided through the reimbursements for indirect costs included in sponsored research agreements. In other departments, the University bears essentially all costs of this kind. Still more generally, we are of course cognizant of our obligation to facilitate the search for new knowledge, as well as to teach students, when we allocate resources for faculty positions. Finally, the University's leave of absence program is designed to give faculty members opportunities to refresh themselves intellectually and to devote concentrated periods of time to research and writing.

In preparing this report, no effort has been made to calculate the sum total of expenditures from endowed funds and general funds that could be attributed to scholarship and research, in large part because such an exercise would almost certainly imply a greater ability to apportion, say, the costs of the library than is in fact possible without being highly arbitrary. Indeed, it should be noted that the greater our success in achieving the goals of integrating teaching and research, the more difficult it becomes to separate out these costs. As a matter of educational philosophy, we try to make it as hard as possible for the cost accountant to disarticulate teaching and research! Nonetheless, even rough inspection of University budgets over the past ten years or so supports the intuitive feeling of many faculty members: the University, like the government, has failed to increase its own support of scholarship and research commensurately with rising costs.

Our overall financial afflictions (declines in the real value of endowment income and growing pressures on general funds) have prevented us from offsetting the fall in the real value of external funding and have in fact aggravated the basic problem of inadequate support. This has been especially true the past few years when inflationary pressure on costs have been particularly strong, teaching obligations have increased appreciably in some departments, and departmental budgets for supporting services have had to be cut back.

The problems of the faculty member doing sponsored research have been exacerbated by significant increases in the portion of a typical grant claimed by personnel benefits and indirect costs. The indirect cost rate has been forced up from roughly 52 percent of direct costs in 1975 to 64 percent in 1979 due to a combination of circumstances: we have experienced both above-average rates of increase in such items of indirect cost as energy and a decline in the rate of growth of the research activities over which the more or less fixed costs of an indirect nature must be distributed.

Coming at the same time as the reductions in the real value of sponsored research grants referred to above, these higher indirect costs have necessarily meant even fewer real resources available for the conduct of research. The University Research Board has been very concerned about this, and has recommended that the University appropriate general funds equivalent to at least a small part of indirect cost recoveries to help finance direct expenditures on research. It has been possible, however, to accede to this request only in part (providing $180,000 to departments in 1977–78) because the costs of heat, light, and administration are none the less real for being indirect, and because the other strains on the University budget have allowed no more generous outcome.

Particular Concerns

Let me now try to describe some particular concerns for the future of scholarship and research that grow out of both limitations on the total resources available, externally and internally, and the forms in which support often comes.

YOUNG SCHOLARS. First on any such list is the discouraging outlook for young scholars in essentially all fields of knowledge. As is well known, a combination of factors—anticipated declines in enrollment, an age distribution of faculties concentrated in the late thirties to early fifties, as well as tight budgets and legislative pressures for later retirement—has drastically diminished opportunities for new people to be appointed and then advanced to permanent positions. This is a very serious matter, not only for the prospective faculty members concerned most directly, and not only for the long-term health of both graduate and undergraduate instruction, but also for the quality and continuity of scholarship and research.

The advancement of knowledge is a cumulative process dependent on the best minds of each generation, and enduring damage can be done if this process is subjected to sharp interruption. The President's Biomedical Research Panel has expressed just this concern in a recent report:

> From the point of view of the youngest people, those just entering scientific careers and those just behind them trying to make up their minds, the future of biomedical science looks bleak indeed. There are few job opportunities, and even fewer visible opportunities for advancement to higher positions in the years ahead. The whole system seems to have become abruptly locked up. Something will have to be done about this situation now, or we will discover sometime in the late 1980s that we have skipped a generation. It hardly needs saying that the scientific enterprise cannot undergo such a loss without serious damage to the future quality of research. It is not widely enough recognized that the youngest people, the ones still in training, are indispensable: they are not only essential for the future, they are also indispensable for the work that has to be done today.

In the humanities, the Andrew W. Mellon Foundation recently made a particularly farsighted attack on this problem by providing grants for the express purpose of creating at least a small number of additional opportunities to advance the most outstanding young scholars. This program requires universities to raise matching funds, and in the case of Princeton the Class of 1922 has provided important leadership by encouraging the University to dedicate the bequest of a classmate, A. Curtis Bogert, to this purpose.

Within the sciences and engineering the problem of the young person seeking to do research is compounded by the need for significant financial support beyond simply the establishment of a position. It is clear that the great pressures on the budgets of grant-making agencies have exacerbated the problems of those seeking to start new projects. In the past, young faculty members—and graduate students—were able to gain experience and establish a reputation by fitting their work into the larger projects of senior faculty. Now, with the funding of projects limited so severely, it is exceedingly difficult to find money for this purpose. Moreover, the universities themselves are extremely hard pressed to find extra funds to help young researchers get started—or, for that matter, to make "seed money" available to either the older investigators who wish to change the direction of their research or graduate students who are seeking funding for promising thesis projects.

Several federal agencies—most especially the Office of Science and Technology Policy and the National Science Foundation—and several members of the Congress have begun to focus attention on these problems and to explore ways to attack them. One set of possibilities is modeled after the Biomedical Research Grants of the National Institutes of Health. This program, which contributed $115,000 to Princeton in 1977–78, is designed to enable the recipient institution "to respond quickly and effectively to emerging opportunities, . . . to enhance creativity, to encourage innovation, to provide for pilot studies, and to improve both physical and human research resources." Each university is responsible for allocating the NIH funds as it sees fit, and Princeton has, over the thirteen years it has been receiving these grants, used a large portion of them as "starter grants" for the projects of young faculty members. One example of a major research accomplishment which began with this type of NIH support is the work of Professors Ulrich Laemmli and Abraham Worcel, of the Biochemistry Department. Their important advances in our understanding of the structure of chromosomes would not have been possible without the use of an extremely sophisticated—and very expensive—microscope, purchased in part by NIH funds.

Clearly, however, the efforts to date to address this set of problems are insufficient. More will have to be done if we are not to endanger the future of scholarship and research by failing to replenish our "intellectual capital," which consists so importantly of the young people who should, in time, become the intellectual leaders of their fields.

LIBRARIES, LABORATORIES, AND INSTRUMENTATION. The major tools of scholarship and research are extraordinarily expensive, as well as extraordinarily important.

Scholars in all fields are dependent on ready access to the holdings of great libraries, and sharp increases in the costs of books and periodicals, while placing great pressures on institutional budgets, have also threatened the quality of libraries. The financing of research libraries, and new proposals for controlling library costs, could be the subject for a separate report. Here it will have to suffice to underscore the seriousness of this particular set of problems and the inability of any one university to solve these problems on its own.

The costs of building new laboratories also have increased dramatically. The decision at Princeton to construct a new Biochemical Sciences Building, at a cost of approximately $6 million, demonstrates the importance that we attach to adequate laboratory facilities for teaching and research. Our general policy is not to spend money on new facilities at a time when other needs are so pressing. In this case, however, we had no choice but to make an exception to that policy. Over the longer term, a major, continuing need is for funds that can be used to renovate and modernize existing facilities. This is a national problem that affects colleges and universities of all kinds, and it is increasingly recognized as such.

The problem of paying for instrumentation is also critical. Today's research in the sciences and engineering is highly dependent on modern, complex, and extremely expensive equipment. Computers, electron microscopes, spectrometers, telescopes, and hundreds of other sophisticated instruments are essential to the day-to-day work of scientists. Not only do they speed investigations, they also determine the quality and precision of the work that can be done. They permit research that simply would not be possible otherwise. Unfortunately, the cost of this instrumentation has been affected dramatically not only by inflation, but by the increasing level of sophistication of the equipment itself. For example, a micro-analytical chemistry lab that could have been fully equipped at a cost of $10,000 in 1960 could not be outfitted today for less than $1 million. This increase in costs, combined with the general weakening of the financial base of universities and inadequate external funding for equipment, has caused a serious deterioration in the instrumentation base at most colleges and universities.

One study, made in 1977 on the basis of site visits to research universities and conversations with faculty, students, and government personnel, found clear evidence of a steadily worsening situation. Institutions were postponing the purchase of new equipment and deferring maintenance on existing facilities. Some had been able to provide no support whatsoever for equipment or instrumentation from their own general funds for the last few years, and many were laboring under the effects of reduced supporting staff, fewer technicians, and less adequate machine shops. Several noted that the typical federal matching grant, which requires a university to pay for one half the cost of needed equipment, was of no use to them since their institutions could not afford even the matching funds.* At Princeton, the accreditation team from the Engineering Council for Professional Development referred explicitly to the inadequacy of laboratory equipment when it reported on its visit in 1977.

Several government agencies have been concerned about this gradual deterioration, and significant efforts have been made to halt this trend, if not to reverse it. In the past year or two, the National Science Foundation has increased the proportion of its research funds spent for equipment from about 7 percent of total funding to almost 15 percent. Although a 15 percent level is thought to be "about right" by a number of knowledgeable people, NSF is well aware that even this higher level of funding will be insufficient to make up for the extremely low level of funding over the past ten years. One rough calculation made recently by the NSF compared the actual funding for instrumentation by all government agencies to an "ideal" level of 12–14 percent of total research spending. The results of this informal comparison showed a cumulative instrumentation deficit for the past ten years of approximately $300 million, without taking into account the equipment in teaching laboratories, where instrumentation is often obsolete and in poor repair. Although documentation of this situation is especially hard to obtain, it does seem clear that all too many recent college graduates—and new

---

* Smith, Bruce L.R. and Karlesky, Joseph J., *The State of Academic Science*, Change Magazine Press, Vol. I, pp. 164–66.

Ph.D's—are entering industry unprepared to use modern research equipment simply because they have never seen it before.

The current system of project support, effective as it is in allocating funds to particular research projects of high quality, cannot finance the costs of this new equipment. Much of it is simply too expensive to be paid for by one project and should be owned communally. However, as less money is available, these communal items suffer what Professor Robert May, the chairman of our University Research Board, has called a "tragedy of the commons." They become dispensable costs for each individual project, sacrificed by each project leader in favor of even more essential personnel costs, for instance. And universities have been unable to fill the financing void.

While wholesale funding for new equipment is clearly not practicable, some judicious replacement of distinctly inferior or outmoded equipment is essential. The effort of NSF to increase the amount of money it spends on equipment and facilities is an important step in the right direction, as is the Foundation's effort to develop regional instrumentation centers, usually located at colleges or universities. It is obvious, however, that, as equipment becomes increasingly complex and expensive, researchers will have to find new ways to share and they will have to learn to deal with the problems that are bound to accompany multiple access. It may also be possible to find ways of facilitating more joint use of expensive equipment by scientists in industry and scientists in universities. This is a problem that is going to have to be met by new organizational arrangements as well as more money.

ADMINISTRATIVE BURDENS. For many members of the research community, one of the most troubling—indeed aggravating—developments of the past decade has been the substantial increase in administrative tasks associated with the performance of sponsored research. This heavier administrative burden takes a variety of forms, and it has evolved for a number of understandable reasons. Many of these obligations represent an inevitable and justifiable consequence of accepting public funds. (Needless to say, recipients of private support also have an obligation to account for those funds, though not usually in anything approaching the same degree of detail.) Whatever the motives, the fact remains that the time and personnel required for these tasks continue to increase; and this trend has had a significant impact on both the time and the funds available to perform the research itself as well as on the general character of the relationships between government agencies and universities.

A part of this larger administrative burden is the greater effort that has to be devoted to the process of seeking grants. The time periods covered by grants have been reduced, thereby requiring frequent applications for renewal. At the same time, increased competition for fewer dollars has made the process of requesting support a more exacting and demanding task—and has served to encourage both much longer and much more specific proposals, with the objective of specificity at least occasionally in conflict with the unpredictable nature of basic research. On the other hand, it is fair to say that in some cases this development has also had a favorable effect by requiring more thoughtful exposition of research plans.

Another source of increased administrative obligations is the fact that many government agencies, in an effort to support more research projects and personnel, are now awarding a larger number of small grants. The trends at Princeton over the past decade illustrate this development. In 1966–67, Princeton received 394 research contracts and grants with an average value of $40,000. In 1977–78, 608 awards were made to project leaders at Princeton, with an average value of $34,000. Therefore, while the number of grants increased by about 50 percent, the value of the average grant declined significantly, especially in real terms. Correcting for the effects of inflation, the average grant in 1977–78 was worth one half the value of the average grant in 1966–67.

Since many of the reporting and processing requirements do not vary appreciably with the size of the grant, at least within this range of expenditure, the clear consequence has been a marked increase in the ratio of administrative work to research performed. While some of the administrative burden can be assumed centrally (as it is at Princeton through the Office of Research and Project Administration), much of the work simply must be done by the project leader and faculty and departmental colleagues.

More generally, the increased uncertainty and unpredictability in funding, and the stop-and-start nature of the granting process, can have serious consequences for the quality of the overall research effort. The following quotation, from an NIH statement on current issues in research, speaks directly to this point:

> Unpredictability in funding probably tops the list. . . . The model of the lone scientist working by himself with equipment put together

with rubber bands and paper clips is no longer valid, if it ever was. Bio-medical science today requires a range of technical support services, complex equipment, often collaboration between a number of scientists and frequently a great deal of time. All of this is expensive. Under these circumstances, uncertainties and interruptions in funding can make it extremely difficult to keep research teams together for the length of time required to complete work on any given problem, or to fully exploit existing leads, with the result that the efficiency of the enterprise is markedly reduced. Any activity which is subjected to a series of arbitrary, externally induced stops and starts is bound to suffer. Basic research, a difficult, often frustrating, long-term endeavor is particularly sensitive to such disturbances.

There has been so much public discussion recently of the last source of increased administrative burdens to be mentioned here—the burgeoning number of regulations and reporting requirements associated with federal funding in any form—that there is no need for much elaboration in this report. It would be misleading, however, to ignore the increased recordkeeping and data collection that are related to federal support (for research, for student assistance, etc.) as a result of governmental initiatives in such areas as affirmative action in hiring, protection of human subjects in research, access to personal records, making programs and facilities accessible to the handicapped, and so on. Demands for increased financial accountability also have resulted in complicated, time-consuming, and frequently duplicative administrative procedures.

It is right that these legitimate concerns be addressed and that funds be accounted for properly. And we should recognize forthrightly that some of the pressures for more complex and more intrusive procedures stem directly from oversights and abuses within higher education itself. Better self-regulation is an important part of the answer to this set of concerns. At the same time, it is very important that contract administration not be pursued as an end in itself, independent of the larger goals to be served. When bureaucratic detail and regulatory zeal begin to crowd out creative effort, the original purpose of the undertaking has been defeated. The support of research in a university environment simply cannot be equated with the purchase of all kinds of other "services" and "products."

What is required is mutual understanding: recognition by those of us in universities of the governmental need for accountability and at least a certain degree of orderliness; and recognition by those in government of the importance of meeting such needs in ways that respect the fundamental character of the university as an educational institution and that interfere as little as possible with the creative process. Required too is recognition that these goals are bound to conflict to some extent, and that in seeking responsible compromises some priority should be given to serving the ultimate purposes for which the support has been provided in the first place.

ASYMMETRIES IN THE SUPPORT OF THE SCIENCES AND THE HUMANITIES. Many of the problems with which this report is concerned relate principally to the support of scientific research, in part because it is so very costly, and in part because it is in the sciences that research support has declined significantly at the same time that costs have risen substantially. In the case of the humanities and many of the social sciences (and even some areas within the natural sciences and engineering), the situation has changed much less dramatically; moreover, the very nature of much of the scholarship in these fields is such that we do not confront the problems of maintaining large research staffs, purchasing and maintaining expensive equipment, and so on. However, as I have noted, many problems are similar (especially opportunities for young scholars, support of graduate students, and the financing of libraries), and it would be an error of the most serious kind to be any less concerned about the future of scholarship in these fields than about the future of research in science, engineering, and those elements of the social sciences that receive project support.

One encouraging sign at the federal level has been the establishment and growth of the National Endowment for the Humanities and the National Endowment for the Arts. Thanks to these initiatives, for which much credit must go to Senator Claiborne Pell '40 and to Congressmen Frank Thompson and John Brademas, the amount of federal funding that has gone into the arts and humanities has increased from $5.8 million in 1966 when the endowments were created to $244.5 million in 1978. While much of this money has been used for disseminating work in these fields to a wider public, significant assistance has been provided for important scholarly projects as well. Private foundations, corporations, and individuals also, of course, have been of great help.

Nonetheless, it is widely recognized that the levels of support in the humanities and in the sciences and engineering are very unequal. It is also true that pressures on faculty members to secure support are in general much greater, for obvious reasons, in the sciences and engineering than in the humanities. The resulting asymmetries are a continuing source of concern, and their nature has been described perceptively by Professor May in the 1977–78 report of the University Research Board:

> The URB was repeatedly drawn to express various unhappinesses about asymmetries in support for research in the humanities versus engineering and the sciences. These asymmetries cut both ways, and, if not sympathetically understood, can be simultaneously a source of dissatisfaction to the humanists (who are relatively impoverished) *and* to the engineers and scientists (whose research is intrinsically more costly, and who often feel exploited). For example, in the humanities graduate students are supported out of general funds, because essentially no other funds are available; in the sciences, graduate education can be, and as a consequence is essentially required to be, supported out of contracted research or training grants. Research in the humanities is sustained (at a modest level, with the conspicuous exception of the library) almost wholly by general funds; in engineering and the sciences it sometimes can appear that all research costs—direct and indirect—must be recovered from outside agencies. Such unfortunate asymmetries are less manifest elsewhere in the western world, where government support for graduate students is usually available on a basis of merit rather than the goal-orientation of the discipline, and where support for basic research is typically less tied to immediately practical ends. At Princeton, as at other universities in the U.S., these asymmetries derive from patterns of federal funding, and we have to operate within the constraints they impose.

On our campus, as in universities generally, there is a long history of concern for such disparities, and I believe Professor May to be right in urging sympathetic understanding all around. It would be exceedingly unfortunate if the all too real problems of inadequate support were exacerbated unnecessarily by divisive disputes within the academic community itself.

INDEPENDENCE AND THE SETTING OF DIRECTIONS. Any time that any activity depends on external support, whether from public or private sources, there is an inherent danger that academic interests will be influenced excessively by the availability of funds and the convictions of donors. At Princeton, concern for the independence and integrity of the institution dates back to the time of President Witherspoon, who was concerned in 1772 that funding from the church not be permitted to determine academic appointments. In the area of research, the availability of substantial amounts of "project" funds following World War II led to the creation at Princeton of an institutional mechanism charged with insuring that sponsored research conducted here be consistent with educational goals.

A Committee on Project Research and Investigations was established in 1946. In 1959, responsibility for the oversight of all externally funded research was assigned to the University Research Board, which today consists of six members of the faculty representing each of the four divisions of the University (humanities, social sciences, natural sciences, engineering), a chairman with the rank of dean, and three members of the administration. All proposals for outside funding of research must be approved by the URB, whose policies require that all projects be consistent with the educational purposes of the University; that their primary goal be a significant contribution to knowledge rather than product development; that they represent the real interests of the faculty member; that they conform with the University's policies governing classified research and patents; and that no funds be accepted whose purpose and the character of whose sponsorship cannot be disclosed publicly.

There is widespread agreement that the URB has been very successful in serving these purposes. But there are more general concerns about research directions and research priorities which no University mechanism can hope to address adequately. They derive from the natural tension between the sometimes highly specific objectives of funding sources and the more general purposes of the University. Professor Robert Jahn, dean of the School of Engineering and Applied Science, has defined one aspect of this problem in terms of a danger that research may be allowed to "drift" along with the currents of federal funding, rather than being based on independent judgments concerning priorities. Another concern is that severe budgetary pressure can all too easily strengthen the inclination of both writers of proposals and reviewers of proposals to prefer "safe" projects that entail relatively little risk of unpredictable outcomes.

Yet, it is often true that the "unpredictable outcomes" are the most significant. It is in this spirit that Lewis Thomas has argued: ". . . the highest yield for the future will come from whatever fields are generating the most interesting, exciting and surprising sorts of information—most of all, surprising.'' Recently, NSF has documented the importance of broadly gauged, flexible research projects through its study (referred to earlier in this report) of the origins and characteristics of the 85 most significant advances in four scientific fields over the past twenty years. It was found that only 43 percent of the projects which led to these advances had actually contained, in the funding proposal, a direct reference to the significant outcome. Forty percent of the advances were derived from grants for broadly defined research in the general area, and 17 percent were related neither directly nor generally to the justification used for requesting support.

Here again, the need is for a balanced approach. Few university representatives would argue against the propriety of public or private funding sources seeking to advance knowledge in areas they believe to be particularly important—provided, of course, that universities continue to decide for themselves whether or not to accept funds offered for particular purposes. Reasonable targeting of limited research funds by those providing the support, with the advice of leaders in the fields being funded, seems eminently sensible—and unavoidable in any event.

However, the word ''reasonable'' should be emphasized. It is critical that there be enough flexibility, and enough support which is untargeted in any narrow sense, to allow the pursuit of the kinds of ''surprises'' to which Lewis Thomas refers. There is an imperative national interest in this kind of investment which permits some significant number of exceptionally creative people to be guided primarily by their own sense of excitement about their fields and which affords the greatest possibility that we will continue to achieve those ''unpredictable outcomes'' that in the long run may be the most important of all.

*   *   *   *   *

Scholarship and research, and our concerns for their future, can be thought of in quite practical, utilitarian terms; and, in one sense, there is nothing wrong with such a conception since these activities do matter so very importantly to our well-being. But such an orientation is, in my view, dangerously incomplete.

Ultimately, our commitment to the advancement of knowledge must be seen at least as much in terms of values that are more easily felt than entered on any ledger of the usual kind. For me at least, the importance of our commitment to scholarship and research transcends measurable ends. It reflects our pressing, irrepressible need as human beings to confront the unknown and to seek understanding for its own sake. It is tied inextricably to the freedom to think freshly, to see propositions of every kind in ever-changing light. And it celebrates the special exhilaration that comes from a new idea.

My greatest personal debt to Princeton as a teaching institution derives from an experience I had as a beginning graduate student in the fall of 1955. As a student in one of the last classes in the history of economic thought taught by Professor Jacob Viner, I was given the privilege of seeing at first hand what constitutes scholarship of a high order, and how the standards and values of scholarship can inform work that otherwise might seem routine or pedestrian. I hope that those who were unable to witness Professor Viner's scholarship, or who do not know the fruits of it, will nonetheless sense the spirit of what I am trying to say through the following comment of his:

> All that I plead on behalf of scholarship is that, once the taste for it has been aroused, it gives a sense of largeness even to one's small quests, and a sense of fullness even to the small answers to problems large or small which it yields, a sense which can never in any other way be attained, for which no other source of human gratification can, to the addict, be a satisfying substitute, which gains instead of loses in quality and quantity and in pleasure-yielding capacity by being shared with others—and which, unlike golf, improves with age.

The Princeton Library

REPORT OF THE PRESIDENT
MARCH 1986

INTRODUCTION

Libraries have a particularly powerful hold on many of us, and in beginning this annual report I wish to acknowledge my own debt to both Firestone Library at Princeton, where I have worked as a graduate student and as a faculty member, and to Doane Library at Denison University, where I studied as an undergraduate.

It has been said that all of us are autobiographical when it comes to writing about education, and I am certainly no exception to that generalization. As an undergraduate, I spent many of my most rewarding hours in the Denison library, and to this day I remember vividly the arrangement of the stacks, the place where I worked, and the inscription that I passed each time I entered the building:

> Books are the treasured wealth of the world
> The fit inheritance of generations and nations.
> —Thoreau

Thus, I do not approach the subject of libraries with the more detached perspective that it is possible to bring to some topics. But then, a certain degree of nostalgic affection may be useful in serving as a partial offset to the tendency for technical issues to dominate so many current discussions of library systems.

Thomas Carlyle once said that the true university is a collection of books. While the spirit of Carlyle's observation remains valid, the information explosion that has occurred in the twentieth century has made it impossible to think of any one library as the repository of all the resources needed by a scholar in pursuit of knowledge. Indeed, the modern research library has reached an important crossroads in evolution. Caught up in the profound changes that are revolutionizing the collection and dissemination of information throughout society, it is compelled to reassess and redefine its role. The library is under significant pressure not only to change, but to accelerate its rate of change; otherwise, it may not remain the vital center of university life.

Although the particular circumstances of Princeton's library system have been determined to no small extent by local history and tradition, they are to a much larger extent a reflection of forces affecting all research libraries. It seems appropriate, therefore, to devote this annual report to the changes that the library has undergone (especially in the past fifteen years) and to the challenges confronting all libraries seeking to address problems that are genuinely complex—that are philosophical no less than financial and technological.

THE ROLE OF THE LIBRARY

As It Reflects a Philosophy of Education

The role of the library within a college or university can be understood only in the context of the institution's philosophy of education. While that statement is no doubt true generally, it merits special emphasis at Princeton. The particular shape and character of our library system reflects this University's distinctive characteristics: the close integration of faculty scholarship and research with graduate and undergraduate teaching, and the heavy emphasis placed on independent work (especially the senior thesis for undergraduates and research papers as well as the Ph.D. dissertation for graduate students).

This same interdependence is evident in even the broadest outline of the evolution of the library and the college from their earliest days. The initial library at Princeton was a personal gift of 474 books made by New Jersey's Royal Governor, Jonathan Belcher, in 1750. A second floor room in Nassau Hall housed the collection, and the educational philosophy of the early college, as it affected the library, was stated eloquently by President Samuel Davies in the first printed catalog (1760), which he compiled himself:

A large and well-sorted Collection of Books on the various Branches of Literature is the most ornamental and useful Furniture of a College, and the most proper and valuable Fund with which it can be endowed. It is one of the best Helps to enrich the Minds both of the Officers and Students with Knowledge; to give them an extensive Acquaintance with Authors; and to lead them beyond the narrow Limits of the Books to which they are confined in their stated Studies and Recitations, that they may expatiate at large thro' the boundless and variegated Fields of [Knowledge]. If they have Books always at Hand to consult upon every Subject that may occur to them, as demanding a more thoro' Discussion, in their public Disputes, in the Course of their private Studies, in Conversation, or their own fortuitous Tho'ts; it will enable them to investigate TRUTH thro' her intricate Recesses; and to guard against the Stratagems and Assaults of Error.

In its emphasis on independent study, an atmosphere of free thought, and the integration of the library into teaching and course work, President Davies' statement captures the ideals that have guided the development of Princeton's library to modern times. Those ideals were, however, far from realized through most of the eighteenth and nineteenth centuries.

After a fire destroyed the interior of Nassau Hall in 1802, the collection was rebuilt, enlarged, and moved to Stanhope Hall when the building was completed the following year. More than fifty years later, a wing was added to the rear of Nassau Hall (now the Faculty Room) specifically for the collections, and the library was thus returned to its original home in 1860.

But progress in developing the library had been excruciatingly slow. Soon after his arrival in 1868 to become president of the college, James McCosh complained to the Trustees that the library was "insufficiently supplied with books and open only once a week . . . for one hour." McCosh is largely credited with creating the modern library at Princeton. Under his administration, the library was open every day except Sunday; the first full-time professional librarian, Frederick Vinton (who was brought from the Library of Congress), was employed; and a new building, Chancellor Green Library, was constructed in 1873 solely for the purpose of housing the expanding library collection. This last event laid the scholarly foundation for the transformation of the College of New Jersey into Princeton University.

As the University developed in the early years of the twentieth century, the establishment and growth of the graduate college under the leadership of Dean Andrew Fleming West required major strengthening of the library collections. In addition, two important innovations in undergraduate instruction had occurred that were to have lasting effects on the library: the introduction of the preceptorial mode of instruction and the development of a new upperclass plan of independent study. Greater emphasis was placed on critical thinking, and students were given more extensive writing assignments that required an appreciation of the nature of scholarship. The consequences were dramatic: Ten years after the introduction of the independent study plan in 1923, for example, the circulation of library books had tripled, and there was a growing demand for work space within the library for both students and faculty.

These trends culminated eventually in a bold new plan for a library that would serve as a "laboratory of the humanities." Until that time, the typical library building was warehouselike in structure, its reading room cavernous and poorly lighted, and its stacks closed to students. In contrast, Firestone Library was planned in the late 1940s as the largest open-stack library in the world, a *teaching* library that would bring students, faculty, and books together in ways that would encourage learning, intensive scholarship, and casual browsing. With more than two thousand study seats dispersed throughout the stacks and in several reading rooms, the plan achieved a functional commingling of space that was part of a revolution in university library architecture at that time. Firestone quickly became a model for other library buildings around the nation.

Princeton's library system has continued to develop in response to the ever-expanding research interests of faculty and graduate students, and the library's collections have become both larger and more distinguished as fields of study have matured. No university of any standing can function at a high level of accomplishment without a strong library. In a famous and oft-quoted statement by the University Grants Committee of Great Britain in 1981, the condition of a university's library was taken to be the most revealing measure of institutional quality: "The character and efficiency of a university may be gauged by its treatment of its central organ—the library. We regard the fullest provision for library maintenance as the primary and most vital need in the equipment of a university." In recent years, meeting that test has proved exceedingly difficult—but certainly no less important.

The present-day importance of the library to the undergraduate program of study at Princeton was stressed by Professor Robert Tignor, chairman of the Department of History, in his most recent annual report:

> Without [the library's] resources in books and guidance we would not be able to offer the kind of senior thesis program we have. Indeed, the high quality of senior theses written in this department reflects the extraordinary manuscript and primary source collections here at Princeton. This year, for instance, I read a prize-winning

thesis on the Alawi group in Syria which drew extensively on Princeton's unexcelled holdings of Near Eastern books and materials in Arabic and European languages.

Graduate students are in many ways especially dependent on the library. It is noteworthy, for instance, that many departments in the humanities and social sciences hold their graduate seminars in Firestone Library. The graduate study rooms are also located there, immediately adjacent to the principal book collections, with the result that in these disciplines the lives of graduate students revolve around the library as completely as those of science students revolve around their laboratories. The blackboards and bulletin boards of the study rooms often provide the common message center for graduate students, and the various areas of Firestone Library have their distinctive cultures.

The Princeton library also attracts visiting faculty and visiting fellows from around the world who value the opportunity to work in such an excellent research facility in close proximity with leading scholars. One professor of military history from England who spent a term in residence as a fellow in the Shelby Cullom Davis Center for Historical Studies paid special tribute to what he called "the treasurehouse of the Firestone Library," and I know he spoke for many in praising the advantages of "so large a library maintaining an open shelf system."

The role of the library and its staff as active participants in the learning process was a favorite theme of William S. Dix, who served with such distinction as head librarian from 1953 to 1975. He once wrote:

> The library lies close to the heart of the University not only as a passive reservoir of ideas and information, but also as an active teaching agency. It seems quite clear that as both the world's society and its knowledge become more complex, the ability to use books effectively becomes an even more essential skill of the educated person. Similarly, as the relative size of personal book collections continues to decline and as public and institutional library resources become progressively richer, the knowledge of how to make effective use of a complex library as an adjunct of private life and professional career must become a more vital part of the education of the Princeton student. Much of this knowledge is gained through formal course work, in support of which the library staff works in close collaboration with the teaching faculty, but a substantial part of it is the independent responsibility of the reference librarian in his teaching role.

*The Princeton Library Today: Essential Facts
and Characteristics*

PRESENT-DAY SIZE AND SCALE. From its original 474 books, Princeton's library has grown to a collection of 3.7 million volumes (including 2.2 million monographs and 1.5 million bound journals), approximately 10 million manuscript items, and smaller but enormously distinguished holdings of prints and coins, as well as phonograph records, microfilms, microfiche, microprints, maps, and various other artifacts, including a superb collection of death masks.

While the Harvey S. Firestone Library is of course the dominant element in Princeton's library system, with fifty-five miles of shelf space, it houses today just two thirds of all items cataloged. There are also twenty-two branch libraries, which have been located throughout the campus in close physical proximity to relevant departments for the convenience of users and to encourage the greatest possible integration of teaching, learning, and research.

Several of these branch libraries, such as the Marquand Library of Art (established in 1908 as the first formal departmental library), the Gest Oriental Library (established in 1971), and the Mathematics/Physics Library in Fine Hall (established in 1931), enjoy international reputations of their own. Other libraries include the Astronomy Library in Peyton Hall; the Biology and Geology Libraries in Guyot; the Chemistry Library in Frick; the Engineering Library; the Forrestal Library; the Near East Collection in Jones-Palmer Hall; the Plasma Physics Library; the Population Research Library in Notestein Hall; the Psychology Library in Green Hall; the Seeley G. Mudd Manuscript Library; the School of Architecture Library; and the Woodrow Wilson School of Public and International Affairs Library. In addition, branch libraries in the residential colleges contain general collections and provide additional study areas.

The library has grown from a staff of eight in 1900 to a full-time complement of about 335, including many highly trained professionals. There are, in addition, 350 part-time staff members, most of whom are students. One person appointed to the staff recently was fluent enough in twenty-two languages to be able to catalog items in each. (The library routinely catalogs in 52 languages.) Advanced and advancing technologies are also having obvious effects on the skills and training needed by library staff members.

Princeton's library ranks eighteenth in total size of collections

The Princeton University library branches on the main campus

Linden Lane
Maple Street
Pine Street
Chestnut Street
Moore Street
Vandeventer Avenue
South Tulane Street
Witherspoon Street
Chambers Street

Palmer Square

Monument Drive
Bayard Lane (Route 206)
Palmer House

Nassau Street (Route 27)
William Street
Olden Street
Roper Lane
Ivy Lane
5 Ivy Lane
Washington Road
Alexander Street
University Place

Psychology
Chemistry
Engineering
Manuscripts, Archives
Public and International Affairs
Population Research
Annex Storage
Mathematics
Physics
Statistics

Laurance S. Rockefeller
Main Library
Urban and Environmental Studies
Art
Phonograph Record
Near Eastern Studies
East Asian Studies
Julian Street
Matthew T. Mellon
Norman Thomas
Biology
Geology
Astronomy

Princeton University

Main Campus

0 50   200   500 feet

Energy Research Lab
Von Neumann
Engineering Quadrangle
Third World Center
Mudd Manuscript Library
Princeton University Press
Elm
Cap & Gown
Coster
Charter
Ivy
Cottage
Colonial
Dial
Tiger
Quadrangle
Campus Tower
Terrace
21 Prospect Avenue
70 Washington Road
Woodrow Wilson School
Corwin
Frick Lab
Bendheim Scientists Lab
IBS Nassau
Burr
Corwin
Fine
Peyton
Jadwin
Armory
Palmer Stadium
Caldwell Field House
Architecture Lab
Jadwin Gymnasium
Elementary Particles Labs.
Lake Carnegie

Henry's House
Nassau Hall
Stanhope
Student Center
West College
Clio
Whig
McCormick
Dod
Brown
Maclean House
Chapel
Firestone Library
Dickinson
McCosh
School of Architecture
Art Museum
Prospect House
Woolworth
Palmer
1879
Guyot
McClellan Library
Eno
Rock Magnetism Lab
Moffett Biology

East Pyne
Madison
Hamilton
Joline
Campbell
Blair
University Store
Witherspoon
1901
Edwards
Laughlin
Holder
Alexander
48 University Place
Little
Pyne
Henry

Dodge-Osborn
Joseph
1937
1903
Walker
Dillon Gymnasium
1939
Cuyler
Patton
1915
Scudder
Foulke
1938
1941
Henry

Tennis
Spelman Halls
McCarter Theater
RR Station
Murray
Dodge
Theater Intime
1922
1940
1942
Baker Rink
Bauer
Roller Rinks

Courts
Lourie-Love

MacMillan
Chilled Water Plant
Cooling Towers
1912 Pavilion
Lenz Tennis Center
Forbes College

among U.S. and Canadian university libraries. But this statistic alone can be misleading because of the absence on our campus of schools of law, medicine, business, or agriculture, each of which requires considerable library holdings. Of particular interest is the fact that Princeton has the highest per student circulation of books of any university in the country (possibly in the world): 113 books per student per year.

A TYPICAL DAY FOR THE LIBRARY. A somewhat sharper sense of the range—and magnitude—of activities at the library can be gleaned from a simple listing of occurrences on an average day. The library system opened its doors at 8:00 A.M., and by 2:00 A.M. the next morning (closing time):

• 3,355 persons entered Firestone;
• 3,993 books were circulated;
• 700 students used some of the 11,000 books on reserve in Firestone;
• 134 questions were answered by librarians on duty in the Reference Room and at the reference desk;
• 222 titles were cataloged;
• 2,663 catalog cards were filed in 40 different public catalogs (which in aggregate already held some 10 million cards);
• 178 books were ordered and 24 books were discarded;
• 11,494 pieces of mail were handled, and 1,341 serial items (books and journals) in many different languages were received;
• 3,529 books were reshelved in 95 distinct sequences;
• 388 books had ownership plates put in them, and 208 books were sent to the bindery;
• 49 books were restored in the Preservation Unit;
• 1.4 hours were spent by reference librarians at terminals connected to computer bases around the country;
• 17,796 pages of photocopy and 438 frames of microfilm were made;
• 27 items were loaned to other libraries and 21 volumes borrowed for Princeton users through the Interlibrary Loan Service.

OTHER CHARACTERISTICS. There are a number of fields in which Princeton's collections are unusually rich, ranking among the best five or six in the country. These include art and archaeology, classics, medieval and Renaissance studies, English and American literature, American and European history (including especially twentieth-century American history), population research, East Asian studies, Near Eastern studies, mathematics, physics, and plasma physics.

The University library also contains several unique collections that have developed over the years into very distinguished holdings deserving of special notice. In almost every instance, the growth of these collections has depended upon specific benefactors. Although it is not possible in this report to do much more than mention their existence, these unique scholarly resources constitute one of the major attractions of Princeton for scholars from all over the world. They include:

• The Graphic Arts Collection, consisting of over 10,000 books and 25,000 prints and drawings. The collection includes the Dard Hunter Archive on the history of paper; the Adler Collection of American prints; the Hamilton Collection of American illustrated books from 1670 to 1870; and the Leonard Milberg Collection of early American city views.

• The Theatre Collection, with 12,000 volumes and 100 current subscriptions. Of special note are the Warner Bros. Archives and Princeton's theatrical archives, which include playbills, broadsides, posters, scrapbooks and photographs, scripts and cassettes of musical shows, set and costume designs, acting scripts, and piano-vocal scores of various productions dating back to the nineteenth century.

• The Pliny Fisk Library of Economics and Finance, containing the original Pliny Fisk Collection of railroad and corporation finance given to the University in 1915, as well as a collection of 5,485 reference books (bibliographies, indexes, statistical handbooks), 6,000 working papers, current issues of 952 journals in economics, and over 800 corporate annual reports.

• Twentieth-Century Manuscripts in the Field of American Statecraft and Public Policy, a collection containing correspondence, speeches, clippings, tape and phonograph recordings, and photographs from, among others, the papers of John Foster Dulles, Adlai E. Stevenson, James V. Forrestal, Allen W. Dulles, Bernard Baruch, John Marshall Harlan, George Kennan, and David E. Lilienthal.

• The Miriam Y. Holden Collection on the history of women, consisting of 3,000 volumes, as well as clippings, photographs and lithographs, cartoons, periodicals, letters, and manuscripts in the field of women's studies.

• The Rare Book Collection, containing 153,000 volumes from all periods, including in the classics the Junius S. Morgan Vergil Collection and the Robert W. Patterson Horace Collection; in American history the Grenville Kane Collection in early voyages and colonization, the Philip A. Rollins Collection of Western Americana, and the John S. Pierson Civil War Collection; in English literature the Morris L. Parrish Collection of Victorian novelists, the Rossetti Collection of Janet Camp Troxell, the J. Harlin O'Connell Nineties Collection, and the Gallatin Beardsley Collection. . . .

• The William H. Scheide '36 Library, comprising 3,000 exceedingly rare books and manuscripts in many fields, including, for example, the Gutenberg Bible, the first edition of *Pilgrim's Progress*, and a pristine copy of the first printing of the Declaration of Independence.

One last characteristic of the Princeton library system has to be mentioned: its extraordinary cost. The annual operating budget of the library this year is $12.9 million. This represents 7.5 percent of the University's entire budget for "educational and general expenditures," and by this measure Princeton ranks highest among 110 research libraries for which comparable data is available. (The corresponding figures at Yale and Rutgers, to take two other examples, were 4.2 percent and 3.3 percent respectively in the most recent Association of Research Libraries report.) The heavy capital costs of space are of course additional—and, at times, daunting in and of themselves.

National and International Dimensions

The Princeton library system operates within a much larger context of scholarly publication, library consortia, and sweeping changes in technology that affect all institutions involved with storing, analyzing, and retrieving information. From every perspective, the events of the last few decades have increased interdependence among libraries concerned with research.

At Princeton, we have long encouraged interlibrary cooperation, and we have participated in many national efforts to extend local collections through shared resources. Julian P. Boyd, Princeton librarian from 1940 to 1952, observed as long ago as 1940: "The fallacy of an impossible completeness in any one library should be abandoned in theory and practice; librarians should now think in terms of 'completeness' for the library resources of the whole country." He was an active member of the group that established the "Farmington Plan," a program designed to bring U.S. libraries one copy of every book of potential research interest that was published anywhere in the world and to make catalog information for all books available through the National Union Catalogue. In the same spirit, Boyd's predecessor, Ernest C. Richardson, had been instrumental in establishing a plan for cooperative cataloging at the Library of Congress; Boyd's successor, William S. Dix, helped create the congressional legislation in 1964 (known as the "Dix Amendment") that funded the national cataloging program that finally achieved Richardson's objective.

Those unfamiliar with Richardson's role in stimulating the development of the Library of Congress system will regard mention of his name in the context of standardization as somewhat ironic. It is, after all, the continuing presence of the unique "Richardson Classification" system in parts of the Princeton library that to this day causes such distress to unwary students as well as established scholars. At about the turn of the century, when there was no standardized system, Librarian Richardson developed a classification tailored specifically to Princeton's needs. When the Library of Congress began producing inexpensive cards carrying its own call numbers, and maintaining complete classification schedules for use in other catalogs (about 1920), that system was adopted generally for its obvious advantages.

At most large research libraries, including Princeton, the Library of Congress system was adopted in selected fields without reclassifying material already on the shelf. New acquisitions were classified using the Library of Congress system, and the two systems were integrated in the catalog. Total reclassification of all books, which would have been costly and slow in a system containing 6 million catalog cards, was not undertaken here (or in a number of other major research libraries) because the cost was thought to be prohibitive.

In the late 1940s, research libraries began working together to develop alternative ways to augment traditional library collections. One of the most impressive early accomplishments was the formation of the Center for Research Libraries (CRL), which was founded in 1949 by ten major midwestern libraries. The CRL is best described as a cooperative library for libraries, intended to supplement member collections. Now an international association, the Center for Research Libraries has more than 180 members, including Princeton, and houses over 3 million research-oriented books and materials that are readily accessible by interlibrary loan.

In 1979 Princeton became the seventh member of the Research Libraries Group (RLG), which was formed in 1974 for the express purpose of exploring ways in which computer-based systems might be used to establish a bibliographic processing system for research libraries. RLG has four main objectives: to ensure that published material of research value will be acquired by at least one member institution; to provide easy access to other collections and to expedite the sharing of resources; to encourage preservation projects among members, including the coordination of advances in preservation technologies; and to provide automated catalog management.

Let me give one specific example of the advantages of this kind of national enterprise. Under a $1 million grant from the Mellon and Ford Foundations and from the National Endowment for the Humanities, RLG undertook a project to develop an integrated component for the Research Libraries Information Network (RLIN) that would have the capacity to handle Chinese, Japanese, and Korean scripts. Since 1983, this first electronic bibliographic system to include the direct use of East Asian characters has been available in Princeton's East Asian Library.

Princeton also participates in the Research Library Centers of New Jersey, a network through which our collections are made available to the population of the state. As a resource center, Princeton's library provides support to local and area libraries, supplying materials that are too infrequently requested to be found elsewhere and providing reference information in specialty areas.

In a further effort to be sure that unique sources of scholarly materials in the library are known to a wider audience, the Friends of the Princeton Library publish the *Princeton University Library Chronicle*. This publication contains full descriptions and comprehensive lists of rare books and esoteric materials acquired by the library. It is sent to some 343 institutions all over the world.

No library can pretend to be totally self-sufficient in today's environment, and interlibrary networking is essential. In conjunction with independent research libraries such as the Morgan, Newberry, and Folger Libraries, major university libraries have begun to think in terms of a "national" library collection. Through cooperative efforts of various kinds, scholars can be assured of access to the fullest possible set of research materials, and libraries can alleviate at least some pressure on tight budgets.

As advances in technology are perfected, the possibilities for cooperation are increased. But whatever our success in developing a national equivalent of Carlyle's "collection of books," there is no way to evade the hard questions that face the Princeton library now, as it works to serve its own community while simultaneously participating actively in national and international efforts that hold great promise for the future.

The remainder of this report discusses four issues that are pressing ones for us: (1) managing the growth of the collections; (2) preserving library materials; (3) incorporating new technologies; and (4) space planning.

ISSUES IN THE 1980s—AND BEYOND

Acquisitions: Managing the Growth of the Collections

LONG-TERM TRENDS. Throughout almost all of the eighteenth and nineteenth centuries, the principal problem for college libraries was the task of increasing their holdings rapidly in order to create at least the nucleus of a collection. Acquisitions problems of course persist: It is critically important today that a library such as Princeton's buy new publications and make retrospective purchases. Our situation is radically different, however, in that a very substantial "nucleus" exists and a reasonable "steady state" of annual purchases is fully maintained. Nonetheless, the accumulated size of the base collection, the current volume of scholarly publication, and the rate of purchases combine to raise difficult problems of how the library can afford—and can manage—ever larger collections.

Some historical perspective is instructive. It took Princeton almost two hundred years to acquire its first million books (in 1947); it took only twenty years to acquire its second million (in 1967); ten years were needed to acquire its third million (in 1977); and we are now about to acquire our four millionth book.

The phenomenal postwar increase in acquisitions—compounded by the still faster growth in other forms of library materials—is in part a reflection of the growth of knowledge and of publications worldwide (see Figure 1). But it also reflects the transformation of Princeton into a major research university with graduate programs as well as undergraduate programs of the highest quality. And it reflects too the importance this University—and its many generous donors—have attached to providing the necessary resources.

Growth in book collections is, by the very nature of scholarship, difficult to contain. Expansion is required by the appointment of a professor with special interests within a particular field, the addition to the

Figure 1
Growth in Book Title Production
in the United States and United Kingdom, 1900-1984

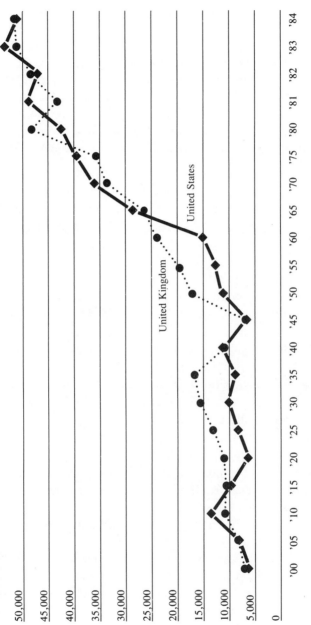

Source: *The Bowker Annual of Library and Book Trade Information*

curriculum of new departments and new programs, and increases in the volume of literature in each field. Consider, for example, the growth of the Gest Oriental Library. In 1957, it had 139,855 volumes; by 1971, when the Program in East Asian Studies was introduced into the curriculum, the collection had almost doubled (248,621 volumes). Now the collection contains almost 400,000 volumes (the fifth largest East Asian collection in the United States), and it is considered by scholars worldwide to be one of the great collections of East Asian works outside of Asia. The richer a library's holdings, the more they contribute to research and to teaching—and that success in turn generates demands for additional volumes from growing numbers of users.

FINANCIAL PRESSURES AND ACQUISITIONS. The general problem of deciding on an appropriate level of acquisitions and of managing the growth of collections can be illustrated by reviewing briefly our experience over the last thirty years or so—the last fifteen of which have been particularly trying and traumatic for librarians and library users alike.

In the 1960s (the "golden days" of university finance, as some refer to the first two thirds of that decade and the latter half of the 1950s), many university budgets were balanced rather comfortably; both private and government support for higher education and for research was burgeoning, real income in the country was rising steadily, and the growth of libraries was taken for granted. Reasonably stable prices facilitated the acquisition of books, and increased resources meant rapid growth—albeit sometimes rather undisciplined growth—in space, in staff, and in collections.

At Princeton, the library system was given exceptionally high marks for its collections, for its acquisition policies, and for essentially all aspects of its operations. In 1968, the Special Committee on University Governance (the "Kelley Committee") found that 78 percent of the faculty rated their degree of satisfaction with the library as "high." In fact, the library received a more favorable rating than any other part of the University.

By 1977, the situation had changed markedly. In the 1970s, libraries were affected severely by the economic pressures that beset universities generally. These pressures mandated reductions in library budgets (or at least slower rates of increase) at the same time that prices of library materials and salaries were escalating in the face of double-digit inflation.

As a result, significant numbers of new books were not acquired because of lack of funds, and retrospective buying to fill in gaps in collections was also restricted. Moreover, the cutbacks in both of these areas were quite unevenly distributed, with several fields of study affected disproportionately. (The informal nature of internal budgeting procedures within the library was one part of the explanation for this unevenness.) In addition, theft and mutilation of books had become serious problems at all major libraries, including ours.

Given this combination of circumstances, it is hardly surprising that satisfaction with the library declined significantly. The situation was so serious that we convened a Special Faculty Committee on Library Acquisitions and Losses to investigate the problems and to make recommendations for addressing them before permanent damage was done to key collections. The committee found that while expenditures for book acquisitions had continued to rise in the early 1970s, the rate of increase had been inadequate to prevent a significant decline in the number of new books added to the collections. The librarian's best estimates show that the annual acquisition levels were fairly steady at about 65,000 to 68,000 books per year until 1976–78, when they suddenly dropped to about 52,000 to 54,000.

The committee observed that changes in publication patterns and in the prices of both books and serials had contributed mightily to Princeton's problems. Whereas the rate of publication of monographs had leveled off in the early 1970s, the number of serials published continued to increase. In the University library, the average price per book rose 75 percent between 1970 and 1976, and the prices of serials rose even more rapidly. The need to maintain an uninterrupted flow of serials purchases, particularly in areas of science and engineering where price increases were especially pronounced, produced a sharp increase in the proportion of the acquisitions budget devoted to serials: from 29 percent to 46 percent. Simultaneously, the proportion of the acquisitions budget used by the humanities and social sciences fell from 77 percent in 1970 to 61 percent in 1976.

Several emergency measures were taken in 1978. The Trustees assigned an additional $3 million of endowment to support acquisitions, and appropriations from general funds were also increased sharply. Two general objectives were to restore book acquisitions to the level that had prevailed earlier and to establish separate budgets for monographs and serials.

It was decided that Princeton would relate its level of acquisitions to the overall volume of book publication in the United States and the United Kingdom, assuming that these publication numbers would serve as a rough index of the world output of scholarly books and that Princeton's "acquisitions share" of this total should not be diminished. These objectives have been accomplished, although at very substantial cost: The acquisitions budget has gone from $1,143,224 in 1971–72 to $3,557,000 in the current year. It is estimated that about 69,000 new monographs will be acquired this year (not including over 6,500 volumes from the private collections of Robert Taylor '30 and Howard Behrman).

Our determination to maintain the policies recommended by the special faculty committee was put to a severe test in 1979–80, when University-wide budget reductions were required. The book budget was protected, although provision was made for a selective reduction in serial acquisitions ($50,000 per year for three years). More recently the budget for 1985–86 provided a 10 percent increase in funds available for acquisitions. The acquisitions budget for 1986–87 will increase at the slightly more modest rate of about 8 percent as a result of a slowing in the rate of increase of book and serials prices. (It should be noted, however, that even this slower rate of increase is twice the rate of increase in the Consumer Price Index and greater than the increase in student charges.)

Of course, Princeton was by no means alone in having to cope with the financial pressures of the 1970s, and in fact this University managed to achieve larger increases in expenditures for acquisitions than did most other research universities. Of the six universities for which data are presented on Table 1, only Harvard increased its acquisitions budget more rapidly than Princeton over the ten years from 1971–72 to 1981–82.

One important, if obvious lesson from Princeton's experience in the 1970s is the changing nature of library management and the need to be every bit as rigorous in allocating funds within the library as within every other organizational unit of the University. All of the struggles with the acquisitions budget that occurred in the 1970s drove home the need for a far more sophisticated budgeting system designed to prevent unintended declines in acquisitions in certain areas and, at the same time, to prevent overbuying in one area at the expense of another.

Under the new system now in place, forty-five full- and part-time selectors (many with advanced degrees) work directly with departments and are responsible for making informed choices and being

Table 1
Acquisitions Expenditures in Selected Libraries*

	1971–72	1981–82	% Change
Chicago	$1,062,121	$2,004,450	88
Columbia	1,132,862	2,672,123	135
Cornell	1,422,690	3,157,799	121
Harvard	1,998,981	5,782,416	189
Princeton	1,143,224	2,898,532	153
Yale	1,641,629	3,425,885	108

* Each of these libraries, except Princeton, also supports a law school and a medical school library.
Source: Association of Research Libraries, *ARL Statistics*, 1971–72 and 1981–82

aware of the particular needs of various fields of study. Fortunately, there is now both greater control and more flexibility in the management of acquisitions, and we can therefore be more confident that every dollar is being used effectively. In this important sense, the real purchasing power of the acquisitions budget has gone up even more significantly than the dollar figures (impressive as they are) would suggest.

THE DECISION TO LIMIT ACCESS TO THE COLLECTIONS. More stringent measures have also been taken in recent years to limit access to the collections. Following a great deal of discussion, the Faculty Committee on the Library issued a report in April 1982 recommending that new steps be taken to limit access to the collections in Firestone to members of the University community and others granted special permission. (Previously the library and its stacks were completely open to anyone.) This recommendation was adopted most reluctantly, because the University has always wanted its collections to be available to a wide array of users. That continues to be an important objective for us. Nonetheless, a combination of considerations led the committee to conclude that the case for imposing some limit on access was compelling.

First, as was mentioned earlier, the problem of providing enough resources to make the requisite number of new acquisitions was compounded in the 1970s by the mounting tide of loss, mutilation, and theft that plagued university research libraries nationwide. The American Library Association estimated the losses for its member libraries to be in excess of $250 million annually in the mid-1970s. A systematic inventory of the Princeton collections made in 1976–77 revealed that 10 percent of the branch collections and 5 percent of the Firestone collections could not be found, with the total of presumed losses amounting to 150,000 volumes ($3 million in replacement costs at that time). Moreover, for reasons no one understood, the losses were very unevenly distributed—with, for example, fully one third of the topology collection in the Mathematics/Physics Library missing.

Careful study persuaded the committee that increased security alone would not correct the situation. Moreover, in addition to the evident problems of theft and mutilation, there was increasing concern over the "intensity of use" of the University's core collections by individuals with no connection to the University. Exit tallies at Firestone Library in the 1970s showed that the number of visitors of all kinds was increasing at the rate of 10 percent per year. The projected growth in the number of research-oriented corporations along the Route One corridor (and the attendant increase in the population in the area) suggested that this set of pressures was likely to become even more acute.

It seemed unwise to delay facing up to this sensitive problem any longer, and the combination of spiraling costs, limited resources, and the virtual absence of user charges made the status quo seem indefensible. Thus the faculty committee decided on a combination of new user charges and rules limiting access for those who were neither members of the University community nor fee-paying card holders (with, of course, provision for exceptions in special circumstances). Fairness in sharing responsibility for meeting costs as well as concern for the long-term condition of the collections argued for this outcome, and while it is still somewhat controversial, it seems to be increasingly understood and accepted. . . .

Preservation of the Collections

At the same time that we worry about acquisitions, we must also pay close attention to the condition of books already on our library shelves. Only in recent years, however, have major research libraries begun to address actively the problem of book preservation or to coordinate preservation efforts. To cite a recent example, last May five major research libraries in our region (Columbia, Cornell, Princeton, the New York Public Library, and the New York State Library) formed the Mid-Atlantic States Cooperative Preservation Service to share information about emerging preservation technology and microfilming for preservation purposes.

But solutions to questions of how best to restore deteriorating materials and to retard the disintegration of books are proving complicated, expensive, and difficult to achieve. Some publishers of academic books continue to use poor quality paper and inferior bindings, while increasing intensity of use puts heavy stress on poorly made books already in our collections. . . .

The scope of the preservation problem is immense nationwide. Our predicament is typical of other research libraries: A survey of Princeton holdings conducted in 1977 revealed that an astounding 42 percent of the 3 million books in the system were deteriorating and badly in need of some type of preservation treatment. Bindings were cracked or tattered, some books were missing spines, the contents were falling out of others, and countless volumes had brittle paper, paper tears, or other evidence of abuse.

In the sciences and social sciences, the books and journals most in demand are generally recent acquisitions that need little or no repair before they become outdated. The situation in the humanities is very different. Many older books in these fields still receive very heavy use, and as a result some three fourths of the items treated come from this division, especially from the fields of English, foreign literature, history, art history, and the classics.

Princeton's program of preservation was initiated in 1978 with the help of a challenge grant of $100,000 from the National Endowment for the Humanities, which was matched by $300,000 in donations from alumni and friends of the library. Because preservation work is extremely labor-intensive, our original objective was limited to hiring additional temporary staff to carry out preservation projects. We found that we could treat more than 17,000 items a year, but even at that rate it would take approximately forty years to review the humanities collection alone. In the beginning, then, we had to limit our preservation program to those items needing immediate attention.

By 1980 it was clear that the task was going to be of such proportions that a long-term commitment on the part of the University would be required. Accordingly, we appointed a preservation officer and several support staff members and purchased technologically advanced equipment to facilitate treatments. These steps have increased productivity, and to date more than 120,000 items have been treated.

A particularly successful part of our preservation program has been the Deacidification Unit, which handles the vexing problem of the high acid content of paper used in many books published from the mid-nineteenth century down to the present day. These volumes are subject to unusually rapid decay and must be deacidified to prolong their otherwise short lives. (Unfortunately, many are already past the point where deacidification is effective.) A national task force on preservation estimated that 25 percent to 60 percent of all research library holdings are too brittle to be circulated routinely and noted that "post-1830 book paper has been notoriously unstable. The life expectancy of a book published today is 300 years shorter than that of a book published in the 16th century."

The library has also been active in preservation microfilming. For example, roughly 12,000 medieval Arabic manuscripts, the largest concentration of such material in this hemisphere, were filmed to ensure preservation of the original documents. This process has enabled us to make copies available in response to frequent requests from scholars all over the world.

New Technologies

Driven by remarkable technological progress and powerful economic pressures, revolutionary changes are occurring that will radically alter the way the research library processes, controls, and disseminates information. For most of its more than two-hundred-year history, the Princeton library has done by hand all of its acquisitions, processing of materials, cataloging, and reference work; by the 1990s there is no doubt that the fundamental operation of the library will be profoundly different. In the past ten years we have already come partly to depend upon computer-based systems developed both locally and nationally to accomplish many key tasks.

While we know that major changes must be made, the terrain that we are entering is both unfamiliar and potentially hazardous, and we believe that the appropriate watchword continues to be "caution." When Librarian William Dix first reported (in his annual report for 1966) on developments in computing for libraries, he recommended strongly that Princeton wait until tested systems proved usable elsewhere. That strategy has worked well, and it continues to guide our actions.

In slightly more than a decade, the University library has made important strides toward automation in four areas: (1) cataloging and interlibrary loan systems using RLIN (Research Libraries Information Network); (2) reference services through PURRS (Princeton University Reference Retrieval Service); (3) acquisition and circulation systems using the Geac system; and (4) a public on-line catalog service using the Carlyle system (TOMUS).

CATALOGING. Princeton made its first move toward automation in 1974 when the Princeton University Library became a member of the Ohio College Library Center (OCLC), a nationwide computer network linking some three hundred libraries of various sizes that was successfully creating computer-produced catalog cards for members. Through this association, we obtained a large amount of derived cataloging and eliminated the costly and burdensome manufacture of original catalog cards. In the process, our cataloging staff also gained valuable experience with the techniques of network processing of library bibliographic records. Unfortunately, structural limitations in the OCLC program prevented full use of the system for many of our cataloging needs or its use as an internal on-line catalog.

In 1978, the Research Libraries Group, described in Part I of this report, developed RLIN, a much more powerful bibliographic network that promises to address specifically the needs of research libraries. This step forward was not without its trials, as might have been expected with a new organization that involved twenty-seven research libraries with aggregate collections of 80 million volumes, aggregate staffs of 10,000 people, and aggregate annual budgets of a quarter of a billion dollars.

Most difficulties were eventually smoothed out, and by 1984 the RLIN system was working well for cataloging (at a level that meets research library standards), for searching and locating books for patrons, and for interlibrary loans among member libraries. The time needed to obtain a book on an interlibrary loan was reduced from two weeks to a matter of days. There are currently twenty-seven RLIN terminals in Firestone and Gest Libraries, and telephone access is available in most branches to the RLIN database, which contains some 20 million items. Princeton staff members have contributed 45,000 records to the database, and almost one fourth of our cataloging production is derived from RLIN entries contributed by other members.

REFERENCE SERVICES. Another early development was a special reference service known as the Princeton University Reference Retrieval Service (PURRS), which the library has offered since 1975. PURRS offers on-line connection with an estimated 110 databases worldwide, including Dialog Information Services, Dow Jones, and Chemical Abstracts. Since understanding the protocols and data structures for various databases often requires special training, experienced reference librarians are available to search for and interpret data. This is a particularly useful tool for comprehensive searches in the sciences and social sciences, but it is considerably more expensive than traditional indexes.

Several smaller local systems were also developed to provide reference information service that was not available through traditional indexes. One of the earliest, known as CONFILE, was developed in 1975 to create a file of bibliographic records relating to conference proceedings in the field of engineering. Previously, such material was rarely cataloged in timely fashion. CONFILE has provided fast and efficient access to this body of information and still works well. Similarly, a three-year grant of $172,000 from the National Endowment for the Humanities in 1982 has enabled the library to undertake the computer indexing of a large arrearage of uncataloged literary manuscripts in Rare Books and Special Collections.

CIRCULATION SYSTEMS. An automated circulation system was another early objective. There was an unsuccessful attempt in 1977 to use a system that was not fully developed; after abandoning that effort, we began over the next few years to develop a database on a system provided by Geac of Toronto, Canada, in preparation for the later introduction of a satisfactory circulation system. This occurred in 1981, when we began use of the Geac circulation control system at Firestone. It was then extended to the Engineering Library last spring.

In 1983 the Geac acquisitions system was also installed, providing an integrated system that has functioned quite well. The combined circulation and acquisitions databases contain over one million items. The Geac methods for searches are easy to use, and Geac works as an online ''finding list'' that can indicate to library users whether a book has been acquired and whether it is on the shelf. For the future, Geac also has the capacity for automating serials check-in, the labor-intensive process by which library staff account for the 300,000 individual issues of serial publications received by subscription each year. At the present time the library is converting its 30,000-plus manual subscription files to Geac.

Our most recent application of technology has been to install (in 1984) an on-line catalog leased from Carlyle, a California firm, to duplicate the ''new catalog,'' which contains items cataloged from January 1981 forward.* Eight public terminals using a Carlyle program

---

* In 1981, the Library of Congress radically changed its rules for cataloging (not to be confused with its classification system). As a result, major research libraries were forced to choose between adding a complex and cumbersome new set of directives to the old catalogs or creating a new card catalog for items acquired after 1981. In libraries that chose to integrate the new cataloging rules

known as TOMUS can search for items by author, title, subject keywords, or call numbers. In contrast, the Geac circulation file is inadequate as an on-line catalog system because entries do not contain full bibliographic data or subject information. TOMUS cannot now do cross-referencing, but our initial experience with the system is otherwise promising.

As technical improvements continue to be made, we look forward to solving some of our most intractable problems. One of these is the need for the "retrospective conversion" of the 3 million earlier catalog cards in the main card catalog (over 6 million in the total library system) into machine-readable form. Only about 300,000 catalog cards in our system have been converted through what is a highly labor-intensive task. It has been estimated that the full conversion of all of our catalog cards into machine-readable cards would take five staff members nine years if done by hand. There is new hope that technology for reading catalog cards and making the conversion automatically may be available in the near future.

Making the right decisions about new systems appropriate for our needs and keeping up with new advances—without inconveniencing users inordinately—are major challenges. The immense costs of the new technologies also force hard choices. But the exciting possibilities continue to push us on in search of the best ways to ensure high-quality library service in a rapidly changing environment.

Space Planning

Providing adequate space for books, readers, staff, and essential library services are preoccupations for American higher education. When Pyne Library opened in 1897, it contained fewer than 200,000 volumes in a space that was expected to be adequate for *200 years*. In the next few decades, some of the more immediate pressure for additional space was relieved with the establishment of the first branch libraries, but by 1928 Librarian James Taylor Gerould announced in his annual report that the library system had reached its full capacity—169 years ahead of schedule!

The period from the late twenties to the late forties was a difficult one for a nation that faced economic collapse and then a world war,

---

with the old, there have been predictable arrearages in cataloging of as much as 300,000–400,000 cards (compared with 30,000 at Princeton), additional staffing expenditures, and the added frustrations of using an overly complex cataloging system. In those libraries, such as Princeton, that have created a second catalog, there is the inconvenience to the user of using two catalogs. Eventually, the Carlyle system is expected to replace the post-1981 card catalog.

and Princeton was not insulated from those events or their repercussions. The library had to cope as best it could. Books were unsystematically stored in cellars and attics; summers were spent shifting books about, in the all but futile effort to accommodate another year's growth. Unfortunately, this unhappy situation took its toll on the library's collections, causing considerable book damage and loss. Some volumes still bear the marks of that trying period.

During those years, extensive planning and fund raising for a new library were undertaken, culminating in the construction of the Harvey S. Firestone Memorial Library in 1947. Some 1,250 groups and individuals contributed to this effort, with a substantial gift from the Firestone family providing the critical funds that enabled the project to succeed.

Even with the rapidly changing requirements of today, Firestone Library continues to accommodate itself to new internal arrangements with remarkable facility. In terms of total space, however, we have already gone beyond the original walls of Firestone four times to create significant additions. . . . There is clearly a limit to how often this kind of expansion can be undertaken, and most of us believe that the Firestone site will not accommodate much more—if any—expansion after a current addition is built. . . .

Many of the issues already identified in this report have obvious bearing upon any discussion of current or future space planning. The growth of the collections, the intensity of their use, our efforts to preserve damaged materials, new methods of storing information, and automation of library systems all have an impact upon the amount of space needed. At the present rate of growth—roughly 100,000 volumes per year, including both books and bound journals—it has been estimated that we would need approximately 10,000 square feet of new space annually merely to keep up. Although new approaches, such as optical disks and cooperative database sharing, offer possibilities for the future, there are no panaceas evident in 1986.

As early as his 1981–82 report to the Trustees, Princeton's librarian, Donald Koepp, observed that the University libraries were essentially at capacity and that existing volumes needed to be moved into storage immediately to make space for new acquisitions. Unfortunately, the Annex storage facility at Forrestal was at that point also full. He described the situation as critical and concluded:

> The lack of adequate capacity to shelve collections is a serious matter with several long-term negative effects. Overcrowding is one

of the most common causes of damage to book collections. Too many books in too little space is one of the main causes of poor shelf order with obvious consequences for the ability of users to find publications we are known to possess. . . . Finally, the attempt to use efficiently the few empty spaces which exist even in crowded collections can become prohibitively costly because shifts of hundreds of thousands of books are usually necessary in order to "move" the empty spaces to where they are most needed.

None of these observations could be called a surprise. Nor has Mr. Koepp been content to "curse the darkness." Rather, he has worked very hard—and very thoughtfully—to develop a closely coordinated plan that is intended to address the space needs of Princeton's libraries until the year 2000. I believe that this plan has a good chance of accomplishing that objective—even as all of us are sobered by the fate of that earlier prediction that the Pyne Library would serve for 200 years!

Mr. Koepp's plan, as endorsed by the Faculty Committee on the Library and the Trustees, assumes a continuation of the current policy concerning new acquisitions (discussed earlier). It then consists of five principal elements: (1) continuing to strengthen branch libraries, but without wishing to "off-load" on them materials that really belong in Firestone; (2) making greater use of compact storage; (3) pursuing a rigorous policy of deaccessioning materials when that can be done responsibly; (4) adopting new, space-efficient technologies for library materials when that is feasible; and (5) pressing ahead with a very carefully considered proposal for an addition of approximately 50,000 square feet of space to Firestone.

STRENGTHENING BRANCH LIBRARIES. One primary response to space problems in the past has been to decentralize holdings. But in recent years several major branches were found to be nearing their capacities, including most particularly engineering, chemistry, and geology. We have several times evaluated the possibilities for expanding those branch libraries most hard pressed, while we have fought for time to develop alternative approaches to the general problem of space for the library system as a whole.

Some pressure was relieved with the construction in 1976 of the Seeley G. Mudd Manuscript Library to house the American statecraft manuscripts and the University Archives. In the following years, several other facilities were modified or expanded, including the Gest Oriental Library in 1980. As the result of generous donations from alumni, especially in the Class of 1945, as well as substantial support by corporations and foundations, the Geology Library underwent major reno- vations in 1979–80 that quadrupled the floor space available in Guyot Hall and added significantly to storage space. Presently, as part of A Campaign for Princeton, work is proceeding to provide a modernized branch library in Frick Chemical Laboratories, at a cost of $750,000.

In addition to work completed or in process, we know that we will need to expand the space for biology and molecular biology in Guyot Hall in the near future. Then, at least two other collections will need attention: the Marquand Library of Art, to provide expanded space for art and archaeology, and Near Eastern studies, where the exceptional level of activity in recent years has outpaced all attempts to accommo- date the collection adequately in Jones-Palmer Hall and in Firestone.

COMPACT STORAGE. A complementary approach, which we have also pursued vigorously in recent years, has been to increase our cen- tralized storage capacity through enlargement of the Forrestal Annex and the creation of compact storage space there and in unoccupied space on the lower level of Fine Hall. Compact shelving refers to spe- cial facilities built for high-density storage; through the use of narrow aisle widths and the placement of the shelving on runners that enable easy retrieval, we can reduce the space needed for aisles to one tenth of the amount needed under more conventional arrangements. This al- lows storage of twice as many books per square foot of space.

Compact shelving is generally most valuable for older, little-used material, and it can reduce our need for space significantly. It does produce additional staffing needs, however, and "open-stack" usage is difficult. At present, we have the capacity to house almost one mil- lion books in this way, including some 600,000 volumes in the storage library on the lower level of Fine Hall, which went into full operation in 1983.

Last year over 60,000 volumes were moved to either the Forrestal or the Fine Hall Annex, and this was the greatest amount of cataloged materials moved to storage libraries in a single year since the Forrestal Annex was first established in 1968. There are now over 400,000 vol- umes in the annexes. In addition, both Mudd Library and the new li- brary in Frick are equipped with compact shelving for some of their holdings. The use of compact storage space for seldom-used materials, with recall available within twenty-four hours, has enabled us to pro- vide a critical margin of breathing space with relatively minor incon- venience to the user.

In our continued planning for growth, we must weigh the economic benefits of compact storage areas against the important benefit of open access to the collections and adjacent study areas. Other universities such as Harvard (where a new "book depository" located approximately twenty-five miles away was recently announced) have also seen the inevitability of this step for the modern library. Even the simplest arithmetic drives one to the conclusion that continuous acquisitions will outrun the availability of any conceivable amount of space on the central campus. By the year 2000, our plan envisions that 30 percent of our total holdings will be in storage areas and that 70 percent will be available in traditional library space. This would be a very favorable ratio for research libraries.

DEACCESSIONING. Librarians have increasingly come to recognize that a policy of holding onto any and all copies of any item previously collected, no matter what, is not rational—especially when the competition for resources, including library space, is so intense. In recent years, the Princeton library staff has given increased attention to evaluating existing holdings and to weeding out and discarding items no longer needed. This is a laborious process, but it is a necessary part of planning for effective use of space into the future. In 1985, approximately 5,000 items were deaccessioned, and it is expected that deaccessioning will continue at approximately this rate.

Space can also be conserved by the careful sorting of gift volumes. This too is being done with ever-increasing care and awareness that gifts of books, however generously intended, are not truly "free" when space implications are considered along with the costs of processing.

NEW TECHNOLOGIES FOR STORING MATERIALS. As was indicated in an earlier part of this report, the library staff continues to use (judiciously) new technologies designed to minimize space demands. These include microforms and laser disks, which offer great promise for the future. A recent visitor to the Classics Department told me how absolutely astonished he was to discover that it is now possible to copy all of the principal texts of classical Greek literature on a single laser disk. Currently, our ratio of new library materials is approximately 85 percent traditional printed materials and approximately 15 percent other mediums. It is expected that as technologies develop and become more cost-effective, this mix may change to 60-40 by the year 2000. Indeed, our plan for the expansion of Firestone is predicated on this key assumption.

THE ADDITION TO FIRESTONE. Underlying all of our concerns about space is this fundamental question: To what lengths are we willing to go to preserve the concept of a library of human dimensions, "a laboratory of the humanities" designed specifically to accommodate the needs of both student and scholar in a working environment that includes attractive study space conveniently located near relevant book stacks? When the cornerstone for Firestone Library was laid in 1947, President Harold Dodds insisted that Princeton's library was not to be "merely another building," not "solely a shelter to books to preserve them against the ravages of time," but rather a symbol of "the inestimable opportunity of intimate association with the thought and experience of the human race." In this conception, ready accessibility to major collections and the setting created by small study spaces, carrels, and seminar rooms dispersed among the stacks are features essential to a broader vision of education.

Today we are just as strongly committed to that vision. In our continuing emphasis on liberal education and on independent work, the library has played a vital role, and we are determined to resist tendencies that would fragment the collections unduly or limit accessibility. Firestone must not be reduced to a mere warehouse for books. Moreover, the Princeton library system must retain its special commitment to accommodate students as well as established scholars. The American Library Association recommends as a standard that a university library have the ability to seat 25 percent of its student population. The Princeton University libraries can seat up to one half of the student population.

From my perspective, retaining the character as well as the quality of the entire library system depends more than anything else on the future of Firestone. Thus, vital as are all of the other aspects of space planning, the addition to Firestone is of preeminent importance. Without the addition, none of our other efforts on behalf of the library system would realize their potential, and the library services provided by Princeton would deteriorate markedly. For this reason the University is committed to pressing ahead with the addition to Firestone as an absolute necessity. . . .

THE LIBRARY OF THE FUTURE: AMBIENCE AND CHARACTER

It would be inappropriate to end this report by inflicting on the reader any "science fiction" view of my own as to the shape of the library of the twenty-first century. There are others much better qualified to speculate in that way.

There is, however, one very general concern that I want to register so that all of us who care about libraries can think about it consciously. For lack of better terms, let me call it a concern about ambience and character.

One of the faculty members at Princeton who has been most concerned with libraries for many years is Robert Gunning, professor of mathematics and former chairman of that most distinguished department. In a thoughtful memorandum to me, Professor Gunning summarized the subtle but clearly perceptible changes in the ethos of the Mathematics Library that have occurred since his days as a student in that department:

> The old Fine Hall library was a great library, almost ideal for its purposes, and recognized as such around the world. Physically it was immediately accessible and always open, with the Common Room, the informal center of mathematical life, as a natural stopping-off place. . . . That design was a lovely bit of applied geometry. . . . I remember with the other students going through the books to read the signatures on the sign-out cards; the Einstein autographs had disappeared by the time I arrived, but there were many names there that we had associated with theorems rather than with mortals. The collection was superb, perhaps the most complete and convenient of all mathematical libraries.
>
> The increase in the size of the department in the 1950s and 1960s . . . and the sometimes daunting increase in the amount of mathematics being produced and published led to the creation of new quarters and vastly different arrangements for the library. . . . It is no longer the center of life for the students; the photoreproduction revolution has even diminished the overall amount of time the faculty spend in the library. . . . [But] the library still works well. . . .

Libraries, and "information systems," have become so complex that I worry about our ability to retain the less tangible attributes that Professor Gunning describes so well in his warm recollection of the old Fine Hall Library. I make no plea for turning our back on new technologies; that would be self-defeating in the extreme and in its own way incompatible with the fundamental purposes for which libraries have existed for so long. On the contrary, we must seize new opportunities to do old tasks better. That itself can be gratifying and rewarding.

At the same time, I think it is exceedingly important to have a conception of the library that stands against allowing it to become too impersonal and too technocratic. Libraries for me, and for many others, have always been places of warmth, of comfort, and of reassurance. This is partly a matter of enjoying books for their aesthetic qualities as well as for what can be gleaned from them. However impressive the capacities of optical disks, they will never, I believe, render obsolete the pure pleasure of being able to hold a copy of Homer's *Iliad* in one's hand.

Libraries are, and should remain, much more than simply "tools." They should be places that are inviting, that themselves are statements of the value of learning, and particularly of the continuity of learning. Thus, in planning the future of our library systems, we should give substantial weight, I believe, to devoting space to quiet corners, to the creation of an ambience and a character that extol the pleasures of learning.

If we succeed in achieving this delicate balance between cheerful—indeed enthusiastic—adaptation of new techniques and respect for old amenities, we will have accomplished a great deal. We will have made it much more likely that future generations of students, when they return to Princeton, will want especially to revisit Firestone Library or the branch library that was such a central part of their lives here. And we will have made it much more likely that libraries will continue to epitomize so much of what is meant by education.

PART FOUR

Faculty

At the center of any great university is its faculty, and one of the central priorities of the Bowen administration was the welfare and effectiveness of the faculty at Princeton. After using his first annual report to review the fifteen-year tenure of his predecessor, Robert F. Goheen, and to identify an initial agenda for his own years in office, President Bowen then devoted his entire second report to issues concerning the faculty.

This chapter reprints that 1974 report in two parts. The first discusses matters related to faculty recruitment and advancement, including tenure, compensation, and the academic job market. The second tackles questions concerning the politics of the faculty that were raised with more than usual vigor in the late 1960s and early 1970s.

Completing this chapter is the 1984 annual report on "Junior Faculty at Princeton." This report includes a description of the role played by junior faculty members, a discussion of major concerns, and suggestions of ways in which the circumstances of junior faculty members might be improved.

Faculty Recruitment and Advancement

REPORT OF THE PRESIDENT, PART I

JANUARY 1974

. . . In a modern university, as in the earlier academies, the effectiveness of the faculty is more important than anything else in determining how fully we achieve our goals as an educational institution. Increased complexity has not changed this basic characteristic of a university. A faculty of high quality and demonstrated commitment to teaching and to scholarship serves directly the purposes for which we are chartered and, at the same time, attracts students, alumni, and others to the cause of the university. . . .

While the central importance of the faculty might seem reason enough for the emphasis of this report, there is a second reason as well. Leaving aside for a moment the overriding problem of finance, which has a pervasive influence on all aspects of the life of the University, there is wide agreement in higher education today that the most difficult questions of the next ten to fifteen years will be faculty-related: what are appropriate policies and procedures regarding promotion and tenure, what opportunities will there be for young faculty members, what is the outlook for faculty compensation, and what kinds of relationships will exist between the faculty and the administration and Trustees. These are the principal questions that I shall be discussing in this report. . . .

THE GENERAL OUTLOOK FOR ACADEMIC SUPPLY AND DEMAND

All of American higher education is now in the early stages of one of the most pronounced shifts in the conditions of faculty recruitment and employment in the history of the academic profession. Whereas the 1950s and most of the 1960s were a period of unprecedented growth in enrollments and in job opportunities for faculty members, the outlook now is very different.*

* The following discussion draws heavily on the excellent paper prepared by Allan M. Cartter for the Carnegie Commission on Higher Education ("Faculty Needs and Resources in American Higher Education," August 1972). Cartter observes that in the fifteen-year period ending in 1970, the age group from which most of our students come increased by more than 60 percent. Enrollments grew even more rapidly because the percentage of the age group enrolled in institutions of higher education rose dramatically. And job opportunities for faculty members in many fields

As we now look ahead to the latter half of the 1970s and to the decade of the 1980s, we have to recognize that each of the factors which made for increased opportunities over the last fifteen years appears to have largely, if not completely, spent its force. Indeed, after some relatively small increases during the rest of this decade, enrollments can be expected to decline markedly in the mid-1980s (probably by more than one million students) as a result of the sharp drop in birth rates in recent years and the probability that further increases in the proportions of young people pursuing higher education will be modest at best. Furthermore, while expenditures on research and development are far harder to forecast, there is no denying that, measured in real terms, the rapid increases experienced earlier have slowed appreciably.

Job opportunities, of course, depend on the number of persons competing for positions as well as on the number of openings. As Figure 1 indicates, there is every reason to expect a gradually widening gap between new doctorates obtained and academic openings available during the early and middle part of the 1970s, and we must expect a greater divergence in the late 1970s and especially in the 1980s as the need for new faculty to meet expansions in enrollment falls essentially to zero.*

These prospects have important implications for the academic profession viewed nationally. At present, for example, American college and university faculties are abnormally "young" because of the large numbers of new faculty members recruited during the 1950s and

---

grew even faster than enrollment because of the unprecedented increase in federal expenditures for research and development: even excluding all expenditures related to the field of medicine and deflating the figures for price rises, there was a fivefold increase between 1955 and 1970.

* This diagram is adapted from the paper by Cartter cited above. Obviously many assumptions have had to be used in deriving these projections, and it would be wrong to attach great importance to the precise position of any of the curves. The striking general conclusion to which this analysis points is not likely to be affected, however, by the substitution of any other set of reasonable assumptions for the ones that lie behind Figure 1.

As a matter of fact, Cartter presents a number of alternative sets of assumptions and shows the sensitivity of his results to variations in the assumptions. It should be noted that the particular set of assumptions that lies behind Figure 1 produces the *least* ominous results, from the standpoint of the outlook for the academic profession, of any of the combinations studied. On the "supply" side, the "low" rather than the "high" projection of the number of doctorates awarded annually is used. And on the "demand" side of the equation, the "total new teachers required" curve assumes no increase in the student-staff ratio in spite of the likelihood that enrollment will increase relatively in those parts of the higher education system (public two- and four-year colleges) where student-staff ratios are well above average now. Also, the assumption that 75 percent of openings will be filled by holders of doctorates represents Cartter's estimate of "the maximum number that can be obtained" (remembering that in some fields of study the doctorate is not the relevant terminal degree, that some young faculty members will always be hired prior to completing this degree, and that in the two-year colleges faculty with Ph.D.'s may not be appropriate in many areas of study). Cartter reports that a 60 percent line would represent the best percentage we have experienced.

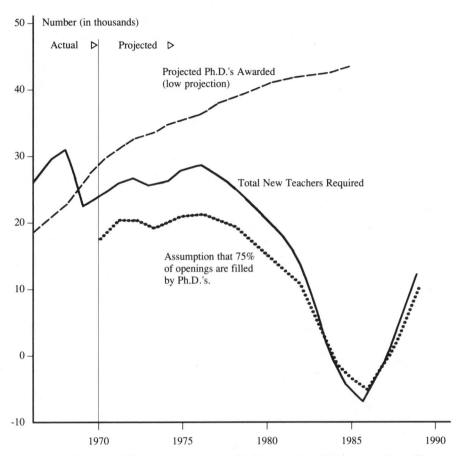

Figure 1
Projections of New College Teachers Required
and Doctorates to be Awarded, 1970-1985

Source: *The Annals of The American Academy of Political and Social Science,* vol. 404, p. 82.

1960s. Assuming no dramatic change in retirement programs and policies, there will be relatively few retirements over the next fifteen years, and this fact, combined with a relatively small number of new positions, means that the average age of faculties is likely to rise appreciably. Cartter calculates that the median age of faculty members nationwide could go up from 39 in 1970 to 42 by 1980 and perhaps to 48 by 1990.

The implications for tenure ratios and for numbers of young faculty members are even more striking. This same study reports that at present roughly 50 percent of all full-time faculty in this country have tenure and roughly 75 percent of faculty over 35 have tenure. If the tenure ratio among those over 35 holds constant, the shifts in the age distribution which Cartter projects would cause the tenure ratio for all faculty to rise to 72 percent by 1990. Given his assumptions, by that year only about 4 percent of all faculty would be under 35 years of age, as contrasted with about 29 percent in 1970.

To call this a serious situation for higher education is, if anything, to understate. As Cartter observes: "A drop to nearly zero in the number of young faculty hired over a ten-year period would have a devastating effect on the educational experience of a generation of undergraduates."

Even if the actual numerical effects are somewhat less dramatic (as Cartter and I both believe they will be, because pressures to alter existing patterns are sure to make themselves felt), the constriction on job opportunities for faculty is sure to be more serious than anything experienced since the depression of the 1930s.

The consequences for efforts to broaden the composition of faculties to include more women and more members of minority groups deserve explicit recognition. First, the extremely limited number of new openings in itself makes it difficult to add significant numbers of new people. Moreover, the intense competition for the few available positions will make it more difficult for institutions of higher education to avoid feelings of suspicion and distrust as efforts are made to reach out more broadly in recruiting faculty members. Such efforts will continue to be very important and must continue to be made.

Another unfortunate effect of an extreme scarcity of openings is that it discourages mobility. It may be true, as some have argued, that during the last ten to fifteen years it has been so easy to move from one place to another that the necessary degree of institutional stability has been endangered. Still, it seems to me that the best interests of individuals and of institutions are served by a degree of mobility which permits initial mismatches between individuals and institutions to be corrected and which allows individuals and institutions to benefit from new experiences and new colleagues.

POSSIBLE RESPONSES NATIONALLY

Plainly the problems posed for higher education by the developing imbalance between supply and demand for faculty need to be addressed at the national level as well as within each college and university. I have no simple solution to propose, and this is not the place for an extended discussion of the many alternative actions that might be taken nationally. I do want, however, to assert as emphatically as I can that further impoverishment of the major graduate schools is not part of an answer. First, well-developed graduate programs, which are integrated with the other activities of a university, simply cannot be turned on and off at short notice—and without affecting significantly the overall educational quality of the institution. At Princeton, as at a number of other leading universities, further reductions in the size of already small and highly selective graduate programs would serve only to push them below their "critical mass" (defined in terms of both educational effectiveness and financial viability) and to divert a good many students to other graduate programs that may be of lower quality.

There is proper national concern with the total number of graduate students and with the total resources devoted to graduate education, but care needs to be taken not to approach this question in ways that serve to undermine the overall quality of graduate education in the United States. Indeed, it may well prove necessary for the nation as a whole to make even stronger efforts to see that a limited number of graduate programs, of demonstrated quality, are supported adequately. (Let me add, parenthetically, that I do not think any of the leading graduate schools, including Princeton, can sit back and assume that their present programs are as well designed as they should be for the period we are now entering—or, indeed, for any period. But it is one thing to seek to make potentially strong programs better; it is quite another to allow strong programs to deteriorate to such a point that their long-term educational effectiveness is impaired.)

Positive steps that may be taken include increasing educational opportunities for individuals beyond the customary school-leaving age (including people in the professions who would benefit from further education). It is estimated that by next year more than 80 million older persons will participate in educational programs, and Princeton, along with many other colleges and universities, is exploring what contributions it can make in this regard. Additional teaching opportunities also could result from a nationwide effort to improve the quality of education by increasing faculty-student ratios where necessary. It is also possible that more changes will occur in retirement programs and in the ease with which holders of doctorates move into non-academic employment. Certainly all of these possibilities—and others—deserve serious study.

No list of possible changes would be complete without mentioning the tenure system itself. In recent years there have been a great many discussions of tenure (defined here simply as an assurance of continuing appointment from the time tenure is conferred until retirement, assuming neither dereliction of duty nor the elimination of the individual's field of study for economic or other reasons). It is a more complex subject than is sometimes realized, and we are fortunate in that just this past year a thorough study of tenure has been published by the Commission on Academic Tenure in Higher Education (a group sponsored jointly by the Association of American Colleges and the American Association of University Professors, constituted to include administrators, faculty members, laymen, and students, and known informally as the "Keast Commission" after its chairman, Professor William R. Keast of the University of Texas at Austin).

After reviewing carefully the pros and cons of tenure systems and of alternative systems (in particular, "contract systems"), the commission concluded that academic tenure

> should continue to be the characteristic form for organizing professional teaching and scholarly service in American higher education. The commission affirms its conviction that academic tenure, rightly understood and properly administered, provides the most reliable means of assuring faculty quality and educational excellence, as well as the best guarantee of academic freedom.

Tenure at Princeton

Our experience with tenure at Princeton supports this central conclusion of the Keast Commission. Dean Lester, in submitting his last annual report as dean of the faculty, noted that the tenure system at Princeton has served a number of important purposes in addition to protecting the freedom of individuals to teach and to write constrained only by their own sense of obligation to the standards of good scholarship.

The tenure system at Princeton, with its requirement that after a certain period an individual either be granted tenure or asked to find a position elsewhere, has served to enhance the quality of the faculty by forcing hard personnel decisions and encouraging a reasonable degree of turnover. In the absence of a tenure system, where there is not the need for hard "up-or-out" decisions, it is all too easy to slip into implied commitments and to keep individuals who are good but not outstanding for too long, as the experience of many companies, governmental bodies, and other organizations indicates. This is neither fair to the individuals concerned nor in the interest of the institution. Thus, I see no reason to believe that, exceptional situations aside, replacement of a tenure system with a contract system would in fact enhance the quality of the faculty or increase our flexibility. The opposite result would seem more likely.

The tenure system also has served to enable senior members of the faculty, who have been granted tenure, to evaluate their younger colleagues without conflicts of interest. In addition, the assurance of a continuing commitment which tenure provides enables individuals to concentrate on long-term teaching and scholarly goals and to feel a loyalty to the University that is hard to attain in a situation in which individuals view their own status in the University as always in doubt.

Of course, in any tenure system some individuals who looked outstanding when appointed will fail to live up to their earlier promise, and some may seek to take improper advantage of the protections tenure offers. Fortunately, a salary system geared heavily to increases based on merit, as ours has been, can be used to recognize outstanding, as contrasted with adequate, performance, and thus, to the extent we are able to distinguish these things, to encourage and reward achievement. Also, departmental colleagues, department chairmen, and the dean of the faculty can and do act to ensure that individual faculty members are faithful to their obligations when this is necessary. Self-discipline is, of course, most important of all. Tenure conveys less "security" in a fundamental sense than is often assumed because of the tensions that continue to exist, particularly for the very best people, between what they have in fact achieved as teachers and as scholars and what they, no less than their colleagues and students, expect of themselves.

The generally good experience that we have had with tenure is directly attributable, I believe, to the way the system has been administered here over the years. The quotation from the Keast Commission report cited earlier endorses the concept of tenure *"rightly understood and properly administered."* These are important words. It is very much to the credit of earlier administrations and the faculty itself that current practices at Princeton conform closely to the major recommendations of the Keast Commission concerning the administration of tenure systems. In particular: (1) our faculty has long felt a direct responsibility for the quality of personnel decisions, and tenure has never been conferred here on anything resembling an automatic basis; (2) formal procedures have been developed to encourage careful scrutiny of an individual's performance and promise as a teacher, as a scholar, and as a member of the University community; (3) the need to achieve a sensible balance between numbers of tenure and nontenure positions has been recognized; and (4) efforts have been made, especially in recent years, to communicate to individuals, and particularly to new members of the faculty, a realistic set of expectations.

I will say more later about the importance of faculty participation and faculty leadership. At that time I also will comment briefly on our formal procedures for reviewing personnel recommendations.*

Perhaps the most frequent criticism of the administration of tenure systems generally has been that in some instances tenure has been conferred automatically, simply as a result of the passage of time. That has certainly not been true at Princeton. In the 1960s and early 1970s, between one quarter and one third of the persons appointed to assistant professorships eventually were promoted to tenure on our faculty. This ratio has, of course, varied significantly among departments and within the same department over different periods of time, depending as it does on the qualifications of individuals and the needs and resources of the University.

It has been understood for some time at Princeton that appointment

---

* A detailed description of procedures can be obtained from the office of the dean of the faculty on request. In brief, openings are approved by the provost and the dean of the faculty in conjunction with the budgetary and planning processes. Specific recommendations for appointment and promotion originate at the departmental level, are transmitted to the dean of the faculty with full documentation of the reasons for the recommendation, are reviewed by the faculty's Advisory Committee on Appointments and Advancements meeting with the president, the provost, and the deans, are transmitted by the president to the Curriculum Committee of the Board of Trustees, and then are acted on by the Board. Candid assessments of candidates by leaders in their fields at other institutions are always required by the Committee on Appointments and Advancements and are often obtained at the departmental level as well. Student assessments of teaching effectiveness also are used by the departments and the central administration in the case of all promotions to tenure from within the University.

to a tenure position, in the words of the *Rules and Procedures of the Faculty*, "must depend both on performance and on the availability of a tenure position." The number of positions filled by persons with tenure must be watched carefully if the University is to retain opportunities to add the most outstanding young faculty members of each generation to its tenure ranks; if there is to be room for the appointment of a sufficient number of new persons, with new perspectives, to the nontenure ranks each year; if the age distribution of the faculty is not to be skewed too heavily in the direction of older faculty members; and if the University is to retain flexibility to respond to changing educational and scholarly needs.

In point of fact, the tenure ratio at Princeton over the last seventeen years has been astonishingly constant—so steady, indeed, as to make one wonder about the reliability of the data! As Figure 2 indicates, approximately two thirds of all persons in the three professorial ranks (professor, associate professor, and assistant professor) have had tenure, and those with tenure have constituted approximately half of the total faculty (including instructors and lecturers).

Over this period it has been possible to maintain a more or less constant tenure ratio and to make a significant number of new appointments to tenure positions (both from outside the University and by promotion from within) in good part because of the substantial increase in the total number of faculty members. However, as can be seen from Figure 2, far and away the largest part of this increase in size occurred before 1968–69; since then the numbers of tenured and nontenured members of the faculty have grown very slightly. (There were 366 faculty members with tenure in 1968–69 and there are 369 this fall; the corresponding figures for the total faculty are 739 and 758.) The principal reason for the sharp slowdown in the growth of the faculty, in spite of increases in enrollment accompanying coeducation, is of course the severe financial squeeze which has affected all of higher education. We simply could not afford many new appointments.

As we now look ahead we would hope to be able to provide for at least a small net increase in the overall size of the faculty. This increase would permit some adjustment in response to the increased undergraduate enrollment, especially as it now is being felt in the junior and senior classes; and it would allow us to approve at least some of the most urgent requests for the strengthening of key disciplines. At the same time, of course, our economic problems continue to be very serious, aggravated now by the inflationary pressures everyone is feeling.

Figure 2
Tenure Ratio at Princeton,
1956-57 to 1973-74

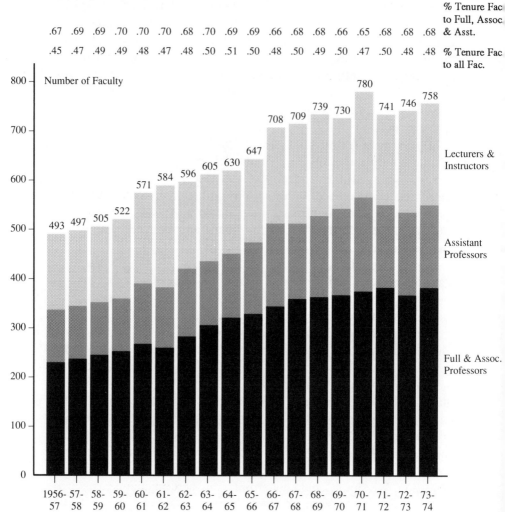

Much depends on our success in attracting financial support, and Trustees, alumni, faculty, and staff are working hard to raise new funds for Princeton, They have been doing a magnificent job; the quality of our educational programs in large measure reflects this effort and the generosity of our alumni and friends. It must be recognized, however, by potential donors and by faculty members, that a major share of the resources we are able to find will have to go to sustain present programs. Thus, while we must continue to make every effort to find that critical margin of support that will enable us to move beyond where we are now, we also must plan realistically. There is no escaping the need to base our plans, for the foreseeable future, on the assumption that at best only very modest growth in the overall size of the faculty can be anticipated. And a continuation of general inflationary pressures, or any number of other difficulties, could make even this goal hard to achieve.

If the tenure ratio is to remain at approximately the present level, and if there is not to be much net growth in the faculty (with some exceptions, including our "targets of opportunity" program), then new tenure openings can come only from (a) resignations; (b) deaths; or (c) retirements.

The dean of the faculty reports that on the average over the last five or six years we have had about ten resignations per year from the tenure ranks. In 1972–73, however, there were only three resignations. It is hard to know whether this marks a new trend, but the national data on likely openings presented earlier (in Figure 1) lead me to expect a somewhat lower rate of resignation over the next fifteen years than during the past fifteen years. While many of our very best people will still receive offers from other universities year in and year out, the scarcity of tenure positions nationwide surely implies some general reduction in opportunities to go elsewhere.

Deaths among tenured faculty members have averaged less than two a year over the last five or six years, and this figure, too, seems more likely to fall than to rise over the next fifteen years, mainly because of the steady decline in the average age of our tenured faculty.

Retirements are somewhat easier to predict since, as Dean Lemonick has observed, the only way to retire from Princeton is to be here and to be of the right age. Whereas retirements, like resignations, have averaged about ten per year over the last five or six years, the dean reports that as of this fall there are sixteen tenured faculty members within five years of retirement and another twenty-six persons within ten years of retirement. Thus, we can expect an average of just over four retirements per year over the next decade. (These figures do not take account of the early retirement plan developed last year under the leadership of Dean Lester. However, while it is too soon to know the full effects of this plan, we do know that it will not have a pronounced effect on the overall retirement rate.)

Taking all of these factors into account, it is clear that tenure openings will be more limited over the next ten to fifteen years than they have been in the recent past. To be sure, the situation at Princeton in this respect is better than the situation at a good many other colleges and universities. Because of careful planning in the past and the insistence on high standards for advancement to tenure, we do not enter this next period with as high a tenure ratio as some other places. Also, having gone through a difficult period of budget tightening and some compression, we do not now have to envision the kind of general contraction in faculty size that otherwise might be necessary. Finally, looking ahead to the 1980s, the size and quality of our pool of undergraduate applicants means that we should be less affected in direct ways than colleges and universities in general by the projected drop in overall enrollment shown so vividly in Figure 1.

Still, the constraints under which we shall have to operate will be tight, and the choices to be made will be extremely difficult, both in terms of general policy and particular personnel decisions. The need to be both sensible and fair, with an eye to the future as well as to the present, puts a premium on good planning. Situations differ markedly from department to department, and it is at the departmental level that much of the detailed planning must occur, albeit in the context of University-wide objectives, limitations, and expectations. This is widely recognized, and several department chairmen, in their annual reports to the president last June, made a point of emphasizing the need they felt for a clearer sense of the number of tenure openings they might expect over, say, the next three to six years. In the absence of such information it is difficult, if not impossible, to know what a decision about any one particular person in a department implies about the future of others, or about the future of an entire field of study.

This fall the dean of the faculty has met with the faculty's Advisory Committee on Appointments and Advancements, the Advisory Committee on Policy, and the department chairmen, as well as the provost and the other deans, in an effort to work out a somewhat more comprehensive set of expectations concerning the likely number of tenure openings over various time periods. This cannot be a mechanical process. Rather, the objective is a set of planning figures tailored to the circumstances of the various departments and, at the same time, consistent with the overall educational and financial outlook for the University. The projections for each department must be definite enough to be of real help to the department in considering priorities and making hard personnel decisions. Yet, there is also a need for sufficient flexibility: (1) to adjust to changes in the relative importance of different fields, (2) to take account of opportunities which new funds may make possible, and (3) to allow temporary ''bulges'' to permit the retention of individuals of absolutely outstanding quality and to provide a reasonably steady influx of new people.

A good start has been made, I believe, in developing plans that will meet these objectives as well as they can be met, and detailed memoranda went out to all departments this fall. There is, in my view, no task before the University more important than addressing this set of issues as intelligently as possible. The choice is between a conscious consideration of alternatives ahead of time and an implicit set of decisions now that will force decisions later that may not be wise. As one considers the implications of Allan Cartter's nationwide figures, it is all too easy to imagine situations in which boards of trustees or regents will feel obliged to impose rigid tenure quotas. The best way to avoid such an outcome, I believe, is by trying to plan sensibly while there is still the opportunity to do so.

COMPENSATION

As a sometime labor economist I approach any discussion of compensation with a certain amount of trepidation. I know how sensitive the subject is, both to the individuals whose compensation is being discussed and to those asked to pay some part of the salary bill, whether through tuition, Annual Giving, other gifts and grants, or some internal act of economizing. I know too how extraordinarily difficult it is to construct aggregate measures of compensation that are useful either in studying trends over time or in making comparisons between institutions or vocations at a single point in time. It is very easy to be misled, even by one's own numbers. Proper comparisons need to take into account not only salary per se but also benefit programs of various kinds; and even when we define ''total compensation'' inclusively we need to relate it to the age, rank, ability, and field of study of the individual, as well as to workload, to living costs in the locality in question, and to all kinds of psychic income—or psychic pain! While several organizations—most notably the American Association of University Professors (AAUP)—have worked hard to improve salary data, and have made real progress, it is still true that the published figures are of limited value.

The complexities of the subject plainly do not justify its neglect, however. As we now look through the 1970s and beyond, there will be no more pressing need than adequate compensation for our faculty and staff. (The words "and staff" deserve some emphasis because the ability of the University to discharge its educational mission depends of course on the quality and the commitment of the staff as well as on the quality and commitment of the faculty. Much of what is said in the rest of this section applies to the staff no less than to the faculty.) We are a highly "labor-intensive" activity. We depend primarily on the efforts of individuals who are expected to think for themselves and to teach others, often in relatively small groups, and our ability to attract and retain the very best people is central to our success as a major university.

After World War II there was widespread agreement that faculty salaries were much too low. Over the last decade and a half salaries have increased significantly, both for faculty members at Princeton and for faculty members throughout the country. The average salary for all ranks at Princeton was 84 percent higher in 1972–73 than in 1959–60; the comparable increase for a fixed sample of all educational institutions used by the AAUP (the so-called "Biennial Survey group") was 94 percent. Over this same period the Consumer Price Index rose 45 percent, and the difference between this rate of increase and the rate of increase in average salaries is a rough—and conservative—measure of the increase in real income.* In 1972–73 the average salaries at Princeton, by rank were as follows: professor, $22,844; associate professor, $15,443; assistant professor, $12,142; and instructor, $9,398. To these salary figures it is necessary to add 15 to 20 percent in the professorial ranks to obtain estimates of total compensation including pension contributions, group insurance, and so on.**

* Comparing changes in average salary with changes in the Consumer Price Index yields a conservative estimate of the increase in real income received by a typical individual because increases in the average salary are damped down by the retirement of senior faculty earning relatively high salaries and their replacement by younger faculty members at lower salaries. Thus, the average increase in salary *for individuals continuing on the faculty* has been appreciably higher than the increase in the average salary paid all faculty members.

** The nature of the University's benefit program currently is being reviewed by a committee chaired by Dean Lemonick. Among the benefits that will be considered are our housing and mortgage programs for faculty and staff. We have invested heavily in housing at Princeton, and we

As we think now about the period ahead, the overall outlook for faculty compensation is a worrying one. The titles of the last several annual reports of the AAUP convey the mood: "At the Brink" (June 1971), "Coping with Adversity" (June 1972), and "Surviving the Seventies" (June 1973). The economic status of the profession is threatened by: (1) the general budgetary and financial problems of colleges and universities, (2) the growing imbalance between the numbers of persons seeking academic positions and the number of positions available, and (3) general inflationary pressures.

This is not the occasion to review again the factors putting severe budgetary pressures on colleges and universities. Suffice it to note that while progress has been made in reducing deficits—and in some cases, as at Princeton, eliminating them, at least temporarily—the underlying problems remain. (In fact, the extraordinarily rapid increases in the prices of food and fuel have caused the treasurer to revise his previous estimate of a balanced budget for the current year to show a projected deficit of about $200,000.) More generally, income from traditional sources has not been rising at a rate fast enough to enable colleges and universities to provide the kinds of salary increases that will be necessary in the long run to maintain the quality of our educational programs. As for the second point noted above, the growing imbalance between demand and supply in the academic labor market depicted so vividly in Figure 1 means of course that salary scales at colleges and universities will not be under the kinds of market pressures that helped boost salaries in the late 1950s and much of the 1960s. Finally, there is ample evidence to indicate that general inflationary pressures, of the kind experienced recently, treat the academic profession even more severely than most other groups.

Let me now consider in slightly more detail the reasons why this outlook seems to me to be worrisome from the standpoint of the long-term interests of the University. After all, one might argue that since

---

will be thinking seriously about further needs in this area as we consider the future use of various land holdings. As has been recognized for a great many years, the availability of housing reasonably near the University, and at prices which faculty and staff can afford, is very important to the success of our educational efforts. In addition to affecting greatly the attractiveness of Princeton, the availability of housing near the campus contributes directly to a sense of academic community: it encourages people in different disciplines and different offices to get to know each other, it encourages people to return to campus at night and on weekends, and it encourages people to invite students and colleagues to their homes. This past year a great deal of time and energy have gone into efforts to adjust some of the provisions of the University's housing program to insure that we are in compliance with the requirements of the Internal Revenue Service while at the same time providing good housing opportunities for our people. At this point we anticipate that these efforts will meet with a larger degree of success than some of us at one time thought possible.

there will be an abundance of candidates for faculty positions there is no need to be greatly concerned about salaries. Indeed, one might ask, why not allow the budget to benefit from lessened salary pressures and, in this respect, take comfort from the market situation?

First, to deal directly with the issue of competition for people, it is essential to recognize that while there may be many potential candidates for positions, there are, almost by definition, very few outstanding candidates. The competition for the very best people is always intense, whatever may be the state of the market in general, and we must meet this competition if we are to function as a major university. We must seek out those relatively few people who already are or will be the intellectual leaders of their fields, as well as excellent teachers, and such people are always in short supply.

During each of the last two fiscal years we have managed to provide salary increases for continuing faculty members slightly higher than those provided by universities generally (just over 5.5 percent at Princeton, on the average, as contrasted with just under 5 percent for all major private universities and 5.2 percent for all universities). Still, over the whole of the last ten to fifteen years, we have lost some ground competitively, as the AAUP figures I cited earlier suggest, and on the basis of the quality of our faculty I believe that our relative position in the salary hierarchy should be somewhat higher than it is.

Having begun by discussing the competitive aspects of salary policy, let me now emphasize as strongly as I can that our concern cannot be measured solely, or even mainly, by the risks of losing people to other institutions. We have an obligation to treat fairly those people who have made commitments to Princeton, and considerations of equity must weigh heavily on us.

Nor is it just a matter of being fair for the sake of being fair, as important as that is. Salary policies have a pronounced effect on morale, and the effectiveness of any organization depends as much on what people *will* do as on what they *can* do. This is especially true in a university where there is relatively little hierarchy and individual faculty members bear such heavy responsibility for what we accomplish in teaching and in scholarship. Moreover, considerations of morale are especially important in a setting in which much also is expected of faculty members by way of general contribution to the University community. It is a great strength of Princeton, I believe, that so many members of the faculty feel a responsibility to participate actively in the general life of the place—advising students in informal as well as formal contexts, serving on committees, meeting with alumni, and so on. Plainly, individuals are much more inclined to contribute in these ways if the University shows that it cares about them and values what they do.

Making a special effort to provide adequate salary pools over the next decade is going to be important for one more reason: the size of the overall pools available for salary increases is directly linked to our ability to apply the merit principle in making salary distributions. When salary pools are relatively small and inflationary pressures intense, it is difficult to save enough money from the general allocations to reward properly those individuals who have made truly outstanding contributions. While adequate data of a comparative sort are hard to find, it is my strong impression that Princeton has put far more emphasis on the merit principle in dividing the money available for salary increases than most other universities. I am a strong believer in this policy. But we also must recognize that our ability to pursue it vigorously does depend on the adequacy of the overall salary allocations.

LEADERSHIP

Good leadership within the faculty is always important, but especially so as we confront the kinds of problems concerning tenure openings and compensation noted above. At Princeton faculty members have not been regarded as "employees," but rather as active participants in the process of formulating policies, applying them to particular cases, and administering the University. The avoidance of the "we-they" syndrome between the faculty and the administration—and between each of these groups and the Trustees—has been important to the general tone of the University and to the willingness of a number of faculty members to serve in administrative capacities. The generally easy and mutually supportive relationship between members of the faculty and members of the administration, which includes recognition of, and respect for, differences of viewpoint within and across both groups, is an important attribute of Princeton. We need to do all that we can to sustain it.

Faculty members who chair departments play a particularly important role in the decision-making process, and I am glad to have this opportunity to say publicly how much I appreciate all that they do for the University—often at considerable personal sacrifice. We provide a modest financial supplement to these individuals (an "administrative override''), but it is only very partial recompense for the time and energy which they devote to their tasks. It is a rare person who can continue to make major progress in scholarly work while serving as chairman, and, generally speaking, individuals are not asked to serve more than two terms in succession. Chairmen are appointed by the president after consultation with members of their departments.

One of the most important responsibilities of the chairman is to see that the department gives careful consideration to the question of whether a particular tenure opening should be filled by promotion from within the ranks or by recruiting someone from another institution. Of course, judgments of this kind are not made in the abstract. They are based on an assessment of the qualifications of particular people—both those already at Princeton in the nontenure ranks and those who might be attracted to Princeton. Also, consideration has to be given to the history and special circumstances of the department—and in this context the desirability of advancing an outstanding person from the nontenure ranks who knows the department and the University and who can be expected to grow and develop with us has to be weighed against the desirability of bringing to the department a person of demonstrated capacities who can provide new perspectives and perhaps even new leadership.

Decisions of this kind are never easy ones, especially when personal friendships are involved, as is so often the case. They are going to be even more difficult in the next ten to fifteen years, however, primarily because of both the limited number of openings likely to be available at Princeton and the even more pronounced lack of good opportunities elsewhere for nontenured members of our faculty who cannot be offered positions here. Certainly we need to be very sensitive to the morale of the nontenured faculty and to be scrupulously fair—as well as candid—in making these judgments and in communicating the decisions reached. We need to be sure that contributions of all kinds to the University are recognized and rewarded—good teaching and contributions to the general life of the University as well as scholarship. We need to consider carefully the contributions that can be made by individuals of diverse backgrounds and points of view. We need to be careful not to become too provincial and ingrown, too ready to make a good though not outstanding appointment. As scores of department chairmen have observed, the most comfortable decisions are not always the best decisions from the standpoint of the long-term interests of the University.

Over the last decade, about half of all new tenure appointments have been promotions from within and about half have come from outside the University. This has not been the result of any conscious policy, but the sum total of many hard decisions made primarily at the departmental level. In my view, we have benefited greatly from both kinds of appointments, and it seems to me important that departments continue to look both within and without for the individuals who can make the most significant contributions.

While it is important to recognize that the initiative for faculty appointments and for salary recommendations rests with the departments in all but the most unusual cases, responsibility for decision-making is by no means confined to the departmental level. A particularly important role is played by the four faculty members, one from each division of the University (humanities, social sciences, natural sciences, engineering and applied science), who are elected each year from among the chairmen by written ballot of the entire faculty, to serve on the Advisory Committee on Appointments and Advancements.* This committee, which is chaired by the president, meets with the provost and other academic officers to review in painstaking detail every departmental recommendation for a new tenure appointment; every recommendation concerning the reappointment, promotion, or termination of an assistant professor; every recommendation for promotion from associate to full professor; and every salary recommendation for faculty members in the professorial ranks. The committee is charged with bringing a University-wide perspective to bear on all recommendations, with insuring that every effort has been made to meet the highest standards, and with protecting the right of each individual to fair and thorough consideration.

The work of this committee has a direct effect on personnel decisions in that the committee can—and does—advise against recommendations brought by the departments. As many chairmen can testify, this committee is not at all easy to satisfy. The committee has, if anything, an even more important indirect effect in that the judgments it makes set a standard that influences subsequent actions taken by the departments. . . .

There is one other group of faculty members that has an important responsibility in this same general area: the Advisory Committee on Policy. This group, which also is elected by written ballot of the entire

* In 1981 this committee was increased to six members, including at least one representative from each of the four divisions of the University and at least two department chairmen.

faculty, meets with the president, either on his initiative or theirs, to consider any matter of general policy. Within the last year and a half the topics discussed have included faculty housing programs, the role of the University in continuing education, and the whole subject of tenure openings and faculty staffing over the next decade and a half. . . . These individuals also serve as the faculty representatives on the Executive Committee of the Council of the Princeton University Community.

The work of these two committees illustrates the important services performed by the faculty beyond their departmental responsibilities. Many members of the faculty serve on other standing and special committees which also contribute importantly to the University.

I think it is appropriate to end this brief account of the leadership role played by the faculty by noting, with more than a little satisfaction and a great deal of appreciation, the work of one faculty member turned administrator: Aaron Lemonick, tenth dean of the faculty. It is of course Dean Lemonick and other members of his office who bear the most direct responsibility for the quality and the welfare of the faculty. There is no more important responsibility to be discharged within the University, and in my view we could not be better served.

The Politics of the Faculty

REPORT OF THE PRESIDENT, PART II
JANUARY 1974

At times of national tension and sharp division, and especially when relationships between campus communities and the society at large are strained, the "politics of the faculty" becomes a widely debated issue—and the debate itself is likely to exacerbate further the tensions that contributed to its prominence. This seems to be one lesson that can be drawn from experiences in this country during such times as the debate over our entry into World War I, the depression of the 1930s, the period immediately prior to the involvement of the United States in World War II, and, of course, the Vietnam War.

Last spring when I wrote to all department chairmen concerning their annual reports to the president, I invited them not only to discuss the affairs of their own departments but also to share with me any thoughts and ideas they had on a number of questions of University-wide import, including this one. The responses were many and varied, and I am including excerpts from several of them in this discussion to give some sense of the way chairmen feel about this topic. One of our most distinguished—and independent-minded—scholars, Professor Frederick Mote of the Department of East Asian Studies, began by commenting: "I feel that we dignify this phony issue by granting it so much attention."

Certainly there have been days when I have felt that more of my own time was being spent responding to questions and allegations dealing with the politics of faculty members than would have been desirable, given the other pressing problems of education and of scholarship before us. Still, I have decided to include a direct and rather lengthy discussion of this topic in a report devoted to issues concerning the faculty because it is a recurring subject and because there are questions of real importance to all of higher education imbedded in it.

A great deal has been said and written already, and I have no very new propositions to state. I would like to try to provide a somewhat broader perspective, however, within which some of the questions that have been raised can be examined a bit more closely. Also, the fact that general interest in the topic appears to have decreased—and that passions have subsided somewhat—may make it possible for all of us to

consider the subject with less reference to particular events and personalities than was possible a few years ago.

THE "LIBERALISM" OF THE FACULTY

To the first question of a political sort commonly asked about the
faculty members at colleges and universities—Are they, as a group,
more liberal in general political orientation than the society at large?—
the answer is surely "yes."

In their excellent study, *Academics, Politics, and the 1972 Election*,
published recently by the American Enterprise Institute, Ladd and Lipset review the various studies of faculty attitudes toward issues and
candidates which have been carried out over the years. Theirs is the
most thorough examination of this general subject to date, and it pulls
together much relevant material. They conclude: "There is by now an
impressive body of empirical data demonstrating that the politics of
American academics, for at least the last half century, have been disproportionately left of center." The table below summarizes the quantitative results obtained by the Carnegie Commission in 1969.

There also is substantial evidence indicating that those individuals
regarded by their peers as the more outstanding members of their disciplines tend to be somewhat more liberal on average than faculty
members in general; that faculty members in the humanities and social
sciences tend to be somewhat more liberal as a general rule than faculty

Political Ideology of Academics and General Public
in the United States (all data presented as percentages)

Political Ideology	Under-graduates*	Graduate Students*	Faculty*	U.S. Public**
Left	5%	5%	5%	4%
Liberal	40	37	41	16
Middle-of-the-road	36	28	27	38
Moderately conservative	17	26	25	32
Strongly conservative	2	4	3	10

* Response to the question "How would you characterize yourself politically at the present time
(left, liberal, middle-of-the-road, moderately conservative, or strongly conservative)?" Data from
1969 Carnegie Commission survey.
** Response to the question "How would you describe yourself (very liberal, fairly liberal, middle-of-the-road, fairly conservative, or very conservative)?" Data from *Gallup Opinion Index*,
Report No. 65 (November 1970), p. 17.

members in most of science and engineering and in most professional schools; and that younger faculty members tend to be somewhat more liberal in general than older faculty members. These patterns are well documented and seem to have existed for a long time.

These general patterns are also evident in voting behavior, but it is necessary to be careful in assessing the significance of any particular election and of attitudes toward any particular set of candidates. For example, Ladd and Lipset emphasize "the predominantly negative cast of much of the voting in the 1972 presidential election" which, in their view, reflected a marked lack of enthusiasm on the part of most faculty members for both candidates. A number of those who supported Mr. Nixon stressed dissatisfaction with Mr. McGovern as the primary reason for their choice, and opposition to the war in Southeast Asia and longstanding anti-Nixon views dominated the reasons given by the significantly larger group which supported McGovern. They sum up: "Reading through the nearly 500 interviews, one is more than struck by the 'anti' character of the 1972 vote—one is almost overwhelmed by it." This is not to argue the absence of ideological considerations in voting behavior; it is to suggest that one ought not to underrate the importance of particular events and particular personalities in drawing inferences from a campaign of the kind waged in 1972.*

Why are faculty members as a group more "oppositionist" and liberal in political orientation than the society at large? A major part of the answer to this question seems to rest in a theme that goes back at least to Tocqueville: the intellectual community in general is inherently questioning, critical, and rather iconoclastic—more inclined than most

* Local polls, conducted without the aid of professional sampling techniques and professional analysis, need to be used with particular caution. There are serious problems of interpretation associated with the rates of response to such polls, and there is a strong possibility of bias in the percentages resulting from different degrees of interest and different attitudes toward polls of this kind which themselves may be associated with differences in voting behavior. Individuals with more moderate views, for example, may be less likely to participate in polls of this kind than others with more pronounced political interest because political questions are of less concern to them or because they consider political preferences to be a private matter. In the faculty preferential poll conducted by the Whig-Cliosophic Society in connection with the 1972 presidential election, ballots were reported to have been addressed to about 500 of the 746 faculty members. The tabulation of 214 responses showed 177 for Senator McGovern, 26 for President Nixon, 6 abstentions, and 5 preferences for others (including one vote for Mickey Mouse). In all likelihood the Princeton faculty, as a group, did prefer Senator McGovern, and by a substantial margin, but we ought not to put great weight on these particular figures or to draw sweeping conclusions from them. The most fundamental point is the one made in the text—namely, that it is dangerous to draw broad inferences about attitudes, and about trends in attitudes, from feelings for and against particular candidates at a particular time and under a particular set of circumstances, especially when those responding to the poll are not asked why they felt as they did.

groups to emphasize differences between the American ideal, as expressed in the Declaration of Independence and other affirmations of principle, and the reality of our life as a people. George Stigler, an able economist at the University of Chicago, known as an eloquent spokesman for the conservative viewpoint on many issues, has written:

> The university is by design and effect the institution and society which creates discontent with the existing moral, social and political institutions and proposes new institutions to replace them. . . . Invited to be learned in the institutions of other times and places, incited to new understandings of the social and physical world, the university faculty is inherently a disruptive force.

These characteristics of the university as an institution help determine the individuals who choose to pursue academic careers, just as the characteristics of other professions lead to similar processes of self-selection. And, as in other professions, the nature of the work itself, with the emphasis in academic life on the search for new ideas and the continuing contact with young people, many of whom are idealistic and questioning, tends to reinforce this same set of values.

Professor Dennis Thompson, chairman last year of our Department of Politics, commented on the connection between the nature of the educational process and the general liberalism of the faculty as follows:

> A good liberal education is, by its nature, one which produces and is conducted by men and women with critical minds who often do not accept prevailing views. In this sense a great deal of what . . . [is seen] as liberal political bias is in fact merely a critical habit of mind that is an essential ingredient in any excellent university. If universities are to perform their traditional function of generating new ideas and knowledge, they are bound to welcome faculty who challenge the conventional wisdom of their society. If the Princeton faculty ceases to be critical in this way, Princeton could no longer claim to be a first-rate university.

The widely observed tendency of academics today in countries operating under a variety of political systems, including the Soviet Union and Greece, to be especially critical of the established society and form of government is no doubt a reflection of these same general tendencies. And, as the studies cited above indicate, there is an abundance of other examples from many periods and societies.

At the same time that we recognize the enduring nature of these general tendencies among academics, we need to be careful not to over-reach ourselves, and, in particular, not to assume the absence of a great diversity of views within faculties, or to confuse a generally liberal outlook with adherence to more activist behavior or more radical views. Ladd and Lipset emphasize the importance of this latter distinction:

> What we have described is a relatively striking commitment by faculty, especially in view of their middle-class standing, to political positions reflective of egalitarian, change-oriented, and generally liberal perspectives. This is not at all the same as a commitment to political radicalism . . . [defined as] a call for sweeping changes in the basic structure of political life. No study of American academics has shown anything more than a small minority inclined to radical politics. . . . *Just as universities have been seen correctly by many outside observers as centers of relatively liberal and critical politics, so they are criticized frequently by radicals within, again correctly, for being generally unsupportive of revolutionary political changes* [emphasis added].

This observation is entirely consistent with my own sense of our situation. More generally, I believe that some people who are not in direct contact with the campus, both alumni and others, have a seriously mistaken impression of the views of the great majority of the faculty because of the natural tendency for the views of those faculty members who are more outspoken to receive more publicity. As Professor Richard Falk, currently the member of our faculty perhaps most widely identified with controversial positions, has said on a number of occasions, he has a far better sense than most people of how many of his colleagues disagree with him! It is all too easy to assume a monolithic character on the part of "the faculty" which simply does not exist.

Let me end this part of the discussion with two observations. The first is an additional comment by Professor Mote:

> What is called "liberalism" by its critics in recent years appears to me to be one doctrinaire group's way of castigating an opposing doctrinaire group's attitudes, and neither can nor should become representative of the faculty. Most members of the faculty known to me seem to hold views on most issues that are as far from a _____ on the one hand as from a _____ on the other, yet for all kinds of fairly obvious reasons, most members of the faculty are more willing to be

labelled "liberal" than "conservative." Most members of the faculty are committed in ideal to thorough learning as a basis for judgment and action, and that not only makes them critics of doctrinaire positions . . . it is in an important sense a "conservative" factor in the shaping of their attitudes. Most of the faculty are conservators of knowledge who derive some of their status and self-respect from their roles as transmitters and preservers of the past's intellectual achievements and values.

The second observation is my own, and it pertains to the degree of importance accorded political questions by members of the faculty. Many faculty members, as citizens, do take an interest in the major questions before the country. In all likelihood, they are more involved in civic affairs than the average citizen. But, whether faculty members take more of an interest than, say, corporate executives, doctors, architects, lawyers, or members of other vocations filled predominantly by college graduates is harder to say. In any event, for most faculty members, as for most other citizens, their interest in public affairs is somewhat sporadic and is clearly subordinate to the concerns of their own professional work, to the needs of their families, and to a great many avocations. Indeed, a number of our faculty have relatively little interest in politics. I make this simple and obvious point in the interest of not allowing the occasionally heated nature of some of the discussion of this topic to fool us into exaggerating the time and energy that faculty members in fact devote to the political questions of the day.

IMPLICATIONS FOR THE UNIVERSITY

Let me now comment more directly on the implications for the University as an educational institution of the tendency for many faculty members to be somewhat more liberal than the population at large. Perhaps the first point to be noted under this heading is the one made just above—namely, that faculty members in general are far less concerned with questions of a political nature than sometimes is thought. The main preoccupation of faculty members is not politics but simply getting on with their own teaching and scholarship.

Moreover, in many disciplines the personal political preferences of the faculty are largely, if not entirely, irrelevant to their subjects. The chairman of our Geology Department, Sheldon Judson, responded to my invitation for comments by observing: "I confess that I can't get very excited about the charges of excessive liberalism of the faculty. This may be because the science faculties, and specifically this faculty, are fairly apolitical. As far as I am concerned the political stance of the individual faculty member is immaterial.'' In the social sciences, and in some of the humanities, the situation is more complex, and it should be recognized that in these fields there is greater potential overlap between an individual's own views on political questions and the substance of the individual's teaching and scholarship.

Appointments and Advancements

In appointing and promoting faculty members at Princeton our objective has been a simple one: to identify and then to attract the very best people, with ''best'' defined in terms of excellence as teachers and scholars and ability to contribute to the overall educational mission of the University. There is—there can be—no political test for appointment to this faculty. In my own conversations with potential appointees, the question of their personal political views simply does not arise. Nor, if I were to learn that a particular person were a Democrat or Republican, would I know what to do with such information in the context of our appointment process.

For the last six and a half years I have met regularly with the faculty's Advisory Committee on Appointments and Advancements. During that time the committee has acted on hundreds of appointments and on thousands of salary recommendations, and in not one single case that I can recall did the politics of an individual enter into the decision-making process of the committee in any way.

As explained in the previous part of this report, recommendations on appointments and advancements originate within departments, and it is, of course, possible that in screening candidates and in arriving at recommendations members of departments might be affected, consciously or unconsciously, by the personal views of candidates on political questions. We are a society of fallible human beings, and I see no way of guaranteeing that no faculty member ever allows his or her judgment to be influenced by such considerations—or, for that matter, by any number of other factors that ought to play no role in our deliberations. I can say, however, and with a great deal of confidence, that department chairmen, and the faculty in general, are fully committed to the principle of basing personnel decisions on the fundamental criteria of academic accomplishment and promise.

Furthermore, Princeton has established procedures for adjudicating questions that may be raised about the application of this principle in particular cases. First, any faculty member can and should go directly to the dean of the faculty if he or she feels that a chairman or a department has behaved improperly. Second, as I pointed out in the previous section of this report, the Committee on Appointments and Advancements reviews every year the salary of each member of the professorial ranks as well as each recommendation for appointment, advancement, or termination of a faculty member above the rank of instructor. Third, the Conference Committee of the Faculty exists as an independent body to hear any and all complaints that may be voiced about unfair treatment, and this committee has direct access to the Board of Trustees if the members should wish to bring a case directly to the Board.

Inevitably certain individuals in universities, as in other organizations, may feel that they are not advancing fast enough in salary or rank, or are not being reappointed, because people disagree with their views, when in fact their disappointment is due to their own shortcomings or to the stronger credentials of other people in what is a highly competitive environment. In view of the concerns that have been expressed about the liberalism of the faculty at Princeton, it is at least mildly ironic to note that the last complaint we received alleging unfair treatment because of ideological bias was from a faculty member who argued that he was being discriminated against because he was a radical. This simply was not true. His case was reviewed by the Conference Committee, which found that he had been denied reappointment for reasons entirely unrelated to his personal political views.

It is highly desirable from the standpoint of our educational mission that a variety of analytical approaches and intellectual positions be represented at Princeton. Departments recognize this, and while they do not base recommendations on the personal political views of potential appointees, they do make positive efforts to recruit qualified individuals with varying approaches to their disciplines who will stimulate students and colleagues alike by providing new perspectives. In parts of certain disciplines, especially within the social sciences, there may be at least a rough correlation between personal political orientation and intellectual approach, but it is the latter and not the former which may properly be taken into account. This is a subtle but important distinction.

In the case of the department at Princeton that I know best, Economics, efforts are made on a continuing basis to identify outstanding individuals who would complement rather than merely duplicate the strengths of persons already on the faculty. In his annual report to the president, the chairman of that department, Professor Albert Rees (who was chairman of the Economics Department at the University of Chicago before coming to Princeton), wrote as follows:

> As you know, the department has been under attack in the past year from conservative alumni for being too liberal and from radical students for being too conservative. The indictments are not inconsistent and may both be true. . . . We are almost uniformly in the mainstream [of American economics].

Professor Rees then went on to describe the positive efforts the department has been making to recruit outstanding individuals who would provide a variety of intellectual perspectives—and the difficulties involved in identifying and attracting strong candidates.*

The effort to include varying perspectives within departments must, of course, stop short of making concessions of quality to achieve this end. There can be no compromise with an insistence on the highest standards. On this point I would hope there is full agreement, both within and without the University. Nor, if we are to attract the best people representing varying points of view, is there any choice. Outstanding academics, whatever their personal politics, do not want to be associated with a university in which intellectual quality is seen as subordinated in any way to ideological considerations.

The implication for the general orientation of the faculty of our insistence on the application of a uniformly high standard of academic achievement needs to be recognized explicitly. The ability of any college or university to have on its faculty individuals representing a variety of viewpoints is affected directly by the characteristics of the pool of people pursuing academic careers. Thus, the best efforts to accommodate varying viewpoints cannot lead to many appointments of individuals with conservative predilections, for example, unless more persons who regard themselves as conservatives go on to graduate schools

---

* Having mentioned Economics, let me also use an example involving that department to suggest, by specific illustration, the dangers of assuming that the general "liberal" orientation of the faculty on some issues (e.g., the war in Vietnam) implies a "liberal" orientation on all other issues as well (e.g., state intervention in economic affairs). The lead letter in the *New York Times* of December 11, 1973, signed by thirteen members of the Economics Department, stated the case against gasoline rationing and the case for using the price system to allocate available supplies. As a further indication that things are not always as they seem, I might note that the response to this letter, criticizing the Princeton economists for overvaluing the market mechanism, came from a faculty member at the Military Academy at West Point—not usually regarded as a center of left-leaning opinion.

in the first place—and then commit themselves to academic careers. It is true, as Dean Lester has observed, that "no intelligent person who is still learning is likely to be consistently progressive or conservative on all matters, and one's views on particular questions are apt to change somewhat with time and experience." In general, however, so long as the academic profession attracts disproportionate numbers of persons with generally liberal orientations (and, as explained above, there are deep-rooted causes of this pattern), faculties in general are bound to be more liberal than the population at large.

The Content and Conduct of the Academic Program

The significance of the personal political views of faculty members for the content and conduct of the educational program depends importantly on the way faculty members see their role and on their commitment to intellectual honesty and fair play. No one would suggest that all members of our faculty, or all members of any group for that matter, meet fully the standards they set for themselves; I do believe, however, that the great majority of our faculty is extremely sensitive to the difference between teaching and indoctrination.

One of our main functions as teachers, I am sure my colleagues would agree, is to encourage students to develop the critical capacities and habits of mind that will help them arrive at *their own values*. To be sure, no one is perfectly objective, but faculty members do take very seriously the obligation to differentiate, as well as they can, between objective analysis and individual preferences. In teaching beginning economics one of the things I always have tried to do is indicate how the same tools of analysis can lead to very different policy conclusions, depending on one's values; that reasonable people can and do differ on the ends of economic and social policy as well as on the most appropriate means of analysis; and that ultimately each person must decide, as a citizen, what he or she believes to be the right course for national policy.

Faculty members pride themselves on encouraging students to think, and many of us routinely argue sides of issues which we do not accept ourselves when that is helpful in prodding students to examine their own assumptions. Some faculty members also make a point of telling their students what their own biases are so that the students can take that into account in listening to what they have to say. Guest lecturers also are used to introduce a variety of points of view into the teaching process.

Plainly the approach to the field of study of the person in charge of a course will affect the list of readings assigned or suggested. The extent to which it is sensible to include a variety of perspectives depends on the level of the course, the amount of background the students can be assumed to bring to it, the nature of the course content, and so on. The general practice, in courses where this is appropriate, is to include materials reflecting more than a single viewpoint, to expect the student to struggle with the contradictions, and to hope that real learning occurs in the process.

This approach has been described recently from the vantage point of the student by Nick Allard, president of this year's senior class and the winner of a Rhodes Scholarship:

> In classes, stereotypes also get knocked sprawling. You take a course in history. There's no textbook. You're given a ton of reading—books that say one thing, and books that say another. And then you discuss them, and the professor doesn't tell you which is right and which is wrong. You yourself have to decide what holds up under analysis and what seems hollow.

Some conservative students and some radical students feel, I know, that the reading lists in certain courses still fail to be as representative of different viewpoints as they think desirable. In some instances they may be right, though this is always a matter of judgment. Students are welcome to discuss reading lists with their instructors and to ask for additional suggestions. Certainly Firestone Library is the repository of a great many viewpoints.

There is one other aspect of this general subject that should be discussed. Students who see themselves as holding views different from the views of the majority of the campus community—whether they be more conservative or more radical or different in some entirely different sense—may feel uncomfortable and even, on occasion, unfairly treated. While a certain number of disputes about grades are inevitable in any academic setting, it is encouraging to note how very infrequent is even the suggestion that a student's ideology was taken into account in the grading process. Certainly individuals at both ends of the ideological spectrum have done extremely well and extremely badly. As in the case of faculty personnel decisions, there are procedures for hearing complaints, and any student who feels unfairly treated should make use of those procedures. Otherwise there is no way of distinguishing between a valid complaint and the natural, human tendency to blame an unsatisfactory result on someone other than one's self.

I have real sympathy for the more general problem of discomfort that can afflict students, especially those who are less secure, when they feel that their own views are not those of many of their compatriots. This is hardly a new problem and both its seriousness and the particular group of individuals most directly affected by it have varied appreciably over our history—from Revolutionary War days to the present. Differences in race, sex, religion, economic and social background, political outlook, career objectives, and life style can lead—indeed have led—to prejudices and forms of treatment that are inconsistent with the ideals of a free society and unacceptable in a university.

Our campus community is a place which encompasses a wide diversity of individuals and fosters opportunities for them to learn from each other. Because of my own convictions concerning the importance of tolerance and mutual respect, I have sought to use the opportunities available to me to ask each member of the University community to do what he or she can to sustain here an atmosphere that encourages individuals to think for themselves, to listen to others, and then, if need be, to change their minds—an atmosphere that stands against any form of intimidation. Every member of the University community needs to feel free to find his or her own way, in dormitory discussions as in the classroom; to feel free to speak out against new as well as old orthodoxies without any fear of being out of step with anyone else.

In seeking to articulate—and to emphasize—this necessary characteristic of any healthy educational institution, I have been expressing what I am confident is a widely shared conviction. Our University today is, I believe, about as tolerant a community as any to be found in this or any other country, and there do not seem to be many instances in which individuals feel aggrieved because of their particular viewpoints. Students and alumni alike should know that the faculty as a body is committed strongly and irrevocably not just to the *right* of each individual to his or her own views, but to the *positive value* of difference of opinion. Tolerance of different points of view is too important to us, as an educational institution, to accept any departures from a deeply felt sense of what is right behavior in this regard.

Fortunately, the great majority of students, as well as other members of the University community, are strong enough people to stand up for their own views. Students are not much inclined these days, if ever they were, to be swayed overly by anyone's pronouncements. More generally, there is a great deal of testimony to the limited effects that colleges and universities historically have had on the values and political preferences of their graduates. Robert Hutchins, when he was president of the University of Chicago, gave a radio address in October 1935 in which he said:

> At every age their elders have a way of overestimating the pliability of the young. As a result many people seem to have the notion that the student comes to college a sort of plastic mass, to be molded by the teacher in whatever likeness he will. But at eighteen, or nineteen, or graduation from high school, it is far too likely that the student has solidified, and too often in more ways than one

One of our faculty members who is also an alumnus, William Moulton, director of the Program in Linguistics, has expressed his own assessment of the situation in the following words:

> Even though I am politically more or less on the "conservative" side, I have absolutely no fear that my more "liberal" colleagues will insidiously infect the political views of our students . . . I can cite a historical example to prove this point. When I was at Princeton as a student in 1931–1935, countless alumni, parents, etc., feared that a "radical" faculty would turn us all into New Dealers, if not into out-and-out Communists. That this did not happen is shown by the "Letters" section of the *Alumni Weekly* ever since then.

Over the years, then, many of our graduates seem to have demonstrated an ability to modify whatever allegiance they might have felt as students to a particular orthodoxy of the time or even to a general political orientation. We hope, of course, that they have retained more fully, and will continue to retain, other kinds of allegiances—to principles of clear thought and conscientious study, to respect for different forms of knowledge as well as differences of opinion, and to a steady, continuing, and open-minded search for truths that are themselves subject to change. For it is in the service of these kinds of goals, not in the interests of any set of political propositions, that the University exists today as in the past.

*   *   *   *   *

If we are to continue to be the kind of University that serves these ends and serves them well, certain things are required of us.

• First, faculty members and administrators responsible for recommending the appointment and advancement of members of the faculty, while welcoming a variety of points of view, must continue to seek out those individuals of the greatest talent and clearest commitment to the ends of the University, without reference to personal political views.

• Second, those of us who teach and study at Princeton must embrace and act out the principles of intellectual integrity that combine the obligation to think and write in accord with one's own conscience with the equally clear obligations to teach rather than to indoctrinate and to learn from, as well as respect, students and colleagues who have different views.

• Third, alumni, Trustees, and other friends of the University need to accept and to practice this same principle of tolerance, to recognize that many faculty members will have personal views that will differ from their own, and to defend vigorously the nature and spirit of a free University.

• Fourth, all of us who care about Princeton and about higher education, and especially those of us inside the academic community, need to take care to protect the true character of the University as an academic institution that is the property of no party or ideology; for only as the University as an institution remains free of partisan obligation can it stand most effectively for the principle of open inquiry and for the right of each of its members to think and to speak as a free and independent person.

Junior Faculty at Princeton

REPORT OF THE PRESIDENT
APRIL 1984

Two of my last three annual reports have been devoted to the broad subject of "opportunity" within higher education—for graduate students (in 1981) and for undergraduates (in 1983). A principal theme of those reports was that the nation, as well as Princeton, has a major stake in ensuring access to educational opportunities for individuals of exceptional talent, whatever their economic circumstances.

In this report, I extend this emphasis on the importance of nurturing talent by discussing the circumstances of junior faculty members. While I shall be concerned most immediately with faculty members at Princeton, I hope that this report will be of at least some help in illuminating concerns that are clearly national in scope.

The first part of the report is devoted to describing the role played by junior faculty members at Princeton in teaching, in research, in advising, and in the overall life of the University. The second section is a discussion of major concerns of these faculty members, with particular attention given to the limited opportunities for advancement in many fields these days, to salary prospects, and to the adequacy of support for scholarship and research. The third section identifies concerns for the University that grow out of these problems. The final section contains a discussion of ways in which the circumstances of this critically important group might be improved.

A final prefatory comment. The problems of junior faculty members are unquestionably real (and, I think, underestimated by many). It is equally clear that the success of the entire academic enterprise depends directly on their contributions. I have come away from the writing of this report with a renewed sense of appreciation for these colleagues of ours—for the important role they play in the University, for the quality that they represent, and for their dedication to teaching and scholarship. They are most remarkable, and they deserve the strongest support that we can give them.

THE ROLE OF JUNIOR FACULTY MEMBERS

Numbers and Characteristics

In the academic year 1982–83, there were 196 full-time assistant professors at Princeton: 62 in the humanities, 48 in the social sciences, 62 in the natural sciences, and 24 in engineering and applied science. The largest departmental contingent by far was in Physics, which had 22 assistant professors, followed by the English Department and the Woodrow Wilson School with 16 each, and Romance Languages with 12. Most departments had between 5 and 10 assistant professors. In some of the smaller departments, such as Astrophysical Sciences, Comparative Literature, and Music, there were only one or two assistant professors.

At present, instructors and assistant professors constitute almost exactly one third of the full-time faculty. For the first thirty years of this century, the ratio of junior to senior faculty members was almost precisely 1:1. By the end of the depression decade of the 1930s, the junior faculty was actually slightly larger than the senior faculty; then, in the period following World War II, the senior faculty grew faster than the junior faculty in every decade. This postwar development was principally a result of the increased emphasis at Princeton on graduate education and research, which require a stronger senior faculty presence. . . .

Between 1970–71 and 1982–83, there has been a further increase in the tenured faculty (from 369 to 387); this has been accompanied by a decrease in the number of junior faculty members (from 252 to 212), with the result that the ratio of senior to junior faculty members has increased from 1.4:1 to 1.8:1. It is important to add, however, that essentially the entire decline in the size of the junior faculty has occurred at the instructor rank. Also, there has been a modest offsetting increase in the number of graduate students engaged in teaching.

One factor explaining part of the increase over the last decade or so in the ratio of senior to junior faculty members has been the widely noted decline in retirements of senior faculty members as a result of both the age structure of the faculty and the change in federal law that increased the retirement age to seventy. There may be some further increase in this ratio over the next few years, but then the temporary "bulge" in the tenure ranks (which is principally demographic in origin) should be corrected, with the "correction" likely to begin in the mid- to late 1990s when retirements will increase significantly.

The main point is that the overall number of assistant professors is not expected to increase over the next decade or so and might even decline slightly as a consequence of these demographic trends. However, the more important developments, in any event, are generally masked by all aggregate statistics of this kind, which tell us nothing about changes within and across fields or about the characteristics of the *individuals* who are the truly important elements in any faculty equation.

As we look beneath the aggregate statistics, we can identify several significant shifts in the composition of the junior faculty at Princeton. The group has become increasingly diverse, and there has also been an increase in average age.

• As recently as fifteen years ago, the junior faculty at Princeton was all male. Today, about 20 percent of assistant professors are women, with the comparable percentages by division ranging from 39 percent in the humanities to 5 percent in the natural sciences. Approximately 10 percent of all current assistant professors are members of minority groups.

• Recruitment is by no means limited to the United States. Today, almost one fifth of our assistant professors are citizens of other countries, including Australia, Brazil, Canada, China, Egypt, England, Greece, Hong Kong, India, Israel, Italy, Japan, Korea, Portugal, and Spain.

• The "aging" of recent cohorts of assistant professors is reflected in figures showing average age at first appointment: age 33 in 1982–83, as compared with 29 to 30 ten and twenty years earlier. It is no longer so exceptional for an assistant professor to be over 40 by the end of the sixth year at Princeton, when a tenure decision is normally required. To some extent, this increase in average age reflects the fact that more assistant professors than ever before come to the University after having had teaching experience at other universities, rather than directly from graduate school. Also, it is taking longer for many candidates to complete their doctoral work.

To provide a sharper perspective on the assistant professors now coming to Princeton, let me comment on some of the characteristics of one group of fourteen individuals who were appointed to the faculty at the Trustees' meeting in April of 1982. Of this group, four were appointed to the Department of History, two each to the Departments of Chemistry and Romance Languages and Literatures, and the others joined the Departments of Art and Archaeology, Biochemical Sciences, Psychology, Near Eastern Studies, Mathematics, and Physics.

As has often been the case in recent years, the age span for this group of newly appointed assistant professors was quite broad: from 25 to 40 years of age. The youngest appointee earned his Ph.D. in 1980 (at age 23!) and held a postdoctoral appointment for two years before coming to Princeton. The senior appointee was a well-experienced teacher who had taught abroad for several years and was already a visiting assistant professor when appointed to the regular faculty.

Six of these fourteen assistant professors had studied abroad, at universities that included the Universidad Complutense in Madrid, the University of Bologna in Italy, the American University of Beirut in Lebanon, Warsaw University in Poland, and Oxford, Cambridge, and the Warburg Institute of the University of London in England. Three are citizens of other countries: one was born in Poland and is now a citizen of Italy, one is Spanish, and one is Lebanese. I might add that one member of this "international contingent" is fluent in five languages.

There are also some general distinctions among these fourteen assistant professors that are related to their fields. Each of the four scientists, for example, has held a postdoctoral research fellowship (one at Massachusetts Institute of Technology, one at California Institute of Technology, and two at the University of California at Berkeley). One also held a research appointment for an additional four years, and one received the Nobel Laureate Signature Award from the American Chemical Society.

In the humanities and social sciences, junior faculty members coming to Princeton these days are quite likely to have had previous full-time teaching experience. Of the nine assistant professors in these divisions, seven had from one to five years of college teaching (more if we include teaching while in graduate school). Only three assistant professors in the entire group of fourteen came to Princeton directly from graduate school (one each in mathematics, history, and art and archaeology). Six were recruited from full-time teaching positions at other universities, including Bard College, the University of California at Berkeley, Northwestern University, Purdue University, the University of Washington, and Yarmouk University.

Equally significant is the publication record that had already been established by members of the group at the time of their appointments. Two assistant professors had books already published or accepted for publication. Others had published articles, book reviews, or translations, and one had published his own poetry.

As we consider the issues discussed in subsequent sections of this report, it is helpful to keep in mind that the junior faculty members in question are individuals whose work has already shown great promise. Moreover, because of the variety of their experiences and the range of their interests, it is very difficult to think of them as a "group."

Teaching Responsibilities

Even before Woodrow Wilson's appointment of the original preceptors, junior faculty members played a significant role in the instruction of Princeton students. That is certainly true today in every dimension of the University's teaching program.

Junior faculty members in the humanities and social sciences usually begin their teaching careers by conducting preceptorials, classes, or drill sections in lecture courses directed by senior members of their departments; in the sciences, assignments to classes in beginning courses and to laboratory sections continue to be a common introduction to teaching at Princeton. The preceptorial mode of instruction is valuable now, as it was in earlier years, not only for the student given the opportunity to benefit from small group discussions, but for the preceptor as well. Preceptorials provide a gradual entry into the teaching craft: the chance to observe experienced lecturers in one's own field and to participate with them in the teaching of their courses can be an invaluable aid to the development of teaching skills.

In the last two or three decades, there has been a general broadening of teaching opportunities for junior faculty members. They now give lecture courses, direct upper-level seminars and classes, and offer graduate seminars, while also precepting in courses led by other faculty members. There is, of course, great variation in patterns of teaching assignments by department and field, with greater flexibility possible in the larger departments. Some departments rotate their members fairly regularly through the basic departmental offerings, while others give certain faculty members continuing responsibility for particular courses. In some departments, the process is modified significantly by the initiative of junior faculty members in requesting certain assignments.

Differences in subject matter, enrollments, research support, and departmental traditions combine to produce so many "unique" sets of teaching assignments that it would be misleading to suggest that there is anything approaching a single norm. Some faculty members are heavily involved in the daily preparation of language "drills," and they may teach a number of language sections (or even courses) with relatively few students in each. Faculty members in the large social science departments such as economics may combine classroom teaching in introductory courses with precepting and supervising of independent work. An assistant professor in mathematics may teach one intermediate level honors course to undergraduates while simultaneously devoting a significant amount of time to research supported by a grant. In engineering, a junior faculty member could well have direct responsibility for a graduate course as well as for an upperclass undergraduate course.

These differences notwithstanding, some broad statistics are revealing—particularly because of the extent to which they indicate that the undergraduate teaching responsibilities of junior faculty members as a group are perhaps surprisingly similar to those of their senior colleagues. In 1982–83, junior faculty members—who constituted 33 percent of the full-time faculty—taught 27 percent of the lecture course "contact hours," conducted 17 percent of the seminars, and did 33 percent of the advising of junior independent work and senior theses. They were responsible for 33 percent of the preceptorials and 29 percent of the laboratory hours assigned to regular members of the faculty. Assistant professors taught just under 20 percent of all "500-level" courses (taken principally by graduate students). Also, junior faculty members supervised a significant number of Ph.D. dissertations.

This increase in the breadth of teaching responsibilities assumed by junior faculty members has come about for several reasons. The most obvious is the expansion of knowledge that has occurred in the past twenty-five years and that has, in turn, required many more courses to be taught within each department. But perhaps the greatest impetus for the change in the nature of teaching responsibilities has come from the assistant professors themselves, who have actively sought opportunities to participate more fully in the teaching activities of their departments. The prospect of a stimulating teaching experience is, in fact, one of the primary attractions for young academics choosing among competing offers of employment.

It is also clear that junior faculty members who have had previous full-time teaching experience—an increasing fraction of all new appointees—are ready to assume greater responsibility for courses. In an era when only one in five or six assistant professors will be promoted to tenure and remain at Princeton, the opportunity to gain a range of teaching experiences is of considerable importance in the development of careers. Also, the junior faculty members themselves recognize the advantage to their own scholarship (as well as to their teaching credentials) of the opportunity to teach upper-level courses and graduate courses related to their scholarly interests.

Of all forms of teaching, the supervision of independent work can be especially demanding. The expectations of students are high, and when all goes well, the results can be very impressive. One senior whose adviser was an assistant professor in a science department offered this commentary:

> The more I became involved in laboratory work, the more I respected A. . . . She finds an immense amount of excitement and enjoyment in her research activities. It seems that every time I walked into her office she had a new piece of data or a new micrograph to show me. This intense interest seems to have paid off as I have read her papers in some of the most highly regarded journals. We have talked often about subjects ranging from her research to my own personal decisions. I began to notice that I was not the only person who enjoyed talking with her. . . . A's most enviable quality is certainly the breadth and depth of her knowledge. This quality was of great value as I pursued my senior thesis. Her ability to criticize my arguments and propose insightful suggestions was extremely helpful.

Another student described the ''less tangible qualities of enthusiasm and critical thinking'' he found in his junior faculty adviser and their profound effect upon him:

> Through the personal efforts of B, my perspective of laboratory work has been completely transformed. Whereas I previously regarded experimentation as a mysterious task to be performed with the aid of textbook procedures, I now consider research as an intriguing and rewarding activity, which I can accomplish with self-reliance and enthusiasm, and which I intend to make a primary focus of my career.

As these letters testify, junior faculty members invest a great deal of time and energy in both teaching and advising. Some of the most highly rated courses in the University are taught by assistant professors. This is one student's description of a course in literature taught by a junior faculty member:

> We came out of the seminar stimulated, thinking about the novel in a different way than we had two hours ago. I remember one seminar went so well that we could hardly believe two hours had gone by so quickly. It was truly an exciting learning experience and perhaps the best class I ever had at Princeton. On the whole, I have never had a more invigorating series of precepts or seminars. . . . The dramatic success of the seminars is mostly attributable to C, whose style encouraged us both to think independently and to think well.

The emphasis upon good teaching at Princeton is a source of significant pressure on junior faculty members. As one assistant professor said succinctly: "You don't want to make a fool of yourself in front of an audience of Princeton undergraduates. You try hard to do your best." At a time when there is great national concern that faculty members (and especially junior faculty members) may neglect teaching to advance narrower research objectives, such indications to the contrary are very encouraging.

The shared commitment of junior and senior faculty members to good teaching also has an important indirect consequence. The greater degree of overlap between the kinds of teaching done by junior and senior faculty members in recent years has meant a greater sense of commonality, of shared goals and joint efforts. Such interactions benefit the intellectual life of departments in many ways and provide direct opportunities for professional cooperation between scholars of different backgrounds, ages, and experiences. While senior faculty members have a special responsibility to provide leadership and continuity, we look to junior faculty members to contribute new ideas and fresh perspectives to teaching at Princeton.

David Bromwich, recently promoted to associate professor in the English Department, wrote me a note this fall that included the following comment about his early experience in the department:

> In English it seems to me . . . the junior faculty are important because they are out of graduate school without yet being "known quantities" in the profession. They do not have the anxious deference that usually handicaps graduate students; they make better teachers, coming into a first job with some classrooom experience

behind them; and they may even be valuable *for* graduate students, when they talk freely without having fixed attitudes to defend. In short they keep the discussion alive. When I was looking for a first job, I chose Princeton in part because I found the junior faculty a lively, varied, and impressive group. Some of these have stayed, others have since gone elsewhere, but the sense of common enterprise from that time still means a good deal to me.

Research Activities

At its best, teaching is an expression of the same fascination with a field of knowledge, the same desire to understand it better, and the same compulsion to communicate ideas to others that make scholarship and research such abiding passions. In a university such as Princeton, research is both exceedingly important in its own right and the primary stimulus to teaching that can remain intellectually alive throughout a person's career. This powerful complementarity between teaching and research is one of Princeton's greatest strengths.

In an academic setting of this kind, junior faculty members are recruited for their research promise as well as for their teaching ability. Our faculty is not split between a "graduate/research" faculty and an "undergraduate/teaching" faculty. It is a single faculty, and an important objective of faculty recruitment at all levels is to achieve the fullest possible integration of the search for new insights and the effective presentation of what is already known.

From the point of view of faculty members, research is generally most productive in departments and in universities that provide both a stimulating environment and tangible forms of support. For a young scholar, the opportunity to do first-rate work seems to be measured, initially at least, by where first-rate work is already being done. Thus, it is not surprising that an outstanding department such as Princeton's Mathematics Department attracts exceptional junior faculty members in large part because of the appeal of working with some of the world's best mathematicians. Physics is an example of a department in which work in many areas is possible only with the collaboration of professors of all ranks, postdoctoral fellows, and graduate students. When Professors Val L. Fitch and James Cronin were recently awarded the Nobel Prize for their groundbreaking research in elementary particle physics, they were eloquent in citing the valuable contributions of their junior colleagues.

In departments where collaborative research is less common than it is in many of the sciences (History and English are examples), the intellectual milieu is still very important. The excitement generated by fine scholarship is contagious, and able senior colleagues can do a great deal to encourage junior members of the department as well as to provide them with useful criticism. One recently appointed assistant professor, who came to Princeton from another department that he liked very much, said that his first year at Princeton was "the most intellectually stimulating year of my life." He believes that he will do better work by being here.

To be fully effective, even a vigorous intellectual atmosphere must be supplemented by tangible support. Indeed, assured support for junior faculty members is absolutely essential, especially in the experimental sciences, if the best candidates are to be attracted. In chemistry, for example, the provision of "start-up" funds has been a crucial element in making strong appointments at the assistant professor level. Without such assistance, a junior faculty member would be unable to undertake a major project and to begin to build what one faculty member aptly called "the momentum of a career." The amounts of money involved are far from trivial, and it is not at all uncommon to have to commit $50,000 or more to support the research of a new assistant professor in one of the experimental sciences.

In the humanities and social sciences, the availability of fully adequate library resources figures prominently in the recruitment of junior faculty members, as does the University's leave of absence policy. Because teaching and advising in these fields so often require an enormous amount of time, the University simply must provide extended periods of relief from these duties if faculty members are to be given a full opportunity to demonstrate their capacity for original work.

For many years, Princeton has had a more generous leave of absence program for the junior faculty than any other major university. In 1949, President Dodds and the Trustees established the Bicentennial Preceptorships—originally ten in number. Awarded competitively to assistant professors in the humanities and social sciences, usually in their second three-year appointments, these preceptorships provide a full year of leave and a modest drawing account for research expenses. In 1963–64, the Trustees instituted a "one-in-six" leave program that assures each assistant professor in these divisions one term of leave in the first three-year appointment. These special opportunities to pursue scholarship in the early stages of one's career have been invaluable to many faculty members, and we wish only that there were still more such opportunities.

Of course, other forms of support for research are also needed. Access to computing facilities is extremely important for some faculty members, while travel funds are crucial for others. In certain departments, sponsored research funds are used to release faculty members from some teaching obligations to devote more time to research; they are also used to purchase equipment, to pay summer salaries, and to help in other ways. More generally, any programs that advance the overall scholarly purposes of a department provide at least indirect help for the scholarly careers of junior faculty members. The Shelby Cullom Davis Center for Historical Studies, which has furthered intellectual exchange both within the Department of History and between the department and visiting scholars, is an excellent example of this kind of supplemental resource. Similarly, the International Finance Section and the Industrial Relations Section in Economics have provided both stimulation and tangible assistance to many assistant professors (including, in the case of the latter, the present writer).

The investments that the University makes in the scholarship and research of junior faculty members pay large dividends. As already noted, the support of research stimulates good teaching and is critically important in attracting (and retaining) outstanding young scholars. Moreover, junior faculty members have been responsible for some extremely important advances in knowledge. Some years ago one of the younger professors in the Mathematics Department, John Fornaess, was the leader of a group of junior faculty members and graduate students that worked very successfully on complex function theory in several variables. A graduate student in this group solved a problem showing—in contrast to what had been almost universally believed—that there existed in higher dimensions some strange functions called "inner functions." This finding in turn opened the way to a fascinating new set of problems.

Professor Dennis Thompson of the Politics Department has observed that junior faculty members, in addition to their specific contributions, provide the intellectual energy and stimulation that keep individuals and departments from becoming too hidebound. They regularly challenge the ideas and research techniques presented to the department by prospective appointees, and they offer perspectives that may differ from those of their senior colleagues. Fresh ideas and new approaches are at the heart of academic life, and junior faculty members often make precisely these contributions.

Other Contributions to Princeton

Along with their teaching and research, many junior faculty members advise students (in addition to supervising independent work), serve on departmental committees, and participate in University governance. Advising takes many forms, ranging from responsibilities as departmental representatives to service as faculty fellows and, in some cases, faculty residents in the five residential colleges that now exist for freshmen and sophomores. In the residential colleges, junior faculty members advise freshmen and sophomores on course selections, attend special receptions and dinners, give informal talks or review sessions, and meet informally with students at meals and other social events. The college environment provides a means of extending formal, departmental teaching activities of faculty members into more informal, less structured situations. In these settings, faculty members often come to know individual students well and are called upon to help with concerns of many kinds.

While junior faculty members have long shared informally in the responsibility for departmental and University governance, they were given more explicit roles to play as a result of the "Kelley Committee" report of 1969. The *Rules and Procedures of the Faculty* now provide for representation of nontenured as well as tenured faculty members on a wide range of faculty committees, including the Faculty's Advisory Committee on Policy and the Committee on Conference and Faculty Appeal. In addition, the *Charter of the Council of the Princeton University Community* specifies that this campus-wide body include at least four nontenured faculty members. At the departmental level practice varies widely, but it has certainly become more common in the last decade to involve junior faculty members in most departmental decisions.

The University benefits immensely from these many forms of service. Of particular importance is the fact that junior faculty members often are able to provide a "bridge" between the perspectives of students and the perspectives of senior colleagues. For junior faculty members, participation in this range of activities provides both an introduction to other faculty members, especially those outside their own fields, and a better understanding of the larger academic community of which they are such an important part.

PROBLEMS AND CONCERNS: FOR THE JUNIOR FACULTY MEMBER

Tenure Prospects at Princeton

Life has always been somewhat uncertain for assistant professors, and for those who would like to make their careers in teaching and scholarship at Princeton, the "tenure hurdle" has always been a major concern. In recent years, however, this concern has become much more pronounced.

Since 1964, tenure decisions at Princeton have been made on a carefully prescribed "up-or-out" basis. In the words of a 1964 faculty report, this rule was instituted to protect faculty members from "overly delayed decisions, with their potential unfairness to individuals." The longer an institution takes to make its decisions, the more difficult it can become for the faculty member not promoted to sever ties and to build a career elsewhere.

In the normal case, an assistant professor is appointed to a three-year term and then reappointed to a second three-year term if scholarship and teaching have been sufficiently promising. No later than the assistant professor's sixth year, the tenured faculty of the individual's department are obligated to make a recommendation for or against promotion to associate professor—and thus, in the Princeton system, for or against a tenure commitment on the part of the University. (Needless to say, not all cases conform to this schedule, and promotion to tenure can be recommended before the sixth year. Also, in very exceptional cases, the appointment as assistant professor can be extended to a maximum of seven to nine years.)

All recommendations concerning reappointment and promotion are reviewed by the faculty's Advisory Committee on Appointments and Advancements which is composed of six elected members of the faculty, is chaired by the president, and includes as nonvoting members the dean of the faculty (who serves as secretary), the provost, the dean of the graduate school, and the dean of the college. In each case, the faculty representatives on the committee make a formal recommendation to the president, who in turn makes a recommendation to the Trustees. This University-wide committee plays a very substantial role in the promotion process at Princeton. It by no means sees its function as ritualistic approval of departmental recommendations. Rather, it seeks to see that University-wide standards are observed and that University-wide contributions are taken into account. In recent years, about three quarters of all departmental recommendations for promotion have been approved by the committee.

The entire tenure review process is an elaborate one, involving the solicitation of outside evaluations from scholars around the world, student evaluations of teaching, and detailed appraisals of all facets of the individual's contributions to Princeton by faculty colleagues. By not allowing decisions to be postponed, the *Rules and Procedures of the Faculty* prevent the creation of presumptions of continuing places at Princeton for assistant professors who may be very good but are not judged to be absolutely outstanding. Through its review process, the University seeks assurance that all promotions to tenure are based on "compelling cases."

To insure careful forward planning, and fair consideration for each individual, departments make their personnel recommendations in the light of "tenure flow plans" that have been developed for each department by the dean of the faculty. These plans indicate how many new appointments to tenure (from outside the University or by promotion from within) departments may expect over the next three years and over the next six years. This system, which was adopted in 1973, assures that departments will approach each tenure decision knowing what effect a recommendation will have on the availability of tenure positions for other candidates over time.

The tenure flow plan helps to prevent situations in which there are no "tenure lines" for which assistant professors can compete. There is also a further degree of flexibility in that the University is always ready to consider exceptional cases—provided that they are truly exceptional—even beyond what the tenure flow plan for a department would allow. So, while there are constraints that are very real, they are not applied so rigidly as to prevent the promotion of candidates with absolutely outstanding qualifications.

As circumstances have changed over the years, the "promotion rate" has varied in response. In the late 1930s (so far as we can tell from available records), approximately half of all assistant professors were eventually promoted. This pattern continued into the latter part of the 1950s when 47 percent of all assistant professors were advanced to tenure. By the late 1960s, however, the promotion rate had dropped to 33 percent; and by the mid-1970s, the rate had fallen to about 20 percent. While the percentage of assistant professors who are promoted obviously varies from year to year, it has continued to hover around the

20 percent level for the last ten years, and there is no reason to expect it either to fall further or to climb again for the foreseeable future.

There is always a temptation to seek too many general explanations for statistics of this kind which are, in the last analysis, the product of many different decisions, made in many different departments (as well as at different levels within the University), in response to many different situations. Nonetheless, the large change from a situation in which roughly one of every two assistant professors was promoted to one in which roughly one of every five is promoted can be attributed to two principal developments at Princeton: (1) a more rigorous effort to protect opportunities for junior faculty members in the future by discouraging departments from becoming "over-tenured," especially given the relatively stable size of the faculty now; and (2) the imposition of a more demanding University-wide standard in considering all tenure decisions.

Job Prospects Elsewhere

The implications of the decline in the promotion rate for assistant professors at Princeton cannot be understood except in the context of the still larger changes that have occurred over the last two or three decades in job prospects generally. Indeed, it is the dramatic contraction in job opportunities throughout American higher education in many fields that is primarily responsible for anxiety among junior faculty members today.

If I may be allowed a personal reference, when I was a beginning assistant professor at Princeton in 1958, the one thing that I never worried about was finding a suitable position somewhere. There was a great shortage of qualified faculty members, and many excellent colleges and universities were competing fiercely to recruit the limited number of candidates who were receiving Ph.D. degrees from leading universities. That terribly comforting reality allowed me and my contemporaries to be relatively relaxed about the question of whether or not we would be offered tenure at Princeton. We were confident that there would be places for us "somewhere," and job security simply was not a major concern.

How lucky we were—and how different the world looks now to many junior faculty members. These days it is not at all uncommon for an opening in, say, English or American literature, to attract more than four hundred applicants. And even in mathematics and the sciences, the advertisement of a junior faculty position can elicit more than a hundred responses. The fact that only about 60 percent of the graduates of Ph.D. programs in the humanities now have firm job offers when they complete their studies has far-reaching implications for young people who are interested in academic careers. The magnitude of this national problem has been discussed at great length, especially as it affects graduate education, and I will not repeat that discussion in any detail here.

Suffice it to note that the twin sources of the problem are the sharp drop in the birth rate, with its attendant effects on enrollments, and the very small number of senior faculty members who can be expected to retire between now and the mid-1990s. To summarize the situation succinctly, we now expect the number of new Ph.D.'s to exceed the number of new faculty positions by somewhere between a 3:1 and 2:1 ratio until at least 1995. Of course, job prospects differ markedly by field, and it is also true that there is always strong interest in the very best people in every field. Still, there is no denying the powerful impact of this general situation on many junior faculty members as they think about the future.

Some of the effects of this national constriction in openings on junior faculty members at Princeton can be read from Table 1, which "tracks" cohorts of assistant professors grouped by the year of initial appointment. For each of three groups, we see the percentage of assistant professors promoted by the end of their first three-year appointment, the percentage who had either resigned by then or been released, and the percentage reappointed for a second three-year term. The last line of the table shows the percentage promoted by the end of the sixth year. (This percentage cannot be given for the last set of cohorts, since decisions have not yet been made in many of these cases.)

The top part of the table reveals a striking change in the pattern of decisions made by the end of the first three-year appointment. There has been a pronounced decline in the percentage of assistant professors promoted this early in their Princeton careers—from 11 percent in the late 1960s to about 3 percent subsequently. There has also been a sharp drop in the percentage of assistant professors leaving Princeton after three years—from 30 percent to 25 percent to 18 percent. Finally, the converse of these first two observations is that there has been a substantial increase in the percentage of assistant professors reappointed to second three-year terms as assistant professors—from 59 percent to 72 percent to 80 percent.

The primary explanation for all of these interrelated changes is

Table 1
Junior Faculty Cohorts, 1964-65 through 1980-81

	Cohorts 1964-65— 1968-69 (5)	Cohorts 1969-70— 1977-78 (9)	Cohorts 1978-79— 1980-81 (3)
Percent promoted by end of third year	11.0	3.0	2.5
Percent leaving by end of third year	30.0	25.0	18.0
Percent reappointed by end of third year	59.0	72.0	80.0
	100.0	100.0	100.0
Percent promoted by end of sixth year	32.0	20.0	N/A

clearly the significant deterioration in the job market for academics, especially in the humanities and social sciences. When positions at other universities were much easier to obtain, assistant professors were naturally more inclined to resign to pursue other opportunities—especially if they did not think that their long-term prospects at Princeton were particularly good. Now, assistant professors are much more inclined—indeed, "forced" may not be too strong a word—to wait for the final decision by Princeton, even if they have good reasons to believe that it will be negative. The much greater availability of attractive opportunities elsewhere in the late 1960s also put pressure on departments at Princeton to make early recommendations for tenure; this pressure is notably absent today except in the most extraordinary cases.

By far the most disturbing consequence of the reduction in job opportunities is that assistant professors at Princeton who wait until the sixth year for a decision about tenure, and who are then disappointed, sometimes face very difficult career choices. These "choices," if they can be called that, can be especially unappealing to those individuals who have already made great sacrifices to pursue academic careers and who must take into account family responsibilities as well as professional considerations.

It is revealing to examine the positions actually taken by assistant professors who did not receive tenure at Princeton. To obtain such information, we have surveyed six large departments at Princeton, chosen to illustrate the sharp differences that exist among fields: Chemistry, English, History, Mathematics, Mechanical and Aerospace Engineering, and Politics.

In Mechanical and Aerospace Engineering, all of the junior faculty who have not received tenure at Princeton during the last two decades have found good positions at other academic institutions (all but one with tenure) or attractive opportunities in industry, research institutes, or government agencies. The universities to which these faculty members went include the University of Kentucky, Rensselaer Polytechnic Institute, Massachusetts Institute of Technology, Cornell, and the University of Hawaii. Positions outside academia have been found in places such as the Brookhaven National Laboratories, the Exxon Research Laboratories, and the National Bureau of Standards.

In the Chemistry Department, too, the situation today is not very different from what it was twenty years ago. Indeed, Professor Thomas Spiro, the current chairman, believes that the improvement in the standing of the department in recent years has, if anything, increased the competitive advantage of junior faculty members here who seek employment elsewhere. As in the case of Mechanical and Aerospace Engineering, good jobs can be found in industry and in national laboratories as well as at other research universities.

There are nineteen junior faculty members who left Princeton's Mathematics Department in 1960, 1970, and 1980 (the three years on which our survey focused). Almost all proceeded to jobs at the next higher academic rank or to full-time research fellowships. The universities that recruited these faculty members include the University of California at Berkeley, the Courant Institute of Mathematics at New York University, Massachusetts Institute of Technology, the University of California at Los Angeles, and the University of Texas at Austin. The excellence of the Princeton department—which was ranked first nationally among mathematics departments in the most recent survey of the quality of graduate programs and faculties—obviously has a great deal to do with this result. It is also true that the "demand" for mathematicians generally has not declined to the same extent as the "demand" for humanists.

The situation in Politics is more mixed. The chairman, Professor Michael Danielson, notes that junior faculty members seeking other academic positions these days clearly have much less choice than they did, say, twenty years ago. This reduction in options has definitely increased the concern of junior faculty members about their prospects. Ultimately, however, sometimes after extensive search and considerable anxiety, most of those who have wanted to continue in academic life have found reasonably attractive positions. So, if we look only at outcomes, the situation does not appear to be so bad. But the process itself has to be considered as well, and the degree of stress associated with job searches has increased significantly.

Another facet of the situation in Politics deserves mention. While there have always been junior faculty members in Politics who have decided that they would prefer careers outside of academia (in, say, government service, public opinion polling, or the law), the number of people electing such "alternate careers" appears to be increasing. There is not enough evidence to support strong generalizations, but there does seem to be something of an emerging pattern. It appears that more junior faculty members deciding on other careers make such decisions before a final tenure determination is made by Princeton—and they do so on the basis of an evaluation of both tenure prospects at Princeton and the outlook for academic employment generally. They may conclude that sufficiently good jobs in academia simply are not available and that they are therefore better off making an "early" decision to pursue other kinds of opportunities.

In the case of the History Department, we see an intensification of the concerns identified in Politics. While all assistant professors (except one) leaving Princeton in the last two decades are now employed, and chiefly in academic positions, there have been increasing difficulties in finding good jobs in recent years. Several assistant professors have found it necessary to spend a "fellowship year" working on their publications while continuing to seek tenured positions. Others have accepted appointments as assistant professors at other institutions where they thought their long-term tenure prospects were reasonably encouraging. While it is recognized that individuals at Princeton and at other universities with strong history departments are more "visible" and in other respects better situated than their counterparts in departments that have less prominence, it is clear that our junior faculty members are now feeling the same pressures that are endemic to young historians all over the country. It is not an easy time to find a tenured position in history.

Job prospects for junior faculty members in English are more discouraging than in any of the other departments included in this small survey. Of the nine assistant professors who have left Princeton since 1980, one has taken a tenured position elsewhere, six have gone to untenured positions at other colleges and universities, and two have enrolled in professional schools.

Of the six who accepted nontenured appointments in academia, one—after completing a one-year appointment which was not renewed—subsequently decided to leave the academic profession entirely. Another has now moved on to a second untenured position. The other four still have the same untenured appointments they received when they left Princeton.

The two former assistant professors who went on to professional schools did so in large measure because they did not find positions at other universities compatible with their interests and needs. In spite of their teaching experience and publications, they decided that they could not afford to invest more time in the scholarly world—especially given the prospect of the kind of uncertainty and vagabond existence described above. Law schools and business schools increasingly receive applications from holders of Ph.D. degrees precisely for these reasons.

Case histories of these kinds often serve as dramatic reminders to junior colleagues that career opportunities in teaching and scholarship are being severely eroded. This increases pressures on junior faculty members to do everything possible to qualify for tenure, and the quest for tenure can become preoccupying to a degree that is unfortunate both for the individual and for the institution.

Salary Levels

The earliest records of colleges and universities reveal concerns about the adequacy of salary levels. The academic profession has always been relatively poorly remunerated, and junior faculty members, in particular, have always had to worry about how to make ends meet. The intrinsic appeal of academic life—the deep commitment of many to teaching and to scholarship—has yielded "psychic income" that has helped to offset the lack of substantial material rewards. But certainly there are limits to the extent to which faculty members can be expected to underwrite the costs of colleges and universities by accepting minimal compensation. And the present lack of anything approaching job security for junior faculty members makes the question of adequate compensation even more pressing.

The recent period of high inflation—which all of us hope is now past—has been a particularly hard one for academics. While this general proposition may surprise few, the *extent* to which faculty salaries have fallen behind other salaries is not well understood and is, in my view, shocking. In January 1983, *Harper's* published a "scorecard" showing real percentage changes in the average salaries of Americans in more than thirty different occupations. College professors ranked dead last, having experienced an average loss of 21 percent in real wages over the decade from 1970 to 1980. This was almost twice the loss of the next lowest-ranking occupation.

Faculty salaries have been, and continue to be, a top priority for Princeton, and we have had reasonable success in maintaining, and even improving somewhat, our relative position within the world of higher education. But we have by no means succeeded in keeping pace with the Consumer Price Index, as Figure 1 reveals all too clearly. Assistant professors at Princeton have seen their average salaries decline by 15.6 percent in real terms between 1970 and 1983.

Many junior faculty members have been able to survive this difficult period in large part because of the simultaneous increase in the number of two-career families. In the nature of things, this is a once-and-for-all kind of adjustment (unless we are to envision a return to child labor!), and it is of course not an option in all cases. Thus it is simply imperative that the academic profession make up some of the ground that it has lost to inflation during the last ten to fifteen years. Otherwise, there is a real risk that we shall revert to a situation in which only individuals of independent means will feel that they can contemplate an academic career. The intellectual and social consequences of such a development would be disastrous.

As already indicated, the academic profession has lost considerable ground not only to inflation, but to other professions, including professions that represent attractive choices for individuals with the interest and the ability to obtain degrees beyond the baccalaureate. According to the most recent data published by the *Chronicle of Higher Education*, the average salary nationally for a newly appointed assistant professor in 1982–83 was $17,061 in English, $18,508 in the social sciences, $18,975 in chemistry, and $26,533 in engineering.

The comparable salary for a beginning attorney—after reducing stated salaries to a ten-month basis—was $23,430 nationally and (to cite what may be an even more relevant comparison) $34,750 in New York City. The average holder of a master's in business administration started at $23,140 in 1982, and health professionals had beginning salaries that averaged $36,406.

Figure 1
Average Salary of Assistant Professors versus the Consumer Price Index

(1967=100)

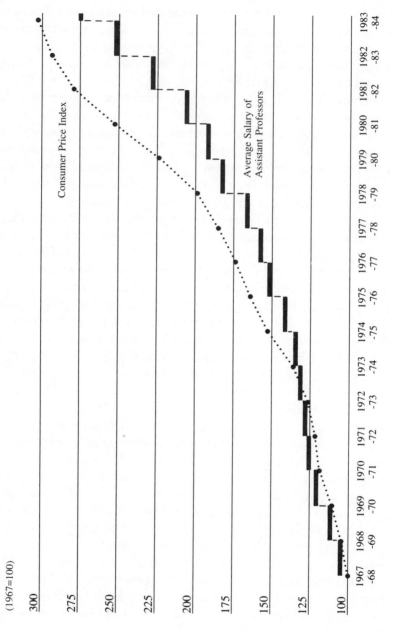

Even in engineering, where beginning salaries in universities must be higher than in other fields to compete with private industry, the gap is wide. At present, the disparity amounts to one third or more of an academic salary, and this is certainly a large enough differential to make the recruitment and retention of junior faculty members exceedingly difficult. One recent example illustrates the problem: An assistant professor at Princeton resigned to accept a position in industry at a salary of $42,000 plus stock options. Robert Jahn, dean of engineering and applied science at Princeton, reports that the graduates of our *bachelor's* program are now receiving offers from industry in the $26,000 to $30,000 range.

The constant pressure to remain at least reasonably competitive in recruiting new assistant professors has made it very difficult to maintain any salary differential among assistant professors related to years of service at Princeton. Generally speaking, we have had to raise starting salaries each year by as large a percentage as overall salary pools were increasing. This has meant that first-year faculty members have received essentially the same salaries as their second-year colleagues . . . and so on right up through what would normally be the assistant professor "scale." The slowing in the rate of inflation should ease this problem somewhat, but it is in large part endemic, since it is rooted in the combination of a generally low level of compensation for junior faculty members and the (associated) need to keep raising starting salaries enough to attract strong candidates.

With salaries as low as they are, junior faculty members often are compelled to supplement their Princeton salaries by accepting outside commitments that may detract from their teaching, scholarship, and University service. Summers, in particular, are frequently devoted to additional teaching or to other pursuits providing compensation, rather than to the scholarship that it was not possible to do during the academic year. This is a particularly acute problem in the humanities and in some of the social sciences, where outside support for summer research is generally less available than in the sciences and engineering.

Perhaps the most debilitating effect of present salary levels is on morale. It is very hard to do one's best, to make the extra effort in teaching or in advising, when personal economic worries loom so large. There is a natural tendency to feel unappreciated, to wonder if it is all worthwhile, and—in the case of assistant professors with families—to ask if it is fair to expect such significant sacrifices on the part of other family members.

Other Pressures

The fact that financial considerations are more easily measurable than many other things does not mean that they are necessarily more important. Any assessment of the current circumstances of junior faculty members has to acknowledge the presence of a number of pressures beyond those related to finances and job security that can interfere with the accomplishment of important professional and personal goals.

Mention has already been made of the greater range of teaching responsibilities assumed by assistant professors today. Overall, this has surely been a favorable development from the standpoint of junior faculty members, and it is most definitely not a source of complaints. It can lead, however, to great pressures on time, especially if a junior faculty member is encouraged to give a lecture course that requires extensive preparation. Assistant professors in the humanities and social sciences often point out how difficult it is to do much scholarship (if any) during the semester in which a lecture course is given for the first time.

The greater degree of participation by junior faculty members in advising, as well as in departmental and University governance, also generates both satisfactions and demands. In some instances, it is necessary for the department to ''protect'' the junior faculty member from too many invitations to serve on committees, to work with student groups, and so on. It is often hard for junior faculty members to know how they should respond to such invitations. They want to be cooperative, they often enjoy such opportunities, and they know that the University values such participation—but they know too that there are only so many hours in the day and that it is also up to them to teach well and to grow as scholars.

Perhaps the most serious new source of pressure on junior faculty members in many fields, including importantly the sciences and engineering, derives from difficulties in obtaining research support. Federal budget constraints have had noticeable effects, even though faculty members at Princeton continue to be more fortunate than those at many other universities in competing for available funds. Until 1981, Princeton's ''success rate'' in applying for federal grants had averaged approximately 71 percent of all proposals submitted during the previous five years. For the past two years, however, Princeton's success rate in obtaining federal grants has decreased, and significantly fewer dollars are being awarded to successful proposals. In 1982, for example, the University achieved 63 percent success in the number of proposals approved, but only 37 percent success in terms of dollars granted in relation to dollars sought. The figures for the previous year were 65 percent and 41 percent respectively.

Although little specific information exists, it is reasonable to assume that the increased competition for research funds has had a greater adverse effect on junior faculty members than on their senior colleagues. The only relevant survey that seems to exist was published by the National Science Foundation in 1980 for the academic year 1978–79. While senior and junior faculty differed very little in the number of proposals they submitted, more requests for support from senior faculty were approved. In engineering, senior faculty had an approval rate of 70 percent as contrasted with 58 percent for junior faculty. In mathematics, the rates were 77 percent for senior faculty and 66 percent for junior faculty. Biological sciences was the one field in which the success rates were the same (74 percent for both junior and senior faculty).

In the humanities and most of the social sciences, junior faculty members have been affected significantly by another pressure: greater competition at university presses for acceptance of manuscripts and increasingly long delays in publication. The traditional expectation at Princeton in these areas of scholarship has been that a young faculty member would have published his or her dissertation and would have embarked upon a second project of significant promise by the end of six years. Now, as one chairman describes the situation, "university presses are in dire economic straits and young professors find it increasingly difficult to get full-length books published by these presses." As a result of these difficulties, he adds, "delays of publication in refereed periodicals have increased inordinately as the pressures to publish radiate down." Publication is, of course, vitally important to junior faculty members, and not just because it enters so significantly into the tenure decision. If tenure is *not* granted, evidence of publication is a necessary credential to compete for academic positions at virtually any other university, and at many colleges as well.

In recent years, yet another set of considerations has increasingly affected the lives and the careers of many junior faculty members. I refer to the choices that must be weighed as a consequence of the marked increased in the number of "dual career" families. Young academics married to other young academics, or to professionals pursuing other careers, naturally want to live and work in areas where the spouse also has ample opportunity for career development. From the standpoint of the junior faculty member, this means that the problem of finding a suitable position becomes the problem of finding *two* suitable positions in the same geographic area.

Nor is this a "one-time" problem. If one person is not reappointed, or fails to receive tenure, the other person may have to decide whether to relinquish a promising position in the uncertain hope of finding something in a new area. Such dilemmas are a major source of added stress, especially when seen in conjunction with the economic pressures that in many situations effectively mandate employment by both husband and wife. There is also often considerable stress, as well as personal sacrifice and a substantial amount of time devoted to travel, in those situations where spouses live apart because the only positions they could find were in communities some distance from each other.

PROBLEMS AND CONCERNS: FOR THE UNIVERSITY

In a fundamental sense, all of the problems and concerns of junior faculty members are simultaneously problems and concerns for the University. Since Princeton depends so much on the contributions made by junior faculty members, anything that makes life difficult for them, or that serves to impede their progress as teachers and scholars, acts directly against the interests of the University. The "identity" between the interests of the junior faculty member and the interests of the University is in this respect total.

There are, however, additional issues for the University over and above the concerns uppermost in the minds of individuals. Specifically, the University has to consider carefully the implications of the current situation for: (1) the quality of the junior faculty members who can be recruited; (2) the diversity of the pool of talent that is available; (3) the promotion/appointment process itself, including the willingness of departments to make "outside" appointments; and (4) the incentives for junior faculty members to value teaching and University citizenship as well as scholarship.

From the perspective of the academic profession generally, there is ample reason for concern about the implications of a depressed (and depressing) job market for the quality of the next generation of scholars. Indeed, it would be astounding if there were not some "response" to such conditions on the part of the most talented undergraduates as they consider a wide range of vocational possibilities.

While qualitative evidence is notoriously difficult to obtain, there is some information that is not merely anecdotal. Since the quality of the pool of potential junior faculty members depends importantly on the quality of the pool of applicants to Ph.D. programs, it is relevant that Ph.D. applications nationally are declining and that "admit rates" (the percentages of applicants to whom institutions offer admission) are rising. At the twenty highly selective universities included in a recent analysis by the Consortium on Financing Higher Education, the admit rate over the last seven years has risen from 35 percent to 43 percent in the humanities and from 25 percent to 33 percent in the social sciences.

President Emeritus Robert Goheen, who now serves as director of the new Mellon Foundation Fellowship Program in the Humanities, has reported on meetings he held with faculty members all across the country last fall:

> With only a very few exceptions, at each place I had confirmed again that many of their brightest undergraduates have not been going on into graduate study recently. Many admitted that they had not been encouraging even the very able to do so. Some said talking down of career prospects in academia was widespread among their colleagues. . . . [There was] a widely shared perception that they are encountering noticeably fewer very bright, very challenging graduate students than ten years ago, and on the whole the quality is down at the graduate level.

A further question is what happens to the many talented individuals who do elect to go to graduate school, this general pattern notwithstanding. There is nothing that can really be called "data" available to answer this question, but there are certainly individual testimonials that are troubling. Earlier this fall, for example, I received the following letter from a former undergraduate who had started out to pursue an academic career:

> I am writing to discuss an issue that I know concerns you deeply: the deterioration of faculty salaries and the consequent decline in academic standards. The recent discovery of a "rising tide of mediocrity" in our nation's schools has brought the problem into sharp focus, but it has troubled me for a number of years. I received a B.A. with highest honors from Princeton . . . took a Ph.D. from Harvard . . . and then went on to a prestigious two-year fellowship. . . . My first book is completed, and I am eager to write a second one. Instead, I will begin a new career on Wall Street in two weeks.
> The reason is money. The salaries of most professors are so low

as to be demeaning. In my mid-thirties, after years of preparation and deferral of income, I stand to earn no more than many [with less education] earn when they are fifteen years younger. As a professor, many of the standard amenities of middle class life would be out of my reach; my family and I would literally be second class citizens.

At the risk of sounding self-serving, I would suggest that my own career path is symptomatic of a general hemorrhaging of talent from the academic world. Very few of the brightest men and women of my generation are attracted to the poverty of academic life. I found, for example, that my peers at graduate school were a less intelligent and dedicated crew than the undergraduates I had known at Princeton. And it was the less impressive graduate students who remained in academe, while the ambitious and venturesome fled to law school, politics, publishing, and business.

There are exceptions, to be sure, and I do not wish to deprecate my many friends who have remained in the academic profession. Nevertheless, the general pattern is clear, and so are its implications: in the years ahead, leading universities will become increasingly mediocre as the great professors who began their careers in the forties, fifties, and sixties are replaced by [their less qualified successors] of the eighties and nineties.

We need to be careful about reading sweeping conclusions into one person's comments, especially when the individual has just made an obviously painful personal decision. Nevertheless, the general concerns that are identified so clearly in this letter certainly demand our attention—and, I think, remedial actions.

At the same time, I want to balance the comments just made by recording my own sense that, by and large, Princeton has been very fortunate in continuing to attract, even under these difficult conditions, unusually able junior faculty members. The attraction of teaching and scholarship is so strong for some people—for some of the ablest people, fortunately—that as long as a university such as Princeton is seeking to make only a few appointments, and as long as it remains competitive, it should be able to attract strong candidates. We have in fact done so, and it would be both unfair and misleading to suggest anything else.

But I do continue to worry about the appeal of the academic profession generally, particularly to those exceedingly capable "generalists" who may feel stronger competing pulls from other professions than do those committed totally to academic pursuits. Universities need both kinds of people, it seems to me, and it would not be healthy to have the intake restricted only to those who will be academics no matter what.

It must also be acknowledged that, even at a university with as much pulling power as Princeton, there have been situations in recent years in which a department has simply been unable to find an outstanding junior faculty member to fill a specific position, and there have been other cases in which searches have gone on for two or three years before a well-qualified candidate could be identified and attracted. The dean of the faculty has also reported more than a few situations in which a department succeeded in identifying one outstanding candidate for an opening at the assistant professor level but was unable to identify other acceptable individuals if the candidate in question could not be persuaded to accept our offer. Thus, there is no doubt about the "shallowness" of the pool, especially in some fields.

In seeking to fill openings, it is also important to the University that there be candidates sufficiently diverse in background and experience that we not fail in our continuing efforts to broaden the composition of the faculty. The problems and concerns cited earlier plainly make it particularly difficult to encourage able minority students to pursue academic careers, and the entire country will lose if it proves impossible for universities to take advantage of the talent that resides in these population groups. At the present time, it is evident that business and other professions are having more success than universities in attracting minority candidates.

Continuing efforts must also be made to recruit able women candidates in all fields, including especially fields in which there have been relatively few women heretofore. This objective, as others, is complicated by the generally discouraging character of the academic labor market as well as by the increasing number of dual-career families. While this presents problems for both sexes, it still seems to create more difficulties in the recruitment of women than in the recruitment of men.

A very different set of potential problems for Princeton is posed by the way our departments sometimes react to the difficulties faced by those younger colleagues who are, in effect, forced out into an inhospitable academic world as a result of nonpromotion at Princeton. When it appears that a junior faculty member is not quite able to surmount the tenure hurdle at Princeton within the requisite six years, it is tempting to give the person more time to make a record that will seem "compelling.'' Nonetheless, the *Rules and Procedures of the Faculty* seem to me right in creating the strongest presumption against extensions of appointments for assistant professors beyond the sixth year. While there are circumstances in which such extensions are clearly justified, they are rare. In general, extensions only prolong the agony of decision for both the faculty member and the University, make relocation more difficult, increase the risk that sentimentality will compromise judgments, and deprive the next generation of scholars of opportunities to demonstrate what they can do.

A related worry is that senior faculty members will care so much about the morale and circumstances of their junior colleagues—who often are, and should be, friends as well as professional associates— that they will be reluctant to ''use'' any of the tenured positions that might go to their junior colleagues for appointments from outside the University. This would have very serious repercussions, of a long-lasting character, since departments need the replenishment of intellectual resources that comes with outside appointments as much as they need to make judicious promotions from the junior ranks. It is often the case that one or two distinguished senior appointments from other universities will rejuvenate a department and, in time, make it a more attractive place for faculty in all ranks, as well as for students. We must not allow ourselves to become timid in making such distinguished appointments because of an altogether commendable desire to advance the careers of our own junior colleagues.

On one very important point of yet another kind, the investigations that preceded the writing of this report are more reassuring than I had expected them to be. I was prepared to believe that the pressures on assistant professors may have already led to some significant diminution in their commitment to teaching, to students, and to the University generally. There is, after all, a cynical view that, in the words of one concerned senior faculty member, ''you only take your scholarship with you''—that time spent on teaching and in working with colleagues and students is ''lost time'' that will not help in securing the ''next job.'' It is to the great credit of the junior faculty now at Princeton that this attitude seems to be held by very few. For most, the internal compass, as well as the direction provided by senior colleagues, seems to point strongly toward a much more balanced sense of responsibilities.

It remains true that, as someone once said, ''machines do what they can, people do what they will.'' Morale, outlook, and enthusiasm matter enormously to the achievement of goals central to Princeton. If junior faculty members find enjoyment and satisfaction in their years at Princeton, their students and their colleagues—the entire University community—will benefit.

The extent to which the morale of junior faculty members has survived various assaults is attested to in moving language by one department chairman who responded to my query on this subject as follows:

> You asked us to say a word about faculty opportunities, especially those of junior faculty roundabout. Let me begin by saying the obvious—namely, that Princeton's junior faculty, at least in the areas where I can measure their strength, is a remarkable group of young people. And they're remarkable not the least, it seems to me, for their grace under pressure, pressure that is fairly staggering when we consider the odds against these people. But still they maintain a healthy group spirit, a camaraderie, not of the aggrieved but rather of the intense, the committed, and the gifted.

WAYS TO HELP

The importance of junior faculty members to every aspect of the life of the University is evident, and we ought not to be reluctant to acknowledge that fact. Words do matter, and expressions of appreciation and encouragement can make a great deal of difference—provided, of course, that they are genuine and that they do not pretend to wish away the hard realities.

It is also important to do what we can about these "hard realities"—softening them, as it were, whenever that is possible. As is true of almost all complex problems, there is no magic wand that can make everything better. But there are things that can be done, both nationally and at the level of the individual college or university.

At the national level, all interested parties—governments (where appropriate), foundations, corporations, and individual donors—need to be encouraged to support the establishment of a modest number of new positions for junior faculty above what might be called for in the short run simply on the basis of enrollment. This is especially important in the humanities because that is where the problem of immediate job opportunities is most acute. Without such positions, the danger is that too many good people, with excellent training and considerable potential, will be lost from the academic profession permanently.

While this may not seem like a serious matter at present, there will be an upturn in enrollments (and larger numbers of retirements) starting in about the mid-1990s, and the country needs to prepare now for the number of able scholars and teachers who will be needed then. Too short-sighted an approach to faculty staffing can create more difficult, and more expensive, problems later on. Thus, for reasons that are in no sense sentimental, there is a compelling national interest in making it possible for exceptional individuals who might otherwise be diverted into other fields to pursue academic careers.

The Mellon Foundation has been a leader in recognizing this problem and in acting to address it. Since 1974, the foundation has initiated several programs at major universities, Princeton among them, for the express purpose of enabling these universities to "add on" several new assistant professorships (and associate professorships) in the humanities. These programs are designed both to increase opportunities for young scholars and to assure a flow of fresh talent into the universities during a period when faculty growth has been sharply curtailed. At Princeton, the Mellon program has enabled us to offer positions to exceptional junior faculty members who would otherwise have been lost to us, and conceivably to the academic profession as a whole.

Of course, individual institutions also have both an opportunity and an obligation to provide positions for talented young faculty members. In planning A Campaign for Princeton, it has been our hope that the clear importance of providing recognition (as well as funding) for exceptional assistant professors would encourage donors to endow junior faculty positions in all fields. The results to date of this particular appeal have not met our expectations fully, but it is encouraging to report the establishment of the American Cyanamid Preceptorship (molecular biology), the Robert Remsen Laidlaw '04 Preceptorship in the Humanities, the Manufacturers Hanover Preceptorship in Economics, the New Jersey Bell Preceptorship (electrical engineering and computer science), and the D. T. Suzuki Preceptorship in Religion.

Research support is another major need, and in this respect the Sloan Foundation has long been known for its support of young faculty in selected scientific fields, including mathematics. Each year, the Sloan Fellowship Program provides technical assistance, summer salaries, professional travel, released time from teaching or leave time for research, and other forms of support for approximately eighty-five young scientists at some forty-five institutions. Through these highly prestigious awards, the foundation seeks both to recognize outstanding young scientists and to stimulate advances in fundamental research.

Federal policy toward the support of young faculty in the humanities, social sciences, natural sciences, and engineering will also play an important role in determining how successfully young academics are able to pursue their own research. In the sciences and engineering, there are several federal programs geared toward the young investigator, especially at the National Science Foundation and the National Institutes of Health. In the humanities, however, there is little federal help available, except for the American Council of Learned Societies Fellowships for recent Ph.D. recipients which are partially funded through the National Endowment for the Humanities.

Engineering is one area where corporate support can be critical in allowing universities and technical institutes to create conditions that will encourage junior faculty members to remain in academic settings. There has been some very enlightened leadership, and special mention should be made of the IBM Faculty Development Program, the Atlantic Richfield Foundation grants in support of junior faculty in science and engineering, the Shell Corporation Faculty Career Initiation Fund, the Faculty Development Program sponsored by the American Electronics Association through which the Hewlett-Packard Company has provided support to junior faculty at Princeton, and the highly significant Exxon Corporation program of grants for support of junior faculty members and graduate students in leading departments of engineering.

Providing adequate salaries for junior faculty members is, of course, essential in all fields. Budgetary constraints facing institutions of higher education make it very hard to do what needs to be done, especially when there are so many competing claims on scarce funds. At Princeton, we have identified the salary needs of faculty at all levels as a top priority in A Campaign for Princeton, and the response to date has been strongly affirmative. Still, it takes so much new endowment to make even a modest difference in the size of salary pools that no campaign, however successful, will address these needs adequately. This is a problem area that will require continuing attention—and a determination to allocate substantial funds from operating budgets, however tight they may be.

It would be highly desirable, as well, to provide targeted financial help for junior faculty members who wish to devote their summers to scholarship but who do not have access to sponsored research funds. This mode of assistance could be provided in such a way as to reward good teaching, thus strengthening the right inclinations at the same time that real needs are being met. Another most welcome form of support (which could also be conditioned on excellent teaching performance) would be supplementary funding for research assistance, travel, and similar expenses associated with scholarly pursuits.

As important as these tangible forms of help are, they are by no means the only ways in which the University shows its concern for junior faculty members. How the University handles personnel decisions is another key determinant of the attitudes of junior faculty members toward their work and themselves. Plainly, the evaluations that lead to recommendations concerning reappointment, advancement, and salary increases must be scrupulously fair. Procedures need to be clearly described and evenhanded.

In addition to being treated fairly, if rigorously, in the review process, assistant professors need to be treated well in all other respects while they are at Princeton. This includes assistance in solving such vexing problems as finding satisfactory housing. It also includes paying reasonable attention to the interests of junior faculty members as well as to the needs of the department in assigning teaching responsibilities.

Under present circumstances especially, generous help with placement when assistant professors are not promoted is also of major importance. Most departments work very hard at this, but there may well be room for further improvement. The various professional associations are much concerned about the effectiveness of recruitment and appointment processes viewed nationally, and we should certainly do all that we can to assist our junior colleagues to cope with what are bound to be difficult and often emotionally draining experiences.

* * * * *

Whatever we can do to improve the lot of assistant professors will serve not only the individuals themselves but also the University and higher education viewed broadly. This is so for many reasons, but in concluding this report perhaps particular mention should be made of the extent to which the mood and morale of junior faculty members affect the ways undergraduates and graduate students perceive the academic profession. If able students, with a wide range of options, are to become interested in academic careers, it will often be because of their admiration for a young faculty member whom they came to know through a class, an advising relationship, or a research project. Attitudes toward teaching and scholarship, and toward academic life more generally, are communicated directly and powerfully by junior faculty members.

Many years ago, Woodrow Wilson saw in this aspect of University life the source of much strength for the process of education. In his annual report to the Board of Trustees in December 1905, President Wilson commented on the rejuvenation in the University that had occurred as a result of the addition of fifty-three new members of the faculty, most of whom were "preceptors":

It is not the amount of work done that pleases us so much as its character and the zest with which it is undertaken. The greater subjects of study pursued at a university, those which constitute the elements of a well-considered course of undergraduate training, are of course intrinsically interesting; but the trouble has been that the undergraduates did not find it out. Our pleasure in observing the change . . . comes from seeing the manifest increase of willingness and interest with which the undergraduates now pursue their studies.

In our day, as in that earlier time, the quality, the commitment, and the good humor of junior faculty members affect greatly the health of the entire academic enterprise.

PART FIVE

Diversity, Opportunity, and Financial Aid

In the context of the eighteenth century, the fledgling college at Princeton was unusually diverse. Its students came from throughout the colonies, not just from New Jersey and its middle Atlantic neighbors. Its graduates entered a variety of professions, not just the ministry. Its charter explicitly protected religious freedom, and its first scholarship (for thirteen pounds) was awarded to a student in the Class of 1759.

Nonetheless, it was not until the late 1960s that Princeton began to reflect the full diversity of American society—women as well as men; racial, religious, and ethnic minorities; the economically disadvantaged and the handicapped; and others of talent and determination for whom an education at Princeton would have been unthinkable in an earlier era.

The Princeton of the 1950s was far removed from the world of a young Ohio tennis player named William G. Bowen, the son of a cash register salesman, who graduated from a public high school in Cincinnati and then enrolled at nearby Denison University in the fall of 1951 to study economics and eventually to succeed Richard Lugar (later mayor of Indianapolis and U.S. Senator) as student body president. His academic accomplishments led to graduate study at Princeton and rapid promotion through its faculty ranks so that only ten years after first arriving as a graduate student he had become, at age thirty-one, one of the youngest full professors in the University's history.

His own experience—in being afforded these opportunities, in adjusting to this unfamiliar environment, in learning from those whose backgrounds and perspectives were so different from his own—nurtured a deep and lasting appreciation for the importance to Princeton, and to the nation, of diversity, of opportunity, and of the financial aid programs that enable students to realize their highest aspirations.

This chapter begins with four Opening Exercises addresses that discuss the educational significance, the tensions, and the rewards of diversity:

• the opportunities that it presents and the obligations that it entails (1977);

• the importance of seeing beyond group labels and stereotypes to the individualism of others, while maintaining a "healthy individualism" of one's own (excerpts, 1978);

• the ways in which campus life is organized, particularly through the residential colleges, to encourage "the difficult unity of inclusion" (excerpts, 1983); and

• respect as the essential bond in any community dedicated to both diversity and freedom (1987).

The concept of opportunity—of what it means for individuals, for the society, and for Princeton—is then developed in remarks from two Commencements, the 1982 remarks on the topic of "No Limits," and the 1984 remarks on the difference between an "elitism of fact" and an "elitism of attitude."

For colleges and universities throughout the country, the commitments to diversity and opportunity of the past two decades have required thoughtful attention to relationships among the races, and to policy questions of various kinds. The chapter continues with the 1982 Opening Exercises address which examined the subject of race and relations among the races at Princeton. Following this address are two documents that focus on major questions of national policy having to do with the relevance of race in admissions and in employment. The first is a 1977 essay on a case then before the U.S. Supreme Court (*The Regents of the University of California v. Allan Bakke*) that asked whether and how considerations of race could properly be taken into account in arriving at admission decisions; this essay was cited at several points in Justice Lewis Powell's pivotal decision upholding policies such as those followed at Princeton. The second is testimony on "Affirmative Action: Purposes, Concepts, Methodologies" that was presented before a Department of Labor hearing in 1975 at the request of the American Council on Education and the Association of American Universities.

The chapter concludes with the 1983 annual report, entitled "Maintaining Opportunity: Undergraduate Financial Aid at Princeton." The report discusses the importance of financial aid and its history at Princeton, current policies and practices, policy alternatives, and concerns about the future.

Diversity: The Opportunities
and the Obligations

OPENING EXERCISES ADDRESS
SEPTEMBER 1977

. . . My subject this morning is a characteristic of our student body that I believe we have come to take too much for granted. To be sure, our neglect is not verbal. We speak about it, and very frequently; but often in what seems to me almost a sloganeering way, and I do not feel that many of us appreciate fully either the opportunities that it affords or the obligations that it entails. I refer to the *diversity* that you represent.

This diversity has many dimensions. It is reflected in the 50 states and approximately 71 countries from which our student body comes; in the varied occupations of your parents; in a wide variety of economic circumstances; in the presence among you of students of both sexes and many races and ethnic groups; of students who are committed strongly to any one of a number of different faiths and students who do not consider themselves religious at all; of students who have a great variety of talents and interests, ranging from the arts to athletics, from chemistry to classics; and, finally, of students with a wide array of viewpoints on questions of every kind, from the literary to the political.

Needless to say, there are even differences among you in academic ability and in the strength of personal qualities. I hope and believe, however, that these differences are all above "threshold." That is, we do not admit anyone who in our judgment lacks the basic qualifications necessary to meet our requirements. We are fortunate in having large numbers of very able applicants from whom to choose, and it would be both unfair to the individual concerned and foolish from the standpoint of the objectives of the University to admit any student who seemed to lack either the academic ability or the character, motivation, and other personal qualities that are important to us. So, I would not want any of you to think that "diversity" extends to including in the student body those who might be expected to disappoint us. None of you was chosen to serve as a horrible example.

There are three respects in which the diversity of the student body of today has roots in the founding in 1746 of what was then called the

College of New Jersey. First, the Charter of the College was quite unusual for its time in promising that students of every religious denomination should have "equal liberty of education"; that all students would be welcome, "any different sentiments in religion notwithstanding." Second, while the main intention of the founders of our College, as of all other American colleges of that time, was to educate ministers, they also declared their hope that the College would be "a means of raising up men that will be useful in the other learned professions. . . ." And, as we know from the recent publication of biographies of the 338 students who attended the College in its first 21 classes, somewhat less than half of the students in these classes in fact became ministers. Even then the prospective doctors and lawyers were much in evidence among us.

Finally, this same study of our earliest students reveals that they came from a surprisingly broad geographical area. We are told that "in these years almost all of William and Mary's students came from Virginia, and perhaps over 90 percent of Harvard's from Massachusetts; . . . Yale drew approximately 75 percent of its students from Connecticut." In striking contrast, only about one quarter of Princeton's students came from New Jersey, and there was a good representation from many of the provinces. James Madison, of the Class of 1771, a Virginian, said that he first learned what it was to be an American as a student in Nassau Hall. The author of the introduction to this biographical dictionary of early Princetonians suggests that the wide geographical dispersion of the alumni may have accounted in some measure for their extraordinary role in the public affairs of their time and even for the fact that by the end of 1775 only 3 percent of living alumni were Loyalists, in contrast to Harvard, where 16 percent of the alumni took the British side. In that important respect, we were less diverse!

In citing these instances of diversity in our early history, I certainly do not mean to suggest that our present conception of the educational values of a diverse student body was present in eighteenth-century Princeton. It was not, even in embryonic form. The diversity that existed in the early years of the College was due in part to a general sense that people of different faiths, living in different provinces, should have a *right* to attend, and in part to a straightforward economic imperative: the College needed students to pay tuition, and for that reason alone it seemed unwise to be too parochial. This is very different from our present view, which I want to discuss more fully in a few minutes, which stresses that differences among students can contribute very positively and very directly to the educational process itself.

The present view could not have prevailed in the eighteenth century, at Princeton or at any other college here or abroad, because it is derived from a philosophy of education which was largely unknown at that time and certainly was not accepted. To believe that students (and faculty) should learn from those who come from different backgrounds, who have had different experiences, and who hold different views, you have to believe that the purpose of education is to open minds and to encourage independent thinking. I wonder how many of us realize what a radical conception of education this is, in how few parts of the world it prevails today, and even how recent it is in countries such as the United States and Great Britain, widely regarded (especially by us) as ancient bastions of free inquiry.

Lawrence Stone, Dodge Professor of History at Princeton and one of the foremost scholars in the history of education, has argued forcefully that from the middle ages through most of the seventeenth, eighteenth, and even nineteenth centuries, a primary purpose of education in Europe and in America was more or less straightforward indoctrination in accepted values as well as in accepted ideas. People who held what were thought to be odd views were often repressed if not dismissed, and academic freedom as we know it now did not exist. In explaining the tenacity of what he calls the "old ideal," Professor Stone writes: "After all, whenever society is precarious—and it usually is—there is inevitably a demand that dissidents and heretics be suppressed. . . . New knowledge disturbs people. . . . For most of recorded history those in authority have thought it wiser to create closed minds than open minds. . . . Accordingly, it was perfectly natural to condemn Socrates to death for asking too many awkward questions."

It took a very long time for "the new ideal of the open mind" to challenge this conventional wisdom. One of the first and clearest statements of this new conception of education was made in the 1830s by Sir William Hamilton, who wrote: "The highest end of education is not to dictate truths but to stimulate exertion. Since the mind is not invigorated or developed—in a word, educated—by the mere possession of truths but by the energy expended in their quest and contemplation." There was then a long period of debate over the right function of universities. Professor Stone tells us that as late as the 1860s, the Trustees of Harvard would not give a chair in history to an avowed agnostic for fear that he would teach his students a "doctrine of despair."

Indeed, it was not until the early 1900s that the twin notions of the open mind as an end of education and of academic freedom as a necessary instrument in pursuit of truth became generally accepted—largely as a consequence of a growing recognition of the need for freedom of inquiry if research and the advancement of knowledge were to be encouraged. Today I suppose it would be widely agreed that the principles of the open mind and freedom of inquiry are fundamental characteristics of American higher education. They are underpinnings of an extraordinary educational system that is an admired model for much of the world. But it is well to remember that these principles are still relatively new—and, as the McCarthy period in the 1950s and the extreme activities of some radical student groups in the late 1960s both remind us, subject to continuing challenge.

In the case of Princeton, Woodrow Wilson signaled the nature of this University's commitment when he made some remarks in 1909 about the purposes of education which have been quoted often since then. He said, "We should seek to impart in our colleges . . . not so much learning itself as the spirit of learning. . . . It consists in the power to distinguish good reasoning from bad, in the power to digest and interpret evidence, and in a habit of catholic observation and preference for a non-partisan point of view, in an addiction to clear and logical processes of thought and yet an instinctive desire to interpret rather than stick in the letter of the reasoning, in a taste for knowledge, and a deep respect for the integrity of the human mind."

This continues to be a fine statement of much of what we intend by liberal education at Princeton. It is particularly valuable for the way in which it expresses the subtle relationship between fundamental values and principles of liberal education that do not change . . . and the ever-changing, ever-developing nature of knowledge itself.

In his time, President Wilson worked hard to give substance to this conception of a liberal education, especially through good faculty appointments and the introduction of the preceptorial method of instruction. I know of no evidence, however, that anyone at that time, at Princeton or elsewhere, thought very consciously about trying to serve these ends through enrolling a diverse student body.

Of course, there was diversity in that there were students from many parts of the country and from some other countries. Also, contrary to some of our current stereotypes of the Princeton of that era, there were students from poor families as well as students of means. (The University's first scholarship fund was established in 1792.) And, campus political opinion was far from monolithic then as now—Norman Thomas, we should remember, was the valedictorian of the Class of 1905. Still, Princeton was all male, overwhelmingly Protestant, and overwhelmingly white. As far as we can tell from the records, there were no black students at Princeton during the period from the Civil War to World War II; and, as we know from some moving testimonials, more than a few of the relatively small number of Jewish students often had reason to feel isolated and unwanted.

I mention these facts not to berate our predecessors. While we need to be aware of our history, little good is accomplished by trying retroactively to hold people who lived in a different era to the standards of today, and both institutions and individuals have difficulty making substantial forward progress if much of their energy goes to flagellating themselves. . . . Yet it is important for all of us to understand where we have been and particularly how the record of the past affects the perceptions of people today—especially those of us who come from groups that were either excluded altogether or not given the opportunity to enjoy a full sense of acceptance.

In more recent years there has of course been a very substantial broadening in the composition of the student body measured along many dimensions. If we had more time together this morning it would be instructive to examine in detail the various considerations that led to these changes and the specific steps that have been important in bringing them about (which include not just the more dramatic and highly publicized events such as the active recruitment of minority students and the admission of women, but also such things as the decision to recruit students in a wide variety of special fields, including the creative arts, the opening of a University kosher dining facility, and increased efforts to enroll students from regions outside the northeast).

What I want to emphasize, however, is not what has happened, but what the changes that have occurred *can* imply for the lives we lead on this campus. I emphasize the word "can" because what is involved here is opportunity, not an assured result. The outcomes for all of us, and for the University, depend greatly on each of you.

How do we learn? In important part from thinking on our own—about what a faculty member has said, about the ideas presented in a book, or about what the results of an experiment seem to imply. But we also learn, and often very powerfully, from our interactions with others, in classroom and laboratory settings to be sure, but also from the myriad contacts that students have with each other in a residential university.

This is hardly a new doctrine at Princeton; but it is only in the last few decades, I think, that we have come to appreciate its full applicability. The learning environment is a far richer one when it contains not only individuals who come from cities and rural areas, from different economic backgrounds, from different regions and countries, and who represent a wide array of academic and extracurricular talents and interests, but also women as well as men, and students who come from a wide variety of religious and cultural backgrounds and who bring with them various senses of what it is like to grow up as a member of a racial or ethnic minority in America. The diverse student body that we have today offers unprecedented opportunities for you to learn from your differences, to stimulate one another to reexamine even your most deeply held assumptions about yourselves and your world.

Taking advantage of these opportunities can be extremely rewarding from the standpoint of the personal growth of each of you individually; and it can be extremely important, too, for the kind of society in which all of us will live. Your ability to make constructive contributions after you leave Princeton, whatever you do, is going to depend significantly on your understanding of other people and your capacity to work sensitively and effectively with them. The diversity of our student body, combined with the small size and residential nature of Princeton, offers greater opportunities for this kind of learning than many of you will ever know again. . . .

To be sure, there are also frustrations—and even dangers—inherent in a diverse student body; and that is one reason why it is important for us to think about our obligations as well as our opportunities. It is easy, for example, to feel keenly frustrated, as I confess I do at times, by the substantial gap that exists between what might be and what actually is. I believe we are only at the beginning of what it ought to be possible for us to accomplish. Thus far we have not succeeded at all fully in obtaining for students or for faculty the educational benefits that should follow from our diversity. Apathy, self-consciousness, misunderstanding, and distrust are hard to overcome.

You can make a difference. I hope that each member of this University community will feel an obligation to do much more than find a comfortable niche here—that you will not be content simply to surround yourself with those who seem most like you. I hope that each of you will feel an obligation to reach out sensitively to others across distances of all kinds—of race, religion, politics, whatever—and to do so without expecting positive results every time. We need to have enough trust in others and in ourselves to be willing to take some risks, to be able to survive an occasional rebuff. We need to be able to learn from our failures to relate successfully to someone else as from the failures of others to understand us. It is, after all, only by taking some chances, by putting ourselves on the line some of the time, that we can hope to enjoy the real satisfactions that come from learning and growing.

If we should be realistic in recognizing that at an individual level trying to form new friendships can be painful as well as exhilarating, we should also be realistic in recognizing that the presence on campus of students of different backgrounds and persuasions can create tensions between groups. It would be astounding if this were not so, and learning to cope with such tensions, rather than trying to assume them away, can be profoundly educational.

To cite just one example of what can happen, a speaker invited by one group may well state views that seem not just wrong but offensive in the extreme to others. We do not believe in censoring ideas, and the University is committed unequivocally to freedom of expression and to the right of any group of students or faculty members to hear speakers of its choice. Accordingly, over the last few years we have had an extraordinary variety of controversial people on the campus, including William Buckley, Amiri Baraka, I. F. Stone, Golda Meir, Sa'adat Hassan, and William Shockley.

The appearances of such individuals can be thought-provoking and stimulating, but they can also be traumatic and disturbing—especially when it is mistakenly thought that an invitation to a speaker implies an institutional endorsement of his or her views (it most emphatically does not), or when the motives of the particular group extending the invitation are themselves a source of controversy. In any event, I am convinced not just that it would be fundamentally wrong to try to limit the viewpoints that are expressed (though I believe that deeply), but, more positively, that real learning often occurs when people with different perspectives confront the most sensitive questions together, openly and directly; when pain, frustration, and even anger can no longer be hidden, creating at least a prospect, though never a promise, that some measure of greater understanding will follow.

In keeping with my theme that diversity entails risks and obligations as well as opportunities, let me add that tensions of this kind, whether growing out of differences in race, sex, religion, background, politics, or simply personal predilections, can also be extremely damaging to individuals and institutions. As one of my faculty colleagues commented earlier this summer in discussing this general topic: "I am suspicious of the idea of the University as encounter group." So am I, and that is not of course what I am advocating.

We need to be careful to keep in mind our own priorities and the priorities of the University. Your first obligation as students is to your academic work, just as the first obligation of the faculty is to their teaching and scholarship. The pressures and tensions to which I have been alluding, along with the many other opportunities for personal growth that follow from our diversity, must not be allowed to become hopelessly distracting or to serve as excuses for failing to meet basic responsibilities.

There is also an even more serious danger for the institution—and thus ultimately for both present and prospective students and faculty members—inherent in the kinds of disagreements and confrontations that can occur so easily in a university that includes many able and energetic people of different persuasions. As can be seen most vividly through the experiences of some universities in other countries, differences can become so pronounced that they lead to the loss of a sense of common purpose and even to the establishment of what are essentially warring camps determined to get their own way no matter what the cost to others or to the institution. The university as we know it is a fragile entity, all too easily damaged by those who would use it for their own ends.

We share an obligation to do all that we can to prevent differences in perspective from degenerating into destructive polarizations. When an academic community becomes polarized in any way, the result can be new forms of intolerance and pressures which work against the spirit of free inquiry and the ability of the institution to get on with its essential business of teaching and scholarship. The West German universities, for example, seem to have suffered seriously as a consequence of political polarization, and their experience suggests anew how important it is for the university as an institution to avoid becoming the captive of any partisan or ideological point of view. Countries as different from each other as Brazil and China offer other examples.

If we are to avoid this kind of outcome, what is required, first of all, is a continuing commitment to the freedom of each individual student and faculty member to think freshly and independently, free of every form of coercion. Required too is a large measure of forbearance on the part of students, faculty, and alumni. The university advances important causes in part by assuring that both their champions *and* their opponents have a full opportunity to argue their cases. This implies a good deal of institutional restraint and an ability to differentiate between the right of the individual to argue vigorously for what he or she believes and the obligation of the institution as such to remain open in fact and in appearance to different points of view.

Thus, the freedom and the diversity of the Princeton of today, which offer such great opportunities to learn, imply a corresponding obligation to respect differences of opinion and to avoid pressing one's own position in ways that could be harmful to the rights of others and to the long-term ability of the University to serve as a center of learning. We need to put ahead of our differences, which in themselves should be healthy, a common commitment to the fundamental values of the University. In the words of a perceptive graduate of ours in the Class of 1976, Eva Lam, we should feel "united in our differences."

There is a final aspect of diversity I want to discuss. It too is a danger, albeit a danger of a quite different kind, associated not so much with the fact of diversity as with the way we approach the subject. Any time that we talk about students in terms of categories—whether defined by sex, race, religion, economics, geography, academic field, or even extracurricular interest—we run a risk of losing sight of the primacy of the individual. It is the unique character and personality of each of you that is most important. There is no set of categories, however complex, that can do anything but injustice to the extraordinary variety of talents, aspirations, attitudes, inclinations—and foibles—that you contribute to this University community.

If so much emphasis is to be given to your individuality, why then talk at all about group attributes, social categories, call them what you will? The answer, it seems clear to me, is that these attributes are relevant precisely because they contribute to the identity of each individual. They contribute to it, but they do not determine it. Thus it is both realistic and right that we be sensitive to all of those aspects of a person's background that make that person what he or she is today. But it is also realistic and right that we not group people together under labels in such a way as to depersonalize them—to deprive them of their right to be different from others who may be given the same label. And it is essential that we not attach undue importance to the labels themselves; that we not let them get in the way of knowing each other as individuals—who laugh and cry, as well as reflect and argue, who share a common humanity.

This too is an obligation, a very important one, which I hope all of us will accept as we celebrate our differences and strive together to learn from them.

A Healthy Individualism

EXCERPTED FROM THE
OPENING EXERCISES ADDRESS
SEPTEMBER 1978

. . . I'm sure many of you are familiar with one educational model often suggested as an ideal: Mark Hopkins on one end of a log, and a single student on the other end. That model minimizes group pressures and distractions and encourages a certain kind of individualism. But it is fraught with obvious dangers of its own and it has never seemed to me to represent anything like an ideal approach to education. There is too much to learn from others, there are too many perspectives to be shared, for us to be content with any educational relationship that is so restricted. As one of my favorite teachers, Professor Jacob Viner, used to say: "There is no limit to the nonsense one may propound if he thinks too long alone."

A principal strength of any great university is precisely the presence of a wide variety of able people who contribute many different viewpoints and experiences. The right kinds of interactions with such people can be the essence of a good education. They can spark one's imagination, broaden one's perceptions, erode one's prejudices, and even help to correct one's most blatant errors. This is of course hardly a new notion, and over 300 years ago Milton wrote: "Where there is much desire to learn, there of necessity will be much arguing, much writing, many opinions: for opinion . . . is but knowledge in the making."

The residential character of Princeton, our relatively small scale, our history and our traditions combine to make strong the "community" aspects of life in this University but these generally beneficent influences create a tension in our pursuit of individuality that I think we do well to examine as candidly as we can. It is a tension between the need to be genuinely independent and comfortable in saying exactly what we believe and the equally clear need for supportive relationships with our peers and others whom we like and admire. These relationships can either help to strengthen our own capacities for independent thought by challenging us to grow, while also comforting us when we falter, or they can envelop us in a kind of group cocoon which is stultifying in the extreme if we allow those who are the most visibly self-assured to do our thinking for us. Possibilities of both kinds are present, especially in this kind of environment, and I believe that the quality of your education, and even your future contributions to society, will depend significantly on which you accentuate.

Satisfying as it can be to enjoy the special pleasure, like no other, that comes from understanding something for yourself, the freedom to do so can be a very frightening freedom—and sometimes intensely painful. Deciding what you believe is, for one thing, extremely hard work. Most interesting, important questions are complex, and the harder one tries to unravel the complexity, the more difficult it becomes to accept simplistic answers. Moreover, thinking for one's self is frequently upsetting and disruptive. It can require giving up cherished certainties and disagreeing with friends who may (however wrongly) interpret such disagreement as disloyalty or rejection of them. It is often so much easier to submerge doubts and disagreements—simply to go along.

There are many countries in which universities avoid imposing such burdens on their students—or on their faculty members, for that matter—by in effect settling many questions of politics, religion, or even literature for them. Our commitment to individualism is in direct conflict with any such approach, and we try hard to minimize the extent to which the University as an institution is seen as taking positions on issues that are not educational in character. It is very important, in our view, that the University be hospitable to the heretic as well as to the sturdiest proponent of the conventional wisdom, that the University be genuinely open to all points of view. Our task is to help you to develop the penchant for coming to your own conclusions, as well as to acquire the knowledge, the skills, the sensitivity, and the values needed to do so responsibly.

Surely one of the most passionate advocates of individualism was the Danish thinker Søren Kierkegaard. Professor Walter Kaufmann, of our Department of Philosophy, notes that in describing himself, Kierkegaard wrote: "If I were to desire an inscription for my tombstone, I should desire none other than 'That Individual.' " On a wall of the library of the president's house at Princeton, there is a medallion of Kierkegaard, in recognition of the fact that it was in that library that the distinguished biographer and translator of Kierkegaard, Walter Lowrie, did so much of his scholarly work. Thus, the subject of individualism is, as it were, constantly before me; and, given the mission of the University, that is as it should be.

In one of the "notes" that he wrote near the end of his life, at the time of his attack on the established church of Denmark, Kierkegaard discussed the relationship of the individual to the group in these terms:

> There is a view of life which conceives that where the crowd is, there also is the truth, and that in truth itself there is need of having the crowd on its side. There is another view of life which conceives that wherever there is a crowd there is untruth, so that (to consider for a moment the extreme case), even if each individual, each for himself in private, were to be in possession of the truth, yet in case they were all to get together in a crowd—a crowd to which any sort of *decisive* significance is attributed, a voting, noisy, audible crowd—untruth would at once be in evidence . . . a crowd in its very concept is the untruth, by reason of the fact that it renders the individual completely impenitent and irresponsible, or at least weakens his sense of responsibility by reducing it to a fraction.

Of course, Kierkegaard recognized that it was often necessary, as a practical matter, to come to decisions through participation in groups—as, for example, in reaching the political decisions that bind all of us. But his concern was particularly for questions of an ethical and religious character—and for the effects on the individual of being part of a group whatever the nature of the issue. In that same essay he describes instances in which crowds performed acts of violence for which no individual would take responsibility, and I am afraid that each of us can cite other examples over the last fifty years more terrifying than anything Kierkegaard envisioned.

Since Kierkegaard's time society has changed in ways that, if anything, make it all the more important to encourage a vigorous individualism. So many pressures have pulled, and continue to pull, in the other direction: the anonymity of bigness, the disintegration caused by specialization, the high degree of organization characteristic of modern life. It is much harder to feel a sense of personal control, or of personal responsibility, when so many aspects of life are determined by powerful external forces that seem impersonal precisely because that is what they are.

Such circumstances put a special premium on the ability—and the willingness—to emphasize first principles; to integrate the elements of life; to try to see the world whole. This is a harder task than ever before. But it is also, for that very reason, more important than ever before. And it is a task that can be performed only by thoughtful *individuals*.

There is another characteristic of the times that underscores the need for renewed emphasis on the individual: the apparently strong tendency for people to think of themselves, and of others, very much in terms of groups of one kind or another—as defined, for example, by occupation, religion, sex, race, or ethnic category. It is an easy tendency to understand—and, for that matter, to defend. The apparent vulnerability of individuals, if left alone, encourages group solidarity. Also, organized groups are often more effective than individuals in addressing important concerns. Much good can come from group efforts, and my intent is not to disparage them; it is rather to urge that we not allow them to depersonalize us, to diminish our responsibility to be ourselves, or to deprive us of the benefits of contacts with individuals outside "our group."

Last June we had the privilege of hearing a remarkable Baccalaureate address in this chapel by Dr. Gerson Cohen, the parent of a graduating senior and the distinguished chancellor of the Jewish Theological Seminary in New York. Near the end of his address, Chancellor Cohen spoke forcefully of the benefits of, in his words, "open and direct dialogue of members of different faiths, not in the spirit of apologetic or disputation but simply out of the desire to learn and to become spiritually enriched." As he said so well, what we must seek is "the kind of pluralistic society that does not level commitments and differences but refines them. . . . It is an atmosphere in which differences can be encountered without fear or threat."

Difficult as it is to foster and to put into practice, that is the spirit that ought to characterize all of our relationships and ought to encourage us especially to reach out to those whose backgrounds are most different from our own. We have so much to learn from each other, so much to give to each other, that we cannot allow ourselves to act or to think in terms of stereotypes. We need to see each other as individuals—each too complex, too rich in detail, too special, to be defined by any group label.

A true commitment to individualism, seen in this light, leads not to self-centeredness or indifference to those around us. It leads rather to the kind of concern for others that is derived from recognition of our diversity and yet awareness of how much we are alike in fundamental respects—from an acceptance of the common humanity which unites us through our differences. Such an attitude of mind—and of spirit—does not just accept the infinite complexity of human beings grudgingly, but rejoices in the uniqueness of each one of us, characterized as all of us are by a mysterious amalgam of great positive possibilities and so many weaknesses and vulnerabilities.

It is, finally, this extraordinary freedom to be an individual, together with the natural extension of this same awesome privilege to others, that is so central to the spirit of the University, and that needs today, as always, to be affirmed and protected, exercised and nurtured.

The Difficult Unity of Inclusion

EXCERPTED FROM THE
OPENING EXERCISES ADDRESS
SEPTEMBER 1983

. . . All of us are inclined to take far too many things for granted—and in this category I would put the very idea of a residential university. To provide dormitories and a campus life for students may seem the most natural thing in the world, but it is, in fact, atypical. The overwhelming majority of students, worldwide, attend universities that are in no sense "residential." Students generally live at home or in non-university dwellings and travel back and forth to classes. Even in the United States, only about 40 percent of all full-time students in four-year colleges and universities live on campus.

The pronounced residential character of Princeton is one of its most distinctive attributes, and it is strongly held educational convictions that have led Princeton to invest so heavily in the many elements that together define a campus community. Residential life here is not an appendage to the academic program, nor simply a convenient way of housing and feeding students. It is a direct expression of a concept of liberal education that seeks to develop *all* of a student's capacities—including the capacities to learn, to live a full life, and to serve others. It is predicated on the assumption that the transactions of the classroom, library, and laboratory, primary as they are, should be complemented by the experience of living with fellow students of many backgrounds and persuasions, and participating actively with faculty members as well as students in the ongoing life of an identifiable academic community.

The contrast with what might be called the continental model of education is striking. In France, Germany, and much of the rest of eastern as well as western Europe, the aims of education are defined more narrowly. And if the main objective is to impart a certain fund of knowledge, then it may well be wise to concentrate resources on conventional classroom activities. Our purposes, however, are broader, and the emphasis we give to residential life follows directly from the same convictions that also shape our course of study. We believe that education should open minds rather than try to fill them up, that it should prepare students to appreciate the beauty of ideas as well as the world around them, to understand both other people and themselves, and to be effective citizens in a democracy. We aim to educate the whole person.

An idealistic conception? Yes. Ambitious? Certainly. Guaranteed to work? Not at all. But rich in possibilities for personal growth as well as for the development of real intellectual muscle? I think so.

The course of study itself is designed for active rather than passive learning, and that is one of the keys to the educational process at Princeton. In doing independent work, including the senior thesis, students are expected to be thoroughly engaged with their subject matter and to be both willing and able to do more than simply repeat what others have said. The preceptorial method of instruction was introduced at Princeton seventy years ago as a reaction against the "learning by rote" mentality, and to this day we encourage the student (in classes, laboratories, and even lectures, as well as in precepts) to be adventuresome—to try out ideas on both teachers and fellow students; to learn to modify opinions; and, at least on occasion, to enjoy the special satisfaction that can come from having made a new idea one's own.

This emphasis on active learning begins, then, in the classroom; but it certainly does not end there. It insinuates itself—and by design—into every niche of campus life. It is evident in the myriad extracurricular activities available here, in the many religious ministries, in athletics, in aspects of the governance of the University (including particularly the character of the disciplinary process), and also in the nature of the living and dining arrangements. The many points of opportunity for interaction with others, for friendship, for the formation of values, for exercising responsibility, for learning to lead, and to be led, can make for complex, and at times frustrating, experiences. But the richness of these experiences is the hallmark of a university that takes seriously the educational values that justify its residential character.

I have time today to illustrate the possibilities inherent in so many of these activities by citing only two comments, both recent, both by alumni. A member of the Class of 1943, Thomas Barbour, reflecting last spring on his days as an undergraduate, paid special tribute to Theatre Intime. Here is what he wrote: "It was—and, I trust, still is—a wholly student run extracurricular affair. I'm mighty glad of that. I learned from Intime by doing, and doing it all myself. . . . Perhaps the greatest thing about Princeton is its dedication to opening up the whole mind and spirit instead of narrowing them down to any special, single skill."

A second alumnus, now the senior Senator from New Jersey, formerly an all-American basketball player and a Rhodes Scholar, described some of the things he has learned from athletic competition in a speech he gave when being inducted into the Basketball Hall of Fame last spring. I refer, of course, to Senator Bill Bradley of the Class of 1965. He first recalled something that a mentor told him: "If you're not practicing, remember that someone, somewhere is. And when you two meet—given about equal ability—he'll win." In all of the things that he has done subsequently, Senator Bradley said, he never wanted to fail to do his best because he didn't make the effort, because he was unprepared. He then spoke of what it had meant to him to be part of "a team of students who played basketball to their collective potential," and he went on to describe the significance of teamwork, in the Senate as well as on the basketball court—of the importance of "getting people with different backgrounds, different experiences, and different personal agendas to agree on a shared goal and to work toward it."

Beyond the way athletic competition and extracurricular activities in general are viewed, the character of any residential community is defined in important respects by how it approaches the necessary tasks of making and enforcing rules. Over the years, many at Princeton have noted the strong interdependence between the Honor System, which asks so much of each student, and membership in a residential community to which individuals feel bound so closely by ties of both responsibility and pride. The Honor System could not function, in my judgment, without the mutual trust and shared commitments of students and faculty here; and the community itself would be very different without the Honor System and all that is implied by its acceptance.

It is far from easy to sustain this sense of institutional character in the face of so many centrifugal pressures. Nor are these pressures to be denigrated, since many are the products of a University that is intellectually alive precisely because it includes many points of view and many conflicting attitudes. Princeton today is a more complex and more interesting place, in this respect as in others, than it was in earlier times. And it is very much to Princeton's credit, I believe, that in the face of the cross-pulls that are generated by its greater intellectual vitality, it has retained a commitment to certain core values.

One of these core values, unquestionably, is academic integrity, which is given direct expression in the explicit nature of the University's rules regarding the taking of examinations and the preparation of papers. The University's commitments to the protection of free speech and of dissenting opinions are equally clear-cut. And we are explicit, too, about regulations having to do with safety and other matters of common concern to the University community. Also, the faculty has never been reluctant to prescribe academic requirements that impose definite obligations on each student—and on each faculty member as well. In short, this is certainly not a community in which "anything goes."

But Princeton also leaves a great deal of responsibility for conduct with each individual and each organization. Ever since the time of President McCosh (in the late 1800s) there has been a trend toward more general standards of conduct and a concomitant reduction in the number of detailed rules and regulations. (The alumni of the 1920s and 1930s would be surprised to see how much more "relaxed" were the regulations of their day, as contrasted with what had been commonplace earlier—when students were even required to have their arrangements for doing laundry in town approved by the college authorities!)

A classic statement of the University's approach to this aspect of residential life was provided by Dean Radcliffe Heermance, who said in a message to parents in 1935:

> We believe that a University, in offering a young [person] training for all his later life, should train him also to rule himself, and to this end it must be an environment of freedom, in which each individual makes his decisions and is responsible for them. This principle is modified only in so far as is necessary to assure the particular type of education to which Princeton is devoted and the general efficiency of the institution. The change from school to university is thus a change from a regulated to a self-regulated existence. . . . It marks the end of a discipline by compulsion and the beginning of a discipline through responsibility.

As Princeton has moved further away from detailed regulation of dormitory hours, use of cars, and other aspects of student life, some have suggested that the University has abdicated its role "*in loco parentis*"—that is, its quasi-parental responsibility for shaping the character of its students. This is, in my judgment, a very wrong inference. On the contrary, the demise of highly particularistic regulations has been accompanied by an *increased* effort on the part of the University to be helpful to students in charting their personal development.

While rules are often necessary, they are rarely a full solution to any problem of importance. Accordingly, in allowing students more freedom from attempts at explicit regulation of their personal lives (often unsuccessful in any case, as many alumni will testify), the University has made ever greater efforts to provide counseling and other forms of assistance as students seek to make frequently difficult adjustments to life away from home—and simply to grow up. In seeking to provide the *positive* assistance that the most sensitive parents provide, the University seems to me more committed to a genuinely *in loco parentis* role today than formerly. It is of course the residential nature of Princeton that permits such a role, as it is Princeton's broad educational objectives that impel the University's acceptance of it.

I turn now to the particular contributions that the establishment of a residential college system for freshmen and sophomores can make to the further evolution of campus life at Princeton. You are familiar with their most obvious purposes. They have been created to provide a structure within which freshmen and sophomores, in particular, can take maximum advantage of the many opportunities at Princeton to learn through associations with other students, through participation in a wide variety of extracurricular activities, and through informal contacts with members of the faculty and staff. In organizational terms, the colleges offer important advantages by providing a focus for a still more vigorous development of intramural athletics, for artistic and cultural activities, for special lectures, for academic advising in a more familiar environment, for personal counseling, and for a range of other events and "happenings" that I am sure will exceed the reaches of my imagination.

In their totality, the residential colleges also provide a "common" experience, or at least a common framework, for all underclass students. In reviewing the history of residential life at Princeton, I have been struck by the recurring nature of this objective. It was *not* achieved during the period from 1843 (when the college refectory was shut down) until the early 1900s, and students of that period complained about the lack of "communality" and about the "rival divisions" and cliques that formed. Subsequent student efforts played a large part in the establishment of the dining halls that we have come to call "Commons," and it is fitting that this splendid set of Tudor-Gothic structures will now serve again their original purposes.

The great dining halls of Commons have served the University well, but over the years since they were built we have become more conscious of the limitations of any arrangement that fails to link living and dining patterns for freshmen and sophomores. Moreover, as a variety of additional dining and social options were developed, especially during the period following the Korean War and then again more recently, it became harder to achieve the goal of "communality." The increase in the size of the undergraduate student body—and of the faculty—brought both greater possibilities for getting to know a fascinating array of individuals and a greater risk of what came to be called "fragmentation" in our dining and living arrangements. The "system" that developed, or really the lack of system, did not encourage interaction either among the students themselves or between faculty and students.

Fortunately, we are now in a position—with your active help—to do much better. Princeton alumni for years have commented on the importance to them, all through their lives, of the friendships formed while they were students and of the learning that occurred in dormitories, dining halls, and clubs. Those opportunities are greater now than ever before, and I think it safe to say that most of us will never again have the privilege—and that is what it is—of living with as varied and as interesting a group of people as are to be found here.

It is tempting, I know, to be satisfied with "easy friendships," formed with those you already know or with whom you obviously have much in common. But I urge you, I challenge you, not to shortchange yourself and Princeton in that way. Reach out, make special efforts to get to know those who seem unlike you—recognizing, and accepting, the risks of being rebuffed or of feeling out of place or inadequate. The rewards can be enormous. Moreover, it is the country, as well as each of you, that has a stake in seeing that you leave Princeton able to appreciate the potential inherent in the pluralism of our society.

This is a general proposition, and it is meant to apply to all of us—to encourage athletes, for example, not to spend all of their free time with teammates. Nor should physicists consort only with other physicists. But what I am trying to say has a special poignancy, I believe, and a special importance, where race is concerned. As some of you who were in this chapel a year ago may recall, I talked then about the sometimes painful, almost always complicated, and tremendously significant issues of race—at Princeton and in America. There is never one "solution" to such complex concerns. But I am persuaded that this is an area in which the residential colleges can make an especially great contribution. There is a common humanity to be served, and I count on each of you to make a maximum effort in this regard.

The vision that I hope we shall keep before us was articulated well by Woodrow Wilson, the thirteenth president of Princeton. In arguing more than seventy years ago for a version of the plan we are now putting into effect for freshmen and sophomores, he said:

> My plea is this: that we now deliberately set ourselves to make a home for the spirit of learning: that we reorganize our lives on the lines of this simple conception, that a college is not only a body of studies, but a mode of association, that its courses are only its formal side, its contacts and contagions its realities. It must become a community of scholars . . . a free community, but a very real one, in which democracy may work its reasonable triumph of accommodation, its vital processes of union. I am suggesting that young [people] . . . be introduced into the high society of university ideals, [and] be exposed to the hazards of stimulating friendships.

It is up to us to give these words meaning in our time.

We must also be realistic, however. Enthusiastic as I am about the residential colleges, I do not think that they will achieve all of our goals. They may not work well in every instance, and they even pose certain potential dangers—well worth accepting, I think, but dangers nonetheless. Perhaps the most serious is that for some of you your college will seem too comfortable, too self-sufficient. Please do not let your friendships be restricted to your own college, wide as the opportunities for friendship will be within it. I am optimistic that class spirit, reaching across all five colleges, will be strengthened, not weakened, by this new departure. But it remains for you to prove me right—in at least this one respect! I count on you also to see that the wide range of friendships formed during freshman and sophomore years carries forward into the upperclass years, and that the "contacts and contagions" to which President Wilson referred not lessen.

If you find aspects of residential life at Princeton—as well as aspects of academic life—confusing and indeterminate at times, do not be surprised. That is characteristic of most interesting aspects of life, and I want to close my part in these Opening Exercises by calling your attention to something said about modern architecture that I think has relevance to our goals for residential life.

It is an observation made by Robert Venturi, a member of the Class of 1947, the architect who has been responsible for Wu Hall at Butler College and for the renovation of both Rockefeller and Mathey Colleges. In his influential book, *Complexity and Contradiction in Architecture*, Mr. Venturi sought to direct modern architects back to historical roots and away from what he described as "the puritanically moral language of orthodox Modern architecture.'' ''I like elements which are hybrid rather than 'pure,' . . . ambiguous rather than 'articulated,' '' he said, as he went on to declare himself for ''messy vitality over obvious unity.'' ''But an architecture of complexity and contradiction,'' he concluded, ''has a special obligation toward the whole: its truth must be in its totality or its implications of totality. It must embody *the difficult unity of inclusion rather than the easy unity of exclusion.*''

Life clearly would be simpler, both on this campus and in the world, if we were somehow to shut out experiences and contacts that were unsettling in one way or another. ''Exclusion,'' whether architectural or personal, is a surer way of obtaining at least one form of ''unity.'' It is also true that contradictions of all kinds, real or only apparent, can be upsetting. ''Contradictions'' in the context of residential life can take the form of tensions between such objectives as finding time to be alone and giving time to others, between wanting to benefit fully from being part of a multifaceted university and also wanting to enjoy the relative simplicities of college life, or between resisting and even resenting what some impossible person is saying while simultaneously insisting on the person's right to say it. But how sad it would be if we were satisfied with an approach to life, in the University or outside it, that failed to exalt Mr. Venturi's ''messy vitality'' over less-demanding aspirations.

As we now start a new year at Princeton, may we be grateful for the stimulation of coping with contradictions. And may we be especially grateful for the rich opportunities to learn that are the reward of pursuing the only unity that I believe is worth having—the difficult unity of inclusion.

The Bond of Respect

OPENING EXERCISES ADDRESS
SEPTEMBER 1987

Today, with these exercises in this chapel, we begin the 242nd year for Princeton. I am pleased once again to have the privilege of welcoming those who are new to the campus and greeting those who are returning. This year I have chosen a complex subject that is, nonetheless, extremely important: the nature and significance of respect on this campus.

"Respect" is a word with many shades of meaning. I am not using it to connote "deference" but rather "to show regard or consideration for"; and as objects of this "regard" and "consideration," I have in mind today especially your fellow students and you, yourself.

We are, first and foremost, a community dedicated to learning. We care deeply about such age-old questions as what it means to be alive in the world, and (as Senator Bill Bradley asks) what we owe a stranger. These are questions with a profound intellectual content, to be studied diligently through curriculum, library, and laboratory. But they are also profoundly personal, and they need to be pursued as well through the fun—and the frictions—associated with being part of a residential university.

The present-day diversity of Princeton has much to contribute to your education here. I am sure you have come not only to explore new fields of knowledge—central as that is—but also to learn about, and from, other ways of thinking, other ways of worshipping, and even other ways of just plain coping. This multiracial community, which includes men and women from many backgrounds and cultures, as well as from more than seventy countries, offers richer opportunities than you may ever experience again to free yourself from some of your own parochialisms—while simultaneously allowing you to deepen values of your own by seeing them in sharper relief than before.

While diversity can be exhilarating, stimulating, and highly educational, it can also create tensions, opportunities for misperceptions, and at times actual conflicts. Let me state my thesis directly: I see "respect" as the essential bond required to avoid fragmentation and, in fact, to realize the true educational possibilities before us.

Of course, differences among people raise issues for institutions of every kind all over the world. But they have, in my view, a special relevance for self-consciously democratic societies. It is the combination of diversity and our commitment to freedom in its many forms that is so significantly American. The French traveler Alexis de Tocqueville, in his prophetic book about America published in 1835, observed:

> In democracies, no such thing as a regular code of . . . [behavior] can be laid down; this has some inconveniences and some advantages. In aristocracies the rules of propriety impose the same demeanor on everyone; they make all the members of the same class appear alike in spite of their private inclinations; they adorn and they conceal the natural man. Among a democratic people manners are neither so tutored nor so uniform, but they are frequently more sincere. They form, as it were, a light and loosely woven veil through which the real feelings and private opinions of each individual are easily discernible. The form and the substance of human actions, therefore, often stand there in closer relation; and if the great picture of human life is less embellished, it is more true.

The strengths noted by Tocqueville are evident today: a greater degree of individuality, of openness, of honesty, than one may find in more homogeneous, more "mannered" societies where behavior is socially and culturally defined to a greater extent. But these same benefits are, as Tocqueville also noted, potential hazards: the lack of a "common language" of behavioral conventions creates risks of miscommunication (at the least), and the wide variety of backgrounds among individuals brought together on a campus such as this may create insecurities and defensiveness that can be expressed in ways that seem to imply a lack of respect for those who are "different."

About half a century later, a very different commentator, Henry James, said: "It's a complex fate, being an American." James was not thinking so much of the diversity of Americans as he was of their penchant for individuality and the willingness of the society to tolerate widely divergent forms of behavior. In a country such as China, for example, there are also many ethnic groups and many other forms of diversity. But the strongly enforced conventions of the society, and the lack of many of the kinds of freedom we take for granted, mean that diversity does not create in that country the same complex choices that are so characteristic of our society.

Henry James' vivid description of Isabel Archer in *Portrait of a Lady* illustrates well his acute sense of the possibilities open to Americans to expand their vistas through the exercise of individuality, but also the dangers attendant on a lack of "training" or discipline. Here is part of James' description of Isabel's upbringing in her grandmother's house:

Her grandmother, old Mrs. Archer, had exercised . . . a large hospitality . . . and the little [girl] often spent weeks under her roof—weeks of which Isabel had the happiest memory . . . . The discipline . . . was delightfully vague. . . . The house offered to a certain extent the appearance of a bustling provincial inn kept by a gentle old landlady who sighed a great deal and never presented a bill. Isabel of course knew nothing about bills; but even as a child she thought her grandmother's home romantic. There was . . . a long garden, sloping down to the stable and containing peach-trees of barely credible familiarity. Isabel had stayed with her grandmother at various seasons, but somehow all her visits had a flavor of peaches. On the other side, across the street, was an old house that was called the Dutch House. . . . It was occupied by a primary school. . . . The little girl had been offered the opportunity of laying a foundation of knowledge in this establishment; but having spent a single day in it, she protested against its laws and had been allowed to stay home. . . . The foundation of her knowledge was really laid in the idleness of her grandmother's house . . . .

We see here a setting with relatively few constraints, and in James' later descriptions of Isabel we see the effects on a young person of having been allowed to avoid the fixed regime of the schoolhouse for the romantic, unstructured riches of her grandmother's home. No "bills to be paid," no reality; only freedom, gardens, peaches. Isabel ends fatally, misperceiving—perhaps for lack of "training" and experience—the reality of the man she marries, as well as the suitors she rejects. She misjudges, in every case, the subtle relationship between external manners and internal substance.

How then, in our day, with a far more differentiated population than Tocqueville or James could have anticipated, are we to educate ourselves so as to make the "right" judgments? How can we benefit as much as possible from our unprecedented degree of freedom—from the virtues associated with the image of the garden—without sacrificing the structure, discipline, and sense of reality that can be provided by the schoolhouse?

A significant part of the answer, I believe, lies in the "bond of respect,'' understood to mean much more than just ''tolerance'' in the weak sense of freedom from bigotry (if that were truly achievable). Put positively, I understand ''respect'' to entail an active regard for others, a desire to understand different ways of thinking and behaving, and a determination to exercise an honest sensitivity that avoids both condescension and indifference.

How is this kind of respect to be achieved? Plainly there are things that the University itself can and should do. First, it must be clear about its own standards. As entering undergraduates know from the letter Dean Lowe mailed earlier this summer, this is not an institution modeled in all respects after Grandmother Archer's house. It is most emphatically not an institution in which ''anything goes.'' We have agreed, as a community, to limitations on the ''freedom'' or ''individuality'' of each of us in order to achieve larger educational goals and to protect communal rights.

Intelligent and fair enforcement of these communal rights is the University's second responsibility. Absent that, any set of regulations is empty of meaning. In seeking to apply rules, we must be concerned with the realities of situations and not merely the appearances; we must act so as to achieve the fullest possible measure of institutional integrity. A single standard for all should be assumed, but also the willingness to make distinctions when they are warranted.

There is a third institutional obligation. It is not enough simply to define key parameters of conduct; the University should also assist each of you to act affirmatively to create an ethos of respect. One part of our responsibility is to educate members of the community about such matters as alcohol abuse, sexual harassment, and subtle as well as overt forms of prejudice and discrimination—all in a larger educational context that stimulates you to think more broadly about the moral, ethical, and spiritual foundations of life in a civilized society. Literature, art, philosophy, history, and, for that matter, all of our subjects have their roles to play—including, I might note, my own field of economics, where values are ever present, whether recognized or not.

While part of your ''education in respect'' will take place at abstract levels, much of it will involve real situations. Those of you who were here last spring will recall a number of serious incidents, many of them involving interactions between men and women, that underscored the importance of an unambiguous reaffirmation of the centrality of respect in the life of this community. It is essential that we learn from these kinds of experiences as well as respond to them—as individuals and as an institution.

I do not mean to exaggerate what the institution can do, or should be expected to do. . . . I am reminded of a wise observation attributed to Dorothy Brown, wife of the late Dean of the Faculty J. Douglas Brown. A young faculty member who had just arrived in Princeton asked Mrs. Brown what people were like here. Mrs. Brown responded by asking what people had been like where the faculty member had been before: "Rather nasty," was the reply. "Well," she said, "I'm afraid you'll find pretty much the same thing here." Another arriving faculty member asked Mrs. Brown the same question, and she responded again by asking about the person's prior experience. This time the reply was: "Very nice; lots of thoughtful, decent people." She then said, "Well, I think you'll find pretty much the same thing here." In large part, we do carry our environments along with us.

It is also worth saying explicitly that this is a university, not a child-care center or a penal institution. We would not regulate your lives in great detail if we could, because part of your education, part of the never-ending process of growing up, involves learning to make responsible decisions—and being accountable for them.

Much of the burden, therefore, of sustaining a climate of respect at Princeton rests squarely with you. But we are all in this together, and I hope you won't think it presumptuous if I now suggest, rather directly, some internal guideposts for you to consider as you decide both how you are to relate to others and what you are to expect of yourself.

First and most obvious: Be your own person. Have the courage to act in ways that express your own convictions, rather than just following the apparent drift of "the crowd." Peer pressure can be hard to handle at any age, but it can be handled, certainly by those who have their own standards and the willingness to stick to them.

As I'm sure you recognize, your own best judgment can be clouded by alcohol and drugs. It is so sad to see otherwise responsible people demean themselves and others—losing both self-respect and the respect of others—by being, in the vernacular, "out of it." I wish the University had a wand that would protect all of you from becoming new casualties of this kind of unthinking behavior that so many seem to associate with college days.

Next, please be alert to the needs, and to the hurts, of those around you. It is a mistake to assume that life is necessarily easy, always, for anyone. Sallie Reynolds Matthews, in her moving chronicle of the pioneer families that established Lambshead Ranch in West Texas in the 1800s, wrote: "Some seem to have more than their share of grief in this life, and we see others who seem to float along on flowery beds of ease, but we do not know; they may be carrying bitter sorrow deep in their hearts."

In making new friends, so that we may learn from them and help them, we also need to remember that relationships of real respect require honesty with others no less than with yourself. Don't be afraid to disagree—perhaps tactfully!—even when disagreement may expose you to the risk of being thought unsympathetic, or worse. Respect for others does not translate into nodding "yes," when you mean "no," "maybe," or "it all depends." There are times when all of us suffer from well-intentioned friends who find it easier, or more comfortable, to agree with whatever is said than to pay a person the compliment of fair argument. Condescension and excessive deference are easily perceived as such, and neither is a foundation on which relationships of respect can be built.

In responding to instances of injustice, or even to acts of simple stupidity, a sense of indignation can be very much in order. Beyond that, it is important to step forward, not aside, when others behave improperly. Victims of assault, and of the subtler kinds of wounds inflicted by racial, sexual, or religious innuendo, are rightfully incensed when indifference seems to be the general response. At the same time, we also know that finger-pointing can be one of the worst forms of self-righteousness, and there is certainly much to be said for suspending judgment until you are sure you really understand the facts. Fairness involves recognizing that relationships between individuals as well as between groups almost always turn out to be more complicated than one first thought. No doubt all of us have had opportunities to learn— sometimes painfully—how complex "the truth" can be.

Respect also needs to grow out of at least some degree of humility. Our emphasis on freedom and individuality (the glories of the garden) can sometimes lead to overconfidence in our own capacity to make judgments. Once again, Henry James' portrait of Isabel is relevant:

It may be affirmed without delay that Isabel was probably very liable to the sin of self-esteem; she often surveyed with complacency the field of her own nature; she was in the habit of taking for granted, on scanty evidence, that she was right. . . . At moments she discovered she was grotesquely wrong, and then she treated herself to a week of passionate humility. After this she held her head higher than ever again; for it was of no use, she had an unquenchable desire to think well of herself.

Finally, I hope you will learn, to the extent possible, to live with ambiguity. Important questions often lack clear answers, and at times it is hard to find any satisfying answer at all. Some of you may have seen the moving Op-Ed piece in the *New York Times* by a woman writing in the aftermath of the Bernhard Goetz incident on the New York subway. She recounted how, years earlier, she had been attacked and injured by black youths who might themselves have been reacting to the death of a black child who was said to have been shot by a white police officer. After raising all the impenetrable questions of guilt and justice, the woman ended by quoting Rilke: "Be patient toward all that is unsolved in your heart." She added: "Learning to live with the questions that have no answers may be the deepest source and greatest power of self-respect."

Enough admonitions. Perhaps more than enough. Do I believe that any of this is easy? Absolutely not. Your generation not only faces all the dilemmas identified by Tocqueville and James decades ago, but must also confront them in a considerably more complicated context. The University is far more diverse than it used to be, and the society has broadened opportunities for self-expression and self-determination—opportunities that fortunately are now much less closely linked than before to gender, race, or religion. Yet such significant changes cannot be expected to happen without stresses and situations that are perplexing to all concerned. As reliance on one set of conventions and expectations is replaced by a greater reliance on personal judgments and the creation of new understandings that are commonly shared, the need for real "respect" becomes even greater than before.

But greater too are the rewards of understanding what respect really means and accepting the obligations that it imposes. Learning to make your own decisions can be excruciating—but it is the path to an earned sense of decency. I envy you your opportunities here. Princeton is—to an extraordinary degree—both schoolhouse and garden. By all means enjoy its beauties and its invigorating freedoms, be as high-spirited as Isabel in extending your own capacities, but learn as well the lessons taught within the schoolhouse, and the disciplines which they instill. Strengthen, together, the bond of respect so that all may benefit from the educational riches of this very special place.

No Limits

EXCERPTED FROM
COMMENCEMENT REMARKS
JUNE 1982

. . . I think it is appropriate—perhaps even obligatory—to say directly what I believe about certain values fundamental to our nation that are at the core of university communities. Specifically, I am concerned about our commitment, as a people, to the idea of opportunity—to the proposition that education of the highest quality ought to be available on the basis of individual qualifications, not simply financial means.

It is surprising, frightening in some respects, to see how fast national moods and norms can change. It wasn't long ago—less than fifteen years—that Edward Levi, then president of the University of Chicago, was warning us not to sacrifice educational quality in our efforts to pursue an overly simple notion of what constitutes "opportunity." Excellence and opportunity were then, and are now, powerfully complementary goals. As John Gardner observed: "The good society is not one that ignores individual differences but one that deals with them wisely and humanely."

Now, just a little more than a decade later, we face a very different kind of danger. There are signs that we risk reverting to a situation in which educational opportunity is more a function of family circumstances than of qualifications. On one of my visits to Washington, I was taken aback when a Congressman told me in almost casual tones that he didn't see that it would matter much if Princeton again became a school attended largely by those of means; others, he suggested, could go elsewhere.

Why do I react so strongly—so negatively—to that way of thinking? In part, I suppose, for personal reasons. It would have been impossible for me to come to Princeton as a graduate student without generous fellowship support; and the education I received here has made an enormous difference in my life. It is for those of you who are graduating today to speak of the difference Princeton continues to make in the lives of individuals, but I shall be very surprised if a number of you in subsequent years do not provide testimony as eloquent as that of your predecessors. Just last week I saw the comment of a member of the Class of 1977 whose education here was made possible through a series of scholarships. She wrote: "I am ready to give life and the world my very best efforts! Thank you, Princeton, for making so many of 'the positives' possible."

From an institutional perspective, this University has a clear interest in continuing to be open to the widest range of talent. The quality of both the undergraduate college and the graduate school depend on our continuing to enroll the most outstanding individuals, whatever their circumstances. Otherwise, our commitment to excellence would be partial at best.

Moreover, we believe that the educational opportunities that Princeton offers are far richer for all because of the variety of students who are here. . . . Differences in background—and therefore in assumptions and in perspectives—can be disturbing and at times profoundly uncomfortable; but it is precisely such interactions that are often educational in the largest sense. The present-day diversity of the student body at Princeton is not something separate from the University's commitment to educational excellence; it is required by it.

I share the view of many that we are only at the beginnings of what it ought to be possible to achieve through personal associations and friendships in a university community that includes students from widely differing backgrounds. Do we do as well now, in these respects, as we should? Of course not. But how far we have come. And the path to further progress surely does not lie in constricting access to Princeton—or to other great universities.

In arguing for efforts—private and governmental—to sustain openness to individuals of talent, I am in no sense urging "handouts." As many here today know so well, at Princeton we expect each person, and each family, to sacrifice—to contribute up to (and some would say beyond) their own capacities before extending scholarship assistance. We do not give anything resembling "free rides." What we do is supplement personal and family contributions with additional resources so that all who qualify for admission are able to come. These institutional contributions accrue to all students, not only scholarship recipients, since even those who pay full tuition receive implicit scholarships equal to the substantial educational costs we incur in excess of the tuition rate. Far from being "handouts," investments in educational opportunity seem to me our best defense—or more properly our best offense—as we work to maintain in this country a belief that opportunity is real; that there is hope for our children, whatever the limitations under which we have lived.

Allow me a personal reminiscence. Some years ago, on the night before Commencement, I was talking with the mother of a senior. She was a woman who I knew had had no schooling beyond the seventh grade. She was surrounded that evening by family who had come from many places to be here for graduation, and in looking at all of those people she said: "You know, Mr. Bowen, my son thinks we are making too much of all this. But you must understand," she went on, "that I knew from an early age that there was a limit on what I could achieve because of my race and my education. I was determined that for my children there would be no limits."

Was her son's presence at Princeton—and his great success here— due in large measure to what she and other members of her family had given to him? Of course. But not even that family could have done it alone. It was—and is—up to all of us to help, not in a patronizing or condescending way, but with a sure sense that we are serving each other, that we are advancing common goals.

The future of this society depends, in my view, on our capacity to continue to call on the idealism of America as well as on the talents of our people. In his recent book, Theodore White has suggested that, in contrast to other, more homogeneous societies, "Americans are held together only by ideas . . . by a culture of hope." Many seem to believe that in America today the idea of opportunity is dead or dying. I don't agree. And I don't think that it will die as long as those fortunate enough to have attended universities such as this one are determined to give it long life.

Princeton is sometimes said, especially by our detractors, to be a place of privilege. In an important sense it is. So much has been given to us here: an idyllic setting, a rich history, substantial material and human resources. Yet I think we recognize that responsibility is the other side of privilege. Each of you graduating today will decide individually what use you are to make of your education. But whatever you do, I hope that you will find time in your own lives to help to build a society in which there are fewer limits on the aspirations of others and to see that Princeton, in particular, remains a place of opportunity as well as a place of privilege.

Elitism

COMMENCEMENT REMARKS
JUNE 1984

. . . This is a time for joy and celebration, not, I think, for overly somber pronouncements. But it is also a time to reflect a bit on our attitudes toward this University and toward ourselves as graduates of it. Today, I have in mind particularly the attitudes associated with a very loaded word: "elitism."

For one graduate alumnus and former Trustee, W. Michael Blumenthal, these attitudes were of such troubling significance that he spoke movingly on the subject when he retired from the Board of Trustees earlier this year. Mr. Blumenthal's personal history is relevant. In the 1930s, he was a refugee from Hitler's Germany. He spent the war years in China before somehow managing to get to this country, arriving in California with no money and no clear path ahead.

But he was very bright, as well as energetic, and he enrolled as an undergraduate in the University of California at Berkeley. He then won a fellowship to Princeton and earned two graduate degrees here, including a Ph.D., in the mid-1950s. He subsequently pursued a career that has included teaching and research, highly significant public service (including a period as Secretary of the Treasury under President Carter), and high-level positions in business.

What Mr. Blumenthal said to his fellow Trustees was that, when he first came to Princeton, it was with a sense that this was an institution foreign to him, that it symbolized many things he disliked intensely: privilege, snobbism, pretentiousness. He would never, he thought, be comfortable here. So, he came intending to take what Princeton had to offer him—an excellent education—and then to leave the place behind.

But things did not turn out exactly that way. Contrary to his initial expectations. Princeton has continued to be an important part of Mr. Blumenthal's life. While he has as little patience today as he had earlier with pomposity, be it institutional or individual, he has come to think somewhat differently about Princeton as an elite institution. His changed attitude is due in part to important changes in the University over the last three decades. But it is also due to a sharper awareness in his own mind of a critical distinction—between what he termed "elitism of fact" (or of accomplishment) and "elitism of attitude."

For my own part, I have always disliked the word "elitism," and I do not use it. I too am bothered by some of its connotations as well as by the quite different meanings and interpretations that can be given to it. But I am persuaded that Mr. Blumenthal is right in acknowledging the reality of an "elitism of fact." The roots of the word "elite" have to do with being selected from among a large number, and there is no denying that those of you receiving degrees today meet that test. The word also implies competence, high achievement, and responsibility. In this sense, elitism of fact is an inescapable objective if you aim to be among the very best. From this perspective, Princeton is without question an elite institution.

How should we respond, as an institution and as individuals, to this reality? Not, I think, by apologizing for the excellence we seek, or for the high standards we set for ourselves. Nor would I recommend the cultivation of what Professor Marion J. Levy, Jr., once called "mock humble arrogance."

What is required, in my view, is sustained effort to avoid as best we can corrosive forms of elitism, including elitism of attitude, while seeking to develop as fully as possible the capacities of the University, and of each of us, to serve the larger society.

This entails, first, continuing to make access to Princeton conditional on qualifications and individual promise, not on family circumstances. While it is undeniably the case that wealth, good schooling, and parental encouragement increase the life chances of children (and can help to improve, among other things, SAT scores), it is also true that this University can—and does—provide a critically important avenue upward for students from all backgrounds.

In this regard, the University's substantial financial aid program is of major significance. It allows the most outstanding candidates to attend Princeton, whatever their economic circumstances: and it also permits Princeton to benefit from the economic, social, and racial diversity so critical to the educational process—including preparation for citizenship in a democracy. Financial aid is important symbolically as well: as a direct statement, made real by the allocation of scarce resources, of principles central to this University.

A second imperative is that we must continue to insist that all students here be treated on their individual merits. As the occasional student who believed that he or she should receive preferential treatment has learned painfully, there is one standard, one set of requirements for all. The degree you receive today certifies achievement, not attendance. Outside the academic arena, there are still, let us acknowledge, forms of snobbism that remain in this all-too-human community. But they diminish, and they will diminish further as we continue to applaud ever more loudly what really matters—the character, and the varied contributions, of each individual.

Third, we must work ever harder to deserve the reputation that Princeton enjoys. Complacency is a deadly ailment, and Mary Kay Ash, founder of Mary Kay Cosmetics, was right when she said: "Nothing wilts faster than a laurel rested upon." Certainly there are many respects in which this could be a far better university than it is today, and it is the shared task of all of us to reach always for that potential, never to be satisfied with what has been achieved. We have to try to push ourselves closer to our standards—and then to be ready to raise the standards once again.

Perhaps most important of all on this list of imperatives is the need to stand squarely against "elitism of attitude." This is partly a matter of recognizing the quality and significance of many other kinds of academic institutions. Our country is fortunate in having an educational system that is itself diverse and that allows many kinds of excellence to flourish. The country depends on the essential contributions of the successful community college and the successful liberal arts college, just as it does on those of the successful research university.

Professor Ezra Suleiman of our Politics Department, in his book on *Elites in French Society*, notes that the most prestigious positions in that society are filled in very large measure by graduates of what are known as The Grandes Ecoles. That kind of pattern is less pervasive in this country. It would be unhealthy for the society, and, in my view, for those of you graduating, if you were somehow assured of a good position or any other lasting mark of success simply as a result of holding a Princeton degree. It is relevant to note—and encouraging to note—the remarkable achievements in this country of individuals who have had very little formal education at all.

But perhaps the most effective way we can discourage an "elitism of attitude" is through the teaching and learning process itself. Paradoxically, the very quality of the institution can protect against some of the worst forms of self-indulgent self-satisfaction on the part of students—and, I might add, faculty members and administrators. I remember well a student who came to Princeton as a highly-touted physics star. At the end of her first semester, I had occasion to ask her father (himself a famous physicist) how his daughter was doing. "Just fine," he said, and then explained: "She decided that she was such a good student she could ignore beginning physics and start right off at the intermediate level. She came home after exams and said, 'I don't know how to tell you this, Dad, but I got a C in physics.' I can't tell you," her father went on to say to me, "how valuable that experience was for her. She learned, for the first time in her life, that there are many smart people in the world, and that she cannot expect always to be first."

There is another form of elitism of attitude that I also hope your liberal arts education will help you to recognize, and then to combat. It is an attitude, or an approach, based on a presumed "expertness" that sometimes results in what I would call arrogant blindness. Some of you may have read Freeman Dyson's exceptionally stimulating essays on the nuclear arms race that appeared in the *New Yorker*. Among his other warnings was a clear injunction against being intimidated by the expert—who, to use another terminology, knows the price of everything and the value of nothing. Again, there are limits to what any university can do. But I believe that there is real advantage—and real protection—in learning the partial character of all forms of knowledge, and in being able to recognize that what the expert may view as decisive from a particular standpoint may actually be of less importance than the larger assumptions about values that are so often unstated.

The truly great leaders have been those who have been both stretched and humbled by education, and I hope that you will contribute to their number. In the Princeton pantheon, one of my great heroes is Adlai Stevenson '22, who once observed: "Many things are revealed to the humble that are hidden from the great."

As a further preventive against elitism of attitude, let me suggest the salutary effects of something else that I hope you have developed here: a capacity to work—to work *very hard*. No one exemplifies that capacity better than a philosopher among us who masquerades as a basketball coach—Pete Carril. Coach Carril is sometimes astonishingly tolerant of missed free throws, but he has no tolerance whatever for errors due to laziness, poor preparation, or inattention. His commitment to making the most of what each person has to offer is total, and his approach represents, I think, an unswerving quest for elitism of fact based on a flat rejection of elitism of attitude. Indeed, I believe that it is precisely rejection of elitism of attitude that often permits the achievement of elitism of fact.

What are you to do with what you have learned at Princeton? That is for each to decide. But I hope that many of you will want to repay the privilege—which is what it is—of having studied here by working even harder in the future, not just to advance personal interests, but to help this country be more than simply a haven for those of us so fortunate as to live comfortably here, to help it be an effective force for the alleviation of the ills of people everywhere. If you live lives dedicated to that end, you certainly need not cringe from elitist labels.

This is a great university. Its achievements, the achievements of its graduates, are many. But it is also a place cognizant of the fact that each of us stands on feet of clay; a place that recognizes that the important tests are always ahead of us, not behind us; and a place determined to avoid the elitism of attitude that defeats every purpose we are here to advance.

Race Relations

OPENING EXERCISES ADDRESS
SEPTEMBER 1982

. . . How good a year it will be—for you and for this University community—will depend in no small degree on the quality of our personal relationships. This afternoon, I would like to ask you to think with me about one dimension of these relationships: the fact that we are a richly diverse community in terms of the races that we represent, as well as in so many other respects.

The subject of race is often a contentious one, not just in this University, and not just in this country, but all over the world. There are those, I know, who believe that we are well advised to leave it alone. That is not my view, however. While I have no panaceas to offer, I believe that we do well to consider questions pertaining to race as openly and as candidly as we can. Plainly there are sensitive—painful—aspects to our experiences at Princeton, but there are also so many positive possibilities. There is so much for us to accomplish, so much for us to learn, together.

Perhaps it is best to begin by reviewing briefly where we have been as a university as far as race is concerned. Princeton, like many colleges and universities, has been through three fairly well defined stages. From the founding of the University through the 1950s, there were very few minority students of any race and almost no black or Hispanic students. Even as recently as twenty years ago, there were only five black students in the entering class of undergraduates.

The second stage can be dated from the mid-1960s through about 1974. It was a period of active recruitment, with dramatic increases in numbers of minority students; those years were marked, too, by a number of group confrontations. It was a time of rapid change and difficult adjustments—for many individuals as well as for the institution.

A third stage started sometime in the mid-1970s and continues today. It can be characterized as a time of greater stability, with modest increases in the overall number of minority students (especially Hispanics and Asian Americans). And while there have been difficult moments, there has been less conflict and tension. This has been, if you will, a period of "consolidation." Yet it certainly does not seem to me to be a time to assume either that all of our major problems have been solved or, at the other extreme, that they are unsolvable.

It is important, I think, to be clear about what we want to achieve. To my way of thinking, there are two complementary goals. The first has to do with what I would call individual fulfillment—providing the best possible learning environment for each student. The second, closely related, goal is the promotion of mutually beneficial interactions among the individuals who compose the University community. These powerfully reinforcing goals are important for several reasons.

One reason is educational in a direct sense. Students and faculty alike testify repeatedly—and eloquently—to the learning that occurs through the diversity of backgrounds and perspectives represented at Princeton today. Such learning occurs both in the classroom and out of it. Some of it is easy and entirely pleasurable, as our eyes are opened to new opportunities for friendship and to new ways of thinking.

But we must recognize that some of the learning that occurs through diversity can also be traumatic. I remember well the invitation extended by the undergraduates of the Whig-Cliosophic Society in 1973 to Dr. William Shockley to come to Princeton to present his views on genetic differences related to race—views exceedingly offensive to many. There was an extended and sometimes angry discussion on campus of the reasons for the invitation, its propriety, and how to respond to it.

By the time Dr. Shockley had come and gone there was a much clearer understanding of why many minority students, in particular, were so offended by the invitation, and of the extent to which a number of their fellow students had displayed insensitivity as well as ignorance. At the same time, there was also a much clearer understanding of why it is so important, especially in a university, that we not censor speakers or disrupt them, however distasteful their views may be to many. Propositions that might have seemed abstract, and that may seem abstract to many of you now, did not seem at all abstract then. Would it have been easier if we had been spared those difficult discussions, many of which occurred between roommates late into the night? Of course. But did learning occur? Absolutely, and in ways that would never have been possible without both the racial diversity of Princeton and the willingness of many to talk honestly about their own feelings, even when it was very painful to do so.

Another reason why pursuit of these goals is so important grows directly out of the first. Our society has a tremendous need not only for individuals of talent from every racial group, but for individuals who understand the diversity of America, who value it, and who can work effectively for ever larger measures of tolerance, mutual understanding, and shared effort on behalf of national goals. I believe that the political and social fabric of this country requires that individuals of different races be educated in settings where they can learn how to learn from each other.

Then there is a final reason that is most fundamental of all, at least for me. It is a moral reason—a spiritual reason for many of us—that has to do with recognizing and honoring the dignity of each person, with what many of us see as the sacred flame inside each human being.

How have we done thus far in pursuing these goals? As Dean Borsch pointed out in a provocative sermon on race last winter, the answer to this question depends very much on the standard that we adopt. In comparison with our own earlier history, or even with the more recent experience of most of the rest of American society, we can say that Princeton has done quite well. Indeed, it would be sad if we were unable to acknowledge the very substantial progress that has been made in promoting both individual fulfillment and constructive interactions.

Yet, if we measure against our ideals, I think we have to conclude that we have fallen well short of what we ought to have accomplished. Many of us, including importantly students, continue to be seriously disappointed with the state of race relations at Princeton. There is much less positive, easy interaction than many of us would like to see; there are instances of discrimination (subtle if not overt) and insensitivity. In the University, our expectations are high—and they ought to be. The frustration that many of us feel, as we confront a reality that does not satisfy our aspirations, is fundamentally healthy. It is testimony to our unwillingness to settle for too little.

If we are to do better, what are the issues we must confront? First of all, we must face the continuing existence of inequality in America, especially in the form of differences in educational backgrounds. Recognition of the long-lasting consequences of generations of discrimination has made it necessary—and profoundly right—for this University to make special efforts to attract minority students.

The fact that we make these special efforts is, we should acknowledge candidly, a source of various stresses and strains. I am not now speaking of the feelings of other well-qualified applicants (and their parents) who see their own chances of admission affected adversely, though such feelings are natural and understandable. I am speaking rather of the feelings of some minority students themselves, and of the perceptions of others in the campus community.

In seeking to understand our situation, all of us should know that, while special attention is given to minority students in admission, the same kind of attention is also given to a number of other groups, including alumni children and students with exceptional talent in athletics and in the arts. It is even more important to recognize that there is no quota system here, and that *all* applicants must be above a very high threshold of qualification to be offered admission.

This basic standard is a most demanding one, and to deviate from it for any candidate would be unfair to the individual as well as to the University. Differences in such measurable (but very partial) indicators of academic potential as College Board scores and rank in class are far greater among the different individuals within every group than they are between groups. Thus, there is no reason to stereotype any group of students according to misperceptions of academic ability.

Of course, insecurities of all kinds, including worries about academic performance, are common to most students at Princeton, whatever their race or academic preparation. A proper humility, if nothing else, should lead each of you to feel at least a modest degree of anxiety. It may be worth remembering that many of our most distinguished graduates had their own academic struggles at Princeton. Adlai Stevenson of the Class of 1922, for example, was fond of noting that he was "never threatened by Phi Beta Kappa." But do not, please, allow a natural concern over your own capacities to lead to self-deprecation or to a kind of defensiveness that makes it hard to accept help.

Perhaps I should note, although it is hardly surprising, that minority students have compiled an enviable record at Princeton. In the last decade and a half, they have won virtually every distinction the University has to confer, including the Pyne Prize on several occasions. Minority students have been active as leaders in class affairs, in student government, in athletics, and in extracurricular activities generally; many have been among the most effective advocates for Princeton.

Similarly, although it is still too soon to appreciate fully the accomplishments of minority alumni, the record to date is most impressive and includes noteworthy contributions to the professions, to business, to education, to government, and to Princeton itself. At last June's reunions, I attended a reception given by the Association of Black Princeton Alumni, and it was one of the highlights of that weekend for me. I was particularly moved by the presentation of an award for distinguished achievement to Dr. Robert Rivers, Class of 1953, one of our early black graduates who is a surgeon and educator in Rochester, New York, who has served on the University's Board of Trustees, and who has had three children attend Princeton.

A second "fact of life" relevant to race relations here also derives from the history of the country, the history of higher education, and the particular history of Princeton: there is a relatively small number of minority faculty members and administrators among us. Here again, we must continue to work hard to recruit outstanding individuals, fully qualified to make their own distinctive contributions as teachers, scholars, and administrators. At the same time, we have to recognize that the very small number of minority candidates, especially in some academic fields important to Princeton, means that progress will inevitably be slow. While it is essential that we make vigorous efforts to identify minority candidates for faculty openings, it is also essential to resist temptations to meet predetermined timetables and purely numerical goals, without regard to qualifications. It would be demeaning in the extreme to suggest by our actions that we have different expectations for minority candidates than for others. We do not.

An implication of the small number of minority faculty members and administrators is that responsibility for being sensitive to questions pertaining to race—questions that are both academic and non-academic in character—cannot possibly be "assigned" only to our colleagues who are themselves members of minority groups. It is a responsibility all of us must accept. But that is, I believe, as it should be in any event.

In thinking about race relations at Princeton, we must also consider this University's unusually strong sense of its own history and traditions. This is a source of great strength, but it can mean that old stereotypes change slowly. As we know, for most of its history Princeton was all male, overwhelmingly Protestant, and almost entirely white. Little is accomplished by trying to judge decisions made in earlier times by present standards, and I am not suggesting that we berate our predecessors—especially since we have so much for which to thank them. But we do need to understand how the University's past affects present-day perceptions. In particular, we should appreciate that it may be difficult for some from groups excluded in the past to feel immediately and fully "at home" here. Fortunately, however, this University also has a great capacity to build on the past, and to improve on it; and it is up to us who are here now to present to those who follow an ever clearer sense of an institution that is warm and welcoming to all.

Another important—and difficult—issue is the balance to be sought between group consciousness and a broader sense of belonging to a single community. Some may think of this as the "integration" versus "separatism" debate, but I find those words so loaded with special meanings as to be unhelpful. I hardly need tell any of you that this is a sensitive topic; it is also a complex one.

It seems to me natural for minority students to want to spend time together—to derive support as well as pleasure from friendships based in part on common backgrounds and concerns. Those of us in the white community are sometimes too quick, in my judgment, to look critically on minority students who wish to be together. Groups of white students may spend just as much time with one another—for largely the same reasons—but with less "visibility" and much less argument over the "correctness" of their actions.

I think it would be extremely unfortunate, however, if the natural desire to form friendships with those who are in some respects most like us should discourage the formation of a wider network of friendships. To the extent that you allow that to happen, your own learning opportunities, and those of others, will be diminished. Most of us will never again live in a setting so rich in opportunities to expand our vistas, to make new friends, to gain new perspectives—even to overturn assumptions about other people that have been comfortable if incorrect. Above all, each person deserves to be seen as a distinct individual, not as a "representative" of any group, however defined. If we fail to take advantage of the privilege of being part of this multiracial community of unique individuals, we will have shortchanged both ourselves and Princeton.

In making this plea for active efforts to form friendships that transcend boundaries of every kind, including the boundaries of race, I know that I am asking you to take risks, to accept the possibility of feeling uncomfortable at times, and even being rebuffed. But I can think of no risks more worth taking. Let me stress that I am addressing these comments to all of us, and certainly not to minority community members alone. Indeed, I believe that it is essential that white students, staff members, and alumni do a great deal of the reaching out; in particular, we should not assume that all interactions should occur in predominantly white settings.

When the Third World Center was established here in 1971, it was intended to serve several important purposes: first, to provide a place where minority students could develop activities especially meaningful to them, a place where they could learn more from and about each other; but also, and equally important, to provide a place where all of us could learn about other cultures and different perspectives. A center of this kind always involves some risks—both for individuals and for the University as a whole. The hope is that we can "have it both ways," at least to some extent—that we can provide a home for a number of minority group activities without thereby cutting minority students off from the rest of the University, or vice versa. Many minority students have in fact succeeded very well in playing active roles within the Third World Center while simultaneously being active in many other areas of campus life. And some white students have taken advantage of the opportunities that the Third World Center offers them. But it should be possible for us to do much better on all counts.

Of course, there are many other organizations on the campus that can foster a wide variety of friendships, and each student should decide individually which activities and which settings are most appealing. The International Center, for example, has enriched the community as a whole by providing opportunities for students from all over the world to meet and get to know each other. The system of residential colleges now being developed has as one of its principal objectives the encouragement of more relaxed and informal associations. Whatever the setting, it is only with trust, and openness, that good relationships can develop. Such attitudes do not, in my experience, grow out of large formal gatherings—nor do they result from presidential pronouncements. Rather, they evolve from friendships formed through shared academic interests, religious associations, athletics, participation in extracurricular activities of all kinds, and college and club involvements. It is the responsibility of the University, I believe, to create opportunities for such interactions, and to encourage them; but we do not, and we cannot, seek to legislate friendships. So much depends, finally, on each of you.

Some of you may have seen the recent television series on the life of J. Robert Oppenheimer, former director of the Institute for Advanced Study here in Princeton. Oppenheimer was a dedicated scientist who also possessed a self-confidence that bordered on arrogance. One of his biographers notes that it was only late in his life that he came to appreciate his need for other people and other perspectives. What he said in one of his last talks seems to me directly relevant to our aspirations for relationships on this campus. He said:

We have, on the one hand, to keep with utmost reverence and devotion and dedication our specialty, our own way, our own life, our own loves. If we do not do that we have no anchor at all in honesty. . . . But we have also, with an equal importance but in a wholly different style, to be responsive to what others have to tell us, to be open to novelty and otherness, to have a sympathy which makes the understanding between men possible. . . . I can think of no greater ideal for the generations whom we in our schools and institutes and universities hope to encourage than to set them an example of people who are trying again to talk to one another, and who are trying again really to listen.

It is my hope that such mutual "listening" will lead to a community at Princeton that is genuinely enriched by both its unity and its diversity. For we ought not, in my judgment, to be thinking in terms of an assimilation of minority students—and minority cultures—into a predetermined set of values and norms that reflect only the contributions of those who happened to be here earlier. The vision to be kept in front of us is of a world of genuine reciprocity.

How are we to move ahead? How are we to come at least somewhat closer to achieving our ideals? In part simply by persevering in the pursuit of objectives already established: by trying to do all that we can to encourage talented students from many backgrounds to come to Princeton as undergraduate and graduate students; by continuing to recruit outstanding minority candidates for faculty and staff openings; and by taking all of the other institutional steps that seem likely to help.

But these institutional actions, important as they are, can do no more than establish a setting. Attitudes, spirit, personal efforts, small steps to be taken by each of us—can mean more in their totality, I suspect, than all of the other options open to us.

We need, in my view, a thoughtful blend of idealism and realism. We must set high standards for ourselves and for our community— being clear, for example, that any racial slurs or innuendoes are unacceptable, and that what we expect, instead, are positive efforts to understand and to reach out. But we also need to recognize that we are no society of paragons, and that there are days when each of us can be remarkably thoughtless. A goodly measure of forgiveness, therefore, and a desire to think the best rather than the worst, will also help.

We all seek, I am confident, that vision of our future that Martin Luther King described so dramatically in his famous speech before the

Lincoln Memorial in August of 1963. "I have a dream," he said, and his dreams then are our dreams now. No one who heard that speech will ever forget the strength of its message of love, of unity, of hope. "We cannot walk alone," he told us, and he went on to speak of working together to transform "the jangling discords of our nation into a beautiful symphony of brotherhood."

The path may be difficult, with steps backward as well as forward. But I am certain of one thing. We shall find fulfillment as individuals—and as a society—only as we recognize our interdependence. . . .

Admissions and the Relevance of Race

ESSAY, 1977*

It is only within the last ten to fifteen years that Princeton, like many other selective colleges and universities, has made deliberate efforts to enroll minority students. As recently as 1962 fewer than 15 black students were attending the undergraduate college and the graduate school combined. We do not have reliable figures for other racial minorities, but there is certainly no reason to believe that, with the possible exception of Asian-Americans, they were enrolled in significant numbers. Since then the situation has changed substantially, partly as a result of many individual and institutional efforts, and partly as a result of the moral concerns and social forces affecting the entire society. In the fall of 1977, for example, we expect to have approximately 340 black students and 300 other minority students in an undergraduate body of 4,400; the comparable figures for the graduate school (again approximate) are expected to be 35 black students and 40 other minority students in a total of about 1,450.

During the same period, similar developments have occurred at most other educational institutions throughout the country. A variety of alternative approaches have been designed to improve the access of minority students, and the issues of principle, policy, and practice raised by these efforts have been discussed widely. Most recently, the case of *The Regents of the University of California v. Allan Bakke*, now before the U.S. Supreme Court, has raised anew—and in the sharpest possible way—the fundamental question of how, if at all, race should be considered relevant in admission decisions.

In a narrower sense, the question before the Court is whether a white applicant, Allan Bakke, was improperly denied admission to the Medical School of the University of California at Davis because of the operation of a special (and separate) admission program that reserved sixteen places out of one hundred in each entering class for minority students. The Supreme Court of California held this admission program to be unconstitutional, and the Regents of the University of California have asked the U.S. Supreme Court to overturn that ruling. Since

* This essay was published in the Summer 1977 issue of *University* magazine and in the *Princeton Alumni Weekly* of September 26, 1977. It was cited on three separate occasions in Justice Lewis Powell's decision on behalf of the Supreme Court.

Princeton does not have a medical school, since we are a private university, and since the admission policies we follow at both undergraduate and graduate levels differ significantly from those in effect at the Davis Medical School (we do not have a separate admission process for minority students nor do we set aside a particular number of places for them), it might be thought that this case has no specific implications for us. That could in fact be right, for no one knows how narrowly or how broadly the Supreme Court will rule. But while we do not expect to be affected directly by the disposition of this case, the language of the majority opinion of the California Supreme Court and the sweeping nature of the arguments advanced in some of the briefs filed in the appeal make it hard to be at all sure that the ruling will be a narrow one.

Moreover, whatever the scope of the Court's decision, the Bakke case has stimulated discussion of such basic questions as: What considerations should be taken into account in deciding which individuals to admit from among the large number who apply? Is it ever proper to consider the race of an applicant, among other attributes? If so, why, and in what ways? Are there significant distinctions to be drawn between the use of quotas and other approaches to the recruitment of minority students?

The answers given to these questions are of obvious importance not only to colleges and universities, but to the country as a whole. They will influence powerfully the opportunities available to individuals to develop their talents to the full; and they will also influence, no less powerfully, both the kind of society to which we aspire and the likelihood of realizing the hopes so many of us share—for a society in which people of many races work together and live together with larger measures of good will and shared respect than exist today.

In stating my own views on some of these questions, I am aware of the different connotations and emotional overtones associated with the very term "race" (which is, nevertheless, unavoidable in this discussion). In addition, it is clear that many of the questions most at issue are sensitive, difficult, and divisive; that good people, with the best possible motives, have come to different conclusions; and that some of the issues are constitutional and involve complex considerations of a legal nature that place them outside the competence of those of us who are not lawyers. Accordingly, this is a personal statement, and it is directed to questions of educational policy rather than to questions of constitutional law. The responsibility for the language and the argu-

ment is mine; at the same time, this statement does reflect substantially
the main policies and rationale followed at Princeton during the last
decade as we have undertaken to make the University more accessible
to minority students as well as to others.

In thinking about this difficult set of questions, one must begin by
considering the broad purposes to be served in making admission decisions—purposes that must themselves reflect the still more fundamental goals of the educational institution as a whole. It is, after all,
only within the context of reasonably well understood objectives that
any particular policy can be assessed. At least part of the disagreement
engendered by discussion of the Bakke case can be attributed, I think,
to differences in assumptions about purpose—differences that are often
implicit. While it may be argued that essentially everything that can be
said about purpose is either so obvious or so general as to be of no help,
there is a basic question to be decided explicitly concerning the nature
of each institution and the group or groups to which those responsible
for it should feel a primary obligation. American higher education is
noted for its healthy diversity, and different approaches to admission
should be expected to follow from different institutional objectives.
Institutional diversity is particularly useful in enabling us to test out
alternative approaches in a relatively new area of activity where there
may be no single "best" approach, and where the best combination of
approaches for the nation as a whole may be known only after considerable time has passed.

In the case of this University, there is a primary commitment to
learning itself, including research as well as liberal education in a wide
variety of disciplines. Thus, our fundamental obligation is not to any
identifiable set of individuals—whether they be applicants, current students, graduates, or faculty members—even though we depend upon
and care greatly about all these groups. Rather, our obligation is to the
society at large over the long run, and, even more generally, to the
pursuit of learning. Amorphous as this way of putting things may
sound, I think there is no escaping our obligation to try to serve the
long-term interests of society defined in the broadest and least parochial
terms, and to do so through two principal activities: advancing knowledge and educating students who will in turn serve others, within this
nation and beyond it, both through their specific vocations and as citizens.

It is clear that admission decisions are critical to our ability to serve
these broad purposes. Accordingly, we invest a great amount of effort

in deciding which individuals to admit from among the large number who apply. While there are many ways of looking at the admission process, for present purposes it may be helpful to distinguish three broad sets of considerations that are involved in choosing among applicants: (1) the basic qualifications of individuals; (2) the composition of the student body; and (3) the potential contributions to society of those applicants possessing the basic qualifications.

Basic Qualifications

It is self-evident that no purpose would be served by admitting students who were unable to take advantage of the educational opportunities offered by a university with demanding academic standards. Every candidate must demonstrate that he or she is capable of doing well at Princeton, and a first obligation of those responsible for admission is, therefore, to decide which applicants have the basic qualifications necessary to satisfy our requirements.

Of course, requirements are different at undergraduate and graduate levels and among graduate programs. At Princeton the graduate admission process is decentralized, with departments and schools accepting responsibility for presenting to the dean of the graduate school recommendations concerning the disposition of each application; the undergraduate college, on the other hand, has a single office of admission which acts on all applications. In the discussion that follows, my main emphasis is on undergraduate admission.

Decisions regarding basic qualifications at the undergraduate level are made on the basis of such evidence as previous academic preparation, including both courses taken and grades earned; recommendations of teachers and others concerning personal qualities as well as academic achievement and promise; aptitude and achievement test scores; the experiences of other students at the University who had similar qualifications; and so on. Reading an applicant's folder to determine even basic qualifications is of course by no means a purely mechanical process. As is well known, there is no perfectly reliable or perfectly "objective" measure of any part of a candidate's credentials, and even such seemingly precise data as grades and test scores have to be examined carefully to determine what actual quality of achievement they reflect and what predictive power they may be thought to have in each instance.

More generally, it is essential to try to understand *why* an applicant has done what he or she has done and then to arrive at a prognosis for the future. While race is not in and of itself a consideration in determining basic qualifications, and while there are obviously significant differences in background and experience among applicants of every race, in some situations race can be helpful information in enabling the admission officer to understand more fully what a particular candidate has accomplished—and against what odds. Similarly, such factors as family circumstances and previous educational opportunities may be relevant, either in conjunction with race or ethnic background (with which they may be associated) or on their own.

Any college or university to which admission is highly competitive has far more applicants who possess all the basic qualifications than it has places. Some candidates (a relatively small number) are so outstanding in every respect that they are obvious choices for admission by any standard. The real problems of choice arise in deciding which individuals to admit from among the large group who also have very strong qualifications, who are thought capable of doing the work and doing it well, but who are not so clearly outstanding as to be placed in the very top category.

In deciding among this group, we do *not* start from the premise that any applicant has a "right" to a place in the University. We start rather from the premise that we have an obligation to make the best possible use of the limited number of places in each entering class so as to advance as effectively as we can the broad purposes we seek to serve. Within the very real limits imposed by the fallibility of any selection process of this kind, we try hard to be fair to every applicant; but the concept of fairness itself has to be understood within the context of our obligations as a university. Accordingly, in making these difficult choices among well-qualified candidates, the second and third sets of considerations come into play.

THE COMPOSITION OF THE STUDENT BODY

The relevance of the second set of considerations is based on the premise that the overall quality of the educational program is affected not only by the academic and personal qualities of the individual students who are enrolled, but also by the characteristics of the entire group of students who share a common educational experience. While I believe this to be true for the graduate program too, it is especially important for undergraduate education and, as a consequence, affects admission decisions much more significantly at that level. The difference is one of degree, related partly to the ages and experiences of the students, partly to the purposes of their educational programs and especially to the emphasis given to academic specialization, and partly to the respective roles of extracurricular and curricular activities.

In a residential college setting, in particular, a great deal of learning occurs informally. It occurs through interactions among students of both sexes; of different races, religions, and backgrounds; who come from cities and rural areas, from various states and countries; who have a wide variety of interests, talents, and perspectives; and who are able, directly or indirectly, to learn from their differences and to stimulate one another to reexamine even their most deeply held assumptions about themselves and their world. As a wise graduate of ours observed in commenting on this aspect of the educational process, "People do not learn very much when they are surrounded only by the likes of themselves."

It follows that if, say, two thousand individuals are to be offered places in an entering undergraduate class, the task of the Admission Office is not simply to decide which applicants offer the strongest credentials as separate candidates for the college; the task, rather, is to assemble a total class of students, all of whom will possess the basic qualifications, but who will also represent, in their totality, an interesting and diverse amalgam of individuals who will contribute through their diversity to the quality and vitality of the overall educational environment.

This concern for the composition of the undergraduate student body, as well as for the qualifications of its individual members, takes many forms. While we are of course interested in enrolling students who are good at a great many things and not one-dimensional in any sense, we also try to enroll students with special interests and talents in the arts and in athletics; we seek a wide geographical representation; we admit foreign students from a variety of countries and cultures; we recognize the special contribution that the sons and daughters of alumni can make by representing and communicating a sense of the traditions and the historical continuity of the University; and we work consciously and deliberately to include minority students, who themselves represent a variety of experiences and viewpoints.

We must accept as a fact of life in contemporary America that the perspectives of individuals are often affected by their race as by other aspects of their background. If the University were unable to take into account the race of candidates, it would be much more difficult to con-sider carefully and conscientiously the composition of an entering class that would offer a rich educational experience to all of its mem-bers.

In the nature of things it is hard to know how, and when, and even if, this informal "learning through diversity" actually occurs. It does not occur for everyone. For many, however, the unplanned, casual en-counters with roommates, fellow sufferers in an organic chemistry class, student workers in the library, teammates on a basketball squad, or other participants in class affairs or student government can be subtle and yet powerful sources of improved understanding and personal growth. . . .

It is of course true—and it should be recognized—that the presence on campus of students of different races sometimes results in tensions and even in hostility. But it is also true that acknowledging this reality, and learning to cope with it, can be profoundly educational. In this as in other respects, we often learn at least as much from our bad days as from our good days.

Perhaps a specific illustration will help make the point. Last October a number of undergraduate dormitories were circulated with leaflets purporting to associate a particular student group with the political and racial views of Lester Maddox. The leaflets called for the exclusion of minority students and other "undesirables" from the University. Not surprisingly, initial reactions were sharp, and the incident quickly gave rise to the expression of bitter feelings on many sides. In some ways these feelings grew even more intense at a later point, when it became clear that the leaflets had been designed as a hoax—and mixed with the sharpness and bitterness was an incredulity that any individuals could be so insensitive to the feelings of others.

This kind of controversy, and the insights it provided, either would not have occurred at all, or would have been far more muted, if there had been fewer minority students at Princeton willing and able to ex-press their reactions, some in quite biting and personal terms. Because of these students, and many others, an experience that was hurtful and disturbing also proved to be very instructive. A number of white stu-dents, caught up in the controversy inadvertently, acquired a deeper understanding of the sensitivities of their fellow students who were members of racial minorities, as well as a new awareness of the seri-ousness of the underlying problem of racism. In addition, a number of minority students learned something about their own insecurities and biases, and about ways of coping with provocations. . . .

These kinds of learning experiences, sometimes very satisfying and sometimes very painful, are important not only for particular students in an immediate sense but also for the entire society over time. Our society—indeed our world— is and will be multiracial. We simply must learn to work more effectively and more sensitively with individuals of other races, and a diverse student body can contribute directly to the achievement of this end. One of the special advantages of a residential college is that it provides unusually good opportunities to learn about other people and their perspectives—better opportunities than many will ever know again. If people of different races are not able to learn together in this kind of setting, and to learn about each other as they study common subjects, share experiences, and debate the most fundamental questions, we shall have lost an important opportunity to contribute to a healthier society—to a society less afflicted by the failure of too many people to understand and respect one another.

POTENTIAL CONTRIBUTIONS TO SOCIETY

The third set of considerations involved in deciding whom to admit from among the large number of qualified candidates also has to do with contributions to the society. Here, however, we are concerned not with the broad educational consequences of a diverse student body but with assessing the potential contributions to the society of each individual candidate following his or her graduation—contributions defined in the broadest way to include the doctor and the poet, the most active participant in business or government affairs and the keenest critic of all things organized, the solitary scholar and the concerned parent.

Assessing the long-range potential of any applicant—trying to determine what the characteristics of individuals can tell us to expect from them beyond their days as students—is, of course, extremely difficult. People change, circumstances change, and there is simply no way of predicting with any great degree of confidence how a particular person will develop as a student in a given educational environment, let alone after he or she has left the University to assume new responsibilities. Nonetheless, if we take seriously our obligation to assign the limited number of places available to us with the ultimate purposes of the institution in mind, we have no alternative but to try to make these assessments of potential, difficult as they may be.

On the basis of our experience, many factors need to be taken into account. A candidate's grade point average and test scores, though significant in assessing potential as well as basic qualifications, are by no means all that are important. It is necessary to try to understand the motivation of the individual, the drive that he or she can be expected to bring to any task at hand, qualities of character and of personality, leadership abilities, skills in relevant non-academic areas, and the personal traits necessary to overcome adversity.

In making such judgments, the race of the individual, as well as many other factors, can be relevant in several respects. It is simply not possible to understand how individuals have come to be the people they are without considering the elements that have shaped them. If two candidates have achieved roughly the same academic results (both meeting fully our basic qualifications), and one has done so in spite of serious difficulties, perhaps including the effects of racial discrimination (or, analogously, the effects of having been disadvantaged in some other way), then that individual may be thought to have demonstrated a degree of drive and determination that should be given weight in the competition for admission.

Race is relevant in another respect. It is a fact of contemporary life, noted by many commentators of quite different persuasions, that our country needs a far larger number of able people from minority groups in leadership positions of all kinds. To put the point bluntly—and to borrow for a moment from the vocabulary of my own discipline of economics—the demand for minority individuals in many professions and fields, compared with the supply, is significantly greater than for the rest of the population. And, I would argue, the true social demand, which should be seen as reflecting the needs of the society as a whole as well as those immediately relevant to its constituent elements, is even greater than the sum total of the perceived demands of individual institutions, businesses, governmental agencies, and the like. It seems to me indisputable that the welfare of the entire society will be advanced through the fuller development and application of the talents of minority members of our population and that this cannot be accomplished without overcoming the substantial disparities that exist now between the races in professional opportunities and attainments.

It is most certainly *not* my view that we should expect—much less try to force—a kind of "proportional representation" of different races or ethnic groups in various professions. But one can stop far short of advocating that kind of statistical outcome and still refuse, as I do, to regard as acceptable the present disparities which are clearly products of generations of unfair treatment.

The substantial public and private support of higher education in this country reflects a longstanding conviction that our institutions of higher learning in all of their forms contribute importantly to the development of what may be called the "social capital" of the nation. We have long believed that the human resources of the society are enhanced enormously by making liberal and humane learning, as well as professional education, available to a large proportion of our people. What is involved here is partly the enhancement of very personal qualities, including the ability to appreciate things of beauty, to develop a set of values, to do nothing less than to lead a full life; and partly the development of talents essential to the social, economic, cultural, and political welfare of the entire society—to the quality of our collective lives, if you will.

If colleges and universities serve these large societal purposes through the individuals they have educated, as well as through scholarship and research, then it seems to me to follow directly that in making admission decisions educational institutions must take into account the needs of the society—including the need for minority persons who can contribute through the law, medicine, the ministry, business, and other professions; who can pursue scholarly careers in the arts and sciences; who can serve in positions of public trust; and who can, in fact, take a full part in every aspect of the life of the nation. If the educational institutions were prevented from being sensitive to race as one factor among others that are relevant in considering the potential contributions of individuals to the society, then it would be far more difficult—indeed impossible—to discharge responsibly the obligation to develop as fully as possible the "social capital" of the country.

In thinking about social capital, it is important to have in mind a very broad concept; we are certainly not talking primarily about economic values or qualities reflected mainly in the marketplace. We mean to include the ability of individuals to contribute through the multitude of informal roles open to the concerned citizen, as well as through vocations and the more formal channels of public service. With this broad conception before us, it is helpful, I think, to view the admission process as involving what are, in one sense, long-term investment decisions. In making its selections, the admission office has to consider which individuals among those with the basic qualifications are most likely over long periods of time to provide what the economist would call the greatest benefit (or highest yield) in terms of contribution to the society.

Thinking in these terms can be useful in part because it allows us to recognize explicitly that risk and potential return are both factors to be taken into account. For reasons that are familiar to all of us, having to do with prior preparation and with the pervasive effects of discrimination, the admission of *some* minority students may entail modestly greater risk than the admission of some non-minority students. But surely it is appropriate to take reasonable risks, remembering that we are talking only about applicants above the "basic qualifications" threshold, in recognition of the very substantial potential returns that may result. (I underscore "some" to emphasize that significant numbers of minority students have had excellent preparation, test well, and have appreciably stronger academic records than many white students who are admitted. One of the discouraging by-products of much of the recent discussion stimulated by the Bakke case is that it seems to have encouraged a certain tendency to assume that all, or nearly all, minority students are less well qualified academically than all, or nearly all, white students. This is not so, and it is unfair to individuals and harmful to our understanding of the real issues to think that it is so.)

Of course, the same considerations apply generally in the admission process. It is often the case that one student with lower test scores than another will seem a better choice to the admission officer because of what appears to be a greater potential, even though the individual may also represent a somewhat greater risk. In short, paying special attention to minority students, because of the barriers many have had to overcome and because of the need society has for larger numbers of well-educated persons from minority groups, is fundamentally only an extension of an important established principle: namely, the need to think hard about every candidate's potential contribution in the light of both what the individual is at the time of application and what he or she may yet become.*

---

* In my view there has been an unfortunate tendency in some of the recent discussion growing out of the Bakke case to assume that arguments pertinent to questions of admission apply without qualification to questions of employment, and vice versa. Thinking about admission decisions as having many of the attributes of a long-term investment decision related to the creation of social capital has the important advantage of suggesting some significant differences (as well as some similarities) between admission decisions and various kinds of university employment decisions. For example, the appointment of a postdoctoral fellow has both some of the attributes of an admission decision (in that one is investing in the further development of an individual's talents and thus trying to develop more social capital for the future) and some of the attributes of an employment decision (in that the person may be expected to contribute immediately and directly to the

For all of the reasons given above, we have concluded, as have many other educational institutions, that in making admission decisions at the present time it is proper to be sensitive to the race of applicants as well as to a great many other characteristics. For my own part, I am convinced, firmly convinced, that this is a correct conclusion. But that is certainly not to say that it is easily reached or that many of us, myself included, reach it without recognizing the substantial and important considerations that pull in the other direction.

There is a real tension, which I think should be acknowledged explicitly, between the strong arguments in favor of being sensitive to race in admission decisions and a deeply felt desire to be free of what is in the ultimate sense a wrong way of distinguishing among human beings. We care finally about what people are and can accomplish as individuals, and not primarily about their race, sex, religion, family background, or politics. To be sure, this is an ideal that we never live up to completely, either individually or institutionally, but it is an ideal nonetheless. And it is largely because of the power of this ideal, and because we are so aware of the abuses that may follow if we depart from it, that one can certainly understand the feelings expressed by one of my colleagues when he said: ''I wish we could wear blindfolds when we admit people.''

Tempting as it may be to base policies on a vision of the world as some of us might wish it to be, it is the present reality that we must address as honestly and as thoughtfully as we can; and I am persuaded that, at this juncture in our history, race *is* relevant. It is relevant because, as I have tried to indicate, ''wearing blindfolds'' would make it harder for us to do three important things in admission: (1) to understand as fully as possible what the record of each applicant really represents in the way of past achievement and future promise as a student; (2) to attain a diversity within the student body that can affect significantly both the quality of the immediate educational experience on the campus and the long-term ability of people of different races to work

---

achievement of a particular research result). At the other end of the spectrum, the appointment of a senior full professor has much less to do with the further development of an individual's talents (though one always hopes that some further learning will occur) and much more to do with trying to put to good use talents that have been developed quite fully already. Of course, there are also other important differences between admission and employment decisions, having to do with the extent and nature of the commitment of the institution to the individual and of the individual to the institution, the risks for both the individual and the institution associated with having one's expectations disappointed, and so on. My general point is simply that the questions of policy concerning admission and the questions of policy concerning employment are both extremely important; each deserves to be considered carefully in its own right.

well with each other; and (3) to assess as thoughtfully as possible every applicant's potential long-run contributions to the society.

The disadvantages of proceeding in this way are obvious. Any time that we allow judgments which are inevitably subjective in more than the usual degree to enter a process of choice, we open up the possibility of abuse—of unwise or wrongful use of discretion. Any time that we allow an attribute such as race to be taken into account at all, we are reminded that too often in the past the consequence has been the arbitrary and unfair limitation of opportunities for particular groups. Moreover, acknowledging the propriety of taking race into account in any way can make it somewhat harder to resist arguments that we should pay more attention to other attributes for which at least some of the same arguments might be advanced but for which, on balance, the case is less persuasive. Taking race into account may also, in the short run at least, exacerbate some antagonisms and generate a new and opposite sense of unfairness, even while contributing to the easing of these same tensions over the long run, as we seek to move through what many of us hope will prove to be a transition period (though quite possibly a long and difficult one). Finally, as I have said, any consideration of race can create a genuine moral dilemma for all of us, of every race, who do not want to think about ourselves or others in such terms.

Conclusions on most important issues are "on balance" conclusions, and those who conclude, as I do, that race does need to be taken into account in admission decisions should not be reluctant to acknowledge the difficulties and the dangers. Indeed, awareness of the full range of concerns is essential if we are to devise sensible methods of translating this general conclusion into specific policies and procedures—policies and procedures that are consistent with the purposes and particular circumstances of each educational institution and that minimize the risk that undesirable results will follow from good intentions.

At Princeton, it has not been our view that sensitivity to race should lead to a quota system, and we have avoided the use of quotas at both undergraduate and graduate levels. We have chosen not to set aside specific numbers of places for minority students or to establish separate admission procedures. Rather, we have made special efforts to identify and attract minority students and we have given them some special consideration in the general admission process, just as we have a number of other groups, including (at the undergraduate level) applicants with artistic and athletic abilities, and children of alumni.

While this approach to the admission of minority students does not imply any formula for determining specific numbers (and in fact the enrollment of minority students has fluctuated appreciably over the last decade or so), it would be quite wrong to suggest that the numbers of those who enroll are irrelevant or unimportant. They matter from the standpoint of the contribution we are able to make to the society through the minority students whom we educate. They matter too from the standpoint of our ability to achieve important educational objectives on the campus. As we have learned from our experience, when there are very few minority students they are apt to feel isolated and unable to make the contributions to the University that we hope and expect them to make; moreover, under such circumstances, particular minority students may also feel especially strong pressure to subordinate some of their own individuality to a perceived need for group identification. Thus, both the importance of encouraging all students to feel free to be themselves and the general case for diversity argue for the desirability of attracting a large enough number of minority students to permit a significant degree of diversity *within* that group as well as within the entire student body.

At the same time, while recognizing that for all of these reasons numbers are significant, we believe strongly that each applicant must be judged as an individual. This is the fundamental reason why the number of minority students should be expected to vary somewhat as the pool of minority applicants changes in size and quality, as other circumstances change (including the number and quality of other applicants), and as experience is gained in admitting and educating a student body that is diverse along many dimensions.

It is for others to decide whether there are differences in constitutional law between these approaches. Whatever the legal distinctions, however, it seems seriously wrong to allow the discussion growing out of the Bakke case to become polarized in the sense of implying that the only alternatives are either adopting quotas based on race or being entirely insensitive to race in making admission decisions. Indeed, in trying to achieve our own educational objectives, we have rejected both of these positions.

Proceeding as we have—taking account of race along with many other factors, but not through the mechanism of a separate admission procedure geared to filling an established number of places—has seemed to us to have two major advantages:

First, it encourages, even forces, comparisons of candidates who present different kinds of special attributes, especially at that point in the process when the most clear-cut admission decisions have been made, and only a relatively small number of places remains for a relatively large number of strong, but not clearly superior, applicants. Making comparisons across various groups, and having them made by a single set of admission personnel, seems fairest to all candidates. This procedure has the advantage of directing attention on a continuing basis to the whole set of considerations that seem relevant in the admission process—and doing so in as consistent a way as possible.

The second advantage of this procedure is, in my judgment, at least as important: It makes clear to the minority students, as to all other students, that everyone who has been admitted has been part of a single admission process, carried out by a single admission staff. An important reason for having a diverse student body is to encourage people who are different from each other to learn from each other and to do so with mutual respect. Any process that separates minority students from other students in terms of perceived criteria or a separate process can work against this objective, in terms of the way minority students see themselves and in terms of the way others see them. Minority students, like all other students, should know that they have been admitted because they have earned admission—because they are expected to do well and to make important contributions to the University and to the society—and not because they are the means whereby we manage to achieve some predetermined numerical result.

In commenting on a draft of a paper I wrote some time ago on affirmative action in employment, a friend of mine said that he thought I had failed to state an important ultimate objective: the desirability of trying to achieve a situation in which every individual, from every background, felt "unselfconsciously included." That states an elusive objective, not attainable for many people in any full sense now, no matter how hard we strive to reach it. But for me it continues to be a phrase full of meaning, indicative of a right direction, and suggestive of a goal worthy of our best efforts.

Affirmative Action: Purposes, Concepts, Methodologies

TESTIMONY BEFORE THE U.S. DEPARTMENT OF LABOR
SEPTEMBER 1975

. . . I would like to begin by associating myself, and, I believe, the overwhelming majority of other college and university presidents, with the positive commitment to equal opportunity which many of us feel so strongly. Historically, colleges and universities have failed to take full advantage of the contributions that women and members of minority groups could have made—could be making now—to higher education in this country. We should recognize explicitly these past deficiencies on our part. We should recognize also that more effective efforts to achieve equality of opportunity will strengthen the ability of our colleges and universities to achieve their educational purposes. Sensible programs of affirmative action can serve this educational purpose as well as the compelling goal of fairness to all concerned.

I hope that in seeking to do better we can approach what are widely shared objectives in a good spirit. One of the more unfortunate consequences, in my view, of the continuing controversy over various aspects of the Executive Order program and its administration is that it has put some unnecessary strains on potentially constructive working relationships. It has led some people of good will to question the motives of other people of good will, and it has diverted far too much time and energy from pursuit of our central purposes to what seem to me to be avoidable problems. The real, substantive problems that we have to surmount in this area are serious ones, and they deserve the best thought and the best effort that all of us can bring to bear on them.

Broadly speaking, the concerns that colleges and universities have had with governmental affirmative action programs to date can be divided into two categories:

1. Concerns over certain administrative requirements and sanctions, including the nature and amount of data required; the slowness of response to plans submitted; the sense that some of those who have been involved in administering the program have not been sufficiently knowledgeable about higher education; the lack, most noticeably this June, of due process in attempting to determine compli-

ance; and the nature of the only sanction available in the event of a finding of non-compliance—termination of federal support for important programs of education and research.

2. Concerns having to do with the basic approach being followed with regard to faculty staffing, including the meaning and measurement of "availability" and "underutilization"; the nature and definition of goals and timetables; the concept of "ultimate goals"; the definition and determination of what constitutes "good faith efforts"; and the emphasis to be given to statistical tests of one kind or another.

Both sets of concerns are extremely important. The first set is being addressed by other speakers, and my task is to consider the second, somewhat broader and more nebulous, set of questions having to do with purposes, concepts, and methodologies.*

As I have reflected on the concerns about basic approach expressed by many people who are extremely sympathetic to the broad intent of the affirmative action effort, it has seemed to me that a good deal of the difficulty resides in what some of the concepts and terminology embedded in Revised Order No. 4 seem to imply about both our real objectives and ways of determining whether or not they are being achieved. I believe we can be rid of some "avoidable" problems by revising certain key concepts, or at least the way we talk about them, seek to translate them into numbers, and try to use them.

To minimize any risk of misunderstanding, it may be helpful to state explicitly certain premises on which my discussion rests. The first is that the fundamental objective of the entire effort is to assure as well as we can that members of both sexes and of all races and ethnic groups have genuinely equal opportunities to be appointed, to be advanced, and to contribute to the fundamental educational purposes of colleges and universities. I believe that active, "affirmative" efforts to deepen and broaden pools of candidates are needed to achieve genuine equality of opportunity; that a passive approach is not sufficient; that we need to work hard to overcome the subtle as well as overt forms that discrim-

---

* There is also a third set of questions, addressed at length in the recent Carnegie Council report on affirmative action, having to do with the supply side of the process of broadening the composition of our faculties. These questions are particularly important in the case of minority groups, and there is considerable agreement that special efforts need to be made to encourage more minority students to pursue academic careers. The generally depressed state of the academic labor market, and the shortage of funds to support graduate students, make this difficult, but the problem seems to many of us important enough to justify a serious search for new approaches that will be both effective and fair to the individuals concerned.

ination can take. But I believe too that, following such efforts at deepening and broadening pools, the individual best qualified to fill each opening, given the needs of the college or university in question, should be appointed regardless of sex, race, or ethnic origin.

This statement of objective is offered here not because I think it is at all original; on the contrary, I believe it is widely shared within both the academic community and the government. But it does provide a crucial point of departure precisely because of the emphasis it gives to ultimate concern for what happens to each individual. The implications of this approach are quite different from those that would follow if our objective were some kind of proportional representation or other form of result defined in terms of groups. This emphasis on the individual is consistent with our two principal, reinforcing concerns: (1) fair treatment of all persons; and (2) strengthening the quality of our educational institutions by trying to make the best possible appointment in every instance.

Notwithstanding the emphasis I have placed on the individual, I believe it is also true that numerical analysis of the circumstances of different groups can be an altogether proper—indeed potentially very helpful—tool in advancing the objective of equality of opportunity. For example, comparisons of the proportions of women and members of minority groups among newly recruited faculty members with their proportions in the pools from which appointments are made can serve to direct our attention to situations in which a detailed review of procedures for recruitment and selection is clearly called for. Colleges and universities have found such comparisons useful in their own efforts, and I believe such comparisons can also be helpful to government agencies in suggesting where more detailed analysis may be appropriate. In addition, nationwide data showing the numbers of individuals from various groups in different disciplines can serve to encourage discussion of realistic possibilities for broadening the composition of faculties and to stimulate longer-run efforts to increase numbers of women and members of minority groups available for appointment.

Since I am testifying here today at the request of the American Council on Education and the Association of American Universities, I should point out that some thoughtful persons in the academic community are not inclined to give numerical analysis much if any role in affirmative action efforts, especially at the level of the individual institution. That is not my position, but I want to emphasize that my own support for certain types of numerical analysis assumes that the concepts will be defined in ways appropriate to our purposes and that the very real limitations of the measures that can be made will be respected. Let me now try to explain in some detail the limitations that must be borne in mind if we are to make proper use of the figures at our disposal.

"AVAILABILITY"

In the existing regulations, a good deal depends on the concept of "availability." "Availability" for faculty positions has usually been measured in terms of the number of holders of doctoral degrees. However, for reasons discussed at considerable length in the recent report of the Carnegie Council (see 5–23 to 5–25), the number of candidates who really might be "available" to fill a particular opening is likely to be very different from (usually much smaller than) the total pool of people with the requisite formal qualifications.

First, among those meeting the basic degree requirements for any given position, there may be important differences, of a more or less systematic kind, in the interests of individuals in teaching versus research, in preferences for different kinds of colleges and universities, in the nature and quality of the graduate training received, in the amount of "human capital" accumulated over time, and in academic standing at the time of completion of graduate work or subsequently.*

It is also necessary to recognize that many people are far from perfectly mobile—and thus are not really available in any meaningful sense even if they have both all of the necessary qualifications and a set of interests that coincides in the abstract with the opening in question. People may already have very attractive jobs, or strong preferences for a certain geographical location, or a commitment to stay in an area where a spouse is employed—and any of these considerations may well

---

* In recognizing the possible existence of potentially important differences of this kind, as it seems to me that we must, we should also recognize that current differences between groups in certain of these respects may themselves be the result, at least in part, of past patterns of discrimination. For example, the finding of Johnson and Stafford ("The Earnings and Promotion of Women Faculty," *American Economic Review*, December 1974) that men have tended to accumulate more "human capital" during their professional lives than women is undoubtedly due in some (unknown) degree to the greater difficulties women have found in obtaining suitable academic employment, to the presence, all too often, of weaker monetary incentives for women than for men to accumulate more human capital, to the lack of policies that would have encouraged more women to continue their employment, and so on. The existence of such relationships should alert us to the need to make changes in those discriminatory factors under our control at the same time that we recognize the present realities. (Plainly social customs and attitudes within the society generally have also played a role in producing such patterns.)

lead individuals to view themselves as unavailable for job openings for which they might otherwise deserve consideration.*

For this combination of reasons the national data on degree recipients with which we must work should not be thought of as measuring, even approximately, the number of candidates actually available for particular openings. The purpose of making this distinction is not to suggest that estimates on a national basis of the numbers of persons with degrees in various disciplines are of no use. Nor is the purpose to imply that the percentages of women and members of minority groups actually available are necessarily larger or smaller than the corresponding percentages of degree recipients. (The evidence on many of these questions is nonexistent, conflicting, or indicative of changing patterns.) The point, rather, is that it is important to be aware of potentially serious shortcomings in a set of numbers of one kind—measuring degrees awarded—when what is sought is something quite different—measures of the number of likely candidates for particular kinds of openings. We need to recognize explicitly the limitations of such data so as not to place too much weight on them or to invest them with a specious precision.

Complications of this kind warn against expecting too much from suggestions that either governmental agencies or educational organizations produce a single set of data that would be thought to indicate, even roughly, the availability of various groups of individuals for various kinds of openings, especially when we take into account the fact that particular openings may be defined in terms of special fields within an academic discipline or may call for interests and talents different from those appropriate to other openings for which the same degree is normally prerequisite. In short, as convenient as it might be to have a single set of national data, we should be aware of the impossibility of reflecting with any appreciable degree of accuracy the actual circumstances that confront the many individual colleges and universities. Fi-

---

* I use the words "view *themselves* as unavailable" in an effort to avoid confusing what are real limits on mobility as the individual concerned sees his or her own situation and perceptions by a college or university of someone else's mobility—perceptions which may well be wrong. In the case of women, in particular, colleges and universities have been guilty on far too many occasions of simply assuming that a potential candidate would not be willing to move to a new location and therefore would not be interested in being considered. Such indefensible practices have made many women very sensitive about any reference to mobility. This sensitivity is entirely understandable, especially when we also recognize that presumed differences in overall degrees of mobility between married men and married women are sometimes used to try to explain away more of the differences in employment patterns than probably should be attributed to this factor; at the same time, there is no denying that willingness to move is a crucially important determinant of availability, and it would be helpful if there were more evidence on this subject.

nally, even if all of the problems referred to above concerning qualifications and preferences of individuals, mobility, and differences among institutions, were to disappear, the availability data relevant to any particular college or university at any particular point in time would still be likely to differ somewhat from the national (or regional) data. The reason is simply the presence of random differences in any set of data drawn from a larger universe.

"UNDERUTILIZATION"

One significant use made of availability data under present regulations is to determine whether or not there is "underutilization" of women or minorities in any job group. The recent directive issued by the Department of Labor applying Revised Order No. 4 to colleges and universities requires that "whenever the percentage of such persons [women and representatives of each minority group] in that job group is less than the percentage available within the applicable labor area, the affirmative action program must specifically state that underutilization exists in that group" (*Federal Register,* August 25, 1975, p. 37066).

This concept of "underutilization" (given the normative connotations of the term) is troubling to many of us, and not just because the data used to measure availability are themselves so imprecise and unreliable. The more fundamental objection is philosophical and is related directly to the question of whether our ultimate objective really is equality of opportunity for individuals. In the minds of most people, "underutilization" surely implies that something is wrong; indeed, Labor Department regulations speak directly of the need to "eliminate" underutilization, and the entire mechanism of goal-setting is rooted in this concept.

Even if it were possible, somehow or other, to obtain perfect availability data, a failure to satisfy the kind of exact "proportional representation" test invoked here need *not* imply that there has been discrimination or that there is "underutilization" in any normative sense. It is very important to be clear why this is so. The reason is that so long as we are meant to fill each position with the best qualified individual, regardless of that individual's race, sex, or ethnic background, the sum total of such decisions in the case of any given department, division, or even college would result only rarely in a distribution of individuals that matched *exactly* the distribution based on availability statistics. Simply because of the presence of random factors, we should expect that sometimes there will be relatively more members of a particular group employed than would be suggested even by perfect availability data, and sometimes relatively fewer members. And, the smaller the hiring unit in question and the smaller the minority group, the greater the importance of random factors.

Focusing so much attention on an exact correspondence between a set of availability data and the current composition of the faculty can also lead departments in which there is no apparent underutilization to believe that they have "done their duty" and therefore have no further obligation to search broadly for talent and to provide full opportunity for women and members of minority groups to compete successfully for all available positions.

The need to think in terms of probability distributions can be seen most easily by considering some simple examples.* Assume that women constitute 25 percent of the (relatively large) pool of candidates for a particular university in a certain discipline. Assume also that there are no differences in the overall distribution of ability between the men and the women and that a strictly non-discriminatory selection process is used. If there are four openings, the probability is 43 percent that exactly one of the four persons appointed will be a woman, 31 percent that none of the four will be a woman, 21 percent that two of the four will be women, 4 percent that three will be women, and 0 percent (rounded to the nearest whole percentage point) that all four will be women. If there are only two positions to be filled, the probability is 56 percent that neither will be a woman, 38 percent that one of the two persons appointed will be a woman, and 6 percent that both will be women.

Suppose now that the number of openings in the particular discipline

---

* I am indebted to Professor Stephen M. Goldfeld of our faculty for these calculations, which are based on conventional probability theory. In the interest of simplicity, we are assuming here that all positions are filled simultaneously.

Unfortunately, we pay a price for the illustrative value of calculations of this kind. All such calculations must of course be based on assumptions that are precise and, as a rule, far simpler than the reality which all of us must confront in making actual personnel decisions. Thus, in considering such calculations (which are meant not to reflect reality but to clarify basic issues) the complexity—and the difficulty—of making the actual decisions may be lost to view. For example, it is assumed in this analysis that the personal attributes of candidates, as they may have been influenced by the sex, race, and ethnic origins of the individuals as well as their personal experiences and perceptions, are irrelevant to the openings in question. That may or may not be true, depending on the field of study, the relation between such attributes and the way individuals approach scholarship and teaching, the educational priorities of the department and of the entire institution, and so on. What is required, I think many of us would agree, is the kind of "wise sensitivity" to the educational implications of personal attributes to which President Bok of Harvard has referred in another context. But I know of no probability calculus that can handle this level of complexity.

is appreciably larger. If there are 64 openings, for example, the probability is 16 percent that the number of women appointed will be equal to or less than 12; 8 percent that it will be 13; 10 percent that it will be 14; 11 percent that it will be 15; 12 percent that it will be 16; 11 percent that it will be 17; 9 percent that it will be 18; 8 percent that it will be 19; and 16 percent that it will be 20 or more. Or, to put the results of these illustrative calculations another way, even when we work with a relatively large number of openings and assume far more precise information about the availability of candidates than is in fact ever going to be at our disposal, there are still only two chances out of three that a perfectly non-discriminatory selection process will result in the appointment of between 13 and 19 women. Of course, relaxing the assumption about the precision of our knowledge of availability could widen this range appreciably.

Ignoring the probabilistic nature of all numbers of this kind, and treating as a shortcoming every departure from exact conformity with the pattern that would be suggested by an ideal set of availability data (even if such data were obtainable), has one absolutely fatal defect at the level of principle: it implies that our objective is what the Carnegie Council has termed "equality of forced results" rather than "equality of actual opportunities" for individuals.

The strength of this objection can be seen clearly when we ask ourselves what conclusion we would draw if the distribution of employment in a college or university were in fact to conform exactly, department by department, to the distribution suggested by availability data. Presumably there would be no "underutilization." However, such a result would be so extraordinarily unlikely if each appointment decision really were being made in a strictly non-discriminatory manner that a pattern of this kind would itself be powerful evidence of the *presence* of discrimination in some employment decisions, not the absence of such discrimination. The probability of such an outcome in the absence of efforts to achieve a certain numerical pattern would be miniscule.

There is a further problem with the availability data themselves when we seek to use them as a benchmark against which to compare not just the kinds of people appointed recently but the composition of the *entire* faculty as it stands at one point in time. The underutilization concept as it is now defined requires that the availability data be used in just this way since the comparison that must be made is between the composition of the entire "job group" and some measure of availability. It is important to note that if we are to make a fair comparison of the entire workforce as it exists at present with an appropriate concept of availability, we have to obtain data on availability *at the different points in time at which each of the positions on the staff was filled.* Also, some account should be taken of the possibility that members of different groups, whatever their initial availability, may have continued to be actively available for different proportions of their lifetimes. Obviously these factors make the task of calculating a correct measure of availability, difficult as that is for current openings, all the harder when the objective is a set of numbers that is to be compared against the present faculty, recruited as it has been over a long period of time.

These considerations—the extraordinary difficulty of obtaining even roughly reliable data that can be used to approximate availability, and the probabilistic nature of any proper test of conformity between whatever availability data can be obtained and observed patterns of employment—lead me to wonder if it is sensible to continue to insist on making use of the "underutilization" concept with respect to faculty staffing. For reasons I shall describe below, I believe that "goals and timetables," properly conceived and used, can serve helpful purposes. But I am not all sure that the same thing can be said about "utilization" analysis. If goals and timetables are to be related to actual openings that occur, as it seems to me they should be if they are to be realistic and effective, they will require estimates of numbers of persons currently available, but they do not need to be derived from utilization analysis. Without in any way suggesting that there is a satisfactory representation of women and minorities now—plainly there is not in many colleges and universities—we may be well advised to focus on the possibilities that exist to improve the situation as it is now rather than on weakly based measures of past deficiencies—measures that are subject to serious challenge. My own preference, in keeping with the theme of this testimony, would be to avoid regulations that require what will be seen by many people as statistical charades.

If, these considerations notwithstanding, "utilization" analysis continues to be thought worthwhile, it seems to me that at the minimum, the concept as it is to be applied to the faculties of colleges and universities should be revised: (1) to recognize the substantial limitations of efforts to estimate "availability" on the basis of data showing numbers of degrees awarded to various groups, and (2) to recognize explicitly that considerable variations between the distribution of availability data and the composition of faculties should be expected in any case.

GOALS AND TIMETABLES

No part of Revised Order No. 4 has resulted in more heated debate than the requirement that goals and timetables be established. There has been more than a little confusion, as well as disagreement, about what is required and what the requirements imply, and it may be that at least part of the difficulty is with the terminology itself.

A common interpretation of the meaning of "goals" in the context of faculty hiring is "normal expectations of what would happen if there were no discrimination" (Carnegie Council, 1975, pp. 1–15). This definition is consistent with our objectives: equality of opportunity for individuals and finding the best possible person for each opening. Moreover, as I indicated earlier, I believe there are important advantages in having rough numerical projections of the likely consequences over time of combining active efforts to broaden and deepen the pool of candidates with a policy of seeking to appoint the best qualified candidate each time there is an opening. Projections of this kind can be very important in stimulating an ongoing commitment to affirmative action—to the fairest and most effective processes of recruitment and advancement that we can devise—throughout the college or university and in directing attention to particular situations in which there may be continuing deficiencies in recruitment or appointment processes which require correction.

But it is not obvious that such projections should be called "goals." Indeed, the word "goal" seems to be something of an inherited misnomer in this particular context. The trouble with referring to projections of what we might reasonably expect to happen as "goals" is that we thereby suggest to a great many people that what we are striving for are the numbers themselves—that is, a particular composition of the faculty, defined in terms of sex, race, and ethnic background. Nor does emphasizing that the "goals" need not be achieved if it can be demonstrated that a good faith effort was made really meet the point of principle. A goal is something for which one strives, and what we are meant to be striving for here is not a particular numerical result, but equality of opportunity for every individual and the best possible appointment in every instance. The aggregate numbers for groups of people should be seen as expected by-products of affirmative action efforts, not as the goals themselves.

The importance of being clear about what we are trying to accomplish stems in no small part from the need to secure and sustain strong support for affirmative action from as many faculty members, administrators, and staff members as possible. The good will and commitment of this large group is at least as important as the visible support of heads of departments and highly-placed central administrators; and to many faculty members and others in the academic community, a key question is whether the numbers are to be seen as ends in themselves. Drawing an explicit and rather sharp distinction between goals and projections can be extremely helpful in allaying fears and in strengthening the desires of a great many people to do what they can to make genuine equality of opportunity more of a reality than it has been. Also important is overcoming any notion that women or individuals from minority groups have been hired because of a need to reach a certain numerical goal. Such an assumption within a university community can quickly result in a condition of second class citizenship for some members of the faculty. The implications for the worth of the individuals concerned obviously are very different when the goal is seen as selecting the best individual, regardless of sex or race, from as broad and deep a pool as possible.

Thus, for all of these reasons, I recommend that we speak explicitly of numerical projections rather than of numerical goals. Also, for reasons that have already been spelled out in discussing availability and underutilization, I would suggest, as a second recommendation, that we recognize explicitly the probabilistic nature of our projections, perhaps even attempting to estimate the standard errors associated with them.

If these two steps were taken we would, I think, have gone a long way to end the controversy over the real nature of our objectives and whether goals will not end up being quotas after all.* And we would not have lost the value of having a set of numerical expectations that can be used, along with a great deal of other information about the processes of recruitment and advancement, to help us evaluate how we are doing over time. As I said at the beginning of this discussion, I

---

* The continuing nature of the controversy over goals versus quotas is indicated by recent remarks of the Attorney General of the United States, Edward Levi. On July 29, 1975, he was quoted as saying: "The country has been on a program where affirmative action requiring the statement of goals is said with great profoundness not to be the setting of quotas. But it is the setting of quotas. So what we have done is to assure ourselves that we are against quotas, and this doesn't involve quotas. And we will call quotas goals, and if we call them goals and swallow hard, or stop thinking until they've appeared on the other side of the argument, then it's okay. And so we have both sides. So we're against quotas and we're for goals. That's really not very good government, in my view. And it means that there are issues that we prefer not to think about. That's really what it means."

believe that numerical projections can be very helpful. Without them, it would be difficult to know where to concentrate our energies in seeking to recruit more broadly and more effectively; and it would be too easy to overlook what may be important and continuing problems. But we should not ask the numbers to do more for us than they can.

Let me now mention rather briefly six other concerns that have been expressed about goals and timetables. First, there has been a concern that the hiring units for which goals (or, as I would much prefer to state it, projections) are to be developed may be defined too narrowly. The case for giving colleges and universities considerable flexibility in determining how broad the unit ought to be seems very strong. As the Carnegie Council argues, the right unit may be the college, a division, a cluster of departments, or a single department—depending on such considerations as the numbers of people involved and the administrative structure of the institution. This principle is accepted in the recent directive issued by the Department of Labor, and that is clear progress. When institutions are required to make projections for very small units, the results can easily be meaningless, and the production of such figures is neither helpful in and of itself nor conducive to building confidence in the common sense and good judgment of those charged with administering the government regulations.

A second, related concern has been that separate projections may be required for minority groups which are themselves so small in terms of the academic discipline in question as to offer no possibility for meaningful analysis. Again, some reasonable degree of aggregation seems sensible, as provided for in the recent Department of Labor directive.

At this point, however, it is necessary to add an important warning concerning pitfalls that can be associated with aggregation—whether the aggregation takes the form of combining departments or minority groups. In an extremely interesting paper on sex bias in graduate admissions published in *Science* magazine in February 1975, Dr. P. J. Bickel and two colleagues at the University of California at Berkeley show dramatically how easy it is to draw wrong conclusions about bias by using aggregate data. In the case they examine, what appears to be substantial bias in one direction turns out to represent, if anything, bias in the opposite direction once the aggregate data are broken down by departments. The problems involved are too complex to describe here, but I think we should be aware that while larger numbers ease some statistical problems, aggregation can create others, especially if, as is often the case, there are differences in either the pools of candidates or the degree of competition for openings among the disciplines or minority groups being combined. This is not an argument against aggregation, but it is a plea for care in aggregation and for care in interpreting the results of aggregation.

Third, there has been concern that colleges and universities may be asked to make projections that extend so far into the future as to be of dubious value for any practical purpose. A good rule of thumb is to relate the time period for which projections are made to: (1) the nature and quality of the statistical data available; and (2) the normal period for faculty planning at the college or university in question. Six years would seem to be a reasonable period, since this is a common period of "probationary" service for newly appointed faculty members at the nontenure levels. Here too, however, some flexibility should be given to institutions.

Fourth, there is a difficult problem in the case of tenure appointments. I do not believe that affirmative action efforts should be concerned only with appointments at the nontenure levels. It is extremely important that women and members of minority groups be given every opportunity to compete fairly for tenure as well as nontenure positions. At the same time, I see no very satisfactory way of developing statistical projections that will be very helpful in connection with most tenure openings. The numbers are often so small, and the range of likely results from a statistical standpoint so wide, that the exercise seems hard to justify. Moreover, since the pool of candidates for a tenure opening often consists of people of widely differing ages, there is an exceedingly difficult practical problem of measuring "availability." Figures for the number of recent recipients of doctoral degrees are of little or no value in this context, attachments of senior people to existing positions and locales are particularly strong, and for these and other reasons, no one seems yet to have made much progress in even approximating availability for this purpose. Perhaps the best approach is to be sure that colleges and universities make special efforts to monitor carefully the processes of promotion and recruitment when a tenure opening is being filled. This is not always easy to do, but I do not believe there is any real alternative.

A fifth concern under this heading has to do with "ultimate goals" and the concept of a kind of final "parity." Unfortunately, Revised Order No. 4 as it now reads has been interpreted as requiring every contractor to establish an "ultimate goal" for each job group in which underutilization exists, and this ultimate goal must apparently be designed to correct fully the alleged underutilization and to achieve a kind of ultimate "parity." As has been recognized, a goal of this kind would often have to be achieved over many decades, and it is hard to see what practical purpose is served by investing a great deal of effort in constructing projections of this kind—especially when it is recognized that the existing data base is inadequate for such a task; that the relative numbers of women and members of minority groups in different disciplines change over time; that the disciplines themselves change in relative importance; that we ought not, in any event, to be so preoccupied with the numbers themselves; and that, finally, no one really can expect to look so far into the future with any reasonable degree of confidence. Requiring projections that look so far ahead has the further disadvantage of suggesting to a number of people that the affirmative action effort consists to too great an extent of playing with numbers rather than working now to improve the lot of real people.

If the concept of underutilization were to be eliminated for faculty positions (and, for reasons noted above, this seems to me worth careful consideration), then this problem would disappear. But even if utilization analyses are retained, I would recommend that the calculation of "ultimate goals" no longer be required.

My final point with respect to goals and timetables is of a rather different sort and is, in the minds of a number of my colleagues in higher education, the most important of all: it has to do with the use that will be made of statistical projections in evaluating good faith efforts. Others can speak more knowledgeably and effectively than I can to the large and important subject of burdens and standards of proof. Let me suggest only that the crudity of the projections of composition of faculty groups by sex, race, and ethnic background, the probabilistic nature of such data, the small numbers often involved, and the appreciable differences among departments within the same institution and across institutions in the definitions of particular personnel needs—all warn strongly against putting much weight on any simple numerical analysis in seeking to determine whether good faith efforts have been made.

Also, it follows directly from what has been said earlier about the statistical improbability of meeting exactly each projection within each hiring unit that actual results in some disciplines exceeding original projections must be seen as offsetting results in other areas that are below projections. Similarly, performance in one time period that was better than anticipated should be offset against performance in another time period that fell short of what was anticipated. These principles are wisely incorporated in the recent Labor Department directive.

A related point concerns the need to be very careful in drawing strong conclusions from "worst cases"—those departments or clusters of departments in which the most disappointing results, compared with expectations, are observed. There is always bound to be, by definition, *a* worst case; and, as Bickel et al. have demonstrated convincingly in the *Science* article cited previously, it is simply wrong to look at the figures for the worst case as if the department or unit in question had been chosen randomly for inspection. Indeed, it has been chosen for scrutiny precisely because it showed the most disappointing results. Therefore, the norm against which such results should be compared is not what we would expect to find on the average in looking at the experiences of all the departments in the institution. Indeed, fairness requires that we examine the probability that the worst case we would expect to observe among all the departments, simply on a chance basis, will be as far from the overall norm as the results we have actually observed for the department in question.

Recognizing the extremely limited degree of assistance in determining "good faith" that can be obtained from statistical tests in most of the situations we are likely to encounter in connection with affirmative action plans is important not only because it reduces the risk that incorrect and unfair judgments will be reached. It is important too because of what it says about the great importance that must therefore be attached to the policies and procedures used to advance the cause of affirmative action and to monitor the results obtained.

All of us have an important stake in ensuring that personnel decisions are made fairly. Unfortunately, however, there is no way of guaranteeing fairness. Just as it is easy to make things seem much worse than they are, and to try to explain away any decisions one does not like on generalized grounds of unfairness, it also is undoubtedly true that the imprecision, variability, and subjectivity inherent in making personnel decisions have been used to mask judgments with discriminatory overtones. Thus, it is not hard to understand the suspicion and distrust felt by some members of groups excluded for too long. Given the many subtle forms that prejudices can take, I certainly would not suggest that the protections afforded by even the soundest policies and the most effective procedures will be infallible—plainly they will not be. But it does seem to me that over time the best protection against discriminatory decisions is likely to come from a combination of sensible policies affecting recruitment, selection, and advancement; better designed procedures allowing individuals who feel aggrieved to receive a full, fair, and expeditious hearing from their peers; and an ever more widely shared commitment to fair play.

I do believe that substantial progress has been made in improving attitudes and perceptions and in designing policies and procedures. I believe, too, that more can be accomplished along these lines—and without substituting new forms of unfairness for old ones. As we seek to assure that "good faith" efforts are being made to achieve the objectives of affirmative action, we do need, ultimately, to count on the many individuals throughout our university communities who are involved in the process of deciding on appointments and advancements. The fact that mechanical tests and statistical measures are of limited value in judging how well we are doing should increase, not lessen, the sense of responsibility all of us feel for doing as much as we can to ensure genuine equality of opportunity.

*   *   *   *   *

I have already exceeded the time that I should have taken today, and rather than comment on the other problems of administration and of sanctions to which I alluded at the outset, I would like to end by restating a theme with which I began these remarks. I think we need to work hard to transform much of the energy now going into disputes of one sort or another into more positive efforts to improve both opportunities for women and members of minority groups in higher education and their relationships with the other members of our academic communities—improving thereby the larger educational enterprise to which all of us are committed.

A better tone and spirit are important to the health of our institutions, and they are also extremely important from the standpoint of the women and members of minority groups being appointed. At the present time it is true all too often that very well qualified individuals are thought—wrongly and unfairly—to have been appointed because of what some think to have been the need of the college or university to achieve a certain numerical result mandated by the federal government. Impressions of this kind can have long-lasting effects on the professional lives of the individuals concerned, can harm relationships with colleagues and others in the institution, and can interfere seriously with the achievement of the broader purposes that affirmative action is meant to serve. Certainly it would be a sad and unfortunate irony if a program designed to bring about greater equality of opportunity inadvertently generated a climate of feelings that made total participation in the academic life of this country more rather than less difficult. . . .

My hope is that we have now learned enough—had enough experience—to do better in pursuit of the always elusive goal of genuine equality. But we need to do better in ways that enhance the dignity and self-respect of each individual, not in ways that subjugate the individual to the group and increase the tendency to think of individuals mainly in terms of sexual, racial, or ethnic categories. That is a tendency that I think should be deplored everywhere, but especially in colleges and universities, meant as they are to celebrate the unique potential that resides in every one of us.

Maintaining Opportunity: Undergraduate Financial Aid at Princeton

REPORT OF THE PRESIDENT
APRIL 1983

Since its earliest days, Princeton has recognized the importance of providing scholarship aid for needy students. At no time, however, has the general subject of financial aid been as complex—or as critical—as it is today. In company with all other colleges and universities, Princeton is faced with difficult choices concerning financial aid policies as it seeks to cope with rising costs and diminishing support from some sources, particularly government programs. Students and their families face equally hard questions as they try, sometimes with considerable anxiety, to meet their share of the costs of a Princeton education. More broadly, the country as a whole must decide what priority is to be given to maintaining access to educational opportunities, what policies and programs are likely to be most effective in promoting this goal, and what degree of responsibility for providing the resources should be assumed by the federal government, state governments, private donors, and individual students and their families.

Because of the long-term importance of these questions, I have decided to devote this annual report to the single subject of undergraduate financial aid. Issues of equal importance exist at the graduate level, but they are different in important respects and require separate treatment (see Report of the President, April 1981).

This report begins with a brief restatement of the reasons why financial aid is so important to the future of Princeton as a university as well as to individual students. Part II provides some history of financial aid at Princeton. Part III consists of a description of current policies and practices. Finally, in Part IV, there is an analysis of the outlook for financial aid, including projected costs, and a discussion of the principal policy alternatives facing both the society as a whole and Princeton in particular.

The Importance of Financial Aid at Princeton

The educational quality of Princeton depends first and foremost on its human material: on the faculty and students who combine to create a genuine community of learning. If we are to continue to aspire to the highest standards of excellence, we must continue to attract the ablest students as well as the ablest faculty members. Since by no means all of the strongest candidates for admission can afford a Princeton education without at least some help, financial aid is as essential to the quality of our student body as adequate salaries are to the quality of our faculty. A central part of the case for financial aid is as simple as that.

Many people who accept this general line of argument will nonetheless be surprised—as I was when I first saw the figures—by how many of our most successful students have received some form of financial aid. Over the last ten years, for example, of the sixty-five Princeton undergraduates who have been valedictorians or who have won Rhodes or Marshall Scholarships, thirty-eight (58 percent) received scholarship or loan assistance. If we go back thirty years, we find that fully 70 percent of all the Princeton valedictorians (the only group for which consistent data exist) received some form of financial aid.

There is, of course, also a broader point to be made about the relationship between financial aid and the educational quality of Princeton. It has often been said that students learn as much from each other as they do from their teachers. Friendships formed through dormitory and social life, athletics, and extracurricular activities generally, as well as through associations growing out of precepts, classes, and time spent together in the library or laboratory, contribute greatly to personal growth as well as to "education" broadly defined. The range of backgrounds, perspectives, and interests that makes Princeton such a stimulating place for so many students simply would not be represented in each entering class without a substantial financial aid program.

As I said at last June's Commencement, the present-day diversity of the student body at Princeton is not something separate from the University's commitment to educational excellence: it is required by it. This view is shared by a great many at Princeton, and it helps to explain why faculty and students who are not themselves scholarship students often support so strongly the University's commitment to financial aid. Michele Warman '82, winner of the Pyne Prize her senior year, spoke to this point at Alumni Day:

> What I treasure most about Princeton is that it is an academic *community* and not merely a narrowly academic institution. What I have learned has come not only from my intellectual pursuits, but from the friendships I have formed with others and from the activities we

have engaged in together. . . . How much I have grown and how much my attitudes have changed since I have had the opportunity to get to know Princeton's people!

There is, finally, an important principle to be reaffirmed: the principle of opportunity. We have been proud to say that the opportunity to study at Princeton depends on an individual's talent, character, determination, and personal qualities—and that no one who is qualified, and who is willing to work and to sacrifice, should be deprived of the opportunity to attend Princeton because of financial circumstances.

This principle is related directly to a broader national goal—to the proposition that in this country individuals should be able to move up the ladder of accomplishment as far as their energies and abilities will take them. It cannot be claimed that, as a nation, we have served this high purpose perfectly, since barriers of many kinds continue to exist; however, we have done better than most other countries in this respect. It is especially important in a country so richly pluralistic that individuals from diverse backgrounds have the opportunity to learn together— and from each other. The ideal of opportunity remains an essential element of our national character, and we must continue to prepare leaders who themselves have seen this ideal given reality in the educational experiences they have shared with others.

SOME HISTORICAL PERSPECTIVE

Contrary to what is sometimes assumed, Princeton's present financial aid policies did not originate in some spontaneous fashion out of events and attitudes of the last two decades. Rather, they have evolved out of values deeply rooted in Princeton's past, and they can be understood fully only in the context of their historical development. More generally, financial aid policies have long been the product of educational philosophies that are themselves derived from the character of the larger society. Thus, any attempt even to sketch the origins of financial aid policies requires at least some attention to the history of higher education in America.

From the arrival of the early settlers, education—including college education—was held in high esteem in America. Massachusetts passed the first school law in 1647 out of a concern that citizens be able to read and understand the laws of the state as well as the principles of their religion. Indeed, with the help of the colonial governments, colleges were established quite early in our nation's history, both for their symbolic value in representing the successful implantation of European culture and for their practical value in replenishing the ranks of ministers and public leaders.

In the immediate aftermath of the American Revolution, difficult issues arose stemming from the principle of separation of church and state and the struggle over the delineation of federal and state authority. Also influencing these early discussions were the ideals of the new democratic republic. The fundamental concept of social justice led many to believe that gifted students should be provided with the opportunity to advance through education. Jefferson was especially adamant on this point, exhorting the republic to nurture at public expense the "natural aristocracy of talent and virtue." In his view, educational opportunity for "poor but worthy" students was a basic necessity in a democratic society, and he observed pointedly that "the mass of mankind has not been born with saddles on their backs nor a favored few booted and spurred, ready to ride them."

The need for educated leaders for the young country led Benjamin Rush, an early graduate of what was then called the College of New Jersey, to publish an essay in 1787 proposing the creation of a national university. The proposal was strongly supported at the Constitutional Convention in 1787 by another distinguished Princeton graduate, James Madison of the Class of 1771. Although it was not officially endorsed, the idea of a national university was favored by the first six presidents of the United States. In fact, George Washington was so convinced of the need for a national university that as President he set aside land in Washington and left a gift for its endowment in his will.

Congressional interest in education is reflected in the Third Article of Compact in the Northwest Ordinance of 1787, which stated: "Religion, morality, and knowledge being necessary to good government and the happiness of mankind, schools and the means of education shall forever be encouraged." But despite this early interest in education, the only significant federal legislation in the years following the Revolutionary War was the Land Ordinance of 1785, which reserved one section in each township in the Northwest Territories for schools. For the most part, education was the sole prerogative of the states, whose focus was on primary and secondary schooling, and of the relatively small number of privately supported colleges.

During most of the early nineteenth century, Princeton's situation was similar to that of other private colleges. Enrollments were small, reaching only 314 at the onset of the Civil War. But students at Princeton came from an unusually wide variety of backgrounds, and the college had a tradition of financial aid for needy students from its earliest years. The first known scholarship was given to James Leslie, Class of 1759, who received thirteen pounds from a "Fund for Pious Youth." Later Mr. Leslie became a schoolteacher in New York and stipulated in his will that a major part of his savings be used to establish a fund "for the education of poor and pious youth" at Princeton. President John Witherspoon designated this fund "The Leslie Fund" in 1792. (Another fund, the Richards Fund, had been established two years earlier for the same purpose.)

The first major appeal for student aid funds at Princeton was initiated by President Maclean in 1853. Maclean's objective was to raise $100,000 to establish 100 scholarships. Historian Thomas Wertenbaker lauds Maclean as a "far-sighted educational leader" for his "initiative in inaugurating a plan which has since been widely adopted and which has had a profound influence upon education in the United States." About 60 scholarships were established between 1853 and 1858. In 1885–86 a second attempt to secure scholarship funds was made, and by 1900 an additional 46 scholarships had been endowed. At this juncture in Princeton's history, there were more than 110 endowed scholarships for an undergraduate body of 1,096 students, and beginning in 1885–86 a statement was added to the catalog affirming that "no candidate for admission to College . . . will be refused admission because of inability to pay the charge for tuition."

In addition to raising scholarship funds, President Maclean organized the Students Aid Association in 1868 to provide loan funds. Hoping to secure endowment for the association, he presented his book *History of the College of New Jersey* to be offered for sale in a fundraising campaign in 1877. In 1899 another fund-raising effort for the association sold the final few hundred sets. One response to the circular announcing the availability of Dr. Maclean's *History* came from Thomas H. Atherton, Class of 1874, a lawyer from Wilkes-Barre, Pennsylvania. He wrote in part: "I enclose my check for Ten Dollars gladly, and will take copies of the history therefor. I wish that I could contribute more largely to the fund. However, aid to deserving students has been a matter commanding my interest and I am free to say that I have no investments which have given me more gratification than the aid I have been able to render a number of young men who have graduated at Princeton with honor. There used to be a slanderous statement in our Church with reference to me as a Sunday School teacher of boys, that 'if Tom Atherton never got his boys into the Kingdom of Heaven, he always got them into Princeton College.' "

Nationally, a new era in American higher education was beginning to emerge at the end of the nineteenth century, stimulated in part by the Morrill "land-grant" Acts of 1862 and 1890. These two pieces of legislation brought America's ideals and the realities of higher education into closer harmony by creating the conditions for broader access to college. To a large extent this development represented a reaction to changes in the society that had occurred over the course of much of the nineteenth century. In the years following the Jacksonian period, the esteem accorded higher education diminished, and despite rapid population growth, college enrollments remained generally static from Jackson's presidency until the end of the century. In 1900, only 4 percent of Americans were attending college. Indeed, higher education appeared to have lost considerable standing: the percentage of congressmen who were college graduates, for example, had fallen below 25 percent by 1885, as compared to 38 percent in 1875.

But by the turn of the century national interest in higher education was reviving with remarkable force. Enrollments increased rapidly from 1900 to 1930—from 156,000 to 1,100,000. Senator Morrill had described his legislation as "designed to largely benefit those at the bottom of the ladder who wanted to climb up," and so it did. For a number of reasons, it was becoming easier for the ablest students to attend college, regardless of their economic circumstances, and higher education was acquiring a renewed prestige that would give the college graduate social status and upward mobility.

When Woodrow Wilson became president of Princeton in 1903, the educational goals and curricula of American universities were being reconsidered and reshaped. Wilson saw Princeton's promise as growing out of the historic role it had played in the nation's service during the Revolutionary War, and he sought to recapture a national purpose for the institution. In one address, he argued that the college is "the root of our intellectual life as a nation . . . our chief means of giving wide-spread stimulation to the whole intellectual life of the country and supplying ourselves with men who shall both comprehend their age and duty and know how to serve supremely well. . . . The college will be found to lie somewhere very near the heart of the American social training and intellectual and moral enlightenment." In this spirit he became not only a leading advocate of liberal education, but a major proponent of a diverse social environment for undergraduates. As he expressed it: "One of the things that makes us unserviceable citizens is that there are certain classes of men with whom we have never been able to associate and whom we have, therefore, never been able to understand. I believe that the process of a university should be a process of unchosen contacts with modern thought and life and particularly with the life of our own country."

Under Wilson's leadership, Princeton's total endowment for scholarships nearly doubled. The scholarship program was reorganized, consistent standards and practices were established, and renewed emphasis was given to the importance of self-help, although that concept was certainly not a new one. It had long been expected that the student would cover as much of his own expenses as possible: In 1886–87, for example, a student on the bare minimum budget of $325 received only $100 from his scholarship; if he were a candidate for the ministry, an additional $30 was deducted from his room rent, still leaving $195 for him to pay out of his own resources, including importantly jobs and some university loans. In Wilson's era a new rule was adopted that gave preference for most scholarships to sophomores, juniors, or seniors who had demonstrated need and who had proved themselves academically. Freshmen were more likely to be granted a Remission of Tuition, which was a kind of no-interest loan (up to $100) that had to be repaid after graduation.

Student employment was an important component of self-help then, as it is now. In 1911 a survey revealed that nineteen members of the senior class at Princeton were "self-made" college graduates, having worked to pay their expenses; another thirty-eight students indicated that they had supported themselves in part. These two groups constituted almost 20 percent of the class. They worked at many kinds of jobs: tending furnaces, washing windows, waiting on tables, baby-sitting, tutoring, selling, typing, and library work. The Princeton University Press Club, which reported this survey, noted that most of these students ranked very high in their class standings at the same time that they worked.

To encourage assistance of this kind, the Student Bureau of Self-Help was established in 1911. Statistics compiled in 1923 showed that one of every five students held a job. An article on self-help in the May 1926 *Princeton Alumni Weekly* explored alumni questions as to whether the student who worked his way through college "nowadays" is "looked down upon, whether opportunities are still afforded for boys to earn money, and whether the self-help student still enjoys the respect and place on the campus he had in their day.'' To answer this inquiry, *PAW* surveyed students who earned at least one fourth of their college costs while at Princeton. Three out of every four students responded that they would urge others of limited means to follow the route they had taken and earn a major part of their expenses at Princeton. In addition, they agreed by a ratio of five to one that working had no effect upon a student's standing among his peers.

In 1931 student employment cushioned the effects of the Great Depression at Princeton. Student employment increased by a third over the previous year, and 617 students were able to earn all or part of their expenses. In an article entitled ''Pity the Poor Collegian'' in May 1939, the *Saturday Evening Post* called Princeton one of the ''hopeful survivals . . . of communities where hard work, frugality, and ambition still rate as virtues and the bootstrap tradition of an older America is still believed in.'' The *Post* also reported the fact that employed students at Princeton were well above average academically and had won eight of the University's thirteen Rhodes Scholarships in the previous five years. By 1934 the University had combined all of the various components of financial aid into a comprehensive program administered by the newly formed Bureau of Appointments and Student Employment.

In 1936 the University described its goals in a statement entitled *A Scholarship Program for Princeton: Designed to Permit a Fuller Realization of the Princeton Ideal That the Students on Its Campus Will Always Represent a Cross-Section of the Best Elements in American Life*. In the words of the document, Princeton's policy was ''to educate the few and to educate them well, . . . but in a democracy it is important that the selection of that few be on a basis of ability and that it not be restricted entirely by economic circumstance.'' At the Bicentennial Convocation on June 17, 1947, President Dodds gave this conviction his firmest endorsement: ''We shall always see to it that our students represent a democratic cross-section of American youth, geographically and with respect to economic circumstance.''

President Dodds presided at Princeton throughout the difficult periods in higher education following the Great Depression and during and after World War II. The war years had a particularly significant impact on higher education—enrollments fluctuated widely, and many campuses (including Princeton's) were converted partly to military training. The enactment of the G.I. Bill also had a profound impact. While the Service Man's Readjustment Act (as the G.I. Bill was officially titled) was intended to solve a unique set of economic and social problems, it had sweeping implications for higher education and particularly for student aid. For the first time, substantial amounts of federal funds were provided directly to individual students. The result was much broader access to higher education and the establishment of a set of national expectations concerning educational opportunity that have continued to this day.

By 1950, the last large group of veterans had graduated from Princeton—bringing to an end the federal support that had buttressed the University's financial aid program during the 1940s. But as the University continued to admit students who could not pay the full charges, pressure for increased financial aid grew rapidly, and for the first time University general funds were used to supplement earnings from endowment for scholarship purposes. Throughout the 1950s, the University raised endowment funds for scholarships, increased self-help requirements for students, and continued to draw upon general funds—yet still fell short of the goal of meeting the full need of all admitted students.

By the 1960s the composition of the student body at Princeton had changed in several respects. The proportion of students drawn from public secondary schools had increased gradually from an average of 17 percent of the entering class in the 1920s to approximately 60 percent in 1963 (where the percentage has remained ever since). Until 1946 the entering class had been largely self-selected. From that year forward, however, Princeton began to receive applications from many more excellent candidates than it could admit. One reason for this was the decision of the College Entrance Examination Board in 1942 to shift from achievement tests (which were based on the fixed syllabi used by the preparatory schools) to the new "aptitude" tests, thereby enabling students from public high schools throughout the country to compete more successfully for places in prestigious colleges. This development, combined with the postwar baby boom, altered dramatically the nature of the competition for admission to Princeton. According to E. Alden Dunham, director of admission from 1962 to 1966, the year 1942 "marks the great divide in the history of college admissions in the nation."

A related change in financial aid policy occurred in 1958. Because the academic qualifications of applicants had improved so markedly, the University Committee on Scholarships amended the regulation on renewal of scholarships to no longer require achievement of a designated grade point average. Instead, a student was entitled to keep his scholarship if he was "making normal progress toward a degree and maintained a satisfactory record in scholarship, attendance, and conduct."

By 1962–63, the selection of the freshman class had become exceedingly difficult, and admission officers were called upon to make fine distinctions among candidates, most of whom were well qualified. The average SAT score for *applicants* in that year was higher than the comparable score for *enrolled* students in any entering class prior to 1958. The average Princeton freshman ranked in the top 2 percent of all high school seniors in the nation on the basis of SAT scores. Under these circumstances, admission itself (rather than any additional criteria) began to be regarded as evidence of sufficient academic accomplishment to merit scholarship aid if need could be demonstrated. Accordingly, the University sought to meet the demonstrated financial need of *all* such students. A report to the faculty from the Committee on Scholarships for 1962 emphasized the continuing commitment of the University to "provide the necessary financial aid so a man's economic situation will not be a barrier to his attending Princeton." However, despite this policy, budget constraints prevented the University in practice from actually providing financial aid sufficient to meet the full need of every admitted student. It was clear that if this goal were to be achieved, the University would have to find additional student aid funds.

Corporations and foundations had, in fact, been helping to meet this rapidly rising need for scholarship funds since the mid-1950s. The National Merit Scholarship and the General Motors Scholarship programs were both begun at that time, and together these two programs provided more than one thousand scholarships nationally each year. Princeton itself was receiving nearly $100,000 a year from these sources by 1960. Union Carbide and Procter and Gamble established scholarships in 1955, and by 1970 thirty corporations were funding scholarships at Princeton.

Then, when the USSR launched Sputnik in 1957, national interest in higher education was sparked as it had not been since the late nineteenth century, and the effects with respect to student aid were nothing short of spectacular. The federal government responded by passing the National Defense Education Act in 1958, which provided loans for college students in areas deemed important to national security. Simultaneously, scholarship programs were established by many states, including New Jersey. The federal government also increased greatly its funding for research and development projects in universities, with significant benefits for graduate education.

Between 1960 and 1980 the federal government took additional steps to assure broader access to higher education. The Higher Education Act of 1965 continued the National Defense Student Loan Program, added a Guaranteed Loan Program, incorporated the Work-Study Program established a year earlier, and introduced scholarships called "Educational Opportunity Grants." The Higher Education Amendments of 1972 established the Basic Educational Opportunity Grant Program (now named Pell Grants in honor of Senator Claiborne Pell '40) and the State Student Incentive Grant Program (directed to state scholarship programs), converted the Opportunity Grant Program to the Supplemental Educational Opportunity Grant Program and the National Defense Student Loan Program to the National Direct Student Loan Program, and reauthorized the Guaranteed Student Loan Program and the College Work-Study Program. Taking into account educational benefits provided through Social Security and the Veterans Administration, the federal government became the single most important source of financial aid funds outside of the colleges and universities themselves.

These federal programs were critical in enabling Princeton (and other colleges and universities) to keep pace with increasing demands for financial aid. By this time, it had become virtually impossible for a student to work his way through a college like Princeton without substantial help, either from family resources or through scholarship assistance. Not only had tuition risen steeply, but academic demands were also so substantial that it was difficult for a student to work more than ten to fifteen hours a week and still meet rigorous requirements. Hence, there was a growing need for the loans and scholarships that were provided in part through federal programs.

In the last fifteen years Princeton, like many other universities, has continued to extend its efforts to attract talented students from diverse backgrounds. President Robert F. Goheen, who played a major role in this development, echoed views expressed by his predecessors when he wrote: "Some of the most important growing and learning in college occurs through the mixing and rubbing of students with one another. It is in these associations no less than in the classroom that future leaders test and enlarge and mature their convictions. This means that a fully healthy collegiate or university community will include students from widely varying socio-economic backgrounds, and will seek to extend its services to a wide cross-section of the American society. Otherwise the institution is bound to be out of touch with both the temper and the needs of the American republic as they present themselves to us now, and as they seem sure to present themselves even more demandingly in the years ahead.''

The percentage of students at Princeton receiving financial aid in some form has fluctuated over the last two decades, but within a narrower range than many assume. In 1962–63, for example, 39 percent of all undergraduates received some form of aid; twenty years later, in 1982–83, 43 percent are receiving such aid. While these percentages have remained relatively stable (with the percentage of students receiving financial aid averaging 42 percent in both the decade of the 1960s and the decade of the 1970s), the absolute numbers of financial aid recipients, of course, increased along with the change in the size of the undergraduate college that accompanied coeducation.

To answer a related question that is asked frequently, there is no evidence of any major change over the last decade in the composition of the student body classified by family income. So far at any rate, the concern expressed by many that rising tuitions would squeeze out the middle class has not come to pass, at least to any substantial degree.

It is clear, however, that recent cutbacks in federal support for student aid—and, to a certain extent, the attendant publicity alone—have made an increasing number of both low- and middle-income students reluctant to apply to colleges and universities with relatively high costs. Princeton has certainly not been immune to this national trend; at the same time, the continued availability of financial aid resources has helped to limit the impact here. Over the last three to four years, the percentage of students from high-income families at Princeton has increased, but only modestly (by no more than five percentage points, according to our estimates). Moreover, if we examine what has happened over a longer time period, we find that students from high-income families constitute a slightly smaller percentage of the student body today than they did fifteen years ago. The representation of students from *both* low- and middle-income families has increased over this period.

Our present financial aid policies (described in detail in the next section of this report) have recognized explicitly that it is not only low-income families who require assistance in financing a Princeton education. Families from a quite wide range of ''middle'' incomes also need help. The objective has been to require a rough ''equality of sacrifice'' at various points along the income scale, and it is encouraging to see that these policies seem to have been effective in allowing students from all economic backgrounds to attend the University.

The application of these policies has led, not surprisingly, to very substantial increases in recent years in funds devoted to student aid. A major driving force behind these large increases, of course, has been the rising cost of attending Princeton, with tuition alone having risen from $2,800 in 1971–72 to $8,380 in 1982–83. At the same time, as already indicated, there have been major shifts in the sources of student aid funds.

The record of expenditures from various sources for scholarships alone over the last twelve years, summarized in Figure I, shows that the total scholarship budget rose from about $3.4 million in 1971–72 to $9.95 million in 1982–83. Even more noteworthy is the relatively recent rise in the dependence on unrestricted University funds for these scholarships, as the increase in the total budget has outstripped available resources designated for this purpose. While there has been a steady increase in income from the University's endowment available for scholarships, the trend in government support has been problematic. There was a rapid rise in federal and state support through 1980–81, but then the funds available from government sources began to decline, and not just relative to other sources of support but in absolute terms. As a result, expenditures from the unrestricted general funds of the University for scholarships increased to about $500,000 in 1980–81, $1.6 million in 1981–82, and $2 million in 1982–83.

Whether the University can continue to increase support for scholarships from general funds at anything like this rate is, of course, a very important question. We shall return to it in Part IV of this report and examine carefully both projections of future costs and policy alternatives. Over almost all of the years since 1970, the University has been able to meet—from one source or another—the demonstrated needs of all undergraduates.* While we remain strongly committed to attempting to sustain this policy, it is by no means certain that ways can in fact be found to do so, and it is this uncertainty that gives such significance to the discussion of student aid policies at this juncture in Princeton's history.

* In 1971, there were insufficient scholarship funds to meet the full needs of all admitted freshmen, and fifty-one students were put on a financial aid waiting list. The Undergraduate Association, led by Mark P. Smith '71, held a fund-raising drive in support of the principle of meeting full need. By September, the UGA scholarships and the normal process of attrition had enabled the University to meet the needs of all eligible students.

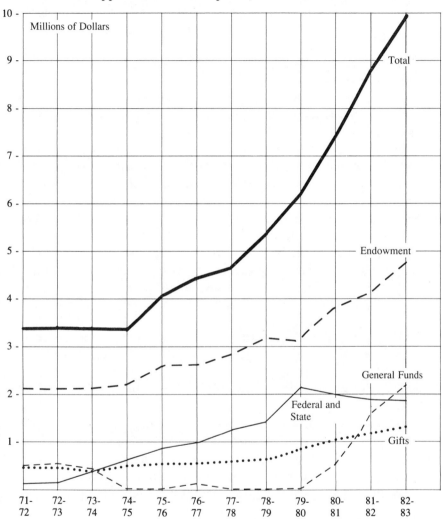

Figure 1
Sources of Support for Scholarship Aid, 1971-72 to 1982-83

FINANCIAL AID AT PRINCETON TODAY

Against this historical background, and as a prelude to a consideration of the choices that we must make as we look ahead, I want now to describe in more detail Princeton's financial aid program as it operates today.

There are four central principles that have governed our financial aid policies for more than a decade:

(1) Admission decisions are made separately from financial aid decisions and without reference to the financial circumstances of applicants.

(2) Eligibility for financial aid is solely a function of the applicant's "need." The family is assumed to have the first responsibility for meeting educational costs, and therefore the expected family contribution is subtracted from the estimated costs of attending Princeton in order to determine "need."

(3) The demonstrated financial need of all those offered admission will be met, and no one will be denied an opportunity to study at Princeton because of inadequate budgetary provision for financial aid on the part of the University. Conversely, no financial aid awards will be made above "need," however impressive the student's academic or extracurricular credentials may be.

(4) Financial aid should consist of a carefully defined combination of "self-help" (work opportunities and access to loan funds) and scholarship assistance. In particular, every student is expected to meet a specified set of self-help expectations before any scholarship aid is provided.

In discussing the application of each of these principles, it is worth emphasizing that they are highly interrelated. For example, the ability of the University to meet all of the demonstrated financial needs of its students depends on a consistent and rigorous application of the policies governing both "needs analysis" and "self-help" expectations.

The Separation between Admission and Financial Aid

At Princeton, the dean of admission and the admission office staff, working within established policy guidelines, are responsible for selecting those students to be offered admission from among the approximately 11,500 candidates who now apply for places in each entering class. An entirely separate undergraduate financial aid office subsequently reviews requests for assistance and prepares the financial award letters that are sent to successful applicants along with notifications of admission. The financial aid office then maintains contact with students throughout their undergraduate years at Princeton, reviewing requests for financial aid and assessing changed circumstances on an annual basis.

Of the 2,069 students offered places in the Class of 1986 last spring, 55 percent applied for financial aid, and 42 percent were found to be eligible. The percentage of "aid" students accepting Princeton's offer of admission (55 percent) was essentially the same as the percentage for all other entering freshmen (56 percent).

Determining "Need"

Each applicant for financial aid is required to submit information on family finances to the independent national College Scholarship Service (css). In turn, the css sends the University a confidential financial need analysis, detailing the student's financial circumstances and estimating the parental contribution that should be anticipated. With this information as a guide, Princeton's financial aid office reviews each individual student's case, making any further adjustments that seem appropriate. The major variables used to determine the parental contribution are family income, assets (including cash, equity in a house, the value of a business or farm, and other financial resources), size of family, number of children in college, and certain extraordinary expenses (such as large medical and dental expenses or private school tuitions).

Determining a fair contribution level for parents has always been a complex and difficult task, but it has been complicated even further in recent years by factors such as a depressed national economy (which has caused concern among families about their future earnings) and an increased number of single-parent families. The effort made to take a number of considerations into account leads to determinations of need that are based on much more than family income alone. . . .

Expected parental contributions for families with incomes in, say, the $15,000 to $20,000 range will vary from about $500 to about $1,500, depending on the other factors listed above. At a somewhat higher income level, a family in which both parents work, with a combined income of $30,000, savings of $10,000, a housing equity of $40,000, and two children (only one of whom is in college), would be asked to contribute roughly $3,000 toward one year's college costs. Families with still higher incomes will, of course, be expected to contribute more; however, some students from families with quite sizable incomes may still qualify for financial aid.

Of course, families differ significantly in the priority they assign to education: in their willingness to make sacrifices, to devote savings as well as current income to educational costs, and to incur debt. Unfortunately, each year we encounter difficult situations in which parents decline to make the contributions that are expected of them. Students themselves sometimes borrow more or work longer hours in such cases to make up the difference, but this is not always possible. While these cases represent some of the most difficult ones for the financial aid office, we have been clear in explaining to students and their families that University financial aid is to be seen as a supplement to what families themselves are able to contribute, not as a substitute for family resources.

The determination of the family's contribution also includes an evaluation of what the student can be expected to contribute from his or her own savings, from such other sources as Social Security or veterans' benefits, and from summer jobs. The final "need" calculation, therefore, is made by subtracting the total family contribution from the projected student budget for the year (including tuition and fees, room and board charges, books and miscellaneous expenses, and, for students who live more than 200 miles from Princeton, a travel allowance).

Meeting Full Need

In constructing the University's budget for each year, a careful estimate is made of the funds that will have to be provided to assure that the full financial need of each student can be met. Needless to say, this is an exceedingly complicated calculation, since it depends on estimates of expected family contributions, determinations concerning the mixture of "self-help" and scholarship dollars, and, very importantly, estimates of the non-University funds that can be expected from private and government sources. A judgment must then be made (first by the Priorities Committee and then by other participants in the budget-making process, including, finally, the Board of Trustees) whether the University can afford such a commitment. Action has just been taken on next year's budget, and it has been possible to retain Princeton's commitment to meeting the full financial need of all admitted students— albeit in the face of difficult budgetary constraints.

Of course, if the University were to offer some students financial aid more generous than their demonstrated need (to compete, for example, with large "merit" scholarships offered by some other colleges or universities), it would be all the more difficult to meet the full needs of students generally. For this reason, as well as because we believe students and families have an obligation to contribute as much as they can, we have declined to enter into "bidding wars" or, for that matter, to give financial aid above need for any reason. This policy has been adopted by all of the Ivy Group institutions, and the decision not to award "athletic scholarships" as such (but rather to meet the needs of athletes to the same degree as the needs of other students) is one consequence of this general approach.

Combining Self-Help and Scholarship Aid

It would be impossible, as a practical matter, to meet the full needs of all students if we were to rely only on scholarship aid. In the current year, term-time jobs and loans for aid students total approximately $4.8 million—33 percent of all financial aid at Princeton. (Jobs and loans for non-aid undergraduate students total an additional $1.4 million.) Self-help is important in principle because of what it says about the willingness of individual students to make commitments—to invest in themselves before asking others to help.

In developing each year's budget proposals, the Priorities Committee begins with recommendations from the faculty and student committees on undergraduate admission and financial aid. In arriving at its estimate of the University funds that will be required for scholarships, the committee first decides what self-help level should be expected. This in turn requires that explicit assumptions be made about both earnings from employment and borrowing levels. In 1982–83, for example, the "average" recipient of financial aid was expected to earn $1,250 during the academic year by working about ten hours per week and to borrow about $1,700; a scholarship of $5,500 was then awarded to complete the financial aid package.

JOB OPPORTUNITIES. As explained earlier in this report, Princeton has a long history of providing job opportunities for students. Today approximately 59 percent of all undergraduates hold jobs, and there is no stigma of any kind associated with working while in college. While aid students are given first priority in the assignment of jobs under the purview of the financial aid office, job opportunities are sufficiently numerous that they have not had to be limited to students receiving aid. Indeed, the University makes a major effort to provide jobs for all students who wish them, and this year approximately 1,150 students not on aid are working.

Many students hold jobs in order to reduce somewhat the financial pressures on their families as well as to earn "pocket money." But financial considerations are by no means the only motivation. A number of students seek employment to gain business experience and to acquire managerial or technical skills; others are stimulated by an entrepreneurial spirit that is very evident in the activities of the myriad of student agencies present on the campus. Among the most successful agencies are the Typewriter Agency, the Souvenir Agency, and the Newspaper Agency. A Personal Computer Agency is at the development stage. (Other unofficial and sometimes less conventional agencies spring up from time to time. In the late 1950s there was an Alligator Agency that guaranteed delivery of a live alligator from Florida for $6.25, and in 1975 a Pie Throwing Agency enjoyed a transitory existence.)

As in years past, students receiving financial aid are employed in large numbers in the library and in food services, and other jobs may be found in such areas of the University as athletics, the security department, and the computer center. One of the most eagerly sought positions is that of research assistant to a faculty member, and students and faculty alike testify to the educational benefits of such associations.

LOANS. As educational costs have risen, as student wages have lagged behind increases in costs, and as academic requirements have limited more severely the hours that can be devoted to term-time employment, it has become less and less practical for students to "work their way through college" in the literal sense of that phrase. Fortunately, however, there has been growing acceptance of loans as a supplementary means of self-help. By taking out loans while they are in college, students are able to accept a significant degree of responsibility for their own educational costs while still having time to study. It seems only sensible that educational costs, like the costs of other sizable investments, should be spread over a number of years and paid when the individual's earning capacity is greater.

The two most important loan programs for students at Princeton, as well as for students at other colleges and universities, are the National Direct Student Loan program (NDSL) and the Guaranteed Student Loan program (GSL). In addition, the University provides a modest amount of money for loans to students—mostly foreign students—who are not eligible for either federal program. Among the members of this year's senior class who have borrowed to finance part of their undergraduate education (roughly 40 percent of the class), the average indebtedness at graduation is expected to be over $6,000; some seniors, however, will have loan obligations closer to $12,000.

There has been a great deal of discussion nationally of default rates on student loans. Princeton has worked hard to impress upon students their responsibilities for repayment, and the results have been very encouraging. As of the end of 1982, the overall repayment rate was between 96 and 97 percent. Moreover, the loans not yet repaid are regarded by Princeton as "delinquent," not in "default," since experience indicates that in many cases repayment will be made at a later date.

Mention should also be made of the availability of two parent loan programs, one sponsored by the University itself and one established by the federal government. Both programs are intended to make it easier for families to spread their own educational payments over more years (eight in the case of the University's program and ten in the case of the federal program). While these programs do not reduce the overall cost of attending Princeton, they do provide important assistance in meeting financing problems.

SCHOLARSHIPS. Last year, 1,817 students (about 40 percent of all undergraduates) held scholarships. Since scholarship awards are set equal to "remaining need," they vary appreciably in size. Some are as small as $300, and some are as large as $8,500. As mentioned earlier, the average scholarship award in 1982–83 was $5,500.

THE OUTLOOK AND THE POLICY CHOICES

While there is never full agreement within a university community on any subject, there is a widespread conviction at Princeton that present financial aid policies are highly desirable and should be continued if at all possible. This view is shared by many students, faculty members, alumni (including, importantly, Schools Committee members), and Trustees. The real question is one of feasibility—of what would happen to other parts of the University if we were to allocate larger and larger sums of money to this particular purpose. There are no easy answers to hard questions of this kind. Much depends on magnitudes—on what "larger and larger sums of money" really implies.

The Federal Role

The federal government and institutions of higher education have become so closely interdependent in providing educational opportunity for undergraduates that it is useful to begin our assessment of the out-look for financial aid with an examination of the federal role.

At the national level, total expenditures for the principal financial aid programs administered by the Department of Education (including the Pell Grant, SEOG, College Work-Study, NDSL, GSL, and SSIG programs) rose from $1 billion in 1972 to $6.3 billion in 1981. This very substantial growth in expenditures reflects at least three phenomena: (1) the double-digit inflation of much of that period, which necessitated significant increases in student charges at many public as well as private colleges and universities; (2) exceptionally high interest rates, which dramatically increased the government's costs under GSL;* and (3) changes in eligibility criteria. The two most important changes in eligibility were enacted in the late 1970s in an effort to address the needs of middle-income families. One of these changes increased the family income ceiling under the Pell Grant program from roughly $16,000 to roughly $25,000. The other made all students eligible for subsidized borrowing under GSL regardless of family income.

The rising costs of student aid at a time of rapidly escalating federal deficits prompted a variety of cost-cutting proposals in the final Carter administration budget and then, more aggressively, in the first year of the Reagan administration. Some of these proposals called for level funding, some sought dramatic cuts, some suggested eliminating particular programs, and most recommended repealing the liberalizations in eligibility enacted just a year or two earlier.

The higher education community in general accepted the need for restraint in the growth of federal spending for student aid, even while recognizing that the cost of education would continue to rise. Many of us felt strongly that it would be wrong in principle, as well as ineffective, to ask that programs supporting higher education be spared the scrutiny being given to all federal programs at a time of budgetary stringency. Thus, there was widespread acceptance of changes in the Guaranteed Student Loan program that restricted subsidized borrowing to those who could demonstrate need. Representatives of higher education also encouraged efforts to improve the administration of the federal programs, to reduce default rates, and to increase somewhat the

---

* Roughly 90 percent of the annual cost of the GSL program is attributable to loans made in previous years. In 1982, approximately half of the federal dollars expended on GSL went to compensate lenders for the difference between the program interest rate and market levels. A 1 percent drop in market interest rates produces an annual reduction in GSL costs of some $200 million. That is why GSL costs in 1983 are projected to decline even though the outstanding loan volume is projected to increase.

level of responsibility assigned to parents when calculating a student's level of need. Finally, although the educational benefits under Social Security served many needy students, there was no "need requirement" in determining eligibility, and thus many in higher education were prepared to see that program phased out (as is now being done) as long as the various need-based programs remained available and were adequately funded to meet projected increases in demand.

Unfortunately, the kinds of proposals to which we could assent were quickly followed by, and in some cases accompanied by, proposals that called into question the basic federal commitment to educational opportunity. Some of these proposals went well beyond tightening up existing programs and restraining their rate of growth; indeed, they would have effectively dismantled the carefully balanced set of programs so painstakingly constructed over the past twenty years. ("Balance" in this context refers both to the mix of grant, loan, and work programs and to attempts to serve equitably the varying interests of the public and private sectors of higher education.) Some of these proposals would have dramatically restricted eligibility, such as the recommendation that graduate students be removed altogether from the guaranteed loan program. Some would have disproportionately affected students interested in private institutions, such as the recommendations to terminate the supplemental grant (SEOG) and direct loan (NDSL) programs that are "campus-based" and thus enable individual institutions to take into account their own costs and any special circumstances of their students in making financial aid awards.

For the most part, these more drastic proposals have not been accepted by the Congress. But it seems likely that further efforts will be made not just to limit federal spending for student aid, but to achieve fundamental changes in the structure and objectives of the programs now in place. The resulting uncertainty makes it extremely difficult to have any confident sense of the extent to which the federal government can be relied on to remain an active partner in the national effort to assure educational opportunity. This uncertainty has important implications not only for institutions, but for students and families throughout the country trying to plan for college.

In relating these national concerns to Princeton, it is essential to recall that federal scholarship support plays a role here that is critically important and yet substantially overshadowed by our own institutional commitment. This year, for example, Princeton students are receiving slightly more than $1.5 million under the Pell Grant and SEOG programs, while our total scholarship budget amounts to about $10 million, or almost seven times the funding available from federal sources.

Since most federal student aid funds are appropriated the year before they are spent, we can make assumptions about federal aid levels for 1983–84 with a fair degree of assurance. Barring unexpected rescisions, we anticipate essentially level funding, except for the further phasing out of the Social Security program. (Had the Congress adopted the administration's request for 1983–84, the $1.5 million available to Princeton students next year under the Pell Grant and SEOG programs probably would have dropped below $400,000.)

Projections for 1984–85 and subsequent years are, of course, far less certain. Figure 2 first illustrates the level of federal funding necessary to keep pace with rising costs. It then presents two projections: one at essentially current levels of support and one assuming modest increases starting in 1984–85. Plainly, under either of these projections federal dollars would cover a significantly smaller fraction each year of a level of need that is expected to rise substantially over this period.

The figure also includes both the proposals submitted to the Congress by the administration last year and the proposals submitted earlier this year. While this year's proposals are less austere, they clearly would have a substantial impact on the levels of federal support that could be expected. More importantly, these proposals would eliminate three of the six existing federal programs (SEOG, NDSL, SSIG), all of which disproportionately affect students attending higher cost institutions. The administration's recent proposals also would increase the cost to graduate students of borrowing under the GSL program.

Even if the Congress chooses to continue current programs at existing levels, it is important to understand that a pattern of level funding over a significant period of time would lead to a progressively diminishing federal role. The amount of federal support must be considered not just in relation to past levels, but in relation to rising costs and rising needs.

Financial Projections for Princeton

The recent report of Princeton's Priorities Committee provides a basis for projecting scholarship needs through 1986–87. The results of this exercise can only be described as sobering (see Table 1). They show that maintaining present policies could well require a commitment of $4.4 million of University general funds for scholarship aid

Figure 2
Federal Support* for Undergraduate Aid at Princeton, 1972-73 to 1986-87

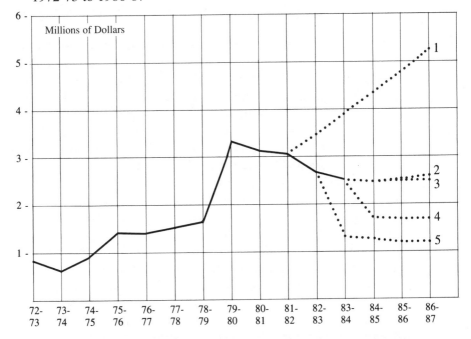

*Federal support includes Pell Grants, Supplemental Educational Opportunity Grants (SEOG), College Work-Study (CWS), National Direct Student Loans (NDSL), and Social Security benefits.

1. Increases in federal programs required to keep pace with increases in Princeton's charges (15% in 1982-83, 12% in 1983-84, and provisionally assumed to be 10% per year thereafter).
2. Assumes level funding in SEOG, CWS, and NDSL, gradual elimination of Social Security benefits (by 1985-86), and 10% per year increases in Pell Grants beyond 1984-85.
3. Assumes level funding (with gradual elimination of Social Security benefits).
4. Reagan administration budget request this year (held level through 1986-87, except for Social Security benefits).
5. Reagan administration request last year (not accepted by the Congress).

just four years from now. This contrasts with an expenditure of about $2 million in the current year.

It should be emphasized that these projections do not assume any increases in the percentage of Princeton students qualifying for financial aid. As our earlier analysis indicated, the percentage of "aid students" has been relatively constant for at least the last decade.

There is another "internal" factor, however, that has a great deal to do with the projected rise in student aid expenditures: projected increases in tuition and other charges. The reasons tuition has been rising so rapidly in recent years are described in detail in the annual reports of the Priorities Committee. Suffice it to say that the nature of the educational enterprise here, and at virtually all major research universities, leads inexorably to relatively rapid increases in our costs. These effects are in some ways intensified at Princeton because, in spite of our small scale, we must nonetheless "carry" the substantial costs of a major research university (including the expenses of an extensive library system, complex scientific laboratories, and so on). Moreover, we also place special emphasis on undergraduate "independent work" and close faculty-student contact. While we hope very much that the national rate of inflation will remain at more acceptable levels, thereby easing somewhat the pressure on the University budget, and while we intend to work hard to moderate increases in student charges, we must recognize that charges could continue to increase in the range of 10 percent per year.*

While increases in student charges lead directly to increases in the overall amount of scholarship aid needed, it would be wrong to conclude that—other things equal—a lower rate of increase in charges would make it easier for the University to meet its financial aid needs. In fact, the opposite conclusion is the correct one. The reason, of course, is that while a lower rate of increase in charges would reduce the amount of University general funds required for scholarships, it

* Fundamentally, the problem facing the University in setting tuition and other fees is that several large categories of expenditures—such as energy costs (with the deregulation of natural gas having a particularly pronounced effect on Princeton), maintenance expenditures, library acquisitions, even scholarships themselves—continue to increase at rates substantially above the rate of inflation in the economy generally. Also, we have thought it essential to continue to make at least some progress in restoring the economic position of our faculty and staff, recognizing that their real incomes have eroded significantly over the last decade. At the same time, revenue sources other than student fees, including federal support for student aid and sponsored research, are now increasing at much lower rates (or even declining). As a result, the University is forced simultaneously to adopt stringent expenditure controls and to increase fees above the general rate of inflation. As inflation moderates, we hope that the rate of fee increases will decline as well, but it is unlikely that the annual rate of increase will fall to the inflation rate.

Table 1

Projected Needs for Scholarship Funds and Sources of Support, 1981-82 through 1986-87

Thousands of Dollars	1981-82 (Actual)	1982-83 (Budget)	1983-84	1984-85	1985-86	1986-87
A. Scholarship Needs[1]	8,844	9,950	11,214	12,366	13,592	14,834
B. Sources and Funds						
1. Federal Government Grants[2] (Pell and SEOG)	1,564	1,545	1,545	1,545	1,606	1,673
2. State Grants[3]	299	310	315	331	347	364
3. Other "Outside" Scholarships[4]	1,191	1,300	1,430	1,573	1,730	1,903
4. University Endowment Income	4,145	4,750	5,180	5,559	6,017	6,512
Subtotal	7,199	7,905	8,470	9,008	9,700	10,452
5. University General Funds	1,645	2,045	2,744	3,358	3,892	4,382

[1] Assumes a 10 percent per year increase in student charges and a 7 to 8 percent per year increase in self-help.
[2] Assumes a 10 percent per year increase in Pell Grants in 1985-86 and 1986-87 and level funding for SEOG.
[3] Assumes a 5 percent per year increase in state grants.
[4] Assumes a 10 percent per year increase in other "outside" scholarships.

would reduce the general funds income available to the University by much more. Roughly speaking, each extra dollar of tuition revenue allows the University both to meet the full costs of the associated increase in financial aid and to devote almost sixty cents of that dollar to such other important purposes as salary increases.

In addition to being affected by tuition rates and room and board charges, scholarship needs depend on decisions made by the University concerning increases in the level of self-help expected of each student. The projections presented here assume an increase in self-help of approximately 7 to 8 percent per year; they also assume that family contributions rise about 10 percent per year.

The projected increases in general funds expenditures for student aid would, of course, be greater yet were it not for projected increases in other sources of scholarship funds. Fortunately, Princeton has very substantial endowment funds designated specifically for financial aid— over $100 million as of June 30, 1982. The income available for scholarships from these endowed funds is expected to continue to increase steadily and very significantly—from $4.7 million in 1982–83 to $6.5 million in 1986–87. Also, gifts and yearly scholarships provided by regional alumni associations, classes, and others are expected to increase from about $1.2 million to almost $2 million over this period.

University general funds devoted to scholarship aid are, then, the "residual" source. To restate our earlier conclusion: The principal implication of these projections is that maintaining present financial aid policies could well require that the general funds spent on scholarships more than double over a period of just four years.

Policy Choices for Princeton

While it is impossible to know with any precision what will in fact happen over this period, these projections clearly indicate that the outlook for financial aid is far from a cheerful one. Princeton is facing a situation in which scholarship needs are rising rapidly and available resources (apart from general funds) are failing to keep pace.

Moreover, this cannot be regarded as a temporary situation. Whatever broad changes may occur in Washington and whatever the near term resolution of the specific questions about the federal role in higher education now being discussed, we would be ill-advised to assume a significant expansion in federal support over the period for which we must now make plans. Nor do I believe that the answer to the attendant dilemmas is likely to be found in some major new departure such as tuition tax credits or the kind of contingent-loan program that has been discussed for a number of years. There may be new ways in which the government can encourage families to save for future educational expenses and assist students to borrow even larger amounts of capital to invest in their own schooling. But so far, the particular proposals that have been developed have not seemed promising. For the short term, at least, I believe we need to examine our principal policy alternatives assuming a rather prolonged period in which gaps between needs and the main sources of money for scholarships will persist.

In this context, the basic choices at Princeton, as I see them, are: (1) to alter admission policy so that we would stop admitting students with financial need at the point in the admission process when some predetermined limit on the University's financial aid budget had been reached; (2) to maintain our present admission policy but to alter our financial aid policy so that we would no longer meet the full demonstrated need of all admitted students; or (3) to seek ways, and probably a combination of ways, to remain on roughly our present course.

LIMITING THE NUMBER OF STUDENTS ADMITTED WITH FINANCIAL NEED. This approach to the problem limits financial aid expenditures by controlling directly the number of students admitted with financial need, and it can be given effect in a variety of ways. For example, it would be possible to continue to make admission decisions without regard to the financial circumstances of applicants throughout most of the admission process and then, for a small percentage of the class, to pass over applicants with need and admit only students who do not apply for financial aid.

The immediate impact on the quality and diversity of the class would depend, of course, on how many applicants were passed over solely on financial grounds. The University might think it important to allow only a minimal impact (for instance, by taking "ability to pay" into account only when filling the last fifty places in the class), but then the relief obtained from the mounting pressures on the scholarship budget would be correspondingly modest.

It must be recognized, however, that *any* departure from the clear separation between admission and financial aid decisions that exists now would have strong—and quite adverse—"announcement effects" for Princeton. It would be interpreted by many prospective students, secondary school counselors, and Alumni Schools Committee members as a retreat from an important principle, as it would be. It is also entirely possible that a number of potential candidates with limited financial resources, however outstanding their credentials for admission, would be dissuaded from applying. While the long-term effects of such a change in policy are hard to predict, many of us would feel that something quite important had been lost—that efforts going back many years to admit the most qualified candidates without regard to economic circumstances had been compromised.

DENYING AID TO SOME ADMITTED STUDENTS WITH DEMONSTRATED NEED. An alternative way of "stretching" the scholarship budget is to continue to make admission decisions on a "need-blind" basis but then to deny aid to some of those admitted who would qualify for it under current policies. In the opinion of some, this approach has the advantage of allowing those who would have been denied admission under the first policy alternative at least an opportunity to try to find a way to attend. In effect, the institution says to this group of candidates: "You qualify for admission, and you deserve to know that; unfortunately, however, we are unable to provide you with the financial aid that we are providing to others in similar circumstances, and you will have to decide whether you are able to come nonetheless." Experience has shown that students sometimes are able to locate additional resources (by obtaining funds from grandparents, for example). There is, however, the worry that such students may be able to pay their bills for a short time only, subsequently finding themselves in desperate straits, with no recourse but to leave school unless additional aid funds somehow become available.

Such situations are made more difficult by feelings of unfairness. Ordinary notions of "equal treatment" are offended when students in essentially the same economic circumstances—and who may be roommates, teammates, or friends—discover that they are receiving significantly different amounts of financial aid from the institution. Nor are appeals to "merit" likely to assuage such feelings when an institution is so selective that it is hard to discern major differences in qualifications (broadly defined) within an entering class.

Moreover, it becomes all the harder to justify not aiding certain deserving students when some who may have been thought to be at least marginally "less qualified" at the time of admission eventually do better than others who were originally thought to be "more qualified" (a far from uncommon situation given the well-known difficulties of predicting relative "success" among an exceptionally talented group of entering students). If, however, an institution were to try to correct for such inevitable failures of prediction by reallocating financial aid over the course of a student's four years, new problems would be presented: First, it would be necessary to agree on criteria. (Many would wonder about the wisdom of making such judgments on the basis of grades alone when we pay such careful attention to other accomplishments, including leadership qualities, when we make admission decisions.) Also, to reallocate aid on the basis of any objective measure of performance would quite probably have some harmful educational effects—by discouraging students, for example, from taking new or intimidating subjects in which they fear they may not do well and by encouraging tendencies to elevate concern for grades over concern for learning. Moreover, such a policy would make it very difficult for families to plan knowledgeably for meeting their share of college expenses since they would not know from year to year whether their child would receive financial aid.

While these problems would exist to some degree on any campus, they would appear in particularly accentuated form at Princeton. The close-knit campus community here, the relatively small size of the college, and the high overall quality of the applicant pool (and of each entering class) make it especially difficult to imagine defining and carrying out a policy that met full need for some while providing less help for others with equal need. Notions of "second-class" citizenship would be hard to lay to rest, and they could be very damaging to morale and to mutual respect.

There is another variant of this general approach that involves reducing the financial aid awards of *all* students by some amount below need. This amounts to increasing self-help expectations and thus merges with the question of what is the appropriate level of self-help under any circumstances. While I think it may be necessary to raise self-help expectations somewhat faster than we have been planning to do, it is necessary to recognize that there is a point at which self-help expectations become so high as to discourage students from attending Princeton (especially those who may qualify for "merit" scholarships at other institutions). The effects of significant increases in self-help expectations would depend, of course, on the self-help expectations of other colleges and universities, and particularly those institutions with which Princeton competes most directly for outstanding candidates.

Finally, mention should be made of the possibility of adopting different self-help expectations for different groups of students. This is being done by some universities now, but such an approach presents the same problems of equity and morale described above.

RETAINING PRESENT PRINCIPLES. Even this brief account of difficulties inherent in alternative approaches—coupled with the positive case for present policies—indicates why it seems so desirable to do all in our power to maintain the principles that have guided us for some years now. I believe that strongly.

But I do not believe that maintaining present admission/financial aid policies can be regarded as our only priority. Princeton has other exceedingly important objectives as well (maintaining salary levels and providing facilities that will allow us to continue to attract and hold an outstanding faculty are obvious examples). In my view, we would have accomplished nothing of value if we succeeded in maintaining access to Princeton for undergraduates from all backgrounds by simultaneously allowing the basic quality of the University to decline. When resources are tight, important principles sometimes collide.

It is for this simple reason that, when I have been asked if I could promise that Princeton would continue present financial aid policies "no matter what," I have said, "No, I can't." In my judgment, it would be irresponsible to make such an absolute promise in the face of so many uncertainties and given so many other compelling needs.

Indeed, an even stronger, if less encouraging, statement can be made: An examination of the projections presented earlier and of the anticipated levels of federal support leads me to conclude that if the federal government were to back away still further from the partnership role that it has come to play in the provision of student aid, we almost certainly could not, as a practical matter, provide enough additional resources of our own to fill the resultant gap. Even at their now reduced levels, federal grant programs for Princeton undergraduates (not counting loan and work-study programs) serve as the equivalent of $30 million of endowment.

As those familiar with the present Campaign for Princeton know, we are already committed to raising a substantial amount of additional private funds to sustain our present policies, *even assuming a continuation of present government programs*. To have an enormous additional demand for private funds imposed on top of existing fund-raising objectives would be overwhelming. Thus, if we are able to have a real chance of continuing to achieve our present objectives in the student aid area, one necessary condition is continued federal participation in the effort to insure educational opportunity.

Allowing ourselves to believe in the more optimistic of the projections presented above for the future of federal support does not, of course, solve our problems by any means. "Optimistic" is a very relative word in this context, and the obvious implication of the (at best) "leveling off" of federal support is that the burden on other sources of support will increase.

Under these circumstances, it seems to me that a somewhat more rapid increase in self-help expectations than we have been projecting may well become a second requirement for continuation of present policies. In recent years, average increases in self-help expectations have lagged behind increases in student charges, putting a relatively heavier burden on scholarship and grant funds. While the reasons for this disparity in rates of increase are easily understood (having to do with limits on how much students should be expected to work and to borrow), I believe that expecting at least somewhat more from students in this regard is preferable to sacrificing the principles on which present financial aid policy is based.

If self-help expectations are to rise more rapidly, it is almost certainly going to have to be the loan component that increases most noticeably. As noted earlier, it does not seem realistic to expect large numbers of students to undertake appreciably more hours of term-work without interfering seriously with their ability to take full advantage of the educational opportunities Princeton offers—including not only academic work, but also participation in extracurricular activities and in campus life outside the confines of library and laboratory. As borrowing increases, the upper limits on funds available to undergraduates under present governmental loan programs ($2,500 per year under the GSL and $6,000 total under NDSL) also will need to increase sufficiently, on a regular basis, to allow students to obtain the capital necessary to meet rising self-help expectations.

Maintaining present financial aid policies may also require that tuition rates rise more rapidly than would be necessary otherwise. Since increases in tuition generate appreciably more income than is needed to offset the higher scholarship needs caused by the tuition increases themselves, this is another way in which the potential gap between scholarship needs and available resources can be narrowed somewhat.

There are, of course, limits to the rate at which tuition can and should be raised, and I am painfully aware of how hard it is now for many families to meet what are already very high charges. Still, it is important to remember that tuition continues to cover only about 50 to 60 percent of the full cost of an undergraduate education at Princeton. In this sense, every Princeton undergraduate is the recipient of a quite substantial implicit scholarship. Using tuition revenues to help meet scholarship needs serves, therefore, to spread more broadly the financial responsibility for maintaining both educational opportunity and a diverse student body at Princeton; it does so by reducing somewhat the size of the implicit scholarship given to every undergraduate.

Whatever success we may have in sustaining a reasonable level of federal support, and whatever can be done to increase self-help expectations and provide at least a modest amount of additional support for scholarships through tuition revenues, the final—heaviest—responsibility is bound to fall on private contributions. This seems to me as it should be. Throughout its history, in seeking support for its scholarship program, Princeton has always looked principally to its alumni and friends—to those who have themselves benefited most directly from the educational opportunities this University offers.

Fortunately, alumni who are active in regional alumni associations recognize clearly, often on the basis of their experience each year with Schools Committee work, how vital it is to maintain a strong scholarship program. For that reason, among others, I believe that we can continue to count on increases in the yearly scholarships provided to Princeton students from such sources. Similarly, it seems likely that corporations, foundations, and other donors will want to continue to do what they can to cushion the effects of recent reductions in the real value of governmental programs. Along with other colleges and universities, Princeton recently received a generous contribution from the Chemical Bank of New York, whose chairman is Donald Platten '40, a Trustee emeritus of Princeton. While the allocation of the contribution was left to the discretion of each institution, Chemical Bank asked specifically that "consideration be given to directing some portion of these contributions toward student aid." In the same generous spirit, the Merlin Foundation made a gift earlier this year that will support undergraduate and graduate students interested in the arts and in music.

It is also encouraging to see how frequently family members and friends choose to establish a scholarship fund as a memorial. When Robert Owen '52 died tragically in January 1981, an effort was mounted by friends to establish a scholarship in his name, with preference to be given to students who came from the West Texas region in which he grew up. . . .

Endowing a scholarship is one extremely satisfying way for alumni and their families to make contact with new generations of Princeton students. The François Louis Chapman Class of 1944 Memorial Scholarship was endowed anonymously by a classmate who asked that each recipient of the scholarship be given a copy of Chapman's memorial in the *PAW* and this statement:

> If you have loved your years at Princeton and the Chapman Fund made this accomplishment partly possible, then as your means allow in later life, make it a point to let someone else love Princeton too by adding what you can to the Chapman Scholarship Fund.

Students often respond in very heartening ways to scholarships that have a personal dimension to them. A member of the Class of 1983 wrote as follows in appreciation of the Richard T. Shelton Class of 1893 St. Louis Regional Scholarship:

> I wanted to express my thanks for making Princeton a dream come true. Perhaps it was best put by a member of the Class of 1933 with whom I was fortunate enough to have brunch recently: "When I was here it cost ten dollars a week for board and room. With the depression I thought I was going to have to drop out because I couldn't pay. Well, they wouldn't let me drop out. They just said to pay what I could and that maybe someday I would be able to help someone else. To this day I'm grateful for that act of generosity." I, too, am grateful and will undoubtedly help someone else someday to attend the greatest university ever.

Beyond the statistics and the seemingly abstract (although very important) propositions about the educational values advanced by financial aid, we come back, always, to individuals. Among the many testimonials from Princetonians who have spoken to the importance of student aid on the basis of their own personal experiences, I would like to conclude this report with a note I received just this winter from a current Trustee of Princeton, William R. Hambrecht '57, a founding partner of Hambrecht and Quist in San Francisco. In asking that his own very generous contribution to our Campaign be credited to scholarship aid, Mr. Hambrecht wrote:

As a former scholarship student myself, I know how important financial aid is. Without scholarship help, I could not have attended Princeton, and I want to do whatever I can to allow other students to have the same kind of educational opportunity that has meant so much to me.

Today's tuition levels already make it difficult for the middle-income family, as well as the lower-income family, to consider Princeton. As the University maintains its commitment to excellence, as it must, costs are bound to rise and increases in tuition are inescapable. Without a proportionate increase in student aid, the student body would inevitably come to represent only the very wealthy. Financial elitism is not only contradictory to the very nature of our political and national heritage but, perhaps more important, would rob students of the rich interchange with the broad range of backgrounds and cultures that is such an important part of the Princeton experience.

There are many others, I know, who share the same values, who are equally determined that Princeton remain a place where dreams can be realized and ideals reaffirmed.

PART SIX

The Economics of the Private Research University

President Bowen's principal scholarly interests have included labor economics, the economics of education, the economics of the performing arts, and problems of stability and growth. His 1968 study for the Carnegie Commission on Higher Education entitled *Economics of the Major Private Universities* remains a standard in the field, and throughout his presidency he was called upon to assess both the economic forces pressing upon the academy and the implications of those forces for quality, for access, for tuition charges, and for the vitality and spirit of the educational enterprise.

The 1976 annual report, "The Economics of Princeton in the 1970s: Some Worrisome Implications of Trying to Make Do with Less," provides a comprehensive overview of this set of issues and constitutes the bulk of this chapter. It is followed by a 1986 essay entitled "Thinking about Tuition" which was prepared at a time of widespread public concern about the rate at which tuitions were increasing throughout the society. A second essay, on "The Student Aid/Tuition Nexus," was prepared a year later to challenge allegations by the U.S. Department of Education that tuition increases were stimulated in part by increases in federal student aid. In fact, the reverse relationship applies at an institution like Princeton: Increases in federal support reduce pressures on the University's budget, while reductions in federal support need to be offset by increased University resources and thus place added pressure on tuition revenues.

The chapter concludes with a discussion of private giving, first through an excerpt from the 1978 annual report entitled "A Perspective on Private Giving," and then through excerpts from two speeches: a 1982 speech at the kickoff event for a five-year campaign to raise $275 million, and a 1986 speech at the closing celebration for the campaign, which had raced well past its revised goal of $330 million to a final total of $410.5 million.

The Economics of Princeton in the 1970s: Some Worrisome Implications of Trying to Make Do with Less

REPORT OF THE PRESIDENT
FEBRUARY 1976

From Princeton's earliest days, when President Burr served for three years without salary, when Benjamin Franklin was called upon to print tickets for a lottery that is reported to have turned a fair profit, and when its leaders were described by one observer as men "whose lives, it is thought, were shortened by their unwearied exertions" at fund raising, finances have been a recurring theme—and a recurring concern.

The current decade is certainly no exception to this rule. The financial pressures that confront us in the 1970s raise fundamental questions related to the very purposes a university like Princeton is meant to serve. Because of the importance of this period, not just for Princeton but for higher education generally and the whole of the society, I have decided to devote the main part of this report to an assessment of where we are, and where we may be heading, in terms of financial realities and major educational objectives. More specifically, I want to discuss, first, potential effects on the *quality* of all that we try to do; second, potential effects on *access* to educational opportunities at Princeton on the part of students from all economic backgrounds; and third, the potential effects on what I can only call our *sense of community*.

THE SETTING

It is not my purpose here to analyze in any detail the economic forces that are basic to our problems, to review systematically our financial history, or to itemize the measures that we have taken and we intend to take to respond to the realities we confront. But some background may be useful.

Following a series of budgets that were mostly (if very narrowly) in surplus during the 1960s, a simultaneous slowing down of the rate of growth of several major sources of income led to deficits of $1 million in 1969–70 and $1.5 million in 1970–71. Thanks in large part to significant reductions in expenditures (especially for administrative and supporting services), the budget was brought back into balance in 1971–72 and 1972–73. Then inflationary increases on the cost side of the ledger, particularly in the prices of energy and food, upset the balance we had worked so hard to achieve, and we ran deficits of $500,000 in 1973–74 and $1 million in 1974–75. Last spring we projected an even larger deficit of $1.7 million for 1975–76, but we now believe that the combination of measures adopted last year, including both very substantial increases in student charges and further significant reductions in expenditures, will enable us to reduce that projected deficit by about $1 million and to end the current year with a shortfall of $700,000. The budget and provisional financial plan for 1976–77 and beyond just submitted to the Board of Trustees envision a further reduction in the deficit next year (to about $250,000) and then a balanced budget in 1977–78. If our experience is consistent with these estimates and projections, our cumulative deficit for the seven-year period from 1969–70 through 1976–77 will be about $5 million.

What is particularly troubling is not so much the size of this figure itself—especially when one recognizes that our total expenditures over this same period have been about $768 million, and that most major private universities have run far larger deficits, both in absolute amounts and relative to total expenditures, when figures are expressed on a comparable basis. More worrisome is the fact that this financial result will have come after, and in spite of, a series of extremely painful decisions concerning both expenditures and charges which I shall discuss later in this report. Inevitably these decisions have affected every aspect of the life of the University, and it is the combination of financial and educational consequences that really has to concern us.

As this year's report of the Priorities Committee says so well:

> Recommending ways to close a deficit or to maintain a balanced budget when we have one is often regarded as the principal or even the only task of the Priorities Committee. This view seems to us to be seriously deficient. Our task is far broader than that. It is nothing less than helping to preserve the health and vigor of the University and helping to insure its survival and continued progress. The bottom line of the operating budget is one indicator, but only one, of the University's health.

From the standpoint of the long-term financial difficulties common to all of higher education, the central economic fact of life is the very nature of the processes of education and scholarship. To be done well, particularly at advanced levels, they require a degree of personal attention, and personal interaction, that simply does not allow the same opportunities for technological change, mechanization, and, if you will, increases in "output per unit of labor input," that characterize the production of such goods as feed grains and calculators. As a result, we must expect the costs and prices of educational services to rise more rapidly than prices in general over the long run. It is all too easy to document this proposition: over the last decade alone, while prices in general have risen about 50 percent, the most widely used price index for higher education has risen over 70 percent—and there are reasons for believing that even this comparison understates the true differential.* As the Priorities Committee notes: "That we all dislike this conclusion does not permit us to escape it."

The extraordinary financial pressures that have beset almost all of higher education these last few years cannot be understood, however, only, or even mainly, in these terms. As everyone is aware, the very high rate of inflation for the economy at large—with the Consumer Price Index rising at an average annual rate of 8.6 percent during 1974 and about 10 percent during 1975—has put particularly severe pressure on our costs and on the living standards of all the people whom we employ. As a reading of Princeton's financial history attests, inflation has always had a particularly harsh effect on university finance, and this recent period has certainly shown the power of that dictum.

Nor has it been inflation alone that has hurt us. What has been really "special" about the recent past is that we have been experiencing both a significant degree of inflation and a substantial amount of unemployment simultaneously—with attendant declines in real income. In my view, the current plight of higher education can be understood only by looking at the effects of this overall economic situation on the revenue as well as the expenditure side of the budget. It is the inflation *cum* recession that has caused such serious difficulties for colleges and universities, as well as for those responsible for making economic pol-

---

* This point is developed further in a talk entitled "The Effects of Inflation/Recession on Higher Education," given before the Regents Eleventh Annual Trustee Conference, New York City, March 13, 1975. Because the factors that cause educational costs to rise faster than costs in general are so deeply embedded in the economic order, we should expect to find similar relationships in other times and places. That this is true can be shown readily. (See, for example, *Economics of the Major Private Universities*, Carnegie Commission on Higher Education, 1968.) As I was just finishing the drafting of this document a friend called to my attention a paper on educational finance in Australia, which shows that between 1965 and 1974 a university cost index rose 105 percent while their consumer price index rose 56 percent and the gross national product deflator rose 77 percent.

icy—and even for those of us still brave enough to continue trying to teach elementary economics.

In addition to the obvious effects on our costs resulting from inflation itself, every source of income available to us has been affected by the accompanying slump in output, employment, and profits. The burden of tuition, for example, is much harder for students and parents to bear in the face of unemployment and reduced real incomes. Federal and state budgets, and thus appropriations for higher education, have been affected adversely by the general fiscal problems that have confronted both Washington and New Jersey. Corporate profits and dividends have not grown at anything like their historic rates, with obvious consequences for earnings from endowment.

Historically, we have been able to count on earnings per unit of endowed funds to increase about 5 percent per year on the average. During the last four fiscal years, however, increases in unit income have averaged only 4 percent; in one of these years there was no increase at all. Declines in the asset values of securities have reduced the value of funds functioning as endowment which Princeton, like other colleges and universities, has used as a reserve. Moreover, depressed securities markets have combined with unsettled economic conditions to make it much harder in recent years for private donors to be as generous as they might have wished to be.

In summary, the impact of the recent inflation has been exceptionally serious because *it has not been accompanied by any of the offsets that we might have anticipated.* On the basis of what all of us were taught, we could have expected rising prices to be accompanied by more rapid increases in money incomes, by rising rather than falling securities prices, and by quite significant increases in the revenues received by state governments as well as by the federal government. These developments in turn should have made it at least somewhat easier to accept rising levels of student charges, to increase income from endowment and from gifts, and to anticipate at least modest help in the form of increased governmental appropriations. It is the absence of these offsets, and the presence in so many instances of their obverse, that has made this such an extraordinarily difficult and threatening period for all of higher education.

What the future holds obviously depends importantly on the national economy. It is not for me to enter the lists of the forecasters. But I can note that even the most optimistic projections envision a continuation of inflation at a rate that is very high historically (say 6 percent) as well as a continuation of unemployment at a level that not so long ago would have been regarded as unacceptable. Levels of output, profits, and dividends are expected to improve significantly, but few if any prognosticators are inclined to think that we shall return to the conditions of the 1950s that we now look back on with such nostalgia. We seem to be in something of a new era so far as the national economy is concerned, and the economy of the University is being, and will be, affected accordingly.

I could try to dramatize the implications of recent trends for the future of our own finances by making some projections for Princeton. Columbia, for example, has projected a deficit of $32 million in 1980 if current trends are not reversed, as they obviously will have to be. M.I.T. estimates a cumulative deficit of $30 million in the five years ending in 1980, if rates of growth of investment income and gifts are not raised to match normal rates of growth in expenditures. Cornell has predicted a cumulative deficit of $36 million through 1980 in the absence of sharp cutbacks in expenditures, which that university is now making. However, while projections of this kind can be very useful in obtaining and communicating a sense of the difficulties ahead, no one would claim that the precise numbers are of any great validity, and I am going to resist the temptation to add my own extrapolations to this list. Suffice it to say that the outlook for Princeton, while not nearly as grim as the outlook for some other universities, is certainly somber enough to justify careful examination of the educational implications of severely straightened circumstances.

IMPLICATIONS FOR QUALITY

It is natural for any organization to think first about its survival, and it is a measure of the seriousness of the financial pressures afflicting higher education that a number of colleges, especially some of the smaller private colleges, are concerned about no less a question than whether they can survive into the 1980s.

For Princeton, survival is clearly not the issue. But I must say that I take very little comfort from that. In my view it is of critical importance to the nation at large that the great universities, public and private, do much more than simply continue to exist. The real question is not, will we survive, but rather, will we be able to continue to aspire to the highest standards of teaching and scholarship—and, on occasion at least, to come close to achieving some of these aspirations.

The only justification for the great resources at the disposal of Princeton, in the form of a remarkable collection of people as well as excellent facilities and a sizable endowment, is that quality matters. I believe that, and I believe too that some of us, especially in recent years, have been overly reluctant to say so. To be sure, the mood of the times has been against "elitism," and no one wants to sound too self-important or too precious. Many of us are aware, fortunately, of our own limitations and the limitations of our institutions. Nor do we— nor should we—want to identify ourselves and our institutions with some of the unfortunate connotations of elitism. As I shall try to say in the next section of this report, I believe that it is crucially important that access to the very best colleges and universities not be limited by the accidents of economic background any more than race, or sex, or religious belief.

I also believe strongly that a great strength of higher education in America is that it encompasses many different kinds of educational institutions, trying to meet a wide variety of important needs. But I do not feel that a commitment to providing equality of opportunity and a broad range of educational opportunities is incompatible in any way with believing deeply in the importance to the entire educational system, and to the society, of a relatively small number of universities which are able to set for themselves the highest standards of achievement. As Philip Handler, president of the National Academy of Sciences, has said: "In science, the best is vastly more important than the next best. One cannot sum several mediocre projects in order to gain the equivalent of one superlative effort."

Quality clearly does not depend on financial resources alone; but it is equally clear that without the funds to make appointments, buy books, assist students, cover indirect costs, provide necessary services, and equip laboratories, quality cannot be sustained. For a very important margin of excellence, Princeton has relied upon its alumni, whose contributions to Annual Giving and development programs have done so much over the years for the University. Such generous support not only has met critical financial needs but has helped immeasurably to build a sense of commitment, which in turn has attracted many of our ablest faculty and students. Alumni volunteers now are working harder than ever, and the response to their efforts will have an important bearing on both the financial capability of the University and our ability to sustain a strong sense of educational momentum.

Much depends upon morale and on a large number of budgetary decisions that, when considered separately, may seem marginal or of no great consequence. The danger is not so much that there will be a sudden, dramatic shift from one level of quality to another but rather that there will be a slow, unspectacular, but cumulative decline in what it is possible to achieve—and then, as a next step in the process, in what one *tries* to achieve. Gradual changes of this sort are, in their nature, impossible to measure with any precision, and they may not even be noticeable to quite experienced observers until some considerable time after they have occurred.

Indications of Financial Pressure

It is possible to indicate, however, what has been happening to the value of the resources we have been able to devote to various programs of education and research at Princeton over the course of the last six or seven years:

• From 1968–69 to 1974–75, total expenditures by the University for all purposes, including sponsored research, increased by 46 percent. The best measure that we have been able to develop of overall inflationary pressures on institutions of higher education rose 52 percent over this same period.* Thus, the total amount of our increase in expenditures was more than offset by rising wages and prices. The real value of the resources devoted to the sum total of our programs of education and research actually declined by about 4 percent over this period. (See Figure 1.)

• We were able to manage a somewhat greater rate of increase in expenditures related directly to our academic program (for academic departments, the library, and the computer center), but even here over three quarters of the total increase was offset by rising wages and prices. This set of expenditures, measured in current dollars, rose 70 percent between 1968–69 and 1974–75; in dollars of constant purchasing power, however, the total increase over this period was only 12 percent. (See Figure 2.)

* This measure is based on the higher education price index developed by D. Kent Halstead. However, we have modified Halstead's index by substituting the data on professional salaries obtained annually by the Bureau of Labor Statistics (U.S. Department of Labor *News*, 75–373, July 9, 1975) for the data on salaries paid to faculty members and administrators used by Halstead. The reason for this substitution is to avoid the understatement of the effects of inflation and other economic pressures on colleges and universities that can result from using a measure of salary increases that has itself been dampened by the very economic pressures we are seeking to measure. Academic salaries are determined in no small part, especially in the short run, by the ability of the institutions to pay, and an externally determined salary measure is freer of this feedback phenomenon.

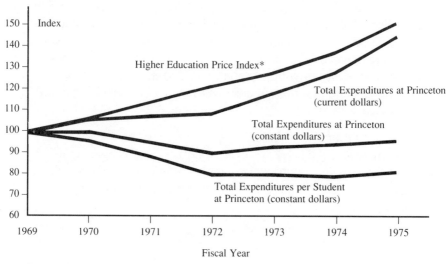

Figure 1
Total Expenditures at Princeton, 1969 to 1975,
in Current and Constant Dollars

*HEPI as modified (see text for further explanation).

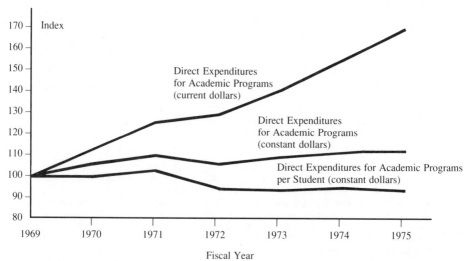

Figure 2
Direct Expenditures for Academic Programs* and Expenditures per
Student, 1969 to 1975, in Current and Constant Dollars

*Defined to include direct expenditures for academic departments, the library, and the computer center.

• Moreover, over the period 1968–69 to 1974–75 there was a substantial increase in enrollment at Princeton, with the advent of coeducation. Not even expenditures related directly to academic programs, when measured in constant dollars, rose in proportion to enrollment, and this set of expenditures per student declined 6 percent over this six-year interval.*

• The effects of inflation can be seen even more clearly if we look specifically at what has happened to the library. Between 1969 and 1975 there was a 60 percent increase in the budgetary allocation for acquisitions. However, even this increase has been insufficient to keep pace with the rising costs of acquiring new books and periodicals. Overall, the inflation rate for materials published in the United States over the past six years has been 60 percent for books and 130 percent for periodicals. But the costs of scholarly books have risen much faster than the costs of other books; and the costs of foreign publications, which comprise a significant proportion of our purchases, have been affected dramatically by currency revaluations as well as by price increases in other countries. Thus, with respect to inflation alone, we have experienced an appreciably greater increase in the costs of published materials than has been recorded generally. In addition, within the past two years, discounts formerly allowed to libraries by publishers and wholesalers, in amounts of 30 percent or more, have been eliminated almost entirely, a development that has had an even more significant effect than the inflation rate. Moreover, the decrease in the purchasing power of funds available for acquisitions has occurred in the face of an increase of over 40 percent during this period in the number of new volumes being published each year.

• To give another specific example: in the sciences and in engineering, where experimental research is particularly costly, the work of many faculty members and students has been hampered by the drastic decline in the purchasing power of funds available for sponsored

* This is not to suggest that the increases in enrollment associated with coeducation aggravated the overall financial position of the University. They did not, for the reason that additional tuition income more than offset marginal increases in expenditures. However, we were able to achieve this favorable overall financial result only by limiting carefully the associated increases in expenditures, thereby accepting the reduction in the real value of expenditures per student indicated in the text and shown in Figures 1 and 2. When the decision was made to admit women undergraduates, we believed that this could be accomplished with a much less than proportionate increase in the size of the faculty, and that has proved to be the case. During the 1950s and 1960s, the faculty was strengthened substantially in terms of both size and quality at the same time that graduate programs were being improved. These developments had much to do with making it possible to increase the undergraduate enrollment in the early 1970s without corresponding increases in the faculty.

research. If we exclude from the overall figures for sponsored research all expenditures for the Plasma Physics Laboratory and the former Princeton-Pennsylvania Accelerator, we find that funds available for all other projects were $12,027,000 in 1968–69 and $12,071,000 in 1974–75. According to one indicator which, in the opinion of several leading people in the field, significantly understates the case, the cost of doing research and development work over this same period is estimated to have increased by 44.3 percent.* As a result, the real value of the sponsored research funds available to Princeton faculty members has declined (in 1968–69 dollars) from just over $12 million to at most about $8.4 million.

Other Implications for the Academic Program

I hope these figures convey at least some overall sense of the pressures on programs of education and research that have been felt in recent years, and some sense too of the degree of retrenchment that has been necessary. What they cannot convey, however, is any sense of the lost opportunities and of the extremely serious threat to the quality of the University—and its ability to serve society—that would result if we should be unable, over some period of time, to respond positively to the most meritorious new ideas and new initiatives. No great university can ever stand still. Disciplines evolve, and the faculty members who are the leading teachers and scholars in their fields need to have opportunities to participate in new developments and to help give them shape. There are always important new challenges to be met, and it is in this context that the hard struggle simply to hold on to what has been achieved to date must be seen.

In short, it is critically important that we retain at least some capacity to strengthen the University, albeit on a necessarily limited and highly selective basis. We have worked hard internally to preserve some flexibility, we have sought to make the most of every opportunity to make a new appointment, and we have been encouraged by our success in attracting and holding outstanding faculty members in a variety of disciplines. This past year we have managed to launch a very promising new Department of Comparative Literature at essentially no cost to the general funds of the University by combining and redeploying existing faculty strengths and taking advantage of an imaginative grant from the

---

* R & D Index of D. Kent Halstead, *Higher Education Prices and Price Indexes*, U.S. Department of Health, Education, and Welfare, Office of Education, U.S. Government Printing Office, Washington, D.C., 1975.

Andrew W. Mellon Foundation. To cite a second example, we are now in the midst of a major effort, as part of our current $125 million development program, to find the funds to house properly our Department of Biochemical Sciences, which contains a number of exceedingly able young faculty members, which is playing an ever more important role in both education and research, and which simply cannot be sacrificed to financial exigency.

Against these instances of forward progress must be weighed, unfortunately, the more frequent decisions either to cut back or simply to refrain from moving ahead. This fall the Executive Committee of the Board of Trustees felt compelled to rule out further consideration of the pros and cons of doing more in the field of law because of the conviction, shared widely on the campus, that our first priority must be to support the core academic disciplines on which the established quality of Princeton rests. Several years ago we were forced to suspend our graduate program in Slavic studies, and the deans and the appropriate faculty bodies are now considering the possible suspension of some small graduate programs.

The case of linguistics illustrates very well one kind of conundrum we have had to face. The growing importance of this discipline is beyond question, and many scholars believe that the field is on the threshold of exciting new developments that will have profound effects on our conception of language. Also, we are already strong at Princeton in certain specialties that complement work in linguistics very well. For these reasons we had hoped, as recently as two years ago, to achieve enough other savings to permit us to make the relatively small number of appointments needed to take our staff in linguistics to a minimum critical size. The worsening of the overall financial situation since then (and the attendant need to reduce the overall size of the faculty somewhat), combined with a sense of somewhat larger minimum needs in linguistics, have forced us to set aside these plans; and if we cannot afford the expenditures that would be needed to build a program of high quality, it may well be wiser in a case of this kind to suspend the program rather than to try to continue it under increasingly difficult circumstances.

Such hard decisions—concerning things not to be done that we would like to do and think we could do well—must be made, and they will be made. But we cannot, responsibly and in good conscience, follow a simple ''cost per student'' test in deciding where to look for savings. There are departments and programs at Princeton which are of outstanding quality, which serve national and even international needs, and yet which do not, and will never, attract enough students to come close to meeting any institutional norm defined in terms of the ratio of faculty per student or cost per student.

One example is astrophysical sciences, in which Princeton has a preeminent reputation for graduate instruction and research—and five undergraduate majors. (An extremely small undergraduate program is inevitable, since even those undergraduates who think they may want to do graduate work in astrophysics are often encouraged to major in mathematics or physics as undergraduates.) East Asian studies and Near Eastern studies are examples of another kind. In both of these fields Princeton has exceptional—and very expensive—library resources, as well as leading teachers and scholars. The importance to the country of a relatively small number of outstanding centers of teaching and research in these areas is evident, but there are never going to be large numbers of students studying advanced Chinese or Arabic.

In allocating faculty positions among departments, the dean of the faculty has to pay a significant amount of attention to enrollment patterns, but he also has to be concerned about coverage of subject matter, and about seeing to it that each department has sufficient strength to sustain the quality of its work and to meet both its teaching and scholarly obligations. (It is because of some of these considerations that crude measures of "productivity" and "efficiency" can be so misleading. In our budgetary and planning process we make use of a great many statistical measures, but we try to interpret data in the light of the purposes we serve and, in particular, in terms of qualitative as well as quantitative criteria.)

In considering possible economies, it is well to recognize that there is a definite limit to the reductions in academic program that are possible at a university already as small and as relatively compact as Princeton without endangering the overall quality of the institution. The report of the Priorities Committee that has just been released envisions a net reduction in the size of the faculty on the teaching budget of ten positions next year and a possible fifteen additional positions over the following two years. In terms of what is happening at many colleges and universities, this may not seem a large number, and we shall of course make every effort to distribute these reductions in a way that will do as little damage as possible to the core of the institution. (We have never believed in across-the-board cuts, attractive as they may seem from the standpoint of administrative convenience.) Still, we must recognize that we are now at a point where further reductions could have significant effects on the quality of what we do.

We continue to put great emphasis on independent work at the undergraduate level, on a highly selective graduate program, and on relatively close contact between faculty members and students. We have worked hard to maintain these special strengths of Princeton, and we shall continue to do so. But it would be disingenuous to claim that further reductions in the size of a faculty that already makes efforts on behalf of undergraduate and graduate students unheard of at many universities would not take some toll in this regard. Also, we have to be concerned about the potential effects of further reductions on the ability of departments to recruit outstanding younger faculty and to make the occasional key senior appointment from outside the University. The widely publicized difficulties experienced by many aspiring faculty members in finding positions does not mean that there has been any appreciable slackening in the intensity of competition for the very best people, at either junior or senior levels.

Student, Administrative, and Supporting Services

I have been discussing the effects of financial constriction on the central academic program of the University because we are beyond the point of being able to make many easier, less painful cuts in the budget. We take great pride in the residential nature of Princeton, and in the many opportunities for personal growth and development that are present here and that complement the academic opportunities that we offer. As I suggested at Opening Exercises last September, it is exceedingly important that the academic pressures which many students feel so acutely not become all-consuming. Partly this is a matter of attitudes and values. But the ability of many students to find a sensible balance between hard academic work, extracurricular pursuits, and informal activities of all kinds also depends on the support that the University gives to the quality of student residential life, student organizations, athletic programs, the work of the chapel, advising, counseling, and other student services. None of these activities has been or can be exempt from budgetary scrutiny, and significant economies have been achieved in these areas; at the same time I want to record here my own conviction that it would be every bit as easy to hurt seriously the overall quality of life at Princeton by seeking substantial additional savings in these areas as by reducing further the expenditures on some academic programs.

As far as administrative and supporting services are concerned, from the beginning of our current effort to control expenditures we have tried consistently to protect the quality of the educational core of the University by looking first for all possible economies in those non-academic areas. In 1970, when the Priorities Committee first had to recommend substantial budget reductions, 80 of the 100 positions eliminated were in administrative and supporting services; last year's Priorities Committee continued the process of attempting to reduce these kinds of expenditures and made recommendations which resulted in an additional saving of about $1.7 million.

These reductions have required both substantial increases in workloads and reductions in services provided, and they have occurred in the face of added pressures on administrative services from within and without the University. Economic difficulties, as they affect individuals in the University, inevitably increase the demands made by students on such offices as those of the dean of student affairs, the dean of the college, and the dean of the graduate school, as well as on the various counseling services and the office of undergraduate financial aid. Tighter budgets increase the pressures exerted by faculty on the office of the dean of the faculty and on the development office, as well as pressures exerted by staff members on the office of personnel services, to cite three other very different examples. Finally, economic difficulties inevitably increase the pressures exerted by my office on the entire budget-making and fund-raising apparatus of the University, just as others, in turn, expect more help from me and my associates. It is ironic but true that it is much easier to make do with a relatively simple and inexpensive administrative structure when financial constraints are relatively loose than when budgets are already very tight.

The added workload created for our supporting staff as a result of requirements originating outside the University has been discussed at length by other people in other places, and I shall not dwell on that subject here, except to note that I hope governmental agencies, in particular, will reduce the burgeoning demands for paperwork on the part of universities that are part of a trend toward increasing regulation that many of us also find extremely worrisome on other, more fundamental, grounds. In addition, like all other segments of society, we have been affected by a general increase in the inclination to litigate issues in the courts.

Reductions in staff and increases in pressures can lead to morale problems. In point of fact, our people have done very well, and I am proud of the positive way in which so many members of the administration and staff have responded to the evident need for savings in these areas. But it must be recognized by all members of the University community that there is a definite limit to the economies that can be achieved along these lines without jeopardizing seriously the ability of the University to serve its many constituencies, to continue to attract able people to administrative as well as faculty ranks, to make effective use of the resources now at our disposal, and to raise new funds for Princeton.

Responsibilities to the Future

There is one other aspect of our current situation that could involve serious long-term dangers to the quality of the University. I refer to the temptation, in any period of financial austerity, to protect the present at the expense of the future. We have been determined not to yield to this temptation by, for instance, deferring needed maintenance. And we have tried to emphasize the importance of being responsible to the future in the way in which we handle the endowment of the University. Let me quote one paragraph from this year's report of the Priorities Committee:

> At one open meeting of the Priorities Committee a student asked why we did not close the deficit by spending some of the endowment rather than by trying to reduce expenditures or by raising tuition. A member of the Priorities Committee replied, emphasizing the importance of preserving the endowment. "Do you mean to tell me," asked the student, "that you expect the University to last *another* two hundred years?" Our answer is "Yes." To answer otherwise would be a betrayal of our predecessors, our colleagues, and our successors.

In the face of the general decline in securities prices, it has not been possible in recent years for any university to maintain even the dollar value of its endowment, and the value in terms of dollars of constant purchasing power has declined even more. Also, operating deficits have required the expenditure of funds that otherwise could have been invested to earn income for the future. We have believed that the further reductions in expenditures that would have been necessary to eliminate these deficits immediately would have done more damage to the

University than the diversion of funds to finance the deficits; but we have also believed that the quality of the University over the years ahead depends importantly on our ability to provide for the increases in costs that are inevitable over time.

There is no easy answer to the question of how we are to hand on to those who come after us the same opportunities that we have been given by our predecessors—how we are to preserve and if possible enhance our educational capital as well as our financial capital, and how we are to do so without sacrificing principles, programs, and people important to us now. The tension between present and future is inevitable, especially under present circumstances, and we should not try to wish it away. It is of course a particular responsibility of the Board of Trustees to take the long view. That is not always easy, and it is not always appreciated, but it is all the more important for those reasons.

It is also incumbent upon the Trustees, and members of the administration, to explore possibilities for increasing income from non-traditional as well as traditional sources. To illustrate what we have been trying to accomplish along these lines, we anticipate additional income in 1976–77, after allowing for all expenses, of $150,000 as a direct result of concerted efforts by the newly established Events Office to make dormitories and other buildings available in the summers to suitable groups. Also, through the development of the Forrestal property, we are engaged in a long-term effort to increase income at the same time that we try to enhance the physical environment of the University.

* * * * *

I do not mean to sound like an educational Cassandra, for that is not how I feel. In fact, to date we have been remarkably successful, I believe, in sustaining the quality of the University—without compromising the interests of future generations. This has been possible in spite of declines in the real value of our resources because of the commitment of many faculty and staff to give even more generously of themselves, because of the loyalty and hard work of Trustees and many volunteers in the alumni ranks, because of the willingness of the entire University community to put preservation of the substance of the educational program ahead of all else, and because of the willingness of so many students and their families to make the sacrifices necessary to enable us to recapture at least part of our rising costs through higher charges. But nothing is helped by pretending that we do not face, in company with all of the other great universities, threats to quality that are unprecedented in modern times.

IMPLICATIONS FOR ACCESS

The steep increases in student charges which we have had to impose in recent years raise important and persistent questions concerning access to the educational opportunities that Princeton offers. In this section of my report, I want to say a few words about these charges, about student aid at Princeton, and also about national policy on student aid as it affects access to Princeton and other private colleges and universities.

The Objective

In my view, it is extremely important that we do all that we can to continue to enroll outstanding individuals without regard to their economic circumstances. The quality of the University, and the value of the educational contribution we are able to make, depend directly on the presence in our student body of applicants who seem to possess the most promising combination of academic and personal qualities and who seem most likely to make a positive difference both to Princeton and to the nation over the years ahead.

This is hardly a new doctrine. The University's first two scholarships were endowed in 1790 and 1792. More than 50 years ago roughly one sixth of the student body was receiving some form of scholarship support, and at the annual meeting of the national alumni association in 1922, John O.H. Pitney '81, chairman of the Trustee Finance Committee, said:

> Princeton is a living thing, and every living thing must grow greater and stronger and larger, and I know that you . . . will require that Princeton someday does meet every claim that can be made on her by young men worthy of her education. . . . My ideal would be . . . [that] those who can't afford tuition fees should be helped by scholarships and a remittance of tuition.

Providing access to Princeton without regard to financial circumstances is an important objective in its own right, in terms of the principle involved; achieving this objective also serves to make Princeton a far better educational institution than it would be otherwise. Students in a university community learn in important ways from each other and from the friction of differing perspectives and conflicting ideas. Accordingly, the University has an educational interest in enrolling students from diverse social, cultural, and economic backgrounds who will bring different insights and experiences to the campus.

This past summer I came upon a 1937 speech by Tyler Dennett, then president of Williams College, before a Williams alumni group, in which he said:

> We need heterogeneity in college to give us an invigorating intellectual and social atmosphere. We need a cosmopolitan group most of all to sharpen our sense of values and to give us understanding.

The case for heterogeneity today is, if anything, even stronger than it was when President Dennett made that statement. Our society has changed significantly and both occupational choice and opportunities to serve in leadership capacities of all kinds are now far less restricted by sex or race or background. It seems clear that without an educational milieu that includes real diversity we would not continue to attract the outstanding students of all races and backgrounds who now come to Princeton, students who appreciate the value of learning with and from a wide variety of people, and who want to be confident that this University, like other great universities, is making a sustained effort to enroll qualified individuals from many backgrounds. It also seems clear that we would not be serving the nation as we should if, in seeking to educate leaders for future generations, we were not to reach out for the best minds and the most promising individuals wherever they may be found.

The Need for Increases in Charges

Between the academic year 1968–69 and the academic year 1975–76, tuition alone has gone up from $2,150 to $3,900, and total charges, for tuition, room, and board, have increased from $3,310 to $5,800. These increases have been adopted most reluctantly by the Trustees, but they have seemed unavoidable under the circumstances.

Earlier in this report I have tried to indicate the pressures on our costs and to note the actual decline in the real value of the resources available to us. Perhaps the clearest way of showing why we have had to increase student charges so significantly is by documenting the extent to which our expenditures, constrained as they have been, nevertheless have risen faster than almost all of our traditional sources of income. (See Figure 3.)

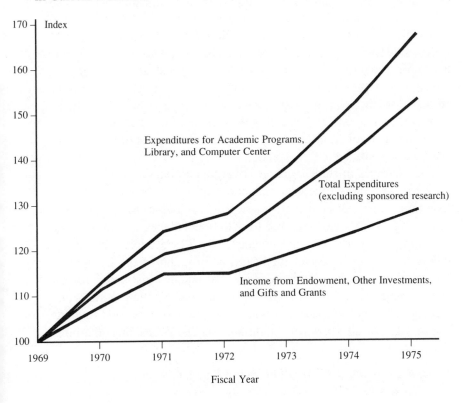

Figure 3
Expenditures and Income at Princeton,
in Current Dollars

For the purposes of this chart I have grouped together endowment income, income from short-term investments, and gifts and grants from private and public sources (excluding sponsored research). These sources of income have risen 29 percent since 1968–69, while total expenditures (excluding direct expenditures for sponsored research) have risen 55 percent, and while expenditures related directly to the academic program (including expenditures by the academic departments and by the library and computer center) have risen 70 percent. In an effort to close the gap, we have had to rely fairly heavily on increases in student charges and other sources of revenue more or less under our control (rents on housing and commercial properties, user fees, and so on).

The increases in student charges over this period have made it possible to avoid more draconian reductions in programs and in services than have occurred. However, it is worth noting that the total amount of the increased income received from tuition and fees at both graduate and undergraduate levels has equaled only 70–75 percent of the increase in the direct cost of the academic program of the University; increased income from tuition and fees has equaled just under 40 percent of the increases in the combined costs of academic programs and student aid, athletics, student services, and administrative and supporting services of all kinds (including admissions, counseling, the infirmary, etc.).

Financial Aid and the Overall Effects of Rising Charges

As successive reports of the Priorities Committee have stated, we have given careful consideration to the effects of increased charges on our students and their families. Approximately 40 percent of all undergraduates at Princeton receive financial aid, and we have undertaken to provide sufficient funds each year in the form of combinations of work opportunities, loans, and scholarships to insure that we will be able to meet the demonstrated financial needs of all students enrolled at Princeton. Also, while it is impossible to make the kind of open-ended commitment that would allow us to guarantee without qualification that we shall always meet these needs for all students offered admission, we have in fact managed to meet the needs of every admitted student in recent years, despite rising charges. We are determined to make every effort to continue this policy, and the projections developed by the Priorities Committee assume that we shall be successful, at least for the next three or four years. We are one of a relatively small number of institutions that have been able to maintain such a policy, and it has not been inexpensive: in the current year we expect the scholarship budget for undergraduates alone to exceed $4 million.

The costs of our program of financial aid would be far greater—in fact prohibitive—if we were not to ask all students and families who request financial aid to join with us in bearing the burden of financing their educations. We allocate scholarship funds only *after* (1) a parental contribution has been determined with the help of a formula developed by the College Scholarship Service (used by all Ivy Group schools); and (2) students have agreed to contribute a certain amount of "self-help" through employment and loans. At present, every student who applies for scholarship assistance is expected to contribute annually about $1,300 toward the cost of his or her education from summer and term-time employment, and also to be willing to finance between $1,000 and $1,200 of the year's expenditures through loans offered at favorable terms. Scholarships are then provided to make up any remaining gap between a student's anticipated total expenses for the year and the sum of the parental contribution and the self-help expectation. The size of the average undergraduate scholarship this year is $2,700.

This policy, which in general outline is common to all of the Ivy Group schools as well as to a number of other selective private colleges and universities, means that every admitted student is expected to demonstrate his or her own commitment to helping defray the costs of a Princeton education. At the same time, the University accepts responsibility for providing enough supplementary funds to enable the student to attend Princeton. This differs significantly from another kind of approach, which provides full scholarships for a considerably smaller number of students thought to merit special consideration because of athletic talent, academic record, or the application of some other criteria. It seems to us fairer to proceed as we do, and more consistent with the objective of making Princeton accessible to significant numbers of students from all backgrounds who meet the standards of the admission office. . . .

In what context are the increased student charges at Princeton to be seen, and what have been the effects on the student body of the combination of increased charges and larger amounts of financial aid that have characterized recent budgets? These questions are easier to pose than to answer definitively. We are all too aware that the burdens are heavy: for students across much of the financial spectrum who have to take out loans; for families, especially in the lower- and middle-income brackets, who may experience real difficulties in meeting the parental contributions expected of them; and for many other families at somewhat higher income levels who must nonetheless make many sacrifices to help with college costs. No one should minimize the all too real human problems that reside not so far below the surface of aggregative statistics. At the same time, as the Priorities Committee reminds us annually, the costs of attending Princeton and similar colleges and universities need to be seen in a realistic perspective.

In determining each year what recommendations to make concerning student charges, the Priorities Committee generally studies four sets of data:

1. It compares increases in charges with economy-wide increases in prices and money incomes. In the most recent two-year period, for example, the rate of increase in charges at Princeton has been somewhat larger than the general increase in both prices and money incomes, but the differences have been less pronounced than many have assumed. Between 1974–75 and 1975–76, our charges increased 12 percent, while the Consumer Price Index rose 7.8 percent and median family income is estimated to have risen between 6 and 7 percent. The increase in student charges for 1976–77 just approved by the Trustees is 8 percent, while prices generally are expected to rise about 6 percent and money incomes perhaps 9 percent over the same period.

What many people do not realize is that over longer periods, such as the last decade and a half, the substantial increases in student charges have been more than matched by increases in money incomes. As Figure 4 indicates, between 1961–62 (when uniform room fees were established) and 1974–75, charges at Princeton increased 102 percent while median family income rose 124 percent. Thus, over this period at least, the income of the average person has kept pace with the increase in charges.* Some of the public discussion of the magnitude of increases in tuition and other charges fails to take into account what economists call "money illusion"—a failure to perceive that increases measured in current dollars must be considered in the context of general changes in prices and incomes if they are not to be misinterpreted.

2. The Priorities Committee also examines admission statistics. Nei-

* The composition of our student body has of course changed over this period, and a somewhat higher percentage of our students now come from lower- and middle-income families. This change, however, has been reflected in substantial increases in our scholarship budget, and does not diminish the force of the point being made in the text—namely, that for families in the same relative position in the national income distribution in 1961 and in 1975, the cost of attending Princeton bears about the same relationship to their income now as before.

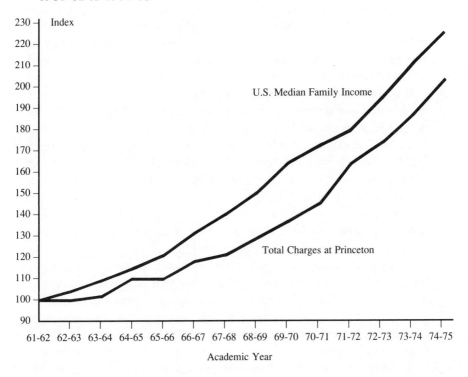

Figure 4
Total Charges at Princeton and U.S. Median Family Income,
1961-62 to 1974-75

ther the number nor the quality of our applications has been affected in any measurable way, even by the sharply increased charges adopted in the last few years. Two years ago our applications rose markedly by some 13 percent, and last year they held steady at a figure of nearly 10,000—which means that we receive roughly nine applications for each place in the entering class. Preliminary figures for the current year suggest no tendency for applications to decline; in fact, they may well set an all-time record.

It is also important to note that the available data on the incomes of the families of entering freshmen do not reveal any clear change in the composition of the student body as a result of increased charges. The fear is often expressed that high charges and scholarships based on need will lead to a student body composed increasingly of the very rich and the very poor. While it is certainly possible that this will prove to be a legitimate worry in the long run, it is encouraging to note that no such tendency towards increased economic polarization is shown by the figures for Princeton to date. To be sure, we continue to attract significant numbers of very able students from families in the professions or in business whose incomes are well above the national average; but, given the high correlation between academic aptitude and socio-economic background that has been found in many studies, it would be surprising if this were not the case. What seems significant is that the percentage of entering students from lower- and middle-income families has not fallen in recent years.

3. The Priorities Committee also analyzes the choices made by students who are offered admission by Princeton but who choose to go elsewhere. Of particular interest is the number who elect to go to public institutions which charge far lower tuition. In 1967, about 9 percent of those declining admission at Princeton chose to attend public institutions; in 1975, the comparable figure was less than 5 percent.

It has been suggested that some outstanding students do not even apply to Princeton or similar schools because of our high costs. This undoubtedly happens on occasion, but there is no evidence—either of a systematic kind or based on the impressions of those who participate actively in our admissions process—that this is a very strong or growing tendency. On the contrary, a study by our assistant provost, Dr. Richard Spies, published in 1973, showed that the quality of an institution's program was a far more important factor than costs in the decisions of the highest quality applicants concerning schools to which to apply. We should recognize explicitly the danger that in cutting back expenditures in an effort to hold down increases in charges, we could sacrifice the quality that attracts the best applicants in the first place. A university that reduces costs at the expense of quality may well lose students who would have been willing to endure real financial hardship for the sake of an uncompromised educational program.

4. Finally, the Priorities Committee compares Princeton's charges with the charges of those schools with which we compete most directly and most vigorously for students. Our tuition this year, at $3,900, falls at about the mid-point of the distribution for the Ivy Group as a whole, between the $3,740 at Harvard and the $4,050 at Yale. It is also worth noting that although Princeton's tuition is comparable to that charged by these other universities, the amount of senior faculty time devoted to teaching undergraduates at Princeton is greater than at most—perhaps all—other Ivy Group universities.

The conclusion to be drawn from this brief review of the available evidence is not that there are no grounds for concern about the effects of costs on access. As I shall point out in a moment, there are difficult and worrisome questions here, especially as we look to the future. But it is important, I think, not to exaggerate the harmful effects to date, and not to minimize the extent to which our scholarship program and the work of our admission officers and Alumni Schools Committees have protected principles important to us in the face of very serious financial pressures.

Concerns for the Future

I want now to express three particular concerns of a long-run nature with respect to the broad question of access.

First, I worry about the special pressures on middle-income families. This is, of course, a problem for all of higher education, not just for Princeton, and it does need to be considered in its proper perspective: depending on the number of dependent children and other factors, a family with a before-tax income of up to $34,000 may qualify for financial aid in some form from Princeton. Nevertheless, it is clear that the burdens on families at or near the edges of eligibility for financial assistance, as well as for those at lower income levels, can be heavy ones. It is very important, for all of the reasons given earlier, to preserve access on the part of this group to the educational opportunities offered by universities such as Princeton, and achieving this objective may well require some fresh thinking about various kinds of state and federal financial incentives for a broad range of students and their families.

Second, I worry, along with many others, about the widening gap between the costs to all students of attending private and public institutions. As Figure 5 illustrates, the gap between tuition charged at Princeton (and other similar private colleges and universities) and tuition charged at state universities has widened dramatically and rather steadily since 1967–68. In that year tuition at Princeton was about $1,600 more than the median tuition charge for residents at a sample of state universities and land-grant colleges (the absolute figures were $1,950 at Princeton and $351 at the state institutions); in 1975–76, the difference was over $3,300 ($3,900 versus $564). While this differential has not grown as much in dollars of constant purchasing power as it has in current dollars, there is no question about the direction in which we are moving.*

As I pointed out above, the effects of this gap on our own admissions seem negligible thus far—in large part, I presume, because of the efforts we have made to provide additional financial aid and to sustain and strengthen the quality of our educational program. As one looks ahead, however, it is hard to be unconcerned about this trend, and about its potential implications, not only for particular private colleges and universities, but for the pluralism of our entire system of higher education, and for the ability of students and their families to feel that they can choose freely among the various kinds of institutions. Some private institutions, of course, are concerned not just with access but with enrollment itself; their overriding concern is whether they can attract enough qualified students to continue to operate effectively, or even at all.

This entire subject can be a highly emotional one, leading to sharp, divisive, and even bitter conflicts between proponents of private and public institutions. My own feeling, shared by many others in both private and public institutions, is that we need to do all in our power to prevent the discussion from taking on that tone. Fortunately, there are ways of addressing this problem, at least in part, which involve public policy proposals that have received broad support within the higher education community. These proposals also address a third concern of mine.

Recognizing that there are real limits on what any one university,

* The corresponding figures for nonresident tuition at the same sample of state universities and colleges were $850 in 1967–68 and $1,438 in 1975–76.

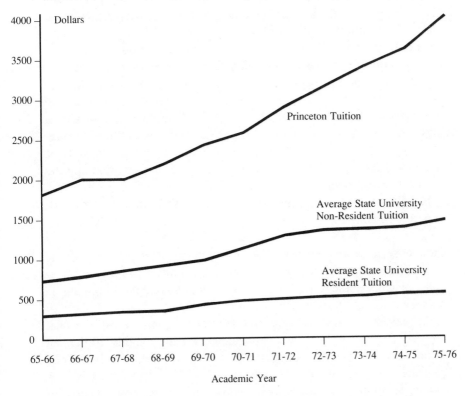

Figure 5
Tuition for Princeton and the Average State University

4000 ┐ Dollars

Princeton Tuition

Average State University
Non-Resident Tuition

Average State University
Resident Tuition

65-66   66-67   67-68   68-69   69-70   70-71   71-72   72-73   73-74   74-75   75-76

Academic Year

acting alone, can do to assure access, I worry about whether we will be able to augment our scholarship funds sufficiently to meet the growing needs of students in the coming years. At present there are approximately 700 named scholarships at Princeton, and this year we have been able to meet the demands on our scholarship budget through a combination of endowed scholarship funds (some of which were restricted by deed of gift and others which we have chosen to allocate to this purpose), private gifts and grants, and a variety of government programs at the state and federal levels. Next year we anticipate that these sources, taken together, will fall short of meeting our requirements by more than half a million dollars—dollars that will have to be provided from general funds. Beyond next year, the situation appears even more worrisome.

Needless to say, we hope that alumni and other friends of the University will continue to provide scholarship support as they have done so generously in the past—and I am confident that they will. At the same time, it seems doubtful that Princeton, or other private colleges and universities, will be able to continue indefinitely to provide financial assistance at the requisite levels without increased help from public sources.

At present, a variety of state and federal programs, most of which are intended to aid the individual student, provide roughly 20 percent of our scholarship funds. In addition, federal loan programs have been of critical importance to our students and to the University. Unfortunately, assistance from various states, which accounted for 60 percent of all of our government support for scholarships last year, declined by 26 percent this year and is expected to drop again next year. Federal support, meanwhile, after growing substantially between 1974–75 and 1975–76 (from $294,000 to about $470,000), is now expected to increase only very modestly next year—less than in proportion to increases in charges.

Obviously budgets are tight everywhere. But there are proposals currently before Congress that would strengthen in important ways both the Basic Educational Opportunity Grant Program (which is designed to provide access to some college or university to every student) and the Supplemental Educational Opportunity Grant Program (which is designed to facilitate individual choice by helping low- and middle-income students meet the costs of moderate and higher priced institutions). This combination of grant programs, directed to the complementary goals of assuring both access and choice, has the strong support of the American Council on Education and the Association of American Universities, both of which represent public and private institutions. Taken together these proposals alleviate somewhat the problems created by the widening gap between private and public tuitions, and they do so by channeling funds through the educational preferences of individual students; thus, they seem less likely to lead to excessive governmental intrusion than would many alternative approaches.

It is my hope that Congress will recognize that the public interest is served, and served importantly, by making it possible for students from all income levels to attend the colleges and universities best able to serve their needs, whether these be private or public institutions. In a pluralistic society, concerned with providing opportunities for promising young people to receive the best possible education, and concerned too with sustaining the ability of colleges and universities generally to offer the educational advantages that come from student bodies that are diverse as well as qualified, we should be unwilling to compromise this important principle.

IMPLICATIONS FOR OUR SENSE OF COMMUNITY

It is important to recognize that the quality of a university—and particularly of a residential university—depends to a significant degree on its sense of community. This sense develops out of a shared commitment to common goals, out of mutual respect, and out of the ability to welcome, and not just to tolerate, different perspectives and differences of opinion. It requires more than a little trust and good will.

No doubt all institutions and all organizations work better if they possess these attributes. For a university, however, a strongly felt sense of community is particularly important because so much of what is accomplished depends on self-motivation and on healthy interactions. The ethos of the university matters enormously. Debate and free expression of conflicting opinion are critical to learning and discovering, and all of us are likely to feel freer to reach out for new understandings in an open way, to test our ideas, and to be willing to correct ourselves and others, if we feel that we are part of a mutually supportive group of people within which it is possible to make mistakes, to be wrong, without being rejected.

Nor is it just students and faculty members who need to feel that they are part of a single community. Administrators and staff members cannot do their jobs well unless they identify closely with the fundamental educational purposes of the institution; at the same time, their morale also depends greatly on their being accepted and respected as persons who are contributing in their own ways to the achievement of common goals. Thus, all of us have a stake in avoiding the "we-they" syndrome that can be so corrosive and debilitating.

It is also vitally important that a genuine sense of community extend beyond the campus to include alumni, parents, Trustees, and other members of the society who care about education. Needless to say, the University benefits immeasurably from the financial support of those who care enough to provide voluntarily the resources that make it possible to do more than meet minimum standards. Equally important, as I have tried to say on other occasions, are the countless other ways in which alumni and others help advance our common purposes: by providing advice and counsel, by working with prospective students, and by representing the interests of the University in the larger society. Nor do the benefits of community extend only in one direction. Those who work so hard on behalf of Princeton are often the same people who enjoy alumni colleges, athletic events, alumni gatherings, and so on. More generally, there is the sense of satisfaction that can come from shared participation in an important undertaking.

While some kinds of adversity serve to strengthen bonds and to build stronger ties, the kind of financial adversity the University confronts today can threaten seriously the sense of community that is so important to us. This is particularly true insofar as the resident university community is concerned. We are faced with the unhappy task of making do with less, and of doing so at the same time that we are asking students and parents to pay more, and members of the faculty, administration, and staff to accept increased workloads. Under these circumstances it is hardly surprising that stresses and strains are felt.

This tendency for scarcity of resources and competing economic claims to exacerbate relationships is of course by no means peculiar to educational institutions. Historians have attributed wars, revolutions, and less dramatic changes in organizations and whole societies to this cause. But the widespread presence of the phenomenon hardly robs it of its significance, and I think we do well to recognize this problem explicitly and to try to address it as sensibly as we can. In my view, this potential consequence of continuing financial stringency could prove to be as serious over the long run as the threats to quality and to access.

The Priorities Committee

The clearest indication of the presence of tensions associated directly with finances has been the procedural difficulties experienced this fall by the Priorities Committee. This committee of the Council of the Princeton University Community (CPUC) is chaired by the provost (ex officio), and is composed of six faculty members, two graduate students, four undergraduates, a member of one of the other groups represented on the CPUC, and the dean of the faculty and the treasurer. It has been in existence since the fall of 1969, and its purpose is to:

> review the current budget as early in the academic year as may be practicable. It shall also consider issues that have arisen in the course of the preparation of the budget and shall review plans for the development of the University in advance of any final decisions with respect to such plans. The committee may advise the president with respect to all these matters and shall from time to time report to the council on the issues before it.

It is fair to say, I think, that over the last six and a half years this committee has functioned exceptionally well. The members have worked hard and have contributed both specific suggestions for coping with our financial problems and a more general sense of priorities as they perceive them. In addition, the committee has served two other very useful purposes: (1) by reviewing presentations and asking hard questions, it has stimulated careful preparation and analysis by the heads of departments and administrative offices; and (2) by being well informed, the members of the committee have helped to increase general understanding throughout the University community of the nature of our problems and the ways in which we are trying to deal with them.

The committee has understood that its role is advisory and that it is responsible for giving advice directly to the president of the University. It has also understood that its effectiveness depends on the willingness of heads of offices to be entirely candid with it, and on the confidence that the president and the Trustees have in its work. The Trustees, as I pointed out earlier, have a particular responsibility for the long-term welfare of the University, and the provost and other representatives of the Priorities Committee have worked closely with representatives of the Finance Committee of the Board so that the two groups would benefit to the maximum degree from each other's thinking. Both Harold Helm '20, who served as chairman of the Finance Committee when the Priorities Committee was established, and H. Chapman Rose '28, who served in that capacity from 1970–71 through 1974–75, have been generous in their praise of its accomplishments, as have representatives of the American Council on Education and other outside groups which have studied the process of budgeting in various universities. While a number of other colleges and universities have moved to establish analogous mechanisms, the Priorities Committee at Princeton continues to be cited as something of a model.

More extensive discussions of the purposes of the Priorities Committee and of its work to date may be found in the reports the committee has issued each January and in the lengthy study of resource allocation at Princeton which a number of us prepared under the auspices of the Ford Foundation. To the very brief background presented here, I would add only that in my judgment a major reason for the success of the committee over the years has been the commitment of the individual members to advancing the welfare of the University viewed as a single, highly interdependent academic community. During the time that I served as provost (and thus as chairman of this committee), I was impressed by the clear sense of the members that they were not on the committee to represent the interests of a particular constituency but rather to bring to bear their best thinking on the problems common to all of us. There was remarkably little special pleading or log-rolling. There was respect for the procedures of the committee, which have included the confidential handling of a great deal of information that is sensitive and the informal interchange of ideas with other members and with Trustees before definite recommendations are framed. Also, there was the kind of camaraderie that comes from working closely together on what is seen as a common task.

It may be that there was no way in which that kind of working relationship among individuals with widely differing perspectives and experiences could have survived the unremitting and increasingly severe pressures on all of us associated with ever more difficult decisions concerning budgetary priorities. In any event, there has been a clear tendency during the last year or so for the work of the Priorities Committee to become more politicized. This fall there also has been a great deal of procedural controversy concerning the degree of "openness" that is desirable or possible for a committee of this kind. There were at least two serious breaches of confidentiality, one by a graduate student who, in resigning from the committee and simultaneously making public materials given to him in confidence, openly stated that he no longer felt bound by his previous promise to follow the rules adopted by the majority of the committee, and the second by a member who later chose anonymously to violate a pledge of confidentiality that had been reaffirmed by all members of the committee.

Actions of this kind inevitably affect not only the procedures of the committee, but also the spirit with which the group is able to work. They also raise questions as to the way in which some members have approached the task of developing recommendations. Most seriously of all, such actions force us to reconsider the kinds of information that can be shared with such a committee, the nature of the discussions that can occur within such a committee, and the future prospects for what has been an important advisory relationship.

More generally, there is an even broader and more troubling question of how such breaches of trust affect the confidence which various members of the community have in one another—and, indeed, how our sense of community itself is affected. The members of the Governance Committee of the CPUC—including faculty, students, and alumni— share fully these concerns, as do many others, and we are going to be discussing them this spring. Needless to say, none of these concerns is peculiar to Princeton, or even to higher education. Similar problems have affected government at all levels, although I should hasten to add that all too often erroneous and misleading analogies are drawn between processes appropriate to an elected government and those relevant to the organization and functioning of a university—a very different institution with a different set of institutional imperatives.

It is my hope that in the course of this discussion constructive proposals can be developed that will enable us to continue to benefit from the evident desires of the overwhelming majority of students, faculty members, staff, and alumni to contribute positively to the discussion of long-term issues which are of great consequence to all of us. Certainly the excellent discussion of the report of the Priorities Committee at the January meeting of the CPUC indicates what can be accomplished along these lines.

In a way it is ironic—though not really surprising—that procedural problems of this kind have arisen at the very time that we have the greatest need for both good ideas and broad understanding of the financial problems that confront us. Optimist that I am, I hope that out of the discussion of these questions will emerge both a clearer sense of how groups of people must work together and a renewed commitment to larger goals that are widely shared.

I have devoted this much space to the Priorities Committee questions because they are current, because they have received a fair amount of attention, particularly on campus, and because they illustrate vividly the broader concerns that I emphasized at the beginning of this section. But I would not want anyone to think that it is only in the context of committees and publicized disputes, whether over procedures or tuition increases, that threats to a sense of community can arise. Indeed, feelings of estrangement and apathy, if not hostility, often seem to be greater on campuses with no regularized process for encouraging broad consultation and participation; although more subtle and less obvious, it may be that a lack of a sense of belonging poses greater threats to educational institutions and the purposes they serve than disagreements among those who share a feeling of institutional attachment.

In general, we continue to be extremely fortunate at Princeton in the extent to which members of this University community genuinely care for each other and for the institution. The task for us is not to create anew a feeling that is lacking, but rather to preserve and sustain what continues to be a special strength of this University. Indeed, my own confidence in what I believe to be the exceptionally positive quality of the underlying attitudes on this campus makes it far easier to discuss this set of concerns candidly than it would be in most other settings.

Relationships with Staff Members

There is one other specific manifestation of the general threat to relationships derived from our economic problems which is common to all educational institutions and which needs to be mentioned. I refer to the growing tensions evident on many campuses between groups of staff members and other elements of the community. The long and in some respects acrimonious labor dispute at the University of Pennsylvania this fall involving its food service and other workers is a dramatic example. Yale experienced a serious work stoppage at Commencement a year and a half ago, and this past summer there was a twelve-day strike by our painters. Also, in September there was an election among our nonprofessional library employees in which the staff members involved voted not to be represented by the Princeton University Library Assistants Association, a group affiliated with the American Federation of State, County, and Municipal Employees.*

The concerns that led to this election are important ones. All colleges and universities, Princeton included, need to be sensitive to the needs

---

* This decision was reversed in 1977 when the nonprofessional library staff voted to be represented by the Princeton University Library Assistants Association.

of staff members, to listen carefully, to respond thoughtfully, and to act fairly. The financial constraints under which all colleges and universities must operate these days do limit what we can do in straight economic terms, but that is certainly not all that matters. Our staff members work hard to serve the University in critical ways, and their effectiveness—and much of our effectiveness as an educational enterprise—depend on their feeling appreciated for the many contributions they make to our common purposes, as well as on their being treated properly in terms of wages and working conditions.

Understanding and Attitude

Adversary relationships tend to grow naturally when we have fewer resources at our disposal than we need to meet all of the legitimate claims that can be made. Plainly we need to do the best we can to allocate the resources that are available to us as sensibly and as fairly as possible. More generally, however, our ability to prevent the all too real financial pressures that confront us from eroding a pervasive sense of educational community seems to me to depend mainly on less tangible qualities of understanding and attitude.

Understanding involves, first, recognizing that there is a greater degree of overlapping interests within the University community than is sometimes perceived—and then reminding ourselves and others that this is so. For example, compensating members of the faculty and staff properly is crucially important, especially in the long run, to the quality of the education that students who come to Princeton can expect to receive. Similarly, the level of student charges and policies governing financial aid are important not only to those now asked to pay those charges but to all of us who have a long-term interest in maintaining the attractiveness of Princeton to students of the highest quality, whatever their economic circumstances.

Understanding also involves, however, being realistic in recognizing that there are limits on what we can do, that principles do collide when resources are scarce, and that trade-offs have to be made. As we look ahead, our situation, like that at most other colleges and universities, is more difficult than before precisely because serious efforts at retrenchment have been going on for the last half dozen years and the relatively easy savings have already been achieved. It seems unlikely that further trimming around the edges of the budget will yield much in the way of additional economies. And in such circumstances it is only fair to recognize that, even though we might wish it were otherwise, there is a close link between such sensitive issues as the level of student charges and the salaries it is possible to pay to members of the faculty and staff.

As far as attitude is concerned, I hope that we can avoid pushing self-interest too hard. To the greatest extent possible, we need to encourage each other to put the general interest ahead of the special interest, and we need to continue to work to structure our procedures to facilitate this result. I hope that we can avoid the temptations to oversimplify, to make what are genuinely hard choices seem easier than they are, to substitute advocacy for analysis and thoughtful consideration. I hope we can emphasize our many areas of agreement and not exaggerate the disagreements that are also bound to be present and, indeed, can be healthy if kept in proper perspective. I hope too that in struggling with what are often unpleasant alternatives we can retain a sense of humor, difficult as that sometimes is for all of us.

Finally, I hope that all of us who care about the future of Princeton, on campus and off campus, will join together to encourage those who can help the University to do so, and to do so as generously as possible. I have deliberately not tried to use this report to state again the fundraising objectives of the University. But I hope it is evident that never before have Annual Giving and our development programs been more important. I believe that there is a widely shared determination that the special characteristics and special qualities of Princeton not be lost. I believe, too, that many people realize that this is a time when all who do share a commitment to the large and long-term purposes we exist to serve will want to put aside whatever smaller differences might divide us and help as they can.

There is, as always, much to be accomplished, and I think the member of the Priorities Committee whom I quoted earlier was entirely right in his affirmative response to the person who asked if we really expected Princeton to last another 200 years. Barring a holocaust, the real questions are not whether there will be a university here, but what it will be like, what purposes it will serve, what it will be able to achieve. It is no exaggeration, I think, to suggest that the answers to these large questions will depend importantly on how well we respond to the financial pressures confronting all of higher education in this difficult decade.

Thinking about Tuition

ESSAY

MAY 1986

In higher education, as elsewhere, everything has its season, and we have just passed through the time of year when tuition increases are announced—and denounced. Parents and students ask: "When will it all stop?" Trustees, alumni, and others worry about colleges "pricing themselves out of the market." For many of us, there is deep concern about maintaining access to higher education for students from middle-income families as well as for those from disadvantaged backgrounds.

It is natural for trustees and presidents to be as apologetic as is seemly about increasing tuition—or sometimes even more apologetic. Unfortunately, this entirely understandable tendency often interferes with direct communication of the realities of the situation in a way that is respectful of *all* the values at risk. The choices are genuinely complex. They must be seen from the perspective of the real options before our society, and they do not lend themselves to simplistic judgments.

Debates—especially in the mass media and in political arenas—are often one-sided because it is so much more popular to inveigh against tuition increases than to argue for their importance. Let me try to redress the balance by examining some of the key questions without assuming that increased charges are automatically grounds for either outrage or apology. This commentary will reflect the situation at Princeton, the university I know best, but the arguments apply to most private research universities and, with some modifications, to other private and public institutions.

Is the Absolute Level of Tuition and Fees Too High?

One obvious standard of reference is costs. Earlier this year a reporter for a national newspaper asked me if it were not true that Princeton students pay a premium above cost for the University's "name" and reputation. To say that I was astonished by the question is an understatement. But then I realized that those of us closely associated with universities are so painfully aware that *tuition does not even come close to covering annual operating costs, much less total costs*, that we fail to recognize that others cannot be expected to know as much about our institutions as we do.

Factoring out the costs of organized research as best we can (in a university that prides itself on mixing teaching and research so thoroughly that the accountant can never hope to assign what are truly joint costs in any precise way), we estimate that our full tuition charge is now about 60 percent of our actual educational cost per undergraduate student. The typical full tuition-paying undergraduate, therefore, receives a "subsidy" of perhaps $7,500 per year—even before taking capital costs into account. And then, of course, the 43 percent of our students on financial aid receive an even greater subsidy that varies with their level of need.

The basic justification for such subsidies is that education confers indirect benefits on the whole society, in addition to direct benefits on individual students, and that therefore "the society" should bear some of the costs. Private donors contribute much of this "societal share," and they are encouraged by the tax laws to do so. Governments are of course also major sources of funding for state and local institutions. The external benefits of education are real, and it is right and proper for there to be a sharing of costs among students, their families, and the society. But no one has been able to measure very precisely how the benefits of education are in fact distributed, and this leaves much room for argument over "fair shares."

What is indisputable is that the direct benefits accruing to the individual student are very considerable. These benefits are in part financial and follow from the higher lifetime earnings of college-educated persons as compared with many others. Here again, precise estimates are hard to obtain, but studies have generally placed the purely monetary return on an individual's investment in education at an average annual rate of something like 9.5 percent.*

It has always seemed to me, however, that the non-monetary benefits are at least as great, since many of us derive so much satisfaction from the vistas opened by education. The ability to choose from a broader range of vocations, even though some may not be tremendously rewarding in financial terms, is but one example. Heightened appreciation of art, music, other cultures, and the world around us is surely extremely important to many people, as are the friendships formed and the expanded opportunities for diverse forms of service.**

* Richard Freeman, "The Facts about the Declining Economic Value of College," *Journal of Human Resources*, Winter 1980.
** In a heroic effort, Robert Haverman and Barbara Wolfe ("Schooling and Economic Well-Being: The Role of Nonmarket Effects," *Journal of Human Resources*, Summer 1984) estimate

Education, then, must be thought of in terms of the benefits it will yield over a lifetime. In this sense it is an *investment*—the most important investment, I would submit, that most people ever make in themselves and on behalf of their children. We are accustomed to paying for other major investments, such as houses, out of savings and future streams of income. How many people expect to pay for a house out of current income? Or even a car? Thus, comparisons of the cost of education (or just the tuition portion of these costs) with median family income can be highly misleading. We need to do a much better job of encouraging students and parents alike to think in terms of a long-range plan for financing education just as they would expect to take out a twenty-five- or thirty-year mortgage on a house.*

Another way of thinking about the level of tuition, and whether it is "too high" in some absolute sense, is by examining not just fairness for an individual student but implications for broader objectives, such as diversity within academic communities and the even larger national goals of promoting equal opportunity, justice, and social harmony. But this set of questions can be addressed only by considering *tuition and financial aid together*, which I will do later, after examining some of the factors responsible for recent increases in tuition.

Why Has Tuition Increased So Rapidly in Recent Years—Significantly Faster Than the General Price Level?

The answer to this question depends on the fundamental economic characteristics of higher education as well as on the particular financial context in which it has been operating in recent years. Broadly speaking, education has many of the attributes of a "handicraft" industry, dominated by salary costs. This is especially true of a university such as Princeton, where great emphasis is placed on close supervision of

---

that the nonmarket effects of schooling may be roughly equal in size to the monetary "investment effects."

* As Dr. Marina Whitman, chairman of the Finance Committee of our Board of Trustees and vice-president and chief economist at General Motors, emphasized in a recent discussion, there is one important respect in which it is more difficult to invest in education than in tangible property such as a house or a business. There is no "equity market" for investments in education because there is no asset that investors can exchange in the way they can buy and sell property. Individuals cannot—fortunately!—"sell themselves." Resulting imperfections in the market for "human capital" are difficult to deal with and can lead to levels of fixed debt that in turn may influence career choices in disturbing ways. The discussion some time ago of contingent-repayment loans (with the amount to be repaid depending on how much one earned) was an attempt to ease this dilemma, but a workable plan was never developed. (One serious problem was defining a "population" over which risk would be shared that would appeal to democratic instincts and yet not fail because of "adverse selection." See D. Bruce Johnstone, *New Patterns for College Lending: Income-Contingent Loans*, New York, Columbia University Press, 1972.)

graduate students and on independent work for all undergraduates, including an ambitious senior thesis. The use of small discussion groups and seminars at the undergraduate level makes the educational process even more "labor intensive."

In the case of all labor-intensive activities of this kind (including, as another example, the performing arts), costs—and prices—rise more rapidly over time than costs and prices in general. The economies of scale and the technological developments that have brought down the unit cost of a hand-held calculator, for example, are simply not available to the members of a string quartet. At universities, studies have shown that the cost per student over rather long periods of time has tended to rise two or three percentage points faster than such economy-wide price indices as the Consumer Price Index.* Thus, it is simply unrealistic to expect tuition to rise no faster than the CPI over any prolonged period—unless educational quality is to be eroded, faculty and staff are to be penalized through below-average increases in salaries, or unexpected new sources of funds are to be found annually.

In recent years, this fundamental problem has been exacerbated by three particular forces that have acted together to push up tuition even faster (in relation to the CPI) than historical experience would suggest.

1. The "internal" inflation rate relevant to higher education has important components that have exceeded the general inflation rate. The prices of library books and periodicals, for example, have been rising at more than twice the rate of increase in the CPI. The average annual increase in the cost of outfitting and maintaining science laboratories and other facilities has escalated dramatically, in our institution rising close to 15 percent a year.

2. Universities often respond slowly, with a considerable lag, to general economic trends that affect them, and in recent years they have been trying to compensate for major economic reversals of the last decade. In the years when the economy at large was suffering from double-digit inflation, tuition rates did not increase as suddenly or as sharply; between 1972–73 and 1981–82, the differential between the CPI and tuition was compressed to about half a percentage point, rather than the "traditional differential" of two or three percentage points. Other parts of the university (especially programmatic elements and salaries of faculty and staff) bore much of the immediate brunt of adjustment. At

---

* See William G. Bowen, *Economics of the Major Private Universities*. Also, see William J. Baumol and William G. Bowen, *Economics of the Performing Arts*, for a fuller discussion of this aspect of the matter.

Princeton, for example, every area of the budget was subjected to three major "base-cuttings" between 1970–71 and 1980–81, with reductions in positions and in other expenditures totaling over $3 million on an annualized basis. Nationally, the real income of faculty members fell almost 22 percent between 1970 and 1980, making them one of the groups most seriously affected by the inflation of that era.

This serious erosion in real income could not be allowed to continue, since it would have had very harmful long-term effects on the quality of teaching and research (with many of the ablest individuals with advanced degrees seeking other opportunities and some of the most promising prospective faculty members dissuaded from even pursuing graduate work in the arts and sciences). Consequently, universities have attempted to correct for at least some of these relative losses in a period when the general inflation rate has been much lower. Over this more recent period, the same lagged relationship between increases in the CPI and in tuition has contributed to a relatively larger differential rate of increase in tuition. This "catching up" process now seems largely complete, however, and in the last year or so the tuition-CPI differential has again become about three percentage points.

3. The intense pressure on tuition in recent years must also be seen in the context of a marked shift in responsibility for certain costs of higher education from the public to the private sector. This is particularly true of student aid and expenditures on science facilities. In 1979–80, the federal government contributed 29 percent of graduate fellowship and undergraduate scholarship outlays at Princeton; in 1985–86, the federal contribution amounted to 16 percent of a total expenditure on fellowships and scholarships that had more than doubled over this period. Endowment income, special gifts, unrestricted gifts, and tuition revenues have all had to help fill the gap created by decisions in Washington to reduce the federal share of student aid expenditures.

Similarly, the pressure on the University's own funds for the purchase of scientific equipment and for the renovation and construction of laboratories has increased tremendously. This is the result of both a steady decline in federal support for such activities and rapid cost increases. Federal obligations to colleges and universities for research and development plant expenditures, when measured in constant dollars, fell from over $200 million in fiscal year 1966 to well under $50 million in fiscal year 1985. The federal share of total expenditures for such purposes has fallen from roughly one third to about one eighth over this period, thereby significantly increasing the burden on private funds. At the same time, the costs of state-of-the-art research equipment have been escalating at an estimated 12–16 percent per year. As a consequence, the pressures on University funds have increased dramatically. In 1966, total University expenditures for equipment and major renovations for academic departments and programs totaled just over $3 million ($9.3 million in 1985 dollars). The comparable figure in 1985 exceeded $25 million. (Both figures exclude the costs of new construction.)

What Trade-offs Are Involved in Making Decisions about Tuition?

It is against this backdrop that the president and trustees of each university have had to make hard choices among competing priorities. At Princeton, we have made determined efforts to retard the rate of increase in student charges, and the annual increases have fallen from a peak of 14.7 percent in 1982–83 (immediately after the high inflation years and the three rounds of budgetary base-cutting) to 12.6 percent, 7.9 percent, 7.25 percent, and 6.96 percent. To have, in effect, "spent" still more resources in pursuit of the objective of moderating tuition increases (by forgoing more tuition revenue) would have meant further compromises on other fronts that have also seemed important: continuing to correct for the relative decline in faculty and staff salaries that occurred earlier, retaining a requisite level of acquisitions for the library, modernizing laboratories, sustaining student aid programs, and making new investments in areas such as computing, the arts, the life sciences, and residential life.*

Budget making necessarily involves balancing many worthwhile objectives in the particular financial context that is created by external as well as internal forces. We have not believed that it was right—or responsible—to elevate any single claim on scarce resources to the status of an absolute priority that had to be served "no matter what." Rather, we have tried to make a coordinated set of careful choices "at the margins," treating no budgetary category—on the expenditure side or on the income side—as either sacrosanct or as "a residual." Thus, proposals for further reductions in the rate of tuition increase have had to

---

* Most of the costs (including all of the capital costs) of these "new investments" have been covered through a major fund-raising campaign. Were it not for the success of this campaign, which has surpassed its $330 million goal, the University would have been unable to make any significant progress in many critical areas without imposing substantial additional burdens on tuition revenues—burdens that almost certainly could not have been sustained. Indeed, were it not for the campaign, it would have been impossible to meet the essential needs of *existing* programs without far greater increases in tuition than those that have been adopted.

compete with proposals to hold salary pools at certain levels, to provide necessary student aid, and so on.

In this complex process of seeking a balance along "all the margins," Princeton's Trustees have been guided by broad principles that inevitably have implications for tuition. Three deserve special mention:

1. A belief that high quality in all University programs is very important, coupled with a recognition that the vigorous pursuit of quality is inevitably an expensive undertaking.

2. A belief that the educational opportunities Princeton offers should be open to the ablest candidates without regard to economic circumstances, that at the undergraduate level this principle requires a strong program of financial aid designed to meet demonstrated need, and that at the graduate level it requires a heavy investment in fellowships as well as assistantships.

3. A belief that commitments made—to programmatic goals and to individuals—must be sustained and nurtured over time; that they cannot be turned on and off based on short-term budget pressures. In part this means protecting the spending power of the endowment and other assets needed to meet future needs in the same way that previous generations have protected our heritage. It also means resisting the temptation to meet budgetary problems by short-term "economies" such as deferred maintenance.

Since the costs of clear commitments both to quality and to student aid rise inexorably over time, adhering to these principles inescapably entails a sustained pattern of budgetary increases. Moreover, progress begets needs, and success in building strength in a field such as computing or the life sciences inevitably entails continuing financial commitments. The most outstanding faculty members quite properly expect to have adequate facilities, competent support staff, and good students. They will do their best work in an environment that says to everyone that "high standards" are real and not just words, that high aspirations are respected.

Rigorous scrutiny of all budgets is much more than simply desirable; it is absolutely essential in a setting where resources always fall well short of exceedingly worthy needs. But there is a critical distinction between economizing in sensible ways versus signaling an unwillingness to make the investments needed to serve high standards. And once there are signs of a shying away from quality—which can take the form of failing to seize opportunities just as surely as allowing existing strengths to erode—it is hard to resist slipping back to a very different, as well as less expensive, set of expectations.

It is unquestionably the case that Princeton could dampen tuition increases further if the Trustees were prepared to modify one or more of the principles stated above. Compelling reasons, financial and other, can impel institutions to adopt more modest goals. But any college or university that has a realistic chance of achieving excellence in teaching and research must consider carefully the long-term consequences of acceding to pressures for lower increases in tuition.

In my view, there should be institutions that charge low tuition, though just how great a subsidy even those institutions should provide to students fully able to pay higher charges is an important question of public policy. Suffice it to say here that many private institutions feel keenly the growing tuition gap between the public and the private sector, and that a number of important goals might well be served by greater efforts on the part of the states to narrow this gap somewhat.

In any case, there is, I believe, wide agreement that the nation benefits greatly from the variety of institutions of higher education that exist. And it seems to me clearly in the national interest *that a number of universities pursue the highest possible quality in teaching and research, even if that is costly and necessitates high tuition charges.* Otherwise, there will be less opportunity for the country to take full advantage of what the ablest faculty can accomplish as teachers, as scholars, and as leaders of demanding research programs. If the university world is unable to provide this kind of setting, there could well be a heightened drain of talent to purely research institutions. This is a pattern characteristic of several other countries—and not, in my view, one to be emulated. Nor would it be desirable to have the kind of homogenization of higher education in this country that has been observed elsewhere.

But What about the Effects of High Tuition on Access to Higher Education and on Family Finances?

Obviously, this is a great worry. The financial aid program in effect at Princeton is entirely need-based, and it is designed explicitly to "equalize" the burdens of student charges over a considerable spectrum of family incomes. *No* student—no matter what his or her academic (or athletic!) attributes—is given a "free ride." All financial aid students are expected to make a "self-help" contribution by working and borrowing. All parents are expected to make a family contribution that is calculated carefully to take into account not only income but also different forms of capital assets, obligations to other children, unusual medical costs, and so on. Generally, the expected family contribution rises with income, but other factors are considered as well. Even families with substantial annual incomes can be eligible for financial assistance from the University, especially if there is more than one child in college at the same time. Also, special loan programs are available to allow parents more flexibility in spreading the expected family contribution over time.

The University's scholarship program is intended to fill the gap that remains after both self-help and family contributions are matched against an estimate of all expenses involved in attending college. Meeting the financial aid requirements of undergraduates is expensive, and this year Princeton has committed approximately $10 million of its own resources to scholarships. Graduate fellowships, which operate on a combination of merit and need, required an additional $11 million of University funds. And, to repeat an important point made earlier, *all* students, including those paying full tuition, receive a large implicit subsidy from other University resources.

How well has this approach worked? The available evidence is at least modestly reassuring.

• Only about 10 percent of all students who decline offers of admission to Princeton go to schools that are significantly less expensive.

• The percentages of students declining Princeton's offers of admission do not vary predictably by income category.

• Even more relevant (because much depends on decisions to *apply* in the first place) are data showing that the income distribution of the entering class was not significantly different in 1985–86 from what it was in 1968. There has been no ascertainable decline over this period of almost two decades in the fraction of the student population coming from low-income families or from what are termed middle-income families in this context.

• There is, however, one worrying development that has become evident more recently. Whereas there was a clear increase in the percentage of the class that came from low- and middle-income families between 1968 and 1980, that increase appears to have been erased in the most recent five years. As noted above, we are now back to approximately the same income distribution that prevailed in the late 1960s, and no one can be sure whether this most recent trend will continue.

It would be helpful if there were current evidence concerning the relationships among academic achievement of students, family income, and application and matriculation decisions of students as these in turn depend on tuition levels, perceived institutional quality, and other variables. One of the most careful existing studies was done by my colleague Richard Spies in 1978, and it concluded that financial considerations do play a part in students' application decisions but that academic factors are much more important for students with the strongest academic records. More specifically, Spies found that, after correcting for differences in academic preparation, students from low- and middle-income families are only slightly less likely to apply to expensive colleges than are their high-income counterparts. An earlier study—in 1973—obtained almost identical results. We are now participating in the planning of a successor study, to see if these basic patterns still hold.

One other important dimension of the problem is what may be called the "pain of coping." It may well be that students from families in the "middle" or "upper-middle" income ranges will continue to attend expensive institutions (as the evidence suggests), but will feel greatly burdened by the sacrifices involved. In terms of morale and feelings of fairness, this is a serious matter, and it too deserves more thought than it has received. Such families may understandably believe that they should be able to do more things, and enjoy a higher standard of living, than high tuitions will allow—especially if the family resists borrowing to finance education. Thus, there can be genuine feelings of resentment and of ill-treatment, even though actual matriculation behavior (where the child in fact goes to school) is unaffected in most cases.

It is far from clear how to respond to this concern. The very real resource constraints faced by all colleges and universities make it hard to "buy out" of this dilemma without doing serious harm to other objectives. Of course, how high up the income scale financial aid programs of various kinds should reach is always an open question, and it may be wise to think further about partial forms of support (conceivably new loan programs) for such families—if relevant criteria for eligibility can be determined. Finding new ways to encourage families to plan ahead, and to finance education as a long-term investment, may be especially important.

About one option, at least, I think we should be clear: it would serve no purpose, in my view, to address this particular problem by significantly lowering tuition charges for all students. Such an approach has three major disadvantages. It would (1) exact too high an institutional price in terms of the resources available over time to support high-quality teaching and research; (2) threaten existing need-based schol-arship programs which themselves depend partly on tuition revenues for funding; and (3) "reward" indiscriminately the very highest in-come families that do not need or seek aid by, in effect, increasing the implicit subsidy they already receive.

My conclusion is that the most productive arena for further discus-sion (and new ideas) involves the character and "reach" of financial aid programs. If I were convinced that present levels of tuition were having serious adverse effects on the diversity of student populations or on opportunities for many talented students to choose the institutions best suited to them, I would want to think hard about tuition increases that might provide the resources needed to enrich financial aid pro-grams. In our setting, at least, reducing rates of increase in tuition is a costly, inefficient, and fundamentally unfair way of addressing the problem of access.*

As I consider the tuition debate, then, my worry is less that we will unthinkingly charge too much than that we will unthinkingly charge too little—and make too small a provision for financial aid. It is some-times necessary to pay for what is really valuable, and it would be a tragedy, in my view, if in an effort to appear "democratic" we were to sacrifice both the unequivocal pursuit of excellence and the real values of democracy itself.

* The situation is much more complex for institutions that must also consider carefully the implications of higher tuition charges for total enrollment (and thus for overall tuition revenues). As mentioned earlier, the "tuition gap" is a major source of concern for many private colleges and universities. This concern reflects both the increasing differential between tuition charges at private as compared to public institutions, and the fact that many potential students are either unaware of the financial aid programs that exist or afraid that these programs—at least at the federal level—are about to be abolished.

Highly selective institutions such as Princeton, which may have five to ten applicants for every place in the entering class, must contend with a similar dilemma. These institutions are of course concerned about attracting the ablest students. If tuition were raised too high, extremely capable students from high-income families, who would not qualify for financial aid even if more re-sources were available, might elect to go to one of the leading public universities or to a private institution that had not opted for such an "egalitarian" tuition/financial aid policy.

The Student Aid/Tuition Nexus

ESSAY

APRIL 1987

In the continuing debate over educational finance, and especially over the relationship between student aid and tuition, there are three types of questions to be distinguished.

First, what are the *facts*? What have been the relative rates of increase in student aid, tuition, educational costs, prices of other things, and disposable personal income over varying periods of time?

Second, what are the *causal connections* between increases in federal student aid and tuition increases, and what are the *consequences* of changes in student aid for tuition and for relevant educational outcomes such as the diversity of student populations and the quality of the education offered?

Third, what is appropriate *public policy* in this area?

This paper deals solely with the "cause-and-effect" and "consequences" questions, and thus leaves to others the tasks of clarifying the (often conflicting) data and evaluating alternative public policies. My goal is a simple one: to sort out, in at least some degree, the confusions that seem to abound at the purely conceptual level and thus to encourage a sharper and more constructive discussion of the real options facing all of us in thinking about the future of higher education in this country.

THE BENNETT MODEL

In a recent background paper circulated by Secretary Bennett to the governors of the states, the Department of Education writes: "Federal student aid is also important in allowing colleges to raise their costs because it constitutes a major subsidy of higher education that insulates them from normal market forces of supply and demand." Later the paper states, "The federal government now provides a subsidy of about $15 billion per year to the higher education industry. It is hard to believe that a $15 billion subsidy of *any* industry would have *no* effect on pricing."

In beginning courses in price theory, students are taught that, *under appropriately defined behavioral assumptions*, subsidies directed to the consumer of a product will shift the demand curve for that product to the right, thereby increasing the equilibrium price and quantity by amounts dependent on the slope of the relevant supply curve.

If the "industry" is education and the price of the "product" is the tuition charge, this is presumably the model that the Secretary has in mind. And if the appropriately defined behavioral assumptions (to which I turn momentarily) were relevant to higher education, we could turn immediately to the next phase of the analysis and ask about the slope of the supply curve. (It would be important to note, even in this case, that the extent of the increase in price stimulated by the subsidy would almost always be significantly less than the subsidy per student and would depend directly on how responsive supply was to price— i.e., how many more student places would be offered at successively higher prices.) But all of this is both rather pedantic and largely beside the point, *because the basic behavioral assumptions of this model bear essentially no relationship to at least that part of the world of higher education that I know best.*

The elementary price theory model illustrated above takes as its "behavioral assumptions" the following:

1. The firms in the industry are profit-maximizers and would have no interest in, and no reason for, holding the price below its profit-maximizing level.

2. In a perfectly functioning market that involves profit-maximizing firms, the market will always clear—that is, there could never be persistent excess demand, with unsatisfied customers still clamoring for "the product" at the stated price, since any (temporary) excess demand would drive up the price until the excess demand was eliminated.

3. Firms have no particular interest in who buys their product—a customer is a customer as long as the bills are paid, and the composition of the clientele is otherwise irrelevant.

This model may apply, in at least a rough sense, to the profit-making, proprietary sector of higher education. The availability of Pell grants and other federal programs to students in this sector may have had some effect on the size of the sector (by stimulating growth) and on prices charged. But this sector is clearly not at the center of the debate the Secretary invites us to join, and it is important to ask directly if the Bennett Model fits at all well the realities of other sectors of higher education—including the private research universities and selective colleges which have been particular targets of the Secretary.

THE RESEARCH UNIVERSITY/SELECTIVE COLLEGE MODEL

In fact, these institutions possess *none* of the attributes of the Bennett Model described above. Moreover, the attributes that these institutions do possess combine to produce a model *in which the relationship between student aid funds and tuition is precisely the opposite of the relationship specified by the Secretary.*

1. The research universities and selective colleges are not profit-maximizers. The budget-making processes in these institutions (which often involve students, faculty members, and administrative staff, as well as trustees) assign a significant weight to the objective of keeping rates of increase in tuition as low as they possibly can be, consistent with the need to offer education of high quality to an appropriately qualified and constituted student population. These institutions care greatly about the all-too-real burdens imposed on their students and parents by the tuition the institutions feel they must charge. Conscious, conscientious efforts are made to moderate rates of increase in tuition.

2. The tuition charged does not come close to "clearing the market." One of the most evident results of this budgeting process, as it is revealed each year to large numbers of disappointed applicants for admission, is that there is a substantial excess demand for places in each entering class. Letters of rejection are sent to large numbers of generally well-qualified applicants, many of whom would be prepared to pay a higher tuition than is being charged, if only they were allowed to bid for places in the entering class. In the case of my own institution, this year we received approximately 13,000 applications for just over 1,100 places in next fall's freshman class.

3. Colleges and universities care intensely about who "consumes their product." A major goal of these institutions is to enable the ablest students, from a wide variety of backgrounds, to attend, whatever their financial circumstances. This goal complements, and is itself part of, the larger institutional commitment to providing excellent educational opportunities for all students, including interaction with a talented and diverse group of classmates. In Princeton's context, this goal is pursued through "need-blind admissions" and a comprehensive need-based financial aid program, which means simply that the University admits the most talented and promising student body that can be identified and then provides the financial aid needed to allow these students to attend (albeit with considerable effort and sacrifice on their part).

In many of these institutions, student aid is based entirely on a family's financial need, and student aid funds available from external sources (the government, company scholarships, etc.) are taken into account in determining what financial aid the University must provide out of its own resources. *Thus, any reduction in federal financial aid going to students at these institutions is translated directly into a need for larger student aid expenditures by the institutions themselves.*

Faced with budgetary pressure of this kind, institutions are compelled, often with the greatest regret, to a combination of actions that include: (1) reduced expenditures for other important purposes such as library acquisitions or modernization of laboratories, all of which affect the quality of education being provided; (2) a compromise with the principle of need-blind admission, which can take the form of a dollar limit on the financial aid offered by the institution and a concomitant limitation on access to the institution by well-qualified students without the requisite funds; and (3) somewhat higher tuition charges. *It is simply a fact that in recent years the declining share of the overall student aid budget coming from federal sources has been one of the main sources of upward pressure on tuition at many colleges and universities.*

Is it any wonder, then, that trustees, administrators, faculty, and students simply shake their heads in disbelief when told that *more* student aid allows (causes) higher tuition charges? On the contrary, it is *reduced* provision for student aid that has not just *"allowed"* but in effect *compelled* higher tuition charges at many institutions.*

THE LESS-SELECTIVE COLLEGE MODEL

Other institutions that deserve careful consideration are the private colleges that are both less selective in their admissions policies and generally in greater financial difficulty. The historically black colleges are important cases in point. These institutions share the objectives of the more selective institutions but do not have the same applicant base or financial capacity. They are often very hard-pressed financially and may well have no excess demand for places at current tuition charges—indeed, enrollment may be below the desired level, and simply maintaining enrollment is often a major concern. Also, potential applicants

---

* There is also a feed-back mechanism at work here. Higher tuition charges resulting (in part) from diminished external support for student aid lead in turn to additional financial aid requirements, which put additional pressure on tuition, and so on. This kind of amplification of initial effects is dampened, however, by the presence of significant numbers of non-aid recipients in the student population.

are generally from significantly less affluent families and thus are much less able to cope with higher tuition unless there is adequate financial aid.

Reductions in federal financial aid are unlikely in these circumstances to lead to higher tuition charges since the institutions simply cannot raise tuition (absent excess demand) without risking further drops in enrollment and perhaps threatening the very survival of the institution. Nor is it likely to be possible to find much if any "replacement money" for student aid by curtailing other expenditures, since these institutions are already operating very close to the margin on all fronts. Further budget reductions could have the effect of crippling the quality of their academic programs. The likely consequence is that reductions in external aid will not be offset, and the increased burdens will be borne directly by needy students. Such reductions in financial aid may in turn curtail enrollments as well as affect the composition of the student body.

The recent report by the United Negro College Fund and the National Institute of Independent Colleges and Universities, titled "Access to College: The Impact of Federal Financial Aid Policies at Private Historically Black Colleges," documents this precise set of events. It also illustrates another dimension of the problem: the tendency under such circumstances to expect students to borrow more and more.

* * * * *

To sum up:

First, the Bennett Model—whereby increases in federal aid stimulate increases in tuition—may apply to profit-making, proprietary institutions, but that is the only sector of higher education to which it applies.

Second, the research university/selective college sector operates under a radically different set of guiding principles that together lead to the conclusion that it is reductions in federal support for student aid, not increases in aid, that are likely to cause higher tuition.

Third, it is a mistake in any event to assume that increases in tuition are necessarily "bad" or in any way inconsistent with national objectives. Reducing institutional expenditures on student aid (or preventing them from rising to meet the requirements of a need-based policy) may be far worse, especially if one believes, as I do, that sustaining opportunity in America is important to both the nurturing of talent and the service of democratic principles. Similarly, reducing expenditures on other valuable educational programs, ranging from basic research to the teaching of foreign languages, may be contrary to the long-term national interest, as well as to the more immediate interests of students themselves.

Fourth, it is more than a little ironic to suggest (as if it were a sin) that selective institutions have "isolated themselves from market forces" when what they have done is to elect deliberately to charge lower tuition rates than the market would bear. (Moreover, educational institutions operate under a set of intense competitive pressures, both within individual institutions and vis-à-vis each other, that are in every way commensurate with what most profit-making firms experience. But that is a subject for a different paper.)

Fifth, for less selective and less well-financed institutions that have no excess demand for places in their classes at current levels of tuition, reductions in federal aid serve mainly to reduce access by needy students.

A Perspective on Private Giving

EXCERPTED FROM THE
REPORT OF THE PRESIDENT
APRIL 1978

. . . The existence of governmental programs providing financial assistance to higher education eases some of the burdens that otherwise would have to be borne by private donors (unless the activities in question were abandoned altogether). In at least three respects, however, governmental programs make private giving all the more essential.

• First, private funding enables us to counterbalance federal funding for specific purposes and thus to ensure that all elements of the University, including importantly the humanities, receive the support that they must have if they are to flourish. Within all areas of the University, including the sciences, private funding provides flexibility; it serves the critically important purpose of permitting us to make our own choices concerning lines of research to be followed and priorities to be established.

• Second, the existence of a strong base of private support provides strength. It keeps us in the position of being able to say ''no'' to governmental initiatives if we believe them to be unsound or to threaten our essential freedoms. It is more than coincidental that in the recent controversy over medical school admissions it was strong private universities that provided much of the leadership in resisting threats to institutional autonomy.

• Third, it is private support that provides—and must continue to provide—the margin of resources necessary to enable us to pursue the highest standards of quality in both teaching and scholarship. It is in the nature of the political process that funds provided through governments will not necessarily be geared to the achievement of objectives that are primarily qualitative. If Princeton is to continue to aspire to excellence, it is almost certainly going to be up to those in the private sector to see that the necessary resources are provided.

This last argument can be seen as parochial, stressing as it does our commitment to the quality of what we try to do at Princeton. But it also has larger dimensions. The chairman of our Department of Politics, Dennis Thompson, wrote to me as follows last summer:

There is a vital place for a university, which, in John Stuart Mill's words, serves as "an example and stimulus to keep others up to a certain standard of excellence," and a private university may now be in a better position to serve this function. Democratic societies desperately need such examples and such stimuli, but democratic governments cannot always provide the kind of support that would accomplish these objectives. Private philanthropy, usually more flexible and more closely tailored to the needs of particular institutions, is therefore essential for the continuing excellence of private institutions.

For these reasons, I believe that we should view governmental and private support as *complementary*, not as a matter of either-or. Indeed, a strong case can be made for the proposition that the strength and the diversity of the overall system of higher education in America are a direct result of our having succeeded in combining direct governmental support with a strong tradition of substantial private support—both serving to advance what are clearly broad public purposes. If we were to rely more exclusively on governmental support for higher education, as do the colleges and universities in essentially all other countries, I believe that the total amount of resources devoted to higher education would almost certainly decline, and that there would be less diversity, a "leveling down" of quality, and an appreciably greater risk of unwise forms of governmental intervention.

TAX INCENTIVES FOR PRIVATE GIVING

The federal government itself affects the prospects for private giving directly through the tax code, and in recent years the tax incentives designed to stimulate giving have come under heavy attack. In a recent statement on this general subject—the best, I might say, that I have seen—John W. Gardner, former Secretary of HEW and former president of Common Cause, has put the matter bluntly: "In the next two or three years the federal government may successfully destroy a unique and fundamental feature of the American system."* In my view, the danger is not so much that bad people will do us in, but that good people, acting on the basis of admirable motives—to simplify the tax system and to make it "fairer," as they judge fairness—will bring about damaging changes in the fundamental nature of the society as a more or less

* John W. Gardner, "The Voluntary Sector and the Tax System," December 1977.

accidental by-product of ''reforms'' designed to achieve other objectives.

It is important to remember that when the federal income tax was enacted in 1913, there was serious concern for the effects it might have on private support of colleges, hospitals, and other private institutions. As a consequence, the Congress devised the charitable deduction as an incentive explicitly intended to encourage the flow of private funds to such institutions—to encourage individuals voluntarily to support a multitude of worthy causes. The objective was not just to provide financial support, important as that was thought to be, but to preserve the peculiarly American notions that considerable initiative for the promotion of good causes should be left in private hands, that there is value in pluralistic efforts to meet community needs, that government need not be given a monopoly in attending to such matters as the care of the sick and the advancement of learning.

This point of view has a venerable history in America, going back to colonial times, and the Filer Commission* quotes historian Richard Boornstein as having noted that our country has been decisively different in this regard ''from the beginning.'' As Boornstein puts it: ''Communities existed before governments were there to care for public needs'' and, as a consequence, ''voluntary collaborative activities'' were set up to provide essential services. Similarly, there is Alexis de Tocqueville's well known observation:

> These Americans are a peculiar people. If, in a local community, a citizen becomes aware of a human need which is not being met, he thereupon discusses the situation with his neighbors. Suddenly a committee comes into existence. The committee thereupon begins to operate on behalf of the need and a new community function is established. It is like watching a miracle, because these citizens perform this act without a single reference to any bureaucracy, or any official agency.

An illustration of the continuing difference in approach between this country and other countries was provided by Frederic Fox '39, who told me of an exchange that took place when his class was visiting Moscow University as part of the celebration of their 30th reunion. A

---

* The privately funded Commission on Private Philanthropy and Public Needs, chaired by John H. Filer, conducted the most comprehensive study ever made of private giving in the United States. It published its findings in 1975 under the title *Giving in America: Toward a Stronger Voluntary Sector.*

Soviet scientist was asked if the graduates of the University of Moscow ever give money to the university. He was astonished by the question and replied, "No, there is no need for such gifts. . . . It would be like giving money to the post office."

The continuing discussion of specific proposals to change tax incentives should respect this distinctively American context, and I want to return shortly to a consideration of some of the general implications of this line of thinking. First, however, let me simply note the special importance to higher education of certain kinds of gifts and of certain provisions in the tax code.

Higher education as a whole receives some 47 percent of its voluntary support from individuals, and the corresponding percentage is even higher for major private universities such as Princeton. In 1973–74, the last year for which data are available, less than one half of one percent of all gifts received by institutions of higher education were for more than $5,000; nevertheless, this relatively small number of large gifts accounted for over 70 percent of the total dollars received from individuals. Bequests typically account for about 30 percent of support received from individual donors, and here too large gifts are tremendously important to higher education, with roughly 98 percent of the total value of all gifts of this kind consisting of legacies of $5,000 or more. A further characteristic of support for higher education worth mention is that major benefactions often come in the form of appreciated securities or other property.

It is easy to deduce from even this cryptic description of the nature of private giving to colleges and universities the kinds of proposed changes in the tax code that are troubling. Major adverse effects would follow from most proposals to introduce tax credits as substitutes for tax deductions (or from any other change which reduced incentives to give for individuals who face high marginal tax rates), from eliminating the deductibility of the appreciated value of gifts or bequests, from limiting the estate tax deduction, or from reconstructing the standard deduction to include more taxpayers within its range (without separating the incentive for charitable giving).

The Filer Commission argued strongly that it was not sufficient simply to preserve existing exemptions. If we wish to increase the number of givers of moderate means, there is an argument for allowing the charitable deduction to become an exemption on top of the standard deduction. Another proposal advanced by the commission would allow families with annual incomes below $15,000 to deduct twice the amount of their giving, with families between $15,000 and $30,000 allowed to deduct 150 percent of their contributions. Suggestions of this kind would narrow significantly the differences in tax savings between these families and those with higher incomes, while at the same time stimulating additional contributions estimated to exceed appreciably the tax revenues that would be lost. Proposals have also been advanced that would encourage larger corporate contributions, and these too deserve consideration.

This is not the place for a detailed analysis of specific proposals, which often raise issues that are highly technical. I would observe, however, that it is all too easy to lose sight of large questions, which are at least as much philosophical as economic or legal, in the natural search on the part of the specialist for an overall tax system that satisfies some test of logical cloture. When it comes to making policy, it is imperative that the full ramifications of all proposals be weighed carefully, bearing in mind not just narrow effects on the tax system itself and on the distribution of the tax burden, but also the long-run implications for our entire conception of American society.

Beneath and behind all of the debate over particular proposals are fundamental questions of purpose. I know of no better way to summarize what many of us believe than by returning to the article by John Gardner to which I referred earlier. He writes:

> The tax deductibility of charitable gifts is a long-established policy designed to further an authentically American idea—that it is a positively good and important thing in American life for a great many people, quite independently, in their capacity as private citizens, to contribute to charitable, religious, scientific, and educational activities of their choice. And we have demonstrated that preserving a role for the private citizen in these matters encourages creativity, and keeps alive in individual citizens the sense of personal caring and concern so essential if a mass society is to retain the element of humaneness.

Mr. Gardner then cites a simple example which puts the central issue in clear perspective:

> But there is a new school of thought which takes a very different view. According to this school of thought, a tax deductible dollar given by Mrs. Jones to a school for the blind children in her neighborhood is a dollar which—but for the deductibility—would have

found its way into the federal treasury, and is therefore to be regarded as government money. It should in fact be labelled a "tax expenditure."

What right, they ask, does Mrs. Jones have to decide that that "government" dollar should go to a school for blind children? The sensible thing to do, they say, is to eliminate the tax deductibility and take Mrs. Jones' dollar (along with all the other tax deductible dollars) into the federal treasury. If the school for blind children needs money, let Congress and the bureaucracy decide whether that's the best use for the money. After all, isn't Congress and the bureaucracy wiser than Mrs. Jones? There's no likelihood that they have seen (or ever will see) the school for the blind she contributed to, so their judgment will not be affected by human sentiment—or firsthand knowledge.

To return to the theme with which I began this discussion, I believe that governmental and private support simply have to be seen as complementary. There are important needs that must be addressed by a vigorous and effective government. But government will function best if it does not try to do everything. It will function best if its own policies encourage the generosity of individuals and thus the vitality of the many voluntary organizations that contribute so much to the general welfare. . . .

A Campaign for Princeton

FEBRUARY 19, 1982

. . . Money is today, as it has always been, what John Stuart Mill referred to as a "veil": what matters is what lies beneath, what the dollars we seek will allow us to accomplish in serving the educational purposes of Princeton. There is no need for me to repeat tonight what I believe—so deeply—about the value of liberal learning in today's world, about the paramount importance of our commitment to the advancement of knowledge, about the unique place Princeton occupies in American higher education, and about the critical importance of this Campaign.

I would like, rather, to provide a broader historical perspective by suggesting some continuities with earlier fund-raising efforts, some differences, and, finally, perhaps some lessons to be learned.

One obvious "continuity" is that there has never been a time in Princeton's history when the need for resources was not a prominent concern. In 1745, before obtaining a charter from the Governor for the College of New Jersey, the seven founders of Princeton took three steps: They determined that they would offer a wide and comprehensive course of instruction; they decided that they would admit students of every religious denomination; and they appointed four representatives to solicit contributions. Subsequently, the first Board of Trustees made the decision to locate the College in Princeton, rather than New Brunswick, only after being assured that "the people of the favored place" would satisfy what was in effect the first campaign goal: "£1,000 New Jersey money, 10 acres of land for the campus, and 200 acres of woodland to provide fuel."

It is also true that fund raising has always been arduous work. But I would remind us that the rigors were even greater in the early days of the College than they are now. The Reverend Charles Beatty expired of yellow fever on a fund-raising mission to the West Indies in 1772, and this was not an isolated incident. History records that Judge John Bryan succumbed to "a violent bilious collic" in the course of a fund-raising trip to Virginia in 1802. Devotion to Princeton clearly knew no bounds, and, as one of my colleagues has observed, "giving one's all for the institution seems to have been taken rather literally in those days."

A third element of continuity can be found in the College's long history of dependence on the special generosity of its alumni. The Alumni Association of Nassau Hall was organized during the Commencement of 1826, and, in the words of Professor Wertenbaker, "the College began to 'capitalize' on its greatest asset—the love and loyalty" of its graduates. While today we work hard to attract contributions from foundations, corporations, parents, and other friends, we continue to look primarily to those who have known Princeton as students. . . .

The fourth and last element of continuity that I shall mention is the objectives for which funds have been sought. The need for a strong endowment became obvious early in the nineteenth century, and the first endowed professorship (the Holmes Professorship of Belles-Lettres, held today by Professor A. Walton Litz of the Department of English) was established in 1857. In the Princeton of pre-Revolutionary times, a "Fund for Pious Youth" provided thirteen pounds to help James Leslie, of the Class of 1759, through college. Years later, Mr. Leslie, then a schoolteacher in New York, gave a large part of his modest savings to establish one of the first permanently endowed scholarship funds at Princeton. Of course, funds have long been sought for libraries, laboratories, classrooms, and dormitories. Nor is the need to purchase scientific equipment (which is so obvious to us now) in any sense new: One very positive result of a generally unsuccessful campaign mounted in 1833 was the acquisition of a large telescope and other apparatus for Professor Joseph Henry.

As for differences, there are many. An obvious one is the fund-raising techniques employed—from lotteries in the early days of the College to lead trusts and life-income agreements today. And then, of course, the amounts of money sought have hardly remained constant. As staggering an amount as it seems to us, imagine how large our $275 million goal would have seemed just twenty years ago, when $53 million represented a tremendous challenge. But we must remember, too, that a dollar today is (regrettably) worth only a little more than a third as much as each dollar raised two decades ago.

The major difference I want to highlight is, I think, much more fundamental. The earliest fund-raising efforts were concerned with the very survival of the College: rebuilding Nassau Hall when it was destroyed by fire in 1802; reclaiming the life of the College, in effect, after the Civil War. Still other campaigns over much of Princeton's history were meant to close deficits in the operating budget or, as in the case of the $53 million campaign, to remedy the effects of long periods of unavoidable deterioration in the University's physical plant. At other times, fund-raising efforts (including President Wilson's campaign to fund fifty new preceptorships) were intended either to enlarge the University in some significant way or to extend its thrust.

This Campaign is, I believe, the first determined, large-scale effort designed primarily to reinforce Princeton's commitment to quality: not to rescue the University from bankruptcy, not to make it bigger or more complex, but to strengthen its capacity to serve its fundamental purposes; to enable it to do better, in difficult times, things that it already does, and does very well. It is our purpose—and our responsibility—to protect against one of the most insidious dangers: the all too real possibility of gradual deterioration in the quality of what we do, and then, if that were allowed to occur, in our very aspirations for Princeton.

Recognizing both continuities and some differences, what can we learn from our predecessors? In particular, what seem to have been the ingredients of earlier successes?

Perhaps it is appropriate—certainly it is sobering—to note that by no means have all of Princeton's fund-raising campaigns had satisfactory outcomes. To cite but one example, the financial problems of the Jackson administration and the ensuing Panic of 1837 wreaked havoc with the first endowment campaign directed principally to alumni: $4,000 was raised out of a total goal of $50,000. Plainly a certain measure of good fortune, and a reasonably satisfactory external environment, are essential to the success of any effort of this kind. That is hardly the only reason—though it is certainly a good one—for wishing wisdom to such graduates of ours as Jim Baker in the White House, Paul Volcker at the Federal Reserve, and Bill Bradley and his colleagues in the Congress.

To speak of matters more under our own control, success clearly depends on having outstanding volunteer leadership. In my view, we will pass this test again, as before, with the highest marks. I want to say now, tonight, personally, how much I admire the ability, and how much I respect the commitment of our Trustees, the members of the National Campaign Committee, and the entire alumni leadership of this University. The presence of all of you at this gathering, the willingness of so many to work so hard and so unselfishly for Princeton, are reassuring beyond my capacity to say so.

There is also something intangible, but very powerful, that speaks to me as I read the accounts of Princeton's determined efforts over so many years to become an ever-stronger university. It has to do with things of the spirit that are never captured fully in words; it is, I think, the source of the loyalty and the dedication so characteristic of Princetonians. And it certainly continues into the present generation. Let me recall what a graduate of the Class of 1980, Ron Lee, observed when he received the Pyne Prize at Alumni Day just two years ago. I'm sure many of you were there to hear these words:

> I would like to suggest that Princeton's most lasting gifts to its students are a sense of joy and a sense of obligation. The joy springs from the beauty of the campus, from the whimsy of countless black and orange tigers, both two-legged and four-legged, and above all, from our unceasing discoveries of the promise within Princeton and within ourselves. Princeton's second gift, a sense of obligation, falls slowly and gently upon us, for the luxury that this university represents to all of us demands repayment to future Princetonians, to society, and to the society of nations.

> Joy and obligation, when fused, can produce extraordinarily effective advocates for Princeton. It has always been so. In reading the Papers of Woodrow Wilson, I found a letter from a Trustee of that time, Cleveland Hoadley Dodge, discussing his various fund-raising projects. Included is a one-sentence paragraph that reads as follows: "Anyhow it's bully fun and the finest sport I know."

*   *   *   *   *

Let me end now with a few words about alchemy. As students of the Middle Ages know, alchemy was an early form of chemistry that had as one of its chief aims the changing of baser metals into gold. It had certain magical overtones and is also defined as "a method or power of transmutation, especially the seemingly miraculous change of a thing into something better." Alchemists also sought to discover the elixir of life.

This Campaign involves applying and extending the alchemists' craft. We seek not to transform other elements into gold; rather, we seek to acquire gold so that it may be transformed, through processes of our own that have their own magical properties, into all the forms, powers, and good works that ought to flow from this University in an unending stream. Education is, I believe, an "elixir of life"—for this nation, and the society of nations, as well as for those of us privileged, as individuals, to partake of it.

This Campaign offers, as well, opportunities for another kind of alchemy. It gives all of us, with our own inadequacies, limitations, and imperfections, the possibility of becoming part of something much larger, much grander, and much more significant than ourselves: part of a shared effort to give continuing life to this great University that—"Dei Sub Numine Viget"—will be a source of light and learning beyond our times and beyond our dreams.

A Campaign for Princeton

OCTOBER 24, 1986

This was not a Campaign that, for me, can be summarized or thought about in terms of statistics, cheering as the final numbers were. It was much too personal for that. If you will allow me, if you will indulge me, I would like to reflect on the Campaign by means of a few reminiscences, a few thoughts on general themes, and then one final thought on the larger significance of what all of you, and so many others, have wrought.

REMINISCENCES

So many vignettes come to mind.
• Bill Bradley launching the Campaign, with a wonderfully warm speech which he started by noting that he was making his first appearance in Dillon Gym in long pants. What a thrill it is to have him back with us tonight.
• By far the most important one-on-one meeting I had pertaining to the Campaign, at the Chicago airport in 1980, when Jim Henderson bravely agreed to be our national chairman. What a stroke of good fortune for Princeton!
• The many times during the Campaign when I thought of Fred Fox '39, that indefatigable free spirit who never tired of reminding one and all that constructive dissent is a form of loyalty and that the real test of one's affection for a place is the capacity to support it even when you disagree with a particular policy or decision. Princeton, he always used to say, is a "given place"—a sentiment so appropriate to this celebration.
• Malcolm Forbes taking me aside after a Trustee dinner, and after he had already made a fine gift to the Campaign for professorships, asking if it would be all right to contribute an additional $3 million to renovate what was then Princeton Inn College in honor of his oldest son, Steve—so that we might, as Malcolm put it, look ahead.
• Gordon Wu greeting me in Hong Kong graciously while asking himself how much our conversation was going to cost—and then, two years later at the dedication of Wu Hall, speaking so eloquently of his desire, as he put it, "simply to do my part."

• All of the lunches that Raleigh Warner arranged for me at Mobil—which I hope will never be brought to the attention of the Mobil shareholders.

• A meeting in my office at which Neil Rudenstine, Van Williams, and I looked at each other and wondered whether we were out of our minds to consider asking the Board of Trustees to raise the goal from $275 million to $330 million.

• Manning Brown volunteering always to do whatever needed doing, and providing right up until his death the quiet strength on which so many of us depended.

• John Weinberg, first contributing a professorship in economics and then being drawn into the intensive recruitment of its first incumbent, Sandy Grossman from the University of Chicago Business School. What an introduction to the complex politics of academia!

• Telephoning John Kenefick on his railroad car in Los Angeles (where he was watching his niece, Joan Benoit, win the marathon at the Olympics) to explain that a brick company in Salt Lake City had somehow made, and delivered, the *wrong* bricks for the molecular biology laboratory, thereby endangering the whole project—and John then marshaling all the resources of the Union Pacific Railroad to rectify the error in record time.

• Lewis Thomas, at the dedication of the laboratory that bears his name (and that, thanks to John Kenefick, is adorned with the "right" bricks), referring to his pleasure in being recognized "pre-humously."

• A trip Charlie Collier and I took to New York on the day of the great blizzard in 1982 to meet Jim Donnell for lunch at the Links Club. We were the only three guests in the dining room, and Jim Donnell must either have felt sorry for us because of the ordeal of the trip or have been moved by the beauty of the snow outside. In any case, he concluded the lunch by establishing the Donnell Scholarship Fund and contributing to the renovation of Little Hall—overall, a $5 million commitment.

• Micky Wolfson meeting with me and with Tom Wright at his home in Miami to discuss his support of the Museum—at the same time that he was introducing this non-swinging person to the wonders of his new Jacuzzi.

• Harold Helm, the father of Annual Giving, Mr. Princeton in the eyes of so many, calling me to be sure that I understood that "Jane" was the niece of "John," who in turn could help us with the "Y" Foundation. What an amazing man he was.

• Arnie Berlin and Joe Bolster agonizing in late June of 1985 as to whether we were in fact going to make that year's enormously aggressive Annual Giving goal . . . which I learned we did by means of a cable sent to Greece, where, in the immediate aftermath of the TWA hijacking, I was attending a meeting of Princeton's Seeger Foundation. (The Greek hotel clerk, incidentally, was quite perplexed by the sender's code on the cable, which was simply ''Tiger.'')

• A longtime member of the staff of the University making a contribution to the Campaign accompanied by a letter that read in part: ''If possible, I would like to have these funds added to the 'Special Landscape Fund.' . . . For almost twenty-five years I have been employed by the University in Planning, Plant, and Properties (now called 'Facilities'). Over those years I have had the opportunity and pleasure to watch the University grow and prosper in many ways, and I can second all the reasons given by her alumni for supporting her now. This truly is a grand old place, and I have grown to love her as much as anyone. Please put this down as a gift from a friend of a great university.''

• An undergraduate on financial aid, who I knew worked easily thirty hours a week to pay her way through Princeton, contributing $50 that she clearly couldn't afford so that she too could be part of an effort in which she believed so strongly . . . and my saying to a group of vastly more affluent Princetonians on the evening following that student's gift that if only each of us would do one tenth of what she had done, in relation to our own resources, the Campaign would be a great success.

• Our good friend Ralph DeNunzio deciding at the very end of the Campaign to see that it ended with a real ''splash.''

THEMES

How are we to ''read'' this Campaign from the standpoint of larger propositions? Let me suggest just five.

First, this was without question the most *broad-based* campaign ever mounted by any major university. While we were fortunate to receive some very generous gifts, it is significant that we did not achieve our overall result through any contribution even one third the size of the Jadwin bequest or the Robertson gift of earlier years. Rather, over forty-four thousand alumni, parents, friends, corporations, and foundations responded to our appeal.

Second, it was tremendously reassuring to see that donors responded so generously to a campaign that stressed *qualitative* objectives and *balanced* support for Princeton: for professorships and scholarships more than for buildings (important as the buildings were and are); for the arts and the humanities as well as for the sciences; for student life, athletics, and religious ministries as well as for research; and, above all, for Annual Giving as the bedrock on which all else must continue to be built.

Third, we learned again and again, as the Trustees have tired of hearing me say, that *"progress begets needs."* Finding the money for professorships (thirty-eight of them) and making superb faculty appointments together have created new challenges by increasing the need to improve faculty salaries, provide excellent laboratories, support graduate students and research, and strengthen the library. Our work, as always, is before us, not behind us. But who would have it any other way? Universities of consequence never stand still, and ours cannot be a quest for an undemanding life—either institutionally or individually.

Fourth, the *loyalty and affection and dedication* of Princetonians is more than legendary; it is there to be seen by all, and it is beyond my power to describe. How often my spirits were raised by some spontaneous act of generosity, by someone I scarcely knew calling and asking how he or she could help, by the constant sense we all had that we were in this together.

Fifth and last, the Campaign for me was inspiring, humbling, and just plain *fun*. What greater privilege is there than to work hard on behalf of something in which you believe so strongly, with so many good friends, surrounded by so much good spirit.

THE IMPORTANCE OF PRIVATE SUPPORT

I could cheerfully end right there, stressing the pure pleasure of having participated in this great effort. But that would be wrong. It would be wrong because it would fail to provoke all of us to think for just a moment—even on an evening that is overwhelmingly for celebration—about the larger significance of this Campaign.

What I have in mind is not so much the powerful new thrust given to the future of this particular University, special as it is to all of us. Nor do I mean to stress—or need to stress—that there are so many respects in which Princeton is not yet close to what it ought to be. Smugness or complacency would be such insults to Princeton that there is surely no need to dwell on that theme. I did bring my hair shirt with me, but not even I could put it on tonight.

Rather, I want to end by saying just a word on behalf of "privateness," of the enormous importance of your having demonstrated, yet again, that voluntarism is far from dead in America, that private resources can in fact be channeled to what are clearly public ends. The excellence to which we aspire, and are sometimes privileged to see at least dimly, would be unthinkable absent private resources. Equally unthinkable would be the luxury of small scale and the still greater luxury of being able to resist pressures to be other than what we are. We have an odd tendency to want to determine our own mission, to define our own character, to say "No" to political and other inducements to conform to someone else's sense of Princeton—and all of these desires, all of these determinations, would be hollow without strong private support.

I regret to say that there is still a tendency, in some quarters, to equate "efficiency," even on occasion to equate "democracy," with public funding. I mean no insult to the appropriations process when I say that it has not always proved capable of assigning resources on the basis of objectives larger than the perceived needs of a particular Congressional district.

To be sure, public support is indispensable to all sectors of higher education, and in no way do I want to demean it. Also we would all agree that our great state-supported colleges and universities make an enormous contribution in higher education and to this country. Those of us at Princeton owe much to them. But I believe that the private universities also serve their counterparts in the public sector—and the nation at large—by setting standards of our own, resisting political pressures that it may be harder for others to resist, and serving complementary ends.

In sum, the variety, the excellence, and the stubborn freedom that characterize our system of higher education owe so much to the willingness of individuals, acting voluntarily, to provide the private support that often distinguishes the exciting from the adequate—and that, in the process, lifts the spirits of both those who give and those who receive.

That is the larger lesson of this Campaign—a lesson that will, I hope, outlive all of us, though not Princeton. We have so much for which to be thankful tonight: perhaps especially the privilege enjoyed by each of us of being part of a university that will exist always, I pray, to correct our errors, to inspire our successors, to make the world a somewhat more humane place.

PART SEVEN

Reflections

At Opening Exercises in 1986, President Bowen looked back over the just completed Campaign for Princeton and at a university that seemed to be "always under construction" and reflected on the "foundation stones"—the essential characteristics of Princeton—that do not change over time.

Those observations begin this chapter. They are followed by remarks (or excerpts) from seven Commencements, beginning with his first and ending with his last. The Commencement ceremony at Princeton takes little more than an hour, and the only speakers are the Latin salutatorian, the valedictorian, and the president. The president's remarks close the ceremony, typically reflecting on the goals of the University and the ways in which those goals have been served during a student's time on campus.

At his fifteenth and final Commencement, President Bowen offered a longer retrospective over his years on campus in the remarks that conclude this collection. Those remarks, like this chapter, are simply titled, "Reflections."

Always Under Construction

EXCERPTED FROM THE
OPENING EXERCISES ADDRESS
SEPTEMBER 1986

. . . I believe that the capacity to take advantage of new ideas and new opportunities is one of the hallmarks of any good university. When trustees, administrators, faculty members, students, or alumni attempt to halt "construction," to encapsulate an institution at any point in its evolution, stagnation is the certain result.

This is, however, hardly a call for mindless change, or for churning about simply to be churning about. The costs of change are real, and they need to be considered particularly carefully in the context of what they portend for the essential character of the institution. Paradoxical as it may at first sound, my own view is that the prospects for successful adaptation are enhanced enormously if there is also a clear sense of what ought *not* to change. In the debate over coeducation in the late 1960s at Princeton, more and more of those originally opposed were won over when they understood that only if Princeton altered one of its characteristics—an all-male student body—could it retain attributes that were much more fundamental: especially a clear commitment to educational opportunities of the highest quality for the very ablest students.

The fact that Princeton has a long history, and that many identify strongly with the traditions of the place, means there is a built-in protection against the temptation to be too trendy, too eager to adopt each new fad. We are compelled to struggle with the weight of the past, and, as one of my colleagues once said, "It is Princeton's hope [that this struggle] will evoke what is most substantial and weighty within us." Trying to identify attributes that really are central, and important to preserve, and distinguishing them from what are no longer compelling expressions of these attributes—that is the challenge before us.

Let me recast the implicit question this way: While the educational structure of Princeton is "always under construction," are there not key "foundation stones," if you will, that ought always to be preserved and built upon? I think there are.

One "cornerstone" is the basic educational mission of Princeton. As you are all aware, this University is firmly committed to the basic arts and sciences, including engineering and applied science; to the pursuit of liberal learning in a quite traditional sense within every division of the University. The absence of professional schools such as business, medicine, education, and law gives sharper focus to the study of subjects such as English, mathematics, history, psychology, electrical engineering, and philosophy, as well as to the interconnections among all of the arts and sciences, than would be possible otherwise. Of the major universities, Princeton is the most clearly dedicated to the arts and sciences per se—and to liberal learning pursued for its own sake.

A second clearly defined part of our foundation is the approach we take to learning. The emphasis here on independent work, on developing your critical capacities and learning to think for yourselves, is perhaps the most distinctive characteristic of Princeton from a pedagogical standpoint. Rote learning has been out of favor at Princeton for many generations, and the preceptorial, the senior thesis, and the doctoral dissertation are specific manifestations of our belief in the active rather than the passive mode of learning.

Third, we hold to a philosophy of education characterized by openness to conflicting points of view, by respect for dissenting viewpoints, and by opposition to efforts from any quarter to impose orthodoxies of any kind, including religious or political orthodoxies. This requires zealous protection of our collective right to hear speakers of every persuasion and an equally clear acceptance of the need for institutional restraint to protect the independence and openness of the University. It is for this reason principally that we try hard to keep the University *as an institution* at some proper remove from the external political and social issues of the day—precisely so that all of you, acting as individuals and in groups, will feel a maximum degree of freedom to be as outspoken and, yes, as political as you wish to be.

A fourth component of Princeton's "foundation," as I perceive it, is an all-out commitment to the highest standards of teaching and scholarship within an institution that retains a scale small enough to give the individual a sense that he or she really counts. While there are at times tensions between the aggressive pursuit of excellence and the desire to remain small enough so that many of us can really know each other, I believe that in most respects our size and our qualitative aspirations reinforce each other rather than conflict.

Fifth on my short list of more or less fixed parameters of Princeton is a deeply ingrained sense of service. We hope that in all kinds of indirect ways, as well as through more formally structured programs, courses, and extracurricular activities, you will be encouraged to share in the view that the learning acquired here ought to be a prelude to service. This University is proud of its graduates who have gone on to make major differences in this country and throughout the world. And we trust that Princeton students will always aspire to that kind of contribution.

Finally, I regard certain values as very strong foundation stones at Princeton. I have alluded to some already in my comments on diversity, respect for the individual, openness to conflicting ideas, and obligations to others. The very act of holding these exercises in this chapel speaks to the importance of religious and spiritual values. Let me add that it is not accidental, or of passing importance, that Princeton is identified in the minds of so many people with the Honor System for examinations. The untrammeled pursuit of truth depends utterly on mutual trust: on confidence that our scientists do not "cook" data, that scholars do not manufacture quotations, and that your answers on an examination are in fact your answers. The larger objective is not so much to curb cheating as it is to establish a climate of intellectual integrity in which real learning can take place.

Perhaps I can sharpen some of what I have been trying to say in these remarks, and even to summarize, by referring to a chance encounter that I had last winter with a faculty member who has come to Princeton within the last decade and who has had a tremendous impact on one of our strongest departments. (I suppress his name only to avoid embarrassing him.) We talked about various aspects of the ever-important task of seeking to make his department stronger yet, and I went away thinking again how fortunate we are to have this professor among us. The next day I was quite surprised to find a hand-written note from him in my mail. After elaborating on some of the points we had discussed the previous evening, he wrote:

> Finally, [this is] a chance to say how privileged I feel to serve on this faculty. I have had every condition and encouragement to do my best. Two aspects deserve special mention. First, the quality of students has meant so much, and I find that its importance to me grows. Second, the scholarly and educational values of the faculty and University community are right for me. I have not felt the need to "advocate" the importance of the best scholarship, recognition of teaching, hard work: these values surround me. They are part of Princeton, and it is easier to maintain the house than to build it.

You can imagine how pleased I was to receive that note. But I wonder if we can extend the last thought somewhat—the suggestion that ''it is easier to maintain the house than to build it.''

In one sense that observation is surely right. Being given a strong institutional structure is a tremendous advantage. As beneficiaries of the past, we can concentrate our energies on making Princeton a better place without always having first to go back and create major pieces of the architecture *de novo*. At the same time, I believe that building and maintaining the house, if that house is a university, are really twin aspects of a single process. Continual building and rebuilding—of the most creative kinds—are essential if the basic structure is itself to be maintained. The capacity to change and the capacity to retain essential characteristics are, finally, utterly dependent on each other. . . .

Preparation for the Possibility of Being Wrong

COMMENCEMENT REMARKS
JUNE 1973

. . . I welcome this chance to share with you a few thoughts on education, indeed on education at Princeton, *as preparation for the possibility of being wrong*, at least on occasion. The points that I want to make are simple ones, obvious, no doubt, to each of us. And yet, somehow, sometimes, we forget. Certainly I know that I do.

For me one of the more troubling characteristics of the period of history through which our society has been moving all during your stay at Princeton has been the widespread presence of a kind of humorless arrogance. Confined not at all to individuals of any particular persuasion, or of any particular generation, or of any particular educational background, it is of course particularly dangerous when if afflicts persons in positions of great responsibility—whether they be in government, in industry, in the churches, in consumer organizations, the media, the universities, or political parties. But it is an ailment that is harmful too when it afflicts all the rest of us, in part because it creates a climate in which learning is made harder and personal relationships, including family relationships, are strained, sometimes to the breaking point. One of the more serious side-effects of this ailment is a willingness to forget all the caveats, to set aside all the restraints, to accept any means to get what one believes to be right. Arrogance unchecked is a frightening thing because it leads so easily to acceptance of the notion that "anything goes"—in support of a "good cause," to be sure, but a good cause defined according to one's own lights.

My hope is that your stay here has provided—and will continue to provide—at least some defenses against a misplaced sense of certainty.

Reading in the history of any subject, including the most exact subjects, or in the history of any people, including the American people, should be warning enough of the possibility of human error. And then, experience with the processes of scholarship and research convinces most of us that truth is rarely a simple thing, simply determined or simply explained. It will be interesting to see how many senior theses, or how many M.A. or Ph.D. theses, produced by those of you graduating this morning, prove impervious to correction. There may be a few beyond redemption, but then that is another thing.

In addition to providing opportunities to study the records of the past and to try your own hand at a serious piece of scholarship, we have sought to prepare you for the possibility of being wrong in one other way—by surrounding you with all sorts of fallible faculty members, administrators, staff members, and, last but by no means least, fallible fellow students. (There are moments, I confess, when I suspect we may have outdone ourselves in this respect, but happily those moments pass.) It is, after all, by forming friendships with a great variety of people, and by trying to see how they think, and what they feel, and why, that we escape to some extent from the natural parochialism that is the lot of each of us as an individual. . . .

In at least one important respect the Class of 1973 has made a distinctive contribution to the variety and quality of our undergraduate population. Yours is, of course, the first class that has included women as well as men from its first days at Princeton. The women among us have now added their gifts for fallibility to our own, and I think that we are a far better university—and a far richer community of people—for it. Among the many contributions of the women students of the Class of 1973 to Princeton let me express my thanks, in particular, for bringing to us the desire simply to be treated like ordinary students, with the same rights, the same obligations, and the same kinds of paranoias (or at least parallel paranoias) as everyone else. . . .

It is, of course, the human material of Princeton that makes it the special place that it is for so many of us, and as you now take that irreversible step of your own into the ranks of the alumni let me warn you, if you did not know it, that there are occasional traces of fallibility in that body too.

One alumnus of Princeton who understood the human proclivity for error—and so many other things—better than most people of his or any other time was Adlai Stevenson. It is particularly appropriate to remember him, I think, in the context of what I have been trying to say this morning about the importance of avoiding arrogance (or at least controlling it) and retaining a sense of humor. As one of his biographers, Herbert Muller, reminds us, he was often criticized as an "indecisive," Hamlet-like person. Yet Archibald MacLeish saw the essential Stevenson in a rather different way and observed that he had "the courage of his doubts"; he was not only willing to consider all possible alternatives, but was unwilling not to consider them.

Stevenson's personal example is relevant this morning in a second sense. He demonstrated that a capacity for thought and reflection was hardly incompatible with an active role in public life. Indeed, I believe that the person who is reflective, who recognizes that there is more than one side to every interesting question, who is prepared for the possibility of being wrong, will prove in most cases to be far more effective— even far more persuasive—than the person who is sure of everything.

In suggesting that a sense of nuance, and an awareness of complexity, are compatible with active participation in public affairs, I do not want to overreach myself and suggest that we try to solve every problem through public action. Following my Stevenson theme, let me recall the message he transmitted as Governor of Illinois in explaining his veto of a bill intended to restrict the freedom of cats:

> I cannot agree that it should be the declared public policy of Illinois that a cat visiting a neighbor's yard or crossing the highway is a public nuisance. It is the nature of cats to do a certain amount of unescorted roaming . . . to escort a cat abroad on a leash is against the nature of the owner. Moreover, cats perform useful service, particularly in the rural areas. The problem of the cat vs. the bird is as old as time. If we attempt to resolve it by legislation, who knows but what we may be called upon to take sides as well in the age-old problems of dog vs. cat, bird vs. bird, or even bird vs. worm. In my opinion, the State of Illinois and its local governing bodies already have enough to do without trying to control feline delinquency.
>
> Judgment still has its role to play. . . .

Generosity of Spirit

EXCERPTED FROM
COMMENCEMENT REMARKS
JUNE 1974

. . . Having decided to try to say only one or two things has not made my task much easier, I confess. I take a certain amount of comfort, however, from a letter I read for the first time this spring, even though it was written some seventy years ago. In fact, by one of those extraordinary coincidences, it was written seventy years ago to the day (May 23) that I was preparing these remarks. It was written by Woodrow Wilson to his wife, and it includes a reference to Mr. Wilson's own efforts to prepare remarks for graduates of the Class of 1904 in which he says "and my! it does go hard." That is one of the elements of continuity that links Princeton presidents at Commencements over the years. . . .

One of the things I hope some of you may have learned here is how much we need each other when we fail as well as when we succeed. As I have tried to say on other occasions, we need to be able to be wrong—and to be held accountable for being wrong—without being rejected at the same time.

This thought has been expressed particularly well by a distinguished member of this faculty, Sir Arthur Lewis, who has just returned this spring from an extended leave of absence devoted to public service. I regret that more of you have not had an opportunity to get to know Professor Lewis, and I want to share with you this morning some remarks he made seven years ago when he was being installed as chancellor of the University of Guyana. He was speaking shortly after returning from a trip to Africa at the time of the bloody conflict between the Hausas and Ibos, and he was speaking in a country which was itself terribly troubled by racial, religious, and class antagonisms. After stressing the need for a passionate concern for social justice on the part of university communities if the values of human civilizations are to be perpetuated, Professor Lewis went on to say:

What distinguishes the civilised man from the barbarian is not that he lacks passion, but that his passion is mingled with compassion. He hates the sin, but not the sinner. He can therefore reach out to exploiter and exploited alike, with understanding and therefore with some chance of reconciliation. The great men of our day, the Hammarskjölds and Bunches and arbitrators of our innumerable disputes, are the men who are welcomed on both sides not because they lack passion—for if they lacked passion they would not care to take on such tasks—but rather because their passion, mingled with compassion, makes them dispassionate. It is hateful that Hausas should murder Ibos, but Hausas are not hateful people, and are indeed no better or worse than the Ibos whom they murder, and who might murder them if their situations were reversed. The civilised man recognises the sin and strives to eliminate the factors which occasion it, without losing his respect and affection for the sinner himself.

As we now leave this lovely place in the company of family and good friends, may you take with you—may you share with others— that generosity of spirit which I know so many of you possess. . . .

The Possibilities You Represent

EXCERPTED FROM
COMMENCEMENT REMARKS
JUNE 1978

. . . While we would not overpraise you, and while we certainly should not claim too much for what we may have done for you (or to you), we are proud of you. We are proud especially of the *possibilities* that you represent.

What are those possibilities? Let me suggest three that need to be seen, in my view, as mutually reinforcing. First is the positive force of what I can call only a fervent discontent. It is fueled by an unwillingness to accept as inevitable the ancient evils: injustice, ignorance, bigotry, exploitation, hunger, and all those tendencies in us that demean the spirit. It is right, indeed essential, that you not be too quick to accommodate yourselves to a world full of imperfection. In a society often marked by apathy and indifference, we need desperately the deep concern and the commitment to a variety of causes that characterize so many of you, as they have characterized university students at many times and in many places.

A fervent discontent is, however, only part of what is needed—as, happily, it is only part of what you offer. Left alone, the passions of discontent can lead too easily to bitterness or even fanaticism, as we are reminded by so much historical experience. If it is to be constructive discontent, it has to be linked strongly to the second possibility you offer: combining deep concern with hard, clear, independent thinking. A primary purpose of the University, of course, is to provide you with some of the tools that facilitate thought; and, more than that, with some sense of their power and especially of your obligation to use them to think for yourself. One of the distinguishing characteristics of education at Princeton, at both undergraduate and graduate levels, is the emphasis given to independent work; and I believe there is very general acceptance of the disciplines of reason and scholarship, however much disagreement there may be from time to time on particular questions. . . .

Accepting an obligation to think carefully and independently about the very subjects one cares about most deeply can be terribly painful. It is, after all, apt to deprive us of the comfort that is to be found in all-embracing dogmas and unmistakable conclusions. But if we are to use the God-given capacity to reason, and if we have any humility, there is really no choice. As Sartre put it: "The rational man seeks the truth gropingly, he knows that his reasoning is only probable, that other considerations will arise to make it doubtful."

If I cannot hold out for you any hope of avoiding the need to wrestle with what will often be conflicting values as well as conflicting feelings within yourself, I can at least remind you that in discharging this obligation to "seek the truth gropingly" you will be in good company. The recently published collection of Isaiah Berlin's essays, *Russian Thinkers*, is full of examples of the moral dilemmas faced by nineteenth-century Russian writers as many of them sought to balance a yearning for absolutes with the complex visions that they simply could not push from their minds—and to do so in a terribly troubled time. Berlin writes with special empathy about Alexander Hertzen and others, "who see, and cannot help seeing, many sides of a case, as well as those who perceive that a humane cause promoted by means that are too ruthless is in danger of turning into its opposite. . . . The middle ground," he writes, "is a notoriously exposed, dangerous, and ungrateful position."

Thus, in our setting, it is my hope—it is my belief—that you offer the possibility of being ardent advocates of large causes without being dogmatic and without being afraid, at least on occasion and when your reason drives you there, to occupy that exposed middle ground. I hope and believe that you offer the possibility of combining deep concern with the courage to think for yourselves, to acknowledge complexity, to correct errors (sometimes your own), to forswear self-righteousness, and to hold off to at least some extent the natural craving for certainty.

Then there is the third possibility which you offer us. It is the possibility of retaining more than a modicum of optimism and trust in a world that is not only imperfect but characterized too often by a destructive cynicism that is not even self-serving. There is a fundamental difference between the cynic and the skeptic. The cynic does not really believe that much good can come from anything or anybody: that, as a friend of mine put it, in every blade of grass there is a snake and in every heart, hypocrisy. The skeptic, on the other hand, while questioning everything and everybody, remains open to encouraging answers as well as disappointing ones. The skeptic can be skeptical even about the degree of his skepticism; and he can recognize that realism need not lead only to negative answers, that it can in fact inspire positive efforts—albeit often modest, humble efforts—to make life at least a little better.

My hope, then, is that you will not be afraid to be *for* some things, as well as against others. I hope you will resist what one of our most distinguished graduates, Adlai Stevenson, once called "the ugly inclinations we as human beings have to believe the worst.". . .

The case for being trusting, for wanting to believe the best rather than the worst, can be made on the pragmatic grounds of effectiveness. But I believe it can be made even more powerfully on moral grounds, on the basis of what it implies about our attitudes toward other human beings. Each of you will have to decide how you want to govern your own life. All I would argue is that there is much to be said for a certain generosity of spirit: for assuming that while perfection is not to be found, most people are well intentioned, however muddleheaded they may seem and in fact may be. Then one can at least hope to be relatively free of the corroding effects of excess suspicion, of the kind of arrogance that can come from assuming, even if only subconsciously, that other people's motives are more suspect than one's own.

These thoughts that I have wanted to share with you this morning reflect my strong belief in the serious purposes this University seeks to serve—in large part through you, as through those who have been here before you and those yet to come. Happily, we can talk about serious purposes and about affirming these purposes through the celebrations of this Commencement period, as Chancellor Cohen said so beautifully on Sunday, while also recognizing that this is an occasion for good cheer, for good humor. How dreary life would be if we were so pretentious, so full of an exaggerated sense of our own importance, that we allowed no time for relaxation, for frivolity, for foolishness. I am all for enjoying the sun and hitting an occasional tennis ball. Our sanity, if nothing else, requires that we retain a healthy capacity to play, to laugh at our foibles, as well as to enjoy Princeton, especially on a day such as this.

But I know too that most of you did not come to Princeton primarily for casual reasons or purely selfish purposes. This University has stood for a broad and expansive commitment to purposes larger than self since its founding, since the time of Witherspoon as well as Wilson. That kind of commitment is by no means out of date. It is the basis for our aspirations today. We thank you for giving life to those aspirations, as we state again our confidence—as I state again my confidence—in the powerful possibilities you represent.

To Be Part of Something Much Larger

COMMENCEMENT REMARKS
JUNE 1986

. . . Memories, recollections, and thoughts of all kinds flood in on us at Commencement time. Many are intensely personal. Some are refreshingly mundane. I remember that a year or two ago, at a Commencement event, I asked a graduating student what he was going to do next. He paused for a moment and then said: "I thought I'd go back to my room."

A rather more general question, which I would like to talk about today, has to do with the relationship between the individual and the institution in what some have described as an age of self-interest in which many have no loyalties that transcend themselves.

There is certainly a general perception within the society that attachments of all kinds are diminishing. Family ties are much looser than in the past, mobility has become a watchword, and changes in both jobs and locales are common. Labor unions, churches, and political parties all worry about their hold on their members.

Within university communities, many commentators have noted forces driving people apart rather than pulling them together. The much greater diversity of students, for example, is often cited as a divisive factor—especially, I might note, by those opposed to what I regard as an absolutely vital effort to enrich our educational life. In the case of faculty, a study released this year by the Carnegie Foundation for the Advancement of Teaching provided further evidence of a tendency for many to identify more strongly with their academic disciplines (as those disciplines become ever more specialized) than with their colleges and universities.

Achieving a strong sense of institutional loyalty is in some ways made more difficult in universities such as this by our own determined efforts to stimulate a kind of ornery individuality. At Princeton, the emphasis given to independent work at both undergraduate and graduate levels is intended precisely to develop the capacity to think for one's self, to take a position and defend it. There is, then, an inherent tension between, on the one hand, our efforts to encourage, almost to compel, critical habits of thought and a fierce independence, and, on the other hand, the complementary need within any institution for at least a minimum degree of collective commitment.

This tension helps to explain the visible stresses and strains that often beset colleges and universities. The delicate but absolutely essential task is to find ways to recognize and respect our collective character while not sacrificing the commitment to the individual that is at the center of our educational philosophy. We sometimes think more about the individualistic side of this relationship than about the communal side, and perhaps today is an appropriate occasion to consider why all of us associated with Princeton—students, faculty, staff, parents, alumni—work so hard, and should work so hard, to nurture an institutional affection that may be considered old-fashioned, if not downright silly, by many others.

It is my conviction, let me say, that the benefits of this kind of attachment are, if anything, even greater for the individuals concerned (for each of us, that is) than for the institution as a whole. But before explaining why I say that, let me comment on the importance of this symbiotic relationship to the University itself.

Those of you graduating today can attest most directly to the tangible consequences of the loyalty of Princetonians. . . . The land on which this Commencement is being held was the gift of Nathaniel Fitz-Randolph, and essentially every aspect of your educational experience here—from physical facilities to professorships, fellowships, and scholarships—can be credited to the commitment of earlier generations. One of my recollections of my own days as a graduate student is working in a carrel in Firestone Library that had been given to honor the memory of an alumnus. You will have your own examples.

But that is by no means all there is to it. This University benefits beyond description from the often intense personal loyalties of present-day faculty and staff. I was moved earlier this year by the lovely tribute by Jon Alterman '87 in the *Daily Princetonian* to three staff members: a DFS supervisor, a janitor, and Larry Dupraz, long-time friend and mentor to *Prince* reporters and editors. So much of the work that has gone into preparing for this Commencement reflects that same kind of dedication. It is a priceless thing.

Fortunately, many of our teachers, including our coaches, feel the same way. It was just over a year ago, if my memory serves me, that I was talking with one of my colleagues who had a very attractive offer to go elsewhere. After giving all the reasons—the *overwhelming* reasons, needless to say—why he should stay, I added that I did not, however, want him to stay out of any misplaced sense of obligation to me. "We take no prisoners," I said, "and you should stay only as long as you feel that this is the right place for you." He thanked me and then added: "But you see, I *am* a prisoner of this institution. It stands for the things that I believe in."

The loyalty that Princeton enjoys also serves the institution in another exceedingly important way. It helps to hold the place together and to protect the University from external threats to its independence and freedom. There is not time today for me to begin to recite the times when exceedingly busy alumni, parents, and friends took time from other tasks to do something important for Princeton, including explain to others why it is in the nature of a university to be at least somewhat cantankerous. Loyalty does not, and cannot, presuppose or depend on agreement with every decision made by the University, never mind every utterance by a faculty member or a student. One test of loyalty is the ability to continue to provide support in difficult and contentious times—including times when you yourself might have favored a different course of action.

I turn now to the proverbial "other side of the coin"—to the basis for my conviction that so often those who give of themselves to a place like Princeton are in fact the principal beneficiaries of their own good spirit. To put the implicit question more directly, why should it matter to those of you graduating that you maintain close ties to a place like this? In the vernacular, what's in it for you?

First, maintaining an affectionate association with Princeton can prove to be a powerful antidote to one of the most pervasive human maladies: loneliness. Thomas Wolfe once wrote: "Loneliness, far from being a rare and curious phenomenon, peculiar to myself and to a few other solitary men, is the central and inevitable fact of human existence."

Friendships formed here, in the camaraderie of learning and growing, playing sports and debating the never-answered questions of life, can sustain you through many dark days if you will let them. Nor is this process over now that you are graduating. Wherever you go, whatever you do, you will be able to turn to fellow Princetonians for encouragement, fellowship, and perhaps an escape from too much preoccupation with yourself. May this campus, and this University community, give to each of you a continuing basis for friendships that will prove to be genuinely sustaining.

Second, your association with Princeton can give you a sense of historical continuity. Whenever I walk into Nassau Hall from either of the side entrances, climbing stairs carved over the years by so many footsteps, I am reminded of how dangerous and even debilitating it is to see yourself only in present time. The fact that students and teachers have studied here, that Commencements have taken place here, over more than two centuries, reminds us that we are parts of a great stream. This can help us see things in better perspective. We can draw strength from the struggles and accomplishments of our predecessors, including the strength of humility. At the same time, we are encouraged as well to think of those who are to come—for whom we are trying to prepare the way.

Finally, and from my perspective most important of all, a continuing allegiance to the University, an active engagement with its purposes, offers a reward beyond all others—the opportunity to be part of something much larger and much more important than any one of us. Harold Helm '20, who died this year after having attended sixty-five consecutive Commencements, always explained his own extraordinary commitment to Princeton in just those terms.

About two weeks ago, I read a column by Ira Berkow in the sports pages of the *New York Times* titled "Is That All There Is?" Berkow reflected on interviews with Chris Evert-Lloyd of tennis fame and Al Kaline, former outfielder for the Detroit Tigers, in which both bemoaned the fact that (in Berkow's words), "despite all the trappings of glamour in their professions, their lives were . . . oddly insular." Chris Evert-Lloyd talked of the unsatisfying rut she felt that she was in, and Al Kaline recalled sitting in the dugout, looking out on the field, and wondering what good it's all done, this "thinking about me, me, me, my batting average, my fielding average. . . ." Both were looking for "something more"—and that is not a concern at all limited to athletes. I have known prominent attorneys and business executives (yes, even an occasional investment banker!) with the same deep sense of unease, of lack of fulfillment.

It is not for me to be so presumptuous as to preach to you about happiness, but I do think that many before you have found that giving something significant of themselves to Princeton, and to other places like it, can add a dimension to life that is otherwise missing. I think that in most of us there is a need that is almost compelling to care about something grander, loftier in its objectives, worthier than the day-to-day pursuits in which it is so easy for all of us to become enmeshed.

Institutions exist to allow us to band together in support of larger purposes; they permit a continuity otherwise impossible to achieve; and they allow a magnification of individual efforts. Learning to make the accommodations that institutional affiliation requires is not always easy, especially for the kinds of ardent individualists we seek to educate here. But there is a need to cooperate and collaborate, as well as to strike out on one's own, if important societal ends are to be served.

Each of us must find his or her own cause, or multiplicity of causes. All that I can tell you is why some of us—why I—identify so powerfully with this University, why I derive such enormous pleasure from my own association with it. It is not, I think, primarily because of its reputation or standing. Indeed, there are many times when I am put off by the snobbishness that we have by no means discarded entirely, hard as we have worked at that task. For me it is the purposes of Princeton that are so "capturing"—the education of students of great promise, the optimistic pursuit of new ideas, the belief that learning is both fun and something important, and the corresponding conviction that education and ideas can make a difference in the world. The blending of a search for light and a commitment to service is right, at least for me, and, I hope, for many of you. Our society has need of what this place, at its best, can be. The pull is finally as simple as that.

This is your University now. You have made it that through your own efforts, which is what we celebrate today. This Commencement is itself an act of further bonding. If Princeton is to become an ever stronger university, with an ever greater capacity to make a difference in the world, that bond must hold. The University needs you. It needs your interest, your affectionate criticism, and your dedication. I think that you need it in turn, and at least as much, as an outlet for the best instincts within you.

Martin Buber once wrote an essay with a title that posed the question: "What Is To Be Done?" His answer was: "You shall not withhold yourself.". . .

Thinking and Caring

EXCERPTED FROM
COMMENCEMENT REMARKS
JUNE 1981

. . . I have often thought of what an odd fact it is that an institution as powerfully committed as this one is to the life of the mind should at the same time have such a strong emotional hold on so many of us. But then, on further reflection, it seems to me that there is a lesson here: of balance and of complementarities.

Sanity, both personal and national, requires a capacity to think clearly; but it requires no less a capacity to care about other people, to acknowledge weakness, to derive strength from friendship and from love, to give as well as to take. It seems to me that the world needs to be saved more or less regularly from both emotional appeals that are essentially content-free and allegedly rational calculations that claim to explain everything while in fact avoiding the most fundamental questions. . . .

As you prepare to take your leave of this place, I hope that each of you will take with you the predilections for both thinking and caring that seem to me so central to Princeton. I hope, very much, that in your own lives you will find ways to blend, and so to make richly human, the powers of the mind and the promptings of the heart. . . .

Roots

EXCERPTED FROM
COMMENCEMENT REMARKS
JUNE 1976

. . . The real roots that you have had an opportunity to develop here are ways of thinking, ideas, values, and the individuals through which these abstractions have been reflected, transmitted, shaped, and brought to life. No list of propositions or people would serve all of you, or even most of you. You have had to pick and choose for yourselves while you have been here, at least within limits, and you will have to pick and choose for yourselves in what you remember after you leave.

If you will allow me to be autobiographical for a moment, when I was a graduate student here in the fall of 1955 I encountered a faculty member named Jacob Viner, who had the most piercing eyes, and the most piercing mind, I have ever encountered. It was from him that I learned for the first time something of what it really meant to be a serious scholar; that there was an appreciable difference between opinion, even informed opinion, and evidence; that it was possible to learn a lot from one's mistakes; and, above all, that there was an excitement and a joy about learning that could be contagious. That was a great gift, which I hope never to lose, and it is in its generality the common property of all of us who have been fortunate enough to study with people like Jack Viner. I hope more than a few of you will carry from here similar recollections. . . .

Reflections

As you will understand, this is for me, as for you, a special day, a day charged with emotion and with feelings that I cannot hope to communicate adequately. One thing at least should be reassuring: I have no sweeping propositions or summary conclusions to impose on you. Rather, I have some personal reflections that I hope will stimulate thoughts of your own about Princeton and your time here.

I wonder how many of you remember your own introductions to Princeton. Most of you, I suspect. In my case, I arrived as a frightened, insecure graduate student at what was for me (a Midwesterner) a distant bastion of the Eastern establishment. Fortunately, I was comforted as well as challenged by wonderful friends and fine teachers.

My first and most lasting lesson, my greatest gift from Princeton, was an at first faint, but then growing, sense of what scholarship entailed; of what it meant to grapple with an idea, or a series of apparently conflicting, seemingly obscure ideas (of the kind expressed in *Value and Capital*, a book used in my first course in economic theory and forever emblazoned on my memory); and then finally to be rewarded by a flash of illumination. It was teachers such as Jacob Viner, Richard Lester, Lester Chandler, William Baumol, and Oskar Morgenstern who taught me that even neophytes, if they were sufficiently determined, could make headway with such materials—and, much more important, that the entire process of studying and of learning was both wonderfully exhilarating and just plain fun.

Professor Viner, one of the greatest scholars of his or any day, was forever arming us with useful warnings such as, "whenever an author writes 'in the last analysis,' you should read 'with no analysis at all.' " Or, " 'virtually' inevitably means 'virtually not.' " In a passage that is a favorite of mine, which I read to the Class of 1987 when I welcomed you in Alexander Hall four years ago, Viner wrote: "All that I plead on behalf of scholarship . . . is that, once the taste for it has been aroused, it gives a sense of largeness even to one's small quests, and a sense of fullness even to the small answers to problems large or small which it yields, a sense which can never in any other way be attained, for which no other source of human gratification can, to the addict, be a satisfying substitute, which gains instead of loses in quality and quantity and in pleasure-yielding capacity by being shared with others—and which, unlike golf, improves with age.''

Having survived my stint as a graduate student, I became a teacher myself, and my students (for almost thirty years now) have certainly been another of my special rewards: which is not to say, as one of my colleagues once observed in another context, that ''all of my ducks have been swans.'' I recall vividly one of the first senior theses that I supervised, in about 1960, which contained a peroration that began: ''We must eliminate poverty within our boarders''—spelled b-o-*a*-r-d-e-r-s!

One of the best students I ever had in Economics 101 is now a colleague of Professor Rawls' in the Philosophy Department at Harvard—as you can see, I managed to drive him from economics forever. A better result was obtained with Alan Blinder, now a leading member of the Princeton Economics Department who gave the lectures in 101 this spring. How enjoyable it has been to teach a section again this term—in spite of the fact that one of my students was overheard to mutter on the day of the final exam: ''I hate this course!''

Teaching is a humbling experience, in part because beginning students, in particular, are often so good at asking the really basic questions that one's graduate students and more sophisticated colleagues would be reluctant to ask—or to answer. And I have noticed that more than a few students are very confident of their own abilities.

One Sunday afternoon last spring I was walking through the Lewis Thomas Laboratory for molecular biology when I encountered an undergraduate reading the *New York Times* in one of the sunny lounges on the second floor. I said that he looked like a student who had just finished his senior thesis, and I asked who had supervised his work. He replied: ''Professor Shenk.'' I then asked if he understood how lucky he was to have had, as an undergraduate, one of the most outstanding scientists in the field as his supervisor. He replied, ''Yes . . . but of course Professor Shenk was pretty lucky too.''

For teachers and students alike, the academic enterprise differs from many others in that greater exposure to it frequently leads to a less certain, rather than more certain, view of the ''right'' answers to many profound questions—and to a deep respect for the limits of our knowledge. I have often thought that one of the real contributions of Princeton is to encourage a greater openness to the all too real possibility of being wrong. There is a wonderful passage from *The Education of*

Henry Adams in which Adams writes about his experiences as a teacher at Harvard College in the 1870s: "A teacher is expected to teach truth, and may perhaps flatter himself that he does so, if he stops with the alphabet or the multiplication table . . . but morals are quite another truth and philosophy is more complex still." Henry Adams would have understood well why some of us today have difficulty with simplistic notions about getting students to "think right."

Another lesson I have learned from colleagues—over and over again—is that success as a scholar is every bit as much a function of character as of intellect. The distinguished demographer Ansley Coale '39 always argued that what really marked the most outstanding academics was not marginal differences in raw brain power but the capacity to work very hard, the ability to benefit from criticism rather than be destroyed by it, the resilience to start again when a paper was clearly confused if not wrong, and the courage to reject what had been a pet idea of one's own—in short, a relentless, but good-humored, integrity. If those of you receiving degrees today take with you some of those qualities, you will have learned much of what Princeton has to teach you.

There is something that can be called institutional integrity as well as personal integrity, and some of the sharpest recollections I have of life in my present office concern efforts to protect the intellectual freedom of this place, to encourage its diversity, to promote respect for the stubborn independence of Princeton. I make no apology for any of that. Real learning can only occur, I believe, where there is genuine freedom to dissent, where no ideology has a special claim on us, and where finally it is the worth of an idea, and of a person, that counts the most— not your background, your religion, or whether you agree or disagree with the prevalent fashions (on or off campus).

I would be less than honest if I did not confess to irritation some days when either the occasional herd instincts of the campus or external voices urged Princeton to conform to some particular view of the world. But far more often I have been heartened by the courage of those who were willing to take unpopular positions, to defend the integrity of the institution against all comers. This is essential if we are to assure, as one eloquent student put it, that "Princetonians of the future have no reason to envy the past."

Trite as it may be to say it, it remains true that much of the most valuable learning at Princeton occurs outside library, laboratory, and classroom. Another of my students, Michele Warman '82, once said:

"What I treasure most about Princeton is that it is an academic *community*, and not merely a narrowly academic *institution*. . . . I recall not only the days spent in the library (and there were many of them), but also the evening rap sessions that began promisingly enough with high-flown debates on free will and determinism and descended by dawn to the inevitable indictment of the frailties of the human male."

We learn too, I believe, from our setting, . . . from the care, dedication, and genius that have formed the beauty of this campus over so many generations. No doubt each of you has a favorite place—a courtyard, a niche, a vista—that you will remember all your life. For me, walking about the spaces of Princeton, watching the interplay of light and shadow on buildings old and new, is always refreshing and, yes, rejuvenating.

I have enjoyed enormously working with architects charged with sustaining and enhancing the special character of the Princeton campus, and I remember particularly an interview with Robert Venturi '47, when we were discussing the renovation of what used to be Commons and is now Rockefeller and Mathey Colleges. Since this was to be a renovation and not a new building, one of the Trustees asked Mr. Venturi why such a famous architect would consider giving so much of his personal time and attention to the project. Mr. Venturi responded by producing a monograph on Holder Tower and the rest of the Commons complex published by Charles Scribner and Sons in 1918 that he had bought while he was a student at Princeton, and that he had kept ever since because, as he put it, "I loved those buildings so much."

That same kind of affection has stimulated generosity to Princeton that is simply extraordinary to behold, and for which all of us should be very grateful. Getting to know a wide array of cheerful donors has been another of my special pleasures. I will mention only one: the late Lev Cartwright of the Class of 1926. Lev was given an Alumni Citation shortly before his death, in part for his very generous contributions to Firestone Library. He responded: "This citation swells the ego and is a far cry from my last citation, which was for a traffic violation in California. . . ." He then continued: "My name is Levering Cartwright. Some friends call me Leverage. Princeton is to me a leverage situation in that it is a rare center of civilization that has the power through the faculty and graduates to radiate civilizing influence. I think . . . [of] the library [as] the kitchen of the University, and I have elected mainly to help fuel the stove."

Let me recall one other memorable example of loyalty, which dates back to an alumni reception held in Maclean House shortly after I was elected president in 1972. I was greeting alumni when a particularly ferocious-looking fellow from the Class of 1912 marched down the hallway toward me, rapping his cane on the floor. His name was Milton King, and as he approached I steeled myself for what I was sure would be an assault on the politics of the faculty, or on any one of a large number of other vexatious issues—perhaps admissions. He looked straight at me and said: "Young man, there is just one thing I want you to understand. There is *nothing* you can do to disaffect me!"

One source, I'm sure, of that kind of loyalty to Princeton is the personal friendships that we form as students, faculty, staff members, Trustees, parents, and alumni. My own reflections would go on too long and become inappropriately personal if I were even to begin to enumerate the individuals who encouraged me whenever I showed any traces of feeling "down," who were always there when I needed them, and who have done so much to imbue my days here with the warmth of friendship. They inhabit not only every academic building on this campus, but other locations as varied as Caldwell Field House, Murray-Dodge, New South, and West College—not to mention Nassau Hall. There are many former students and alumni among them, residing all over the world.

But perhaps I can be allowed to mention three individuals: my predecessor in this office, Robert F. Goheen '40; R. Manning Brown '36, chairman of the Executive Committee of the Board of Trustees during almost all of my tenure as provost and president; and Neil Rudenstine '56, my close colleague for nearly two decades, who is now to move with me to the Mellon Foundation. How much Princeton owes to these three—and how much I have valued, and will always value, their friendship! I can say no more than that.

Fred Fox '39, Keeper of Princetoniana, exemplified in his person much of what I am trying to say about affection for Princeton. I regret that those of you who came to Princeton after Fred's death in 1981 had no opportunity to know him. Perhaps you will be able to gain at least some sense of what a rare person he was if I tell you that, when we once made the dreadful mistake of asking him to write a "position description," he listed 161 separate activities. About halfway down his list was: "Soothed Yale Professor whose bulldog was stolen by our undergraduates. Petted his dog."

Fred believed that association with Princeton was something like a marriage, meant to be lifelong. When I became president he decided that I should receive "something old, something new, something borrowed, and something blue." He proceeded to give me a sword from the House of Nassau, a new Princeton umbrella (in case it ever rained), a quarter that he had somehow managed to borrow from Ricardo Mestres '31 (the notoriously parsimonious financial vice-president of the University), and—finally—a jar containing a strange-smelling liquid and a blue cloth object soaked in it. On examination, the object turned out to be a pickled Yale banner, which resides to this day on my mantel at home.

There is, I believe, another source of the extraordinary hold that Princeton has on so many diverse people. It has to do with a widely shared sense of commitment to others: to causes—and institutions—larger than any of us. Princeton is one such place.

Harold H. Helm '20, long-time Trustee and Princetonian extraordinaire, certainly lived that philosophy. In thinking about Harold, and his irrepressible urge to be useful, I remember him once saying: "It's healthy to spend some time with other people's problems." It was as if he had ingrained within him Woodrow Wilson's charge to the Princeton Class of 1909: "Set out to fulfill obligations, to do what you must and exact of others what they owe you, and all your days alike will end in weariness of spirit. . . . There is no pleasure to be had from the fulfillment of obligations, from doing what you know you ought to do. Nothing but what you volunteer has the essence of life, the springs of pleasure in it. These are the things you do because you want to do them, the things your spirit has chosen for its satisfaction."

I want to conclude these reflections by remembering Adlai Stevenson '22, one of the true statesmen of our time and someone appropriate to recall as our country prepares for another election campaign. Governor Stevenson returned to Princeton in the spring of 1954 to speak at a senior class banquet. He observed, "I came here last night in darkness, after not having been here for some four or five years. I came with an old friend and an old classmate. We drove a little through the campus after dusk. It was soft, the air fresh, the beginning of spring." After quoting a poem by Alfred Noyes that he had read as an undergraduate, he said to the seniors:

This is the last of your springs. And now in the serenity and quiet of this lovely place, touch the depths of truth, feel the hem. You will go away with old, good friends. Don't forget when you leave why you came.

To each of you, congratulations, best wishes, and Godspeed.

Memorial Tributes

On a number of occasions, President Bowen was asked to speak at memorial services for especially beloved Princetonians. While of a different nature than his other writings, these tributes reveal dimensions of the man who composed them that complement the more institutional materials reprinted elsewhere in this volume.

The four tributes selected for inclusion are from the services for:

• Harold W. Dodds *14, who served as the fifteenth President of Princeton University from 1933 to 1957;

• Frederic E. Fox '39, legendary alumnus, class secretary, Recording Secretary of the University for twelve years, and Keeper of Princetoniana (1976–81);

• R. Manning Brown '36, a Trustee for twenty-two years, including fifteen years as chairman of the Board's Executive Committee; and

• Harold H. Helm '20, first chairman of Annual Giving, longtime Trustee and chairman of the committee that recommended coeducation, chairman of the Board's Commencement Committee, and a participant in more than sixty-five Princeton Commencements.

Memorial Service for Harold W. Dodds

NOVEMBER 7, 1980

We have come together today, in this chapel, to remember Harold Willis Dodds, fifteenth President of Princeton, and a dear friend of many of us. We are grateful for his life; we mourn his death; and we offer our sympathy to those nearest to him, especially to Margaret, his wife.

When Margaret and I spoke about this service, she expressed her wishes—and Harold's—with customary clarity: "No eulogy," she said, and no eulogy this will be. These remarks will be more in the nature of an appreciation, with some special attention to Harold's own words.

Since this is not a eulogy, I feel no call to recite all the facts of Harold Dodds' presidency of Princeton or, for that matter, the facts of his life. The historians of the University will do that, and they will add sufficient interpretative material, I am confident, to make plain the extraordinary accomplishments of President Dodds. All of us privileged to share in the life of this place today are in his debt for his service as president during twenty-four difficult and demanding years—from 1933 to 1957. My intent, rather, is to say a few words about Harold Dodds as a person—about the qualities that endeared him to so many, about the values for which he stood.

I begin with a factual observation, in part to note its irony—a quality Harold always appreciated. It was given to him to preside over a period of substantial growth at Princeton: in faculty, in students (especially graduate students), and in the size of the campus; and all of this in the face of depression and war. The irony is that President Dodds valued smallness so much. He once said: "We have no illusions of grandeur that bigness will satisfy." Yet he was wise enough to recognize that not even that principle was an absolute, and that some increase in size was necessary to achieve other goals—including importantly the strengthening of the intellectual capacities of Princeton. He would want us to remember, I feel confident, the distinguished appointments he made to this faculty. Many of us owe to him the presence at Princeton of teachers, scholars, colleagues, and friends who have shaped our lives. Certainly I do.

Harold Dodds believed strongly, devoutly, in the power of the mind;

he knew well from his study of politics that good intentions are not enough. In its cover story of June 18, 1934, written at the time of his first Commencement as president, *Time* magazine quoted Dr. Dodds as observing: "A thick head can do as much harm as a hard heart."

In his leadership of Princeton, President Dodds always sought what he called "the education of the broad reaches of the mind." A staunch believer in scholarship and independent work, he saw the need for a modern open-stack library, and it is mainly to him that we owe Firestone Library. He began working for it in 1933, and when its cornerstone was laid fourteen years later he said: "Within the walls of this building the miracle will constantly occur that we take for granted, because the process is quiet and continuous rather than spectacular and instantaneous; the miracle of the imagination kindled, prejudice thrown overboard, dogma rejected, conviction strengthened, perspective lengthened. This miracle is performed by teachers and students together through the instrumentality of books."

Before Firestone Library could be built, America had to overcome the dangers and agonies of World War II. Harold Dodds, normally a quiet man, knew that there was a time for passion too, and he was a passionate defender of democracy, of democratic processes and attitudes complete with all their imperfections. It is hardly surprising, then, that his was one of the strongest voices for active resistance to totalitarianism—and at a time when isolationism was still widely advocated. In rereading his talks this week, I was struck again by the force of what he said three months before Pearl Harbor: "The moment has arrived to realize that, for those who believe in America, the range of debate is narrowing. . . . The time has come to forgo our cherished habits of leisurely criticism of tangential matters, in the interest of conserving our full national potential for self-preservation. If our democracy cannot discipline itself to this truth, Hitler's contempt for us will be well-founded."

The democratic processes in which he believed so wholeheartedly had no place for privilege. As he spoke to generations of Princetonians about leadership, he was always sure to emphasize that he was talking about a "leadership earned by ability, not conferred by circumstance of wealth or birth." "Privilege," he said, "rots the privileged."

The theme of Princeton's bicentennial, celebrated in 1946, was "Education for Freedom." President Dodds' understanding of the meaning of freedom was tested shortly thereafter when Alger Hiss was invited to speak here by the Whig-Cliosophic Society. Many of you will recall the fierce national reaction to this invitation, complete with pumpkins strewn about the campus. Protesters and reporters were present in what seemed almost equal numbers. But President Dodds was steadfast in refusing to rescind the invitation, even though he personally disapproved of it, and he kept reminding all who would listen that "education includes the freedom to make mistakes."

Harold Dodds combined so many qualities; he was a man of remarkable balance. An idealist, he was always concerned for practical results. He knew that the University had to have resources in order to remain strong and to remain free. A principal founder of Annual Giving, he told me only last year how absolutely delighted he was to see what has been built on the foundations established so laboriously in 1940. He added: "I'll admit that it did not begin easily. . . . When I think of the arguments we used to justify it, I smile."

He had a great capacity for friendship, as so many here today can attest. I first came to know him in 1958, when I was doing research on higher education in Britain, and I remember so well both the good advice he gave me and the exceptional efforts he made to smooth my way in England, taking advantage of his many friendships there. Over the years he has been a constant source of wise counsel and encouragement, always anxious to do whatever he could to be useful, as he indicated just this last summer by offering to put into perspective problems related to intercollegiate athletics—a subject familiar to all university presidents. Mary Ellen and I are more grateful than we can say for the gift of friendship that Harold and Margaret have bestowed on us, as on so many others, with an exceptional generosity.

Harold was also a man of deep and abiding religious faith—a faith that was secure enough that he never felt an obligation to impose it on others, much as it meant to him. It is another indication of his balance, and his wisdom, that he combined such a strong personal faith with an insistent affirmation of the virtues of tolerance. Indeed, he devoted his last Baccalaureate sermon to that topic, saying: "The hallmark of civilization is the acquired capacity of men to respect the convictions of others without compromising their own."

Let me end by noting two testimonials to President Dodds, one from a somewhat unlikely source, and then a final comment of his. We remember Harold Dodds each year at Commencement through the Harold Willis Dodds Achievement Award, presented to a graduating senior. What some may not know is that this award was established by the 1957 Board of the *Daily Princetonian*, a publication that was, in the nature of things, of more than occasional annoyance to President Dodds. He once told me (with that wry humor of his) that he knew he was recovering from an ailment when his doctor informed him that he could resume reading the *Prince* before breakfast. The award is given to that senior who best exemplifies President Dodds' qualities of "clear thinking, moral courage, a patient and judicious regard for the opinion of others, and a thoroughgoing devotion to the welfare of the University and to the life of the mind." The students who established the award must have known him well.

And the Trustees did too. At his final Commencement, Harold Dodds received an honorary L.L.D., and the citation included this phrase: "A man of honor and courage, integrity and humor, he has served us well with the infinite labors of a lifetime. His name will be forever associated with a great epoch in the annals of Princeton University."

But President Dodds had the last word then, as he should this afternoon. In bidding farewell to the graduating class at that Commencement, the Class of 1957, he said: "My fondest wish for every member of the Class is that each one of you will have an experience similar to mine: that you will find a work which you love above everything else under circumstances which spell fulfillment; and that you may have the good fortune to find it in a place which you love above all other places on earth."

We have lost a great leader and a warm friend. We are grateful for his life, for his work, and for his presence among us through these years.

Memorial Service for Frederic E. Fox

FEBRUARY 25, 1981

This service, in memory of Frederic E. Fox '39, is his in more than the usual sense: in his characteristic way, he planned it, even to the extent of choosing the hymns and scriptures and asking his friends in the Band to be present and to play a medley of Princeton songs as a postlude. He made provision in the Order of Service for "Personal Remarks," but I think I should say (for otherwise legitimate doubt might exist) that he did not draft them—an exercise of what must have been, for Fred, remarkable restraint!

How much I loved him. How much so many loved him: for himself, of course, but also for what he represented. In coming together today, we cannot conceal the loss we have suffered, the loss we feel so deeply. It would be dishonest to try too hard to do so. But we come primarily to celebrate his life among us, to give thanks, and then to go forward in song and in his good spirit to serve the causes so dear to him, including of course the cause of Princeton.

Words can illuminate; they can help to define; they can offer some comfort. Fred himself was a master with words—written on paper, inscribed on bronze and stone. He was a skillful editor; drawing his inspiration from gardening, he used to tell me that editing was like weeding. But there are no words I can find that will do justice to Fred's life and works; to his devotion to Hannah and his family, classmates, and friends all over the world; to his responsiveness to others; to the texture, the tone, and the substance of all that he did.

Fred loved fairy tales, and he once wrote one about himself that provides the best short description of the long sweep of his activities. It reads as follows:

> Once upon a time, there was a little boy who came to Princeton and lived happily ever after.
>
> As an undergraduate, dressed up in a tiger skin, he crashed the gates of Palmer Stadium and cavorted on the field with the Band.
>
> During the war, dressed up like a soldier, he gathered a helmetful of invasion currency from a group of alumni on board a landing ship off the Normandy coast, and sent it back to the University to build a new gym and library.

When Peace came, dressed up like a clergyman, he helped edit the hymnbook now used in the Chapel, making sure it contained at least three hymns written by Princetonians: Nos. 8, 170 and 444.

In the White House, dressed up like a Republican, he drafted messages for D. D. Eisenhower L.L.D. '47 in the nation's service.

Finally, returning home as Secretary of the Distinguished Class of 1939, he became the only man in history to climb *above* the belfry of Nassau Hall, and put a 1939 nickel in the gold ball at the top of the pole just below the weather vane.

ɔn, in 1976, after having served for twelve years as recording sec- .y of the University, Fred became, in his words: "Keeper of Princeton's legends, songs and symbols."

His office, he said, was "a showroom for Archives, a variety store of orange and black, an historical hangout, an information booth, a one-man speakers bureau, ombudsman, post office, bank, bar, and pastor's study." As many will testify, the most extraordinary array of people sought him out: to present a gift, to ask advice, to gather information, or simply to be with him. They were of all ages and persuasions, some of them the most unlikely visitors to 1 Nassau Hall (which Fred once described as "the ultimate address"). And of course students, alumni, and friends also enjoyed the warmest hospitality at the Foxes' home at 28 Vandeventer. Life was for Fred, and his family, a whole cloth.

Fred was once prevailed upon to complete—of all things antithetical to his character—a "position description and analysis form" that provided fascinating insights into the work of our illustrious Keeper of Princetoniana. A colleague, in reviewing the form, had the good sense to observe: "In significant respects, the position and the incumbent defy classification, and that is as it should be." Fred's submission was also described as "an awesome illustration of the difference that one dedicated individual can make to the life of an institution." Fred listed 161 separate functions involving students, faculty, alumni, and friends, written material of all kinds, and an indescribable assortment of memorabilia. Included on his list was "Soothed Yale Professor whose bulldog was stolen by our undergraduates. Petted his dog." Also: "Barraged various offices with suggestions . . . on how to run the University." And: "Sent Princeton University Press book on the birds of Venezuela to amateur ornithologist, Robert Keeley '51, the new Ambassador to Zimbabwe." The final item on his list was: "Planted a few zinnias and marigolds alongside Nassau Hall. Keep watering them.''

Fred was unfailingly colorful, and two particular colors were of course his favorites. ''Obviously I can't touch everyone, every event, with my magic wand dipped in orange and black,'' he said, ''but as long as I'm Keeper of Princetoniana, I'm sure going to try. I hope I don't tip over the paint in the process.''

Over the years, his orange and black magic wand assumed international, indeed extraterrestrial, proportions. With Hannah's help, he sent a homemade Princeton banner to the moon with our alumnus Pete Conrad ('53) as a way, he said, of putting Princeton 239,000 miles ahead of Harvard and Yale. While in Red Square in Moscow with other members of his class, he painted two cobblestones orange and black. When Japanese visitors came to campus he taught them the words to ''Old Nassau,'' substituting ''banzai, banzai, banzai'' for ''hurrah, hurrah, hurrah''; and he inspired them to sing with as much enthusiasm as he elicited from entering students each fall in Alexander Hall and from alumni at the conclusion of each P-rade.

Although he considered himself the vice-president for intangibles, Fred made the traditions and the legends of Princeton come alive in decidedly tangible ways. As he had done in the White House, so too at Princeton he seldom let anyone leave his office without carrying away some remembrance. When our daughter, Karen, went to interview him about his experiences in World War II for a high school social sciences project, she came home with a packet of sand from the beaches of Normandy. When Nassau Hall was being remodeled, he ''rescued'' a steel crossbeam and dragged it behind his bike to the physics workshop to have it sliced into paper weights. I have one on my desk. He had bricks and mortar and pieces of old fireplaces, and orange and black lollipops, and orange and black balloons which he gave to young and old alike. And he sent packages of Food Services Tiger sugar to occasionally bitter correspondents to sweeten their dispositions.

Certainly one of Fred's most remarkable qualities was the way in which he provided a link among the generations. He was loved and respected in all the Princeton classes. At the same time, it is only fair to acknowledge his special relationship with his own class, which he served as secretary for seventeen years. It is those in '39, of course, who knew Fred first and longest, and who remember with particular clarity the impression he made on this campus from the moment he arrived: the time he agreed to have his head shaved as a walking advertisement for Jack Honore's barber shop; the time he sneaked into the Junior Prom through steam pipes; and the time he made his way past the ticket-taker at a Theatre Intime production in the garb of a Western Union messenger. Fred always insisted that his name was Frederic Fox *'39*, and that any Princeton name was incomplete without its numerals.

The picture of Fred that emerges from such wonderful stories—and there are so many more that could be told—is of a colorful, delightful person who cheered all who passed his way. It is a true picture; but it is also only a partial one. He was so much more than that.

Within the University, he was especially valuable in insisting on the human scale of the place, in resisting bureaucratic tendencies even as he understood the need for orderly procedures. When asked to draw an organization chart that would place his activities in their right structural context, he did just that—but he did it by drawing arrows to all sorts of colleagues, allies, and semi-supervisors, and his chart culminated in clear pictorial recognition of Hannah's overarching role and the special place of his family in his life. He had a clear sense of his own priorities.

He also had a much more subtle sense of tradition than all the orange and black trappings might have suggested to some. His symbol of tradition, of continuity, was the river, because it was never stagnant, never still, always moving. He believed so deeply in the core values of Princeton that he became incensed when people mistook the trappings for the real thing and tried to preserve the form at the expense of the substance.

He was a person of real depth, and one of his greatest gifts was the ability to make important points with such a deceptively light touch that his students—and we were all his students—learned lessons without ever knowing that any "teaching" had occurred. It is no accident that he taught "Old Nassau" to the freshmen in Alexander Hall as part of a presentation on the Honor System, and his inimitable description of the song as reflecting Princeton's commitment to musical as well as intellectual integrity made a lasting impression on many.

He and I talked often about religion at Princeton. Characteristically, he brought to these discussions his understanding of the views of others as well as his own clear convictions. I know how hard he worked to encourage a larger range of opportunities for religious observance, a broader conception of the role of religion in the life of the University, at the same time that he was so faithful to his own beliefs as an ordained minister and a devout Christian. He had no use for bigotry in any form. His sense of this University's religious tradition was secure enough and generous enough to infuse his view of the chapel and its place on this campus with a broad perspective.

As many current students and graduates in all classes will testify, Fred was also deeply committed to extracurricular activities of many kinds—especially to Triangle and the Band. He saw these activities not just as opportunities for fun—much as he approved of having fun—but as unifying elements, as carriers of the right kind of spirit, and as learning opportunities. He was a strong supporter of recent efforts to improve residential life, believing as he did in the value of friendships that include all within what must be finally a single community.

Fred could of course be wrong—a trait he shared with each of us. In fact, I think he had the capacity to be even more outrageously wrong than most, perhaps because he was more creative and less inhibited. In any event, he knew full well that certain of his judgments had to be checked from time to time, and Dennis Sullivan in my office used to exercise what he called his "desk drawer veto" of some of Fred's proposals. But if he could be wrong, he could not be arrogant; and so another lesson he taught us was humility.

At the same time, he was also, on occasion, a very tough adversary. This past weekend, I read again copies of some of his letters, generally written to critics of Princeton whom Fred regarded as not only backward-looking but, far worse from his standpoint, unloving.

One of Fred's strongest qualities was his unremitting desire to be constructive: to build, not to tear down. He was in his person a great antidote to the occasional waves of cynicism that can wash over all of us, and he always tried to find a graceful way to aim concern in a positive direction. He buoyed our spirits, he breathed his zest for life into us, and he quickened our steps along the way. I think of Fred particularly as I remember what Adlai Stevenson once said of Eleanor Roosevelt: "She would rather light a candle than curse the darkness."

I have left to the last that characteristic of Fred that I think was most important. He was, for me and so many others, a pastor. A member of his class observed, "he baptized us, he married us, he buried us." As others, from all classes, will testify, he helped us celebrate our joys and he comforted us at times of distress. We always knew he was there. He could listen, and laugh, and cry. He taught by example that no small act of kindness is too small to count. The notes he has sent me, over the years, are among my special treasures. I know I am not alone in that regard.

Fred has also been described, especially these last few days, as

"irreplaceable." In a real sense he is. But he would have been offended, I think, disappointed in us, if we could not, together, sustain
the infectious enthusiasm for Princeton that is surely a large part of his
legacy. That is a charge for each of us—not to copy Fred (an effort
certain to fail)—but in our own ways, within our own capacities, to
carry forward his vision of Princeton as a place of learning, and of the
spirit, a human place, where each person is in the care of all.

Finally, as we commemorate Fred's life today, we should remember
his efforts to commemorate the lives of others. Fred always sent each
class memorial in the *Princeton Alumni Weekly* to the spouse or next of
kin with a personal note. When he was Recording Secretary, he wrote
the words that I still use frequently to conclude letters of condolence.
Now it is our turn to say good-bye to him. He was our pastor, he was
our friend, he was a light to our lives and to the life of this University.
To use again his words, most appropriately of all applied to him:
"Princeton holds in honor and affection the name of Frederic E. Fox,
Class of 1939."

Memorial Service
for R. Manning Brown, Jr.

OCTOBER 25, 1985

R. Manning Brown was born on July 1, 1915, in Elizabeth, New Jersey. He died on October 19, 1985, in Princeton.

Of those seventy years, over fifty were shared with this University, which his father had attended before him as a member of the Class of 1907. All these years of direct association with Princeton created a relationship so special that it had a character all its own. That is why it seems particularly appropriate that we assemble here today, in this chapel on this campus.

We have not come to "pay our respects" to Manning. How inadequate that phrase sounds. Rather, we are here to give thanks for his life, for all that he gave of himself to so many. And we are here too to remember those special qualities of his that will always exert such powerful "pulls" on the institutions he served and the individuals who were privileged to know him.

My own association with Manning was of course centered on Princeton, and I hope that those of you who knew him principally in other contexts will understand that I mean no disrespect to any of his other activities in talking principally about his life as it intersected the life of this University. I also hope—and believe—that in describing those qualities most evident here, I will be recalling the same qualities most evident in other settings. He was a person of such wholeness, so remarkably consistent in his attributes, that it could not be otherwise.

The list of his other important roles and contributions is so long that I cannot even begin an enumeration without taking too much time and risking an inadvertent omission. But special mention must be made of his strong leadership of the New York Life Insurance Company, which he served from 1951 until his death, as Chairman and Chief Executive Officer from 1972 to 1981. He developed—earned—the same fierce loyalty there that is so characteristic of all of his associations.

Many other companies, foundations, and organizations enlisted Manning's services as director or trustee, and they did so because of another of his most obvious qualities: predictably good judgment. Having served with him on some of those other boards and committees, I know how good he always was at distinguishing the truly important questions from the underbrush.

The generosity of the New York Life Insurance Company, and numerous other organizations, in contributing to the scholarship fund established last winter in Manning's honor, and the content of the retirement resolutions adopted by boards on which he served, speak eloquently to the esteem in which he was held. Perhaps someday I shall meet a representative of an organization that felt poorly served by Manning; that would be a new experience!

Another dimension of Manning's life was his service in the United States Army during World War II. It was really only during these last months that he talked very much to me about those wartime years, but they plainly stamped his life and character. The official record of his service speaks for itself: He attained the rank of major and commanded an infantry company in Italy. He was decorated five times, receiving the Purple Heart and a Bronze Star with three clusters. As he reflected with me last spring on his illness, he observed that he had learned a long time ago, in Italy, the limits of fear. He was, I am sure, as brave a man in Italy as he was in the Princeton Medical Center.

Manning was in many ways a private person, and he would not want anyone to dwell on his personal life. But since I have been fortunate enough to be treated "like family" by Marnie Brown and the children, Ralph and Anne, I think it is in place to recognize them and their relationship with Manning. Manning's devotion to his family was as extraordinary as everything else about him, and there was nothing he would not do for them. I know how proud he was of their accomplishments—and of their personal qualities. Marnie, let me say, has provided her own example of faith and courage these last nine months.

With respect to the University, and Manning's association with it, it is hard to know where to begin—and, for me at least, impossible to know where to end. It is, in fact, an association that, while it had a beginning, will have no ending. Princeton University will *always* reflect Manning's spirit and his incalculable contributions.

As one alumnus wrote to me just this week: "I shall always think of Manning when I think of Princeton. . . . Now that I am a Princeton parent, I am struck with how much stronger the place is . . . than it was as recently as those seemingly few years ago when I was an undergraduate. . . . The University can serve as a living memorial to Manning."

Among the many "marks" that Manning left on Princeton, there is at least one that I suspect he would have preferred to forget. I refer to the famous black eye he gave to President Goheen on the Dillon Gym squash courts just before a series of speaking engagements that elicited, no doubt, more than a few queries about the extent of student activism. That incident aside, President Goheen would also want to attest, I know, to Manning's indelible impression on Princeton.

Most people think of Manning as, in the words of one student, "Princeton's top Trustee." Natural as that characterization is, it would be terribly misleading if it were to suggest that he always held grand positions—or that prestigious positions mattered particularly to him. I believe it is fitting to record that his first "position" at Princeton, held as an undergraduate, was assistant football manager.

Following graduation with the Class of 1936, having earned honors in Politics, Manning served in such roles as assistant secretary of his class, president of his class, and as a member of various Alumni Council committees. He was Princeton area regional chairman of the $53 million campaign from 1959 through 1962, and on and on went his service to Princeton.

But it was of course Manning's twenty-two years on the Board of Trustees that left the greatest imprint. It is generally known that he served for fifteen years as chairman of the Executive Committee of the Board—the longest term in that demanding position in the modern history of Princeton. He tried repeatedly to step aside, insisting that others should have their turn, but his fellow Trustees were much too wise to accede to any such proposal. As one person put it, "Why replace the best?"—a sentiment I echoed emphatically. What an extraordinary privilege it has been for me—and what a pleasure—to work alongside him. I cannot imagine that the president of any other university has been as fortunate. I shall miss him, as colleague and as friend, more than I can possibly say.

Many people have commented on the unerring skill with which Manning led the Board. He taught us how a Board of Trustees should function. He had a kind of sixth sense as to when a discussion was about to get off the tracks, and when the Trustees were about to do something that they might later regret. His capacity for reconciling differences, for bringing people together, was so great that it seemed to be exercised effortlessly.

In commenting on his own work as a Trustee, Manning once said, "The pay is lousy but the rewards are great." For his colleagues, one of the greatest rewards was the opportunity to work so closely with him.

Less well known than Manning's leadership of the Board was the extent of his involvement with the work of the Board at all levels, and, for that matter, with countless other aspects of the University. He served on every Board committee, and he would ask no one to do anything that he was not prepared to do first. I estimate that he participated in a minimum of 600 meetings of Trustee committees. I am totally incapable of estimating how many questions he answered from student reporters, how many letters he wrote, how many speeches he delivered, how many University events he attended, how many gifts he solicited, how many football practices he witnessed, how many alumni he could call by name, how many times he simply said an encouraging word to a student, a staff member, a professor, or a fellow member of the Board.

It would be staggering to know how many lives he touched directly, quite apart from the even larger effects of policy decisions—such as coeducation, equal access, or the more recent commitments to the residential colleges and the life sciences—in which he played such a major role. As one of my colleagues observed just this week: "He treated everyone alike, with kindness and respect." Another person observed that Manning simply couldn't bring himself to hurt anyone's feelings. As far as he was concerned, there were no junior members of the Board, no junior members of the University's staff, no junior partners in any enterprise of which he was a part. No wonder he had so many friends.

Manning always said that the excellence of the faculty was the most important thing about Princeton, and that is what he believed. But no faculty member will take offense (I hope) if I suggest that of his list of favorite things, the football team, and especially the players, may have ranked even a shade higher—especially on certain fall days. The character of his relationship with the football team always seemed to me to reveal much about him, as well as about how one ought to view athletics in a university setting.

As anyone who ever played tennis with Manning will attest, he was a fiercely competitive—and highly skilled—athlete. He won something on the order of seventeen championships at the Pretty Brook Tennis Club, and I sat next to him at enough football games to know how much he wanted to win. I saw him this fall right after the Dartmouth game at Hanover, and—ill as he was—he treated himself to a victory cigar.

But that dedication to competitive success would not alone have earned him the affection of the team that has been so noticeable, especially in recent years. It was reflected in the decision by the team to give Manning the game ball following the win over Dartmouth. That ball, signed by all the members of the team, was in the window sill by his bed last Friday, when I saw him for the last time. What mattered so much to the players, let me suggest, were the same qualities I have already alluded to: his total commitment to them as individuals, not just as football players, his presence and support on the "down" days as well as when the ball bounced right, his real understanding of what the team was going through, his empathy for them.

He had such a special feeling for young people, and such an appreciation for the opportunities that a Princeton education offers, that it seems exactly right that the R. Manning Brown Scholarship Fund was established last winter—before any of us knew of the disease that would claim him. That was especially fortunate timing, since nothing gave Manning more pleasure than learning of the growth of the fund and, later, of the first six students chosen to hold his scholarships. Having been a scholarship student himself, and having worked in the Commons dining halls, he knew at first hand how important such assistance could be. Marnie took special pleasure, she told me, in reading Manning letters from two of the recipients not long before his death.

There are so many other memories; so many vignettes. I think that a careful historian, assessing Manning's role at Princeton, would note how pervasive, how all encompassing, it was. That itself says a great deal. But there are also central threads of personality and of character that tie all of the bits and pieces together, and strongly so. I have already mentioned some, and I would like to end by identifying others that seem especially significant to me.

In forming any such list, I keep coming back to Manning's modesty, his genuine humility, the unassuming, unprepossessing way in which he accomplished so much. He never wanted to "be in the way," as he never was, or to take credit, which he always resisted (usually successfully). His example is a direct challenge to any students of leadership who believe that a "high profile" is necessary to make a difference.

He was also unbelievably conscientious, never too busy or too self-important to attend to the smallest matter (including setting the table for a breakfast meeting of the Trustees held during the 1978 blizzard, a day when he also stepped in to chair six different committee meetings). Yet, at the same time, he had such a clear vision of this University and its future. There are not many people, in my experience, with that ability simultaneously to "think big" and to attend to details.

I should also underscore his ability to think rigorously. He had an exceptionally good mind, and one of the most important lessons Manning taught was the need always to do things for reasons and to be prepared to give reasons for what you do. His self-effacing gentleness never translated into sloppy thinking. While he was tolerant of others (sometimes almost to a fault), willing always to listen to different points of view, he had no difficulty finally coming to his own conclusion.

It was, I think, his *thoughtful steadiness* that made so much difference on so many occasions.

I mention, finally. the three qualities that I think were displayed so powerfully during the last period of his life: his integrity, his capacity for friendship, and his courage.

As Manning's classmate and close friend John Coburn observed just the other day, "integrity" was a big word for Manning. It comes close to defining him, and he possessed it to such degree that it gave him both dignity and a capacity to accept things that he could not change.

Many here today will know precisely what I mean when I speak of Manning's personal warmth, compassion, and concern for others. His loyalty to individuals, as to institutions, was so evident that it almost goes without saying. You always knew that he would be there when you needed him. I can put it simply: His was one of the great friendships of my life.

As for courage, I do not mean just pressing ahead when it would have been so easy to yield to self-pity or simply to give up. Nor do I mean just standing up to personal abuse, as he did so regularly during contentious times. I mean something larger than that, something that I referred to at last June's Commencement when I quoted a poem by Jack Gilbert entitled "The Abnormal is Not Courage." The poem reminds us that courage is not "the bounty of impulse," but rather

> . . . The beauty
> That is of many days. Steady and
> 　clear.
> It is the normal excellence, of long
> 　accomplishment.

So it was with Manning: "Steady and clear . . . the normal excellence of long accomplishment."

Memorial Service for Harold H. Helm

NOVEMBER 22, 1985

Harold H. Helm ("Triple H" or simply "Harold" as he was known to legions of friends of every age and station) always seemed to encourage the rest of us to do things we never thought possible. But I do not think I have ever attempted a more impossible task than trying to convey in a brief time some sense of why Harold was such a truly remarkable man: why so many of us, knowing him from so many different perspectives, admired him so much, respected him so much, loved him so much.

If I were simply to read a list of his activities, accomplishments, and honors, we would be fortunate to reach "H" in the alphabet before the doors of the church were closed for the night. His remarkable career at the Chemical Bank—where he was a vice-president at the age of 28 and an honorary director at the age of 84—is a story all its own. So too is his work on behalf of (it almost seems) every good cause in America: the American Red Cross, the USO, the Community Chest, his church, the Columbia Presbyterian Hospital, local schools, clubs, and on and on, including—you must allow me—Princeton University. He served on at least twenty-five corporate and foundation boards. I was never quite sure if he actually slept—though I can report that, with characteristically good judgment, he did manage an occasional nap at some meetings and dinners that we attended together!

His honors included the designation of "Kentucky Colonel," various funds and prizes established to recognize him, numerous honorary degrees, decoration by the King of Norway, an oil tanker that bears his name, and—I discovered recently—a citation by Governor Nelson Rockefeller for his work to reduce traffic fatalities. Harold, and his good works, were hard to miss—and will be missed very greatly!

But I am sure I speak for many when I say that all of these things, enormously impressive as they are, were really incidental. It was Harold himself that mattered; it was Harold himself who was the message. It wasn't just that I admired him, though I certainly did; it was that I was inordinately, outrageously fond of him. What fun it was to be with him, how inspiring it was to know him. He was a genuine person, a genuinely great man, who spoke to values by living them. He often referred to the "power of example." And what an example he was.

From his days as a student in the Class of 1920 at Princeton (when he was known, at least for a time, as "Judge"), Harold was always seen as a person of exceptional judgment, very "level-headed" as one person put it. Early in his career at the Chemical Bank, he was described by Percy H. Johnston as having "an old head on young shoulders."

I first came to know Harold well in the late 1960s, when campus protest was so widespread. I remember vividly a Princeton Board meeting when angry students were harassing the Trustees, and person after person entered Nassau Hall sputtering and visibly upset. That was certainly my condition. Harold, in sharp contrast, came into the room with his usual bounce, smiling and in good humor. "How can you be so cheerful?" I asked him. He gave a reply that I have recalled many times since: "The fact that every one else is losing his head is no reason for me to lose mine." How unflappable—how steady—he was. And how generous in his assessments of others. He was always ready to overlook aberrations in behavior, always eager to assume the best about everyone.

This is certainly not to suggest that he was any Pollyanna. He was smart and shrewd, a leader and a strong one. Before enrolling at Princeton as an undergraduate, he spent two years at Ogden College in Kentucky, and there is a wonderful picture of Harold as a member of the Ogden basketball team below which someone at Chemical Bank noted perceptively: "In this team photo, Captain Helm is shown in the center foreground, carrying the ball as usual."

His success was attributable in part to his enormous energy, hard work, and attention to detail—all combined with a gift for making friends that I have never seen matched.

How could anyone possibly remember so many names? One of my colleagues suggested that so long as Harold was abroad in the land, there was really no need for an Alumni Directory. There has never been another Trustee emeritus as active as Harold (and I'm not sure how many that active we could accommodate!). If a month passed without several phone calls from Harold and at least two or three of his famous half-page memos, I thought that something was amiss.

The memos and letters were gems. Just this fall, Harold wrote to Congressman Bill Natcher of Bowling Green, Kentucky, urging him to come to Princeton for a football game. He ended with one of his characteristic personal touches: "In the meantime, keep up the fine job you are doing for our nation, for Kentucky, and for higher education. I am also glad that you have excused me for having made a contribution sometime ago to my nephew . . . when he sought to succeed you in Congress. I think he soon realized that to beat you was a hopeless task, which I am sure it continues to be.''

A copy of another letter in my file, this one addressed to the manager of the Links Club, tells us about Harold's love of fishing, his generosity to his friends, and his grasp of detail. The letter begins: ''I would like to give you the following instructions in regard to the fish being held in the deep freeze . . . belonging to me.'' There follow four numbered paragraphs in which elaborate particulars of distribution are given for a 32 lb. fresh salmon, two single sides of smoked salmon, one double side of smoked salmon, and a 27 lb. salmon that had been cut up into steaks. The letter concludes: ''You may want to use tags to distinguish these fish for delivery.''

Harold's dedication and perseverance were especially evident in all the fund raising that he did for so many institutions. A young Princetonian who observed the Helm *modus operandi* described it as follows: ''Mr. Helm [is] the most 'do-it-now' man I have ever had the privilege of observing in action. . . . He took about five telephone calls, dictated a memo for me to take to Nassau Hall, asked me to take a letter he had recently received to the financial vice-president for discussion next Friday, and dictated a long letter to a fellow alumnus—all in my presence.'' Harold's willingness to do anything, go anywhere, talk with anyone was simply overwhelming (as long as there was no conflict with the Kentucky Derby!). He thought—optimistic soul that he was—that everyone else should be, or could be, equally supportive, and one of his most remarkable qualities was that he never gave up on anyone.

Friendship was such an important thing for Harold and for all who knew him. I think that the secret of his gift for friendship was that he genuinely liked people so much and always took the time to get to know them. He cared about them as individuals, and when he asked about someone's children, it was because he really wanted to know how they were doing, not because he thought he should be polite. Harold made so many of us feel that we were his intimate friends—because that was just the way he felt about us.

He was also, for all of his accomplishments, unpretentious, sensitive to other people and their contributions. This quality, and his self-deprecating sense of humor, are revealed by Harold's characterization of his role in inaugurating Annual Giving at Princeton in 1940. Whenever anyone would refer to Harold as the ''father of Annual Giving,'' Harold would say: "If I was the first chairman of Annual Giving, I was also the worst. We raised only $80,000 with 18 percent participation." But what a seed he planted.

From my perspective, one of Harold's most important contributions to Princeton was serving as chairman of the committee that proposed the election of Robert F. Goheen as sixteenth president. It was a courageous choice, in that Robert Goheen was then an assistant professor of classics; it was also an absolutely inspired choice. Harold had the vision, and the capacity to look ahead, that made all the difference. And yet, in that instance too, he insisted on giving others much of the credit, emphasizing the important role that another Trustee, Chick Belknap, played in that decision.

Harold's ability to think freshly, to combine the best of the past with the requirements of the future, was evident to all who knew him, whatever the setting. In the Princeton context, this quality was demonstrated most strongly by his leadership of the Board at the time the decision was made to admit women undergraduates. When President Goheen asked Harold to chair the committee charged with examining the question, Harold, direct and honest as always, first demurred, telling Bob that he was "not for it." But Bob knew how to appeal to Harold, and he responded: "I'm not asking you to be for it, I'm asking you to *study* it." As Harold recalled just last spring in retelling this story, he didn't see how any Princetonian could reject a proposal to study something. So, he accepted the charge. Months later, as the facts became clear, there was no holding back, and no one stood more firmly for coeducation at Princeton than Harold.

There are so many revealing anecdotes, and all of us have our favorites. We could go on and on. Let me conclude by noting three general qualities of Harold's that were, at least to my way of thinking, particularly powerful in their impact: his capacity to link generations, his sense of institutional loyalty, and his unquenchable desire to make things better.

Harold was, as one colleague put it, a "thread" running through the entire alumni body of Princeton (and, by extension, through other groups as well) linking disparate elements, fusing energies, bringing people together. Young and old, north and south, liberal and conservative, business and academic, all were "connected" to one another by Harold. He made so many different Princetons into one Princeton.

His impact was so great in large measure because he believed so wholeheartedly in the causes that he served. He was especially good at distinguishing what was truly important, and lasting, from what was transitory. That is one reason, I think, why he had such a strong appeal to both the oldest, most nostalgic alumnus, and the youngest graduate. As chairman of the Commencement Committee—and as a participant in over sixty-five Princeton Commencements—he saw so clearly the bond between tradition and change. He was revered by generations of Princeton students, in part because they instinctively knew that he was at least as young at heart as they were.

Loyalty is a concept in some disarray these days. But Harold did not merely understand it; he lived it. Can we think of anyone more constant in his affections and commitments? Harold and Mary have been married for more than sixty years, and we are proud that there is a maple tree dedicated to them next to the chapel on our campus. Whereas today the ablest young people are taught that they should expect to change employers with regularity, Harold's entire career was with one institution: the Chemical Bank. The sixty-five Princeton Commencements to which I referred a moment ago speak for themselves. Institutions, like individuals, derive strength from those few who *always* support them, in hard times as in times of celebration.

Finally, there is Harold and what I call, clumsily I fear, "volunteerism." He had a zest for life that was combined with an irrepressible urge to be useful. Harold himself was once quoted as saying: "It's healthy to spend some time with other people's problems." It was as if he had had ingrained within him Woodrow Wilson's charge to the Princeton Class of 1909:

> Set out to fulfill obligations, to do what you must and exact of others what they owe you, and all your days alike will end in weariness of spirit. The road of life will be long and very dreary. . . . There is no pleasure to be had from the fulfilment of obligations, from doing what you know you ought to do. Nothing but what you volunteer has the essence of life, the springs of pleasure in it. These are the things you do because you want to do them, the things your spirit has chosen for its satisfaction.

I know of no one who gave greater heed to that admonition than Harold Helm. He lived life to the full because he lived it for others. His own cup was always at least half full, and if you thought that your cup was at all close to empty, Harold had the capacity to fill it—or, to help you to help yourself to fill it.

We come together today to give thanks for Harold's life, for his bounteous spirit, for his cheerfulness, for his kindness, for his care for each of us—as for causes which transcend all of us. He had the "essence of life" in him, and he imparted the "springs of pleasure" to each of us privileged to know him.

An Annotated List of Annual Reports, Opening Exercises Addresses, and Commencement Remarks

Annual Reports

1972 (November)

A review of the Goheen presidency (1957–72), with sections on the faculty, undergraduate education, graduate education, scholarship and research, educational resources, physical and financial resources, and governance and administration. Also, a look ahead at general directions for Princeton, at needs, and at policy questions concerning the size and composition of the undergraduate college, the nature of the undergraduate program, the future of the graduate school, equal opportunity, the role of Princeton in the professions, continuing education, Princeton in the larger community, and internal governance. The report is dedicated to Harold H. Helm '20, who had chaired the Trustee committee that recommended Dr. Goheen as Princeton's sixteenth president.

1974 (January)   See pages 303–36

Faculty recruitment and advancement, with sections on the general outlook for academic supply and demand, possible responses nationally, tenure, compensation, and leadership. Also, **the politics of the faculty,** with sections on the "liberalism" of the faculty and on implications for the University in the areas of appointments, advancements, and the content and conduct of the academic program. The report is dedicated to J. Douglas Brown '19, dean of the faculty from 1946 to 1967 as well as the University's first provost, and Richard A. Lester, dean of the faculty from 1968 to 1973.

1975 (January)   See pages 13–19

A review of academic year 1973–74, with particular emphasis on three major issues: (1) the presence of Army ROTC at Princeton; (2) a visit to campus by Dr. William Shockley at the invitation of the Whig-Cliosophic Society; and (3) the adoption of an admission policy of equal access with regard to men and women. The report also includes remarks on "Alumni and Princeton" from an October 1974 conference of alumni leaders.

1976   (February)   See pages 491–526

The Economics of Princeton in the 1970s: Some Worrisome Implications of Trying to Make Do with Less, with sections on the implications for quality, for access, and for the University's sense of community. The report is dedicated to Ricardo A. Mestres '31, Princeton's financial vice president and treasurer from 1953 until 1972.

1977   (March)   See pages 75–118

Liberal Education at Princeton, with sections on the historical context, undergraduate education in the 1970s, liberal education as preparation for careers and later life, and concerns for the future. The report is dedicated to the eight deans of the college since that office was created in 1909.

1978   (April)   See pages 544–49

A Perspective on Private Giving, with sections on national trends, tax incentives, the importance of private giving to Princeton, and a look ahead. The report is dedicated to "the volunteers who have worked so hard to build and sustain Princeton through private giving."

1979   (April)   See pages 238–69

Scholarship and Research, with an opening section on their importance in the society and on campus, followed by a discussion of concerns for the future at universities generally and at Princeton. These concerns include support for young scholars; libraries, laboratories, and instrumentation; administrative burdens; assymmetries in the support of the sciences and the humanities; and independence and the setting of directions.

1980   (April)

Coeducation at Princeton, with sections on the size, composition, and quality of the student body; academic life, including course enrollments, the curriculum, the general character and quality of the academic program, and faculty recruitment; campus life, including athletics and other activities as well as patterns of residential and social life; and career plans and commitment to Princeton.

1981   (April)   See pages 189–237

Graduate Education in the Arts and Sciences: Prospects for the Future, with sections on the "defining characteristics" of the Princeton graduate school; national trends threatening graduate education, including the outlook for academic employment, rising costs and changing patterns of financial support for graduate students, and the problem of specialization; and questions of policy for Princeton, for universities generally, for the government, and for private sources of support.

1982 (March)

A Campaign for Princeton, the "prospectus" for a five-year fundraising program whose initial goal of $275 million was later revised to $330 million, and whose final total was in excess of $410.5 million. The prospectus describes the reasons for the campaign and the needs that it was designed to address. The first draft of the prospectus, along with the 1981 annual report, was prepared at the Center for Advanced Study in the Behavioral Sciences in Stanford, California, while President Bowen was on leave there in the fall of 1980. The prospectus was extensively reviewed both on campus and at meetings with alumni around the country before being issued in final form as the 1982 annual report.

1983 (April)   See pages 454–88

Maintaining Opportunity: Undergraduate Financial Aid at Princeton, with sections on the importance of financial aid at Princeton, some historical perspective, current financial aid policies and practices, and policy choices both for the society as a whole and for Princeton.

1984 (April)   See pages 337–71

Junior Faculty at Princeton, with sections on the role of junior faculty members, including their numbers and characteristics, teaching responsibilities, research activities, and other contributions to Princeton; problems and concerns for the junior faculty member, including tenure prospects at Princeton, job prospects elsewhere, salary levels, and other pressures; problems and concerns for the University; and ways to help.

1985 (April)   See pages 136–49

The Creative Arts at Princeton, with sections on the history of the creative arts at Princeton; the creative arts today, including creative writing, theater and dance, visual arts, music, and architecture; the role of the creative arts in a liberal arts curriculum; and needs for facilities and program support. The report is dedicated to the memory of two faculty members: Professor Rensselaer Wright Lee '20 *26 of the Department of Art and Archaeology, who chaired the 1965 committee that provided guidelines for the future development of the Creative Arts Program at Princeton, and Professor Daniel Seltzer '54 of the Department of English, who served as the first director of the Program in Theater and Dance.

1986   (March)   See pages 270–300

The Princeton Library, with sections on the role of the library as it reflects a philosophy of education, as it has evolved over time, and in its national and international dimensions; such pressing issues as acquisitions, preservation, new technologies, and space planning; and the ambience and character of the library of the future. The report is dedicated to five longtime benefactors of the Princeton library: Howard Behrman, Levering Cartwright '26, William H. Scheide '36, Robert Taylor '30, and the Firestone family for whom the University's principal library is named.

1987   (May)   See pages 157–66

International Studies at Princeton, with sections on international and regional studies activities at Princeton, the increasing internationalization of Princeton's faculty and student body, and two challenges for the years ahead: the intellectual challenge of fusing ancient and modern, cultural and economic/political; and the financial challenge of paying for intrinsically expensive programs.

Opening Exercises

1972
Climate for Learning
"My subject is attitudes and values in the setting of a university viewed first and foremost as a center of learning. . . . It is as a center of learning, and not as a political instrument, that the university, as an institution, serves best."

1973   See pages 126–32
The University and Moral Values
"I believe that both the substance of the curriculum and, even more importantly, the ways in which we teach and learn can have profound effects on moral development."

1974

Ends and Means: The University in Society and the Individual in the University

"Recognizing the limitations of an institution represents, if you will, institutional humility; and recognizing our limitations as terribly fallible human beings represents that personal humility without which no real learning can occur and precious little, if any, development as a person."

1975   See pages 133–35

Academic Pressures and Purposes

"It is my hope . . . that by considering together this general subject [of 'academic pressure'] we may at least come to understand somewhat better what it is that concerns us, what choices we need to be prepared to make, and perhaps how we can help others—and ourselves—to cope more sensibly with the pressures that are an inescapable part of our life here."

1976

Liberal Education at Princeton

"I want to discuss with you one of the oldest subjects, and yet also, I think, one of the most timely: the commitment of this University to liberal education in the arts and sciences and the implications of that commitment for your own education here."

1977   See pages 375–84

Diversity: The Opportunities and the Obligations

"The freedom and the diversity of the Princeton of today, which offer such great opportunities to learn, imply a corresponding obligation to respect differences of opinion and to avoid pressing one's own position in ways that could be harmful to the rights of others."

1978   See pages 385–89

A Healthy Individualism

"A true commitment to individualism . . . leads not to self-centeredness or indifference to those around us. It leads rather to the kind of concern for others that is derived from recognition of our diversity and yet awareness of how much we are alike in fundamental respects— from an acceptance of the common humanity which unites us through our differences."

1979   See pages 119–25
The Skills of Freedom
    "My subject this morning is your education here seen as preparation for citizenship."

1980

(President Bowen was on leave in the fall of 1980 at the Center for Advanced Study in the Behavioral Sciences, Stanford, California. The Opening Exercises address was delivered by Provost Neil L. Rudenstine.)

1981   See pages 179–85
Ithaka
    "You are beginning an entirely new journey, and no doubt many of you are thinking about where it will lead—about the goals that will give direction to your own days at Princeton. . . . 'As you set out for Ithaka, hope your road is a long one, full of adventure, full of discovery.' "

1982   See pages 413–21
Race Relations
    "While I have no panaceas to offer, I believe that we do well to consider questions pertaining to race as openly and as candidly as we can. Plainly there are sensitive—painful—aspects to our experiences at Princeton, but there are also many positive possibilities. There is so much for us to accomplish, so much for us to learn, together."

1983   See pages 390–97
The Difficult Unity of Inclusion
    "How sad it would be if we were satisfied with an approach to life, in the University or outside it, that failed to exalt Mr. Venturi's 'messy vitality' over less-demanding aspirations."

1984   See pages 150–156
Capturing "Otherness"
    "Given broad definition—to encompass not only other times but also other cultures in our own time, other disciplines, other groups within our own society, and other individuals within one's own group (however specified)—an appreciation for 'otherness' is central to the very idea of liberal education."

1985   See pages 5–12
At a Slight Angle to the World
    "The University as an institution must exercise a significant degree

of institutional restraint if its individual members are to enjoy the maximum degree of freedom.''

1986 See pages 563–66

Always Under Construction

"Let me recast the implicit question this way: While the educational structure of Princeton is 'always under construction,' are there not key 'foundation stones,' if you will, that ought always to be preserved and built upon? I think there are.''

1987 See pages 398–404

The Bond of Respect

"While diversity can be exhilarating, stimulating, and highly educational, it can also create tensions, opportunities for misperceptions, and at times actual conflicts. Let me state my thesis directly: I see 'respect' as the essential bond required to avoid fragmentation and, in fact, to realize the true educational possibilities before us.''

Commencement

1973 See pages 567–69

Preparation for the Possibility of Being Wrong

"My hope is that your stay here has provided—and will continue to provide—at least some defenses against a misplaced sense of certainty.''

1974 See pages 570–71

Generosity of Spirit

"I hope too that the exercise of your critical capacities will be characterized by generosity of spirit in a second, slightly more personal form—through the ability to be critical without being unloving.''

1975

The University as Partnership

"In my view a university has a particularly great need to bridge generations, to reach both backward and forward in time.''

1976 See page 581

Roots

"I hope . . . that the roots you have put down on this campus will prove to be long-lived, capable of providing continuing nourishment.''

1977   See pages 170–73

A Quiet Confidence

"There is something in the ethos of this place that many of us internalize quite powerfully—and which gives us a confidence, a strength, many of us never knew we could possess."

1978   See pages 572–74

The Possibilities You Represent

"I hope and believe that you offer the possibility of combining deep concern with the courage to think for yourselves, to acknowledge complexity, to correct errors (sometimes your own), to forswear self-righteousness, and to hold off to at least some extent the natural craving for certainty."

1979

Why You Came

(Quoting Adlai Stevenson): "Don't forget when you leave why you came."

1980   See pages 167–69

The Texture of the Effort

"What counts for so much is what . . . George Kennan of the Class of 1925 once called 'the texture of the effort.' "

1981   See page 580

Thinking and Caring

"I hope . . . that in your own lives you will find ways to blend, and so to make richly human, the powers of the mind and the promptings of the heart."

1982   See pages 405–07

No Limits

"I hope that you will find time in your own lives to help to build a society in which there are fewer limits on the aspirations of others— and to see that Princeton, in particular, remains a place of opportunity as well as a place of privilege."

1983

A Tradition of Service

"You will find, I know, countless ways to give new life to what I trust will always be one of Princeton's most important traditions: a tradition of service."

1984   See pages 408–12

Elitism

"What is required, in my view, is sustained effort to avoid as best we can corrosive forms of elitism, including elitism of attitude, while seeking to develop as fully as possible the capacities of the University, and of each of us, to serve the larger society."

1985   See pages 174–78

OTSOG (On the Shoulders of Giants)

"What is required, then, if you are to use your education to the full? A blend, I believe, of continuing respect for learning, a capacity to take the long view, and the courage of persistence."

1986   See pages 575–79

To Be Part of Something Much Larger

"The University needs you. It needs your interest, your affectionate criticism, and your dedication. I think that you need it in turn, and at least as much, as an outlet for the best instincts within you."

1987   See pages 582–87

Reflections

"My greatest gift from Princeton was an at first faint, but then growing, sense of what scholarship entailed; of what it meant to grapple with an idea, or a series of apparently conflicting, seemingly obscure ideas . . . ; and then finally to be rewarded by a flash of illumination."

Biographical Information

William Gordon Bowen was born in Cincinnati, Ohio, on October 6, 1933. A son of the late Albert Andrew Bowen and Mrs. Bernice Catherine Bowen and a graduate of Cincinnati's Wyoming High School, he received his A.B. degree from Denison University in 1955 with highest honors in economics and was awarded fellowships from the Danforth, Woodrow Wilson, and Woodland Foundations for graduate study at Princeton University. At Denison he was the ranking member of the varsity tennis team and for two years swept top honors in both singles and doubles in the Ohio conference. He also was elected student body president.

Upon receiving his Ph.D. in economics from Princeton in 1958, he was appointed an assistant professor. He was promoted to associate professor in 1961 and full professor in 1965 with a joint appointment in the Department of Economics and the Woodrow Wilson School of Public and International Affairs. In 1962-63 he served as acting director of the Economics Department's Industrial Relations Section, and from 1964 to 1966 he was director of graduate studies for the Woodrow Wilson School.

Elected provost in 1967, he served for five years as the general deputy to the president. On June 30, 1972, at age 38, he became Princeton's seventeenth president, succeeding Robert F. Goheen, a classicist and later Ambassador to India. In January 1988, Dr. Bowen became president of the New York-based Andrew W. Mellon Foundation. He was succeeded at Princeton by Dr. Harold T. Shapiro, an economist who received his Ph.D. from Princeton in 1964 and most recently had served as president of the University of Michigan.

Dr. Bowen's scholarly interests are in the fields of labor economics, the economics of education, the economics of the performing arts, and problems of stability and growth. He has authored and coauthored seven volumes, as well as numerous articles, essays, and reviews. His principal publications are: *The Wage Price Issue: A Theoretical Analysis* (1960), *Wage Behavior in the Post-War Period: An Empirical Analysis* (1960), *The Federal Government and Princeton University* (1962), *Economic Aspects of Education* (1964), *Economics of the Ma-*

jor Private Universities (1968), *Performing Arts: The Economic Dilemma* (with W. J. Baumol, 1966), and *The Economics of Labor Force Participation* (with T. A. Finegan, 1969).

An enthusiastic teacher, Dr. Bowen taught a section of the basic economics course, Economics 101, almost every year of his presidency.

Dr. Bowen is a Regent of the Smithsonian Institution, a Director of Merck and Company, NCR Corporation, and Reader's Digest, Inc., and a Trustee of the Center for Advanced Study in the Behavioral Sciences. In 1977-78 he served as Chairman of the Board of the American Council on Education. He is a member of Phi Beta Kappa, the American Academy of Arts and Sciences, the American Economic Association, and the American Philosophical Association.

In 1956 he was married to the former Mary Ellen Maxwell of Cincinnati. The Bowens have a son, David Alan (born August 30, 1958), and a daughter, Karen Lee (born October 5, 1964).

At his final Princeton Commencement as president, Dr. Bowen was presented with a surprise honorary degree. The text of the citation was as follows:

> As graduate student, faculty member, provost, and president, you have invigorated this community with your talents, your energies, and your vision for Princeton. You have led us, prodded us, befriended us, inspired us—teaching us always, in Adlai Stevenson's words, how much better to light a candle than to curse the darkness. Reaching well beyond this campus whose beauty has moved you so deeply, you have been an eloquent and effective advocate for excellence, opportunity, and independence in this nation's institutions of learning. We salute your leadership and love of this University, and we send you on to new challenges with our appreciation, our affection, and your favorite injunction, "Onward."